The Theater in Its Time

THE THEATER
IN ITS TIME
An Introduction

Peter Arnott
TUFTS UNIVERSITY

 **LITTLE, BROWN and COMPANY**
BOSTON   TORONTO

Library of Congress Catalog Card No. 80-82163

ISBN 0-316-051942

9 8 7 6 5 4 3 2 1

HAL

Published simultaneously in Canada
by Little, Brown & Company (Canada) Limited

Printed in the United States of America

The photograph facing the title page is the theater of Epidaurus, Greece.

Acknowledgments

We are grateful to the following individuals and institutions for permission to reprint their
photographs.

Greek National Tourist Organization, pp. ii, 14
The Guthrie Theatre, pp. 41, 42
The Cleveland Museum of Art, pp. 67, 119, 131 (top), 132 (top), 165, 202 (top), 215, 259
    (bottom), 305 (top), 355 (bottom), 399 (top), 407 (bottom), 489 (top)
Thaddeus Torp, pp. 70, 88, 89, 398

(continued on page 550)

A fact is like a sack which won't stand up when it's empty.
In order that it may stand up, one has to put into it
the reason and sentiment which have caused it to exist.

Luigi Pirandello

Preface

The purpose of this book is to consider both the theory and practice of the theater, and to illuminate the more important principles that control its operation through a study of the theater's past. Of all the lively arts, the theater offers the clearest demonstration of the folly of attempting to separate past from present. Greek plays over two thousand years old exercise modern minds and provide star vehicles for twentieth-century actors. Molière's comedies have enjoyed a continuous performance history of three hundred years, and Shakespeare is the greatest box-office success on record. But the theater preserves ideas as well as examples. Contemporary controversy about what the stage should properly show, and the rights and responsibilities of the dramatist, merely reformulates arguments that were old in Plato's time. The censorship of Puritan London or feudal Japan brought the same charges against the theater that we are still hearing today. Though the language has changed, certain attitudes remain constant.

Thus the history of the theater offers a series of examples, drawn from a range of local situations, of phenomena that are still with us, and makes it easier for us to consider and evaluate them because they are at some remove from us and can be judged more objectively. In the chapters that follow I have tried to stress the debt that the modern theater owes to a past off which it is continually feeding. In its cyclical history, the theater shows a pattern of constant rediscovery. Techniques discarded as outmoded in the fifteenth century are exhumed and hailed as innovations in our own. Actors, in their ceaseless re-examination of the basis of their art, talk to one another across the gap of many years.

As the emphasis is on how the theater's past feeds into, and to a large extent controls, the theater's present, this history is inevitably selective. Greater consideration has been given to those periods or works which have had a demonstrable effect on the developing pattern of the theater and its present manifestations, or which embody fundamental attitudes still evident today. Less attention has been paid to periods that are dramatic cul-de-sacs or have had little impact on the modern repertory. Thus, the classical theater of Japan has been discussed in some detail as one of the clearest examples of a particular conception of the art that has influenced many artists elsewhere, although the Japanese plays themselves have never been widely seen outside their own country. The theater of the Spanish Golden Age, by contrast, has been summarily (and, some are bound to feel, unfairly) treated, both because its plays have made little impact on the main body of drama and because its basic principles are illustrated in the more familiar products of its historical contemporary, the public playhouse of Elizabethan London.

The sheer mass of material makes further selection obligatory. Theater is an integrative art. It involves writers, singers, actors, dancers, composers, scene designers, costumers, makers of props and lighting technicians, administrators and business people, critics, censors, and audiences. A systematic study of any *one* of these groups would run into several volumes. My method, therefore, has been to illustrate the most significant characteristics of a given period by examples drawn selectively from all of them, as each seems appropriate, and to suggest the flavor of an age sometimes by the description of a building, sometimes by the synopsis of a play, now by an actor's or a playwright's life, now by a study of audience behavior. In the early chapters, which deal with periods and styles now remote from us, I have from time to time attempted to make the reconstruction more alive and meaningful through a description of a play in performance. Although these descriptions, for the sake of simplicity and vividness, are presented as fact, it must be emphasized that many details are hypothetical. We shall never know exactly what the medieval audience saw when the *Second Shepherds' Play* was given in the streets of Wakefield or the positioning of actors at the first performances of *Doctor Faustus*. The descriptions represent intelligent surmise based on available evidence.

It remains for me to record some special debts: to my editor Charles Christensen, who suggested that this book be written; to my daughter Catherine, who typed the greater part of the manuscript and whose criticism has improved it in many places; to my son Christopher, who undertook several portions of the research when my own time was lacking; to Patricia Sankus and Renata Sorkin, who assisted in the work's preparation; and to my colleague, Professor

Sylvan Barnet, whose comments have saved me from many errors. Above all, my thanks must go the the audiences throughout Great Britain and North America before who, for the past thirty years, I have directed or acted in most of the plays used as examples in this book, and whose approval has encouraged me in the conviction that old plays can still speak with a modern tongue.

Contents

The Theater in Its Time

1
The Study of Theater

What Is Theater?

To anyone writing such a book as this, even as recently as fifty years ago, this question would have seemed to have an easy and obvious answer. It would have been taken for granted that theater involved a script — which had an independent literary existence, over and above the fact of its performance — designed to be given life, by actors, in a place specially built for, or at least adapted for, its presentation. Thus for the Western world the history of the theater was assumed to begin with the earliest known playscript, and this was thought to be a largely choral drama called *The Suppliant Women,* by the Greek playwright Aeschylus (525–456 B.C.). The scanty evidence for plays and theaters from before this time was of interest only to specialists. The script was the thing, and from Aeschylus the study proceeded methodically from text to text, with an emphasis on the plays as literature. Such things as acting, music, scene design, and audience reaction, when they were considered at all, were viewed as secondary considerations, providing the milieu in which the script could operate.

This literary emphasis (which to some extent is still with us) meant two

3

things. First, whole areas of theater in which there was no script, or where the script was of minimal importance, were neglected. A conspicuous example is the popular comedy of the Italian Renaissance, known to us as the commedia dell'arte. This form was not merely beloved in its own time but had a vast influence on other times and countries. However, these plays were virtually scriptless. The actors worked from a scenario, which they embellished from their stock of traditional gags and business; and so conventional theater histories either ignored them or dismissed them with a passing mention. Second, scripts that lacked conspicuous literary merit were passed over. This attitude virtually obliterated the nineteenth century — apart from studies of a few key authors — although this was a period of intense theatrical activity. Even for the works of a major author the same principle of literary selectivity applied. Studies of Molière, for example, spent a great deal of time on the longer, more obviously literary works — *The Misanthrope, The Learned Ladies, Tartuffe* — and very little on the shorter, action-packed farces that were the author's bread and butter. Criticism of individual works showed the same prejudice. The continuing argument that Christopher Marlowe did not write the comic scenes in *The Tragical History of Doctor Faustus* (see p. 192) is based on the fact that these do not *read* so well as the tragic scenes and were therefore considered to be by an inferior hand. Always the proper work of scholarship was thought to be the text. The remaining apparatus of the theater was left to the antiquarian.

But things have changed. The fact that we now know that *The Suppliant Women* was not Aeschylus's first play, and thus the beginning of European dramatic literature, is trivial beside the wholesale reappraisal of what theater is and what its study should properly involve. This change has been marked by the rapid development in American universities since the 1930s of departments of drama as distinct from departments of literature — a development paralleled, but more slowly and reluctantly, in Great Britain and Europe. It has involved a growing rapprochement between those who write about the theater and those who perform in it. It has encouraged a scholarly awareness of what actors have always known — that the text is not the sum of the theater but merely one of its component parts, and not necessarily the most important. The theater is now seen as a composite of diverse skills, illuminating and inspiring one another; and even purely textual scholars are now prepared to admit the extent to which the published script was shaped and influenced by the practical necessities of stage performance.

Our assessment of the nature of theater has thus been both deepened and broadened. Aristotle (384–322 B.C.), the first known theorist of the drama, defined it as "an imitation of an action," and this definition is now interpreted in the widest possible sense. Books about the theater now start not with Aeschylus, or even with the Greeks, but with magico-religious rites of remote antiquity, with priests or dancers dressed as animals or gods, or with "green men" hung with leaves and processing through the European woodlands to bring blessings on the cottages and farms. They consider folk forms, whose scripts have evolved not from the conscious creative act of a single individual but from generations of collaboration among amateur performers. Due attention is now paid to that vast subculture of paradramatic activity — rites, games, feasts, shows, sports — that bridges the gap between known scripts — and, in fact, helped to bring those scripts into being. In considering the Elizabethan theater, we now look not only at the plays of Shakespeare and his contemporaries, not only at the working conditions of his playhouse, but at contemporary popular entertainments that influenced those conditions and help to illuminate them for us — at bearbaiting, jigs, and juggling, at fairground shows, at social dances and public executions. No study of Molière can now be complete without a survey of that popular, nonliterary Italian comedy that was once so despised but that so heavily influenced Molière's written work. The burlesques, melodramas, and spectacular extravaganzas of the nineteenth century are now considered as works of importance in their own right. Studies of the modern theater now include phenomena that stretch the definition of drama to its widest extent: the tightly organized mass spectacles of Hitler's Nuremburg rallies, for example; or the happening that subjects unprepared participants to a series of partially prearranged events and considers the drama to be the sum of their unpredictable reactions; or even the speaking, moving figures whose automated playlets delight visitors to Disneyland. Contemporary critics link dramatic theory with games theory. It is not enough now for theater scholars to be textual critics merely. They must be archaeologists, sociologists, and psychologists, too.

Why Did Theater Develop?

What brought this form of art into being in the first place? Here we are dealing with a period so long before the beginning of recorded history that we can only work by speculation and analogy. An analogy from the visual arts may be particularly useful. The earliest paintings we know are those perishable but miraculously preserved relics found on cave walls at Lascaux and elsewhere. They bear mute witness to primitive people's desire to reproduce an experience and show things of importance to the tribe, particularly the hunt, on which survival depended. We see the outline of the quarry surrounded by figures representing hunters, whose spears are piercing it. What motivated these paintings? Art historians have proposed various explanations. They may have been a form of pictorial record keeping, showing successful hunts that had already taken place and of which the tribe was proud to be reminded. They may have been magical in nature, showing the desired result of a hunt that had yet to happen, in the hope that the representation would influence the event. They may have served as instructional charts, showing novice hunters where best to aim their spears. Or they may have been purely decorative. Perhaps the unknown artist merely saw a lump of rock that recalled an animal shape, and he drew his picture for the joy of it.

Equally diverse claims have been made for the origin of drama. Most of these arguments revolve around the Greek theater, which remains the earliest fully organized drama form that we know and the first substantial body of material that we have access to. It has been variously suggested that these plays came into existence to record the lives and achievements of recently dead kings; that they were offshoots of, and elaborations upon, primitive fertility rites celebrating the annual cycle of death and regeneration in nature; or that they were from the beginning strictly civic celebrations, dedicated to the instruction of the citizen body by dramatizing issues vital to their interests. Each of these theories claims to find support in certain distinctive features of the plays themselves.

We cannot, at this remove, prove that any theory is true. They may *all* be partly true. And certainly all the explanations — record keeping, magico-religious, art for art's sake, or art for diversion — can be shown to be true of different kinds of theater at different periods of time. A medieval audience, watching the performance of a religious play in the square of an English market town, would have taken it for granted that it was participating in a pious, though enjoyable, devotional exercise. A Paris audience of the mid nineteenth century took it equally for granted that the theater's prime function was to entertain. The theater speaks in diverse ways. Its uses are as varied as the communities that have employed it, and all these uses may derive from some part of the theater's earliest beginnings.

The most persuasive source theory, however, remains the magico-religious. Some anthropologists have traced the roots of *all* drama to seasonal celebrations marking the end of the old year and the beginning of the new, the triumph of spring over winter. It is argued that this symbolic enactment of a critical time in the lives of early peoples either celebrated the event or was believed to induce the event, like the ancient custom of lighting bonfires to lure the sun back after the winter solstice. This protodrama, then, would have been a ritual combat between two figures, one representing the Old Year, one the New, culminating in the mimic death — perhaps, originally, the *actual* death — of the former. This type of conflict has been seen in sublimated form in the clashes between opposing forces that characterize Greek tragedy. It can be clearly observed in the very early type of folk drama, ultimately given a Christian coloration, that we know as the English mummers' play (see p. 113). It can still be observed in surviving cultures that have retained their primitive patterns. Even in societies that have lost these patterns, the connection between drama and religious ritual is demonstrable, and the dividing line is often unclear.

In different cultures at different times, the earliest actors have been shamans or priests. Even when the theater has established itself as a separate and secular activity, it has often retained vestiges of ritual speech and behavior that have proven themselves to be dramatically useful. Some plays even retain formulaic expressions, incantations whose original meaning has been long forgotten. The English mummers' play provides one example, the early Japanese theater another; and the sacramental associations of church Latin lingered in English plays long after the theater had turned secular. This is not to say that there has to be religion before there can be drama. Aristotle remarked that the impulse to imitate is innate in all of us. Religious ritual simply provided an obvious, and forceful, way in which this impulse could be harnessed. And if the early priest-actors turned to drama because they thought it could, by sympathetic magic, help them to control, or at least comprehend, the superhuman forces with which they had to deal, they touched on a quality that has been vested in the theater ever since. The theater acts as a focusing glass. It reduces complex and momentous issues to manageable proportions, and it allows us to discern patterns that, in the tangle of everyday life, are less clearly visible. If drama began as an expression of human need, it remains as a mirror of humanity's state of mind.

Theater and Society

As noted above, the earliest forms of drama that we know all seem to have been by-products of other activities. As long as the theater has been content with this subservient relationship, it has enjoyed a considerable measure of protection. In any culture where the theater has functioned as an adjunct of the religious, political, or even educational establishment, it has been at least tolerated and often cherished. In this aspect it has normally not employed professional performers in the sense of actors who make their living by their occupation. The earliest actors of whom we have record were usually priests or laymen temporarily serving in a priestly function and returning to their normal occupations afterward. As long as the theater remained a function of the community as a whole and its performers were, in the noblest sense of the word, amateurs, the participants gained honor from the association.

Inevitably, however, whenever the theater has severed its religious ties and established itself as a secular, independent, and professional venture, its social status has fallen and its personnel have suffered from the change. We shall see many examples of this as we proceed through the history of the theater: how the Greek amateurs of the fifth century B.C. received some of the highest honors in the state, while the fourth-century professionals were considered disreputable; how medieval craftsmen who took time from their work to play religious drama were esteemed, while their successors in the Elizabethan public theater were harassed by legal restrictions and social prejudice; how Louis XIV and his court could dance in ballet with propriety, while Molière, the leading actor-playwright of the time, was denied burial in consecrated ground. Wherever the professional theater has emerged, it has been subject to attack; and the periodic viciousness of this attack testifies to the power that the art, even by its sternest critics, was admitted to possess.

Why does this happen? There seem to be several reasons.

First, once the theater has divorced itself from other institutions, it stands revealed as a social oddity. Though acting may answer a deeply felt human need — to imitate and by imitating possibly to control — and though we all at times act sentiments we do not really feel, the *profession* of acting as a full-time occupation stands apart from any other category of human labor. Its skills are more esoteric, less easily discernible to the untrained eye. Indeed, most actors would argue that their art is to conceal art, to make their performance *seem* simple, easy, and natural, no matter how much labor has gone into its preparation. It is amazing how many people assume that theater somehow just happens. Most audiences, and many tyro performers, have no comprehension of how much mental and physical effort is involved in actor training or play rehearsal and how time-consuming these things are. And, of course, there is no tangible end product. We may not understand how a computer scientist works, or a poet, but the printout or poem is there for us to read. Once the actor's performance is finished, nothing is left but a memory of an impression:

> Nor pen nor pencil can the actor save;
> The art and artist share one common grave.

For this reason the playwright, who writes the words, has usually been accorded higher status than the actor, who merely speaks them. Acting is a human activity like no other, and popular response has run the predictable gamut from awe to derision. The Greeks seem to have perceived this when, perhaps more wisely than they knew, they made Dionysus the god of the theater; for Dionysus was an outlandish god, a foreigner, whose ceremonies had no known parallel in Greek worship. He was an intruder, representing a power that forced itself upon unbelievers: a power founded in the irrational but still irresistible.

Second, the profession has often been considered frivolous, unworthy of the attention of a mature adult who should have more important concerns. The semantic confusion is indicative: English is not the only language using the same word for the play that takes place on the stage and the play that children indulge in. As the material rewards of the theater, below the highest levels, are demonstrably few, its practitioners have been charged with frittering away their time when they could be "holding down an honest job." Elizabethan England was not the only society that officially classified actors with rogues and vagabonds. Unfortunately, there is a grain of truth in these charges. Many have been attracted to the theater by its supposed glamor and romance and the chance of an easy success. They have soon found out their mistake; but there have been enough of them to support the accusation of frivolity. The Royal Academy of Dramatic Art (RADA), Great Britain's senior conservatory, was for years little more than a finishing school for debutantes. Those days have happily passed, but the different requirements of filmdom have encouraged another, equally damning legend: that you do not need to work for a cinematic career; you only need to have the looks and the luck to be discovered. And, as in all the arts, where standards of apprenticeship and training are so diverse and ill defined, it is all too easy for poseurs and dilettantes to enter the profession and even to flourish.

Third, and much more seriously, the profession has periodically been condemned for immorality. It has been labeled not merely frivolous but evil. We have a hint of this in what may be the earliest piece of dramatic criticism to come down to us, a dialogue put into the mouths of Solon, the legendary Greek lawgiver, and Thespis, the traditional first actor, both men who have bequeathed their names to their professions. Solon condemns Thespis's art as immoral because it is a living lie. A man who represents himself as someone else is perpetrating a falsehood all the more insidious because of the power that drama exercises over the imagination. Plato elaborated on this view in his *Republic* when he dismissed drama from the Ideal State on the grounds that it so often portrayed unworthy sentiments and actions morally detrimental to actors and audience alike.

In the continuing history of hostility toward the theater, the Christian church must take much of the blame. Growing up under the disapproval of Roman society, the emergent religion was burlesqued on the contemporary stage. Christianity, being new, outlandish, and potentially subversive, was an easy and popular target. As soon as Christian writers acquired a voice, they took their revenge by condemning not merely the burlesques but the theater as a whole. This legacy of odium was bequeathed to posterity. Later critics found ready-made material in the diatribes of the church fathers. Paradoxically, the medieval church developed a form of theater as a devotional aid, which it cherished as long as it retained control; but as soon as the theater reverted to the secular, the attacks resumed. The actors suffered by association. Periodically the charge has been made, either openly or by insinuation, that all actors are scoundrels and all actresses prostitutes. Even when the art has enjoyed great popularity, and individual performers have been idolized, the rank and file have had to bear the stigma. The history of the theater is full of tales of persecution, of actors run out of town because their very presence was offensive. Today one may still meet people who refuse to go to the theater because it is against their principles. It is sometimes argued that respectability returned to the English-speaking theater with the knighting of Henry Irving in 1895 and the accompanying assumption that an actor could still be, in contemporary terms, a gentleman; but one need only apply for car insurance and list one's profession as actor to find out how false this assumption is.

Fourth, the theater has often suffered because authority has found it abrasive. It is recognized that this art form has power to move and excite as no other can, and along with this recognition has gone a fear that in the wrong hands it may prove inflammatory, subversive, revolutionary. Whether the theater has ever, in fact, provoked political action, or merely reflected it, is a debatable point. But the fear has remained. Shakespeare's theater suffered harassment from magistrates who, in a politically sensitive time, distrusted any kind of public assembly, and particularly those where some two thousand people were hanging on words delivered with trained skill and theatrical passion. In Japan the shogunate continually regarded the theater as a social and political menace (and with some reason; a famous play about a suicide pact, performed in 1720, started a rash of actual suicides throughout the capital). Thus there were continual pressures and closures, often for political reasons masquerading as public morality. Political satire on the London stage provoked a stringent censorship that remained in force, incredibly, from 1737 to 1969. When the military junta took power in Greece in 1967, one of its first acts was to censor the program of the annual festival of ancient drama. Plays over two thousand years old still had uncomfortably modern things to say about tyrants.

And yet the theater has proved ineradicable. The Broadway theater has long enjoyed the title of "the fabulous invalid" — always ailing, never dead. This title merely reflects the general condition. The same deep wellspring of emotional need that brought the theater into existence has ensured its continuation. Whatever pressures have been laid upon it, it has always reemerged, sometimes in disguise but always very much alive. Loved or hated, it can never be ignored.

Why Study Theater History?

As a good deal of this book is concerned with the theater's past, the question "Why study theater history?" demands an answer, for theater is very much a thing of the present. Its impact is immediate and direct. It speaks to the audience before it, and it can assume little from them in the way of foreknowledge and preparation. A play that needs to be explained perhaps no longer deserves to be performed. Playwrights and actors are more concerned with the here and now than the hereafter. Though the former may hope that they are writing for the ages, and the latter that their work will be remembered, they are more immediately concerned with the effect they will have on a particular audience, in a particular kind of theater, and with a particular set of preconceptions. And theaters and audiences change. The *Hamlet* we see can never be the same that Shakespeare's audience saw because of the transformations that have occurred in the theater and in us. Why, then, bother with what was? Why not simply concern ourselves with what is?

The problem is compounded when we confront the difficulties of reconstructing any theater of the past. The literary bias of traditional theater studies seems more excusable, even inevitable, when we consider that the text is often the only element of the production to survive. Performance is transitory. Acting has been called "sculpting in snow." It exists for the moment and vanishes at curtain fall, leaving no mark except in the memories of those who saw it, and memories differ. No two audiences are ever the same, and no actor ever gives exactly the same performance twice. And over a period of time acting styles change substantially. The Greek actor's skills and expectations were not those of his Elizabethan or modern counterpart. Critics of all ages have praised actors' performances as highly realistic, true to life; but what an eighteenth-century audience meant by *realism* is not what we mean. If we want to reconstruct these vanished performances, we usually have to do it on the basis of fragmentary evidence — a hint in a review, a personal anecdote, a clue in a stage direction.

We can never be sure that our picture is accurate. The American star Joseph Jefferson III summed it up cruelly but accurately when he said, "There is nothing as dead as a dead actor."

What is true of acting is hardly less true of stages and their settings. Though some Greek theaters have survived in their original stone, we lack the detailed knowledge to make a sure interpretation of what we see. In other cases firsthand evidence has disappeared entirely, leaving us (if we are lucky) with a few pictures, verbal descriptions, and, once again, stage directions in plays. For the Elizabethan theater, for example, the surviving evidence is so scanty that it has been interpreted with equal conviction in diametrically opposite ways. Pictures are not always as helpful as we might expect. The visual arts have their own conventions; these, too, change, and the painter may be an interpreter rather than a recorder. He may distort, compress, or rearrange for compositional values. A vase painting or an etching is not a photograph. And even photographs are fallible. Publicity shots of a stage scene often rearrange the elements to give a more vivid impression. A film of a stage production is never the same as the real thing.

So — to return to our original question — why bother? First, because theater history has value to the practitioner, not merely out of sentiment but as a useful tool. Any role acquires a patina of use over the centuries. It becomes a composite of different interpretations: not merely what the author put in it but what generations of actors have seen in it. The role is larger than the script, and we profit from having as many different points of view as possible. An actor playing Hamlet in 1981 will want to know *something* about how Betterton played it three hundred years, and Irving a hundred years, before. Even though their techniques may be discarded, their perceptions may sharpen or augment his own. This interest goes beyond the actor to embrace other theater practitioners: directors, designers, technicians. The theater tends to feed upon itself and, periodically, will draw upon its own past. The following chapters will point out some of these recurring cycles of theatrical behavior. When all is said and done, the range of theatrical possibilities is finite, and most of these possibilities had already been explored in the early stages of the art. There are only a few ways of arranging an audience in relation to the performance or of defining the actor's relationship to his or her role. Later theater tends to look back to earlier practices and revive those that, for new reasons, have once again become useful. Bertolt Brecht, hailed as a revolutionary in the modern theater, was in fact using devices familiar to Greek and Chinese audiences centuries ago. A recent staging of Lodovico Ariosto's (1474–1533) *Orlando Furioso,* which let the audience wander at will about the dispersed setting, was considered an avant-garde triumph; in fact, it reflected practices well known in the Middle Ages. Theater history is a history of rediscoveries, and the practitioner who knows the past will be well equipped to utilize the present.

There is, however, a wider justification for studying theater history, extending beyond the practitioner or theater student to embrace those who are concerned with history in *any* form: the simple fact that the theater provides a shortcut to history. It is a microcosm of its time. By its nature it responds to all contemporary trends, often before they are completely discernible in society at large. It seizes the moment. It echoes contemporary politics and philosophy. It reflects the language and class structure of its time. It takes whatever is urgent, or relevant, or even merely fashionable and dramatizes it. It has an eye for novelty. It exploits whatever is new and exciting in painting, music, dance, the written word. Even scientific and technological discoveries make an early entrance on the stage, often before the wider world is fully aware of them — either as the subject matter for plays or as part of the apparatus for staging them. London's Savoy Theatre, built in 1881, was fully lit by electric light when most private homes still made do with gas, and the manager appeared before the curtain nightly to reassure the audience that there was no danger.

The following chapters, therefore, will try to trace the development of the theater in place and time and to say what we know, or can reasonably conjecture, about what the buildings looked like, what sorts of audiences came to them, what kinds of plays they could expect to see, and how these plays, both in form and content, reflected the currents of contemporary life. There is much we do not know and probably never shall know. This survey will therefore also indicate what the principal sources of evidence are and where hard fact must be supplemented by intelligent guesswork based on practical theater experience. You may be surprised to learn how much of the theater of the past is still modern.

The Theater in Its Place

The following chapters will survey many different theater buildings and various ways of placing the audience in relation to the performance. Certain basic considerations, however, deserve attention here.

Any kind of performance needs a special place, a center of focus that will draw attention and distinguish it from other activities. In the early history of the theater this focal point may have involved nothing more elaborate than clearing a space for the actors to work in. The English mummers' play opens with the traditional cry of "Make room!" while a player with a broom sweeps out a circle on the floor. The act of sweeping here has obvious magical, purificatory associations, but, more practically, it also distinguishes the audience's space from the actors' space. In Japan sacred dances in the early shrines took place on a square of ground marked off by paper streamers. Often the performers set up a platform to give both height and focus; in its most elementary form this platform is the box from which the showman makes his spiel in the marketplace. Thus at a primitive level we already have the basic components of any theater building: a place where the audience sits or stands (and spectators could not expect to be comfortably accommodated for a long time) and another place, usually a raised area, where the performers are.

The specific form that these arrangements took, and the more elaborate structures into which the permanent theaters developed, varied according to time and circumstance. As a general rule the development of *plays* preceded the development of *theaters*. Since drama in any culture usually emerged as an offshoot of some other activity, the earliest performances tended to be given in surroundings designed for other purposes. The performers used whatever location they found suitable in buildings available to them, either as it was or with a minimum of adaptation. In the course of time, as drama became a regular feature of community life and demanded attention in its own right, special places were built to house it; and these theaters usually retained the features of the temporary structures that earlier generations had grown used to.

We can trace examples of this development from country to country and from age to age. The first theater is no more than a space, indoor or outdoor, where people are accustomed to assemble for other reasons. Into this the actors bring their simple portable stage. And the combination dictates the shape of the permanent theater that eventually appears. The characteristic structure of the Greek theater can be seen as deriving from the stone circle built for sacred dances in the open air, on the rim of which the actors set their temporary platform. In the Middle Ages the staging of religious drama continued to be influenced by memories of the earliest performances in churches. The stage that Shakespeare knew may have been influenced by the strolling players' custom of setting up their platform in an inn yard open to the sky. And the typical long, narrow shape of the French playhouse of the seventeenth century recalls the early practice of acting in an indoor tennis court. Since plays are usually written with a specific building in mind, the characteristic features of any drama may find their distant origin in buildings that originally had no connection with the drama at all.

2
A Theater for the Gods: Festival Drama in the Mediterranean World

The Origins

RITUAL DRAMA IN EGYPT

Examples of ritual drama, or ritual becoming drama, may be found world-wide. The most impressive body of evidence comes from the Mediterranean, where so many other features of our civilization began. Several examples may be found in Egypt. The Greek historian Herodotus (fifth century B.C.), who had traveled there, records a ritual combat over a sacred image, in which one band of priests tries to drag the cart containing the statue into its temple, while another band opposes them with sticks and clubs. Apparently the combat was real enough to produce many broken heads. This bloody ritual may well have come into being to preserve the memory of an earlier religious war, and short

Greek drama as a living festival. Revivals of the ancient plays are presented annually at the ancient theater of Epidaurus.

15

Rectangular "theatral areas" in Crete, such as those at Knossos (*below left*) or Phaistos (*left*) may have accommodated dramatic spectacles themselves, and may also have served as models for the earliest theaters on the Greek mainland. (*below*) The circular stone threshing floors still found throughout the Greek countryside may have inspired the circular orchestra of the Greek theater.

though it is, it already possesses features that we shall come to recognize as constants of drama: the element of conflict and the ability to summarize, reducing to one brief, dramatic encounter what may have taken many years in actual experience.

A much more elaborate Egyptian example is the *Triumph of Horus*, a ritual text perhaps at least as old as 1300 B.C. Some scholars argue that this was conceived from the beginning as a ceremonial play to be performed by priest-actors in the temple compound. It is the formalized reenactment of the victory of the god Horus over his rival Seth, in the shape of a hippopotamus, and his coronation as King of Upper and Lower Egypt. Modern reconstruction suggests that there was a reader, who provided the linking narration, and a chorus, who sang in the triumph. Whether it was actually a play in the strict sense is still disputed; but its dramatic qualities are evident, and that it can be acted has been proved by modern revivals. Its most interesting quality, from the standpoint of later drama, is the way in which language can be used to create setting and action. The word is the deed. When the chorus tells us we are at the Sacred Lake, we suppose ourselves there; and the excitement of the sacred hippopotamus hunt is brought before us by evocative language and symbolic gesture.

CRETE AND EARLY GREECE

As the center of power shifted from the southern to the northern shores of the Mediterranean, other manifestations dimly appear. The island kingdom of Crete, which provided a stepping-stone between Egypt and the emergent cities of Greece, had its own outdoor ritual celebrations. Excavations in the main towns have uncovered what archaeologists cautiously call "theatral areas" — rectangular stone-paved courtyards surrounded by tiers of steps or seats. The most impressive, in the Cretan capital of Knossos, lies within the palace complex, with a broad processional avenue leading into it and what may well have been a royal box, a dais for important spectators. What kinds of spectacles were offered in these places we do not know. Though we can now read Cretan writing, we have so far found no religious or dramatic literature. A surviving fragmentary picture shows us a crowd on bleachers, watching — but watching what? We are shown the spectators only, not the performance. Perhaps these were religious ceremonies, perhaps processions, perhaps the acrobatic bull-fights which played an important part in Cretan ritual. But though we know so little about its contents, the shape of the playing space is important. It is argued to have had an important influence on the theaters of the culture that followed.

As Crete declined in importance, the cities of mainland Greece grew, and this area is where our first systematic records of the history of the theater begin. This society was still an outdoor one; that is, most important public activities took place in the open air. It was a society of small city-states, where the mass of the population could assemble in the same place to participate in rites and ceremonies and perform their civic functions. It was a culture, too, where a sense of the dramatic marked many of the occasions of everyday life. Greek religion offers many examples. At a local festival of Artemis, the huntress goddess, young girls dressed up as bears, to be hunted by the citizenry. At the shrine of Eleusis, a few miles from Athens, initiates seem to have watched every year a sacred passion play about the goddess Demeter and her daughter Persephone. In myth Demeter was goddess of the crops. Her daughter was kidnapped by Hades, god of the underworld, and in her sorrow she so neglected her duties that the world was starving. A reconciliation was finally worked out whereby Persephone spent six months in the upper world and six in the world below. This was the story that seems to have been celebrated at Eleusis, with priests playing the roles in a symbolic drama of the seasons. Drama even infiltrated politics. The tyrant Peisistratus, returning to Athens from exile in 555 B.C., had himself accompanied by a woman dressed as the city's patron deity Athena, and the public was so impressed that they restored him to power. In a country whose life-style was public and extrovert, where emotions were freely displayed and argument was considered a fine art, it is not surprising that we find the flowering of a formal drama.

One word of caution is needed here. *Greek drama* is a misleading term. With brief exceptions there has never been a Greece, in the sense of a unified country with national aims and ambitions, until the modern era. Classical Greece was made up of a number of small, fiercely independent city-states, separated geographically by the mountains and temperamentally by local pride. Though sharing a few common assumptions, these cities had distinct dialects, patron deities, constitutions, and cultural patterns. Most of what we now call Greek art and literature comes from one city only, Athens; and this situation is particularly true of the drama. Though most communities had theaters of their own, the only plays we have come from Athens. Not Greek drama, then, but Athenian drama; and even here our evidence is only partial. Surviving scripts represent the work of only five major dramatists. Of their contemporaries and rivals — some of whom were judged to be better playwrights at the time — we have only scattered fragments. And for the five we have, we see but a fraction of their output. Euripides, for example, wrote some ninety plays; nineteen have survived. Thus we have to make judgments based on evidence that no statistician would consider a significant sample, and these judgments are always liable to be upset by the discovery of new evidence.

RELIGION AND DRAMA IN ATHENS

Such evidence as we have, in the plays themselves and in statements made by the Athenians about them, suggests that Greek drama took its beginnings from the religious ceremonies of the community and retained *some* religious connections for most of its history. Another caution is necessary here. With centuries of other traditions behind us, we have come to regard religious ceremonies as occasions for quiet observance rather than active participation and for hearing an inspirational message delivered by a member of the priestly caste. To talk of Greek drama as part of a religious ceremony, therefore, sometimes induces the feeling that the plays were intended to be like sermons, for edification rather than enjoyment. Nothing could be more misleading. Though various cults had their appointed priests, there was no such thing as a priestly caste, nor was there a sacred book. The Greeks worshiped their gods in diverse ways, most of them involving exuberant community participation and displays of physical or artistic skill. In Greece gods could be worshiped with a boxing matcn, with chariot races, with feats of arms, with poems, songs, and dances, and, eventually, with plays. Regular religious festivals brought such activities together, attracting tumultuous holiday crowds from both the host community and abroad, and those who were spectators on one occasion might well be participants in the next. This is the context out of which Greek drama evolved and in which it should properly be seen, though modern revivals can never come close to re-creating the festival atmosphere that the Greeks knew or the massive public celebrations involving song, dance, music, and the spoken word that they identified as drama. In the surviving plays the religious connection often seems tenuous at best. Gods usually appear in them, of course, and some of them explore, profoundly, the nature of the divine order and the ways of god with humanity. But some of the most powerful dramas are also the most humanistic, and others, particularly the later ones, are openly derisive of established notions of divinity. All these could still be embraced within the Greek concept of a religious festival, some to be applauded and some to be booed off the stage.

We noted earlier some general theories about the origin of drama, and we must now consider their specific relevance to Greece. As we have seen, the Mediterranean temperament created a climate in which various minor forms of dramatic activity already flourished. For the establishment of the theater as a major and increasingly independent art, we must look to Athens in the sixth century B.C.; a time when that city, under a succession of powerful leaders, was already showing signs of asserting the leadership in Greek affairs that was to mark its history for the next hundred years.

The Greeks had their own theory about how the drama started. They derived it from an already long-established tradition of choral songs and dances celebrating the major deities and local heroes and presumably already involving some mimic action, performed as festival events by groups drawn from the community. Enough evidence for these choruses survives to show that, though still narration, they were clearly on the verge of becoming drama proper. The Greeks, who liked to see their history in terms of single, dominant personalities rather than trends or social movements, attributed to one man the decisive step that transformed choral song into acted drama. This man was Thespis, the legendary first actor, who is said to have stepped out of the chorus, taken a solo role, and for the first time sang *as* the god rather than *about* the god.

How much truth lies in this legend we cannot now say. Undoubtedly it represents a simplification of what was in actuality a long and complex process. There does seem to have been a historical figure called Thespis, who engaged in various kinds of dramatic activity around the Greek countryside before making his first impact on Athens about 534 B.C. But no drama form has simple origins, and Thespis, though he has bequeathed his name to actors ever since, may have been only a catalyst in the process.

Certainly we know of other aspects of Greek ceremony that were also, like the choruses, on the verge of becoming drama. We know of the regular public recitals by trained bards of the poems of Homer. Both the *Iliad* and the *Odyssey* are, by their nature, very close to drama. They embody numerous first-person speeches, and the bards, as we know from Plato's later descriptions of them, were to all intents and purposes actors. In more modern times these epics have often been dramatized, with little effort. For the Greeks they may have made their own contribution to the evolutionary drama, particularly in the long narrative speeches that remain a notable characteristic of Greek tragedy. We have hints also of various experiments in lyric drama conducted by early poets who are now little more than names to us; and it is reasonable to assume that, as the Athenian festivals grew in complexity and importance, each of these activities influenced the others as well as having its own contribution to make.

The importance of the choral tradition in determining the shape of Greek drama, however, is supported by its continuing presence. Throughout the fifth century the chorus remained as the characteristic feature of both tragedy and comedy and as a valuable and versatile instrument for the dramatist. Once the actor had established himself as a performer distinct from the chorus, playing the role of god or hero as the story demanded, it was possible for the chorus to take roles, too, as worshipers, soldiers, citizens, or whatever was appropriate. The range of dramatic possibilities had increased, for actor and chorus could now engage in dialogue. But the chorus could still, at need, retain its original narrative function. Thus it could be in the play or out of it; the choral group could either participate in the action, as characters, or stand outside the action and comment upon it, as observers. This double function, which continued for most of the fifth century, gave Greek drama a distinctive quality that no subsequent drama form has quite been able to duplicate.

Deriving as they did from features of existing festivals, the plays were naturally assumed into the festivals themselves. In Athens the festivals involving drama were three in number, all honoring the god Dionysus. This deity was a latecomer into the Olympian pantheon and represented a type of religion that was in many ways oriental rather than Greek. His devotees engaged in mystical rites in which they claimed — under the influence of wine or self-hypnosis — to transcend their normal personalities and identify themselves with the godhead. (Our word *ecstasy* comes from the Greek *ek-stasis,* "standing outside oneself"; our *enthusiasm* means literally "having the god inside one.") Though exotic, Dionysus was a forceful god who infiltrated a number of exist-

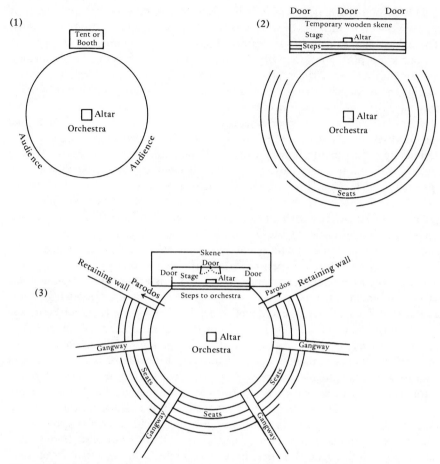

The development of the Greek theater of the fifth century B.C. (1) The simplest elements: dancing-floor and tent for changing. (2) Beginnings of an architectural form: wooden skene of stone foundations, wood seats. (3) The theater in stone.

ing cults as well as creating major festivals of his own. In Athens his temple stood at the foot of the Acropolis and probably served as the background for the earliest theatrical performances.

The Great or City Dionysia, his principal festival, occurred in late March and rapidly grew into an international event, attracting audiences not merely from Athens itself and its widespread network of tributary states but from important foreign powers besides. The Lenaea, held a couple of months earlier when it was still unwise to sail, was a Dionysiac festival of more local importance, while the Rural Dionysia, variable in date, carried the celebrations outside the city walls into the Attic countryside. In these celebrations the fledgling drama found a natural home, though history records one anonymous, early critic who complained that the plays had "nothing to do with Dionysus" and did not belong there. Other commentators, whether friendly or hostile, have pointed out the obvious affinity between the Dionysiac worshiper whose personality merges with that of the god and the actor who casts off his own character to assume another.

The Greek Theater: Its Components and Relationships

THE THEATER AND THE COMMUNITY

The Dionysiac performances, like the festivals out of which they grew, remained part of the community enterprise. A professional theater with a continuous, year-round organization was still far in the future. With performances confined to some three weeks in every year, each play was a special event, to be anticipated with pleasure, watched with attention, and treasured in memory. Significant passages were learned by heart. Striking sentiments from the plays became embedded in the language as proverbs, serving as a starting point for argument and discussion. Many of the audience had already served as performers or could expect to do so in the future. Thus the Athenian theater developed an audience that was not merely knowledgeable but personally involved, and that soon acquired for plays the kind of memory that Americans have for baseball scores or Australians have for cricket scores. In such an atmosphere the drama soon began to feed upon itself. Virtually every play we have contains echoes from, or allusions to, some other play that has gone before. Aristophanes, writing a comedy in 405 B.C., can base a key joke on a line written in a tragedy twenty-three years before in the certainty that his audience will catch the reference.

Like other forms of civic duty, the theater was the work of amateurs, volunteers. There was no such thing, as yet, as a professional playwright, no way a person could make a living in the theater by the pen. The plays were written by Athenian citizens who spent most of their time in other activities and could earn little from the theater but esteem. Aeschylus (525–456 B.C.), the earliest Greek playwright whose works have been preserved, was regarded as the greatest poet of his age; but when he died, his tombstone recorded the battles in which he had fought against the Persians and said nothing of his dramatic career at all. Sophocles (496–406 B.C.) held office as general (tradition says he was appointed because of the success of his *Antigone*) and as treasurer of the tribute money paid by dependent states to Athens. Even Euripides (480–406 B.C.), who seems to have come nearer to being a full-time playwright than any other ancient figure we know, held his share of public offices. This was no more than was expected in a community where the state came first and private interests second. But since each festival was also a competition, the author whose work was judged to be the best would have the satisfaction of knowing that his victory was inscribed on stone in the city archives and that in the streets around the theater some monument would rise that bore his name.

ACTOR AND CHORUS

Just as there were no professional playwrights, so there were no professional actors, though the number of trained personnel rapidly increased. Once the initial distinction between actor and chorus had been made, it was logical and inevitable that the development should continue. For some time the playwright was also his own chief actor. Aeschylus, we are told, added a second actor to assist him, and Sophocles added a third. During the fifth century the number never rose above three, at least in tragedy. This restriction may have been due to the competitive nature of the event and the need to impose some limits on the contestants. It may also have been urged by financial considerations, since the festivals were supported by the state and actors were paid for their services. In 431 B.C. Athens entered into a costly, and ultimately disastrous, war with Sparta, which enforced increasing economies at home. The three-actor limit, however, did not imply a limitation of roles. As the drama grew increasingly complex, the actor could expect to play several parts in the same work, though there could never be more than three speaking characters on stage at the same time.

At first the actor seems to have had no status as an independent artist. He functioned merely as the mouthpiece of the poet. The institution of a separate prize for actors, as distinct from that for playwrights, at the festival of 449 B.C. suggests that actors were beginning to assert their independence and demand that their own contribution should be recognized. Certainly as the fifth century proceeds, we become increasingly aware of actors as personalities in their own right. Sophocles is said to have been the first to write plays with specific actors in mind, and Euripides too seems to have had his favorites.

Although actors became increasingly important to the festival activities, there was still no large body of professionals. We can detect a continuing history of a master-disciple relationship in which the playwright first trained his own assistants and they, in time, passed on their accumulated expertise to others; but though the actors were paid for their festival services, there was still no way in which they could earn a full-time living from the theater. Performers of note might be invited to appear at local festivals, just as dramatists were occasionally asked to produce their works in other cities, but there were too few opportunities to justify, or sustain, an acting profession. Probably many of the part-time actors spent the balance of the year teaching public speaking. A Greek actor was by definition a skilled orator, and in a society where most decisions were made by the citizen assembly in public debate, formal rhetoric was a necessary art. We know of several actors entrusted with missions of high diplomatic importance because they could deliver a speech more impressively than anybody else. We cannot speak of actresses, however, for there were none. In a male-dominated society it was unthinkable that women should participate in drama. The great female roles of Greek drama — Hecuba, Jocasta, Antigone, Medea, even Lysistrata — were written to be played by men.

Choruses, unpaid, were drawn from the citizen body at large. Each festival needed a considerable number. In the early theater, up to the last years of Aeschylus's career, each chorus seems to have numbered fifty, a figure already established in mythology as the canonical number for large groups — fifty Argonauts, fifty daughters of Danaus, fifty children of Hecuba, and so on. In later years this number was reduced to either twelve or fifteen (the evidence, as on so many important issues of Greek theater practice, is unclear); this reduction may have stemmed from a desire to simplify the administrative problems of the festival or from the increasing financial stringency brought on by the war. Though the chorus members contributed their services free, they still had to be costumed and trained. Costuming was an expensive business, usually imposed on some rich citizen as a form of taxation, and men were rumored to have bankrupted themselves in the process.

Even with the reduced numbers, however, a good proportion of the citizen body was involved each year, and this in time created a knowledgeable and critical audience well equipped to judge the subtleties and intricacies of an art in which they had participated. Choruses were trained by the poets themselves or by specialists who, like the actors, became increasingly professional as the century wore on. This high level of public involvement was consistent with the spirit of the time. To perform in the chorus was no less a civic duty than voting in the assembly or serving on a jury; and it is noteworthy that when the temper of the age changed after Athens lost the war, and the traditional democratic institutions went into a decline, the chorus rapidly disappeared from the plays.

THEATER AND POLITICS

Although the theater grew out of, and continued to be attached to, the religious festivals, it acquired increasing secular importance as a political weapon and a focus for public discussion. The concept of art for art's sake had little meaning in fifth-century Greece. Any art was expected to serve a social function. The Greek vases we now hail as masterpieces and place in museums were originally made for everyday use, statues were made for worship, and plays were expected to provide instruction and example. In a community where most of the population could assemble in one place at the same time, the plays offered a powerful and immediate way of bringing important issues to the public attention. The playwright was a *didaskalos,* "teacher," not merely of his actors and chorus but of the public at large. His plays were expected not only to provide entertainment (which they did; if he fails to do this, a playwright can do nothing else) but to contribute to the common good. Thus such early examples of dramatic criticism as we have ask not "Is the play good?" but "What is it good for?" and it was not until a century later that Aristotle could write dramatic criticism based solely on dramatic merit.

It follows inevitably that Athenian plays have a strong patriotic slant. The appearance of local deities could be counted on to produce applause, and a city that gloried in its democracy continued to enshrine its legendary kings and aristocratic heroes in affectionate memory. The goddess Athena, Athens's patroness and founder, plays a dominant part in Aeschylus's *Oresteia,* and in other plays Athenian kings regularly appear as savior figures. In Sophocles' *Oedipus at Colonus* it is Theseus, the legendary unifier of Attica and liberator of Athens from foreign rule, who gives sanctuary to the old blind outcast when all the rest have turned against him. In Euripides' *The Madness of Heracles* the same Theseus offers hope and comfort to the protagonist, who has killed his own wife and children in delirium, and persuades him to restore himself to the living world. Euripides was the most caustic of the tragedians and, for most of his career, a relentless critic of Athenian pretensions; but even he, in *Medea,* could write a paean of praise to the glories of Athens and introduce King Aigeus, Theseus's father and hardly less revered, as the savior of his heroine in distress.

Conversely, the Spartans, with whom the Athenians were at war from 431 on, and who had been viewed with strong suspicion long before that, tend to be cast as villains. Several tragedies, whatever their main theme, have political side issues dealing with the relationship between Athens and other states. Aeschylus's mammoth *Oresteia,* whose theme is nothing less than the relationship between gods and men, takes time to reflect on the desirability of keeping on friendly terms with the city of Argos. Orestes the Argive, acquitted by an Athenian court for the murder of his mother, makes his farewell with a speech of obvious relevance to the contemporary political situation:

> No governor of Argos
> Shall come with warlike preparation to this land.
> For if any are unmindful of the oaths we swear,
> We, who shall then be buried in our graves,
> Shall frustrate them and bring all their works to nothing,
> Confound their marches, cast the evil eye upon
> Their goings, so they count the work ill-spent.

Thus a dramatic character speaks to the actual political situation, and contemporary expediency is given legendary sanction.

It must be noted, too, that while Athenian drama deals plentifully with the misfortunes of other royal houses — particularly those of Argos and Thebes — there are few surviving plays about Athenian disasters. We distinguish between legend and history, but the Greeks did not. For them the Homeric poems were authentic historical documents, and the outbreak of the war with

Sparta was accompanied by accusations dredged up from the remote mythology of both sides. In this context plays, which took the bulk of their material from legend, could still speak with an urgent, contemporary voice and use the past to illustrate and justify the present.

Characteristics of Greek Tragedy

Though the Greek tragedies we have cover some three-quarters of a century and reflect widely differing points of view, they all share certain common features.

First is the pro-Athenian bias, not merely in the obvious sense of flattering Athenian claims and pretensions but in the more important aspect of dealing with issues of immediate public concern. Virtually every tragedy we possess can be shown to touch on some contemporary question. What keeps the plays alive is the fact that these questions have turned out to have continuing significance, and their implications are still valid in the modern world.

Second, the plays take their material from the common store of myth and legend. (Aeschylus's *The Persians,* now recognized as the first Greek tragedy we have, and dealing with a battle only eight years old, is a unique exception.) This body of traditional material was a great aid to dramatic economy. The poet could assume a basic knowledge of the general situation and spend a minimum of time in exposition. Surely, too, the Greeks knew what many later playwrights have recognized: that delicate contemporary issues can be more safely dealt with in historical guise.

Third, because of the compressed nature of the festivals, Greek tragedies were short. Though each playwright was required to submit three tragedies, the total playing time was not much more than four and a half hours. For all that happens in *Oedipus the King,* the play is only ninety minutes long and brief by comparison with most later drama. Much of the power of Greek tragedy lies in this compression.

Fourth, certain structural constants embrace the century. All tragedies are composed as an alternation of acted scenes (*episodes*) and choruses, though the way in which these elements are interwoven, and the relative time and importance attributed to each, may vary widely according to the year of composition, the inclinations of the playwright, and his choice of subject.

Fifth, the emotional impact of the music and dance out of which the drama began continued as an integral component of the art throughout the century. Greek tragedy was a *musical* performance to an extent inaccessible to us now, for all but a fragment of the music has been lost. Language, however, preserves a memory of the fact: ancient Greek *tragōdia,* "tragedy," yields modern Greek *tragoudi,* "song."

THE PERFORMING SPACE

In their presentation all Greek plays had certain common features. In its general outline the Greek theater changed little over the course of the century. The architectural features that Euripides knew at the end of his career were virtually the same as those that Aeschylus knew at the beginning of his. Few fundamental changes occurred for centuries after this, and a citizen of the later Roman Empire transplanted back to the theater of Sophocles would soon have made himself at home. Of course, a few changes did occur, but the limited nature of the festival offerings acted as a brake upon experiment. Many features of the performances continued to be dictated by tradition, and any innovation, however small, was widely commented upon and often censured.

The origins of any drama form influence the shape of the theater no less than the shape of the play. This fact is particularly important in Greek drama, where fifth-century theater building seems to show clear marks of the drama's hypothetical beginnings. Just as the most distinctive feature of the drama was the chorus, so the central component of the theater building was the place where the chorus sang and danced: a circular, stone-paved floor called the *orchestra,* which means, simply, "dancing place." Some scholars see this component as clear evidence for the evolution of the drama, as the Greeks themselves believed, from the earlier choral dances. They suggest that in the primitive rural communities the most obvious sites for such dances would have been the stone threshing floors, examples of which may still be seen about the Greek countryside. The space available indeed may have dictated the pattern of the dances. There is continuing evidence for circular folk dances in Greece from ancient through to modern times. Thus it is argued that when choral dances became a regular part of the religious festivals, a special dancing place, in the now traditional shape, was built in front of the temple or shrine, and this in turn became the orchestra of the Greek theater. Another theory, however, which has increasing archaeological support, suggests that the earliest Greek orchestras were not circular but rectangular and influenced directly by the "theatral areas" we have noted in the palaces of Crete. By the time Aeschylus wrote, however, the orchestra had certainly assumed a circular form. We can trace a few stones marking the earliest rim of such an orchestra in the precinct of the Temple of Dionysus in Athens, and this shape remained the typical one for more than a century.

In the ordinary Greek theater audiences sat on the steep hillside, which gave a good view of the performance below. At first there were no seats at all; local Athenian tradition remembered a favorite tree in which spectators perched to watch the dancing. Later, wooden benches were built, which in time were replaced by stone. The characteristic bowl shape, with the circular orchestra surrounded by tiers of seats rising far up the slope, became the model for other Greek communities, and it was naturally suited to the hilly terrain.

Thus the fifth-century theater had an organic relationship to the country that produced it; it was not imposed upon the terrain but grew out of it, and in a climate that encouraged outdoor activity, there was no effective limit upon size. In Athens the Theater of Dionysus held about fifteen thousand spectators, perhaps about half the city's total population, so that most of the fully franchised citizen body who wished to see a play could do so at one sitting. Other important sites, such as Corinth and Syracuse, had theaters of similar capacity, and though smaller structures were built for local audiences at the rural festivals, it was the large theaters that the playwrights wrote their plays for. This situation had obvious implications for the way in which Greek drama had to be written and performed. It had implications for the audience, too. Even though the ancients were smaller than we are, and though many brought their own cushions, the seating was hard, cramped, and uncomfortable. A full day at the festival must have been a test of endurance. Small wonder that crowds often grew restive — when bored, they drummed their feet, en masse, against the benches and were known to pelt the actors with fruit and pebbles — or that the plays contain so many devices to catch their attention and maintain their interest.

The earliest orchestra at Athens was set in front of the Temple of Dionysus, and the wall of this temple was probably the first stage setting, providing both a sounding board for the actors' voices and a place where they could wait between entrances. By the middle of the fifth century a special background had been built, of which the stone foundation can still be seen. It was made of wood and so could be dismantled between festivals, when the orchestra was used for other purposes. It was still little more than a simple wall with painted architectural decoration, providing a central entrance and a neutral, all-purpose background. Probably, too, a low platform was added at this time to give the actors prominence and to distinguish them from the chorus singing and dancing in the orchestra. The chorus normally entered the orchestra in procession down a broad aisle (*parodos*) on each side. The actors could move down into the orchestra, by steps or ramps, when the action demanded, and the chorus could occasionally move up onto the stage; yet the plays show a desire to keep the two groups separate, with the chorus moving as a complex unit on the level floor and the actors playing their episodes on the platform.

The vocabulary of the Greek theater suggests its simple beginnings. *Skene,* the Greek word for the stage house, means literally "hut" or "tent," and this is presumably what it originally was: a simple, temporary structure erected as the actors' place on the rim of the orchestra circle. Even after it grew larger and more complex, it continued to be known by its original name; the theater has a way of preserving words long after their literal meaning has vanished. *Skene,* by way of the Latin *scaena,* gives us our word *scene;* but it is important to realize that the Greek theater had no illusionistic scene painting in our sense of the word. No attempt was made to change the background to suit the particular location demanded by the play, and our first evidence for such scene changing does not appear until a century later. The *skene* merely provided a formal background; the indication of the setting was left to the audience's imagination

The Theater of Dionysus in Athens as it stands today. Here the works of Aeschylus, Sophocles, Euripides, Aristophanes, and Menander were performed for the first time.

The Theater of Dionysus: stone foundation of the wooden *skene* used in the fifth century B.C. Note the slots in the stone to hold wooden uprights. The small projection may have served as a basis for the *ekkyklema*.

Orchestra, seating, and remains of *skene* of the theater at Apollo's shrine at Delphi.

Though the plays were written with the larger centers in mind, smaller communities had their own theaters. The theater at Oropus, cramped for space, has a tiny orchestra and a *parodos* stepped into the hillside. Seats within the rim of the orchestra were later additions for important spectators.

and the language of the dramatist. In the earlier plays, at least, the roof of the *skene* conventionally represented heaven, in which the gods could appear.

This extreme simplicity was not a disadvantage but an asset. It freed the way for the creative use of language and left it to the dramatist to create his own environment. The poet's words provided appropriate scenic identification and local color. A number of the plays we have take place in front of a house or a palace. The entire action of Sophocles' *Oedipus the King* unfolds before the palace of Oedipus in Thebes, and that of Euripides' *Medea* occurs before Medea's house in Corinth. For such works the *skene,* which already provided an architectural facade, would obviously serve with a minimum of explanation.

In plays that are set elsewhere, however, the author is careful from the beginning to let us know where we are and to paint a word picture that will take the place of realistic scenery. Here, clearly, the theater retains one important element of ritual. To say something is to make it so. Thus the neutral background of the Greek theater became a blank slate on which the audience could see anything the author cared to indicate. Aeschylus's *Prometheus Bound,* for example, is set on a mountain peak in some forgotten corner at the end of the world. The theater did not *show* this, nor did it care to. Everything is in the language, and the play opens with an evocative description of place:

> *Strength.* Now we have reached our journey's end, land's end,
>> The Scythian wasteland, the untrodden desert.
>> Hephaestus, you must look to the instructions
>> The Father issued you. The offender here
>> Must be pinioned to a mountaintop, held high
>> In chains of adamant that never shall be broken.

And Hephaestus, in reply, makes clear the barrenness and desolation of the place:

> Son of Themis who spoke true, my high-minded friend,
> Against my will and yours I have to rivet you
> In brazen chains unbreakable upon this rock
> Where no man walks, where you will know no voice,
> No human face. You will be roasted by the sun
> Till bloom of skin is gone. And you will have two pleasures:
> When night drapes her starry robe across the sun
> And when the sun returns to chase the night-chill.
> As each comes round in season you will feel its sting
> And smart, for your deliverer has not been born.

This description brings Prometheus's place of joyless confinement before us more vividly than a painted setting could do, for it leaves room for the imagination to work. Similarly, at the end of the play, when Prometheus is swept down to the underworld in a cataclysmic storm, language does simply and effectively what could hardly be accomplished even by modern stage mechanics:

> Now it is no longer talk
> But happening; earth pulses;

> Out of the deep the thunder
> Rolls around me, lightning writhes
> And flashes fire, dust dances
> High on the whirling air, and there
> Is contest in heaven, as the winds
> Blow at variance together.
> Sky and water are one.

In a later play, and a different mood, Sophocles sketches, at the beginning of *Oedipus at Colonus,* a charming word picture of the countryside near Athens where the blind king ends his days:

> Father, poor father. We are coming to a city,
> There, in the distance. I can see the watchtowers.
> And this is surely sacred ground, where vines and laurels
> And olive trees grow wild; a haunt of birds
> Where nightingales make music in the coverts.
> And here there is a shelf of rock. Sit down.
> It has been a long day's journey for an old man.

SPACE AND TIME IN GREEK DRAMA

The verbal scene painting done by early Greek dramatists has another great advantage. Settings established by language alone last only as long as the author wishes them to. There is no painted scenery to limit the action. Once the ambience has been established and the dramatic point made, the details can be allowed to lapse from mind if they are no longer relevant; or the imagined setting may be changed in a moment, in major or minor ways, provided that the necessary verbal cues are given. We are dealing, in fact, with a kind of theater that is very similar to radio drama, where the author's imagination can flow freely, unimpeded by technical limitations, as long as the author is careful to take the audience along. The enormous flexibility this gives to the play is one of the Greek theater's most valuable assets and is particularly obvious in comedy, where the action may jump from one supposed location to another at a second's notice and range with equal freedom over earth, heaven, and the underworld.

In this scenic void the normal laws of time, like those of space, also may be suspended. Events that would be separated by hours or days in real time may follow each other in rapid succession. In Aeschylus's *Agamemnon* the chorus, representing old men of Argos, first learn of the fall of Troy from a chain of beacon fires from the captive city across the island stepping-stones to mainland Greece. This first news is almost immediately reinforced by a herald who has traveled from Troy by ship — a journey that in real time would have taken days.

In the drama there is no incongruity in this compression of time. We accept that time is manipulable if it serves the dramatic effect. Conversely, events that would occupy only a few moments of real time may be extended to increase their dramatic impact. In Sophocles' *Antigone* the desperate heroine goes to perform the final rites over her brother's body, which has been denied burial by law. She sprinkles dust over him, is caught by the guards, and is brought back for punishment. In real time those events are consecutive. In the drama we are shown them piecemeal, in three scenes punctuated by choral interludes, for the sake of the cumulative effect.

This freedom with time shows itself in another important way. We have seen how the dramatists wrote plays that, though based on legendary material, still spoke to the immediate situation. In Greek tragedy one is always conscious of a double time standard, the fictitious time of a drama set in the remote past and the real time of the audience sitting in the theater to watch the play. These two times may meet and merge; the plays may contain direct allusions to the audience's present experience, apparent anachronisms justified by the loose time convention of the theater.

WORDS AND ACTION

Later critics have often commented upon the apparent lack of action, and particularly violent action, in Greek tragedy. They have sometimes professed to find the plays overly cold and formal, showing characters who talk a great deal about violent actions and emotions but are rarely seen indulging in them. Although the plays concern themselves with death, madness, battle, murder, and mutilation, the bloodier events take place offstage. We are led up to them; we see the results in dead bodies or blinded eyes. But we do not see the events themselves. Rhetoric substitutes for action.

It is perfectly true that rhetoric is the single most powerful component of Greek tragedy and that we hear more than we see. But there are good reasons for this, some deriving from the physical nature of the theater, others from the playwrights themselves and what they considered drama to be. One of these reasons was undoubtedly aesthetic. The Greeks, like any good writer of ghost stories and like Alfred Hitchcock in the movies, clearly understood that horror hinted at is more disturbing than horror seen. Occasionally a modern revival, succumbing to the contemporary taste for stage violence, attempts to bring these horrors into full view. There have been productions of *Oedipus the King* in which Oedipus has been shown plunging the points of his wife's brooches into his eyes, and modern stage technology can produce convincing blood. Film, especially, is able to be graphic. But none of these effects quite equals the horror that Sophocles produces, not by showing the effect but by bringing on a messenger to tell about it — a description so vivid, so compelling, that audiences regularly leave the theater convinced that they have seen what they have merely heard. The Greek theater provides room for the imagination to work. We become willing accomplices in the dramatic event. Just as the word

The three acting levels of the Greek theater, showing the ekkyklema in position: chorus in orchestra, actor on stage, god on roof.

is the stage setting, so too the word is the deed. We see what the poet tells us to see.

Similarly, in Greek plays stage death is conspicuously avoided. Although the plays are full of death and dying, on only two occasions in the whole of Greek tragedy does death actually occur on stage. There seem to be more pragmatic, but no less cogent, reasons for this. Greek tragedy, as we have seen, restricted itself to a maximum of three speaking actors. In many plays when a leading character is killed, his body is exposed as a focal point for subsequent lament or discussion. If the character died in full view of the audience and his body continued to lie on stage, the play lost an actor. (It is instructive to see how often in Greek tragedy exits are abruptly manipulated simply because the actor is needed to play someone else in the next scene.) Thus the customary practice was to have the character die offstage and his body replaced by a dummy. The body was displayed to the audience by one of the few pieces of mechanical equipment the Greek theater had, a small rolling platform called the *ekkyklema* (literally, "something that is rolled out"), which was pushed into view through the central door. The actor was then free to change his mask and costume and reappear as another character. Occasionally the *ekkyklema* was used to reveal other tableaux, things that were supposed to have happened inside the house but whose results needed to be seen. In Euripides' *The Madness of Heracles* we have such a tableau of Heracles in a coma after the murder of his wife and children; he gradually comes to his senses, sees the wreckage and the slaughtered bodies, and realizes what he has done.

Even the most casual reading, however, shows that the Greeks did not avoid scenes of violence totally. We have Oedipus lurching blindly from the doorway, reaching for the saving hands of the chorus; blinded Polymestor in Euripides' *Hecuba* groping in vain for the bodies of his murdered children; the chorus of slave women in Aeschylus's *Libation Bearers* tearing their faces and their clothes in mourning; Philoctetes, in Sophocles' tragedy of that name, succumbing to spasms of wrenching agony from the festering wound in his foot. These are but a few examples. We must remember, too, that what we read by necessity as pure *description* may have been made *visual* in the original production by the pantomimic dancing of the chorus. In Aeschylus's *Agamemnon,* for example, the chorus sing at length of the sacrifice of Iphigeneia by her father to secure the gods' favor for the Greek armada against Troy. It is more than likely that when Aeschylus staged the first performance, the narration was illustrated by dance, and the sacrifice of Iphigeneia was seen as a ballet. This device has been used convincingly in modern revivals. On numerous occasions, even in the actors' speeches, evocative dance movement could have illustrated the narrative or given metaphors a visual form. The Greek temperament, always prone to histrionic display, would certainly suggest this effect, and the supposed coldness of Greek tragedy may lie not in the works themselves but in their commentators. We need to remind ourselves that the Greeks were, then as now, vivid, excitable, prone to rapid anger and equally rapid appeasement, and given to loud, colorful talk and emotional display. Read in the right light, the plays reveal this temperament, even though the passions are harnessed into formal verse or, too often, obscured under pompous translation.

The impact of the plays, however, remains largely rhetorical, a fact that is explicable, and indeed inevitable, when we consider the conditions in which the actors worked. Here the dominant factor was the theater's size. We have already noted that the principal Greek theaters were far larger than any modern equivalent. Statistics, perhaps, only become fully meaningful when one sees them at work; for instance, when one sits in the theater at Epidarus, the finest surviving example of a Greek theater and home of an annual festival of ancient drama, and sees a crowd of fourteen thousand people filling up the tiers of seats. The acting area is dwarfed by the auditorium. Detail is lost. At such a remove from the action most of the audience are conscious only of the large, sweeping gestures, the mass effects. They see the chorus as Americans see a football game, and from the same angle, looking down on a pattern of colored dots deployed across the stone face of the orchestra. It has been calculated that to the spectator in the back row of the Theater of Dionysus, the actor looked about three-quarters of an inch high. In such a theater visual detail counted for little. It is noticeable that at no moment in extant Greek tragedy is any vital point of dramatic information conveyed by sight alone. The dramatists could not rely on the audience's sight. The audience was always *told* what was happening, and the telling was safe, for the theaters were acoustically superb. The natural bowl shape lay like an ear on the ground. Every word carried, and a competent actor could make himself heard without artificial aids in the furthest reaches of the auditorium. Thus although the Greek word *drama* means "something done," for most of the audience a play was something heard. Words were the dramatists' principal medium.

In Greek plays, then, the ear is more important than the eye. We are told everything we need to know, often, we may think — for we are accustomed to more intimate theaters — *more* than we need to know. Characters almost invariably tell us who they are within half-a-dozen lines of their first appearances. They identify other characters as they enter. They tell us what they are doing themselves, as they do it, and what the others are doing. They tell us what they are thinking and feeling and what emotions they detect in others. In Euripides' *Hecuba* the captive Trojan princess Polyxena pleads with her Greek captor Odysseus to spare her life. She turns to appeal to him, and he rebuffs her. We know exactly what happens here because it is all in the words:

> Odysseus, I can see you hide your hand
> Under your cloak, and turn away your face
> To stop me touching you. You need not worry.

If this were a modern script, these lines would be unnecessary; a simple stage direction would suffice. But in the Greek theater the actor has to show *and* tell. Similarly, in Euripides' *Medea* Jason asks his wife, "Why do you hide your face, begin to weep?" He has to ask this because there is no other way the audience could know that Medea was crying. A modern dramatist would simply use a stage direction, *Medea weeps;* and any actress worth her salary can cry on cue.

This reliance on the spoken word extends to other aspects of the plays. From necessity and convenience the playwrights' favored devices were rhetorical. They wrote for an audience accustomed to listen, in a way that a modern audience is not, and for a community used to conducting its public affairs in open, formal debate. Tragedy thus fell naturally into the rhetorical patterns already familiar in the assembly and the law courts — and the influence of the latter was powerful. Although the plays were religious in the sense that they were part of a religious festival, they took the secular assemblies as their model. Characters addressed each other in long, elaborate speeches framed according to the customary rules of formal rhetoric. Often these addresses, particularly the messenger's speeches recounting a violent offstage event, became forceful, self-contained set pieces, and they were favored by actors who knew what a powerful effect they made on the audience. In the later Greek theater when the star system had developed, some leading actors openly preferred the messenger's roles. They knew these gave them the best moments of the play.

Similarly, at moments of high crisis the action in a Greek tragedy tends to fall into the pattern of a formal debate. This device may seem strange to us because debating is no longer part of our social pattern. For the Greeks it was a natural and acceptable way of marshaling arguments on both sides of a case, a wavelength to which the audience was instinctively attuned. In *Medea* the first encounter between Jason, the husband who is deserting his wife to make a better match, and Medea, the wife faced with the loss of home, fortune, and security, takes a pattern obviously shaped by law court practice, with speeches of exactly equal length delivered on each side and each accusation met by a rebuttal. Medea enumerates all the sacrifices she has made for Jason and argues that he cannot, in all conscience, reject her now. Jason replies to her case point by point, arguing that, far from betraying her, he has benefited her immeasurably by bringing her from her barbaric land to enjoy Greek law and Greek society.

In many plays the debate is the nucleus of the drama; in some the whole play is framed as a debate, with the audience sitting as judges to award praise or blame. Once again, therefore, we recognize that given the physical conditions of the Greek theater, the dividing line between drama and reality was a thin one that could easily be crossed. In the public assembly, which met in a structure very similar to the theater, the citizens heard opposing politicians argue their ideas. In the theater they heard the same issues thinly disguised as dramatic fiction. Though the characters might represent Oedipus, Hecuba, or Agamemnon, the sentiments expressed and the means used to express them came very close to the realities of everyday life.

DRAMATIC VERSE

Greek plays were written in verse, the customary medium for ceremonial performances, and several different verse forms were used within the play. The actors' parts were normally composed in iambic trimeters, a rhythm adopted by the ancients as the closest poetic equivalent to the rhythm of ordinary speech. This form gave a line of six metrical feet based on the iambus (a short syllable followed by a long), though various substitutions were permitted for variety. The closest English equivalent is Shakespeare's iambic pentameter, which employs the same basic rhythm; most translators use English iambics to reproduce the Greek.

At moments of high emotion the actor could burst into song. This transition is clearly marked in the Greek, and usually in the English translations also, by a change of meter. These sung, or lyric, portions used a variety of meters, the exact structure of which is not always entirely clear to us. The choral songs (*stasima*) that punctuated the episodes were in lyric meters also, and they often had a balanced structure in which one portion of the chorus answered another in metrical responses. These choral lyrics are often extremely intricate. Greek musical theory recognized several musical modes, each with its own emotional connotations, and we can similarly detect certain metrical patterns recurring in the choruses for similar types of effect. Greek dramatists had a strong tendency, for example, to use a marching rhythm for the *parodos,* or processional entrance of the chorus into the orchestra, which marks the true beginning of the play. *Parodos* thus means both the aisle down which the chorus enters and the opening song. Greek plays were thus closer to opera than spoken drama, and it is possible that there was a musical accompaniment to what we now usually refer to as the spoken portions, turning them into a kind of recitative. We know that flutes provided the principal accompaniment, but other instruments occasionally appear in the plays, such as trumpets, drums, and tambourines.

When actors converse with each other, Greek tragedy regularly uses a strict form of dialogue called *stichomythia,* in which one character speaks a complete verse line, to be answered by another complete verse line from the other. A typical example comes from Aeschylus's *The Libation Bearers,* as Orestes, home from exile, steels himself to kill his mother:

> *Clytemnestra.* You took my youth. Should I not share your age?
> *Orestes.* You killed my father. Would you share my house?
> *Clytemnestra.* Have you no terror of a mother's curse?
> *Orestes.* You bore me, and then cast me out to sorrow!
> *Clytemnestra.* Gave you to friends! This was no casting out!
> *Orestes.* I was born of a free father, and you sold me.

The pattern is rhythmical and regular, and lines are rarely split between speakers, as they so often are in later verse drama.

The formality of this device has caused translators, readers, and modern actors some problems, as it seems oddly stilted, even in an already highly formal context. Though some scholars have derived it from a question-and-answer pattern used in earlier religious ritual and remaining embedded in the drama, its retention may have had more practical uses. We come back to the size of the Greek theater and how little most of the audience could see. They certainly could not see lips moving. The actors were, in any case, masked; and though the chorus was probably usually maskless, their faces would have been little more than blurs in such a setting. Without clear *visual* identification of the speaker, therefore, random dialogue, in the manner of everyday conversation or even of realistic stage practice, could have been dangerously misleading. The audience could never have been sure which character was saying which line, particularly if, as seems to be the case, all actors used a standardized tragic chant with minimal vocal differentiation between one character and another. With stichomythic dialogue, however, a regular and predictable pattern was provided. The audience knew that at the end of the verse line the speaker changed, and dialogue became a verbal Ping-Pong with lines thrown regularly and rhythmically from one character to another. One notices how, even in the alternation of long speeches, such as in the debates that we have noted as the nucleus of many tragedies, the author is usually careful (as in radio drama) to make clear who is saying what. Often the chorus is used as a form of verbal punctuation to mark a change of speaker, but even without these the change is usually quite clear. For example, the earliest Greek manuscripts made no identification of speaker at all; they used a mark to indicate a change of speaker but did not note the character's name. Later editors have had to do this for themselves, and they usually found no difficulty in doing so.

So once again we see how the physical features of the theater dictated certain literary features of the play. Some of these, hallowed by classical tradition, remained in use long after the Greek period, when the physical features of the theater had changed. For example, stichomythic dialogue continued to appear in drama for centuries afterward.

MOVEMENT AND CHARACTERIZATION

It follows from the points emphasized above that a Greek actor had first and foremost to be a good speaker. His voice, in this theater and with this kind of play, was his most important instrument. Aristotle, writing in the fourth century, couples acting and music as arts chiefly appreciable by the ear. Our information about actors' training throughout classical antiquity relates chiefly to the voice.

But, of course, the actor had a physical presence, too. Movement and gesture were still components of his art, though less important ones than they are today. Our information on fifth-century acting technique is scanty; yet we can make some reasonable conjectures. The actor's stage behavior was conditioned by both his theater and his costume.

Open-air acting has its own laws; it must always be bigger and broader than that in the more confined and intimate surroundings of an indoor playhouse. Costuming also had a broadening, generalizing effect, and the primary way this generalizing effect was brought about was through the use of masks for the actors. The device probably had its origin in predramatic ritual, where the priest-performer concealed his face for two reasons: to inspire awe in the congregation by persuading them that he was something other than an ordinary human being, and to protect himself from the divine resentment of the gods he was impersonating by avoiding recognition. The clearest historical illustration of this dichotomy comes from Roman rather than from Greek sources and from ceremonial rather than from dramatic behavior. For the triumphal procession that escorted a victorious Roman general through the city streets (the ancient version of the ticker tape parade, familiar to all, if not from Roman history at least from historical movies), the general had his face painted bright red in the likeness of the statue of Jupiter that stood on the Capitol. Behind him stood a

In its production of *The House of Atreus,* John Lewin's modern version of Aeschylus's *Oresteia,* the Guthrie Theater, Minneapolis, sought to recapture the appearance of ancient masks and costumes. (*above*) Clytemnestra confronts Agamemnon, the husband she is about to murder. (*right*) Orestes prepares to murder his mother in vengeance for his father's death.

(*left*) The goddess Athena sits in judgment.
(*below*) The trial before the gods. In the rear
Hermes, Athena, Apollo; in the foreground,
the chorus of Furies.

slave endlessly reiterating the cautionary whisper: "Remember, you are still a man."

Whatever the origins of the mask, its use in the theater had obvious practical advantages. The mask not only provides greater visibility, but it generalizes the character. It suggests that we are looking not merely at a single individual called Oedipus, who was king of Thebes at some fixed point in the historical past, but at Everyman faced with an irreconcilable conflict between what he hopes and desires and what his destiny has appointed for him.

Just as the neutrality of the stage setting broadens the play's message, so, too, does the lack of specific facial features. The open, pictorially undefined stage can assume any coloration the author cares to suggest; and the mask can be a blank slate on which is written any kind of emotion that the author describes. It is a well-known phenomenon of mask theater in all cultures, and one often remarked on with wonder by audiences, that masks *do* change. Emotive language works so strongly on the spectator that the mask may be seen to age, to blush, or to weep.

Finally, the mask limits the personal element in the performance by standing between the interpreter and his audience. The audience sees the mask, not the actor. The mask and the costume are the character, and the individual personality of the actor who wears them is of comparatively little importance. Thus in Greek terms it was possible for one role in the same play to be taken by two, or even three, actors in succession, if the complexity of the script and the restrictions of the three-actor rule required it. It was equally possible for one actor to diversify himself by taking several different roles in the same play. And among the other uses of masks we may note that in the Greek theater they removed certain problems that modern, maskless revivals find extremely difficult to solve. For instance, Sophocles' *Oedipus the King* is a play about a man who marries his own mother. The actress who plays Jocasta must be equally convincing both as wife and mother, a double role that few actresses can carry off. For the Greeks there was no problem. The mask generalized and depersonalized; questions of relative age became insignificant. Oedipus wore a mask that said "man," Jocasta one that said "woman"; and the masks conveyed the various possible relationships that these words imply: mother-son, husband-wife. The mask was not an incidental ornament of the Greek drama but an integral part of it. Where we list on our programs "Characters in order of appearance," the Greeks prefaced their manuscripts with *ta tou dramatos prosopa,* "the masks of the play."

Costumes, similarly, seem to have been conceived in general rather than specific terms. They were formal robes for acting in rather than detailed reproductions of real life garments. Our evidence for this conclusion comes partly from vases, on which Greek painters loved to reproduce things they saw on the stage, and partly from occasional comments. The plays themselves suggest that types of characters were distinguished not so much by what they wore as by what they carried. Different roles were marked by easily recognizable props. A herald wore a wreath. A traveler wore the *petasos,* a broad-brimmed hat that shaded the face from the Greek sun. A king carried a scepter; a warrior, a spear.

Costume *color* must also have been important, though we know few specifics. We tend to have a monochrome view of ancient Greece today because we see the ancient ruins as bleached white columns against a blue sky. In antiquity those columns and the statues were painted, apparently in a range of hues and metallic overlays that rivaled the gaudiness of the later Byzantine church. The same must have been true of the staging of Greek drama. Though we lack positive evidence (the vase paintings are monochrome), we can safely assume a simple, obvious color symbolism that would tell the audience, as soon as an actor appeared on the stage, what kind of character he was.

Character in the Greek plays is thus *visually* established in broad and general terms, and we may notice how the same tendency works to establish the *age* of characters. Age distinctions in Greek tragedy are not subtle. One cannot look at a character and say, "He is thirty-eight." Rather, characters fall into broad groups. The old, like the prophet Teiresias in *Oedipus the King* and *Antigone,* or Hecuba in *Hecuba* and *The Trojan Women,* are very old indeed. They need sticks to walk. They complain of weakness and fatigue. Any calamity is likely to prostrate them. Then there are the characters, the majority of the dramatis personae in a Greek play, who are in the prime of life. Finally there are children, played presumably by real children. They are normally silent characters on stage, possibly because their voices had not yet developed to the point where they would be audible in a theater. These roles may have provided a start in the business for would-be actors who would thus have their first taste of performance as the children who are murdered in *Medea* or as the infant Astyanax in *The Trojan Women.*

We have some evidence that describes how Greek actors comported themselves on the stage and the kind of movements they used. We can detect certain stock gestures used to convey specific emotions — all of them large and easily comprehensible, in keeping with the size of the theater and the audience. Grief, inevitably one of the most frequent emotions in Greek tragedy, was shown by lowering the head, perhaps with one hand to the brow (when an actor is masked, the angle of the head becomes far more significant than when he is not), or in extreme cases by throwing the cloak over the head and concealing the face completely. Mourning, another well-attested tragic emotion, was signified by gestures stylized from those of real life. Greek mourning was (and still, to some extent, is) a violent business; in the sixth century B.C. grief-stricken relatives were doing themselves so much harm by self-mutilation that the practice had to be stopped by law. But the gestures survived, in an abstract form, on the stage; in Aeschylus's *The Libation Bearers* the whole chorus go through the motions of tearing their faces with their nails, beating their breasts, and rending their clothes.

Another common stage gesture was that of supplication, or appeal; the petitioner knelt at his interlocutor's feet, threw his arms around the latter's leg, and reached up with his other hand to grasp his chin. This is what the phrase

"I beg you by your beard" or "by your chin," so often found in Greek tragedy, refers to; it is often puzzling to readers who do not have the stage picture in their minds. Prayer to the gods of heaven was conducted with the arms outstretched and the palms upward, to the infernal gods with the palms downward — sometimes accompanied by a stamp of the foot to force the underworld to listen. Long narrative or hortatory speeches undoubtedly used the extensive repertory of hand gestures listed in ancient rhetorical manuals: enumerating successive points on the fingers, spreading the arms wide to indicate a swelling peroration, drawing the hand to the breast to show diffidence, and so forth. Writers on oratory are our best guide to early acting, for the two arts were kin; and though the most complete surveys of speakers' practices date from long after the fifth century B.C., they embody a long and virtually unchanging tradition.

We are clearly talking here about actors who used a system of studied, patterned movements that communicated instantly with the audience and could, at any moment, be heightened into dance, just as the strong rhythmical base of the actors'-verse speech could, at moments of heightened emotion, make the transition into song. This system was, in fact, closely akin to classical ballet, with rhythm and expressiveness taking precedence over naturalistic probability. It does not bother a ballet audience that Doctor Coppelius, in *Coppelia,* having been established as a doddering old man, can dance as nimbly as a young one. By the same token, the old Jocasta, in Euripides' *The Phoenician Women,* can dance her joy at seeing her grown-up son again.

ROLE STRUCTURE AND PLAY STRUCTURE

In approaching the play, the Greek actor's attention was necessarily fragmented. A modern actor normally expects to take one role in a play and to remain with it to the end. Though doubling, and even tripling, of roles is not unknown in the modern theater, the roles concerned are usually small, and the actor may expect one to finish before the next begins. In the Greek theater, because of the limited number of actors, role distribution was considerably more complex. Sometimes an actor could count on carrying one role, and one role only, through the play; more usually he would divide himself between two or three, and these roles might be alternating rather than sequential.

Consider, for example, Sophocles' *Antigone.* Let us assume that in the prologue actor A plays Antigone, actor B, Ismene. There follows the *parodos* (chorus entry); actor C enters as Creon to address the chorus; he is in turn addressed by the entering Guard, who reports that the body of Polyneices has been buried. If the same actor plays Antigone throughout, then the Guard must be played by B, who has just finished playing Ismene. The next episode involves Creon, Guard, and Antigone (C, B, A), at the end of which the Guard (B) exits; but the next brings Creon face to face with Antigone and Ismene, so actor B has to resort to his first role again. (Other permutations are possible, and you may like to work them out for yourself; it makes an interesting exercise in stage logistics. But however the pattern is arranged, one actor has to vacillate between two important roles.)

Two conclusions are evident from this discussion. First, the Greek actor had to be extremely versatile, switching from one role to another with a minimum of delay. The time needed to change mask and costume is very short, but the temperamental strain of continual role shifting is more than most modern actors would care to undertake. Second, there is no such thing as a small part in Greek tragedy. An actor might well end up with a collection of small parts, which would add up to more than what we would now label the leading role.

An even more important conclusion can be drawn: actors became accustomed to viewing the play in segments rather than as a continuum, and to thinking of a number of roles in relation to one another rather than of one role in its entirety. There is some evidence that this attitude communicated itself to the writing of the plays. Often a Greek tragedy makes its impact scene by scene rather than by linear development through a series of scenes. Often, too, the point of the play resides in the way scenes are related to each other — like speech and rebuttal in a debate. In other words, the *structure* of a Greek tragedy is often more important than the *story*. Euripides, in particular, was fond of writing plays in which the first half presents a case from one point of view, the second from a diametrically opposed point of view; and the play makes its point by an antithetical balance often supported by direct repetition of lines, situation, and imagery. Consistency and logical development, therefore, are often subordinated to the requirements of structure. One scene may not exactly cohere in detail with the next. Characters may seem not to know what logically they should know — or to know what logically they should not. Modern critics, influenced by ideas of psychological continuity, which belong to a far later theater, have sometimes dismissed these features as lapses on the part of the dramatist. In truth they stem from a different idea of what a play is and how it should proceed.

THE INVOLVED AUDIENCE

One other important component of the performance needs to be considered here: the audience. We, who are accustomed to think of the audience in a passive sense, may not find it easy to consider them as part of the totality of the production. But in the Greek theater they were often involved not merely as spectators but as participants. From the beginning the Greek audience were more closely integrated with the action than is the case in modern theaters. They surrounded it and were lit by the same light. Through the chorus, which was a representative selection of the citizen body, the whole vast audience was linked closely with the action of the drama, and the plays emphasized this link by having the chorus at one moment address the actors, at another, the audience.

The actors could recognize the audience, too. Aeschylus's *Seven Against Thebes* is set in a beleaguered city. The enemy is at the gates, and King Eteocles appears to calm the population:

> Men of Cadmus; citizens; in time of crisis
> It is my duty, as the pilot of the state
> Who keeps a sleepless vigil, to address you,
> . . . you, with but a step
> To crowning manhood; you, who are past your prime
> But working still to keep your vigor ripening;
> And you, at the perfect age, the peak of youth;
> Your city needs you.

Who is he talking to? Not the chorus, for this is the very beginning of the play, the prologue, and the chorus has not yet entered — and, anyway, the chorus in this play is composed of women. There is no need to assume a crowd of extras here, for Eteocles has the whole audience in front of him, and it is surely they who are for the moment assumed into the action as citizens of Thebes.

Such occasions are common in Greek tragedy. They are even more common in Greek comedy, where, besides the collective appeals to the audience as a whole, individual members of it may be pointed out and identified by name. Often the playwrights use devices that obliterate the gap between fact and fiction. At the close of his *Oresteia* Aeschylus reconstructs in the orchestra the songs and processions of the quadrennial Panathenaia, Athens's proudest civic festival, turning a legendary drama into actuality through the collective experience of his audience. At the end of his *Persians* protagonist and chorus join in a dirge over the Persian dead, but they use the familiar patterns of Athenian dirges so that the audience, while watching the feigned representation of an alien disaster, are simultaneously reminded of their own mortality; and the action has a universal application.

Presentational Theater

The characteristics we have described above are not peculiar to the Greek theater, although the Greek theater demonstrates their earliest known application. They belong rather to a whole genre of theater of which we shall see further examples in other times and places, usually, but not invariably, in the early stages of any theater culture. Critics have distinguished this genre by various names; *formal* or *conventional* were once used, though perhaps the currently fashionable *presentational* is a happier choice. Presentational theater, as opposed to representational (see p. 79), signifies a kind of theater that makes no attempt to offer a plausible and realistic illusion or representation of everyday life, or to make the audience believe that it is watching a real action happening in a real time or place. Rather, it communicates with the audience by a series of agreed conventions, by developing a symbolic or emblematic theatrical vocabulary, which has meaning only within the confines of the theater and nowhere else.

We use *convention* here in the original Latin sense of the word, as a coming together, a meeting: a meeting of minds, in this case, a compact, an agreement between the playwright and his audience over the rules by which they will play the game. All theater, of course, involves conventions, even when it professes to be realistic. It is a fixed convention of the illusionistic theater that the auditorium lights darken and a curtain rises to signify the beginning of the play. It is no less a convention when the curtain rises again after the end of the play to show the cast assembled for a curtain call — even those who have died during the preceding action. We shall explore other implicit conventions of the illusionistic theater later. What distinguishes presentational theater is that the conventions are openly admitted and become the primary language of the play.

Different cultures evolve different sets of conventions. A Greek audience of the fifth century B.C. would have had as much initial difficulty in understanding a Noh play of fifteenth-century A.D. Japan as we do, though both are examples of presentational theater. The same general characteristics, however, are usually present. First, the presence of the audience is openly acknowledged, even utilized. The actors do not pretend that the spectators are not there; on the contrary, characters may address them directly and in various ways involve them in the action. Second, the actors wear types of costume (in the Greek theater, obviously, the mask) that are clearly theatrical costumes and not real clothes; they proclaim throughout that the actor is an actor, using those various blatant devices to show the audience that for the moment he is standing for somebody else. Third, setting is left largely or wholly to the imagination; the actual furnishings of the stage may be, at most, a few permanent architectural set pieces. Fourth, the characters use modes of speech and behavior that set the action apart from real life. In our everyday existence we do not communicate in formal verse; nor do we dance, individually or collectively, to express high emotion; nor do we fall into the pattern of a formal debate at moments of stress; nor is a chorus continually present to comment and moralize upon our behavior. The presentational theater offers a world that is set apart from the world of real life, that is an abstraction from it, a heightening of it; but a world that is perfectly self-consistent within its own terms and one that works as long as everyone abides by the rules that have been laid down. As soon as a proportion of the audience, or the actors, fail to do this, the self-contained world disintegrates. You may have noted that the laws of presentational theater have much in common with the way team games work, and this bond has led to a surge of modern interest in the similarity between dramatic theory and games theory. The object of a football game is for each team to score as many touchdowns as possible. An elaborate system of rules has been formulated to control the ways in which this can be done, and these apply within the confines of the football field. If one player appeared on a motorbike, he might make a number of easy touchdowns, but the game would cease to exist.

It is the critics who make categories, not the practitioners, and thus we must beware of applying the labels too arbitrarily. The term *presentational theater* has a number of subtle shadings. We must emphasize again that the difference between presentational and illusionistic (or representational) theater is one of degree rather than kind. At one end of the spectrum presentational theater is barely removed from ritual; indeed, religious ritual is often, in a very real sense, presentational theater. At the other end it may involve some elements that are highly realistic. But presentational theater tends to be distinguished by its subject matter as well as by its form. At its purest it is obviously suitable for displaying, through symbolic or emblematic means, dramatic actions that, in a more realistic theater, could not be shown at all.

The Writers of Greek Tragedy

In a survey that covers over two thousand years of dramatic achievement, it is not possible to look in detail at every dramatist, much less at every play. With the Greeks, however, it is possible to go into more detail, because the body of surviving material is small. And it is desirable to do so because so many aspects of Greek drama were taken over and built upon by later ages. We see the Greek playwrights developing themes, plots, and technical devices that become a permanent part of the theatrical vocabulary. We see, too, the formulation of distinct attitudes toward the theater and what it should do, attitudes that will be repeated over and over again in the centuries that follow.

AESCHYLUS

Aeschylus (525–456 B.C.) used the presentational techniques of his theater to handle vast subjects, though what is now universally agreed to be his first surviving play, *The Persians* (472 B.C.), seems to be an exception to his usual practice. It celebrates a local event, the battle of Salamis fought eight years earlier, in which a small, well-led fleet of Athenian ships had smashed the Persian armada, freeing Greece from the threat of foreign invasion and establishing Athens as de facto leader of the city-states. The play is set in the Persian court, with the chorus representing the council of elders. It is largely choral, beginning with a proud recital of the forces that have gone to subdue Greece. Hopes of victory are first disturbed by the queen's premonitions of disaster and then shattered by the arrival of a messenger to recount the naval defeat and subsequent expulsion of the land army. The play ends with the return of King Xerxes in rags, symbolic of the ruin of Persian ambitions, and a prolonged dirge for the fallen.

The Persians, with its topical appeal, is unique in Greek tragedy. It can still bring a Greek audience cheering to its feet. But its message is not limited to the moment. Aeschylus uses the events of Salamis to draw a moral about the folly of human pride and to press home the recurrent Greek message that we bring disaster upon ourselves when we venture further than we should.

Aeschylus's later plays employ a wider canvas. They range across the universe, finding their protagonists in gods, demigods, or heroes, mail-clad supermen from myth or distant past. They concern themselves with such vast questions as the nature of justice, human and divine responsibility, the growth of civilization, and the nature of the gods themselves. And they use the emblematic techniques of the presentational theater to bring these lofty issues to the stage. Aeschylus enlarges his scope still further by his preference for submitting the required three festival entries as a trilogy, in which each play, though self-contained and performable by itself, forms one act of a larger drama, and the whole is greater than the sum of its parts. Only one complete trilogy, the *Oresteia* (*The Story of Orestes*) has survived. Written in 458 B.C., it is based on a familiar story of the curse on the royal family of Argos, and it shows the working out of the curse over successive generations.

Agamemnon, the first play, opens with the end of the Trojan War and the prospect of Agamemnon's triumphal return. But we learn that he has estranged his wife, Clytemnestra, by the sacrifice of their daughter Iphigeneia to secure divine favor; that Clytemnestra has taken a lover, Aegisthus; and that Agamemnon has lost all his followers, so that no one remains in the city but men and boys. He enters his palace, Clytemnestra murders him in his bath, and the city succumbs to tyranny.

The second play, *The Libation Bearers,* begins years later, when Agamemnon's son, Orestes, who has grown up in exile, returns to avenge his father. Despite his mother's pleas, he murders her, and for this he is haunted by the Furies, supernatural pursuers of the wrongdoer. This play — which, though short, is packed with incident and is the most obviously exciting of the trilogy — had an immense influence on later playwrights. Orestes coming home to kill his father's murderer begat a whole series of revenge plays, which were particularly prolific in Elizabethan England.

In the wider context of the trilogy, *Agamemnon* and *The Libation Bearers* work in antithesis to each other. The first pleads Clytemnestra's justification, the second that of Orestes. The trilogy assumes the familiar Greek pattern of debate. In the third play, *The Eumenides,* the issue has come to transcend the family feud and involve the notion of cosmic justice. Orestes is put on trial by the deities. The Furies, who represent the primitive code of bloodguilt, accuse him. Apollo — who stands for a more civilized concept of justice, one that recognizes extenuating circumstances and regards the marriage tie as no less important than the blood-tie — defends him. And the trial is presided over by Athena, who champions the new order of godhead over the old. Orestes is exonerated, the Furies are transformed into benevolent spirits, and the play ends in celebration.

In the *Oresteia* Aeschylus has transformed a primitive revenge tale into an allegory of civilization. Feud and blood lust are replaced by law and trial by jury. Ostensibly the action of the *Oresteia* covers two generations. In actuality it celebrates centuries of human progress and social evolution. Although the immediate action is limited (the only thing that happens in *Agamemnon* is that the king's wife kills him, offstage), the playwright gives it universal scope through prophets, ghosts, and deities who can range backward and forward in time and project the drama onto a larger screen. His most useful vehicle is his chorus, sometimes drawn into the action as participants but at other times serving as commentator to alert the audience to the wider reverberations of what they have just seen. In a drama of such scope individual characterization counts for comparatively little. This is still theater dominated by one man: we hear the poet's single voice, disseminated through his chosen agents; and the characters, larger than life, are used as symbols, abstractions of certain human qualities, rather than flesh-and-blood human beings. Some of the smaller roles have great humanity, however, especially the earthy, garrulous old nurse of Orestes in *The Libation Bearers*, who foreshadows a long line of such characters — including Juliet's nurse — in the later theater.

SOPHOCLES

With Sophocles (496–406 B.C.) tragedy began to come down to earth. In 468 B.C. he competed against Aeschylus and won, the neophyte defeating the old master. This is, perhaps, not surprising; the Athenians admired Aeschylus, but they could not always understand him. Sophocles wrote simpler Greek (a fact often carefully concealed by translators) and dealt with more immediate themes. In the hands of Aeschylus the Greek theater could still be called a religious institution: the gods were at the center of the plays. Sophocles wrote for a generation whose religious faith was waning, and in his work the gods are shifted to the periphery. His characters, too, become recognizably more human. We know a great deal more about Oedipus as a man than we know about Agamemnon. In fact, Sophocles is said to have been the first to write plays with specific actors in mind.

Most of Sophocles' plays were written under the tension of war and have a desperation that Aeschylus's lack. In Aeschylus's plays, though people may die and cities be destroyed, there is always a sense of cyclic regeneration: the bare fields will grow again, the rain will water them, new children will be born, the persecutions will somehow, sometime, end. Sophocles' most famous plays are set in crisis situations from which almost all hope and human comfort have been withdrawn, and they examine how people behave under stress. *Oedipus the King* is set in a city that has been ravaged by plague, *Antigone* in one prostrated by war, *Philoctetes* on a barren island, *Electra* in a household devoured by guilt and festering from within. The gods are present, but only to provide the datum, the starting point. Most of the action is worked out in purely human terms.

Aeschylus had written a trilogy about the royal house of Thebes in which, as in the *Oresteia,* he studied the workings of a curse upon successive generations. If we had the complete work — only the last, *Seven Against Thebes,* has survived — we should undoubtedly see that Aeschylus was enquiring why the curse existed and what forces had brought it about. Sophocles, using the same story in *Oedipus the King* about 429 B.C., asks none of these questions (though critics have sometimes tried to pretend that he did). Rather, he sets up the curse as a framework. It is ordained that a man shall murder his father and marry his own mother. What does he then do? How does he try to escape, and how does he react when he finds he has not escaped? Are there any admirable, purely human qualities that man can develop in the face of divine intransigence?

In the earlier *Antigone* (ca. 441), too, we are presented for most of the play with a purely human confrontation. Eteocles and Polyneices, Oedipus's sons, have died in mutual combat during the civil war for the Theban throne. Creon, their uncle, now comes to power and decrees that Eteocles shall receive a hero's funeral while Polyneices' body is to lie unburied as an object lesson to all traitors. Antigone is determined that her brother, whatever he has done, shall have the burial that is the common right of all men. However, in the play Creon is not represented as a heartless tyrant. His opening speech to the chorus, justifying his action on the grounds of political expediency, would have fallen on sympathetic ears; Athenians were brought up to believe that the individual must be subordinated to the state. Nor is Antigone a totally sympathetic character. She is hard and dispassionate; she refuses even to consider the idea of compromise. *Antigone* reminds us, too, of how often the concept of debate is not merely part of, but the whole of, Greek tragedy. This play is not Antigone's, nor is it Creon's play. It is a play about both of them, about contrasting value systems in opposition.

Aeschylus was interested in the grand design, and he saw individual persons as insignificant parts of that design — hence his comparative lack of interest in characterization. His work reminds us of archaic Greek sculpture, in which the form, the mass, takes precedence over the subject matter and details may be compressed or distorted to fit the pattern. While Sophocles still believes in a grand design, he does not try to explain it. For him there is a power that shapes our ends; we may dimly perceive it, we may, with suffering, partially understand it, but we are measured by the grace with which we respond to it. "Be resilient" is the abiding message of Sophocles' plays; "take what comes, and do not become so hardened in your attitudes that you snap under pressure." Oedipus comes to understand this at the end:

> But I am sure of one thing; nothing,
> No disease can touch me now.
> I would not have been saved from death
> Unless it were for some strange destiny.
> But let my destiny go where it will.

And Creon, when he prays for death at the end of *Antigone,* is reminded that this is too easy a solution:

> All in good time. There are other things
> To be seen to here and now. The future is
> In other hands. . . .
> Save your prayers. Whatever will come to pass
> Has already been appointed. Nobody can change it.

This new stress on individual humanity diminishes the importance of the chorus. When the protagonists are no longer gods but men, the chorus are reduced to lesser men. Thus for much of *Oedipus the King* we see them as ordinary human beings caught in a dilemma. Whom are they to believe? Their king, whose wisdom has been proved in the test, or the prophet who accuses him? There are moments when they are completely wrong, when they know less about the action than we, the audience. Only once do they rise to the old Aeschylean omniscience: when they sing an ode on the unwritten laws that dominate mankind, and that we ignore at our peril.

EURIPIDES

We often talk of Euripides as if he were Sophocles' successor. In fact, he was his near contemporary and competitor (480–406 B.C.), and he died first. But his work represents, in many ways, an extension of what Sophocles was doing; he introduced so many changes in the traditonal forms and concepts that by his death the mold was shattered and could not be reformed.

Euripides, like his predecessors, believed that drama should be an educative force. It was incumbent upon him to do so. He sought to instruct his public, however, not by holding up illustrious example but by forcing them to think for themselves about matters they had taken for granted. This was the age of Socrates, who was applying the same techniques to philosophical enquiry; and both Euripides and Socrates were children of their time, made skeptical, or at least inquisitive, by the erosion of traditional values under stress of war. There were others like them, but not, as yet, enough for Euripides to be greeted with the applause of the majority. He fared poorly in the festivals; his plays were often booed on the stage for their alleged atheism and immorality, and his private life was blemished with slander. He brought much of this on himself, by going out of his way to annoy people and challenge conventional prejudices, shocking his audiences so that he could stimulate them.

Superficially his plays belong to the traditional pattern. They take their subject matter from myth and legend, they employ the conventional verse forms, they use a chorus. But once we look closer, all is different. Though Euripides takes his stories from myth, he selects unfamiliar versions and brings them together in new combinations. He came closer than any Greek tragedian to writing original plots; probably for the first time in their theater, Athenian audiences did not know what they were going to see. We sometimes fail to make allowance for this originality, for Euripides' versions have, in many cases, become canonical. It is usually said that Greek tragedy is based on myth. It would be more accurate to say that the tragedies are part of the creative process by which the myth has reached us. The story of Medea's killing of her own children to revenge herself on her husband is, even now, one of the most familiar in the Greek corpus, but the story seems not to have existed in this form until Euripides wrote his play in 431 B.C.

As well as manipulating his material, Euripides adopts a critical attitude toward it. Divesting his characters of their mythic grandeur, he depicts them as ordinary, fallible human beings forced into desperate situations and responding in quite unheroic ways. Orestes in Euripides' *Electra* sneaks back into Argos with one eye on his escape route. In *Orestes,* which deals with the aftermath of Clytemnestra's murder (roughly the same situation treated by Aeschylus in *The Eumenides*), Orestes is put on trial by a human, not a divine, court; he is treated as a pariah and his only recourse lies in further plots of murder and revenge. In *The Madness of Heracles* the celebrated hero and savior suddenly, unpredictably goes mad and slaughters his own wife and children.

Euripides shows us an arid, blighted world where morality has abdicated, and chance and expediency determine human life. The traditional gods suffer most from this treatment. Euripides shows them as callous and selfish or, worse, as meaningless. In this chaotic world one of Euripides' favorite devices is to reverse the popular image and attribute to barbarians — by which the Greeks meant all non-Greek peoples — all the traditional Greek virtues, while showing the Greeks themselves as contemptible. In *Hecuba* and *The Trojan Women* it is the foreigners, the Trojans, who show grace, nobility, and resignation, while their Greek captors practice atrocities in the name of statecraft.

Above all, Euripides was concerned with humanizing his characters, showing them not as remote figures from another age but as people with problems to which the audience could relate on a personal level. To this end, though he used the old conventional devices, he modified them until they verged on a more realistic kind of theater. His characters often wore costumes that appeared to be real clothes — rags in some cases, which his audiences condemned as lowering the status of tragedy. His verse, though still in iambics, allowed so many variations that it became almost conversational. His music was drawn from popular sources. His vocabulary used more ordinary words, and his descriptions contained more domestic detail. And he was a supreme showman; his plays are full of violence, spectacle, and noise, and any excuse served for a procession. Audiences detested and were fascinated by him. It says much for this fascination, and for official tolerance, that though his work eroded many of the traditional values of Athenian society, not one of his plays was ever refused a hearing. In the tragedies of Euripides we see a sick society scratching its own sores.

A Greek Tragedy in Performance

So far we have been looking at various aspects of the Greek theater in isolation. But theater is a multiple and complex art, and it is necessary to consider how these various factors and the wide range of performing skills were harnessed to the production of a specific play. The work we shall look at is Euripides' *The Bacchae,* one of the last fifth-century tragedies that we have — its author died before it saw production in Athens — but still one of the most illuminating in terms of the content and the practice of the Greek theater.

It is a spring morning in 406 B.C. Although Athens is in the last stages of a calamitous war, and lies under the shadow of imminent defeat, the dramatic festivals are held as usual — perhaps the more eagerly because a series of military reverses have returned the audience to an older, half-forgotten piety. Into the Theater of Dionysus are packed all those citizens who are not serving with the fleet; they still fill the theater. They sit on the stone benches in the sunshine; some have brought leather cushions — many, food and wineskins — for the celebrations go on all day. In the front tier sit the priests and officials, with the priest of Dionysus, whose festival this is, in the center. Ritual offerings have been performed, and the altar in the center of the orchestra circle still smolders. After the usual preliminary trumpet calls and ceremonies, there is an expectant hush; the audience knows, from prefestival proclamations, that it is about to see something unusual, a play whose protagonist is Dionysus himself. And Euripides, though recently dead, still inspires a lively interest.

The prologue begins. In Greek terms this is the part of the play preceding the chorus entrance. It may be a complete scene with several characters or an introductory monologue; *The Bacchae* gives us the latter. Through the *skene* (stage house) doors Dionysus advances onto the low raised stage. His identity is apparent from his costume: a pale, smiling mask, a long, womanish yellow robe with a fawnskin draped over it — the traditional costume of the Bacchic rites. In his hand is a *thyrsus,* the tufted pine branch carried by his devotees. If these clues are not enough, he makes himself known in his first lines to the audience:

> People of Thebes, prepare to meet your god,
> Dionysus, son of Zeus and Semele,
> Of God the Father and a mortal woman,
> Daughter of Cadmus, ruler of this land.

With a gesture Dionysus indicates that the *skene* represents the palace of Thebes. He makes it clear that we are in the early years of that proud city's legendary history. Cadmus, the founder, is still alive; Dionysus was born to Cadmus's daughter Semele, and his father is Zeus himself. He has come back to Thebes with his Asian followers to punish the Thebans for their refusal to acknowledge his divinity — particularly Pentheus, Cadmus's grandson, the present king. All the Theban women, including Agave, Pentheus's mother, have been ensnared in the Dionysiac spell and are dancing in ecstasy on the mountains. At the close of the prologue he summons the chorus:

> And now, my band of worshippers, who leave
> The savage peaks of Phrygia to come
> As handmaids and companions on my journey,
> Beat on your timbrels, make the strange wild music
> That I and the mountain mother gave the world!

The *parodos* now begins. As Dionysus leaves the stage, the chorus pour down the twin aisles leading into the orchestra. This is not the solemn, processional entry familiar in other tragedies but a wild dance, a stage version of an actual Bacchic ritual that many of the audience would have known from experience. The chorus members are dressed in exotic costumes; they carry drums and tambourines. Their song is of the exultation of the Bacchic rite and the way in which the worshipers are transported to a pitch of ecstasy.

In the first episode two old men appear. Their age is denoted by their white-haired masks, but their costume is strange, for they wear, like the Bacchic women, the skins of beasts, and they carry wands tipped with ivy, the symbol of the new god. They are Cadmus, the founder of Thebes and grandfather of the present king, and Teiresias, the blind prophet, long familiar to the audience from his appearance in other plays. In a scene that is half-comic, half-pathetic, they tell of their joy in the new worship; they are the only men in Thebes to be infected. Their patterned movement transforms itself into dance steps like those of the women; they are old men infected by the god with an illusion of youth.

Pentheus, the present king, enters, identified by his costume and scepter. He wears a young man's mask and begins with an angry soliloquy about the new god:

> They say there is a stranger in the land,
> A wizard, a magician from the East
> With wanton looks, with scented golden curls,
> Who moves among our women night and day
> With promise of mysterious delights.
> If once I catch this man within our walls
> He'll wave his wand and shake his golden locks
> No more; I'll have his head upon the block!

Not until the end of this speech does he notice the old men; in presentational theater characters see only what the author wants them to see. He pleads with his grandfather to abandon this foolishness, and accuses Teiresias of mercenary interests:

> This is your work, Teiresias. You hope
> By introducing this new deity, to earn
> More profit from your auguries and omens.
> If your gray hair did not prohibit me

> I'd lock you up among the Bacchic women
> And teach you rites you would be sorry for!

Teiresias responds with a long and carefully constructed speech, formulated according to the regular rules of oratory, in which he puts the case for Dionysus. Pentheus refuses to listen, and orders the new god arrested.

Now the first *stasimon* (formal choral song) begins. The chorus, stirring once more into life, sing and dance in praise of Dionysus. They contrast the joys of acceptance with the foolish recalcitrance offered by Pentheus, who stands before them:

> His joy is in the feast,
> The chosen one, the son of god,
> And hand in hand he walks
> With Peace, who gives our sons
> Long life, and sweet prosperity.
> To rich and poor alike he gives the boon
> Of wine to comfort them
> And bring them ease. His hatred is for those
> Who do not hold this truth in heart:
> To count the blessings of this life
> Under sun and grace of night.
> All who question, all who doubt,
> Purge them from your heart and mind,
> For blessed are the simple, who accept,
> As may I do, the common law.

Up to this point the action has been largely static and rhetorical; there has been a good deal of necessary exposition to encompass. Now, with the beginning of the second episode, the action moves more rapidly. A guard enters with Dionysus, who has been taken prisoner. A rapid stichomythic exchange ensues between god and king, Pentheus asking about these new and strange rites, Dionysus, in his human guise, giving only half answers that whet the king's curiosity further. Pentheus ends with threats of imprisonment, and Dionysus is dragged from the stage.

In the second *stasimon* and third episode, the musical continuum is now so strong and the involvement of the chorus with the action so intense that any division becomes arbitrary. The chorus again sing of the god and the unbeliever, and they lament the punishment about to fall on them. Their song is interrupted by an offstage voice, which they identify as that of Dionysus. (A further technical point: offstage voices always have to be identified in the Greek theater to make it quite clear that it is not someone on the stage who is speaking.) Music and voices rise and fall in an antiphonal, liturgical pattern; Dionysus summons up an earthquake to devastate the palace, and through the choral responses we see its effect:

> *Dionysus (off)*. Spirit of earthquake, come, uproot the earth!
> *Chorus*. In a second Pentheus's palace

> Will be shaken to its fall;
> See, the columns shake, the great stone doors
> Tremble and shatter; the Thunder-god
> Is bellowing within the house.

This visual moment is one of the most exciting that the Greek theater has to offer, yet it is accomplished with extraordinarily simple means. There is, of course, no real earthquake in the sense that the *skene* is literally shaken to the ground. We get that impression, however, from the song of the chorus as it rises to a crescendo. We get it too from their evocative dance movement, showing the shaking of the ground. In presentational theater such as this, what you are told is always true: when Greek characters are going to lie, they always prepare the audience for this well in advance. What we *see,* therefore, is spirited dance and gesture, ending with the chorus prostrating themselves on the orchestra floor. What we *imagine* is the whole palace splitting, reeling, and crumbling. It is typical of presentational theater, too, that once this scene has made its dramatic impact, the earthquake is never mentioned again. Characters entering subsequently do not comment on the fact that the palace is lying in shambles (and, in fact, by the end of the play, characters can still talk about the "palace walls" as though the earthquake had never happened.) This is pure dramatic economy. In realistic theater any effect has to be considered to remain in force until the next convenient stopping place — the end of the scene or the act. In presentational theater an effect is only considered to be in force as long as it is dramatically valuable; after that it can be ignored.

Freed by the earthquake from his prison, Dionysus reappears and comforts the chorus. Here, significantly, the meter changes from the customary iambic ($\smile$ -) to a longer trochaic line (- $\smile$), which gives a different, almost magical sense to the dialogue. (Euripides exploits this device elsewhere to emphasize moments of special note.) Pentheus, entering from the palace, confronts his enemy again; but their encounter is interrupted by a messenger from the mountain, who tells what the women of Thebes are doing.

The messenger's speech is typical of its kind. It is pure narrative (and we should note that though the speaker is characterized as a simple rustic, he uses the same formal tragic language as everyone else in the play; even in Euripides realism of characterization does not go very far). It is a set speech, a showstopper in its own right, and greeted, like an operatic aria, with applause; and it enlarges the immediate boundaries of the action by transporting the audience out to the mountainside.

The messenger's speech also marks the mathematical center of the play. Significantly it begins by showing the Bacchae as peaceful, enjoying a simple harmony with nature:

> When the herds were out to pasture, moving up
> Towards the hilltop, as the morning sun
> First came to kiss the fields with warmth and light,
> We saw three bands of women from the dance. . . .

> Each lay where she had dropped, exhausted; but
> Still kept her modesty. They were not drunk
> With wine, as you had told us, or with music.
> Nor were they making love there, in the woods.

It goes on to show how, when threatened and disturbed, they grow violent, irresistible:

> They fell
> Upon a heifer, lowing, with her udders full of milk
> And rent her limb from limb, while other women
> Fell on our cows, and tore them apart. . . .
> To Hysiae and Erythrae they came,
> The hamlets shadowed by Cithairon's summit,
> Like an invading hoard, to sack and pillage
> Creating havoc, snatching children from their homes,
> Piling their backs with plunder. . . .

The play now follows the reversal implicit in this speech. Pentheus, from being the master and the hunter, now becomes the slave and the victim; the persecuted Dionysus becomes the persecutor. This transition is accomplished with a rapidity that is implausible by any naturalistic standard. Pentheus threatens to march against the women in vengeance; Dionysus tempts him with the prospect of seeing them asleep, with the proviso that he dress as a woman to ensure his safety; and Pentheus accepts with "You speak good sense as always; I believe you." All this has taken twenty-five lines of dialogue! But as we have seen, psychological consistency is often forfeited in Greek tragedy to the needs of the dramatic moment. The structure of the play is paramount here; the reversal must take place; and Euripides uses a kind of dramatic shorthand to bring it about.

Next comes the fourth *stasimon*. After the preceding excitement, this is a sober, reflective chorus on the human condition. We cannot hope to know our lot; we can only accept what comes.

> Happy the man who from storm at sea
> Comes safe to harbor.
> Happy the man who has risen clear
> Of the turmoil of this life.
> Different men, by different ways,
> Attain power and prosperity.
> For every man, there is a different dream,
> For every dream, a different ending:
> For some fulfillment, and for some denial.
> The man who finds his happiness
> From day to day, I count as blessed.

The next scene brings in the fourth episode. During the chorus Pentheus has changed into Bacchic costume — women's dress, long wig, pine branch; he is, almost, the simulacrum of Dionysus. This episode introduces a key costume convention of Greek tragedy. As we have seen, the Greek actor reveals himself to the audience entirely in terms of externals — the mask, the costume, the stylized gesture. The costume *is* the persona, the character; the individual actor is simply the mechanism that gives the costume temporary life. Thus evolves a simple and recurrent convention that when something happens to the costume, something happens to the character; the chance or disintegration of the one foreshadows the disintegration of the other. Thus Pentheus's change of costume, and the shattering of his former personality, looks forward to his forthcoming fate.

The scene is both ludicrous and pathetic. Dionysus has told us that he will make Pentheus a laughingstock and then destroy him. Here we see the first half of the threat carried out. Laughter is expected from the audience — but it will soon turn to shock and outrage.

In the fifth *stasimon* the chorus once again extends the action beyond the boundaries of the orchestra. They speak as the Bacchae on the mountain; the onstage chorus becomes a second, offstage chorus. And we see, at secondhand, the reaction of the worshipers to the intruder.

In the fifth episode the choral pronouncement is reinforced by another messenger speech, of great length, relating how Pentheus was trapped by the frenzied women and torn apart by them. In a culmination of visual horror Agave, Pentheus's mother, appears on the stage; in her hands she holds her son's bleeding head — perhaps the empty mask. In her delirium she has taken him for a lion. She and the chorus join in a lyric duologue in which the head is displayed.

Cadmus enters, followed by servants carrying a bier on which lie the rest of Pentheus's remains. In a stichomythic passage Cadmus brings Agave to her senses, and she recognizes her son. On the roof of the *skene* — heaven — appears Dionysus, now clearly recognizable as a god. He pronounces judgment on the city: Pentheus is already dead; Agave and her sisters, as murderers, must go into exile; Cadmus must go into exile elsewhere; the city itself will fall into foreign hands and its people be driven abroad. Thus the motif of disintegration that has run through the play has reached its culmination. First the palace was torn apart by the earthquake; then the cattle, as described in the messenger's speech; then Pentheus himself; and finally Thebes. We see this disintegration in the theater by the orchestra slowly emptying. Cadmus goes off in one direction, Agave, supported by the chorus, in another. All that is left in the empty space is the dummy representing Pentheus's broken, fragmented body. Euripides ends the play with lines he has used before, lines expressive of a person's helplessness in the face of what life may hold in store:

> The gods wear many faces for mankind
> And heaven works much beyond human imagining.
> The looked-for result will fail to materialize
> While heaven finds ways to achieve the unexpected.
> So has it happened in this our story.

Greek Comedy

So far we have said nothing about comedy. Although tragedy remained the staple of the fifth-century festivals, comedies were first given in 486 B.C. and enjoyed a large share of the public attention. It is often stated that the Greek writers were specialists in a way that those of later ages were not; and it is true that Athens produced no fifth-century Shakespeare whose genius could encompass both the high tragedy of *King Lear* and the broad farce of *The Merry Wives of Windsor*. Some of Euripides' plays conventionally listed as tragedies, however, might more appropriately be called high comedies.

In Greek theater a meeting ground of the two forms is found in the minor genre known as the *satyr play*. These were brief entertainments that each tragic poet was expected to offer as an afterpiece to his three tragedies. Though we have only one complete example — *Cyclops* by Euripides — and a few fragments from Aeschylus and Sophocles, some generalizations about the form can safely be made. A satyr play had, as the name implies, a chorus of satyrs — half men, half goats, the buffoons of Greek mythology, regularly characterized as drunken, greedy, cowardly, and lecherous. Some scholars, indeed, have argued that just as the kind of animal and nature worship implied by the existence of the satyr was one of the earliest strata in Greek religion, so the satyr play may have been the origin of all Greek drama; but this conclusion is uncertain. The plots of satyr plays, like those of tragedy, were taken from myth and legend. Euripides bases his *Cyclops* on the well-known story in the *Odyssey* of the encounter between Odysseus and the cannibalistic, one-eyed giant. In satyr plays, however, these stories were burlesqued. It is likely that the satyr play took one of the same stories, or at least one of the same themes, that had been treated seriously in the preceding tragedies. This device both gave the audience some necessary light relief and tested the author's skill in another field entirely. The inclusion of comic material in a primarily tragic bill is a phenomenon we shall see elsewhere in the history of the theater, and it seems to answer a universal human need for respite from considering the sterner aspects of life.

CHARACTERISTICS OF GREEK COMEDY

About comedy proper we have even less evidence than for tragedy. Complete plays by only one author, Aristophanes (450–385 B.C.), have survived, and these represent only a quarter of his output. They exhibit recurrent features, however, which seem likely to belong to all Greek comedy. They suggest that the form developed from an amalgam of choral and other elements that left their mark on the literary works: elements that may, in part, have been vestiges of predramatic ritual preserved for their dramatic values. For example, most of the plays end with a revel or a banquet — sometimes a marriage feast, but

almost invariably with strong sexual overtones — which may look back to
fertility rites of great antiquity, the sacred marriage performed annually to
bring blessings on the fields. They usually embody a choral *agon,* or conflict
— sometimes physical, sometimes merely verbal — which may, again, recall
the kind of ritual combat described by Herodotus among the Egyptians (see p.
15). There is usually a *parabasis,* an extended passage in which the chorus,
either in or out of character, step outside the context of the action and address
the audience on some matter of immediate topical importance. Smaller, formally distinct recurrent features occur also, such as the *pnigos* (literally,
"choker"), a kind of patter song in which the chorus reels off a long line
sequence in one breath. Around these elements were added a number of stock
jokes and familiar bits of comic business, perhaps derived from improvised,
rustic folk entertainment. Aristophanes lists a number of them: slaves scatter-
ing nuts and fruit among the audience, beating scenes, slapstick with burning
torches. (To give another character a hot seat with a torch was Greek comedy's
equivalent of the silent movies custard pie.)

The form of comedy, however, is much less rigid than that of tragedy. In
the latter the chorus intervenes at regular and predictable moments. In the
former the chorus may be all-important in some parts of the play and do
virtually nothing for the rest. A similar looseness is observable in the subject
matter, which derives from a variety of sources. Tragedy preferred familiar
subjects hallowed by mythology, but comedy invented its own.

CHARACTERS IN GREEK COMEDY

If we look at Aristophanes' lists of characters, we normally find that they
divide into three types. The first consists of gods, heroes, and other well-known
figures from myth and legend — though in comedy they are, of course, traves-
ties of their more serious selves. In *The Bacchae* Euripides offers a savage,
sensual portrayal of the god Dionysus. In *The Frogs,* written almost at the same
time, Aristophanes gives us a Dionysus who is both a screaming coward and a
parody of a literary poseur. The tragic Dionysus works devastation on a city
that has rejected him, while his comic counterpart dresses in absurd costumes,
runs from imaginary monsters, shows ludicrous incompetence in the simple art
of oarsmanship, and makes coarse jokes. That two such disparate portraits could
be offered side by side tells us much about the freedom of the Greek theater
and of Greek religion. In two plays Aristophanes gives us a comic Heracles, no
longer the great warrior, sufferer, and champion of humanity, but a muscle-
bound buffoon who thinks and talks only of food. Aeschylus's tormented Prometheus is reduced in comedy to a sniveling little man creeping about under
an umbrella so that the gods will not see him.

A second class of character is drawn from contemporary life. We see on the
Aristophanic stage slanderous caricatures of the playwright's contemporaries,
men who were presumably sitting in the audience and, with mixed emotions,

seeing themselves lampooned in public. Euripides is there, together with Cleon the politician, Socrates the philosopher, and others hardly less distinguished. Cleon tried to silence Aristophanes by law and failed. Plato, on the other hand, shows Socrates and Aristophanes on excellent terms. The pervasiveness and virulence of this humor seems surprising today. But Athens was, by modern standards, a small town. Everyone knew everyone. Without protection of libel laws, personal foibles became common gossip. Any citizen possessing a distinguishing eccentricity — the too fat and the too thin, the adulterers and the homosexuals, the cowards and the saber rattlers, the general who had lost a campaign and the soldier who had lost a helmet on parade — was liable to see himself caricatured on stage or at least hear his name treated with irreverence.

The third class of character that makes up comedy is fictional, though usually based on well-known Athenian types. Their names indicate the roles they will play in the plot: Pisthetairus (Blarney), Strepsiades (Twister), Lysistrata (she who sends the armies home). One of Aristophanes' favorite characters is the old Athenian countryman, who looks with a cynical eye on the follies of the city.

These characters are enmeshed in preposterous plots. In *The Acharnians* (425 B.C.), his first extant play, written in a time of war, Aristophanes fantasizes the desire of the average citizen for peace. His leading character, Dikaiopolis (Honest John Q. Public), attends a meeting of the public assembly. He is so offended by the politicians and ambassadors who, in the manner of their kind, attempt to rob the public blind that he decides on a one-man secession and makes a private peace with the warring powers. He sets up his own common market to which representatives of several states come. The play ends with, on one side of the stage, a battered general weeping over his discomfiture in war and, on the other, a happy and well-fed Dikaiopolis flanked by dancing girls and enjoying the bounty of peace.

In *The Clouds* (423 B.C.) Aristophanes satirizes the new philosophy. Old Strepsiades, desperate to dodge his debts, enrolls as a pupil of Socrates, expecting to graduate in lying, trickery, and evasion. Socrates is shown as the high priest of humbug, conducting pseudoscientific experiments, worshiping strange and fallacious gods, and growing fat on his pupils' credulity. As an exposé of the Socratic method of education, the play is grossly unfair, which did not bother the audience as long as it was funny. *The Clouds* does, however, end with a moral twist. Strepsiades, having learned how to duck his obligations to others, is appalled to find the same subterfuges used against him. The clouds, Socrates' deities, reveal themselves as impostors, and the philosopher himself is driven out of town as punishment for corrupting the community — an uncanny presentiment of Socrates' actual fate many years later.

The Frogs (405 B.C.) is a play about tragedy and tragedians. Its first half shows the comic misadventures of Dionysus on his journey to the underworld to resurrect the dead spirit of Greek drama. In the second half Aeschylus, a generation dead, and Euripides, only recently deceased, debate the proper ends and methods of tragedy. Underneath the humor is a comment on the importance of drama to the Athenians and on the playwright's role as public spokesman.

Aristophanes' fifth-century work is anarchic in form. We look in vain for order and consistency, for the logic and symmetry that mark Greek tragedy. Each play is based on a central comic idea, but the individual scenes tend to be self-contained, illustrating various aspects of this idea and showing little coherence with what precedes or follows. Major changes in plot occur without warning. Characters come and go without notice. Even physical details may change. In *The Wasps* the old man who early in the play is described as toothless, later on has somehow grown teeth to bite through the ropes that bind him. In this kind of comedy we see an amplification of a tendency we have already noticed in tragedy: that the immediate dramatic moment is the important thing, and the context may change at will to accommodate the particular joke. Once again we see that the concept of drama is suggested to the author by the medium for which he is writing. He creates in a scenic void, and he suggests to the audience what they need to imagine. In this context it is not surprising that characterization should be as malleable as scenery. Perhaps the ideal medium for re-creating Aristophanes in our time is the animated cartoon.

WORDS AND HUMOR

The language and the humor of the comedy reveal the same wild fluctuations. Aristophanes vacillates between sublime poetry — some of his lyrics are among the most beautiful in the Greek language — and four-letter-word obscenity. A parody of Greek tragedy may be followed by a knockabout beating scene, intellectual teasing by an outrageous pun. Aristophanes' humor is all-embracing and explosive, as though the author's mind was so fecund that he never needed to pursue one idea to the end; there was always some new joke crowding in. The ancients found this versatility (*eutrapelia*) to be Aristophanes' most admirable characteristic. His plays offered something for everybody: a strong vein of political and social satire, escapist fantasy, and a leavening of pure clowning. Those whom the subtle jokes passed by found plenty to be amused by in the robust fare. Later, more timid ages, who preferred to categorize their comedies more precisely, found this fusion unacceptable and often incomprehensible. The Western comic tradition has followed other models (see Chapter 3), and it took centuries for audiences to rediscover Aristophanes. It was not until our own time that the comic formulations of radio and film, with their rapid pace and uninhibited changes of subject and scene, began to create an environment in which he could once more be appreciated.

In another sense Aristophanes was not anarchic at all. Greek comedy, like tragedy, was expected to be functional. However funny, it had to serve some purpose other than mere entertainment. In subjecting contemporary issues and personalities to the blast of his ridicule, Aristophanes worked as a cartoonist of the political, social, and artistic scene in dramatic form. Anything strange, abnormal, or even merely different that was at that moment in the public eye was liable to find its way into his plays. Thus his works acted as a safety valve for public emotion. Laughter could deflate personalities and defuse potential danger. Comedy, in its annual tongue-in-cheek scrutiny of men and events, cut both down to size. Underlying Aristophanes' wildest fantasies and most outrageous jokes we see a deep and sensitive concern for the well-being of Athens. The comedies combine the raunchiness of the burlesque show with the acuity and worldly-wiseness of the intimate revue.

But only a society outwardly secure could tolerate such outspokenness from within. As the fifth century drew to a close, Athens lost the war and with it most of the old independence of thought and action. Aristophanes' last plays grew tame. It was no longer safe to utter the frank political criticism of the earlier works, and the new leaders of the state, more precariously established, were less inclined to see themselves treated frivolously. In the closing years of his life we see Aristophanes transformed from an uninhibited satirist to a composer of timid allegories. The pattern of the comedies remains the same, but their force is gone. In *Plutus* (*Wealth;* 388 B.C.), which marks the end of his creative life, Aristophanes restricts himself to a gentle comedy about the blind god of wealth who has his sight restored and thereupon distributes money only to the deserving, instead of haphazardly as before. Though it has its moments of fanciful charm, *Wealth* is still a sad, thin work, whose only contact with social reality lies in its comment on the economic depression that followed the war. It is written out of the financial and artistic poverty of a battle-weary and depleted age.

Survivals

The literary influence of Greek tragedy has been enormous. Many examples of imitations and borrowings will be found in the chapters that follow. Its performance history, however, has been scanty.

Normally the Greek tragedians could expect only one performance of each work during their lifetimes. The fourth century B.C. saw many revivals, but these were selective. Aeschylus largely vanished from the repertoire. Plays that stressed a large, well-trained chorus were impractical in an age that was straitened financially and had lost the old sense of community responsibility. Some plays of Sophocles could still be seen, but it was Euripides, suspect in his lifetime, who was the prime favorite after his death. Star actors found that his plays provided their most powerful roles. Adapted by generations of actors, however, the texts became corrupt. In the late fourth century B.C. an attempt was made to compile a definitive corpus of the three great writers' works for the Athenian archives. This collection, purloined by the library at Alexandria, became the basis for school editions that circulated throughout the Mediterranean and were the source of the medieval manuscripts through which the plays

(*left*) Chorus from a modern revival of Aristophanes' *The Frogs*. The bird and animal choruses of Greek comedy may recall an earlier nature worship. (*right*) Greek comedy was all-inclusive in its mockery. In *The Frogs*, the god Dionysus is beaten by the doorkeeper of Hades.

The Theater of Dionysus in its later, more permanent form.

The Odeion of Herodes Atticus, Athens, used for modern revivals of ancient plays.

are known to us. For centuries these plays were studied in schools and universities, but they were only rarely performed, and then more as educational aids than as dramatic experiences.

It was not until the late nineteenth century that the public theater began to rediscover Greek drama. Mendelssohn wrote incidental music for a London production of *Antigone;* the newly formed Oxford University Dramatic Society performed *Oedipus the King;* and the success of this production, though still in Greek, inspired a Harvard *Agamemnon* (a sellout in its enormous stadium) and a similar venture at Princeton. Gilbert Murray in the commercial theater began to bring the plays to a wider public by offering, for the first time, a number of actable translations into English, staged by the innovative director Harley Granville Barker. Murray's work opened the way for subsequent commercial presentations, and several of the tragedies now form part of the modern repertory. Commercial pressures, however, have reduced the number seen today to even less than the total selected by the Alexandrian scholars. We can expect to see fairly regularly *Oedipus the King, Antigone, Medea,* and *The Trojan Women;* occasionally, *Agamemnon;* the complete *Oresteia,* perhaps once in a generation.

In Greece the situation is better. Most of the ancient repertory has been performed by the Greek National Theater either at its winter indoor house or in the annual summer festivals of Epidaurus and Athens. The enormous popularity of Epidaurus has made it possible for hundreds of thousands of Greeks and foreigners to see Greek plays in a setting as close to the original as we can now get — though women now act women's parts, and the performances are given after dark, with artificial light. Some of these productions tend to be overly reverential and ponderous, though more experimental staging has been offered by such smaller groups as the Piraeus Theater. A touring company, the Nea Skini, has performed in the ruined sites of ancient theaters across the country. In the United States a festival on Greek lines planned as an annual event at Ypsilanti, Michigan, failed to survive an economically disastrous first season.

Aristophanes has fared even worse. His topicalities had little appeal for the wider Greek audience of Alexander's world, and his frequently obscene and scatological humor did not endear him to schoolmasters careful of the morals of their young. Translators, for the same reason, found him impossible; the ingenious Victorian versions by B. B. Rogers resort to asterisks for long passages. Only recently has it been possible to translate Aristophanes into the sort of language in which he wrote. Several revivals have appeared in recent years, and they have often attempted to recapture the freshness of the originals by replacing ancient with modern topicalities.

3
The First Professional Theater

The End of an Age

Century dates are only a historian's convenience. They rarely relate to the cycle of human activity. For the theater, however, the end of the fifth century B.C. was a date of major significance, marking a substantial change of organization, repertoire, and attitudes. Up to this time the theater had been communal, amateur, local, celebratory. From the beginning of the fourth century it rapidly became secular and professional, offering an entirely different caliber of plays to a much wider audience. Its production methods changed also, moving from performances presentationally conceived to something much closer to stage realism. These changes are important, not merely to the ancient theater but to the theater generally, for they represent the first instance of a cyclical pattern that we shall see repeated in other cultures.

The closing decade of the fifth century was one of loss and decline. Athens said farewell to its major playwrights. Aeschylus, revered in memory though

Sponge, the parasite, from a modern revival of Plautus's *The Twin Menaechmi.*

infrequently revived in performance, had already been dead for nearly two generations. Euripides died in exile in 406 B.C.; Sophocles died in the same year. Aristophanes, though he lived on into the next century, was only a shadow of his former outspoken, satirical self. But these losses were overshadowed by the defeat of Athens at the hands of Sparta in 404. Its wealth and political prestige were gone, its walls destroyed, and its people, for a while, subjected to Spartan rule.

In the turmoil of Greek politics this state of affairs did not endure for long, and Athens soon regained a vestige of her former independence. But although she remained the cultural leader of Greece, and her works set the standard by which those of other cities were judged, she was never able to assert her old imperial dominance. And the artistic achievements of the fourth century reflect this: they are shabby by comparison with those of the fifth, content to live in the reflection of past glory.

There were wider political changes. The days of the city-state were numbered. In the fourth century the dominant power was Macedon in the north, a state previously derided as semibarbaric but that now, first under Philip and then under his son Alexander the Great, subjugated the earlier centers of power and imposed an unwilling cohesion on most of the country. Pressing further, Alexander reversed the previous pattern of history by leading Greek armies against the East. He conquered Egypt and Persia, the greatest empires of the ancient world up to his time, imposing on them not merely Greek rule but the Greek language, Greek customs, and Greek cultural patterns. He led his forces as far as India, and on his death he bequeathed his conquests to Greek dynasties.

This enormous geographical expansion, however, was not matched by any creative surge in literature and the arts. What happened to Athens was true of the Greek world generally. The new age lived off borrowed glories. Hellenistic Greek was the old Athenian dialect simplified. Poetry and drama either repeated the themes of the past or contented themselves with more mundane issues. The new city center was no longer the temple with its associated festivals but the administrative building. Increasingly controlled by a bureaucracy, the people relinquished the sense of community involvement that had characterized the century before.

The Theater in the New Age

The theater, as it always does, reflected the changing mood. As the Greek world expanded, the theater expanded, and it was no longer confined within the bounds of the local civic festival. The more important festivals, of course, continued to exist. Some were still in operation through Roman times. But they were differently administered and could no longer count on wholehearted citizen participation. Increasingly we see the performances turned over to visiting professionals, who toured the major festivals as opera singers do today, bringing their own musicians and assistants and relying on a locally trained chorus, which, in the changing shape of the drama, had less and less importance. But now other outlets existed for performers. The theaters followed the armies, and it was possible, for the first time, for touring companies to perform year round for a living.

THE TOURING STAGE

Most cities already had their own theaters that the touring actors could use. When they did not, the companies brought their own portable trestle stages that could be set up anywhere an audience could be found. These provided the bare necessities of performance and reproduced the essentials of the permanent structures that the actors were used to. They are illustrated on vases, mostly from the independent, prosperous Greek colonies in South Italy, where the actors found rich pickings. We see, normally, a platform stage, with steps connecting it to the ground level, which served as an orchestra for what was left of the chorus. The stage is no more than a bare platform, although sometimes it is more elaborate, with supports designed like pillars. Behind it is an approximation to the *skene* of the permanent theaters, either a hanging curtain or panels decorated with an architectural design. Such were the stages that, we may surmise, were carried around the rural districts of Greece and far into the East: it is probably through direct influence that the rear hanging in the early theater of India was known as the Greek curtain.

THE PROFESSIONAL COMPANIES

The actors who used these stages were the new professionals. As most of the tragedies they played were fifth-century revivals and originally composed for three actors, casting posed minimal problems. A company of three, usually a star and two assistants, could present the standard repertoire.

The chorus, however, was another matter, and it had to be pared down in response to the economic pressures of touring. In the fourth century the number seems to have been reduced to nine, and we can assume that extras, and even chorus members, were often jobbed in from local talent in much the same way that touring opera companies operate today. Certainly the chorus problem dictated the repertory. Aeschylus, whose plays depend on a large, intricate, and highly trained chorus, was virtually unstageable in this new environment. But Euripides was another matter. His impatience with tradition had often led him to minimize the importance of the chorus; often in his plays the chorus is little more than a crowd scene, and some modern revivals have gone so far as to cut the choral passages altogether, insisting that the meat of the play lies with the actors. Undoubtedly the fourth-century actors felt this. Euripides, who had been the most controversial dramatist of the fifth century, was the most frequently revived in the fourth. His personal unpopularity was long forgotten, overridden by the fact that he wrote stunning parts and magnificent speeches in which a star actor could make a great appeal.

So for whatever reason the chorus was fast disappearing as a feature of drama. Its decline was not merely due to financial stringency but reflected the growing detachment of the average citizen from community affairs. Even in the later comedies of Aristophanes we see the choruses dwindling to the point where nothing special was written for them. The manuscripts only bear the notation "chorus" at appropriate intervals, signifying that though something is sung, it does not matter what. The chorus was no longer an integral part of the play, any more than the citizen assembly was at the heart of public affairs.

Thus the plays fell into the hands of the actors, who often adapted them to exploit their particular talents. Lines were cut or rearranged, and additional scenes or entrances inserted. We begin to be aware of a *performance* tradition, distinct from the *literary* tradition, which altered and embellished the texts at will, passing them on to future generations in a form quite different from what the original authors had had in mind. As scripts were still carried, largely, in the actors' heads, and as human memory is fallible, words were changed and lines omitted, by accident as well as by design. When, in a desperate attempt to reclaim the vanishing scripts, the Athenian authorities had written copies made from actors' memories, these were often faulty. Indeed, a major part of modern scholarship has been concerned with trying to restore what the ancient playwrights actually said.

ACTORS' GUILD

Though expansion brought the actors profit, the new professionalism had its dangers. We remarked in Chapter 1 that professionalism in the theater is invariably stigmatized, and hireling actors no longer commanded prestige in the state. Individual stars could attract large followings and handsome incomes, but the rank and file lost status. The fourth-century politician Demosthenes (384–322 B.C.) could vilify an opponent by dredging up his theatrical past and reminding his audience with glee of how the man played small parts on the touring circuit and was pelted by the audience for his pains. By this time, clearly, *actor* was on its way to becoming a term of abuse.

It was undoubtedly in self-defense against social ostracism as well as in acknowledgment of their new professional status that actors began to form their own associations. The Artists of Dionysus, forerunner of Actors' Equity, had their headquarters on the prosperous island of Delos. This island was sacred to Apollo, a god with an interest in the arts, and was an important commercial center; in Roman times it was a major market for the slave trade. It had its own theater, which still stands and which housed an annual festival. Excavations have uncovered a house that was probably the guild headquarters and may also have provided rehearsal space; it is handsomely ornamented with mosaics of Dionysus, tragic masks, and other dramatic illustrations. The guild regulated the activities of its members and handled contracts, which could be very elaborate indeed. Its members made names for themselves throughout the Mediterranean world.

The New Drama

Changing tastes in the expanding Greek world called into being a new kind of play. The pro-Athenian bias of fifth-century drama was less appealing to the cosmopolitan audiences of the Hellenistic age. We have noted that the old tragedies, and particularly those of Euripides, were still frequently revived. Little evidence of fourth-century tragedy has survived. What we have suggests that the later playwrights were content merely to reproduce the superficialities of Euripides' style — spectacle, horror, domestic detail, violence — without understanding the philosophical basis that supported such devices.

But the new, more placid age was not primarily interested in tragedy. Audiences no longer sought plays that would tax, challenge, or affront them. Works that dramatized significant public issues were no longer desirable, or acceptable, when the public was not involved in the decisions. It is indicative of the softening of the age that the favored form was now comedy — but not the old, hard-hitting, festival comedy of Aristophanes.. Audiences sought milder amusement in works to which they would not be asked to contribute physically, financially, or intellectually; a theater for diversion rather than involvement, and an ornament to society rather than an integral part of it.

MIDDLE AND NEW COMEDY

Although audiences now preferred comedy, the conditions of touring made Aristophanes unsuitable for revival. Apart from the constant problem of the chorus, Aristophanes' best material was topical. He had written for a specific community at a specific point in time, and what was funny in Athens would not necessarily raise a laugh in Ephesus, Alexandria, or Tarentum. The changing conditions of the theater demanded a kind of comedy that would present few production problems and have a universal appeal: a comedy dealing in generalities rather than specifics, founded on characters and situations comprehensible to anyone who spoke Greek.

We can see this change even in the late work of Aristophanes himself. His fifth-century works are usually classified as Old Comedy, plays characterized by the loose plot structure, freedom of comment, and personal attacks that we noted in Chapter 2. His last play, *Plutus* (*Wealth*), is assigned by most critics to a different genre, Middle Comedy. *Plutus* retains some connections with the past. It has a vestigial chorus. It is still conceived within a framework of mythological burlesque. But the old pungency and topicality have vanished. Though set in Athens, its story is no more than a gentle allegory, which loses in sharpness what it gains in broadness of appeal. It is a harmless moral tale of the god of wealth, who is traditionally represented as blind and thus distributes his favors haphazardly. In the play an impoverished Athenian finds the blind god and takes him to a healing shrine to have his sight restored. Once Plutus can see again, he begins to bestow money only on the deserving, so that the virtuous grow rich and the corrupt are bankrupted. Even the gods are affected and forsake Olympus to join the earthly party. It is a sad play for a comedy. It mirrors the Athenian financial depression that followed the war; it foreshadows the desperate gaiety of the animated cartoons of the American depression years and "Who's afraid of the big bad wolf?" In showing the gods abdicating their position in favor of worldly riches, it also marks the declining religious standards of an increasingly materialistic age.

Middle Comedy led to New Comedy, the characteristic fourth-century form. This genre clearly signaled its abandonment of larger issues by turning from myth and legend to the domestic and mundane. It was situation comedy involving the kinds of family conflict common to all eras and all societies: father versus son, husband versus wife, lover versus lover in rivalry for the girl's hand. Relinquishing more complex issues, New Comedy virtually discovered the romantic love plot, so that a theme that scarcely appears in fifth-century drama — where it would have been considered too trivial and personal to concern the theater — became dominant in the fourth. In New Comedy the few gods who appear are simply part of the traditional literary machinery and reduced to the status of prologue speakers. If there is any higher power, it is only the force of chance, accident, or circumstance, which brings characters into involuntary collision. It is significant, too, that in a world where the personality of the individual now counted for much less, mistaken identity was another favorite theme: the child abandoned as a baby and finally recognized through a chain of improbable events, by his parents; brother and sister reunited after years of separation and many misunderstandings.

With the range of plot material so limited and the demand for material increasing, playwrights inevitably fell back on tried and tested formulas. This situation is characteristic not merely of Greek New Comedy but of other, later periods of theater and can be seen recurring whenever the growth of the potential audience outpaces the amount of original creative talent, which never increases in the same proportion. We see it in England when the establishment of the professional theater in the sixteenth century attracts a whole new public; we see it in the eighteenth century in both England and France when a large middle-class audience suddenly starts to patronize a theater it had previously conspicuously avoided; we see it most obviously in our own time with the vast audience expansion that accompanied the development first of film and later of television. In all these cases the theater's response has been the same. Increased pressure means that there is no longer time to prepare fresh and original material; the market must be served. A few basic elements serve for a whole range of plays; the same familiar situations are served up in different combinations. The Greek New Comedy is our earliest instance of this phenomenon, whereby playwriting is virtually reduced to a mathematical formula.

CHARACTERS AND COSTUMES

The characters of New Comedy were no less stereotypical than the plots. Certain stock characters reappeared in play after play with nothing changed but the name. This concept was made easier in the theater by the continuing use of the mask, which by the fourth century had become more realistic. Masks and costumes were now labels that defined a character type as soon as he appeared on the stage, so that the audience could predict, from his first entrance, not merely how he would walk, talk, and behave, but what would happen to him. There were no shocks, no surprises. Furthermore, costumes, in keeping with the changing substance of drama, had also grown more realistic. They were no longer the formal robes of tragedy or the padded, often obscene extravagances of Old Comedy but were closer to the garments of everyday life. Audiences could distinguish at a glance the angry old man and the placid old man; the playboy, invariably at odds with his father, in constant need of money and always reconciled at the end; the prostitute, sometimes with, but usually without, a heart of gold; the innocent virgin — usually offstage and silent when on, for this was still a male chauvinist society — and a whole gallery of comic slaves, rascals, simpletons, cooks, and porters, each with his distinctive attributes and vocabulary. Characteristic no less of the new society than of its theater was the *parasite,* a professional sponger, an uprooted, classless individual living by his wits. Having no social status himself, the parasite moves freely between different classes and generations. He is thus often used as the living embodiment of chance, the motivating force of the plot, and he often precipitates collisions between other characters.

FEATURES OF NEW COMEDY

It is perhaps unnecessary to discuss the characteristics of New Comedy at length. They will be familiar to anyone who has ever watched a situation comedy on television. The same factors operate, and mostly for the same reasons. Interest is in the manipulation of events rather than in the development of character. Characters, in fact, rarely develop or change at all. Each has certain strong, well-defined personality traits. They do not influence one another to the extent that these personalities change. Rather, they bounce off each other, and the fun lies in the manipulation and the collisions.

This kind of play has been aptly compared to a game of pool. The balls, of known colors and numbers (the characters), are arranged on the table (the stage). An external, arbitrary force (the pool cue, chance) puts them in motion.

They set off on their courses, striking each other, going off at tangents; they finally come to rest in a different combination. But the balls have not changed. They are still the same colors as when they started on their collision course; they have not melded or changed shape from sphere to cube.

Greek New Comedy is, indeed, the spiritual ancestor of modern situation comedy. Its authors would have recognized Oscar Wilde, Noel Coward, Neil Simon, and most television scriptwriters as kin. When later comic playwrights talked of classical models, it was the Greek New Comedy and its immediate Roman descendants that they meant, not Aristophanes; he was already forgotten, consigned to the limbo of scholarship and revived, if at all, by literary societies conscientiously resurrecting a dead master. It was not until the twentieth century that Aristophanes was truly rediscovered and his vastly different comic techniques recognized for what they were.

THEATER ARCHITECTURE

Theater buildings accommodated themselves, by changes more or less subtle, to the new kind of play. With the chorus no longer part of the drama, the full orchestra was not necessary. As theaters were rebuilt, therefore, the orchestras were truncated to a semicircle, diminished in size, or impinged upon by a deeper, higher stage on one side and extra seats for privileged spectators on the other. *Skene* buildings became more elaborate, decorated with columns and statuary.

More important than any structural change, however, was the new use to which the old architectural elements were put. In the fifth century the *skene* was merely a conventional background, a sounding board against which the action took place. It looked like a house facade, and so, at need, it could function as a house, but it could also be imagined as anything else the author's fancy dictated or imagined away altogether. Even before the end of the fifth century, however, this situation had begun to change. Euripides, for instance, was more literal about his stage settings. (The *Bacchae*, p. 55, is a conspicuous exception.) For him the *skene* facade was a solid, tangible presence that could not be imagined away; his plays tend to be set in front of specific and clearly identified buildings, and the locale does not shift for the whole action of the play. In this Euripides was probably motivated by his own desire to draw tragedy into closer contact with his audience's everyday lives — to show *real* happenings in *real* surroundings — and also by the influence of comedy, which is always, by its nature, closer to the everyday. And in Aristophanes the *skene* is normally used as a real housefront, and the upper level is not always heaven but at times a prosaic roof over which characters can chase and scramble. This tendency continues in New Comedy to the point where the *skene,* now with three doors, comes to be regarded as a quasi-realistic setting of a street frontage, and various rationales are given in the dialogue for bringing situations that would normally take place inside the house into the open air.

Thus although the physical appurtenances of the theater remain more or less the same, the whole concept has shifted from presentational to representational theater. The action no longer controls the setting; the setting dominates the action. Although some conventional techniques remain, the masks, the costumes, and the acting have grown so realistic that the audience are being given something much closer to a slice of life. They are also distanced from the action in a way they never were in the fifth century. The orchestra, which had been the center of the drama, now becomes, for most of the play, an unpopulated void across which the spectators view an elaborately, realistically composed picture. As the professional actor has estranged himself from his society, so the stage action has distanced itself from the audience.

The Playwrights: Menander

Many theaters of this period have survived. In Athens the Theater of Dionysus was rebuilt to conform to the new principles. Similar structures can be seen in Greece, Italy, and Turkey.

The same is not true of the plays. The three most distinguished playwrights of the period were Diphilus (ca. 340–289 B.C.), Philemon, (ca. 361–262 B.C.), and Menander (342–290 B.C.). Works of the first two are known to us only from fragments and scattered references. Menander, who enjoyed an enormous, perhaps extravagant, reputation in antiquity, was hardly known to us at all until very recently. In 1905 substantial fragments of his plays began to turn up on papyri found in Egypt. (Most of our papyrus discoveries of ancient authors come from this country, where the dry climate has preserved them.) These were still not complete plays, but enough remained to give an idea of what they were like. Then in 1955 a virtually complete comedy was discovered on Egyptian mummy wrappings: *Dyskolos,* variously translated as *The Grouch, The Man Who Hated People,* or *The Misanthrope.* This discovery caused a sensation. It was not merely the first new Greek play to be found for centuries; it offered, at last, a chance to match an actual work against the almost legendary reputation that Menander had enjoyed since his own time.

Dyskolos is a pastoral comedy set in the rocky, inhospitable fields of Attica. The prologue is spoken by the god Pan, who identifies the central door of the *skene* as his shrine, the other doors as the house of Knemon, the "grouch" of the title who lives alone with his beautiful daughter, and that of Gorgias, his estranged son. Pure chance precipitates the plot. A well-brought-up young Athenian, while hunting in the country, sees Knemon's daughter and falls in love with her. (Love at first sight is axiomatic to these comedies.) Her father, however, has turned his back on the human race — particularly on those he considers effeminate city dwellers — and will have nothing to do with him. The young man tries to work in the fields, but he ends up with only blisters and an aching back for his pains. Then — chance again — Knemon falls down a well. His son and his daughter's suitor run to his aid, and he begins to realize that no man can live entirely alone. His reintegration into society is not complete, however, until the servants drag him out forcibly, on his mattress, to join in the feast.

Such is the play. There is a relic of the old Aristophanic spirit in the city-country controversy, but the chorus has vanished, except for a band of revelers who punctuate the action with songs before Pan's shrine. Modern critics have found it flat and disappointing. Ancient writers applauded Menander's fidelity to nature: "O Menander and life, which of you imitated the other?" *Dyskolos,* on the contrary, shows stereotypical characters and arbitrarily contrived situations. Knemon's change of heart comes from no inner motivation but simply from the accident of falling down the well.

We must remember, however, that Menander was at the beginning of a comic tradition of which we now stand near the end. What we consider clichés were, in his time, new. Menander and his contemporaries developed a repertory of situations and devices that later comedy, through Plautus, Shakespeare, Molière, Sheridan, Wilde, and Coward, has continued to exploit. By comparison with his later imitators, Menander's comedy is indeed artificial and contrived. By comparison with Aristophanes, it is not. The fifth-century writers' comic figures were exaggerated grotesques, chameleon characters changing according to the whim of the dramatist and the exigencies of the situation. Menander's are consistent; though they divide human nature into arbitrary types, they are much closer to the world as we know it.

In summary, then, the later Greek theater retained many features of the old, but it turned them to new uses. In many of its aspects the staging became more representational, more realistic. The subject matter of the plays showed a similar trend, moving from the dramatizing of abstract issues to more immediate and personal affairs, from myth and legend to domestic narrative. We may remind ourselves here, as the theater frequently asks us to do, of how intimately form and subject matter are connected. Presentational theater commonly concerns itself with issues that cannot be *shown* but only *symbolized* or *suggested.* Representational theater portrays the texture of everyday life. A similar change reveals itself in language. New Comedy was still written in verse, and it retained the iambic trimeter that had become traditional for actors' roles. It was now, however, much more fluid, colloquial, conversational, and closer to the irregular speech patterns of everyday life. In New Comedy we find fewer formal orations, and the debate format, though it may still underlie key scenes, is no longer so apparent.

Above all, this was now an actors' theater, as its contemporaries recognized. "In the last century the theater belonged to the poets," mourns Aristotle; "now it belongs to the actors." Such evidence as we have for Greek New Comedy suggests that the plays were elegant in manner but trivial in content; their art lay in their construction, and they needed the actors' personalities to give them warmth and life. Thus scholars who merely *read* plays have been less than enthusiastic about the newly discovered Menander: the play does not read well.

On the stage, however, it is an hour's good entertainment. We might note that here we touch on another recurring pattern in theater history. An age of creators tends to be followed by an age of interpreters, a playwright's theater by an actor's theater.

The Critics

Among interpreters we must also number critics, and the fourth century produced its own, giving us our first extended critical writing on the theater as a genre.

PLATO

First came Plato, whose philosophical inquiries brought him into contact with the theater from several points of view. His attitude is generally unsympathetic, surprisingly so from one who had such dramatic skill himself. Plato's philosophical works are written in dialogue form, to recapture the freshness and spontaneity of living discourse. They are distributed among characters, the most prominent of whom is usually Socrates, Plato's old mentor. They are composed with considerable dramatic skill, giving us a vivid sense not merely of the idiosyncratic characters of the participants but of the environment in which they move. And they can easily be, and frequently have been, dramatized. Perhaps it was Plato's awareness of his own dramatic power that made him sensitive to its potentialities for abuse in others. Certainly, though he is drawn back to the theater again and again, and discusses it in various dialogues, his approach is at least cautionary, and sometimes downright prohibitive.

Plato offers his most extensive consideration of the theater in Book X of his *Republic,* which was probably written in the early fourth century B.C. In this work he develops his concept of an ideal state, naturally colored by his experience of the institutions of his own city-state of Athens. Among these he could hardly fail to include the theater, and his unsympathetic treatment must be seen as influenced both by his overriding philosophical beliefs and by the state of the art as he was able to observe it.

Theater is imitative art, and imitative art is something of which Plato's grand philosophical design causes him to be deeply suspicious. He posits an ideal world of ideas, of "forms," of which the phenomena of this world are imperfect copies. In the ideal world there is an ideal chair, which the actual chairs of this world strive, and fail, to imitate. The artist who paints a picture of a chair is therefore producing an imitation of an already flawed imitation. Representational art is thus at two removes from the truth.

We must remind ourselves that when Plato went to the theater, he was no longer watching the tragedies of Aeschylus. He was experiencing a form of drama that had become much more realistic and prided itself on reproducing the details of everyday life. Plato complains about this. He points out that the actors of his day are largely concerned with meaningless impersonations. They like to demonstrate how cleverly they can imitate the squeal of a pig or the squeak of a windlass. Their concern is with displays of technical virtuosity, regardless of content.

This criticism could be leveled at fourth-century art in general. Painters and sculptors had abandoned pure form for graphic skill in reproducing detail, and they had become obsessed with the problems of reproducing the texture of fabric in marble or reproducing painted fruit that could be taken for real. This concern for technicalities led Plato to argue for a visual art that concentrated on the underlying shape of things rather than on their superficial detail, and it made him, with uncanny prescience, an early spokesman for the abstract painting that the art world did not begin to see until the early twentieth century: Plato is the first theorist for the kind of art that the cubists put into practice. It also led him to denigrate the representational theater, which was the only kind of theater that he knew.

Though he distrusts imitation, Plato has to admit its utility. He argues elsewhere, in fact, that the only way we can learn is *by* imitation. If we model ourselves on what we hear, it is crucially important that we see and hear the right things. We learn virtue by imitating the good. And as theater is not only an imitation of an action but is so persuasive that it inspires others to imitate, the subject matter of drama is of great concern. Here Plato becomes censorious, and he applies rigid strictures not merely to drama but to the content of epic poetry also. Homer is argued to be as misleading as the playwrights. Audiences should not be shown a hero weeping, for such unmanly behavior betrays the ideal of the true heroic character. They should not be presented with examples of human vice and corruption, for if we learn by imitation, such things are doubly dangerous — for the actor who imitates them in performance and for the audience that watches him. Both may be led into harmful courses. Plato is thus forced, with regret, to suggest that there is no place for the theater, for actors or for dancers, in his Ideal State. Whatever their attractions, they are potentially too powerful an instrument for harm.

Plato's criticisms, though directed at his own theater, extended far beyond his time. We should note that they embody two fundamental principles. One of them, traditionally Greek and accepted long before Plato's time, is the assumption that art should be useful. We should ask not merely is a play good, but what is it good for? The other is the fallacy, still met with all too frequently in censorship, that the moral value of a work is determined by the morality of its characters and of the individual incidents it represents. Or, to put this concept specifically, critics might argue that Henrik Ibsen's *Ghosts* (1881), a play that deals by implication with venereal disease and incest, is an immoral play because venereal disease and incest are immoral. Plato is blind to the fact that although Euripides' plays — which he presumably saw, though he does not discuss them in detail — are full of characters who commit treason, adultery, rape, and murder, the focus of the plays is not on these incidents for their own sake but on the wider scheme of morality in which they must be seen. He ignores the fact that when Achilles is shown weeping in the *Iliad* — which he *does* discuss in detail — this unmanliness is part of a greater design that shows Achilles restored to heroic stature.

Though Plato's criticisms were conceived in a pagan world, they later fell on willing Christian ears. The Christian church was quite ready to countenance a form of drama that was good for something — in this case, for the instruction of the unlettered and the advancement of the faith. When theater began to sever itself from the church and establish itself as an art worthy of attention in its own right, the church at once began to level strictures against it. And censorship, in whatever period, has always tended to concern itself with *what* is shown rather than *why* it is shown. Plato was quoted appreciatively by self-appointed censors of later ages, and even those who had never read him unquestioningly accepted his assumptions.

ARISTOTLE

The second critic who emerges from this period is Aristotle (384–322 B.C.), a writer of a very different nature. Born to a family of physicians, he was a scientist by training but a polymath by profession. As tutor to the young Alexander, shortly to be called the Great, he could not fail to be aware of the way in which the horizons of the Greek world were expanding. His investigative spirit led him to found a school in Athens that concerned itself with virtually every branch of human enquiry, and his own writings reveal the breadth of his studies. He wrote on physics and metaphysics (it was Aristotle who coined the term *metaphysics*), on rhetoric and politics, on ethics and poetry. His *Poetics,* which treated epic poetry, tragedy, and comedy, has proved to be one of the most influential, as well as one of the most troublesome, works that have come down to us from classical antiquity.

The importance of the *Poetics* lies in the fact that, so far as we know, it is the first work ever to treat drama as a genre in its own right. Aristotle conspicuously does not ask, "What is a play good for?" In this he was probably — as in other aspects of his thought and teaching — consciously opposing Plato, whose influence he both respected and resented. He asks, rather, "What makes a play good?" And he proceeds, like a scientist, inductively, examining the available evidence and drawing conclusions from it. Where Plato was concerned with what should be, Aristotle was concerned with what was; and he had available to him, presumably, a mass of fifth-century drama that no longer survives as well as the lists of prize-winning poets and actors in the Athenian archives that have similarly failed to come down to us. Although he was even further removed from the fifth-century tradition than Plato, clearly he had read plays that he could no longer see, and his conclusions, though they may lack eyewitness validity, are marked by the scrupulousness of the conscientious scholar.

The *Poetics,* therefore, should be of enormous value to us. The value, unfortunately, is flawed by the nature of the work itself and the tricks that time and circumstance have played on it. First, it is incomplete. We have only about a third of the original. The section on epic poetry is largely, and that on comedy completely, lost. We are left with the section on tragedy. Second, even this section is of less use to us than it might be because of the way in which it is composed. It is densely written and often cryptic to a degree that suggests it was never intended, in its present state, for publication at all. Scholars have been forced to the conclusion that it represents Aristotle's lecture notes, intended to be expanded upon in class, or perhaps, even worse, a student's notes from Aristotle's lectures — and anyone who has tried to compensate for a missed lecture by borrowing a fellow student's notes will know how misleading these can be. What we are left with, then, is a text that seems at times to be almost willfully obscure; that leaves key terms undefined or takes them for granted; and that appears to be a kind of shorthand, intelligible to the initiated but, at a remove of centuries, often baffling. The burden of understanding Aristotle has thus been thrust upon his interpreters, and the centuries have seen a number of widely different interpretations based on the same elusive text. In most modern editions of the *Poetics,* much more space is taken up by notes and commentary than by the slim text itself.

Some ideas, however, are reasonably clear. Aristotle's favorite dramatist is Sophocles, and his model tragedy is *Oedipus the King.* (A strange choice, perhaps, for there is no other play quite like it in the canon that we know.) He conspicuously fails to understand Euripides, and he seems vague about Aeschylus. On the basis of *Oedipus* he constructs an ideal scheme of what a tragedy should be, and he uses several technical terms that have remained embedded in the theater's critical vocabulary. Tragedy, he says, should deal with a great man who suffers a fall from greatness or a reversal of fortune (*peripeteia*) through *hamartia.* Precisely what Aristotle meant by *hamartia* has been disputed. The word used to be translated as "fatal flaw," with the supposition that Aristotle was referring to some basic weakness of character in the protagonist that made him susceptible to error. According to this view, Oedipus is accused of rashness, with the implication that to some extent he gets what he deserves. More recent scholarship suggests that this is too elaborate an interpretation, pointing out that in Greek the word may mean simply "missing the mark," "making a mistake." It could certainly be applied to *Oedipus the King* in this sense. Oedipus is a great man who makes a mistake, who eventually faces his moment of truth, the recognition of his situation (*anagnorisis*), and falls.

Aristotle also made some remarks on the desirable effects of tragedy: that it should bring about a purgation (*katharsis*) of pity and terror. He uses a medical word that clearly occurs to him from his own training. It has usually been assumed that when Aristotle speaks of purgation, he is referring to the *audience:* by watching the enactment of tragic happenings on the stage, they are purged, vicariously, of undesirable and unhealthy emotions in themselves. A variant, and more modern, view would argue that Aristotle is referring to the *actor,* who effects a purgation in himself by acting out the misfortunes of others. Or perhaps Aristotle is saying that the *character* is purged by recognizing his error.

Aristotle also makes some observations on the desirable economy of tragedy by pointing out certain features of fifth-century drama. He stresses the need for simplicity of action. There should be one plot, with no side issues or irrelevancies. This situation is what *most* Greek tragedies (not all) give us. The plot of a play can usually be expressed in one short, simple, declarative sentence. Oedipus seeks the cause of the plague that has fallen on Thebes and discovers that it is himself. Orestes returns from exile to avenge his father's death by killing his mother.

Aristotle stresses also the compactness of the action. In Greek tragedy dramatic time is, for the most part, approximately equal to real time, or at least seems to be. In *Oedipus the King* the immediate dramatic action occupies an hour or so of Oedipus's life, which is also the length of the play. Again, though this is often true, it is not always true. We pointed out in Chapter 2 that given the performance conditions of the fifth-century theater and its preference for suggestion over realistic depiction, time is often flexible and can be extended or curtailed according to dramatic expediency. Particularly, the timing of individual incidents within the general scheme can be speeded up to make the plot work faster. In *Oedipus the King* Oedipus sends for the old herdsman who knows the secret of his birth; the man appears almost immediately, though we have earlier been told that he is living "as far as possible from the sight of Thebes." Nevertheless, by and large the observation about compactness of time is valid.

But the most important consequence of Aristotle's statements lies not in how they related to the plays he knew but in how they were interpreted — or misinterpreted — to guide playwrights of later ages. We shall see how, in the seventeenth century, the *Poetics* became virtually the playwright's bible and was used to enforce a pattern of drama far stricter, and far more exclusive, than anything the Greeks themselves knew.

Drama in Italy

In the cultural history of the Western world, the Greeks are usually regarded as inventors and creators, the Romans as copyists and propagators. Though this criticism is often unfair, in the theater it is certainly true. The Romans took over the Greek theater and its plays and made them available, in Latin translation, to a much larger audience.

EARLY INFLUENCES

When the expanding power of Rome made contact with the Greek world, it had had little time to develop cultural traditions of its own. Such native drama forms as had emerged were still in the rudimentary stages and could not compete with the more sophisticated products of an older civilization. It is interesting, however, to look at these indigenous products and see what features they have in common with early drama elsewhere.

Rome was founded, according to tradition, in 753 B.C., on an unpropitious site, volcanic, marsh-bound, and without a good natural harbor. In its early years it was heavily influenced by neighboring powers. Prominent among these were the Etruscans, who inhabited a region approximately denoted by modern Tuscany and who supplied Rome with some of its earliest kings. Roman tradition also derived from the Etruscans the beginnings of Roman theater. The historian Livy (59 B.C.–A.D. 17) relates how, when the city was plague-stricken in 364–363 B.C., Etruscan dancers and musicians were imported to appease the anger of the gods. These performances remained as fixtures in Roman life and were gradually embroidered upon by the Roman youth until they became the nucleus of a drama. Though the story may not be true in detail, it indicates the same connection between drama and music, and drama and religion, that we have seen in other places; and certainly other features of Roman public entertainment can be shown to derive from Etruria. It is suggested that the Latin *histrio,* "actor" (hence our *histrionic*), and *persona,* "mask," were originally Etruscan words.

We know indirectly of another kind of native drama, a rustic comedy associated with the town of Atella, in Campania, and so known as the *fabula Atellana,* "Atellan farce." These seem to have been a series of skits built around such stock characters as the oafish Maccus, the old man Pappus, Bucco ("fat-face"), Dossennus ("hunchback"), and Manducus ("bigmouth"); however, most of these attributions are only conjectural. The Atellan farce survived as a popular folk entertainment for centuries. There are records of its survival long after the more sophisticated theater had come and gone. In trying to exhume it, however, we are hampered by a recurrent problem in Roman studies.

Rome had two cultures and, one might almost say, two languages. What we know through the works of Latin literature is primarily the elitist culture, heavily Greek-influenced and expressed in an elegant language. Of the popular culture and the Latin of the streets we know relatively little. Much of it was never written down — was, indeed, despised as unworthy of polite attention. Only by occasional hints and quotations are we aware of its pervasive, tenacious existence. The main reason we know of the Atellan farces at all is that the form was taken up by *littérateurs* of the late Roman Republic who patronized it and made it temporarily fashionable.

It is likely, though not certain, that the titles of these literary Atellanae reflect the content of the earlier folk form. Thus we have suggestions of domestic situations in comedy (*Sponsa Pappi,* "*Grandpa Takes a Wife*") and of identical twin plays (*Gemini Dossenni,* "*The Dossennus Twins*"). Plays of the latter type may indicate that the actors wore masks and that, as in the Greek New Comedy, a physical feature of the theater facilitated this sort of plot material. Some would posit an even closer connection, arguing that the Atellan farces were not native at all but already influenced by New Comedy through the Greek colonies in the south. This view is supported by the obvious similarity of the stock characters on both sides of the Adriatic. Similarity, however, does not necessarily imply influence. We can say, only in general terms, that popular culture had evolved the same kind of comedy on both sides of the sea. Stock characters appeal to an unsophisticated audience because they are easily comprehensible. If the stock characters tend to repeat themselves from one culture to another, it is because human nature tends to remain the same.

GREEK PLAYS IN ROMAN DRESS

The Romans readily acknowledged that their greatest dramatic influence came from Greece. While Rome was still a huddle of shacks along the marshy banks of the Tiber, Greece was insinuating itself in all directions. As early as the eighth century B.C. waves of colonists were spreading throughout the Mediterranean. They infiltrated Italy to such an extent that the lower half of the peninsula, from Naples southward, became known as *magna Graecia,* Greater Greece. Naples itself (Neapolis, the New City), with a far better harbor than Rome's, was one of the more important of their colonies; so was Taras (Roman Tarentum, modern Taranto) in the very south, a vital center of culture and trade. In these cities the Greek theater, imported from the mainland, flourished; when Rome first threw off the domination of Etruria and then took over the other Italian powers piecemeal, it found a ready-made theater waiting. Rome, as a later poet was to put it, was subdued by the cities it had conquered.

Livy acknowledges this debt in his history of the Roman theater. He states that a Greek, captured in the Roman siege of Tarentum, proved himself so adept at literary matters that he was adopted by the family that owned him, and that, taking the name of Livius Andronicus, he became the first to stage Greek plays at Rome in Latin translation. The date given for this innovation is 240 B.C. The story itself is open to question, as the possible dates for the siege of Tarentum and the principal events of Livius Andronicus's life do not agree. In recounting the story Livy may have been influenced by family pride, for he was a later descendant of the man who had supposedly adopted the Greek actor-playwright. Furthermore, this kind of adoption story turns up so frequently in Roman literary history as to suggest that it may be a metaphor for cultural transmission, not an actuality. The Romans, no less than the Greeks, liked to individualize their history, and we may surmise that the Roman absorption of Greek theater was a far more complex process than the story suggests. Nevertheless, Livius Andronicus became for the Romans what Thespis had been for the Greeks, the legendary father of the theater. He was, undoubtedly, a historical figure, and several titles of his plays have survived, both tragedy and comedy.

His successors are, for us, more concrete figures. Naevius and Ennius also wrote both tragedy and comedy. The surviving tragic fragments reveal them-

Typical characters of Roman comedy from a modern revival of
Plautus' *The Twin Menaechmi*. (*above*) Nagging wife and parasite.
(*below*) Slave, doctor, old man, henpecked husband.

(*right*) Prostitute and one of the identical twins. (*below*) Old man and his daughter, the nagging wife.

selves as rather heavy-handed adaptations of Greek originals, with variations in treatment that may have been influenced by generations of actors' improvisations and additions: a performance, rather than a literary, tradition. Titles, of which we have many, suggest a preoccupation with plays about the Trojan War, which, for Rome, was beginning to assume the proportions of a national saga. One of Rome's foundation legends traced the origin of the city to Aeneas, exiled Prince of Troy.

Rome's continuing foreign involvements carried it beyond the Greek colonies in Italy to other bastions of the earlier civilization: first to Sicily, during a series of wars against the North African power of Carthage, and subsequently to Greece itself. Macedon became a Roman province in 148 B.C. In the maturing Roman Republic, therefore, Greek influences continued to predominate.

They were not, however, unanimously welcomed. A puritanical core of the Senate held out against Hellenism as decadent and corrupt, with important consequences for the theater, as we shall see. But playwrights continued to adapt Greek plays for the entertainment of the Roman populace, and it is noticeable that tragedy rapidly gave place to New Comedy. This was, perhaps, inevitable. Once the novelty had worn off, popular taste asserted itself, and the Roman public was on the whole unsophisticated in its tastes, lacking the traditions that, for the Greeks, had made tragedy a living reality.

PLAUTUS

The most important comic writer was Titus Maccius Plautus (ca. 251–184 B.C.), whose name, meaning "Titus, the Flatfooted Clown," may indicate a theatrical ancestry; the similarity to the name of one of the Atellan farce characters will be noticed. Twenty-one of his plays have been preserved. He undoubtedly wrote many more. He was so well liked that after his death, theater managers unhesitatingly added his name to other people's plays with the assurance that this would draw the crowds. By the first century B.C. so many works were attributed to him that Varro, a friend of Cicero and the leading antiquarian of his day, sat down to compile a list of those works undoubtedly Plautine. His total of twenty-one certainties is probably represented by the surviving corpus.

These short comedies (average running time, one hour) show a remarkably effective compromise between the spirit of Greek New Comedy and popular Roman taste. The plots are Greek; the names of many of the characters remain Greek; the action is still laid in Greek cities. But the language, of course, is Latin — the Latin of the streets, one of the few extended examples we have — and the action is enlivened with local allusions and Roman topicalities. This compromise produces a never-never world, half Greek, half Roman, in which the stock themes and characters of New Comedy make an impudent comment on the cherished values of Roman society, while remaining sufficiently distanced to avoid serious offense. In the Roman family the father's word was law; in the plays he is regularly deceived and robbed by sons and slaves alike. The

Roman matron, whose power was only slightly less awesome, is portrayed in comedy as a nagging virago. Slaves, classified as goods and chattels under Roman law, appear in Plautus as wittier, braver, more resourceful, and often more moral than their masters. This reversal becomes, of course, a commonplace of comedy, but in Roman society it touched upon a sociological truth: as long-established civilizations fell to upstart Rome, slaves often were more cultivated than their masters and occupied what we should now call the learned professions. The story of Livius Adronicus, true or not, illustrates this phenomenon.

Plautus happily rang the changes on formulas that, by his time, were tried and true. A few synopses will give the character of the whole. In *The Twin Menaechmi* identical twins cause confusion among wife, mistress, father-in-law, and servants, until they are at last brought face to face by a loyal slave. In *The Pot of Gold* an old man is driven nearly berserk by a hoard of buried treasure, which is constantly slipping from his grasp. In *Prisoners of War,* slightly more serious, a father discovers that a slave purchased from foreign conquests and working in his house is really his own long-lost son. *Amphitryo* is unique in that it represents a return to an older comic tradition of myth parody. Jupiter, the king and father of the Roman gods, disguises himself as a mortal to seduce that mortal's wife.

These plays are fine works of stage carpentry, put together by an expert hand. They are not great literature, nor did they ever pretend to be; they were written for a mass market, and Plautus would be surprised to find them being read now in universities. Like many good situation comedies, they do not read well. They need the actor's personality to bring them to life; they need slapstick, music, gymnastics, and tumbling. Plautus clearly wrote for an audience that lacked theatrical sophistication. His humor is broad; the plot is usually explained by the Prologue in advance, and any vital piece of information is given several times to ensure that no one misses the point.

One thing the plays conspicuously lack is pointed political allusion. The day for this was past. Naevius, Plautus's contemporary, risked one such attack and was imprisoned for his pains. Even the general parodies of Roman life and institutions are clearly signaled as "only in fun." The plays come back to a sense of reality at the end. The father is reestablished in his authority; errant sons and slaves are formally pardoned; the girl without birth or fortune whom the son has married without his father's knowledge or consent turns out to be the long-lost daughter of respectable parents. The audience can go home, after an hour of licensed laughter, secure in the knowledge that the fundamental values of family and state are unassailed.

TERENCE

Plautus represents the mainstream of Roman comedy. His successor, Terence (ca. 195–159 B.C.), moves in a more rarefied world. His full name, Publius Terentius Afer, gave rise to the story that, like Livius Andronicus, he had originally been a slave — in this case an African — who gained his freedom and rose to eminence through his literary abilities. He admitted to having patrons, who presumably assisted him financially, and his limited output — only six comedies — suggests that he did not need to rely on the stage for his livelihood.

Although he, too, takes the Greek New Comedy for his source, Terence clearly writes for a different clientele. His prologues take a superior tone. They spurn the mere explanation of the plot — as one of them says, "the old men coming on to the stage will tell you all this themselves" — and serve, instead, as literary manifestoes, defending the author against his critics. Terence can assume that his audience has read the plays in the original Greek; it is doubtful whether Plautus could assume that his audience could read. And in Terence the Greek atmosphere is preserved inviolate; there are no Roman jokes, no compromises with local mores; even the titles are transliterated Greek. All this suggests a privileged writer composing for an upper-class literary coterie; there were many such in republican Rome.

Terence's comedies also show a delicacy and sensitivity that Plautus's more robust humor avoids; a delicacy perhaps present in the Greek originals, did they but survive for us to read them. The plots are the same — intrigues, family misunderstandings, mistaken identities — and the characters are drawn from the same range of familiar types. But in Terence these characters tend to have hearts and consciences. The son still deceives his father but feels pangs of conscience about doing so. The old father's traditional sternness is motivated by a genuine concern for his son's well-being. Physical humor is largely eliminated. These comedies are refined to the point where tears are apparent behind the laughter; they have been called Chekhovian in the subtlety of their nuances.

Within his own circle Terence presumably enjoyed some success. With the general public, brought up on more substantial fare, he had little. One of his plays failed twice before it won acceptance. He complains that the public walked out of the theater, preferring to see a ropedancer. Perhaps this neglect bespoke a deeper malaise, for Terence's plays close the age of Roman play writing. Drama in Rome was never the abiding passion it had been for the Greeks. Popular audiences were turning to other kinds of entertainment, spectacular, brutal, or a combination of both. Though plays continued to be performed and theaters proliferated, the drama as such was more and more an art of limited appeal.

The Roman Theater

Of the physical conditions in which Plautus and Terence worked we know far less than we should like. For this the blame rests with that residual Roman conservatism that, while permitting the performance of Greek-inspired plays, did its best to restrict the opportunities for staging them. In Rome, as in

Greece, performances were limited to public festivals. In Rome, however, these festivals multiplied till they took up a large part of the year. Special occasions could also be found, such as the inauguration of a new temple, for Rome even in the Republic was prone to introduce new gods. Some of Plautus's work was first performed at such events. In addition, private ceremonials could turn into public holidays: Terence's work was seen at funeral games for departed members of illustrious Roman families. In practice, therefore, opportunities for play performance were far more frequent than in fifth-century Greece. And as in the earlier civilization they were supervised and financed by the city magistrates. Increasingly, however, Roman officials seeking new office looked on the theater as a vote-catching device and were lavish in their private funding to provide a good show.

ACTORS AND AUTHORS

The acting companies hired for these occasions were professionals, with the low social status that this implied. The troupe (*grex,* a word that, significantly, has another meaning in Latin, "flock of sheep") was led by the actor-manager (*dominus*) and its members could be expected to double or triple in roles. Some actors clearly were slaves, educated in professional skills to increase their value, but even the freeborn actors ranked little higher in prestige. One or two in the later Republic gained enormous followings and were taken up by the nobility. Roscius, traditionally known as the greatest Roman actor of all time, was a personal friend of Cicero. But these were unusual cases. The average actor's life was hard and unrewarding.

So was the author's. Terence was an exception. One or two others, in the early period when theater was still something new and exciting, enjoyed official esteem. Livius Andronicus was called upon to compose a song for one of the most solemn state occasions. Ennius was the leader of an artist's guild in the Temple of Minerva. But the average writer, represented by Plautus, could expect little reverence and much drudgery. Plays were bought outright by the company. There was no royalty system; this system would not appear in the theater for more than a thousand years. Once his script was sold, the author had no further financial or artistic control over it. If he needed more money, he had to write another play. There is evidence that Plautus was not always on good terms with Pellio, his principal actor-manager, though Ambivius Turpio, in the next generation, seems to have gone beyond the call of duty to get Terence's plays some measure of public appreciation.

STAGING THE PLAY

The opposition of the puritanical element in the Roman Senate to the whole concept of the theater was most forcibly expressed in its continued refusal to permit a permanent theater building. Rome, incredibly, had no stone theater until 55 B.C., though Italian cities originally Greek had been enjoying such buildings for centuries.

Plautus and Terence saw their work performed on temporary stages, set up against temple walls, or in stadiums where there was existing stone seating for the audience. Naturally no evidence of these structures has survived. We can reasonably assume, however, that they followed the pattern of the Hellenistic theater, providing a platform for the actors backed by a wall with three doors. In the prologues these are usually identified with their appropriate characters. Characters could appear on the roof: in *Amphitryo,* a slave pours water from the roof onto the head of an intruder. Occasional traces of fifth-century practice remain; the imaginative flexibility of the older stage has not completely died away. In Plautus's *The Rope* one of the entrance doors represents the seashore, through which fishermen net and haul a floating chest. In the same play there is even a vestigial chorus.

One of the most argued questions about the Roman theater of this time is whether or not the actors still wore masks. The difficulty is caused by some firm statements that the mask was first introduced by Roscius, long after Terence was dead. But it would be strange if the Romans, who took over every other aspect of the Greek theater — its stage, its plays, its verse forms, even its technical vocabulary — did not also inherit the mask, which was its most characteristic feature. Indeed, the number of identical-twin plays suggests it. Though one does not *need* masks to show identical twins (Shakespeare, for instance, does not in *Twelfth Night* and *The Comedy of Errors*), the frequency of the device in Roman comedy suggests that it was facilitated by the convention.

Roman acting seems, generally, to have followed later Greek principles in using broad, pantomimic gestures. Literary and pictorial sources suggest that acting was primarily frontal, with characters facing the audience directly even when they were supposed to be addressing each other — thus making more plausible the frequent scenes where a conversation is overheard by a third, unseen party who is standing only a few feet away. Recognizable comic routines reappear: the beating scenes, for example, and the "running slave" who is so obsessed with the necessity of delivering a message to his master that he cannot see him, even when he is under his nose.

Music, which had played so large a part in the Greek performance, was still present, in truncated form, in the Roman. Most of the dialogue was written in the iambic or trochaic meters, but the action was punctuated with solos (*cantica*); the total effect must have been something like musical comedy.

THE THEATER BUILDING

In the last century of the Republic temporary theaters grew increasingly elaborate. On one occasion the contractors had to take out special insurance against damaging the underground sewers, so heavy were the structures they

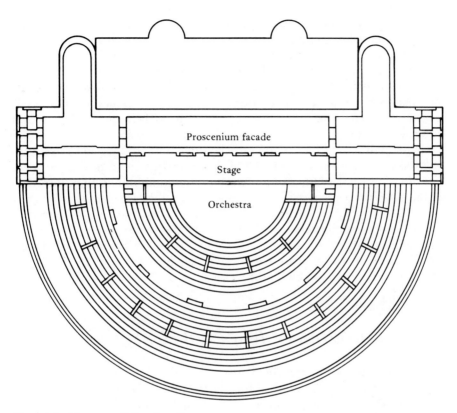

Proscenium facade

Stage

Orchestra

Plan of the Theater of Marcellus, Rome.

had to cart through the streets. Finally, in 55 B.C. Rome acquired its first permanent theater. It was built by Gnaeus Pompeius Magnus (Pompey the Great), who, returning from a series of foreign triumphs, used his enormous political prestige to override senatorial objections. Pompey's theater no longer stands, though its outlines may be traced in later street patterns near Rome's Largo Argentina and its shape is known from a surviving map. Built in imitation of the theater at Mitylene, on the island of Lesbos, it had the habitual Greek features and was the center of a much larger complex. An adjacent piazza provided shelter and accommodation for the waiting crowds; a temple to Venus rose behind the *cavea* (auditorium); and a new Senate House stood nearby.

With the change from Republic to Empire under Augustus (31 B.C.–A.D. 14), Rome saw a spate of theater buildings, for monumental construction became a mark of imperial prestige. Rome itself saw the Theater of Marcellus, still standing, built to honor Augustus's heir designate, who died young; Augustus's second-in-command, Agrippa, built another bearing his own name. During the Empire any provincial city of importance, from Britain to North Africa, had its own theater.

Vitruvius, who wrote a treatise on architecture in the first century A.D., laid down basic principles for builders to follow. Though these structures were still built on Greek models, they were conceived on a different premise. Greek theaters had been built in hollows in the existing terrain; they were at one with their environment. The Romans often built on flatland, as if to demonstrate their dominance of nature. Innovations in building techniques (the full development of the arch, the discovery of concrete) made these enormous buildings freestanding, rising like islands on the plain.

Significantly, the *scaena* (the Latin transliteration of *skene*) and *cavea* were now linked by containing walls. Once in, the citizen could not see out. We have already seen the fifth-century Greek theater as an architectural metaphor for the society that produced it. The same is true of the Roman. The theater is now self-contained, cut off from real life; the audience attends, not to hear discussion of contemporary issues but to enter a fantasy world, dominated increasingly by spectacle and violence. Pompey's Theater was inaugurated with animal shows in which exotic beasts were slaughtered. On this occasion, at least, public sympathy was with the victims.

Entertainments of Imperial Rome

In the Empire other forms of dramatic entertainment became prominent. Popular audiences were entertained by troupes of mimes (*mimi*) presenting what were virtually vaudeville performances: mélanges of music, dance, skits, and acrobatics. Here for the first time women began to enter the theater. Some imperial ladies, enjoying the thrill of slumming, performed as *mimae*. Some centuries later a female mime, a child of the streets, rose to become empress of Byzantium. Her name was Theodora, and contemporary gossips have left us information about her performances that probably represent the state of the art as a whole. One of her popular acts was to lie naked under a pile of birdseed and let the birds slowly peck the seed off her. A more elegant form of the art was represented by the *pantomimus,* who performed, to musical accompaniment, solo dance recitals of Greek myth and tragedy, playing every character in turn.

Tragedy itself had almost entirely disappeared. Plays were still written, but as an intellectual diversion only, with no prospect of performance. Revivals of older tragedies were still given at the surviving dramatic festivals; these revivals, however, tended increasingly to the pompous and grotesque, with elaborately padded costumes to give the actor superhuman stature and with frightening, distorted masks. For the intelligentsia Emperor Nero (A.D. 54–68), who saw himself as a born artist, performed frequently on the Greek festival circuit and in his own palace theater, using masks, it is said, modeled after his family. Such a domestic performance may be the ultimate source of the famous, and anachronistic, story of Nero fiddling while Rome burned.

Nero's sensational private life, lavishly reported by historians, has left us much information on the actor's training that the emperor underwent. Clearly, even at this late date, the actor's prime instrument was still the voice, and Nero exercised as strenuously as any opera singer, declaiming with weights on his chest to improve his breath control and taking potions for his vocal cords.

TRAGEDY: SENECA

The only original tragedies from the imperial period have come down to us under the name of Seneca (ca. 5 B.C.–A.D. 65), Nero's tutor and one of his chief ministers. There is a partial mystery here, as no contemporary allusion to these tragedies has been found, and Seneca himself, in all his voluminous writings, makes no mention of them. With one exception they are based on Greek tragedies, mostly on plays that we still have and mostly on Euripides.

Comparisons are instructive. Seneca (let us assume it was he) has taken the rhetorical quality already present in Greek tragedy and enlarged upon it till it completely dominates the play. By this time rhetoric, shorn of its practical applicability — the emperor, not the public assembly, now made the decisions — had become an elaborate and formal art. Seneca's father had composed rhetorical treatises; Seneca himself was Nero's ghost-writer. In one aspect, then, the plays are rhetorical textbooks, compendia of every kind of stock speech and oratorical device taught in the schools. They may have been composed for this purpose, to be declaimed for specialist audiences in the academies and not for public performance at all.

In another sense they show what aspects of Greek tragedy appealed to the later Roman world. They are morbid and violent; they exaggerate the sensationalism to which Euripides was already prone; they deal with the psychology of guilt and perversion; they show a world very like that in which Seneca lived, selfish, corrupt, and where the autocrat's whim could destroy the innocent. *Phaedra,* based on Euripides' *Hippolytus,* shows a woman driven insane by unrequited incestuous passion and bringing about the death of the youth who has rejected her slanderous accusation. At the play's conclusion Hippolytus's broken body is reassembled by his repentant father in a ghastly jigsaw puzzle. *Thyestes* begins with a prologue by a monster from the underworld and relates how the name character was deceived by his brother into making a cannibalistic feast of his own children's flesh. *Oedipus* dwells gloatingly on incest and the more picturesque forms of suicide and self-multilation. Only *Octavia* deals with a contemporary subject. It gives a picture of Nero's relations with his wife, so grossly unflattering that if Seneca did write it, he must have kept it very carefully hidden.

Choruses are used in these plays, but as literary adjuncts only, embroidering the action with recondite mythology. Often the stage action — exits, entrances, movements — is completely unclear, and the elaborate nature of some of the effects suggests that these tragedies were meant to be read, not seen. In *Oedipus* a cow is slaughtered to reveal a calf inside the womb; in *The Trojan Women* the walls of Troy fall down. The plays may even have been intended as scripts for a *pantomimus,* where such practical difficulties would have no relevance.

Though we know nothing about their performance in their own time, these plays were to have a major effect on later generations. Characteristic Senecan devices such as the revenge plot, the long internal monologue, the horror and the violence, were to be picked up eagerly by Renaissance dramatists, many of whom were to know Greek tragedy only through the Senecan adaptations.

THE AMPHITHEATER: A ROMAN HOLIDAY

The entertainment center of the imperial world was not the theater but the amphitheater. This word means literally "double theater": as though two Hellenistic orchestras were placed face to face, forming an elliptical arena completely surrounded by tiered seats. Numerous examples survive in Europe, but the largest and most famous remains Rome's own Colosseum.

This amphitheater was built as a political gesture. Nero's fire (A.D. 64) had devastated much of the city's heart. One of his more grandiose and obnoxious actions was to seize the abandoned land for a sprawling new palace, the Golden House. After Nero's death (A.D. 68), which brought about a change of dynasty, the new regime sought popular favor by converting the hated site into a pleasure palace for the people. From the statue (*colossus*) of Nero, which it replaced, the new building took its name. Its foundations, laid over a former artificial lake, allowed the arena to be flooded at will for mimic sea battles — though this practice proved inconvenient and was soon abandoned.

The Colosseum, holding forty-five thousand spectators, was a masterpiece of crowd control. A network of entrance ways (*vomitoria*) led under the seats to separate sections; mass rioting, therefore, was automatically contained. At one end was the imperial box; overhead stretched awnings controlled on ropes by sailors from the imperial fleet (the notches worn in the stone may still be seen); and under the arena floor, now exposed to view, was a labyrinth of passages, cages, dressing rooms, and elevators for bringing men, beasts, and scenery to the surface. The Colosseum and its provincial imitators were massive sops to the popular demand for distraction, showplaces designed to focus the attention of the mob upon the person of the ruler and the magnificent entertainment he was providing for them.

The entertainment consisted of gladiatorial fights varied with the slaughter of wild beasts. Ritual human combat was one of the more offensive traditions that Rome had acquired, centuries before, from the Etruscans. At first appearing only in connection with funeral games, it soon became a popular mode of entertainment. Captives from foreign wars were brought home to fight with

Gladiatorial amphitheaters:
(*above*) Pompeii. (*right*)
Capua: a more elaborate
building with a complex
substructure.

Capua: (*left*) Underground passage for the movement of men and animals. (*above*) Gladiators' greenroom. The walls bear graffiti scribbled by fighters waiting their turn.

The strange beasts slaughtered in the arena appealed to the Romans' love of the exotic: they were brought from the furthest regions of the Empire. A mosaic from Praeneste (ancient Palestrina) shows an expedition on the Nile.

Entertainment centers of Rome: the Theater of Pompey (*left*), the Circus Flaminius (*center*), and the Theater of Marcellus (*right*).

their exotic and specialized equipment; trained slaves formed professional teams with the hope of freedom if they survived; freeborn Romans (including one emperor) fought as amateurs or professionals. Crowds followed the favorites as avidly as fans follow their favorites at football games today. At Pompeii in A.D. 59, squabbling between the home and visiting supporters broke out into riots that closed the amphitheater for years.

But human combat, plain and unadorned, began to pall. To keep the public interest, the shows had to contain spectacles and beasts. Exotic animals gathered from the widest extent of the Roman dominions — giraffes, rhinoceroses, panthers, hippopotamuses, even, once, a polar bear — were hunted down and killed. At Ostia, the port of Rome at the mouth of the Tiber, surviving mosaics still advertise the importers of these beasts. Often the combats and hunts (*venationes*) were given scripts, costumes, and settings from mythology. In the Colosseum a condemned criminal, representing Orpheus, was torn to pieces after signally failing to charm the beasts with his lyre; others received picturesque punishments drawn from stories of the underworld. Late classical sources indicate the elaborate stage settings for these shows: trees and mountains sprouting from the floor (brought up, presumably, by the same elevators used for beast cages); rivers made to flow; enormous corps de ballet. But this whole era of Roman theater technology has been lost to us through lack of evidence. Memories of these shows were passed down to the Middle Ages and provided one of the byways by which the theater was transmitted, even though formal drama had ceased to exist.

The death blow to Roman drama, and most of the Greek drama that remained, was dealt by Christianity. When the new religion began to show itself in Roman society, its adherents were regarded as, at best, eccentric and, at worst, subversive. They were therefore natural targets both for persecutions, at first sporadic but later highly organized, and for ridicule on the public platform. Christian ceremonies were mocked by the mimes; Christian martyrs were thrown to beasts in the arenas — never provably, however, in the Colosseum, though this site was enshrined by later popes as a Christian memorial. These persecutions gave the acting profession its Catholic saint, Genesius, a mime who in the reign of Maxentius was converted in the midst of a parody of Christian rites. As the faith became stronger and acquired a voice, its apologists, notably Tertullian, the fiery African Christian, and Augustine, turned on the institution that had mocked them.

Some of these propagandists made a distinction between the abuses of the gladiatorial arena and such writers as Menander, in whom no harm could be found. Others, however, were insistent on eradicating the theater in all its manifestations, root and branch, as a work of the Devil. Christian humanity, in the person of Emperor Constantine, banned human combat in A.D. 404. *Venationes* lingered somewhat longer, finally ending in Rome in 523. As the new spirit triumphed, theaters and amphitheaters all over the Roman world fell into disuse and finally into decay.

(*below*) Ruins throughout the former Roman Empire show the characteristic features of the later classical theater: an elaborately ornamented stage house, the orchestra reduced to a semicircle, and the complete enclosure of the auditorium. (*left*) Reconstructed wooden stage and audience entrance from the Roman theater at Benevento (ancient Beneventum), southern Italy.

(*above*) Auditorium with aisles
and *vomitoria*, Beneventum.
(*right*) Tragic mask reproduced
in stone, decorating the theater
at Ostia, the port of Rome.

Roman theater, Arles, in use for a modern festival.

Arles: another view of the auditorium.

Small Roman theater, Byblos, Lebanon.

The entertainment centers of the Roman world took up vast spaces. The Piazza Navona in Rome was once an imperial stadium.

Upper tiers of the Colosseum, which once supported awnings over the crowd. Holes for the metal braces that originally bound the stonework can still be seen.

Rome: the Colosseum (*upper left*) and the Circus Maximus flank the palace area.

Survivals

Plautus, whose plays for a while vanished from sight and were rediscovered largely by accident (see p. 212), has reestablished himself in the modern theater. Regularly performed since the Renaissance in schools and colleges, as educational exercises calculated to encourage the study of Latin, his comedies have also contained enough of the enduring spirit of farce to justify themselves commercially. One of Plautus's most recent incarnations has been as musical comedy in the stage and film versions of A *Funny Thing Happened on the Way to the Forum;* these inspired a BBC television series, which in turn inspired another film. The modern mass media take happily to the ancient material.

Terence is another story. His works never faded from sight. Cherished as masterpieces of Latin verse style and also for their wealth of moral apothegms, they were used as schoolbooks for centuries. Only in the nineteenth century did teachers begin to feel that the subject matter was, perhaps, unfit for the young, and they substituted Caesar (an inferior and far duller writer) as the first Latin reader. Their stage history has been negligible. Though every year sees numerous Plautine revivals, Terence, significantly, is hardly ever done.

Seneca, whose literary influence was enormous (see pp. 183, 238), has recently had a new vogue in performance. Ted Hughes's version of Seneca's *Oedipus,* first produced by the National Theatre of Great Britain, has been seen widely elsewhere. Others of his plays have been given in Italy and France.

Of the Roman theaters, several are still in use for performance. Ostia, at the mouth of the Tiber, and Benevento (Roman Beneventum), not far from Naples, house annual festivals of Roman comedy. The Roman theaters at Arles and Avignon have been restored to hold modern festivals of drama, opera, and ballet. At Nîmes the amphitheater does duty as a bullring and occasionally serves for such Americanized entertainments as ice shows. In Rome the Colosseum, of course, still stands, though robbed of its supporting ironwork in the Middle Ages and menaced by earthquakes, traffic, and pollution. The most theatrical sight to be seen there now is the cosmopolitan visiting public.

4
The Theater and the Church: Types of Religious Drama

<hr>

The Classical Theater Forgotten

The Christian Church, which had originally declared its hostility to the theater, eventually became its advocate and sponsor. This paradox repays study, not merely because of the enduring quality of the plays that the Church produced, but as an illustration of how deep-rooted the performing impulse is and how vigorously it resists any attempt to suppress it.

As the Western Roman Empire fragmented into smaller communities, with new national identities and new languages, memories of the classical theater faded, either from outright opposition or from disuse. In Rome itself the theaters served as fortresses during the feudal brawls of the Middle Ages, and the Colosseum, denuded of its ironwork, was shunned by the superstitious as an anteroom of hell. At Nîmes in the south of France, a substantial village grew up within the amphitheater's protective walls, and the same thing hap-

The Church as patron of the theater: York Minster.

111

pened elsewhere. For the most part only vague and distorted memories of the ancient glories survived. There was, for example, a widespread medieval misconception that classical plays had not been performed by actors but had been recited by the author from a pulpit with the assistance of nonspeaking performers who mimed the action to his reading. By another misapprehension the ancient theaters were often represented as roofed. Some places were in closer touch with the ancient tradition than others, but on the whole Roman theaters, like Roman bathhouses and palaces, stood as crumbling, unintelligible relics of a vanished age.

Though the Eastern or Byzantine Empire remained Greek-speaking and cohesive, succumbing to the Turks only in 1453, its theatrical accomplishments were slight. Now that Christian humanity had eliminated the gladiatorial games, the center of public interest, in Constantinople as elsewhere, was the Hippodrome, where the populace expended on charioteers the frenzy they might have otherwise unleashed, more disastrously, in politics. Of original drama, however, there seems to have been little. It has been suggested that the complex rituals and ceremonies that permeated Byzantine life were themselves so elaborate and so theatrical as to make the theater unnecessary. As in the West, the ancient theaters fell into disuse; some of the more important were buried, not to be disinterred until the late nineteenth century. After the Turkish conquest the libraries preserved the only memorials of Greek drama, and the rediscovery of classical Greek was a lengthy and laborious process. Only in a few popular forms did any vestige of the ancient drama survive. It has been suggested that the plots and characters of New Comedy, long familiar in the Greek-speaking East, remained in the repertoire of the Greco-Turkish shadow puppet play. Living examples of these puppet plays can still be seen in Greece today.

Christian Compromise

The Byzantine Empire was Christian from its inception, and Christianity rapidly became the religion of the West. The Church soon came to realize, however, that it could not eradicate pagan sympathies entirely. Some things were too firmly embedded in the public mind; the best the Church could hope for was to compromise and to give these things a Christian coloration. This compromise is apparent, for instance, in the major Church festivals. The day chosen to celebrate the birth of Christ marks a festival of immemorial antiquity, the recognition of the winter solstice. The date of Easter is calculated from the phases of the moon, and it shows how the Church overlaid a much older fertility rite with its own symbolism. In the Mediterranean, saints are often recognizably the pagan gods in disguise; the Virgin Mary took over various traditional functions of the goddess Aphrodite.

GRECO-ROMAN DRAMA

We find the same spirit of compromise and adaptation in the theater. The more sensitive spirits in the early Church were torn by a dilemma. They were taught to consider a pagan work as bad by definition. Considerations of artistic merit suggested otherwise. Sometimes, therefore, we see an attempt to have the best of both worlds in the Christianizing of Greco-Roman drama. Music that Euripides had written for his choruses was preserved for centuries, with new words, in the hymnology of the Byzantine Church. Ironically it was swept away in one of the liturgical purges to which the Eastern rite was prone: there are tantalizing hints that fragments may survive in Russia. We have a curious playlet, known to scholars as the *Christus Patiens* (*The Passion of Christ*), that consists of lines taken from *The Bacchae* and other Euripidean plays and rearticulated to give a Christian message. Lines originally spoken by Agave over the ravaged body of Pentheus are in this version given to Mary at the cross. In the tenth century the nun Hroswitha, of the convent of Gandersheim in Saxony (in Germany), wrote a number of plays based on the comedies of Terence, which were still in use as schoolbooks. The resemblance is slight; the plays combine ponderous lessons in Christian morality with an unsavory prurience. They were probably never intended to be acted. They survive, however, as some of the few examples we have of transitional drama, foreshadowing the morality plays of the later Middle Ages.

RITUAL COMBAT DRAMA

Another kind of drama that the Church had to deal with went back far beyond the Greeks and Romans. It was the seasonal enactment of a ritual combat that we have already suggested as one of the many possible sources of Greek tragedy. Though the Church applied a Christian veneer to these performances, the original nature worship remains apparent. Originally the combatants had been New Year versus Old Year, Spring against Winter, with the symbolic death of the latter. In the Christian versions New Year becomes a champion of Christendom — normally St. George, a notable dragon slayer — and his opponent an infidel, normally one of those Turks whose invasions for a long time seemed likely to supplant Christianity in the East.

Other elements and characters grew up around this nucleus. In the versions that we have, known as the English mummers' plays, the pattern is usually as follows. First comes a ceremonial clearing of the space, the marking out of a special, sacred place for playing. A prologue, often spoken by Father Christmas, introduces the characters. Then comes the fight. St. George is wounded but rejuvenated by a doctor (the nature worship theme of death and regeneration) so that he can ultimately kill the Turk. Finally the characters ask the audience for money (the *quête*) and go on their way. Numerous local variations were introduced. The hobbyhorse was a favorite character. Sometimes the antagonists are replaced by other opponents more in the public eye. One version from the 1770s turns the Turk into an American colonist. Another from a generation later matches Lord Nelson against Napoleon. Some examples contain lines now totally meaningless — dialectal jokes or even ritual invocations — fossilized in the plays long after their meaning had been forgotten. It has been suggested that the Punch-and-Judy puppet show, which derives from unknown origins and reached its apogee of popularity in the nineteenth century, reflects the same primitive dramatic pattern. It shows a series of combats in which the hero, part villainous, part sympathetic, triumphs over wife, neighbors, various representatives of authority, and finally the Devil himself.

CHURCH PARODIES

There were other forms of secular diversion over which the Church exercised only limited control. Although the Dark Ages (from, say, A.D. 500 to A.D. 900) produced no plays, we have evidence of anonymous individual performers, or perhaps small itinerant troupes, who were linear descendants of the Greco-Roman mimes, offering songs, dances, and skits to village audiences. Some of these were clearly parodies of Church institutions. The Church was forced to accept them, as a necessary release and diversion, to such an extent that some were given houseroom within the fabric of ecclesiastical life. We have several examples of the Feast of the Boy Bishop, in which a selected youth, bishop for a day, assumed licensed authority; various types of the Feast of Misrule, limited holidays in which the customary taboos could be broken; and even, more grossly, the Feast of the Ass, in which an animal, vested in ecclesiastical robes, was given a seat of honor in the church. Even after the Church had developed its own drama in the later Middle Ages, this secular spirit often intruded to temper the doctrinaire solemnity of the plays.

Liturgy as Theater: Christian Drama Develops

In its own way the Church was itself a focus of show and spectacle. At Mass the people could enjoy rich vestments, colorful ceremonial, and sonorous language and music, which made a powerful contrast to the toil and drabness of their own lives — lives all too likely to be cut short by death in unpleasant forms. The Mass, in a real sense, was a dramatic performance, a symbolic reenactment of Christ's Passion and Resurrection. Even in the modern church, for all the changes of language and liturgical revisions, this sense of drama persists, particularly at the great feasts of the Christian year. The decoration of the Christmas crèche within the context of the service and the veiling of the crucifix and images on Good Friday are pure examples of presentational theater. In the medieval church, therefore, a sense of drama was already latent and was fostered by missionary zeal. Most of the worshipers were illiterate; most were ignorant of Latin. They had, however, that strongly developed visual sense that is the common concomitant of illiteracy, as the elaborate symbolism of church sculpture testifies. The beginnings of Christian drama seem to have come from a desire to bridge the gap between clergy and laity and to bring the Scriptures closer to the congregation by means of illustration.

EARLY ORIGINS

The earliest experiments in Christian drama were local and sporadic. Though the universal language of the Church was Latin, and its procedures were regulated by a central authority, it addressed itself to a variety of cultures and was subject to as many local influences. Our information is sadly incomplete, yet we have enough to suggest a general pattern of development in English and European examples. The Easter ceremonies, for long not merely the principal but the only high festival of the Church, offered a natural starting point. And we seem to have, as with the Greeks, another example of drama originating spontaneously in the receptive climate already created by ceremonial acts of worship.

From the beginning of the ninth century the services of the Church, including their music, underwent a process of increasing liturgical elaboration. The existing Gregorian texts were supplemented by other chants, originally wordless but, by the end of the ninth century, already having words of their own; these chants (*tropes*) provided a natural basis for a Church drama. From the monastery of St. Gall in Switzerland comes the earliest example that we know. Dating from about A.D. 923, it is a simple transposition into dialogue form of the visit of the Marys to the holy sepulcher. Finding that Christ's body has vanished, they are informed that he has risen — *non est hic, sed resurrexit.* The opening words of the dialogue, *Quem quaeritis,* give the title by which this nuclear drama is now known. An English source, the *Concordia Regularis,* drawn up by St. Ethelwold, Bishop of Winchester (959–ca. 979), gives elementary directions for the staging of such playlets within the context of the Mass, indicating a combination of chanted dialogue and mimetic action. Using regular church vestments and furnishings, the plays must at this point still have been little more than extensions of the Mass itself, scarcely separable as drama.

SECULAR INFLUENCES

Other evidence suggests the gradual extension of the Easter tropes to include additional scenes. The visit of the apostles Peter and John to the sepulcher is seen mainly in German texts but in some French versions also. Congregations in Italian, French, and German churches saw the representation of the risen Christ. Other incidents were the journey to Emmaus and the incredulity of Thomas. At a fairly early stage episodes began to creep in that had no scriptural basis. One such was the incident of the Marys stopping on the way to the sepulcher to buy spices from a merchant. This kind of episode set an important precedent for the later development of Church drama; it freely embroidered on scriptural themes, adding imaginative and purely secular flourishes to the sacred material. The spice seller himself (in Latin, *unguentarius*) was destined to become an important comic relief character. All these scenes gradually merged into a connected Easter narrative.

A similar pattern emerged from the Christmas celebrations, which contained equally dramatic material. First seems to have come the obvious choice, the *Officium Pastorum,* the visit of the shepherds to the manger, with a crib made ready behind the altar. Here the staging could take advantage of the popular custom of dressing the church with the *praesepe,* the Christmas crib, and its attendant figures. This custom is, of course, still with us. In Italy, and particularly in Naples, such Christmas cribs have become works of art deemed worthy of exhibition, out of season, in their own right. Other incidents from the Christmas story suggested themselves for dramatization, especially those involving the Three Kings, their encounter with Herod, and their following the star to the East. Eventually the Christmas scenes, like the Easter scenes, coalesced. We have from Freising, just north of Munich in Germany, a list of scenes including the announcement to the shepherds by the angel, the encounter of the Magi with Herod, their warning from the angel not to return, the report to Herod that the Magi have escaped, the flight of the Holy Family to Egypt, and Herod's massacre of the innocents.

THE ACTORS AND THE CHURCH STAGE

For these plays it is almost certain that the parts were still played by clerics, priests turned actors; that the costumes were church vestments, perhaps slightly adapted; and that the settings were provided by the existing church architecture. Here we must remind ourselves that medieval churches were different in many ways from the buildings we are accustomed to today. Many elements we now consider indispensable elements of church architecture were not finally fixed until the nineteenth century. In the Middle Ages there was more open space. There were no pews, so the priest-actors and audience-congregation could move about more freely. Nor did nave, chancel, and choir stalls automatically lead the eye to the apse. The altar, centrally located in the cruciform shape of the church, offered itself as a natural focal point. It was also a natural stage property. In Christian symbolism the altar was already understood to represent the tomb of Christ; in actuality it usually enfolded the relic of some long-dead martyr. In dramatic use, therefore, it could easily represent the holy sepulcher in the Easter plays. Or, as it was customary for benefactors and dignitaries to be buried within the church walls, an actual tomb could often be found. For the Christmas plays the altar could do double duty as the manger, sometimes dressed up with prayer books, sometimes with the miniature Christmas crib and mannequins representing the Holy Family. Hence, supposedly, is derived the word *marionette,* from the French for "little Mary."

THE PLAY MOVES OUTSIDE

The final step in the development of Christian drama involved the combination of the seasonal plays into a larger drama, amplified from other sources. A good deal of Old Testament material now came to be included, showing the prophets as precursors of the ministry of Christ. Other stories were also added whose interest was more secular than sacred: Daniel in the lions' den, the raising of Lazarus, and various stories, biblical or apocryphal, connected with the saints.

At about the same time the plays began to move outside the church. There must have been mixed motives for this. One was the increasing elaboration of staging; the plays had now developed to the point where they could no longer be comfortably accommodated inside the church walls. Another factor may have been religious sensitivity to the kind of material now being presented. As we have seen, there was an early tendency for secular scenes and incidents to be incorporated into the performance — a tendency that becomes more obvious as time goes on and that clearly endeared itself to the audiences, who welcomed a respite from the more serious material, and to the anonymous playwrights, who were able to indulge in flights of fancy not permitted by strict adherence to the Bible. There may well have been a feeling that certain elements were no longer sufficiently decorous to be performed in church. The movement outside, then, is symbolic. When the play is acted against the church facade, the link with the sponsoring authority is still apparent, and the clerics still retain control. In a more open environment, however, the drama exercises a different kind of appeal. It is no longer part of the church ritual but has become a performance in its own right; and it is now more susceptible to secular influences.

A surviving example from this period is the Norman-French *Jeu d'Adam (The Play of Adam),* dating from the end of the twelfth century and played in either France or England, which had been brought under Norman domination. This story of the expulsion from paradise is remarkable in that it shows a transition to the vernacular. The appropriate scriptural passages are still read by a cantor in Latin, assisted by a choir apparently seated within the main doorway of the church. But the actors illustrate the story in their own language, thus providing a living translation of the Bible long before the Church condoned the translation of the sacred text. The copious stage directions indicate a platform for God, attired appropriately in ecclesiastical vestments, another platform curtained off at waist height for the garden of Eden — thus making the convention of stage nudity more acceptable — and a third scenic unit destined to be highly popular in the medieval drama, a huge gaping mouth representing hell, from which issued devils, noise, and explosions.

DRAMA EMERGES

Le Jeu d'Adam is a fascinating example of how the sense of drama was beginning to take precedence over the mere elucidation of the text. This play not only expounds the sacred word but embroiders on it. One of the key scenes is pure mime. Adam and Eve, driven out of paradise to labor in the world, till the field and plant corn; when they retire, the devils appear and sow thorns. We also see the beginnings of medieval delight in elaborate stage mechanics, both in the hell mouth and in what is, apparently, a cleverly articulated serpent.

This play is still presentational theater, in that it involves the use of ritual language, suggestion, and symbolic gesture. And it fulfills one of the prime purposes of presentational theater, that of realizing the unrealizable: how can one realistically depict God? Impossible; we do not know what he looks like. But we can suggest him. At the same time there are individual moments of pure realism; and this mixture continues to characterize the plays that follow.

English Cycle Dramas

In the full flowering of medieval drama, national practice diverges, though the desire of the Church to retain control and to ensure adequate standards of performance remains a common factor. In England, once the plays had moved outdoors, the notorious vagaries of the climate had to be taken into account. Fortunately the performances could be grafted onto an established festival. In 1311 Pope Urban had inaugurated the Feast of Corpus Christi, a celebration, like Easter, of varying date; it could fall any time between May 23 and June 24. As one cynic has remarked, this date represents about the earliest point in the English calendar at which outdoor events can be held without too much fear of rain. Corpus Christi was a feast in which the Church went out to meet the laity, and a procession of priests and citizens carried the Sacred Host through the town. It won rapid acceptance, and by 1318 it was established throughout England. By its nature it provided an opportunity for the performance of religious plays, and the date became a favorite one for such performances; our records of Corpus Christi drama date from 1377.

ORIGINS

The English plays of this period are known to us primarily through four great play cycles associated with this festival, which were performed in major

(*above*) Platform stage for performances of sacred drama in church, from
Germany. (*below*) The medieval conception of the classical theater: platform stage
for a revival of Terence.

The environment of the English cycle plays. (*left*) The substantial organization provided by the guilds and the alliance between church and commerce are shown in this surviving guild hall, with attached chapel, belonging originally to the Mercers and later to the Merchant Adventurers of York. (*above*) The streets through which the York plays passed: the Shambles, or butchers' quarter, in a reconstruction of its medieval appearance (*right*) and as seen today (*left*).

population centers of a country that was still fragmented, diverse, and primarily rural. One comes from York, a city in the northeast that had grown from a Roman garrison town to become a center of the wool trade. Its medieval pattern is still evident today; the protective walls still stand, the city is dominated by its magnificent medieval cathedral built on Roman foundations, and some streets have survived virtually unchanged. Another cycle comes from Chester on the Welsh border, which had also, as the name shows (Latin *castra,* "camp"), begun as a Roman garrison town and later developed into an important commercial center. Some parts of medieval Chester still survive, though the pattern is less evident than it is at York. The third group is usually known as the Towneley cycle, from the name of the family that owned the manuscript; the plays were in fact performed at Wakefield in Yorkshire. Fourth is the cycle described for convenience as the *ludus Coventriae,* the Coventry play, though this traditional attribution is known to be false; the cycle was given somewhere in the East Midlands, but the exact location remains debatable. In addition to these there are several individual plays from other English towns, which may either represent various parts of complete cycles or, with equal probability, have been given as isolated works. Among these are a highly colorful version of the *Noah* play from, appropriately, the great shipbuilding town of Newcastle-upon-Tyne, and one of the most famous, the play of *Abraham and Isaac* from the Suffolk village of Brome.

It is with the cycles, however, that we must be chiefly concerned, as these show the magnitude of the annual operation and the immense amount of time, money, and labor contributed by the townspeople to the church drama. Our manuscripts date, at the earliest, from the mid fifteenth century. But these are merely the written records of plays that had been in existence considerably earlier, plays that may originally not have been written down at all and must have gone through many changes as they developed from their simple beginnings to the complexity of the literary text as we now see it.

We do not know who wrote these plays. Undoubtedly a succession of authors contributed as the plays were handed down through the years and each generation made its changes and additions. Like excavations, the cycles reveal strata, marked by shifts of emphasis and rhyme scheme. Clearly there were borrowings, as one town sent representatives to see what the others were doing. There are also near duplications, representing variants in the performance tradition eventually combined in the manuscript. But one common factor remains: the vernacular is used almost entirely. In dramatic form, at least, the Bible had now become fully accessible to the public. Latin is retained only for moments of importance, to give the full weight of ecclesiastical authority to key pronouncements. God occasionally uses Latin; thus the York play of the Creation begins:

Ego sum Alpha et O, vita, via,
Veritas, primus et novissimus

(I am Alpha and Omega, the way and the life,
the truth, the first and the last)

Similarly, in the Towneley *Second Shepherds' Play,* the shepherds combine Latin and dialectal English when they announce the mystery of Christ's birth.

CYCLE STRUCTURE

Each cycle, too, has a similar structure. It is composed of a number of short plays, each of which relates an incident in the Bible story. These plays vary in length: the Towneley *Second Shepherds' Play* runs for about fifty minutes, the Brome *Abraham and Isaac* for half that time. They also vary in dramatic content. Some are packed with incident; others are little more than a series of narrative speeches. Collectively, however, each cycle covers the principal incidents of both Old and New Testaments, together with some apocryphal and some purely invented material, with a total playing time of some two days in a massive community celebration that could not be lightly undertaken or too frequently repeated. As with early Greek drama, we are talking here not of a permanent professional theater but of an annual festival event that strained the time and resources of the participants.

The plays are written in the familiar form of the age, rhymed alliterative verse, as in the speech of God preparing the Creation:

> I am gracious and great; I am God without beginning;
> I am maker unmade, and all might is in me;
> I am life and way unto weal winning;
> I am foremost and first; as I bid shall it be.

The rhyme pattern changes from time to time, responding either to the needs of the immediate dramatic situation or to the period in which a scene was written into the whole. But, in general, the form has one valuable feature, which must have endeared itself to generations of amateur performers: it is extremely easy to memorize. And despite the mass of disparate material that they contain, the cycles show an overall artistic unity — either from a conscious artistic design imposing a shape on the cycle at a fairly late stage in its development, or from an unconscious process of assimilation and adaptation over a long period of time. Though the cycles may appear episodic and fragmentary, they contain recognizable rhythms and balances, in which themes and motifs from the Old Testament look forward to the New.

ANACHRONISMS

In more ways than one the cycle plays brought the Christian message home and made it comprehensible. They presented the Bible story not as some remote event taking place centuries ago and thousands of miles away but as vivid and contemporary. As we see or read the plays now, however, we are often conscious of what appear to be anachronisms. Old Testament characters, living long before the birth of Christ, swear constantly by Christ and Mary. Abraham and Isaac talk of the Holy Trinity. Herod, a favorite comic character, swears by "Mahound," Mahomet. Personal names given to minor characters are often not biblical but contemporary. Local place-names appear in a biblical setting.

Scholars used to amuse themselves — and some still do — by citing such things, condescendingly, as examples of the naiveté of the rustic writers and performers. It was suggested that the anachronisms occurred because the authors did not know any better. Growing familiarity with the works, however, has taught us to be more humble. It is now recognized that the cycles were not crude products of the rustic imagination but highly sophisticated works whose complexities are still revealing themselves to us. The anachronisms now appear as a conscious device to unite the past and present in the same way that the combination of myth and contemporary reference worked for Greek tragedy.

In the medieval view history was not linear. Space and time were obliterated in the mind of God. Past and present ran parallel, and the audience, for whom the presence of the Deity was a daily reality, saw the evolution of his will against a background they recognized as their own. This sense of a double time is one of the prime constituents of presentational theater, and we recognize one of its strongest manifestations here. While watching events purporting to occur in the past, the audience is continually aware, both through the words spoken and the techniques of performance, of its present environment.

The so-called anachronisms of medieval drama do not confine themselves to single words and phrases. They embrace the whole social situation. Though the characters and incidents are biblical, the local color is contemporary. The shepherds in the fields near Bethlehem have problems and complaints all too familiar to a fourteenth-century peasant, and Noah uses the shipbuilding techniques of his audiences' time.

We must remind ourselves, too, just who the actors were. They were drawn from the population at large. Much has been written about the anonymity of the medieval artist. It has often been suggested that he was content to subjugate his own personality to the greater glory of his work for God and was too humble to obtrude his name on the spectators' attention. In many cases this was probably true. In the drama, for example, the playwrights are anonymous; probably, as we have suggested, there never was a single playwright. And to us the actors of the time are virtually anonymous, though we do have a few names from the cycle records, which list the roles played and the amount of money paid the actors for an honest job well done. But for their audiences the actors were not anonymous at all. We are still talking of small towns here; and when the public turned out to see the plays, they were watching, in performance, people they knew very well in ordinary life, people they saw every day in their farms and businesses and with whom they went to Mass on Sunday. The conditions of performance created the same combination of reverence and familiarity that we observe in the writing: familiar faces seen in biblical roles, reminding ·the audience once again that the Bible story was a living and continuous experience.

ORGANIZATION AND STAGING

For practical purposes the staging of the plays was entrusted to an organization that already permeated medieval society, the guilds. These guilds — part trade union, part benevolent association, part fraternal order — were the economic backbone of the time. Each reputable craft or trade had its own guild whose purposes were to regulate the practice and privileges of the craft, to supervise apprenticeship requirements, and to control prices. (One of the problems that beset actors when they began to emerge as professionals was that they had no guild; from the beginning they were outsiders, classless people in a society still bound by medieval traditions.)

Some of the guilds were extremely rich and powerful, with their own assembly halls and churches. They all liked to put themselves on display, and they were already familiar in civic pageantry. Thus if Corpus Christi provided an appropriate religious occasion for the plays, the guilds offered a ready-made mechanism for their production.

Each guild undertook one play in the cycle. These medieval plays are often known as *mysteries,* and the word has a double sense. First, the plays were mysteries in the religious meaning, in that they represented the mystery of Christ's Passion. Second, they were mysteries in the technical, medieval sense of the word, a mystery being an art or craft, a *métier.* There seems to have been some rough correspondence between the particular expertise of the guild and the play it performed. At York the armorers presented the expulsion of Adam and Eve from the garden of Eden — the point of reference here being the sword with which the angel guards the forbidden paradise. The shipwrights, appropriately, performed the building of Noah's ark. The goldsmiths undertook the presentation of gifts by the Magi. Though such accurate correspondence was not always possible, we have more than a hint that the guilds seized the opportunity to display their skills and their wares (the bakers their loaves, for example), thus giving a religious and theatrical occasion some of the overtones of a trade fair. Those who complain, today, that the modern revivals of the cycles at York and Chester have lost all religious sense and become merely a tourist event forget that in the original performances it must have been highly desirable to attract the tourist trade also. The whole town was putting itself on display. The cycle plays, then, availed themselves of a secular organization, which undoubtedly increased the presence of secular elements in the plays themselves.

HUMOR AND BIBLICAL ADHERENCE

We have noted the contemporaneity of the works. We must also note their humor — often broad humor — and the way in which the Bible narrative is regularly enlivened by the addition of material that had nothing to do with the Bible at all. No longer quarantined within the church walls, they were susceptible to elements of folk play and mumming, to other aspects of the civil pageantry in which the guilds indulged, to observations and characters drawn from street life or the mercantile activity that was the daily round of the performers. And one can sense from the scripts how eagerly the dramatists fell upon these devices and wove them into the fabric of their plays.

Any writer, however humble, however anonymous, likes to feel that he is contributing something of his own, but in many ways the medieval writers were far more restricted in their dramas than the Greeks had been in theirs. As we saw, the Greeks wrote many plays dealing with the workings of the gods with man. But the Greeks had no sacred book; they had myths, which, though familiar, did not possess the authority of Holy Writ. Myths could be adapted and interpreted; the same basic story could produce a variety of interpretations. In dramatizations of the Bible such freedom was not available. The Bible *was* Holy Writ. It depicted its principal characters in ways that could not, without danger of blasphemy, be changed. It gave substantial portions of dialogue that had to be used. We find, therefore, that the sacred narrative is used more or less as it stands. In the Chester play of the *Purification,* for example, we find Simeon speaking an alliterative verse translation of the Nunc Dimittis.

Sometimes, of course, there are changes of detail to suit the new form and to give greater dramatic emphasis. As the Old Testament relates the Abraham and Isaac story, the two principals are accompanied by attendants when they go to the mountain, and Abraham offers to sacrifice his son with a knife. In the Brome play the attendants are omitted as dramatically irrelevant, and Abraham uses, with much greater theatrical effect, a sword. But these are minor matters. By and large the plays say what the Bible says; and we know from contemporary French examples how careful the ecclesiastical authorities were to preserve the fidelity of the text.

There are many things, however, that the Bible does *not* say or at least does not spell out in full — things that are merely hinted at but must be fleshed out in detail if a complete play is to emerge. Here the writers' invention could have full rein, and it usually took the form of comic relief. Characters who are little more than names in the Bible emerge as fully developed personalities in the plays. Sometimes whole episodes are woven round them; and it is here that the sense of contemporary observation comes through most strongly, giving the plays a warm humanity. Herod, though he has his tragic moments, is developed largely as a seriocomic ogre. One of the most famous stage directions in the cycles is "Herod rageth in the pageant [i.e., on the wagon stage], and in the street also." Here the actor was presumably allowed to improvise; and the audiences loved his bluster, especially when it was directed straight at them. Noah's wife, who has a small role in the Bible, is developed in the plays as a nagging shrew, refusing to board the ark until her husband drags her on by brute force. In the lone Newcastle version she is wooed by the Devil and ends by slapping his face. The Devil himself becomes a comic. Probably this characterization was influenced by a sense of fear no less than a sense of fun. This was an age that firmly believed in corporal punishment in a material hell, and the farcical devils, with their grotesque masks and costumes and fondness for fireworks, offered laughter as a palliative to anxiety.

Sometimes these comic attitudes wash over onto the major biblical characters. Joseph is portrayed, in very human guise, as a husband who suspects he has been cuckolded and needs convincing of the truth of Mary's pregnancy; in the Wakefield *Annunciation* he wonders if she has been seduced by "a younger man." Cain, in the York Glovers' version, works as a comic foil to a somewhat sanctimonious Abel, though after the murder he switches rapidly to a tragic figure. In his pathetic final speech we see not merely a character leaving the action but a beloved comic making his farewell to the audience:

> Alas, alas, whither may I go?
> I dare never see man in the visage.
> I am wounded as a wretch in woe
> And cursed of God for my fleshage.
> Unprofitable and vain also
> In field and town, in street and stage,
> I may never make mirth more.
> I know never whither take passage;
> I dare not here abide.

STAGING: THE PROCESSIONAL METHOD

Our information about how the plays were presented is not as complete as we would like. We have one description from the Reverend David Rogers, son of the Archdeacon of Chester, who wrote in his *Breviary* that the players acted on "a big scaffold with two rooms, a higher and a lower, upon four [or possibly six; the reading is dubious] wheels. In the lower they apparelled themselves, and in the higher room they played." Similarly, Sir William Dugdale, in his *Antiquities of Warwickshire,* writes of "theatres for the several scenes, very large and high, placed upon wheels." There is some supporting evidence from other sources, enough to give us the picture of each play within the cycle being staged on its own *pageant,* or wagon. The pageants trundled through the streets on a predetermined route, stopping at fixed points for the performance of the play. Thus each play was given several times during the festival, and the audience that gathered at each stopping place saw the whole cycle pass before it. At York the final location was the field used for public executions — a cruelly appropriate setting for the Crucifixion. It was a mobile production with a stationary audience.

In its general outlines this description is undoubtedly true. The technique of using carts, as American college towns now use floats for a homecoming parade, is familiar from other countries. Spain used its *carros* for sacred processions, and scenically decorated carts were seen in the streets of medieval Rome. In England enough of the pattern of medieval York survives for us to follow the processional route and identify the stopping places. It is clear that the cycle plays had adapted themselves to processional methods familiar in secular uses. In the sixteenth century we shall become familiar with the "royal entry," an elaborate procession escorting the monarch, by a familiar route, into the capital and stopping periodically for speeches to be recited or congratulatory plays to be performed. The cycle plays, then, fitted neatly into this traditional pattern.

In its detail, however, the processional method has raised some questions. The trouble is that what looks like our best evidence is very late. Rogers finished his *Breviary* in 1609, but the last Chester cycle took place in 1575. Dugdale's *Antiquities* was not published until 1656. Both men, therefore, were relying on reminiscences of others, and memory is prone to exaggeration with time. It has rightly been asked how the description of these huge, two-story wagons can be reconciled with the notoriously narrow, winding, and badly paved medieval streets, with houses overhanging to such an extent that they almost cut off the sky. A reasonable compromise suggests that though wagons were used, they were not so cumbersome as the description makes them; that each cart contained the scenic units necessary for the play but was not the *whole* playing space; and that when the carts stopped, the action spread over any convenient playing space — perhaps the steps of a building, perhaps the ornamental base of a monument or fountain, perhaps simply the street itself. It is further suggested that Rogers's reference to "upper" and "lower" rooms may mean not two levels, one on top of the other, but two separate carts, one behind the other, the rearmost serving for a dressing room, much as we use the terms *upstage* and *downstage* now.

The technical vocabulary of the medieval drama suggests that the argument for a small wagon forming the focus of a larger playing area is substantially true. Here the key words are in Latin: *domus,* which means simply "house" and indicates the main scenic structure, or, as it was elsewhere called, the "mansion"; and *platea,* which means a large open space and gives us French *place,* Italian *piazza,* and Spanish *plaza.* Thus the *domus-platea* combination offers a convenient theatrical ambiguity. The pageant, the *domus,* is a setting indicated with some degree of realism. Medieval illustrations and carved panels give an idea of how these locations could have been portrayed. The *platea,* on the other hand, is neutral space, which can become anything that the action requires. We may imagine the pageants as little islands of floating realism, moving through the everyday space of the city streets. Here, then, we have the same kind of constructive ambiguity that we have noted in the performance of biblical characters by actors well known to the audience in their everyday aspects.

THE CYCLE IN PRODUCTION

The same kind of ambiguity extends itself to the details of production. As we know from the surviving stage directions, many of the effects were presentational, working with emblem and symbol, by suggestion rather than depiction. They had to be. The cinema, when it offers films of the Bible, can *show* God creating and destroying the world, the building of the tower of Babel, the crossing of the Red Sea. The stage cannot. But the medieval theater could *suggest* these things very effectively. In the *Play of the Creation* God's division between night and day was shown by a curtain half white, half black. In the play of *Noah* the animals were represented by painted panels that stood around the cart, which thus became the ark. In the play of *Exodus* a strip of red fabric represented the Red Sea. Held by stagehands, it dropped to allow the Israelites to pass and rose to envelop the pursuing Egyptians. Thus the pageant plays secured cheaply, simply, and effectively an impression for which Cecil B. de Mille had to use crowds of extras, trick photography, and a vast quantity of liquid Jell-O.

Within this presentational framework, however, were moments of vivid realism, graphic to the point where they might disturb the squeamish. Medieval audiences loved stage blood — bladders that could squirt realistically when pierced. Many of the audience would have responded, as fellow professionals, to the technical details of the building of the ark or to the discussion between the two Torturers on how most effectively to fasten Christ to the cross. This realistic detail in a generally presentational format was something that communicated itself to the later Elizabethan theater, where we shall see many of the features of the medieval performance translated into a more permanent setting.

THE ACTORS

We know even less about the acting than about the performance conditions, but we can make some intelligent guesses based on the artwork of the period and on the obvious requirements of the cycle structure. The characters wore contemporary dress; that is, the shepherds were costumed as European peasants, not as robed Palestinians, and Pontius Pilate wore the dress of a medieval governor. Thus the costuming once again reinforced the contemporaneity of the plays' message. Actors were still, in England at least, all male. The conditions of guild membership must have enforced this, and the medieval housewife had other things to do. Particular characters and functions were indicated by a symbolism drawn from that of the statues and stained glass in the churches — an often elaborate symbolism, distinguishing disciple from disciple and saint from saint, which the medieval audience was trained to read in ways we can only reconstruct painstakingly from scholarship. It is important to remember here that major roles were played by a number of different people. Each play in which Christ appeared used a different actor; there were several Virgin Marys. This situation must have enforced a consistency of symbolism. The costumers could not risk a radical departure from established conventions any more than the medieval artist could break from tradition in portraying a saint. The audience would merely have been confused.

Thus we see the cycle plays: a combination of devotional exercise and public holiday; a productive mixture of theatrical styles, rigidly traditional in some ways, freewheeling in others; and above all a massive community operation in which the whole populace felt itself involved. To get the flavor of this mixture, we now look at one play in more detail.

IN PERFORMANCE: THE TOWNELEY SECOND SHEPHERDS' PLAY

This play is one of the most frequently discussed cycle plays, and with good reason. It is not only, even in reading, one of the most obviously dramatically effective, it also illustrates how powerfully the secular influence had insinuated itself into the dramatization of the Bible, influencing not merely the content but the whole form of the work. The title (in Latin, *Secunda Pastorum*) indicates that it is preceded in the manuscript by another shepherds' play, covering the same basic material — the annunciation of Christ's birth — but with different treatment and characters.

Though we have no specific directions, the staging requirements suggest that the wagon is divided. At one end a section of fence suggests a sheepfold. At the other are a few items of household furniture — a stool, a cradle, a rough bed.

The three shepherds enter individually. Each has an opening monologue; these set the time, place, and mood. The mood is not a happy one. In typical English fashion the First Shepherd complains about the weather:

> Lord, how these weathers are cold! And I am ill happed;
> I am near numb of hand, so long have I napped.
> My legs bend and fold, my fingers are chapped;
> It is not as I would, for I am all wrapped
> In sorrow.
> In storm and tempest
> Now in East, now in West.
> Woe to him who has no rest
> Midday nor morrow!

This view of the harsh climate is underscored by the Second Shepherd. "When the shoes freeze to your feet," he says with endearing understatement, "it is not all easy." "Never since Noah's flood were such floods seen." In this unnatural turbulence something portentous is brewing.

The shepherds have other complaints, too. The first grumbles about taxes and the arrogance of the "gentlery men" toward the impoverished peasantry. The second is troubled with a nagging wife. The third — the boy — is weary of the hardships of his serfdom and wants to run away. The audience listens with sympathy. Though these are, nominally, the biblical shepherds, they talk of all too familiar medieval hardships. They bear medieval names: Gib, Col, and Daw. They refer to landmarks familiar on the Yorkshire moors. The biblical setting is vividly equated with the local landscape and the rhythm of the audience's daily life: in an action purporting to happen before the birth of Christ, the boy tells the time by the church bells as they ring matins and lauds.

Enter now Mak, the comic villain of the piece. His name is meaningful: it is cognate with Latin *magus,* "wizard," and Mak is known to steal. "Let every man now take care of his thing!" But Mak pleads poverty, starvation, and a wife at home about to add to an already large brood ("Every year comes a baby — and some of them, two!"), and they reluctantly allow him to sleep with them. As soon as their eyes close, he casts a spell: "But about you a circle as round as the moon . . ." and steals a lamb from the fold. Jumping from the cart, he makes a circuit through the street, the *platea,* indicating a journey, and returns to the other end of the cart, which he identifies as his house. His wife, Gill, the archteypal shrew, appears. She is delighted with the lamb but fearful of the consequences; sheep stealing then was punishable by hanging. They devise a plan to hide the lamb in a cradle, should the shepherds come looking for it, and pretend it is a newborn child. Mak reverses his journey, lies down again beside the shepherds, and sleeps.

They all rise, stiff and aching from the cold ground. Mak takes his leave, with thanks. He has dreamt, he says, that his wife has given birth and he must run home to see. Discovering the loss of their lamb, the shepherds go to Mak's cottage. Gill goes through the pretence as arranged, claiming to be so weak from her labor that she cannot stand. Reluctantly persuaded, the shepherds take their leave. But one, moved by goodwill, returns with a present for the baby. Drawing back the covers, he finds the lamb. "What the devil is this! He has a long snout!" Gill runs screaming from the stage, and Mak is dragged out and tossed in a blanket. His punishment is both funny in itself and in the spirit of a play with a happy ending, as hanging would not be.

So far the tone has been largely secular and farcical. Apart from the passing reference to church bells, and a few anachronistic oaths, there has been no mention of Christianity. The play might have been, and probably was, a rustic, homegrown entertainment with its roots in a pagan, superstition-ridden society. But now the mood abruptly changes — abruptly enough to disconcert some modern readers who are used to more gradual development in the theater.

In one important respect this kind of drama has a similarity with the Greek. The imaginative flexibility of the setting induces a corresponding flexibility in mood and characterization; plot and character may change in ways that would seem arbitrary in a drama more realistically conceived, and the point of the play is in the way in which its sections relate to each other. In addition, the episodic structure of the cycle induces a similar episodic tendency within individual plays. Linear continuity is often sacrificed for a moment-by-moment effect. (We have already noted how the character of Cain changes from low comic to tragic figure in a few lines.)

Thus as soon as the shepherds have returned to sleep, we move into another world, that of the biblical narrative. The Angel appears — perhaps on the

(*above*) Medieval pageant wagon, a self-contained, mobile stage on which the plays were drawn through the streets. (*right*) Pageant wagons as used for modern revivals of the York cycle. Note the hell mouth.

(*top*) Simultaneous staging as practiced in Europe: setting for the Valenciennes Passion Play. (*above*) Simultaneous staging as revived in modern America: permanent setting for the Black Hills Passion Play, Spearfish, South Dakota.

(*top left*) Medieval arena theater: model of Piran Round, Cornwall, set up for a production of the Cornish cycle. (*top right*) The Cornish cycle: Noah's Ark. Note the animals and birds represented by painted panels. (*above*) Hell mouth with devils.

The Cornish cycle: (*below*) the trial of Christ. (*left*) One of the stage mansions, with the four torturers.

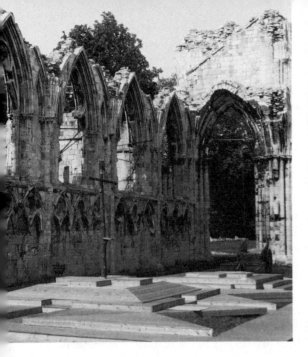

Modern revival of the York cycle: two views of the setting against the ruined walls of St. Mary's Abbey.

Actors wearing medieval costume in procession through the streets of York. God leads, flanked by two angels.

wagon, perhaps on a platform above it, perhaps from some convenient point on the surrounding buildings — and announces the birth of Christ. Waking, the shepherds decide to go to seek him. Their tone is now completely serious, and the unlettered hirelings of the first part of the play now make theological pronouncements in Latin.

They undertake another journey, a circuit in the street to the other end of the wagon, which before had represented Mak's house. It is now occupied by a familiar tableau, Mary, Joseph, and the baby Jesus in the cradle. Kneeling, the shepherds present gifts drawn from the audience's own time — a bird, a ball "to play at the tennis," a bob of cherries — and, at Mary's injunction, they go forth with song to relate the joyous news to the world. Thus a play that seems divided reveals a profound unity of purpose. The power of pagan magic and the lamb that is false are contrasted with Christianity and the Lamb that is true. Guile is replaced by God's word; and the shepherds who began the play with discontent and bickering end in joy and harmony. The *Second Shepherds' Play* is a capsule version of how the whole cycle blends secular and sacred elements, entertainment and instruction, for the more effective propagation of Christian doctrine.

Religious Drama in Europe

The processional method was not confined to England. It was used in Italy, Spain, and even on the remote island of Crete. But the European countries generally preferred a more static mode of presentation. Our most complete information comes from France, where a number of scripts survive together with production records, notably the *Livre du conduite* of the town of Mons. As in England the productions were important civic enterprises, though organized on a different pattern. Management was normally in the hands of a syndicate representing the chief men of the town, who selected a script, arranged for the building of sets and costumes, and cast the play from the local population.

SIMULTANEOUS STAGING

Script writing in France attained a degree of professionalism unrecorded in England, and some famous names have come down to us. Also more apparent from France is something that was surely true in England also: the extent to which the productions served as trade fairs as well as religious exercises. They were major festivals that drew thousands of people from the surrounding countryside and offered a natural opportunity for the local craftsmen to put their wares on show. A good example comes late in the period, from Bourges. This area was a center of the weaving trade; the costumes were made locally, and it is not surprising that we hear a great deal about their sumptuousness. The script, by Simon Greban, was *The Mystery of the Acts of the Apostles.* Though chiefly concerned with the missions of St. Paul, it drew heavily on the colorful, often apocryphal lives of other saints.

Opening the performance was a procession, in the English manner, of wheeled tableaux and characters. The play itself, however, took place outside the city, in what the locals knew as *les Arènes* — a Roman theater, or amphitheater, we do not know which, as the evidence has vanished. Here the audience sat on the Roman benches with the carts drawn up in front of them. Thus the successive settings required for the action were on view simultaneously, side by side. Common practice was to set heaven at the right, hell mouth on the left, an ancient association still remembered in language: the right hand (*dextrous,* from Latin *dexter, adroit* from French *droit,* and the various uses of *right* in English) was the good side, and the left (French/English *gauche,* Latin/English *sinister*) was the bad. Between them were framed the various other locations required for the long play. Some, like the prison, were neutral enough to serve in several roles; others, designed more specifically, could be changed at the end of the day's playing.

This method of simultaneous staging is a theatrical version of a familiar convention of medieval art, of which an early and famous example is the Bayeux Tapestry: as in a modern strip cartoon, actions supposedly happening consecutively are arranged side by side. In the performance of religious drama this convention acquired deeper implications. These plays were panoramic, covering a large portion of the known world and many years in time. The audience, however, was presented with a God's-eye view, in which miles were compressed to feet and centuries to hours. On this stage Rome stood next to Jerusalem, and the characters needed only a few paces to get from one to the other. Although all the locations were on view simultaneously, the action brought each into prominence as required.

When we compare the medieval theater with the Greek, it will be obvious that though both may be classified as presentational, they are vastly different in scope and character, and the difference resides in much more than the change of subject matter. The Greek theater was compressed, economical, and selective, deliberately restricting its range of technical possibilities to secure the maximum of intensity. The medieval theater was extravagant, sprawling, and episodic, cramming the stage with a mass of detail always of interest for its own sake, quite apart from its contribution to the whole. We get the same effect if we compare the simple austerity of the Parthenon to the complexity of Chartres Cathedral or York Minster. It is important to note these divergent approaches, as they beget rival traditions that will divide the theater for centuries to come.

ALLEGORY PLAYS

Simultaneous staging appeared in England, too, not in the cycle plays but in another type of religious drama that developed during the late Middle Ages, probably in the mid fifteenth century. These were no longer dramatizations of the Scriptures but allegorical portrayals of the Christian message; their informing image was not the Bible but the sermon; and their characters were personifications of various aspects of the human condition. *Everyman,* the most famous, is of disputed date and provenance. Its patent similarity to a Dutch play, *Elckerlijk,* has provoked discussion as to which came first — English scholars have, predictably, argued that the Dutch version is a translation of the English, and Dutch scholars the reverse — and some of its comments on the abuses of the priesthood suggest a Catholicism that had already been touched by the cold wind of the Reformation.

God, in a prologue, deplores the condition of mankind and announces his intention of sending Death to Everyman and asking for a reckoning. Death interrupts Everyman among his worldly pleasures. Everyman begs for a respite, to set his account straight, but is given none; he then goes in turn to Good Fellowship, Kindred and Cousin, and Worldly Goods to implore their company and assistance. Rejected by all, he turns to his Good Deeds, who is weak from lack of nourishment. Fortified by Knowledge, he restores Good Deeds by a visit to Confession. Then, accompanied by Beauty, Strength, Five-wits (i.e., the senses), and Discretion, he makes the journey to the grave. All fly from him in turn, except Good Deeds and Knowledge, who rejoice with the angels as they tell us that Everyman's soul will ascend to heaven.

We have no evidence of the play's original staging, but it clearly demands a set of units in simultaneous view. God is presumably on an upper platform, surrounded by his angels, where Everyman joins him at the end. Death comes from a grave trap, probably also used for Good Deeds, who is specified as lying "cold in the ground" at first appearance, and for the moment of Everyman's death. The other units would be a house for Everyman, another (perhaps a tavern?) for Fellowship, a third for Kindred and Cousin, and a church for Confession.

Although the play's methods have changed from those of earlier medieval drama, the prime function is still to teach. A Messenger demands the audience's attention at the beginning; a Doctor — perhaps of theology, perhaps a vestige of the spirit of regeneration seen in the mummers' play — sums up the action at the end; and Everyman's progress is divided by soliloquies in which he sums up, so clearly as to appeal to the dullest observer, "the story so far."

A more complex allegory was offered by *The Castle of Perseverance* (possibly late fifteenth century). Here Mankind was represented as torn between the opposing forces of Good and Evil, who fought a battle for his soul. The staging of this play shows the influence of another favorite form of secular entertainment, the tournament.

Displays of martial prowess were one of the medieval world's legacies from the ancient, though tournaments were war games rather than slaughter. Originally conceived as providing training for armored knights, they turned into public spectacles. The simple combats evolved into elaborate shows, staged in rectangular or elliptical arenas protected by a ramp or moat and surrounded by

tiered seats, like the Roman amphitheaters. Here, as in the gladiatorial combats, the familiarity of repetition brought the need for picturesque variations.
In France a mounted knight fought a dog. Scripts evolved in which the com-
petitors took part in a mimic battle, often ending with the siege of a scenic
castle in which sat the ladies of the court; the victorious party was duly crowned
by the rescued maidens. Chaucer, who had been responsible for organizing such
affairs at the court of Richard II, gives, in *The Knight's Tale,* a description of an
arena with shrines and other buildings constructed at points around the perimeter.

A surviving stage plan for *The Castle of Perseverance* shows how this concept
has been extended to the religious drama. The circular playing space is surrounded by a moat and ditch; a castle marks the center; and around the
perimeter stand the mansions of God, the World, the Flesh, and the Devil.
Spectators either sat on the sloping banks or — in one theory — stood in the
arena itself, moving with the action from mansion to mansion under the guidance of marshals with wands. Essentially the play *is* a tournament, culminating
in the siege of the central castle by the forces of evil and their repulse, a forcible
illustration of how much of the theater, even in a church-controlled drama, was
conditioned by secular factors. Where *The Castle of Perseverance* was staged we
do not know; but in the west of England there still exist circular earthworks
— the Cornish rounds — that could have been used equally well for tournaments or plays and have been used for the revival of medieval drama in modern
times.

Other types of medieval setting were even more complex. For example, at
Lucerne the town square and its adjoining buildings were turned into a theater.

DECLINE OF RELIGIOUS DRAMA

As the overwhelming power of the Church declined, so, inevitably, did the
religious drama. In England, Henry VIII's break with Rome diminished the
appeal of plays that had developed under Catholic authority. In France, though
Catholicism continued supreme, the enormous, costly productions succumbed
to a growing lack of interest and the incompetence of the players.

This trend may be seen most graphically in the history of the most famous
French producing organization, the Confrérie de la Passion (Confraternity of
Christ's Passion), founded in Paris in 1398. So successful was this group with
performances in and around the capital that in 1402 it was granted a virtual
monopoly of religious drama by royal charter. The charter was renewed by a
succession of monarchs, and the monopoly proved both lucrative and prestigious. In 1540 the Confrérie appealed to the king to build them a new theater;
in the next year they produced, with great success, the same *Acts of the Apostles*
that had recently been performed at Bourges.

But complaints were already beginning to be heard. It was objected that the
plays were emptying the churches at Mass and that far from inspiring devotion,

the Confrérie was actually bringing religion into disrepute. Abruptly the organization found its material taken away: in 1548 there was a ban on religious drama. This action must have come as a particular shock to the Confrérie, as it had recently taken new premises, the disused town house of the Dukes of Burgundy, for conversion into an indoor theater. That they had hoped to continue their former repertoire may be assumed from the carving, over the door, of the symbols of Christ's Passion. This was now denied them, but a sympathetic monarchy provided compensations. The Confrérie was now given control over secular drama, and their new house, the Hôtel de Bourgogne, inaugurated a new era of the French theater.

Religious Drama in Japan

Contemporaneously with these European developments, on the other side of the world another type of religious drama had originated, which in time would exercise its own influence on the theater of the West. This was the Noh drama of Japan. Like its Western counterparts, it had been called into being to expound and illustrate religious precepts, in this case those of Buddhism, which had exercised a major hold on Japan since the mid sixth century A.D. Like the western plays, too, it found its starting point in religious ritual, which in Japan meant primarily the sacred dance. In a Noh play the dance remains the nucleus of the drama, the climax around which the purely narrative elements are built. Noh's first playwrights were the monks Kwanami (1333–1384) and his son Zeami (1363–1444). The latter laid down the theoretical principles of the art, which his successors accepted as incontrovertible. Because of the unique social conditions under which Noh developed, most of these early plays survive; never permitted to disappear from sight, they may still be seen today in a form Zeami would recognize.

NOH AND CLASSICAL GREEK THEATER

Between the Greek drama and the Japanese, though there can be no provable historical influence, there are remarkable similarities. Both are highly presentational; they share the same premises and evolved, independently, similar conventions of costume and stage action.

We have seen Greek drama deliberately limiting its stage effects; Noh works under even stricter limits. It has only one principal actor, the *shite* (pronounced "sh'tay"), who takes the main role and performs the climactic dance. Normally he is the only masked player: as in the Greek theater the mask confers theatrical reality, and the unmasked figures are denoted as having lesser importance. A secondary actor, the *waki,* acts as support and feed to the *shite.* His questions customarily provoke the main action. Other supporting figures (*shite-tsure, waki-tsure*) may be used at need, in silent roles. A chorus provides a linking narrative and illuminating commentary. Consisting of eight members, the chorus is immobile, but the actor-chorus relationship is far more complex than that in Greek tragedy. The *shite* may speak in the first person as the character; he may speak of himself in the third person, functioning as his own chorus; the chorus may speak of him or in his person. Thus the play provides a fluid concept of personality in which, even with such simple technical means, the point of view constantly changes. The disorienting effect of the split focus has been compared to the use of drugs in the trancelike state it induces in the actors and the audience. Part of the fascination of a Noh play is its hypnotic quality.

The most familiar pattern of the Noh play is presented in the form of a journey. It begins with the entry of the *waki* as a traveler to some shrine or historic spot. He meets the *shite,* who appears to him first as a local resident. By his questions the *waki* elicits the history of the place, involving some local hero or legendary figure of Buddhist tradition. With a change of costume the *shite* then reveals himself as the ghost of the hero or priest and dances for the *waki.*

We have seen Greek tragedy as largely actionless. Even from this elementary description it will be seen that Noh is even more so. It is retrospective drama, dealing in reminiscence and allusion; the leading figure is usually a revenant, recalling actions long since vanished into the past — as though the messenger speech in Greek tragedy had expanded to take over the play. Even where physical action is involved, it is refined to such a great degree of stylization that the untrained observer may miss it altogether.

STAGING

The Noh theater remains the extreme example of a theater designed *not* to imitate the exterior surface of life. Its characteristic stage, originally outdoors, evolved from the buildings of the Buddhist shrine. A low platform, protected by a canopy against the elements, holds the main action. The platform is connected by a long runway to the dressing rooms. This runway also forms a valuable acting area; the *shite* pauses frequently on it, striking attitudes during his long ceremonial progress to the stage. As the Noh assumed the status of a protected art, its buildings were transported indoors, though retaining their initial shape. The original open-air vista was replaced by a stylized painting of a gnarled pine tree — as in the Greek theater, not illusionistic scenery but a conventional background against which the action could proceed. The original environment was remembered, too, in the gravel path bordering the stage. Down one side of the stage in two ranks sits the chorus, along the back are the musicians, four in number, who accompany the chanting and action on flute and drums. Space for action, therefore, is restricted, but the tightly patterned, rigidly controlled movements of the actors are easily contained within it.

Properties are called for, often large ones, but these are only suggestions of

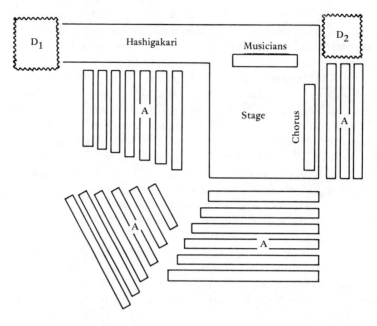

A = Audience

D₁-D₂ = Tent dressing-rooms for
actors and chorus

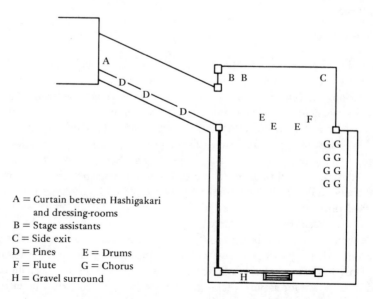

A = Curtain between Hashigakari
and dressing-rooms
B = Stage assistants
C = Side exit
D = Pines   E = Drums
F = Flute   G = Chorus
H = Gravel surround

The development of the Noh stage. (*top*) Open-air Noh stage, early period.
(*bottom*) Open-air Noh stage, later period.

the actual objects. Typical is the Noh boat, frequently called for in the journey plays; it shows merely the outline, shaped from bamboo, and the actors stand within it and pantomime the motion of rowing. Trees, rocks, and buildings are similarly suggested by skeleton shapes, light enough to be carried on at need. For smaller props the fan often suffices. In the actor's hands it can suggest a cup or a sword — in samurai Japan the iron-ribbed fan was often, in any case, employed as an offensive weapon. Any additional small props necessary are handed in through a small sliding door in the side of the stage behind the chorus.

PRESENTATIONAL ASPECTS

The actors' movements are refined from real life, just as the props are sketches of actual objects. To the original audience the movements and gestures of Noh would probably have seemed much more realistic than they do to us now. Noh was originally popular drama, designed to expound the sacred message to as wide a public as possible and in language they could understand; there was no point in being willfully esoteric. Even at this early date, however, the behavior of the ruling and priestly classes was highly studied and formal, and real life actions were choreographed to a degree that no longer exists. Society moved on, however, while the gestures of Noh did not; they gradually evolved into a subtle language intelligible only to the initiated and within the context of the theater. Any resemblance between these gestures and those of real life that had suggested them was vestigial.

We have spoken of presentational theater as setting up, like a game, a code of rules that players and spectators must abide by if the performance is to be meaningful. Any performance exacts a contribution from its audience — if only, at the minimal level, the act of walking across the room to turn on the television set. But the rules set up by Noh are perhaps the most specialized and intricate of any theater in the world. It is quite possible for the uninitiated spectator to watch a complex drama unfolding before his eyes and to have no comprehension of what is happening. The audience is expected to go more than halfway to meet the performers and learn the code of actions that make the play meaningful.

The aesthetic basis of Noh acting may be perceived most simply, perhaps, in the typical Noh walk, which is a balletic abstraction of normal motion. It is a slow, gliding step in which the sole of the foot normally never leaves the ground. When it does, it signifies a moment of high crisis: the vigorous stamp is often the culminating moment of the climactic dance and has as much power, in this rarefied context, as a massive stage spectacle would have in a Broadway musical. Noh refines away *all* the irrelevancies, *all* the excess, to concentrate on the essence of the action. Long journeys on the Noh stage can be expressed by a walk around the platform, or even by a single step. A motion of the hand toward the body can express a suicidal blow.

(*left*) Outdoor Japanese Noh stage. From left to right, the dressing room, the connecting walkway (*hashigakari*), and the stage platform. (*below*) Noh play in performance. Note the masked *shite* (leading actor) and his maskless colleagues; also the musicians seated in a row at the rear.

Just as in the Greek theater, within this formal context the normal laws of time and place can be suspended. A real life action taking hours or days may be compressed into a few seconds. A momentary action can be extended to infinitely longer than its normal duration if it is dramatically important to do so. The language of the plays is medieval court Japanese, which has survived as stage language long after it had fallen out of use elsewhere. Delivered in a singsong chant, it has reality only within the theatrical context; like the gestures, it demands a knowledgeable audience before it can be meaningful.

LATER DEVELOPMENTS

We can speak of Noh in the present tense, because it still exists in a form very close to what its original audiences knew, a conspicuous exception to the rule that the theater is a thing of change. But this survival has been artificial. There are signs in the late Noh plays that the form was about to change, to enlarge its casts and involve more spectacular action. But before these changes could materialize, the form was frozen by the society that gave it birth. What had originally been designed as popular, doctrinaire drama was taken up by the ruling class of feudal Japan, the warrior caste of the samurai. It became fossilized, a deliberately preserved relic of the past to which the greater public was increasingly denied access. (How the public retaliated with a drama form of their own will be seen in the next chapter.)

By cutting itself off from foreign contact, Japan preserved its social structure unchanged for centuries, and the traditional art enjoyed a protected existence within this artificial environment. The Noh stage gives us a further example of the theater building as a metaphor for its society: the outdoor stage brought indoors, the stage canopy made redundant by the roof over its head, sums up perfectly the state of the art as a living museum piece artificially preserved and cherished. Those few families entrusted with the performance passed down the knowledge to subsequent generations; most of the Noh performers in Japan today are direct descendants of the progenitors of the art. When Japan was finally forced in the 1860s to establish contact with the world at large, it seemed at first as though Noh would wither and die; but a series of protective measures have kept it in continued, though limited, currency. When Noh was finally revealed to the Western theater, it was seized on with delight as a total contrast to the heavily illusionistic theater of the time. The impact of this discovery will be discussed in Chapter 10.

Survivals

Several of the early liturgical dramas, after being neglected for centuries, have been successfully revived in our time, often in the context for which they were created. The best known is the twelfth-century *Play of Daniel,* available, with the original instrumentation, on records. The English cycle plays, after their demise, were similarly neglected and preserved only as quaint curiosities, precursors of Shakespeare in anthologies of English drama. They remain some of the most conspicuous examples of plays that act better than they read, and it was not until the twentieth century that their dramatic merits began again to be fully appreciated. In York the original cycle is periodically revived, though no longer in processional form; it is now staged, still with much community participation, against the ruins of a disused abbey. In conjunction with this major festival, however, performances of individual plays are still given on carts, along the original processional route, by local groups. More recently the Chester cycle has been similarly revived in its own city. The commercial theater in London has seen a shortened version of the Wakefield plays and a reworking of a medieval cycle by John Bowen, under the title *The Fall and Redemption of Man.*

Of the later medieval plays *Everyman* is by far the most frequently performed. It is so familiar now that it comes as a surprise to realize that it was only rediscovered, and restored to the stage, early in the present century, by William Poel, whose name will reappear in connection with Shakespearean revivals. *Jedermann,* Hugo von Hoffmansthal's modern version of the same theme, is given every summer in Salzburg, Austria, on a stage built against the wall of the cathedral. This staging gives a glimpse of what the plays must have been like when the Church first brought them outdoors and the town center became a theater for the occasion. The Passion play of Oberammergau, in the Bavarian Alps, performed every ten years, preserves a medieval tradition of family participation, with the same roles being passed on from one generation to another.

Revivals in North America have been slower to appear and more sporadic — largely, perhaps, because this part of the world had no Middle Ages. Now they appear in unlikely places. The small town of Humboldt, Kansas, has an annual procession of religious floats, scriptless, but still conveying the feeling that a cycle play must have had. Spearfish, South Dakota, hosts an annual Passion play based on German sources, using the simultaneous staging principle. Mansions are constructed the length of a huge stage, which allows plenty of room for long processions; the action moves back and forth from mansion to mansion (Herod's palace, Pilate's house, the sepulcher, etc.) exactly on medieval lines. For the Crucifixion and Deposition the action even spills over onto a hill beyond, so that the audience can see, at a distance, the erection of the three crosses. There are some compromises with modernity: full theatrical lighting is used, and the central mansion is a proscenium stage with drop curtains, which allows for changing sets to stage such tableaux as the Ascension. But the Spearfish experience still provides the closest modern approximation to the colossal enterprises of the French medieval theater. In Canada the University of Toronto, using a diversity of local groups, has produced a full processional cycle, which lasted for two days.

Some Conclusions

As we have now surveyed several centuries of theatrical activity, a few generalizations emerge.

First, in any culture there is a noticeable movement from presentational theater, dealing in suggestion and symbol, to a theater that is more realistic, a change that accompanies the shift from sacramental to secular. The subject matter of presentational theater tends to be abstract and metaphysical, dealing with things that cannot be realistically represented — with the hereafter; representational theater deals with the here and now. In this shift the impulse comes from comedy, which is by its nature more inclined to the mundane. The principles of presentational theater, however, though temporarily abandoned, are not forgotten; we will see how theaters of other periods return to them.

Second, we see a shift from amateur theater, pursued either as a collective civic responsibility or as a sideline by those whose main activity is elsewhere, to a theater controlled by professional groups, who pursue this as their full-time occupation, for pay. As noted in Chapter 1, this change usually precedes theater buildings. The first performances are given in whatever surroundings are at hand. As the theater begins to assume a permanent and independent existence, special buildings are constructed, but these tend to retain the features of the temporary theaters that gave them birth.

Third, a recurrent cycle begins to appear in theatrical activity: an age of creative talent (the playwright) is followed by one of interpretive talent (the actor). We shall see other examples of this in the periods that follow.

All these conclusions, of course, admit of exceptions. The theater refuses to work to formulas, and nothing is cut and dried. But the cycle established from the first emergence of the Greek theater to the decline of the Roman sets up a pattern clearly discernible in other countries and other ages.

5
A Theater for the People

Elizabethan London

In the latter part of the sixteenth century there occurred a theatrical explosion whose center was the capital of England. Though exciting things were happening elsewhere, and though there were parallel developments in Spain, in Italy, and as far away as Japan, the extent, the vitality, and the far-reaching consequences of the London experience had no real equal anywhere else in the world.

THE EARLY CITY

To understand the development of the London theater, we must know something about London, for the city was already ancient, with local taboos and traditions that molded the shape the theater was to take. London lay on the

A working reconstruction of an Elizabethan theater; Ashland, Oregon.

north bank of the long, slow curve of the Thames, a river originally gentler, broader, and shallower than it is now. A series of embankments have confined and hastened it; the building of the original London Bridge created a major navigational hazard as the water raced through the arches. But it was deep enough to permit access to shipping and still shallow enough, in its upper reaches, to be fordable; it could once be crossed, on foot, near where the Houses of Parliament now stand.

North of the river by two small hills, now known as Ludgate and Cornhill, in the area crowned by St. Paul's Cathedral, other rivers flowed down from the north. We now think only of the Thames, but earlier Londoners knew the Fleet and the Walbrook also. The Walbrook continued to flow through medieval times, after which it was gradually filled in until it became a covered sewer; its line is still marked by Walbrook Street. The Fleet, which has left its name to Fleet Street, originally marked the city's western boundary; it too has now been covered and lost.

Already settled in early British times, London acquired great importance during the Roman conquest. Colchester, the first capital of the Roman province of Britain, was destroyed in a native rebellion. The seat of power was then transferred to London, which developed as a typical Roman town. Roman merchant ships anchored at the spot that remains the city's dockside area to this day; Roman walls enclosed the two hills, demarcating the area known now as "the square mile," London's commercial heart. A fortress rose in the southeast corner. Traces of the Roman walls have been found in the underwork of the Tower of London, which later rose on the same site; Shakespeare remembered the Roman origins when, in *Richard III,* he referred to it as "great Caesar's tower." Remains of other typical Roman structures have been discovered in the southeast area, though so far no trace of a Roman theater, which is strange, as any Roman city with pretensions to importance had one. A fine example, for instance, may be seen at St. Alban's (Roman Verulamium) only a few miles away. This building passed through several reconstructions, serving variously as theater and amphitheater for beast shows and games.

It has been conjectured that the London theater of Roman times stood on the south bank of the Thames, an area now so densely overbuilt as to make excavation impossible. If this is true, it provides a striking illustration of London's tendency to perpetuate activities in traditional places. The South Bank became Elizabethan London's principal theater area, and Shakespeare's Globe may have been built on the same ground where Roman soldiers laughed at Plautus. The same area in more recent times has held the South Bank Festival Site, a major pleasure resort developed in 1951, the National Film Theatre, and, most recently, the National Theatre of Great Britain. We shall see other examples of how specific areas of London came to acquire traditional associations, some working for the good of the theater, and some working to its detriment.

London became the center of the system of Roman roads that stretched throughout the conquered country. Thus when the Romans left Britain in A.D. 410 to concern themselves with problems nearer home, and the country was left to its own devices, London was already well established as a trading center, and was able to hold its own in the impoverished, invasion-ridden years that followed.

A significant new development came in 1065 when Edward the Confessor, who had his own reasons for disliking London, built a new abbey and an adjoining palace some miles upriver at Westminster. Westminster Abbey became the seat of coronation for all subsequent monarchs as well as the seat of government. He who held London, however, still held England, and in the following year when Edward's successor was swept from his throne by the Norman invasion, William the Conqueror was formally presented with the keys of the city.

The new regime inaugurated a spurt of building. Along the river the docks grew. In the angle of the Roman walls, which still contained a medieval town of wattle-and-daub houses, rose the Tower of London. It contained, among other things, the Royal Menagery, an important center of popular entertainment, which remained there until 1834, when it shifted to the present London Zoo site at Regent's Park. The west end of the walls, overlooking the Fleet, was protected by another fortification, Baynard's Castle. Shakespeare sets part of *Richard III* here; the castle, now vanished, has left its name to a tavern on the site. Religious foundations began to multiply and spread outside the walls. Most important of all, the year 1176 saw the beginning of a new stone London Bridge, destined to last until 1831 — the London Bridge that is falling down in the nursery rhyme. It had nineteen stone arches and a drawbridge that could be raised in case of attack, and gatehouses guarded each end. More than just a bridge, it grew into a street thrown across the river. Medieval travelers passed between overhanging shops and private houses and by a chapel erected in memory of St. Thomas More. For travelers crossing from the south the first sight of London was the grisly array of traitors' heads impaled on pikes above the gatehouse.

The religious and quasi-religious orders proliferated during these years. One of the more important was the Order of Knights Templar, founded during the Crusades to make the roads to Jerusalem safe for pilgrims and quartered in that city on the site of Solomon's Temple. Made up of soldiers, priests, and laity, it grew wealthy and highly privileged; it established centers in various European cities. In 1184 the London headquarters moved to Fleet Street (the Temple Church there still stands) and established a district later to be of great theatrical importance; in Paris, too, a theater was to grow up under the shadow of the temple. In the late thirteenth century the Black, Preaching, or Dominican Friars moved from the adjacent countryside into London, finally settling in the ward of Baynard's Castle. The city wall was rebuilt here to enlarge the original boundaries and to make room for the new foundation — a symptomatic change, for the city was bursting its boundaries.

THE CITY GROWS

In the late thirteenth century London and Westminster were still separate and distinct, joined by a country road, but this road was beginning to be filled by imposing buildings. London was a walled, gated city (the names of some of these gates, as in Paris, are still remembered in the subway stations), but people were spilling outside into the "liberties," as they were known, which did not come under the jurisdiction of the city magistrates. Although London, Westminster, and the liberties have now been swallowed up in the vast urban conglomerate, some traditional divisions persist. Temple Bar (where the Knights settled) remains the official boundary between the City of London and Westminster. The actual barrier was removed in the nineteenth century as a traffic hazard, but the monarch is still greeted with full ceremony by the Lord Mayor of London when crossing the symbolic line.

Tudor London saw the old religious orders collapse. The Order of Knights Templar had already vanished by 1313. Although the church remained, other property was secularized and leased to students of common law, creating two of the Inns of Court where English lawyers are trained and practice — the Inner Temple and Middle Temple. There is a traditional, and strong, connection between law and the theater, and the Middle Temple sponsored many theatrical performances. In 1602 Shakespeare's *Twelfth Night* was seen there. The change to the secular was furthered by Henry VIII's break with the Church of Rome. In Westminster the palace built by Henry's Cardinal Wolsey was taken over and renamed Whitehall; it became a seat of government and plays. The Blackfriars property eventually became a theater too.

The London that Queen Elizabeth knew was still surrounded by greenery. Henry VIII had been able to hunt partridge, pheasant, and heron around Westminster, and citizens did not have to go far from the city walls to find open land where they could practice archery. But the city itself was overcrowded. In 1590 the population was about one hundred sixty thousand, four times larger than that of Paris. The Thames still froze over periodically, so that people could skate on it, but most of the time it was a running sewer, whose malodorousness offended the citizens, though they did nothing to prevent it.

For all its offensiveness, the Thames was a major avenue for processions, which could not progress through the crowded, jostling streets. On ceremonial occasions strings of barges moved upriver from the Tower past Westminster to the palace that Henry VIII had constructed at Hampton Court. When Elizabeth of York married Henry VII in a coronation that marked the end of the Wars of the Roses, she sailed upstream from Greenwich to be met by the Lord Mayor, with barges holding both civic dignitaries and set pieces — including a dragon that spouted flames on the water. Years later a similar pageant celebrated the marriage between Henry VIII and Anne Boleyn. The dragon float appeared again; it was obviously a stock item of Tudor pageantry, an aquatic hell's mouth propelled by a crew of terrible monsters and "wild men" shooting fire.

Despite the traffic problems there had to be some street pageants, too. Most

Inn yards housed the first English professional
companies. (*above*) The surviving Eagle Tavern,
Cambridge, shows the narrow courtyard entrance
useful for audience control; and (*right*) the George,
Southwark, the balconied walls that may have inspired
the seating arrangements of the public playhouses.

Both before and after the
building of theaters, companies
played interludes and longer
works in such settings as the
great banqueting hall at
Hampton Court (*above*).
(*right*) The serving screens in
such halls, often elaborately
decorated, provided a
background for the action, and
may have influenced the tiring-
house facade of the public
playhouse. This example from
Trinity College, Cambridge,
has two large doors and an
upper balcony.

The Elizabethan theater in its social context. Model of a "frost fair" on the frozen Thames, looking toward the theater district of Bankside. Note the various entertainments on the river itself, including an open bearbaiting ring, the row of brothels flanking the river, and the Globe playhouse just behind them.

notable of these were the "royal entries" to mark the new monarch's official possession of the capital. Triumphal arches were erected along the streets, adorned with allegorical tableaux, and speeches and playlets were presented, often composed by professional writers. Ben Jonson, Shakespeare's contemporary, made several contributions of this sort. Congestion and inadequate sanitation made plague a frequent hazard, threatening such ceremonial occasions. In 1603 when James I ascended to the throne, 30,578 people died, and conditions were so dangerous that the new monarch had to postpone his coronation procession until March of the following year.

For all its disadvantages, however, London was where people wanted to be. It was the center of an England that had established itself as a major power; it was a city of great wealth pouring in from the new explorations. Like Rome in antiquity, London was a magnet that drew the talented and adventurous, and one of the things it attracted was the theater.

Our information about the performance of religious drama in London is curiously scanty. Part of the blame may lie with the anti-Catholic movement, during which many church records must have been destroyed. William Fitz-stephen, in a description of London toward the end of the twelfth century, remarks on how many sacred performances there were. The fact remains that, though we know a great deal about what went on in York and Chester, we have virtually no word about the capital. In 1378 the clergy of St. Paul's were giving Old Testament plays at Christmas and objecting the laity was performing bad imitations of them. From the year 1384 we have a record of an extravagant performance lasting five days in August and September. In 1409 Henry V saw a play of the Creation; in 1411 a seven-day performance "from the beginning of the world" was held. These plays were given by clerics, near Smithfield (originally Smooth Field) north of Blackfriars. This place was famous as a horse market, and it was used also for tournaments; there may thus be a familiar connection (see p. 138).

Also near London stood St. Bartholomew's, both a religious foundation and a hospital. Familiarly known as Bart's, it is still one of the major teaching hospitals of London. Around this structure grew up one of London's major fairs. First held about 1123, it accommodated traders, jugglers, acrobats, wrestlers, and what seem to have been miracle plays, which used real animals for the Creation. Bartholomew's Fair was immortalized by Ben Jonson in his play of that name (1614), which gives a panorama of the entertainment offered and the public that patronized it. The fair continued as an annual event until 1855.

The Beginnings of the Professional Theater in England

Out of the debris of the Middle Ages professional companies had begun to emerge. Their standing was precarious, for they pursued no recognized trades; as we have already noted (p. 124), there was no guild of actors. By enrolling themselves in the household of a member of the aristocracy, however, they gained some measure of protection.

THE PLAYS

The material the professional companies performed often contained vestiges and echoes of the old religious drama. "Interludes" were given at banquets and ceremonial occasions. Here the staging was improvised in the banquet hall of a great house. Surviving examples of this type of architecture show a standard pattern: a long hall, down the length of which the tables were set, and a screen at one end, separating the hall from the kitchen. A platform could be set against the screen; the regular access doors served for stage entrances; and normally there was a minstrel's gallery, which could be used for musicians or, at need, for scenes to be played from above. We have seen (p. 13) how the theater's temporary surroundings often suggest a shape for the permanent building; the architecture of the banquet hall probably influenced some features of the Elizabethan public playhouse.

The interludes were, by the nature of their presentation, compact and made few demands on stage resources. Some of the best known have come down to us under the name of John Heywood, who was born in 1497 and died in the last quarter of the sixteenth century; his life thus spans the gap between the decline of the cycle plays and the establishment of the professional theater. In *The Four P's* Heywood sets up four characters, a Pardoner, a Palmer, a Pedlar and a Pothecary, who engage in a lie-telling contest. His treatment of the first two — representatives of the old Catholic order — is symptomatic of his time; post-Reformation England loved stage burlesques of figures from the Roman church. Similarly, Heywood's *Johan, the Husband,* which has much more stage action, treats with frank obscenity the relationship between a cuckolded husband, his wife, and their priest.

Although few of the actual interludes survive — they were occasional pieces, intended for diversion only, not for posterity — echoes of them remain in Elizabethan drama. Into *Love's Labour's Lost* Shakespeare inserts the "Pageant of the Nine Worthies," which is in effect an interlude given as a play within a play and performed by amateurs for the amusement of an aristocratic audience who comment noisily and rudely on the action. The "Pyramus and Thisbe" interlude in *A Midsummer Night's Dream* offers another example, and it allows

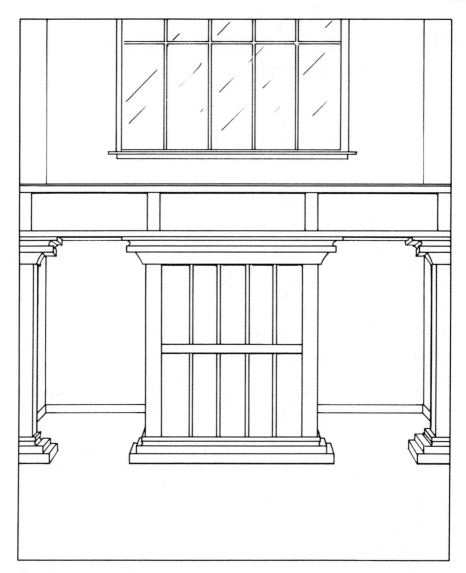

Great banqueting hall, Hampton Court: serving screen and balcony.

us to see what the original interludes must have been like when played between courses of a banquet at the Inns of Court or at one of the royal residences.

THE PERFORMING SPACE

The most common sites for the public performance of plays were offered by inns, in both London and the provinces. These were not only hostelries but termini for coach journeys, and though it is perhaps exaggerating to compare them to the railway stations that rewrote the map of London in the nineteenth century, they were still important centers of comings, goings, and meetings, and many acquired strong literary associations. It has been suggested that the practice began when one of the medieval pageants pulled into the inn to let its players act in a more exclusive spot. Chaucer immortalized one, the Tabard, as the starting point for his Canterbury pilgrims. It stood in Southwark, south of London across the river (a district about which much more will be said presently).

An old view shows the typical structure of the time: a large open courtyard fronting onto the street, with a sign on a beam across the thoroughfare, marking it as a place of no small importance. One surviving inn in Southwark — the George, first mentioned in 1554 — still shows the old pattern. Burnt in one of the district's frequent fires, it was subsequently rebuilt, and one can still see the original layout of the courtyard surrounded by tiered galleries along the enclosing inn walls. Even today plays are occasionally given here, on a straw-covered platform set up at one end of the courtyard.

In the university town of Cambridge, opposite Corpus Christi College where the playwright Christopher Marlowe was a student, stands the Eagle, another surviving inn of the same type. This too is still occasionally used for the performance of plays today, and it shows how easily the combination of open courtyard and surrounding galleries could be adapted for theatrical performances.

We know of several theatrical inns in Tudor times. In Stepney, outside London's city limits, stood the Red Lion. The books of the Carpenters' Company (i.e., the trade guild) record a contract between John Brayne, grocer, and William Sylvester, carpenter, for the building of a "scaffold" (platform) for a "play of Sampson" here. John Brayne was probably the brother-in-law of the more famous James Burbage, who financed the construction of London's first professional theater building in 1576. In Bishopsgate the Bull Inn had a courtyard used first for prizefights and later, from about 1575, for plays. A perplexing reference from 1579 notes a play called *The Jew and Ptolone.* Is this somehow connected with Shakespeare's *The Merchant of Venice,* and is the Jew Shylock? Is Ptolone the Pantaloon who was a leading character in the popular Italian comedy (see p. 199)? Other identifications have been suggested, all debatable. Richard Tarleton, the famous clown, is said to have played at Bishopsgate; and from 1594 we have a letter from an anxious mother who feared the corrupting influence of the plays on her son who was living in Bishopsgate. It was an objection that would be often repeated by the stern voice of officialdom.

In Fleet Street stood the Bel Savage, first noted as an inn in 1453. Its name, like those of many London taverns, derives from a series of confusions. Savage seems originally to have been a family name, but Princess Pocahontas, who stayed there in 1616–1617, gave it a new meaning; the sign was a painting of her holding an arrow. In its early history the inn was used for fencing matches; one in 1599, between two English and two Italian guardsmen, was held on a "scaffold," with some apprehension that the contestants would fall off. Edward Alleyn, one of the most famous actors of his time, who created leading roles for Christopher Marlowe, was associated with this inn. The Cross Keys in Grace-church Street exhibited a famous performing horse, and there were companies of players here from 1579 on. This frequent association of actors and other more robust types of entertainment is significant. The theater was considered part of the whole complex of the popular arts, and when permanent theaters came to be built, they were frequently designed as multipurpose structures to accom-modate other types of shows if public interest in the drama waned.

One kind of show that had a continuing popularity was the baiting of bears, bulls, or other animals — a relic in spirit of the vanished Roman *venationes*. These bloody entertainments are important to the theater; commentators, both Elizabethan and modern, have pointed out the resemblance in shape between the bear pit and the public playhouse. A German visitor, writing of Southwark in 1584, mentions that he saw bears fighting with dogs in a round building three stories high. The show included a shower of fruit falling on the spectators and a fireworks display. Another visitor writes in 1598 of a "place . . . in the shape of a theatre, designed for the baiting of dogs and bears." The same vocabulary tends to be used for both types of structure, and it is sometimes surmised that the first professional theaters took the shape of the already famil-iar bear pits. The question is a complex one, as it is impossible to give the relative dates of theaters and bear pits with any accuracy; it may even be that the theaters influenced bear pit structures rather than the reverse. It is probably safer to say that both types of buildings found a common solution to the problem of housing as large an audience as possible to see the show, and that the theaters retained traces of all the various types of buildings in which players had been accustomed to perform.

London's Playhouses

The building of permanent theaters was a businesslike response to an obvious public demand. The builders were not benefactors of the arts but hardheaded entrepreneurs interested in the best returns on their investments and careful to provide for alternatives if the plays should fail. In selecting sites they were torn between economic considerations and a desire to avoid official prejudice. While the city center was the most advantageous location, building land was scarce, and bad feeling ran high. Apart from the general prejudice against actors as "guildless men," the city magistrates had what seemed to them good and valid arguments against having a theater on their doorstep.

THEATER AND POLITICS

Though history has recorded the Elizabethan period as marking a great surge in national strength and prosperity, it was riddled with doubts, fears, and

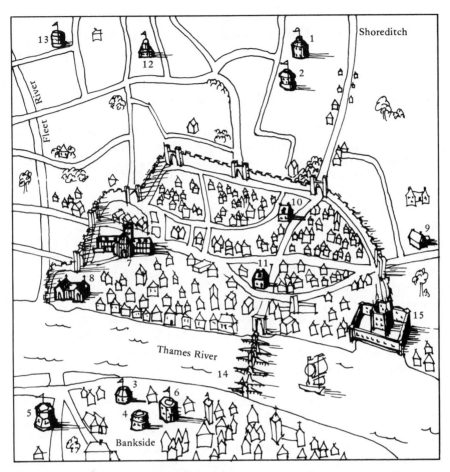

Map of London showing the principal Elizabethan and Jacobean theaters. (1) The Theatre, (2) the Curtain, (3) the Rose, (4) the Globe, (5) the Hope, (6) the Bear Ring, (7) St. Paul's, (8) Blackfriars private theater, (9) the Boar's Head Inn, (10) the Bull Inn, (11) the Bell Inn, (12) the Fortune, (13) the Red Bull. Also shown are (14) London Bridge and (15) the Tower of London.

uncertainties. The question of the succession had been a difficult one. And Elizabeth's position, never totally secure, was threatened by religious difficulties, for Catholics were still suspect, and their challenge to the queen's legitimacy carried a related fear of foreign invasion. The authorities were security conscious to a degree that bordered on paranoia, and their feelings were shared by many private citizens. Ben Jonson, in his comedy *Volpone* (1606), caricatures the Englishman traveling in Italy who sees spies under every bed and conspiracies on each street corner: the picture is hardly exaggerated.

Officialdom was most distrustful of public assemblies — any assemblies — and particularly those where, as in the theater, a crowd could be inflamed to passion by a provocative theme. History shows that these fears were not ill founded. In 1601 the Earl of Essex, Elizabeth's favorite, attempted a political coup. His abortive march on London was preceded by a specially commissioned performance of Shakespeare's *Richard II,* a play conspicuously dealing with the deposition of a monarch. It was clearly hoped that the public would be urged to bring about in fact what they had just seen in mimic action. The coup failed, but it had its effect on the earliest printed versions of the play, which omit the deposition scene.

The prevailing political sensitivity made its mark on the writing of plays, which were scrutinized for revolutionary sentiments; several playwrights were imprisoned for real or imagined offenses. And it suggested that theaters should be built outside the city limits, where they fell under jurisdictions more sympathetic than the London magistrates.

While suburban location helped in some ways, it hurt in others. The outlying areas were already occupied by those who, for less valid reasons, wished to evade the official eye, and to set the theater among them invited guilt by association. Nevertheless, London's first professional theater was built in Shoreditch, one of the liberties, in 1576. It was called simply the Theatre; no need for further distinction for it was the only one there was. Land that had formerly belonged to a priory was taken on a twenty-one-year lease, and in spite of the unattractive surroundings — Shoreditch was one of London's red-light districts — the venture was clearly profitable. In the following year a second theater was built about two hundred yards from the first; it was called the Curtain. Its name did not come from the theater drop curtain because that did not yet exist; perhaps it came from a family name connected with the estate. The Theatre stood until 1598, when it was moved; the Curtain remained in operation well into the seventeenth century, when it was apparently used by prizefighters. Shoreditch, now part of the great urban sprawl, still retains a Curtain Road and a plaque to commemorate the builders of the Theatre.

SOUTHWARK THEATERS

If we could return in time and take a fast-action film of London at this period, we should see the theaters rising — and sometimes falling — like the mushrooms they somewhat resembled. Once the first two were established, a spurt of building followed, though now across the Thames, on the south bank of the river. This location shared the advantage of Shoreditch in that it was outside the grasp of the city magistrates; there were, however, corresponding disadvantages. Southwark had grown up with a shady reputation as a haven for those who could not enter London once the bridge gates had closed for the night or who, for reasons of their own, were afraid to. In addition, the new theater district was inconvenient to reach. One could take the long way around, by London Bridge, or cross by ferry. Boatmen regularly plied the Thames, calling "Eastward Ho" or "Westward Ho" to indicate their direction; this call provided the titles for two popular plays. Thames tour guides still point out a flight of stone steps where, so legend says, theatergoers disembarked. Once there, they found themselves in a district raffish enough to be slightly hazardous. The South Bank was lined with brothels, many built, paradoxically, on land owned by the Church; many had picturesque names: the Cardinal's Cap, the Ape and Urinal. Elizabeth had closed the brothels in 1563, but like most such laws, the ban did not work and merely forced the trade elsewhere.

Thus in Southwark as in Shoreditch, the theaters found themselves forced into association with undesirable companions. This situation gave fuel to public complaints about the immorality of the theater, complaints that grew louder as the age progressed.

Nevertheless, a theater opened about 1580 in Southwark itself, at Newington Butts, which, as the name implies (*butts* means "target range"), was an archery ground. It lasted some twenty years; the site is now occupied by the Elephant and Castle pub. In the district known as Bankside the Rose was built in 1587. It was the work of Philip Henslowe, one of the most active entrepreneurs of the day, who had a finger in many pies and whose *Diaries* (more properly, account books) give a fascinating account of day-by-day expenditures in the theater. It disappeared by 1606, when it was either demolished or converted into tenements.

The Swan was built in the same district about 1595; by unfortunate association it had the same name as one of the local brothels, which augmented the ire of the magistrates; there was a threat to pull it down in 1596. The Swan was several times in trouble. In 1597 a performance of *The Isle of Dogs,* held to be seditious, landed the authors in prison. In 1602 it was the scene of a notable fiasco. The theater advertised a production of *England's Joy,* promising a pageant of Elizabeth's coronation and the Spanish Armada and an ending with fireworks and a display of the torments of hell. This description gives us a good idea of what the paying public would turn out in large numbers to see. But the production was a hoax, the backers absconded with the takings, and the audience vented their frustration by tearing the theater apart. After 1611 it was used by various companies and then gradually fell into decay; it was probably demolished some time after 1632.

The Globe, which went up on Bankside in 1599, was the original Theatre under a new name, transported piecemeal across the river and reerected. This building practice was not an unusual one, and it was made easier by the fact that the original structure was built in "frames" and so could be broken down for transport; we have records of a house being moved onto London Bridge itself in similar fashion. The Globe was the theater chiefly associated with Shakespeare's company, and its sign showed Hercules bearing the world on his shoulders. In 1613 it burned down as a result of badly managed stage effects during a production, probably of Shakespeare's *Henry VIII.* A new Globe rose, more splendidly, on the site and remained in operation until it was closed by the Puritans in 1642. It was demolished two years later, and a brewery now stands where Shakespeare's works were acted.

Some later theaters went back to the north bank: the Fortune (1600–1662) in Smithfield and the Red Bull, which had a low reputation, nearby (ca. 1600–1665). There was also Blackfriars on the property of the old monastery, within the city limits; this theater was of notably different character, being an indoor theater, and deserves a separate discussion (see p. 223). Back on Bankside, a bear pit was converted to the Hope in 1613, later reverting to "wild beasts and gladiators."

THE EVIDENCE FOR PHYSICAL FEATURES

What did these theaters look like? No question in the history of the theater has produced such a vast amount of controversy. The difficulty arises from the remarkable lack of evidence. (It is a paradox of theater history that in the periods that produced the greatest plays, we know least about the theaters that staged them.) The Elizabethans did not trouble to write detailed descriptions of buildings that were as familiar to them as movie houses are to us. Some of our most useful information comes from foreigners who were struck by the contrast between what they saw in London and what they knew at home.

We have four principal sources that give us information about Elizabethan theaters. The first source is a drawing of the Swan theater by, or inspired by, a Dutch visitor, Johannes (Jan) de Witt. Discovered in a commonplace book belonging to a friend in Holland, it is an amateur's view of the principal elements of the structure, with actors in place and perhaps some of the audience. The drawing is labeled, and there is an accompanying but unsatisfactory description. This drawing is the only contemporaneous view of a theater interior that we have. Some frontispiece illustrations to later published texts of plays show the same kind of structure, though differing in detail; these, however, are too late to be taken as firm evidence for the theater that Shakespeare knew.

The second major sources are builder's contracts for the Hope and Fortune theaters, which are informative on some matters, infuriatingly incomplete in others. They assume a knowledge of contemporary theater practice, which the builders would have had as a matter of course, but which the modern would-be reconstructor does not. Our third sources are pictorial view maps of the city and its environs, which offer qualified evidence for theater sites and exteriors. Unfortunately the dates are dubious, and some of the attributions and details are demonstrably wrong. Fourth, we have original stage directions in the plays themselves, which offer hints of the equipment that theaters provided and how it could be used.

There is much we do not know and shall never know. The evidence is so scanty that totally diverse interpretations have been built on it, and the following survey can only indicate some lines of general agreement. It is important to keep in mind that no two theaters would have been the same. Each must have varied with the skill and resources of the builder, the company that occupied it, and the particular requirements of the repertory that was performed there.

The Globe Playhouse, interior and exterior. Reconstruction by John Cranford Adams.

(*below*) The Swan playhouse, reconstructed by Richard Southern from our only contemporary drawing. (*left*) The Swan: the veiled-off stage; the tiring-house wall with twin entrances and hanging arras for concealment, and upper balcony; heavy "Roman" pillars supporting the stage canopy.

(*right*) The Swan: the open
courtyard gives standing room
for the groundlings, while the
three tiers of galleries, at
graduated prices, provide
seats, shelter, and some
comfort to more prosperous
patrons. (*above*) The Globe:
the protective canopy over the
stage decorated with signs of
the zodiac and thus a
conventional "heaven."

THE EXTERIOR

Even the details of the exterior cause problems. The pictorial maps indicate a circular shape, and so does the de Witt drawing; the narrative accompanying the latter makes a comparison to the Roman theater, which, of course, had a circular design. A passage often quoted in this connection is Shakespeare's prologue to *Henry V*, where the Chorus describes the theater as "a wooden O." The trouble is that, as intensive architectural studies have shown, the circular shape would be extremely difficult to construct in wood, particularly when it was built in frames that could be taken down and reassembled, as was the Theatre. Constructional feasibility, then, suggests a multisided building — an octagon or hexadecagon — which, from a distance, would look circular and, by artist's shorthand, be so shown. As for the *Henry V* prologue, one may beg leave to doubt whether Shakespeare or any poet, even in the interests of accuracy, would have specified "this wooden octagon." The loose description suffices.

One exception to the general pattern of theater building must also be noted, the Fortune, which so far as we know was unique in being rectangular. This shape posed some construction problems, which are noted in the contract.

THE INTERIOR

Once inside the theater we are, for a while, on safer ground. The walls enclosed a central courtyard, open to the skies, in which part of the audience — the "groundlings" — stood. Although the Fortune was, unusually, rectangular, its contract gives dimensions that may indicate the space available in most theaters: the internal dimensions of the courtyard were 55 feet square, of which half was taken up by the stage buildings and the stage itself. Within the depth of the walls were three tiers of galleries (clearly shown in the de Witt drawing), to accommodate higher-paying spectators under cover. The Fortune contract specifies the heights of these as 12, 11, and 9 feet, respectively, and other references suggest that the top tier was the least comfortable. De Witt labels the lowest tier *orchestra,* which in the Greco-Roman theater, as we have seen, meant "dancing place"; but the sketch probably uses the word in the different sense it had already begun to acquire in later antiquity, when seats for privileged spectators were placed within the orchestra circle. Thus *orchestra* here must mean no more than best seats.

The tiered seats, the central, open area (*arena* in de Witt's drawing), and the coincidence of vocabulary suggests a further analogy with Roman stage building, which has not escaped the notice of commentators. Was there any deliberate influence? This is not impossible. Vitruvius's work on theater architecture had already been rediscovered. In contemporary Paris, where Roman models lay more readily to hand, the Confrérie de la Passion had petitioned the king to build them a theater "in the Roman manner." Some scholars have carried this argument so far as to suggest that the central courtyard was a playing, rather than an audience, space, and that the public theaters represented a translation of the Roman stage into an Elizabethan idiom. It is more likely, however, that the resemblance was only superficial and that the Roman parallels derive from the contemporary fancy of seeing England as a new Rome: popular tradition traced the name and origins of Britain from Brutus, descendant of Rome's founder Aeneas. It is clear, though, that in some theaters the stage work could be removed at need to make an arena in the Roman sense, for prizefights or beast shows.

Thrusting into the standing audience, and taking up a large part of the courtyard space, was the stage. Evidence suggests that this was high, perhaps 5½ feet, and mounted on trestles, which may be indicated, rather clumsily, in the de Witt sketch. This height, placing the actors' feet at the groundlings' eye level, allowed for understage mechanics and trapdoor entrances. A lower stage would have made it necessary to excavate, which underground springs sometimes made impossible and which would have created difficulties for multipurpose buildings where the stage was periodically removed. The stage underpinnings were probably concealed by hangings — suggesting an analogy with the draped scaffolds for public executions, referred to also as "stages." The absence of such drapes in the de Witt sketch suggests that it may represent a rehearsal rather than a performance.

Some evidence suggests that the stage was tapered; other, that it was rectangular; some, that the edge was bare; other, that it was protected by spikes or railings — presumably from unruly spectators who threatened to climb on it. Obviously individual practice varied. Trapdoors were a practical necessity, and the plays suggest many uses for them. *Hamlet* needs a large trap to represent Ophelia's grave, in which Hamlet and Laertes fight. In Shakespeare's *Pericles, Prince of Tyre,* a suit of rusty armor is fished out of a trap representing the sea. In Middleton's *Women Beware Women* a character falls through a trap that has been devised as a devilish machine to end his life. One bizarre interpretation of the de Witt drawing argues that the Elizabethan theater was completely theater in the round, that characters made their regular entrances and exits through trapdoors, and that what we have identified as stage supports are in fact intended to represent windows lighting an underground greenroom. This theory need not be taken too seriously; it is quoted here simply as an example of the diverse reconstructions that can be founded on the same piece of evidence.

Behind the stage was the "tiring-house," the attiring house, or dressing rooms, with doors providing entrances to the stage. What else occupied this rear wall has been a major source of controversy. The de Witt drawing shows a blank. Later illustrations show a curtain, which appears to cover an alcove or recess. The plays, and their stage directions, show a frequent need for a place of concealment in which characters could hide or from which sudden discoveries of characters or props could be made to the audience. *Hamlet* provides an obvious instance: Polonius hides behind the arras (wall hanging) to overhear Hamlet's conversation with his mother, is himself overheard, and is stabbed through the curtain. The curtained alcove, then, would offer the most convenient way of showing such scenes.

One theory, which remained popular until comparatively recently, argued that there was in fact a whole inner stage — the "inner below" — in which one scene could be set while another was being played on the main stage. It was held, indeed, that many Elizabethan plays suggest an alternation of inner- and main-stage scenes, and several Shakespearean productions of the 1920s and 1930s were designed on this principle. In the Elizabethan theater, however, a deep inner stage would have been impossible because the sight lines would have cut the action off from a large part of the audience. More probably the curtain concealed only a shallow recess in which large and cumbersome items could be preset or a character discovered; the action would then spill out onto the main stage, as usual. Where there was no alcove, as apparently at the Swan, a curtain could have been hung from the balcony overhead or a freestanding pavilion erected, rather like a medieval mansion given a new lease of life on the platform stage.

The stage balcony continued the line of the second audience gallery, providing an "inner above" as an additional upper acting level and perhaps for other purposes also. In the de Witt drawing figures are seen in this balcony. Are they actors or audience? If the sketch shows a rehearsal, as is possible, they may be actors watching their fellows on stage. The possibility that they are audience is suggested by references to higher-priced seats for privileged spectators in the "lord's rooms" — though we do not know where these were located. Spectators in the balcony, of course, would have a backward view of the stage, but there has always been a class of playgoer who attends the theater not to see but to be seen. Probably the use of the balcony was flexible. It could be used for scenes if the play so demanded; if not, it could be used for additional seating or for the musicians who provided a regular accompaniment to the performances and were sometimes (as in *Romeo and Juliet*) involved as characters in the plays. Some theaters may have provided additional balconies above the first. And above all rose the loft that held winches and pulleys for flying mechanisms and the lowering of large properties, such as thrones.

The upstage area, as shown on the de Witt drawing and substantiated elsewhere, was protected by a canopy or "heavens"; the underside of the canopy was probably decorated with the signs of the zodiac. The canopy made a conventional sky; it also served a vital practical function in protecting the actors from the rain, a frequent annoyance of the English climate. Groundlings in the courtyard were not sheltered, but the actors had to be; their costumes were the most expensive item of their professional equipment. This canopy was supported on posts. The de Witt drawing shows these as rather clumsy and ornate — perhaps simply bad drawing, perhaps an attempt to emphasize the Roman theme. The necessity for good sight lines would suggest that the columns be as slender as possible. Some theaters — the Hope and the second Globe — dispensed with them altogether, supporting the canopy on a massive beam bridging the interior walls. A reconstruction of the latter theater suggests that it may also have had an ingenious light well to help illuminate the rear section of the stage. It is likely that the stage posts could have served as scenic elements at need — to represent, for instance, the trees in the forest of Arden in Shakespeare's *As You Like It* or the ship's masts in his *Pericles*.

Production Values of the Public Playhouse

The Elizabethan public theater, then, whose use continued, effectively, for over two generations — 1576 to 1642 — was a complex architectural construction providing a highly sophisticated machine for the production of plays. When later theater scholars and practitioners, around the turn of our century, began seriously to investigate and reconstruct Elizabethan performance conditions, they chose to think of Shakespeare's stage as rudimentary in its simplicity, perhaps even crude: little more than a rush-strewn platform, a balcony, and a series of lettered signs identifying where the action was supposed to be taking place. But this concept was itself an overreaction against the heavily pictorial production of Shakespeare that the Victorians knew. It is now clear that the Elizabethan theater could be highly spectacular when it so wished; it employed machinery, pageantry, and elaborately built scenic units. But these were merely elements of a production style that was imaginative, flexible, and organically related to the building that housed it.

INFLUENCES FROM EARLIER PRACTICES

We can surmise — and only surmise — some of the earlier practices that suggested the various components of the playhouse: the high platform may retain memories of the medieval wagon; the staging of interludes in banquet halls may have urged the convenience of an upper balcony; the bear pits may have suggested a pattern of audience seating. We can see much more clearly that when all these elements were finally put together, they retained the essential spirit of the medieval pageants, now cast into a solid, permanent architectural form. The three-tiered structure of the medieval universe remains: an upper level for celestial action (though this may now be put to more mundane purposes), a ground level for human action, and a subterranean world of pits, devils, and spitting fire. Notice that this tiered structure is now carried through into an auditorium whose stratification reflects the class structure of Elizabethan society, rising from the groundlings in the pit to the more well-to-do in the galleries, on rising price levels.

The medieval spirit is retained, too, in the combination of individual set pieces to give specific location to a scene with a larger, undifferentiated open area that may change, in the imagination, at will — as though the old relationship of mansion and *platea* had been retained in a different guise. We may refer again to Shakespeare's prologue to *Henry V:*

> But pardon, gentles all,
> The flat unraised spirit that hath dared
> On this unworthy scaffold to bring forth
> So great an object: can this cockpit hold
> The vasty fields of France? . . .
> Piece out our imperfections with your thoughts;
> Into a thousand parts divide one man
> And make imaginary puissance.

This speech has often been interpreted as the playwright's apology for his theater's inadequacy. But what author would begin by admitting failure? Rather, it is a statement of the theater's means, which are emblematic and symbolic rather than realistic: a part is to be taken for the whole; and if this is simplicity, it is the simplicity not of poverty but of sophisticated art.

THE SETTINGS

For many scenes the specific location does not matter at all. Directions offered in the usual reading texts of the plays are misleading, stemming not from the original but from later scholars' editions. It is the editors, not Shakespeare, who have labeled scenes as taking place in "another part of the forest" or "a room in the palace." Often the setting is neutral, indeterminate; the action takes place on the blank main stage, the characters exit, others enter, a new scene begins.

When the location *does* matter, it is indicated verbally, more often than not. For example, in *Macbeth* the opening dialogue between the three witches is not localized; it is the more effective for being left in limbo. We know where they meet Macbeth, however, for they tell us — "upon the heath"; and so the open stage becomes the heath. Later when Duncan and his party enter Macbeth's castle, it is important for us to know this, for Duncan will never emerge again, and an appropriate speech is put into Duncan's mouth:

> This castle hath a pleasant seat: the air
> Nimbly and sweetly recommends itself
> Unto our gentle senses.

Thus the tiring house door becomes, for the moment, the castle gates, which shut behind Duncan as he goes unknowingly to his doom. The same door will be reidentified as other places later on.

But as we have indicated previously, elaborate and specially designed set pieces could be introduced at need. It is obvious from Henslowe's *Diaries* that many of these were stock pieces. We hear of a hell mouth for Marlowe's *Doctor*

Faustus (another medieval survival) and an arbor for Thomas Kyd's *Spanish Tragedy* sturdy enough for a character to hang himself. Shakespeare's *Richard III* needs two tents for the battle scene, one for Richard and one for his opponent Richmond; the ghosts of those whom Richard has murdered pass from tent to tent, cursing the one, encouraging the other. This staging again is suggestive of medieval mansions reerected in a new environment, and it is interesting to notice that when the professional companies played away from home, in covered halls for private gatherings, they reverted, for practical reasons, to the old mansion structure. In the French theater also, as we shall see, mansions took a long while to disappear.

TIME AND SPACE

The flexibility of the stage induced an expansiveness of space and time, which, again, was reminiscent of the medieval cycles and remote from the compactness and economy of classical drama. With the rediscovery of Greek and Roman literature in the Renaissance, Seneca, at least, was becoming widely known; the first English translation appeared in 1559. Some critics of the time advocated the use of classical models for English tragedy. Sir Philip Sidney urged the retention of the unities, objecting to plays in which "you shall have Asia of the one side, and Africk of the other," and which asked the audience to believe that the same stage was, successively, a garden, a rocky island, a cave, and a battlefield. Some writers even attempted works that reflected the old economy. For example, Ben Jonson wrote *Catiline* and *Sejanus,* both based on episodes of Roman history, though these met with little popular success. But the vast bulk of Elizabethan and Jacobean drama remained faithful to the swirl and scope of its medieval forebears. The geographical range is enormous. Shakespeare's *King John* and *Henry V* move between England and France. His *Antony and Cleopatra* is located over most of the Roman world — to such an extent that modern productions have sometimes set the play in front of a huge map of the Mediterranean to aid audiences who may find the geography confusing. His *Henry VI* embraces the whole sweep of the Wars of the Roses. The time span, too, may be great. Marlowe's *Doctor Faustus* covers a period of "four-and-twenty years" as well as moving among the principal cities of Europe and from heaven to hell.

STAGING

Some devices automatically suggest themselves whereby such vast actions could be made coherent and comprehensible. Different stage doors could be identified with different armies or opposing houses (the Shakespearean historical plays; *Romeo and Juliet*), providing quick identification of the appropriate parties. Obviously this device could not work in every case, and studies of individ-

The public playhouse offered scope for ample stage pageantry, as seen in this Ashland production (*below*). (*left*) An aerial view of the Ashland theater.

Woodcut of Dr. Faustus conjuring up the devil, from the 1631 edition of Marlowe's play. The actor represented is probably Edward Alleyn, who created the role.

English history provided material for many Elizabethan and Jacobean plays. Shakespeare's *Henry VIII*, as performed at Ashland.

ual theaters suggest that each worked out its own patterns of action, presenting easily recognizable movements and groupings for its own audiences.

The upper level could be used in a variety of ways; it could be brought into play as needed, forgotten when not. In *Romeo and Juliet* it is used for Juliet's balcony, up to which Romeo climbs. In *King John* it becomes the prison walls from which the boy-prince Arthur leaps to escape his uncle and dies:

> *Enter ARTHUR, on the Walls.*
>
> *Arthur.* The wall is high, and yet will I leap down: —
> Good ground, be pitiful, and hurt me not! —
>
> . . .
>
> If I get down, and do not break my limbs,
> I'll find a thousand shifts to get away:
> As good to die and go, as die and stay.
>
>   (*Leaps down.*)
>
> O me! My uncle's spirit is in these stones: —
> Heaven take my soul, and England keep my bones!
>
>   (*Dies.*)

In *Richard II* the upper level becomes the walls of Pomfret Castle from which the beleaguered monarch speaks to his usurper. In Marlowe's *The Jew of Malta* it becomes part of a devilish device through which the protagonist plans to hurl his victims to death in a vat of boiling oil; the plan misfires; he falls through and is discovered (presumably by the drawing of the inner-below curtain), making his death speech in the caldron. In *Henry VI*, part 1, various levels of the stage are clearly used to suggest various spots around a besieged castle; a gun fired from one point hits a man standing in another. In Robert Greene's *Friar Bacon and Friar Bungay* upper level and main stage are used to suggest simultaneous action in two places separated by a considerable distance. Two uncles, above, peer into a magic glass, which shows their nephews, miles away, fighting a duel. The duel takes place on the main stage, both nephews die, and one uncle cries out, as well he might, "Oh strange coincidence!"

But the upper level could also be used thematically to move the scene from the realm of the actual into the allegorical. Laurence Olivier's film of *Henry V*, with its first scenes set in a reconstruction of the Globe theater, demonstrated brilliantly how effective this device could be. The play's first scene shows the dignitaries of the church devising ways of urging the king into a French war. They were set above; when the inner-below curtain opened to reveal Henry on his throne, the implication was clear that he was subjected to pressures from above. A similar device is used in *Henry VI*, part 3, which deals with the interminable twists and turns, wastage, and slaughter of civil war. After we have been almost sickened by the individual deaths, the action moves into another plane. King Henry, above, soliloquizes on the joys of the simple life, free from cares and responsibility. Below him, a son who has killed his father meets a father who has killed his son. The action moves from the particular to the universal, freezing into an allegorical tableau that the Middle Ages would have recognized and that speaks not only for this but for all war.

The theater could also delight in spectacle for its own sake. Popular audiences reveled in such things. They enjoyed the sword play, which so frequently occurs and in which the actors had to be expert. They loved processions. Shakespeare's *Henry VIII* reconstructs a coronation procession in exact detail, calling for two Judges, the Lord Chancellor "with the purse and mace before him," choristers singing, the Lord Mayor of London, several members of the nobility bearing heraldic emblems, the Queen under a canopy borne by four dignitaries, the Bishops of London and Winchester, the Duchess of Norfolk "in a coronel of gold, wrought with flowers, bearing the Queen's train," and "certain Ladies or Countesses, with plain circlets of gold." *The Tempest* introduces elaborate masques and dances. Marlowe's *Doctor Faustus* gives us stage magic and a papal banquet. Shakespeare's *Cymbeline* introduces a flying eagle and a descending throne; his *Pericles,* the figure of the goddess Diana descending in a cloud.

Elizabethan Playwrights and Plays

The authors who wrote for this theater were beleaguered men. We are so accustomed to regarding Elizabethan and Jacobean drama as one of the world's great bodies of literary masterpieces that it comes as a shock to learn how little esteem the dramatist enjoyed in his own time. The drain upon their energies was vast; the theater consumed material. New plays could expect only a few days' run, though they might be revived later and some of them could go on, sporadically, for years. But the audience craved novelty, and the playwright was more a purveyor of material than a literary artist.

WORKING CONDITIONS FOR THE WRITERS

Shakespeare's lifetime output of at least thirty-seven plays — an average of a play a year during his active career, while he was also busy as an actor — has been considered by some scholars as phenomenal. It may more properly be regarded as an active response to the pressures of the commercial theater. Plays were merchandise in keen demand. It was to the playwright's advantage to be prolific, for, as in Rome, once the work had been purchased by a company, the author had no further artistic or financial interest in it. It would be another century before the first traces of a royalty system appeared. Speed of composition was made more desirable by the fickle interest of the public. Subjects of urgent topical importance had to be dramatized while they were still fashionable. Thus playwrights often had to forgo total control of their material in the interest of expediency.

Collaboration was common during this period: an attractive subject might be farmed out, so that one man would prepare the scenario while others did the actual writing. Plays that were already company property might need reworking for revival, with scenes cut or changed, or new material added, to suit the public whim. This work was given to any playwright who happened to be available, not necessarily the original author. Thus popular works that remained in the repertory for years changed their shape so much that it is impossible, now, to decipher how much of the original remains. Marlowe's *Doctor Faustus* has survived in two texts, differing in significant ways; probably neither represents exactly what Marlowe originally wrote. (Henslowe's *Diaries* contain an entry for "additions to *Faustus.*") *The Spanish Tragedy,* by Thomas Kyd, Marlowe's contemporary and sometime roommate, was another popular play which suffered the same fate.

A further complication occurred when plays from the public theater were commanded for performances at court. Neither Elizabeth nor James visited the playhouse. The plays were brought to them, carefully scrutinized first for anything that might give offense and, where necessary, altered — by a playwright employed by the Office of Revels, which supervised such things, not by the original author. When eventually published, the work would appear, for reasons of prestige, in the version performed at court. It seems clear, for example, that Shakespeare's *Henry VIII* is the product of such forced collaboration.

Texts of the plays were carefully guarded, as the lack of adequate copyright protection meant that they could be stolen and performed by a rival company. Unscrupulous impresarios kept pirates who took down shorthand versions in performance or bought scripts from treacherous actors who wrote them down from memory. We owe some of our bad Shakespearean texts to such sources. From surviving scripts it appears that even the actors did not have a complete text of the play but merely their own parts ("sides") and the appropriate cues. (This situation, incidentally, tells us something about rehearsal conditions in the Elizabethan theater; given the pressures under which plays had to be mounted, many actors must have gone on without ever having seen the play whole.) Scripts were hoarded until their value had been exhausted, and only then were they published; entries in the *Stationer's Register* gave notice of intent to publish. When the first Globe burnt down in 1613, many scripts that had yet to see print must have perished in the blaze.

THE PLAYWRIGHT'S LIFE

Small wonder, in these circumstances, that the playwright was regarded more as a hack than as a literary artist. Financial rewards were small, and playwrights normally supplemented their income from other sources. Shakespeare was in a privileged position, being a shareholder in the Globe company. He also worked as an actor; tradition credits him with small roles in his own plays — Adam in *As You Like It* and the Ghost in *Hamlet* — and he is known to have acted in plays by other men. Ben Jonson, known to us now primarily as a comic playwright, was a literary jack-of-all-trades. Christopher Marlowe was in government service. Henslowe's accounts show that his company kept a stable of playwrights on hand, feeding them advances, paying their debts, sometimes rescuing them from prison. Some of these men achieved literary reputations but not, originally, as playwrights. Shakespeare first enjoyed critical esteem from his nondramatic poems. It was not until 1616 (the year of Shakespeare's death) that Ben Jonson had the effrontery to publish a folio collection of his own work, including some plays, thereby demanding that they be considered as literature. Editors Hemings and Condell followed suit after Shakespeare's death with the First Folio of his plays. It is likely that some of these plays were edited for publication, thereby making reconstruction of the original even more difficult.

Uncertain though the playwright's life was, it exercised an undeniable fascination. The almost spontaneous generation of a professional theater and its extraordinarily rapid development responded to a lively public demand; theater was, for a while, *the* art and a magnet that attracted talent from every walk of society. Some of the playwrights were self-made men who learned their trade the hard way. Others were refugees from the learned professions, including a whole coterie of playwrights known as the "University Wits." And though Ben Jonson, among others, disparages the young gentleman scholars who dabble in the drama, there can be no doubt that the major centers of higher learning fed into the theater in a way that has scarcely been equaled until the present day.

LANGUAGE OF THE PLAYS

The most common medium for drama was blank verse; specifically, the iambic pentameter, which, in English as in Greek and Latin, preserved the rhythms of ordinary speech in heightened poetical form. Several examples have already been quoted (see pp. 172–176). Marlowe established the pattern, and successive dramatists refined and perfected it to the point where it became a uniquely flexible instrument, serving as the standard for nearly all English verse drama since. It has been argued, indeed, that the development of an English opera was preempted by the musical use of the language in English drama.

In its language, however, Elizabethan drama was much less rigid than the Greek; here, as in other ways, it was closer in spirit to the Middle Ages. Rhyming verse could be used; so could prose; and there is often a social differentiation, verse denoting the upper, prose the lower, classes. In *A Midsummer Night's Dream* Shakespeare employs all three forms to show a tripartite world. His courtly characters, Theseus and Hippolyta, use blank verse; his lovers, rhyme; his "mechanicals" (clowns), prose. The fairies use all three. A change of verse style, too, may have an immediate practical function. Shakespeare commonly ends a blank verse scene with a rhyming couplet. This device acts as a kind of verbal punctuation, indicating that one scene is over and another about to start — an indication perhaps not so much for the audience, who would already have a visual cue, as for the actors waiting offstage for their entrance: even subconsciously the change makes itself felt.

The language of the plays showed an exuberance, an inventiveness, a vitality, a sheer joy in the use of words for their own sake, that was very much part of the spirit of the times. Shakespeare's plays conspicuously delight in word play, elaborate figures, flights of rhetorical fancy, and particularly puns, many of which are lost on modern audiences because words have become obsolete or pronunciations have changed. Ben Jonson's scripts, too, are so densely packed with imagery, allusion, and literary conceits that they are often cryptic to the modern ear (and extremely difficult for modern actors to learn). The Elizabethan ear, however, was quick. Here, as in Greece, we are talking of a society that was largely illiterate and thereby accustomed to *listen* in a way that we are not.

PLAY STRUCTURE

In structure, too, the plays retained a medieval flexibility. They are diverse. Tragic scenes intermingle with comic; scenes from high and low life are interposed. The subplot makes its appearance, and different actions intertwine. In Greene's *James IV,* for example, scene 1 takes place at the court, and scene 2 shows fairies dancing in a churchyard. Sometimes the subplots seem irrelevant, but the irrelevancy is more apparent than real; closer study shows that they are normally closely articulated with the main theme, reiterating it in a minor, comic key. We shall see this more clearly when we look at *Doctor Faustus* (pp. 192–196). But the playwrights were well aware of the practical necessities of appealing to a diverse audience. A comic scene follows a serious one as light relief. The clowns were dearly loved and enjoyed considerable license. There is evidence of a good deal of ad-libbing: "Enter Clown, saying anything."

One vestige of the classical theater in Elizabethan drama is the retention of the chorus, now dwindled to a single figure, as a linking device. He may, as in *Henry V* or *Doctor Faustus,* be anonymous; he may be an allegorical figure, as in *Henry IV,* part 2, where he is "Rumour, painted full of tongues"; he may be a historical figure, like Machiavelli in Marlowe's *The Jew of Malta* or the poet Gower in Shakespeare's *Pericles.* He serves to fill in gaps in time and place, with a linking narrative; to give a focus, at the play's beginning, for the audience's attention; and sometimes, in the manner of a medieval presenter, to moralize on the action.

From Seneca, studied in Latin at the universities and after 1559 available in English translation, the theater picked up the device of the internalizing monologue, the soliloquy, which punctuates the action and which, in performance, probably carried the actor out to the tip of the thrust stage, where his communings were surrounded by the standing audience. The formality of stichomythic dialogue (alternating one-line speeches; see p. 39), another classical device, also reappears from time to time; and some playwrights loved to display their learning by extended references to Seneca or other Roman authors, even including whole sections in Latin. In no sense, however, did the playwrights see themselves as writing neoclassical plays. They were eclectic; they took their material where they found it and adapted anything they saw as useful. These classical devices are only one element in the vast melting pot of Elizabethan drama.

ETHNIC INFLUENCES

Any national drama reveals national preoccupations. For the English, who were rapidly being taught to regard themselves as the center of the universe, it was natural that foreigners should be portrayed as comic, eccentric, or sinister. In Elizabethan plays the French are usually funny, the Spanish fantastic, Moors exotic, Italians treacherous and corrupt. For a Protestant audience representatives of the Catholic hierarchy had a special fascination. In *Doctor Faustus* Marlowe wins easy laughs with a slapstick banquet involving the pope, a cardinal, and a chorus of comic friars. Shakespeare presents a scheming papal legate in *King John* and a disgraced cardinal in *Henry VIII*. John Webster shows an unbelievably devious and sinister cardinal who is elevated to the papacy in *The White Devil*.

Jews in England had always been regarded with suspicion. Their life there had been as miserable as it was in most of Europe. Forced by church policies out of the usual trades and handicrafts, they were crowded into ghettos — a memory preserved in the London district still known as Old Jewry — loaded with punitive taxes, and slandered with tales of infanticide and well poisoning. As in Hitler's Europe, they were forced to wear badges and eventually, in 1290, were expelled from England by royal command. By Tudor times they had started to trickle back, though still few in number. Some were important as physicians, others as moneylenders, a trade that had now been legalized. They remained suspect, however, and the execution of the Spanish Jew Roderigo Lopez for allegedly attempting to poison Queen Elizabeth inflamed popular feeling against them. The plays reflect this feeling. Marlowe's *The Jew of Malta* shows a villainous Jew exacting a revenge from a Christian society hardly less villainous; Shakespeare's more complex Shylock may have been directly influenced by the Lopez case.

Other ethnic stereotypes are nearer home. In *Henry V* we have a comic Irishman, Welshman, and Scotsman to match against the honest homespun Englishman. Anti-Scottish jokes became touchy after 1604, when James I, who had been James VI of Scotland, ascended the English throne. He filled many court posts with his own nobles, causing so much bitterness among the deposed English aristocracy that Scottish references in plays suddenly became suspected treason. Ben Jonson suffered from this attitude. The jokes, however, were still made. Shakespeare even ventures a few jokes about Scottish meanness in *Macbeth*.

More generally, the habit of looking at the world through English eyes gave a contemporary local color even to plays supposedly set in countries far away and in ages long past. Shakespeare's Athens in *A Midsummer Night's Dream* has no connection with the ancient city. Theseus and Hippolyta engage in activities and voice sentiments fully familiar to Elizabeth's court. The clowns are drawn directly from English life; the wood in which the characters lose themselves could be located in Shakespeare's native Warwickshire; and the fairies are not classical nymphs but familiar English sprites. The brawling crowds of *Julius Caesar* are taken straight from the London milieu. Just as the cycle plays had placed the biblical story in a contemporary English landscape, so the Elizabethan drama translates the past into a world familiar to the London audience — together with the inevitable anachronisms, of which the striking clock in *Julius Caesar* is merely the most famous example and to which the spectators would not have given a thought.

INFLUENCE OF HISTORY

English pride stimulated an interest in English history. The popular audience liked to see its own past reevoked on the stage, and chronicle or history plays made up a large part of the dramatic output. It is significant that when a benefit performance was organized for the Master of the Revels, a history was chosen: it was clearly expected to do well at the box office. George Peele, who died about 1598, wrote an *Edward I,* Marlowe an *Edward II,* and Greene a *James IV*.

Shakespeare composed two major cycles of historical works. The first cycle included the three parts of *Henry VI* (about whom a play had already existed) and *Richard III,* beginning with the accession of a weak king and working through the chaos of the Wars of the Roses. Though the four plays were written to be performed separately, they offer, collectively, a vivid panorama of one of the most troubled periods of English history: they have been given in our time, in cut and rearticulated fashion, as one long play. Great figures flash before our eyes; they rise and fall; and the chaos spreads from the rivalry of nobles to engulf every level of society. Often the swift-moving pattern of political events reaches out to embrace the spectator. In the physical conditions of the theater, a character delivering a harangue on the stage might have a token crowd of extras around him but a real crowd of groundlings at his very feet: the deep thrust stage carried him into their midst, and they were assumed into the production much as a Greek audience was at the Theater of Dionysus. This situation was precisely what the authorities were afraid of, the sort of mass feeling that Essex's supporters hoped would give fuel to his rebellion; and Shakespeare is notably cautious on historical issues that might be construed as attacks on the current regime. Elizabeth took her stand on the divine right of kings, but the wars had shown what a shaky foundation this was.

Shakespeare's second cycle goes back in time to begin, once again, with a weak king. *Richard II,* in 1595 — as we have seen (p. 162), a politically touchy play — was followed by *Henry IV,* parts 1 and 2, in 1597 and 1598, with *Henry V* (on whom, again, a play already existed) completing the sequence in the following year. Flattery of the reigning monarch, direct or oblique, was inevitable.

Henry VIII was a particularly touchy play, dealing as it did with Elizabeth's father, still alive in the memories of many of the audience. Shakespeare is careful to attribute Henry's principal failings to Cardinal Wolsey, who is established in the play as his monarch's evil genius and properly deposed by the end; and the play concludes with the christening of the baby Elizabeth amid appropriately flattering prognostications. *Macbeth,* one of several plays that exploited the interest in things Scottish following the accession of James I, contrives to be uncomplimentary about Scotland while still flattering the new monarch. In this tragedy the northern kingdom is seen as a dark, murky place, full of witches and horrors, while England, under a saintly king, becomes the place of refuge for Scottish exiles. As a counterbalance to this picture, we are shown a vision of Scottish kings, ending with James himself.

FOREIGN SOURCES

When we turn from homegrown to foreign sources, we find one conspicuous gap. Greek and Roman drama do not provide as many models as we would expect in an age that was proud of having rediscovered the classics. Ancient history provides some plot material: Sir Thomas North's translation of Plutarch's *Parallel Lives,* paired biographies of illustrious Greeks and Romans, gave Shakespeare several plays. Marlowe wrote *Dido, Queen of Carthage.* But although Seneca, Plautus, and Terence were well known, works that were simply anglicized versions of classical plays seem to have had small popular appeal. In 1561–1562 Thomas Norton and Thomas Sackville wrote *Gorboduc,* or *Ferrex and Porrex,* for lawyers of the Inner Temple. It is a play of mostly talk and little action, with a chorus of old Britons and with messenger scenes. It has passed into history as one of the more tedious examples of one age imitating another and has, deservedly, remained unrevived. Ben Jonson's unhappy explorations in the classical mode have already been mentioned.

What Seneca did bequeath to the English stage, however, was a tremendous repertory of plot devices; the new authors took the substance while rejecting the classical form. Thus play after play borrows such familiar Senecan motifs as ghosts, bloody murders, and revenge plots: the murder of Clytemnestra by Orestes, as redramatized by Seneca, begets a whole series of Elizabethan revenge plays, of which *Hamlet* is simply one of the more distinguished examples. Kyd's *The Spanish Tragedy,* one of the most successful potboilers of the time, shows many Senecan influences. It has a ghost, a chorus, a messenger, and a revenge. Like many of its contemporaries, it was larded with Latin quotations. Scholar-playwrights were proud of their learning, and though Elizabethan plays owe little to classical form, the Latin language is used for decorative and imposing effect — perhaps a relic of the cycle plays where, as we have seen, Latin was still retained for authoritative moments.

OTHER INFLUENCES

Also popular with Elizabethans was what we might designate generally as the wonder play. The era was a time of urgent geographical and intellectual exploration. New worlds were being discovered, old barriers broken down. We have this sense of exploration and the exotic appeal of distant lands in such works as Peele's *The Battle of Alcazar,* a topical work dealing with the war in Morocco; Marlowe's *Tamburlaine,* a massive two-part work that dramatizes the rise and fall of an Eastern potentate, full of strange-sounding names and oriental pomp; Shakespeare's *Pericles,* a great deal of which takes place on the high seas; and, of course, his *Tempest,* which borrows color from contemporary explorations of the American continent. Intellectual exploration is present in Greene's *Friar Bacon and Friar Bungay,* treating of alchemy and science, and Marlowe's *Doctor Faustus.* In an age still riddled with superstition, traffic with other worlds beyond our own exercised a horrific fascination. Witchcraft, astrology, and fairy lore found a large place on the stage. Nearer home were plays dramatizing contemporary episodes in foreign life, like Marlowe's *The Massacre at Paris,* and those with a strong vein of domestic tragedy, often based on actual events of the time. The theater had something of the quality of a living newspaper, picking up any story that was current and making dramatic capital from it.

As we have already noted, the Elizabethan age was obsessed with politics. The concept of power was important: who had it, how it was acquired, and what happened when power was lost. *Macbeth* is such a play; so is *Julius Caesar.* Shakespeare's *King Lear,* which begins with the subdivision of a kingdom whose monarch no longer desires to rule, must have touched a chord in many who were speculating about what would happen when Queen Elizabeth died, and the chaos of the Wars of the Roses had a distinctly contemporary application.

THE COMEDY

Comedy drew material from many sources. Here the effect of the classics is more readily apparent. Plautus and Terence were easily accessible; at Westminster School the pupils performed a Latin comedy regularly. One of the earliest comedies we have, *Ralph Roister Doister* (1553–1554), a neo-Plautine comedy using the character type *miles gloriosus* (boastful soldier), was written by a schoolmaster, Nicholas Udall, for performance by his pupils. Shakespeare compounded the mistaken identity plot by using double sets of twins in *The Comedy of Errors,* based on Plautus's *The Twin Menaechmi.* Ben Jonson wrote a series of classically conscious comedies, both directly — his plays are full of Plautine echoes and quotations — and indirectly, by way of medieval psychology.

What passed for science at that time decreed that human temperament and behavior were determined by the balance or imbalance of four fluids in the body: blood, which produces a sanguine (optimistic) nature (from Latin *sanguis,* "blood"); bile, bilious or choleric (hot-tempered); black bile, melancholic; and phlegm, phlegmatic (unresponsive). These fluids were known technically as *humors.* By the end of the sixteenth century this word had become little more than a catchword — producing, in a more limited sense, our own use of the term. Jonson picked it up as his trademark and was jealous of everyone else who used it, particularly those who used it incorrectly. In the Induction to *Every Man out of His Humour* (1599) he writes:

> When some one peculiar quality
> Doth so possess a man that it doth draw
> All his effects, his spirits and his powers
> In their confluctions all to run one way
> This may be truly said to be a humour.

For Jonson, then, a humor is an imbalance, an eccentricity, not a mere external affectation but a disposition of the whole person in one particular direction. Two of his plays use the word in their titles. In all his works Jonson's use of this device produces a series of boldly conceived types, each characteristic of some folly or vice and thus strongly akin, in spirit, to the type characters of Roman comedy. Shakespearean comedy, on the other hand, relies much more heavily on the infinite variety of observable rather than idealized human nature and takes its plots from an extraordinary range of sources, domestic anecdotes as well as continental romances.

Components of the Elizabethan Theater

THE ACTORS

The actors who performed these works were as hard pressed as the dramatists who wrote them. Acting in the Middle Ages, as we have seen, was primarily amateur. The Elizabethan period created and stabilized the profession in the face of a good deal of public and official hostility. Amateur acting still continued, especially in the schools, and Shakespeare makes gentle fun of such performances in *A Midsummer Night's Dream* and *Love's Labour's Lost.* In 1607 Francis

Beaumont and John Fletcher wrote *The Knight of the Burning Pestle,* which satirizes the practice of some hard-pressed companies of drafting amateurs into their ranks.

The new professionalism, however, created closely knit groups who were expected to be industrious, versatile, and adept in speech, song, and movement. They were still all-male. Actresses did not appear on the English public stage until the 1660s. Female roles were played by boys or young men. Shakespeare, in *Antony and Cleopatra,* makes daring allusion to this convention when he has his Cleopatra fear that, if she is taken captive to Rome, she will have to watch "some squeaking player boy her greatness." Corvino, the jealous husband in Jonson's *Volpone,* accuses his wife of having been "an actor with your handkerchief"; even the word *actress* did not then exist. This all-male ensemble undoubtedly created some difficulties, and the dramatists were adept at getting their girls, on some pretext, into boy's clothes and avoiding the more obvious embarrassments of all-male love scenes — it has been well noted that the most passionate love scene in all Shakespeare takes place with Juliet at a window and Romeo on the ground below. All-male revivals of Elizabethan drama are still occasionally tried, with success: the National Theatre of Great Britain has recently staged such a revival of *As You Like It.*

As noted before, the companies sought some measure of security by enrolling themselves in a noble household. What saved the theater at this period was the simple fact that Queen Elizabeth liked plays. What she liked, her courtiers liked; and with the actors so protected, the local magistrates, however hard they tried, could not eradicate them.

Official objections on the pretext of protecting public morals were not entirely groundless. The private lives of many actors and playwrights were hardly models of order and sobriety. Shakespeare's life, so far as we know, was blameless: he ended it in comfortable middle-class retirement in a substantial house purchased in his native Stratford. But Jonson was several times in prison, and in his later years he was a notable drunkard. Greene died repentant after a lifetime of excesses. Marlowe was accused of atheism and homosexuality, and he died in a tavern brawl after a shady career that involved work in the secret service, possibly as a double agent. Kyd was once arrested.

The objections against the immorality of the stage would be heard with increasing force after the turn of the century. During the reigns of Elizabeth and James, the authorities sought to harass what they could not prohibit. Actors were legally classed with "rogues and vagabonds" — hence the necessity for noble patronage. Plays were censored and permitted only in an authorized text; theater licensees were compelled to pay sums to charity. And plays could be forbidden entirely for what the authorities deemed "adequate reason." This usually meant plague, when it was reasonable that public assemblies of any sort should be discouraged, but the ban seems sometimes to have been invoked even when the danger was slight. Actors hated it. They were then forced to tour in the provinces, making do, as in the early days, with whatever makeshift theaters came to hand and often facing the outright hostility of rural prejudice.

There are some disheartening notes of payments made to traveling companies *not* to play — in other words, they were bought off and asked to move to another town.

The acting companies apparently consisted of some twelve to fifteen men. They were organized on lines similar to the guilds, perhaps as protective coloration. The control was vested in the shareholders, who divided the take among themselves when expenses had been met. Then came the hireling actors, who were paid a wage; finally came the apprentices, boys playing female parts, who, as in any other trade, were taken into their master's household and learned their craft as one of the family.

Two companies stand out in this period. One was the Earl of Leicester's Men, who after several changes of name became, in 1603, the King's Majesty's Servants, a title they retained until the closing of the theaters in 1642. Its rival was the Lord Admiral's Men, after 1603 known as Prince Henry's and Queen Anne's Men. Some scholars have assumed that this progression from noble to royal patronage marks the growing prestige of the theater. Others have suggested a less honorable interpretation: that the political power of the stage was so distrusted that James I and his successor, Charles I, preferred to keep the companies under their own eye rather than to leave them, as potential fomenters of revolt, in the hands of the aristocracy. These companies were well matched. The King's Men had Shakespeare and Richard Burbage, reckoned to be the finest actor of his time; the Queen's Men, controlled by Henslowe, had Marlowe to write for them and Edward Alleyn, a great "roaring" actor, to play the titanic roles that Marlowe created. Alleyn showed considerable astuteness by marrying the manager's daughter. We have some of the family correspondence, written when Alleyn was on tour, that gives a charming, intimate view of life in a theatrical household.

With companies so small, and casts so large, doubling and tripling of roles was common. One of the reasons that, in Shakespeare's histories, lords address each other with such continual formality of title is the necessity for keeping these roles straight in the audience's mind. The pressures of an ever-changing repertory also placed great burdens on the actor. He needed a prodigious memory, which was not always infallible; lines from previous productions, still embedded in the actor's memory, tend to crop up in later scripts. Many actors, it has been surmised, could not read; most people could not at the time. The actors learned their roles by ear, a method surprisingly effective once one is used to it.

The nature of Elizabethan acting has provoked as much controversy as the reconstruction of the stage, and for the same reason: a substantial lack of evidence. It is generally agreed that the actor's most important instrument was his voice; theater at this time was still chiefly rhetorical. Beyond this agreement, however, interpretations differ.

One school of thought holds that Elizabethan acting was highly realistic as we now understand the term. It bases its argument on such statements as a eulogy written on the death of Burbage:

He's gone, and with him what a world are dead
Which he revived, to be revived so;
No more young Hamlet, old Hieronymo;
King Lear, the grieved Moor, and more beside,
That lived in him, have now forever died.
Oft have I seen him leap into the grave,
Suiting the person which he seemed to have,
Of a sad lover, with so true an eye,
That there I would have sworn he meant to die.
Oft have I seen him play this part in jest,
So lively that spectators and the rest
Of his sad crew, whilst he but seemed to bleed,
Amazed, thought even then he died indeed.

But such tributes are not necessarily evidence. What one generation considers lifelike, the next may think artificial, and a formally conceived performance may be realistic within its own context.

A rival school of thought sees the acting of the period as a highly stylized art, using a code of gestures and postures closely akin to those found in the rhetorical manuals of the day — which themselves derived from Quintilian, thereby perhaps establishing a continuity of the presentational acting tradition from the Greeks through the sixteenth century. Certainty is impossible, though.

Perhaps it is safest to assume that acting followed the mode of stage setting: though formally conceived and responding to certain agreed conventions, it contained highly realistic individual moments. For the comics we can identify a style of broad horseplay, with considerably more liberty in text and interpretation than the serious actors enjoyed. Richard Tarleton served at various times as actor and the Queen's Jester; he was famous for his extemporized doggerel. Tarleton's successor was William Kemp, whose travels took him as far as Germany. He was still a broad comic, working with Shakespeare's company till about 1598. He, in his turn, was succeeded by Robert Armin, who played a more serious, pathetic type of comedy: the change of fools is marked in the plays that Shakespeare created for them.

A LIFE IN THE THEATER: BEN JONSON

For an illustration of the kind of career that a professional could expect in the theater, and the rewards, dangers, and uncertainties that might come his way, we look not at Shakespeare — whose life has too many gaps and who is too encrusted with legend — but at his contemporary and rival, Ben Jonson. About him we know a good deal. As a self-made, largely self-educated man, he was proud of his accomplishments and left much information about them. His spectacularly checkered career may not be typical, but most of his profession shared at least part of his experiences.

Ben Jonson was born just outside Westminster in 1572 or early 1573, a few years before the public theater itself came to birth. His father, a minister of the church, died a month before he was born. His mother was remarried to a bricklayer, then a highly skilled trade with its own guild. Elizabethan spelling was notoriously variable, and the family name was written as both Jonson and Johnson; it was not until the eighteenth century that literary historians settled on Jonson, to distinguish the playwright from the famous lexicographer. The boy was educated at Westminster School, one of the best of its time. Jonson's education consisted largely of the classics, and their influence continued to appear in his work. He must also have been exposed to the performances of Roman comedy in Latin, which were part of the school's tradition (and continue to be so to this day). Then came a disappointment; he failed to obtain a university scholarship, and the family was too poor to send him as a paying student. He therefore followed his stepfather's profession and bound himself as apprentice to a bricklayer for seven years. The year 1585 saw him on military service in the Low Countries; in 1594 he married Anne Lewis, by whom he had a number of children, most dying young. In 1597 he accepted a job as an actor with the Earl of Pembroke's company at the Swan.

What took Jonson to the theater we shall never know, any more than we know for Shakespeare. It is impossible to overemphasize, however, the magnetism that this fledgling profession had for men from all walks of life. It was new, vibrant, and exciting; it offered the most powerful and immediate means of communication that society had yet developed; it had glamor and the irresistible fascination of semi-illegality; and it drew people from the universities and from the London streets alike.

Jonson's first attempts at play writing were unfortunate; he collaborated with another author on *The Isle of Dogs,* which was suspected of being seditious; he went to prison for his efforts. On release, he went to work for Henslowe at the Rose. This occupation did not prevent him from selling his work to other companies. In the fall of 1598 the Lord Chamberlain's Men produced his first great success: *Every Man in His Humour,* with Shakespeare as one of the actors. His acquaintance with Shakespeare probably began at this time. Meanwhile, Jonson co-authored, with two collaborators, another play for Henslowe and sold plots to the same company.

He also found time to brawl. Gabriel Spencer, one of Henslowe's actors, fought a duel with Jonson and was killed. Back he went to prison, and this time he escaped by the curious legal survival of pleading "benefit of clergy." This provision was left over from the Middle Ages, when priests had exemption from common punishments; the proof of priesthood, in an illiterate age, was the ability to read and write. Jonson, as a playwright, could do both. He was, however, branded; and in the same confinement he was converted to Roman

Catholicism. This step was unwise. Catholics were still suspect, and Jonson was to pay for his change of faith later on. Perhaps the greatest index of the uncertainties of the theatrical life is that at this date, when he was already established as a playwright, he chose to serve out his apprenticeship and become a full-fledged member of the Bricklayers' Guild.

In 1599 he was in prison again, this time for debt; possibly Henslowe bailed him out, for Jonson returned to his employ. In the same year the Globe produced his *Every Man out of His Humour,* the first of his plays to be printed. His work was now beginning to diversify. In 1600 he started to write for the "private" theaters, which catered to a smaller, more exclusive clientele. (These theaters belong to a different stratum of English theater and will be discussed at greater length in the following chapter.) He still worked for the public theater, sometimes as a hack writer; Henslowe's *Diaries* show payments to him for additions to *The Spanish Tragedy* and an advance on a script about Richard III. His nondramatic verse began to appear in poetic anthologies and gained him a patron.

In 1603 Elizabeth died and was succeeded by James VI of Scotland, who became James I of England. Jonson, presumably through his new connections, quickly found favor with the new regime. He was commissioned to write an entertainment for James's formal entry into London, and shortly after he wrote the first of the many masques that occupied his later years. These lavish verse-and-dance spectacles, designed to be presented by and to the Court, will be discussed in Chapter 6.

The public theater next saw his *Volpone,* which has remained in the modern repertory as his most frequently revived play. Written in five weeks, it was dedicated to the universities of Oxford and Cambridge that Jonson had never been able to enter. *Eastward Ho,* another collaborative work, followed; this play was frowned on as an anti-Scottish satire, and Jonson found himself once again in prison. He may have won release by working as a government agent among his fellow Catholics. This year was a disastrous one for Catholicism in England. A plot to blow up King James on his visit to Parliament had failed, through the ineptness of the conspirators, but it brought about a purge of suspected dissidents. In some way, however, Jonson was able to redeem himself, and he pursued his interrupted career, writing for the court and the private theaters on the one hand, the public playhouse on the other, and producing a stream of works.

In 1616 Jonson received the first of a string of honors when he was made England's first Poet Laureate, a position still in existence. For a pension of one hundred marks a year, he was expected to produce appropriate verse on official occasions. In the same year he challenged the world of criticism by publishing a collection of his plays and poetry in the same anthology. The year 1619 brought an honorary degree from Oxford, 1621 the promise of succession to the office of Master of the Revels, and 1623 his contribution to the memorial folio edition of Shakespeare. In 1626, however, with James now dead and

Charles I on the throne, he was still vulnerable enough to be questioned in connection with the murder of the Duke of Buckingham, again a suspected Catholic plot.

His last years were passed in drunkenness and convivial disorder. Charles I was not as interested in the theater, or in masques, as his predecessors had been; the clouds of civil war were gathering; Puritan protests against the immorality of the theater were beginning to take effect; and Jonson fell on hard times. In 1629 Charles appointed him City Chronologer, the assumption being that he would write an ongoing London history. Jonson regarded the position as a sinecure and wrote nothing. Charles did not take the same view and discontinued payment two years later. So Jonson rolled into an impoverished but honorable grave. His life ended with a practical joke. One of his last requests was to be buried in two square feet of earth of his own choosing. This request was treated as a jest and granted. He promptly asked to be buried in Westminster Abbey, England's most hallowed site, standing upright. He was, and recent excavations in the crypt have proven the truth of the legend by uncovering the playwright's vertical remains.

THE AUDIENCE

Of the other essential component of the theater, the audience, we know far less than we should like. Much of our information comes from sources hostile to the theater and is therefore unreliable.

Estimates of theater capacities vary greatly. The Swan has been conjectured to have held as many as 2350 spectators, the Rose, 2500, though the average daily attendance would have been about half this. The first performance of a new work always drew a larger crowd, and so it was in the theater's interest to make additions to the bill as often as possible.

One of the inhibitions on theatergoing — and one of the objections voiced by the theater's critics — was that performances, by necessity, took place during daylight working hours. The artisans and craftsmen who attended therefore did so at the cost of their labor, though they had good value — a two-hour entertainment at the least for a penny, which was the price of a loaf of bread. The more leisured classes would have had no problem attending, and at least a sprinkling of the nobility would usually be present.

How long did a play take? This information too is dubious. Shakespeare, in his prologue to *Romeo and Juliet,* speaks of the "two hours' traffic of our stage." In the modern theater this tragedy cannot be performed uncut in anywhere near this time. Shakespeare may have been guided more by alliteration than chronological accuracy. There are grounds for believing, however, that the rate of verse speaking then was far faster than we are used to; and though two hours is probably too short, we may suspect that Elizabethans were never exposed to a four-and-a-half-hour *Hamlet.*

A Play in Performance: Christopher Marlowe, The Tragical History of Doctor Faustus

We have this play in two texts, dating from 1604 and 1616; it was continually popular and much altered. Like many Elizabethan plays, it is based on historical fact overlaid and embroidered by popular tradition. There was a real Faustus, a German scholar-scientist believed to dabble in alchemy and magic. Stories about him grew, and his name was confused with Johann Fust, one of the earliest German printers (printing itself was a suspect art in the illiterate mind). The German *Faustbuch* had been translated into English in 1592; Marlowe takes this as the source for his play.

The theater is full. The trumpets have sounded on the London afternoon, and overhead, from the theater's summit, a flag flies to announce that a performance is in progress. Onto the open stage strides the Chorus. His voice cuts through the chatter of the audience; in ringing tones he unfolds the play's subject. Faustus is set before us as a self-made man, not unlike Marlowe himself, supported in his education by relatives. He has so distinguished himself at the University of Wittenberg (not far from Berlin, one of the most famous universities of the time and alma mater of Hamlet and Martin Luther) that he has become the leading scholar of his age. But now:

> He surfeits upon cursed necromancy.
> Nothing so sweet as magic is to him,
> Which he prefers before his chiefest bliss;
> And this the man that in his study sits.

With a sweeping gesture the Chorus parts the alcove curtain and leaves the stage. Faustus is discovered in his chair, books about him. Advancing on to the main stage, he begins a long monologue in which he examines all the traditional disciplines — philosophy, medicine, law, theology — and finds them too circumscribing for his powerful, questing mind. This speech gives us a good example of how the Elizabethan theater condensed time; Faustus's whole academic career up to this point is crammed into a few minutes. He finally resolves to study magic, tempted by the powers it can confer. His servant, or graduate assistant, Wagner (a comic role, giving the audience a foretaste of the subplot to come) is sent to summon other magicians to a conference.

Then follows a purely medieval device. Above Faustus's head, on the balcony, appear his Good Angel on the right, and his Evil Angel on the left. It is an allegorical tableau of a divided mind. The Good Angel remonstrates; the Evil Angel tempts. Faustus succumbs and is further persuaded by the blandishments of Valdes and Cornelius, two friends who promise that magic will bring him fame and worldly riches. The curtain closes again on Faustus as he makes his promise: "This night, I'll conjure, though I die therefore!" And the actors playing his colleagues run off to change their costumes because this play has many roles.

Two scholars pass across the main stage, voicing their fears for Faustus. They meet Wagner, who ridicules them. This scene, the first of many comic episodes interwoven with the main action, serves obviously as light relief. On another level it reinforces the main theme. In the opening scene we saw Faustus confronting established authority; Wagner's impertinence repeats the challenge. The scene is only a brief one; as soon as the stage is clear Faustus reenters. Though nothing on the stage has changed, his opening words make it clear that it is now night:

> Now that the gloomy shadow of the earth,
> Longing to view Orion's drizzling look,
> Leaps from the Antarctic world unto the sky
> And dims the welkin with her pitchy breath,
> Faustus, begin thy incantations,
> And try if devils will obey thy hest,
> Seeing thou hast prayed and sacrificed to them.

He performs, in Latin, his magic incantations to raise the Devil. *Doctor Faustus* has been, traditionally, an unlucky play over the centuries; it shares this dubious honor with *Macbeth,* and for the same reason: the aura of black magic that hangs over both. The superstition began in the case of *Doctor Faustus* from the fact that Marlowe uses incantations drawn from authentic books of sorcery of the time. An audience that still believed in witchcraft found this effect terrifying. Edward Alleyn, who created the main role, was convinced that the Devil had actually visited one performance, conjured up by the spells in the script, and he founded Dulwich as a college of Christian education to expiate his offense. Dulwich still stands and houses the Alleyn papers. Similar stories of diabolical visitations haunted *Doctor Faustus* over the years.

The spell works; there is an apparition, one of the theater's gaudy pasteboard monsters accompanied by smoke and flame from under the stage. (Henslowe's *Diaries* contain an entry for "a dragon in Faustus.") Faustus, in terror, commands him to return in more acceptable form:

> Go and return an old Franciscan friar;
> That holy shape becomes a devil best!

The anti-Catholic joke will be noted.

Mephistopheles obeys; he is shrouded for most of the rest of the play in monk's habit. This device is one of Marlowe's daring innovations. He takes one of the stock conventions of the medieval stage and turns it into a study of hell that is psychologically more acute than the original convention. This devil is a tragic figure in his own right. Mephistopheles speaks of the sense of loss that the fallen angels must forever feel. He tries to dissuade Faustus from following his error. It is useless; convinced of his own power and invulnerability, Faustus offers his soul for "four and twenty years" in which all things will be granted to him. What is so impressive about this scene is its simplicity. We watch only two characters on an empty stage. Marlowe's language conjures up for us the dead of night and a desolate place; looming behind the dialogue, we sense the rival forces of heaven and hell.

Now we have another swift change of mood to a comic scene, which again echoes the scene preceding. Wagner tries to conjure up devils on his own account. He does, but these are comic devils in the medieval style, leaping out of the trap and scampering over the stage. The audience laughs with greater reassurance.

The curtain parts, reestablishing the scene in the study. Faustus and Mephistopheles meet to sign the bond. Marlowe makes the scene uncannily plausible by having Faustus go through the same steps that any merchant in the audience would have known from signing his own contracts; it brings the matter unpleasantly close to home. Faustus wavers; the two angels reappear, repeating the tableau seen earlier. He wavers again; Mephistopheles tempts him with "a show of spirits" who dance — the Elizabethan stage took every opportunity to introduce music, dance, and spectacle. Faustus signs, in his own blood; when the blood congeals Mephistopheles brings "fire, to dissolve it straight," the kind of realistic stage moment familiar from the Middle Ages and appealing to an audience who, though they appreciated beauty, had a relish also for the grotesque, the cruel, and the bizarre. The bill is signed. Faustus proceeds to question Mephistopheles about hell, and he receives another tragic answer.

> Hell hath no limits, nor is circumscribed
> In one self place; for where we are is hell,
> And where hell is, there must we ever be,
> And, to conclude, when all the world dissolves,
> And every creature shall be purified,
> All places shall be hell that is not Heaven.

Asking for a wife, Faustus is put off; marriage is a Christian sacrament, with which the Devil does not meddle. Insisting, Faustus is presented with "a devil, dressed like a woman, with fireworks" and, rejecting this apparition, with a magic book that gives him all kinds of power and knowledge.

A brief pause occurs; a musical interlude marks the passage of time; the dialogue resumes. Faustus is wavering again. Once more the Good and Evil angels appear, and Faustus is swayed toward repentance.

Now the theater brings out all its armory, and the full panoply of hell appears to terrify him into submission. Backstage, cannonballs roll in a wooden trough to simulate the sound of thunder; stagehands fire off powder flashes. How the Elizabethan theater loved explosions! It is small wonder that the

Globe burned down, surprising that more theaters did not. Up through the traps rise the princes of hell, Lucifer and Beelzebub. Dominating the cowering scholar, they appease him with another show, a parade of the seven deadly sins; a motif familiar in art and literature is brought to life on the stage. As Faustus sits in his chair to watch, the sins, in appropriate allegorical costume, emerge one by one from the trap — Pride, Covetousness, Wrath, Envy, Gluttony, Sloth, and Lechery. They both provide the audience with a moment of rich pageantry and mirror Faustus's fall. His first sin, like Lucifer's, was pride; we shall see him in the later scenes of the play run the gamut of the carnal vices, for the power he has bought so dearly has not enriched but coarsened him.

The central section of the play is a series of spectacular scenes interwoven with the comic subplot. Literary critics find it wanting, a sequence of pointless displays that lack the majesty of the opening. But the pointlessness, surely, is the point. Faustus has bought power at the cost of his immortal soul. We now see him frittering away this power in mindless conjuring.

The Chorus is resurrected for a linking geographical commentary, so that our imagination may whisk Faustus from place to place. What little furniture is necessary is brought on stage by the actors and removed by them when they leave the scene. A scene in Rome strikes a popular anti-Catholic note. Faustus, invisible, interrupts a papal banquet and throws dishes to the ground. A chorus of monks trying to exorcize this malevolent spirit is scattered with fireworks (fireworks again!). Hardly have stagehands removed the banquet table when we have another rich spectacular scene at the court of the Emperor of Germany; an impertinent knight has a pair of horns clapped on his head. In another scene the Duchess of Vanholt is magically presented with grapes, out of season. In and out of these scenes scamper the clowns, trying their own experiments with Faustus's magic book.

These passages do not read well. Some scholars have gone so far as to suggest that Marlowe could not have written them; they are unworthy. But they stage splendidly. Obvious crowd pleasers, they show the necessity of the playwright to appeal to every level of his audience. Those who had no taste for Latin and theology could be reached with show and noise. The diversity of the Elizabethan cast list, running the gamut from clowns to monarchs, matches the social diversity of the audience it had to appeal to.

No one has found fault with the closing sections of the play. It gives us one of the theater's grandest moments. Faustus, sated, hovers near repentance once again. And once again the stage picture takes the form of an allegorical tableau, but larger in scope than the one featuring the two angels. In the center stands Faustus; on stage right, an anonymous Old Man, who might have walked straight out of a medieval miracle play, urging Faustus to return to God; on the left, Mephistopheles, urging Faustus to suicide. Over Faustus's head, on the balcony, an angel is offering a vial of grace. The grace is rejected, and Faustus succumbs to his last temptation, the spirit of Helen of Troy. Her beauty is ambiguous. She is presented, in one of the most famous speeches in all drama, as both a vision of perfect loveliness and a succubus, sucking out Faustus's soul.

> Was this the face that launched a thousand ships,
> And burnt the topless towers of Ilium?
> Sweet Helen, make me immortal with a kiss!
> Her lips pluck forth my soul; see where it flies.

He leaves the stage with her. The devils advance on the Old Man, but his faith drives them off.

The last scene of the play is built around a single speech, the monologue in which Faustus takes leave of life. His four and twenty years are over. Bidding farewell to the scholars, he takes the stage for his last hour on earth. Once again the Elizabethan theater compresses time. This last hour, though measured by a clock that strikes eleven, eleven thirty, and finally twelve, has a playing time of some three minutes. Faustus appeals to the stars, to God, to Christ; no use. He must pay his bargain. As the clock strikes midnight, the stage trap opens. He plunges into a gaping hell mouth and vanishes from sight, leaving the Chorus to speak his epitaph.

Thus ends *Doctor Faustus*. It has been described as a play about "a Renaissance man who pays a medieval price for being one"; and no play shows more clearly the transition from the medieval to the Elizabethan theater or from the medieval to the Renaissance frame of mind. It begins in a way that audiences a century before would have recognized: with a Presenter offering, with appropriate moral reflections, the story of a human being's fall from grace. It carries many of the trappings of the medieval stage: the fiery devils, the emblematic figures of Good and Evil, the pageant of sins, the hell mouth. Apart from Mephistopheles and Faustus, the characters are two-dimensional, moral qualities given names, like the figures in *Everyman*.

But as the play proceeds, we can see another world evolving almost before our eyes. Marlowe offers a parallel vision of hell, more terrible because it is more subtle, suggesting that it lies in the torment of the inner being rather than in the affliction of the outer man. Faustus's moral crisis, represented in the early stages of the play by the externalizing device of the two angels, is shown in the latter by self-lacerating monologues in which the anguish of the spirit is explored.

The play begins with medieval symbolism. It ends with a man, alone, on an empty stage. And the play is dressed in a conscious richness of language that medieval drama could not have conceived. We see the splendor of the age in the restless urge that drives Faustus to explore realms yet unknown. We see its ambiguity in the dark underside of beauty. And we see its dangers in the waste that is Faustus's personal tragedy: the accomplishment that is rendered fruitless because it is self-defeating, deprived of spiritual purpose. It is incredible that the man who wrote this play could ever have been charged with atheism. But he was; antagonism to the theater knew no logic.

The Spanish Theater

The magnitude of the English achievement tends to overshadow the spate of similar activity elsewhere, but it is important to remember that other countries were simultaneously establishing a popular theater culture. In Spain a continuing tradition of religious tableau dramas on moving wagons (*carros*) was supplemented by a secular theater remarkably similar in its plays and staging to what was happening in contemporary London. As the English players had found a temporary haven in inn yards, which eventually contributed to the shape of the permanent playhouse, so the Spanish troupes set up their trestle stages in the open spaces framed by the backs of houses (*corrales*). This habit gave birth to more enduring structures that unconsciously duplicated English principles. An open platform provided the main acting area. Behind this stood a wall with an entrance at either end and a curtain in the center opening onto an inner stage. A balcony provided for any upper level needed in the action, and freestanding scenic units could be introduced as required. Spectators were accommodated on benches, in the windows of the adjoining houses, and in a special gallery reserved, with strict Spanish propriety, for women.

The first permanent Spanish theater was established in Madrid in 1579, but the playhouses continued to be known as *corrales* for long afterward; as we have seen elsewhere, the theater has a way of preserving technical terms long after their literal significance has vanished. In Spain the theater did not have to face the animosity it knew in England. Moral justification was provided by a levy on the theater's income to support hospitals and charities.

The Spanish dramatists were even more prolific than their English counterparts. Lope de Vega, who was born two years earlier than Shakespeare and entered the theater at the same time, wrote some 1700 plays, of which 470 survive. Like Shakespeare's, his work shows admixtures of various genres and social levels. Much of the action springs from the rigid Spanish code of honor and social propriety, something that intrigued dramatists in England and France and led to many borrowings.

This period still remains, however, one of the great unexplored periods of world drama. The vast bulk of the material remains untranslated. In the late 1960s the National Theatre of Great Britain commissioned new versions of some Spanish plays that had been unperformed for centuries, but these translations represent only a minute amount of what still remains. Perhaps the lack of interest in the Spanish theater is due to the fact that it was, historically, a dead end: it had no repercussions, no wider influence, on the European scene.

Italian Popular Theater: Commedia dell'arte

In Italy, however, the sixteenth century saw the emergence of a form of popular theater that had a very wide impact indeed. This was the commedia dell'arte, or professional comedy, distinctive because it was actor- rather than poet-centered. The plays were improvised in the sense that there was no written script, only at best a working scenario giving the outline of the action, which might be changed, even in midperformance, as the immediate situation suggested. Each actor, however, had a large and growing repertoire of comic routines (*lazzi*) developed to suit his or her chosen character — and we may begin to use the feminine pronoun here, for in Italy, as in Spain and soon in France, actresses began to appear regularly on the stage long before they were tolerated in England. There existed, then, a large repertoire of comic scenes and business (for instance, a young man courting a pretty woman behind her old husband's back), which could be linked in various combinations.

The prevailing spirit of the commedia was very similar to that of American burlesque in its heyday: performers could draw on a vast stock of common material known not only to them but to those they worked with, so that one skit could merge into another and a whole pattern of action be set up by a few simple cues. Actors who worked together over long periods of time — and these companies were, often literally, families — learned to respond instantaneously to one another's suggestions, to take a comic idea and expand it, or to protract or curtail a scene at need. The element of improvisation, then, lay not so much in creation as in selection — the same kind of improvisation that is offered in the United States today by such groups as the Proposition and the Second City, who rehearse long hours to evolve material that they may bring into play according to the audience's suggestions.

CHARACTERS AND FORM

The commedia used a range of stock characters, each with distinctive costume, speech, and a line of comic business, which normally had strong local affinities. There are obvious similarities to earlier types of performance in the Italian peninsula, and historians have gone to great lengths to draw up a family tree of the commedia, tracing its origins back to preclassical antiquity. One must ask, however, to what extent it was the product of earlier influences and how much an independently evolving form. Certainly after the disappearance of formal drama in the decline of the Roman world, the stereotype comedy of Plautus and Terence must have left many memories and echoes behind. Favorite characters, bits of comic business, perhaps even whole scenes and plays must have survived as an oral tradition among the traveling mimes and minstrels who kept the spirit of entertainment alive until the theater regrouped. Certainly, too, some vestige of the Greco-Roman mimes, which had been a contributory influence on those comedies and of whose existence we have only the barest hint, must have survived for centuries in the walled, isolated Italian communities and fostered local comic traditions. On the other hand, we notice how the theater frequently reverts to a pattern of comic stereotypes, normally to provide an easy means of identification for a popular audience; and we notice, too, that whatever the period and place, these stereotypes always seem to be the same. Though human nature offers an infinite number of individual variations, only a limited range of basic types is broad enough, and distinct enough, to be usefully exploited for comic purposes. It is not impossible, therefore, that the commedia types evolved independently, and though they show obvious affinities with their classical predecessors, there need be no direct influence.

The comic characters were normally masked, the straight characters — of minor importance and necessary only to carry on the slim plot line — not. Once again we see the mask, as in the Greek theater, as a device to fix the role and give it an existence over and above that of the actor who played it. Though generations of actors might play the same part, its main lines were defined by long tradition, and the actor inherited the role together with the costume. One did not interpret Pantalone, or the Doctor, or the Captain, but merely displayed one's skill in executing the interpretation that had already been designed.

The comic characters break down, like the cast lists of later Greek and Roman comedy, according to age and social standing. The crotchety old father was Pantalone, whose name one theory derived from a Sicilian mime, Pantaleon. He was characterized as bad-tempered, avaricious, exercising a despotism over his son, in which he was continually frustrated, and given to spasms of senile lechery. Local Italian color was given by his costume (and probably, also, by a distinctive dialect), which identified him as a Venetian merchant: a tight red tunic and breeches with a black cloak, a brown, wrinkled three-quarter mask, scanty white hair, and a skullcap. Anglicized as Pantaloon, his name has become identified with an item of clothing.

Pantalone's frequent companion is the Dottore (Doctor), often of Bologna, Italy's senior university. He is the familiar type of the comic learned man; the reponse of an unlettered public to erudition has always been a mixture of awe, fear, and derision. We find this type of character as early as Aristophanes in the person of Socrates in *The Clouds*. Plautus gives us the doctor of medicine, with his incomprehensible jargon, in *The Twin Menaechmi*, and Terence gives us a collection of muddled lawyers in *Phormio*. In the Italian comedy, the figure appears either as a scholar or a medical doctor; the latter found particular favor as the type of learned man with whom the public most frequently comes into contact. The Dottore's costume was a burlesque version of academic robes: black coat, cloak and breeches, a floppy black hat, and a black half mask.

The Capitano (Captain) was the comic soldier. He belongs in the same family as Aristophanes' fire-eating generals and Plautus's *miles gloriosus,* or braggart warrior. His identification as a Spaniard stems from Italian resentment of foreign mercenaries in their interminable little wars. His names, like Cocodrillo and Rinoceronte, which are self-explanatory, and Spezzafer, which means "spitfire," express his character. Arrogant, boastful, and pugnacious, he always runs from a real fight. He wears a burlesque of the warrior's costume, and his long-nosed mask is graced with an extravagant, spreading mustache.

Of the servant group the most prominent of the clowns (*zanni*, "zanies," or crazy men) is Arlecchino, black-masked with a costume of patches. He was identified with the northern Italian hill town of Bergamo — though some scholars trace him back to the satyrs of the Greek farce afterpieces, suggesting that the lumps on the mask's forehead represent vestigial horns. His less savory companion is his fellow Bergamese, Brighella, with wide trousers, a short jacket, and a short cloak. The hook-nosed, hump-backed Pulcinella has been identified as one of the ancestors of the puppet Punch (though he is only one of the candidates for the honor). Scapino had baggy clothes, a slapstick, and a huge, floppy hat with feathers. Other minor servant figures acquired greater importance when the commedia infiltrated into other cultures; we shall meet with them later.

The straight characters, maskless, change their names from play to play and, beside the clowns, have only a pallid identity. The young man in love and the girl he wants to marry are there only to keep the plot going. In our time the Marx brothers have revived the commedia on film: Groucho, Chico, and Harpo are invariably defined by mustache, hat, and wig, and they always perform their familiar *lazzi,* while the romantic hero and heroine vary from film to film and are instantly forgotten.

What started as a rough entertainment was gradually refined. Our earliest pictures show peasant faces peering from crude costumes. Though these works were, by definition, scriptless, the legacy of comic business inherited by the literary drama suggests that the *lazzi* were broad, obscene, and scatological. The stage was the actor's basic necessity, a trestle platform, which could be erected in town square, marketplace, or any open area, backed at best by a curtain to serve as a screen for changes. Portability was the commedia's greatest asset. Its troupes traveled throughout Europe. In Spain the visit of a commedia company to Madrid, setting up its platform in a *corral,* helped provide the impetus to establish a professional theater there. They were widely known in the south of France, and eventually they were brought to the capital, where they settled for long enough to have a powerful effect on French comedy. Their influence was felt in England, Germany, and as far north as Scandinavia.

INFLUENCES ON OTHER THEATERS

It is worth anticipating here to see some of the forms their influence took. Though somewhat domesticated from its rough-and-tumble beginnings, the commedia remained a violent, anarchic comedy, which sometimes offended the

Two of the earliest illustrations of the *commedia dell'arte* while it was still in its rustic phase. The pictures were constructed from birds' feathers by a gardener in a noble Italian household.

(*right*) Portable *commedia* stage. (*below*) *Commedia* characters in their later, more sophisticated masks and costumes. From left to right Brighella, one of the comic servants; Pantalone; maidservant; Dottore; young lovers.

(*left*) Kabuki actors frozen in a tableau.
(*above*) Kabuki actor making up. (*below*)
Kabuki actors on *hanamichi*.

moralists but escaped censure through being both foreign and scriptless. The Paris audiences, even at their most censorious, tolerated in Italian what they would not have permitted in French, and in any event, it is easier to censor words than gestures. However, the Italian comedy was sufficiently housebroken to remain in polite society. The change is noticeable in the illustrations of the stock characters from various periods. Costumes become more elegant, notably that of Arlecchino, which changes from its original rough patchwork to the more sophisticated diamond pattern with which we are more familiar.

Arlecchino, anglicized as Harlequin, became the favorite English character, and by the eighteenth century the Harlequinade was a familiar feature of the London theater bill. Resuming the function of the Greek satyr play, it offered light relief from the major tragic offerings, and it often burlesqued the tragic subjects, with Harlequin, as magician, effecting wondrous scenic transformations.

In France the plots and characters of the commedia were assumed en bloc into the literary comedy. A number of Molière's plays, particularly the earlier pieces, are commedia farces given French names and purged of their grossness. The later French theater cultivated one of the minor commedia servants, Pedrolino (Little Peter), as a silent, pathetic clown. As the white-faced Pierrot he established a new mime tradition, achieving his final incarnation in the pierrot troupes that were a feature of English seaside entertainment until after the First World War. Neglected for years because it was not literary, the commedia achieved a spectacular revival, especially in France, in the 1920s, as part of the "pure theater" movement that was attempting to discount the text in favor of the purely actorly qualities of mime, gymnastics, and tumbling.

Popular Theater in Japan: Kabuki

In Japan another theater movement was evolving, which, like Noh, independently paralleled contemporary developments in the West. As we have seen, Noh, which began as popular, expositional theater, was increasingly confined to the upper orders, where it survived as a badge of class. Popular resentment at this deprivation called into being a new kind of theater, Kabuki, which served both as an entertainment and as an oblique political protest.

ORIGINS

The word *kabuki* means something like "deviant," "not quite straight." It has connotations of sexual irregularity, and the first Kabuki performance was a series of erotic dances given by a woman, Okuni, in the dry bed of the Kamo River at the imperial capital of Kyoto. Okuni was partnered first by her lover

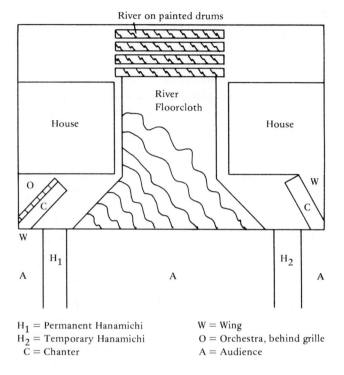

H₁ = Permanent Hanamichi
H₂ = Temporary Hanamichi
C = Chanter

W = Wing
O = Orchestra, behind grille
A = Audience

Kabuki stage as set for *Yoshinogawa*, a play about rival households. The drums at the rear of the stage revolve to represent a flowing river. A second *hanamichi* has been added

and later by a whole troupe of female dancers. Okuni died in about 1610, but her successors were popular enough to arouse the alarm of the shogunate (officials), which, like the London magistrates, distrusted assemblies and outbursts of public feeling. The women were declared a danger to public morals, and in 1629 their performances were banned. An attempt to evade the censorship by creating troupes of young men and boys met with a similar fate; this time the charge was homosexuality.

Finally, in 1654 a third form was born, using robust, mature male performers against whom the former charges could not plausibly be brought. This troupe was reluctantly allowed to continue, though the authorities hampered it at every turn with bureaucratic restrictions; they limited the places where it could be seen, censored the subject matter, and frequently closed the theaters as fire hazards. (Fire, it must be admitted, was as real a danger in Japan, where houses were built only of wood, not stone, as plague was in contemporary

London.) Thus Japan created, though somewhat later than England, its own all-male theater and, as dramatic action began to supplement the original dances, evolved plays that an Elizabethan audience could have watched with some understanding.

Kabuki borrowed much from the senior drama form against which it was ostensibly protesting. Its early performers worked where they could, usually on existing Noh stages or the bare dance platforms of religious shrines. As so often happens in the theater, these temporary accommodations influenced the shape of the later, permanent buildings. The Kabuki stage is basically an expanded and reoriented version of the Noh counterpart. A large platform provided the main acting area: the Noh *hashigakari* (a bridge between dressing-room and stage) was retained in the form of a long, narrow walkway running from the back of the theater right through the audience to the forestage. This walkway was known as the *hanamichi* ("flower path"); it made possible the long, colorful processions that became a characteristic of Kabuki and also allowed the leading actors to make extended entrances, pausing frequently to strike an attitude for the admiration of their fans seated on the floor around them. The early Kabuki stage even retained, for a while, the Noh canopy, though this was soon reduced to a mere decorative appendage and finally disappeared altogether.

Several of the plays were taken over from Noh, also, sometimes to the extent of retaining the Noh chorus and the traditional Noh pine tree background. Increasingly, however, the chorus came to be replaced by a single chanter (*joruri*), a device already familiar from other forms of popular entertainment, notably the puppet show, which grew into esteem side by side with Kabuki; the two forms were mutually influential. In Kabuki the *joruri* functions variously as narrator and chorus: seated in a niche at stage left, he chants both for the characters and about them — though the characters can also, of course, speak for themselves.

CHARACTERISTICS

Kabuki, whether adapting its material from Noh or developing its own plots, demonstrated a flamboyance antithetical to the older form and much more to the popular taste. Noh was beautiful but chaste and austere, refining actors' movements and stage spectacle to the irreducible minimum: the emphasis was on the transcendent thought, the essential idea. Kabuki, by deliberate contrast, displayed a showmanship of the most extravagant kind. Its action is violent and spectacular. It loves fights, whether single combats or pitched battles; the Kabuki actor, like his English contemporary, had to be an expert swordsman. Kabuki cultivates the gruesome and macabre, showing violent deaths, tortures, and beheadings. Its long and physically draining performances involve chases, dancing, and acrobatics — present-day Kabuki actors find a lucrative sideline as film stunt men. Its costumes are sumptuous, and its props are built with a lavish expenditure of money and energy. Kabuki eventually developed, also, an elaborate system of painted scenery and stage mechanics that anticipated by many years similar developments in the West, though the pictorialization of the stage, in Japan as in Europe, belongs to a later period and will be discussed in its appropriate place.

PRESENTATIONAL THEATER

Kabuki, however, for all its love of stage spectacle, retained the principal characteristics of presentational theater. Though Kabuki actors are maskless, they wear an elaborate formal makeup that has the same qualities as the mask and confers the same style on the acting. Kabuki costumes, though closer to actuality than those of Noh, are still demonstrably stage costumes, not real clothes, responding to an elaborate system of conventions that enables an experienced audience to read a great deal about the character from his first appearance. In Kabuki, as in the Greek theater, the actor reveals himself to the audience by externals, and what happens to the costume suggests what is happening to the character. For example, the loosening of the obi, the sash that binds a woman's kimono, is an action of sexual significance; a character dying, or being progressively more seriously wounded in a sword fight, is successively stripped of layers of clothing; a character stripped of his costume entirely becomes nothing, displaced from the action and from society. The Greek and Japanese theater, though totally unconnected and separated by a considerable period of time, started from similar aesthetic premises and evolved a remarkably similar set of conventions.

Though the action of Kabuki is realistic enough to be meaningful, a good deal of the time, to the untrained observer, it is still founded on the same presentational premises that we have seen elsewhere. Time is fluid. Important moments may be prolonged far beyond their normal duration. Moments of crisis are signaled to the audience by a freeze in which the principal actor assumes a contorted posture known as a *mie*: eyes rolling and limbs locked in a resemblance to the violent attitudes of Buddha's guardians as represented in statuary. The freeze is accompanied by a prolonged rattle on wooden clapper blocks wielded by a stage assistant. Thus the moments of high tension tend not to evolve from the action by the sort of buildup that we are accustomed to in the Western theater; rather they are applied from the outside.

The introduction of important properties also is conventionally handled. They are brought on by a black-robed assistant, the *kurombo* ("invisible man") of Kabuki. Though the audience can clearly see him, his presence is conventionally ignored. Discarded properties are similarly picked up and taken away. Here we have an example of the same kind of dramatic economy we have seen in the Greek theater, though there it manifested itself in rather different ways. An effect is only prolonged for the time that it has dramatic validity; after that it is expendable. The props are only important while they are being used. How they get there or what happens to them afterward is, dramatically, irrelevant. It is not necessary that their introduction or disappearance be realistically motivated. Perhaps the clearest illustration of this concept comes from the Kabuki battles, which leave the scene littered with dead and dying. As soon as the battle is over, they rise and leave the stage. The dramatic point has been made; to keep the dead in view would be merely untidy.

Thus the Kabuki theater presents a more advanced case of what we have already seen in the Greek; namely, the tendency of the presentational theater to work from moment to moment without the necessity that the representational theater insists on for a logical and plausible connection with what precedes and follows. Each scene, each vignette, is self-contained and self-complete; and this idea is reinforced by the aesthetic principle of Kabuki, which demands that an audience be able to enter the theater at any time and see a perfectly composed stage picture and a self-explanatory dramatic moment. Hence Kabuki performances, which are extraordinarily long by modern Western standards, are not so grueling a test of endurance as they may at first seem to be. The audience is free to come and go as they please — to leave for a meal and then return later on with the assurance that they can pick up the thread of the action at any point.

THEATER AND POLITICS

In its relations with officialdom, Kabuki provides an extreme example of the universal malaise. After the initial hostility, the authorities and the theater settled down to an uneasy truce. Kabuki was permitted to continue but under stringent conditions. It was grudgingly tolerated, in much the same way that other cultures have tolerated their theater, as a safety valve for emotions that might otherwise have found a more dangerous vent elsewhere. Every precaution was taken, however, to ensure that the danger was contained.

In the earlier theater direct access from the auditorium to backstage was prohibited for fear the spectators might be contaminated by physical contact with the actors. Later theaters were located, along with brothels, geisha houses, and other places of ill repute, in walled-off sections of the city, which the samurai (warrior aristocracy) were forbidden to enter (though many did in disguise).

Some subject matter was rigidly proscribed. Nothing that even hinted at political commentary was tolerated. Kabuki, therefore, concerns itself with chronicles of the early, and therefore safe, periods of legendary history or melodramas that are soap operas in gaudy disguise. Kabuki, however, is less concerned with the script than with the production values. Thus the art remains, like commedia, as an example of pure theater, in which the literary element is subordinated to actorly and scenic skills.

Survivals

Shakespeare, of course, is legion. Over the centuries he has proved the biggest box office draw in the world. His contemporaries are seen less often, though the Shakespeare Quatercentennial in 1964 produced a spate of revivals of both major and minor works, some of which had hardly been performed since their original appearance. Marlowe's *Doctor Faustus* often achieves professional production. His *Tamburlaine* — which has an enormous cast — is seen more rarely; modern theater economics are more stringent than they were in the Elizabethan period, when actors were plentiful and cheap. Ben Jonson remains popular, particularly his *Volpone* and *The Alchemist*. There are signs, though, with Jonson as with some of his contemporaries, that we may be reaching a point where Elizabethan drama needs to be translated, as Chaucer does; too many words and phrases are outside the reach of the modern popular audience.

Shakespearean plays, though continually in the repertoire, have usually been presented according to the changing theatrical fashions of the time; we shall see many examples of this situation in the chapters that follow. The present century, however, has seen a remarkable attempt to reconstruct the basic features of Shakespeare's stage and to restore the plays to the environment for which they were designed. Audiences in North America today may see a working reconstruction of the Elizabethan playhouse at the annual Shakespeare Festival in Ashland, Oregon. The Festival Theatre in Stratford, Ontario, approximates in a modern architectural vocabulary the basic spatial relationships of the Elizabethan stage. Laurence Olivier's film of *Henry V* (1944) begins and ends in a reconstruction of the Globe Playhouse, with boy players in girls' roles, a courtyard open to the skies, and groundlings standing in the pit.

The theater of the Spanish Golden Age remains almost totally ignored in the modern repertory. Commedia dell'arte is known chiefly by its offshoots: Molière's shorter comedies, which are frequently staged with commedia costumes and in the Italian manner, and the later, more decorous works in the commedia style by Gozzi and Goldoni (see pp. 286–287). Kabuki is still, of course, a living art, though it is slowly being endangered by rising prices and dwindling audiences. The Kabuki-za in Tokyo preserves a full repertory of plays from the early pieces onward, handed down from generation to generation of actors who, as in Noh, live and work in families. Troupes have toured widely in the United States, giving performances made more accessible to a Western audience by simultaneous translations.

6
The Theater and the Courtly Arts

The New Playhouses

REDISCOVERY OF THE CLASSICS

Side by side with the popular theater movements described in the preceding chapter, another view of the stage came into being that was much more closely related to classical concepts. This approach, the court theater, was born of scholarship and fostered chiefly by the European aristocracy, which had time, space, and money at its disposal — and, paradoxically enough, it called into existence a theater functionary we have not seen so far: the scenic artist.

We have seen the Elizabethan drama, with its expansiveness and surging vitality, as the natural heir of the cycle dramas of the Middle Ages. Although Elizabethan writers were schooled in the Latin classics, or at least aware of some of them, their debt to them was limited. *Doctor Faustus* begins with an allusion to Roman history and an invocation of the Muse; Faustus, in his terminal

Monsieur Jourdain, from Molière's *Le Bourgeois Gentilhomme.*

agonies, quotes from Ovid, whose erotic works Marlowe had translated; Helen of Troy, the paragon of classical beauty, appears as the model of *all* beauty. But in its form the play is totally anticlassical. A medieval spectator, though he might have disapproved of it, would have understood it. A Greek spectator would not have accepted it as a play at all.

The Renaissance was, of course, literally a rebirth of classical studies. Works that had disappeared from the general view for years were exhumed from the monastic libraries, studied, and, above all, printed. Some things were imperfectly understood, and much remained inaccessible to all except a few specialists. When Aeschylus's *Oresteia* was first printed, for example, scholars were confused by the shortness of *The Libation Bearers,* the second play, and published it as part of *Agamemnon.* Greek was not yet widely studied. It took a long time to reach the universities, and when it did, it occasioned a major dispute between the "Greeks," who supported this new discipline, and the "Trojans," who clung to the traditional Latin.

Latin, however, was well known, and the reconsideration of existing works and the rediscovery of lost ones caused a flurry of excitement in which the theater had a part. This excitement was most evident in Italy, where men still lived among the ruins of the classical past — mutilated, for the most part, by time, neglect, and the metal-and-stone-hungry Middle Ages but still decipherable. Here statues and buildings could be studied and copied. One of the most exciting discoveries of the time consisted of several plays by Plautus, the manuscripts of which had been reused by medieval copyists for biblical texts.

We have remarked on the tendency, almost inevitable in theater scholars, to see the theater of past ages in the image of their own. Illustrations of the new editions of plays by Plautus and Terence showed a Roman stage reconceived in medieval terms, with the three doors of the *scaena* transformed into separate "mansions" labeled with the names of the characters. Several productions took place, not following the Roman simplicity but with the wealth of painterly scenic effects that the Italians were already using in their religious plays. In the late fifteenth century the Roman Academy offered productions of Seneca and Plautus. The year 1486 saw a revival of Plautus's *The Twin Menaechmi* on a wooden platform stage with a row of five battlemented houses — the mansion principle again — and an actual ship with sails, which crossed the courtyard in which the play was presented to bring the visiting Menaechmus onto the stage. Mansion staging was not antithetic to the scenic compression of the Roman *scaena;* in a sense it is merely an extension of it. But the ship was something new, deriving from the technical inventiveness of medieval producers with a touch of Renaissance flamboyance, and it pointed to the shape of things to come. In 1487 came Plautus's *Amphitryo,* the comedy in which Jupiter assumes mortal shape to seduce a mortal's wife and with a prologue spoken by the god Mercury. This production was set in "a paradise, with stars and other devices" — an element of scenic splendor, which would have surprised, but probably delighted, Plautus.

VITRUVIUS AND THEATER STRUCTURE

An even more important rediscovery had been made in 1414, though its full impact was not felt until the work was published seventy years later: the Latin manuscript of Vitruvius's treatise on Roman architecture, which included detailed specifications for constructing a theater. The treatise had a widespread effect on the theatrical world, particularly after its reissuance, with illustrations, in 1513. In an age that was vastly interested in technology, Vitruvius's intriguing though sometimes incomplete descriptions were eagerly speculated on and put into practice, often with ramifications in remote areas. For example, Vitruvius describes a practice, familiar in the theaters he knew, of using large empty vessels, placed at key points in the auditorium and tuned to resonate to certain pitches of the actor's voice — a kind of preelectrical amplification system, used, curiously enough, in the Japanese theater also, where jars were set under the Noh platform to magnify the stamps of the climactic dance. We find this device taken up and used in English parish churches, with vessels set in appropriate niches to amplify the preacher's voice.

Reading Vitruvius after so long a gap of time, however, induced certain misconceptions. He describes both Greek and Roman theaters, and his account of the former was accepted by generations of scholars as applicable to the kind of stage that Aeschylus, Sophocles, and Euripides knew. It was not until the nineteenth century, when Greek theaters began to be excavated and dated by the new scientific techniques of archaeology, that Vitruvius's description was more correctly interpreted as pertaining to the Greek theaters he knew in his own time — which had changed considerably since the fifth century B.C.

Other misconceptions involved his account of the Roman theater, despite the fact that the shells of these buildings still stood; and these misconceptions assumed solid form when scholars began to construct what they considered to be a working replica of the classical Roman playhouse. The year 1580 saw the beginning of such a building at Vicenza, not far inland from Venice and just south of the mountain district of northern Italy. Known as the Teatro Olimpico, after the Olympic Academy, which sponsored the project, it was entrusted to the architect Andrea Palladio. With his death a few months later, the project passed to Vincenzo Scamozzi, who completed it in 1584. The theater still stands, a living, working example of what Renaissance scholars thought a Roman theater looked like. The merest glance shows one way in which they went wrong: they put a roof on it, combining stage and auditorium in one enclosed complex.

But we should not sneer with the wisdom of hindsight. Vitruvius was writing for those already familiar on an everyday basis with the general shape of the theaters he was describing and for whom a covered performance space was the exception rather than the rule. He does not trouble to specify what for him was obvious and elementary. It is not difficult to see how scholars coming to the study after a gap of centuries, and with only an imperfect knowledge of ancient architecture and traditions, could have made this basic mistake. In any case, the open-air theater belonged to a period when performances were limited and could be arranged to suit the weather. For professional theaters performing continuously some form of cover was essential. Even the Elizabethan public playhouse, which still left its groundlings unprotected, had to shelter its actors; and in the period that followed, covered theaters became the rule.

Under its roof the Teatro Olimpico contained features with which a Roman would have been comfortable: an auditorium arranged on a semicircular basis, an elevated stage, and a *scaena* with three openings. Behind these openings was something he might have recognized less easily. Vitruvius, describing the theater he knew, wrote of devices called *periaktoi*. These devices certainly existed in the later classical theater; they present a problem because we cannot be sure what they were. From the text they seem to have been revolving units capable of presenting a choice of three faces to the audience. Vitruvius describes them, loosely, as being used when a change is made in the play or when a god appears, to "alter the appearance in front." What exactly does this mean? The language is vague: once again, Vitruvius was writing for people who knew his subject more precisely than we do.

It is difficult, in terms of the Roman theater as we have reconstructed it, to think of the *periaktoi* as a device for changing whole painted sets — though it is true that the basic principle has been used for large-scale set changes in the later theater and may most commonly be seen today in moving billboard advertising. Most scholars believe that *periaktoi* in the classical theater were used only for symbolic purposes, to display an appropriate emblem to accompany the appearance of a god or to suggest a change of locale. The Italians, however, expanded the notion of a changeable, painted set to embrace the whole stage picture; and through the archways of the Olimpico *scaena* the audience could see architectural vistas in diminishing perspective. One can see how even this limited opportunity to pictorialize the stage must have appealed to an age that was exploring the mathematics and practice of perspective painting and delighting in trompe l'oeil (realistic) effects.

SERLIAN RECONSTRUCTIONS

The Teatro Olimpico was not unique. It was simply one of the more elaborate examples of the classical revival; it has received a good deal of attention because it is still there to be viewed and used. Theaters created in the Italian palazzi for the entertainment of princes and scholars followed the same general plan. Within this format architects experimented with ways of augmenting the pictorial effects, giving the designer a place on the stage while remaining faithful to the spirit of the classical theater.

In 1551 Sebastiano Serlio (1475–1554), who had studied Vitruvius deeply and illustrated the work, published his treatise on architecture. Here he set out typical scenes for the three genres of ancient drama: tragedy, comedy, and satyr play. These, it must be emphasized, are full-stage scenes. The *scaena,* with its

Scene for tragedy designed by Sebastiano Serlio: a late renaissance interpretation of classical motifs in false perspective.

Teatro Olimpico, Vicenza: a renaissance interpretation of a Roman theater.

doorways, has disappeared. In its place are half-modeled, half-painted backgrounds, which are still, for tragedy and comedy, composed of architectural motifs but now provide a complete picture in cleverly contrived receding perspective. A street, leading from front to back of the stage, is flanked by houses; those nearest the spectator are three-dimensional, to give the illusion of depth, and blend into the painted houses on the backdrop. *Scaena* has become, in our sense of the word, *scenery*.

It must be emphasized also that these effects are strictly backgrounds. The actors played against the setting, not within it. They could not; they would have appeared as giants against the perspective houses. It would be a long time before the set reached around to enfold the actor. Some have therefore seen the earlier settings as a compromise between three modes of thought: the classical impulses that set the play against an architectural facade; the medieval practice that used a mansion to define the locale but set most of the action in the open space before it; and the pictorial emphasis of the Renaissance.

The subject matter of Serlio's settings is also worth attention, for they define genres as well as decorating them. The tragic scene is made up of imposing palaces, leading back to a triumphal arch with an obelisk in the far distance. The comic scene shows ordinary houses with balconies and chimneys. To the front is the house of a courtesan, to the rear a ruined church — a pictorial footnote on the shift of values from the Middle Ages to the Renaissance. This scenery shows a cast of mind that the theater was going to find hard to break: tragedy is about kings, queens, and princes; comedy, about ordinary people. Serlio's third scene, the satyric, shows scattered huts and cottages and a semi-formal arrangement of trees. This scene was to become familiar as the pastoral mode.

THE EVOLUTION OF THE PROSCENIUM ARCH

Pictures need frames. The development of the pictorial element called for a means of cutting off the view at the sides and from above, bringing a new architectural unit, the proscenium arch, into the theater and giving an old word a new meaning. The Greeks, who had coined it, used it ambiguously. *Proskenion,* the Greek word, derives from *pro-,* "in front of," *skene,* and *-ion,* a diminutive suffix. The word therefore means, literally, "a little something in front of the *skene.*" In one usage it applied to decorative panels set, in the Hellenistic theater, against the *skene* facade (in this sense, too, it was used figuratively of a notorious prostitute, who was all makeup with nothing behind it). In another usage it referred to the raised stage, which could also be called, in a different sense, something in front of the *skene.* Latin naturalized the word as *proscaenium,* and in Plautus it means, indisputably, the raised stage. Renaissance usage initiated the sense in which we now employ it. As the meaning of *scene* changed, so did the meaning of *proscenium,* which now implied "something in front of the scenery"; and so the framing arch with which we are still familiar in most of our theaters. It has been argued that the practice of using the proscenium arch began with the design of the Teatro Olimpico, in which the doors framed individual architectural vistas: the full proscenium arch was thus seen as a simple expansion of this device. There is evidence, however, of proscenium arches being used some time before the Teatro Olimpico was built.

Once the proscenium became a fact, it changed the actor-audience relationship. For the first time the audience was segregated from the stage. This segregation was not immediate, nor was it for a long time complete. In the court theaters of Italy — and in France and England, where courtly ballet spectacles were presented in the Italian manner — it was still possible, at need, for the action to spill out of the proscenium into the main body of the hall. In the French public theaters of the seventeenth century — and in the English theaters of the Restoration (the period beginning in 1660), where the proscenium arch became a fixture — the audience could still infiltrate the backstage, pack the wings, and use the stage as an intermission lobby to meet friends and occasionally interfere with the action. Not until the eighteenth century were they banished from the stage.

But even as early as the Renaissance, the emergence of the proscenium clearly began the division of the theater building into two separate worlds, that of the audience and that of the play. Actors still played as far forward as possible, for the reason cited above — to avoid violating the architectural perspective. In the English Restoration theaters still had apron stages, protruding from the proscenium, which retained some of the old imaginative flexibility of the Elizabethan open stage. For a long time, too, the auditorium remained fully lit during the performance, providing another inducement for the actors to play forward, as they were better lit by the spill from the audience lights than by the scanty illumination provided on the stage. But the old, creative fusion of actors and audience so characteristic of the Greek and Elizabethan theaters was beginning to disappear.

The proscenium arch is the most characteristic device of the representational theater. It induces the feeling that the audience is watching a moving picture of a slice of the real world. It further induces the convention that, so far as the performers are concerned, the audience does not exist. The audience is in another place, another realm of being: it can no longer be used, or regularly referred to, with the casual frequency that we find in the earlier drama. This feeling finally hardens into what the nineteenth century knew as the "fourth wall" convention: the assumption that the proscenium represented a transparent wall of the stage room, through which the audience could observe the action without being observed themselves.

THE ROYAL SEAT

In the auditorium the Renaissance court theaters provided one feature in particular that was to have its effect elsewhere. This was the royal seat, which accommodated the noble patron of the performance and was placed dead center, opposite the stage. To this seat the lines of the stage perspective were accommodated, so that one person, and one only, had a perfect view of the stage picture: for the rest of the audience filling the curved tiers, the perspective was progressively distorted according to their distance from the center. Once again the theater provides an architectural metaphor for the society that produced it. The world is seen perfectly through one person's eyes alone; the king forms the apex of the social pyramid, with the lesser ranks of society filling in the sides in descending order.

This attitude is reflected also in the social orientation of the dramatic genres to which we have already referred. In a world of authoritarian monarchies the lofty issues of tragedy should properly be performed by, and addressed to, the nobility and presented with appropriate language and behavior. Comedy is about, for, and by the common people, though the aristocracy may go slumming and enjoy it. You will recall that the Japanese theater had already become one of clearly marked social distinctions, with Noh reserved for the samurai and Kabuki for the commoners. In Europe such social distinctions manifested themselves in major and minor ways. In France the cast lists of tragedy were regularly given with the characters in order of rank, not of appearance or dramatic importance. The king was always listed first, however small a part he might play in the action. For a long time, too, the arrangement of the stage groupings was controlled by the rank the actor played rather than by the necessities of the action: kings took stage center.

MECHANICAL WONDERS AND THE DROP CURTAIN

Behind the proscenium the Renaissance stage was increasingly dominated by the designer, who rapidly established himself not merely as a partner but as a superior partner in the enterprise. We have extensive documentation of this relationship in the works of Serlio himself and other designers, who give detailed specifications not only for perspective scene building but for a whole range of mechanical contrivances to make the stage a place of scenic wonder. Flying machines, for which these men claimed classical authority in the Greek *mechane,* were of primary concern. What evolved was something far more elaborate than the Greeks could have envisioned: intricate arrangements of ropes and pulleys for lowering a character and moving him across the stage simultaneously; ways of parting painted clouds to show a god descending from the sky; ways of moving the clouds themselves to let them mass or scatter. Instructions are given for changing scenery by mechanical means, so that one set of painted frames gives place to another. There are ways of showing seas in motion, by means of painted waves turning on rollers, and swimming, spouting sea monsters moving above them. Simultaneously, and inevitably, a system of lighting the stage developed to throw these mechanical marvels into sharp focus and augment them with shadows and transparencies.

The stage thus became an architect's paradise in which the text was relegated to second rank. And now that all attention was on the scenery, the designer needed a means to conceal the change from one setting to another. This concealment could no longer be done merely by language and imagination, and the designers felt an obvious desire not to let the machinery show. Thus we see the inevitable concomitant of the proscenium arch, the proscenium curtain.

Here again the designers could quote classical authority. Because so little was known about the workings of the Roman theater, and what was known was imperfectly understood, appropriate authority could be found for virtually anything. There had, indeed, been a Roman stage curtain, at least in the later, more lavish period of the classical theater. Little is known about it; it is mentioned in late sources, and a trifle of supporting archaeological evidence has been found. What seems certain is that the Roman *siparium* fell, not rose, to disclose the performance, descending into a trough in the ground, though how this was mechanically possible in an open-air theater without overhead support from which the curtain could be hung is much debated.

The Renaissance curtain also originally fell, though with much greater ease in an indoor theater that had a roof from which to support it. Such a curtain existed in the Teatro Olimpico; and perhaps the most vivid illustration of the way in which the theater had changed comes from comparing the original production of *Oedipus the King* given about 429 B.C. at Athens with the revival in 1585 at Vicenza. The Greek production opened in a bare theater before an audience representing most of the city's population, with illumination by the sun and with a single actor on stage conjuring up a plague-stricken Thebes by his language. The Italian revival played to an exclusive, scholarly, and aristocratic clientele; it flooded the theater with perfume and set off fireworks; and by dropping the curtain, it revealed a stage crowd set against an elaborately painted architectural vista.

THE COURT THEATER

Thus the Renaissance Italian stage, while ostensibly basing itself on classical practice, set off on an orgy of spectacular scenic effect and established, in the principal cities of Europe, a form of theater based on totally different aesthetic principles from the popular art. In most places the two forms could be seen simultaneously, though on different social levels. Sometimes they met and mingled. Some authors worked for both; from time to time the popular theater obviously sought prestige by borrowing devices from the courts; and there are obvious compromises, some examples of which we shall consider below. Court and popular theaters were not, therefore, mutually exclusive; but the pictorial stage, produced, endorsed, and made financially possible by the court theater system, was in the end to dominate its rival and establish the picture stage for popular audiences also.

The Ballet Spectacles

FRENCH COURT BALLETS

The French equivalent of the Italian spectacles, inspired by their example and using many imported personnel, was the *ballet de cour,* the court ballet. Though we call these works *ballets,* they were not pure dance in the sense we use the word today. Rather they were combinations of song, dance, spectacle, and the spoken word, with spectacle tending to predominate as it did in Italy. Even the dance element was not what we should now call ballet proper, for the basic techniques of what we know as classical ballet were not formulated till the latter part of the seventeenth century.

Originally the ballet consisted of a combination of marching to music and patterned groupings with social dances of the period. We are talking here of a time when the upper classes were taught to sing and dance as we are taught to read and write. Dancing was a social necessity, and the ballet master could assume a knowledge of the basic repertoire from which he could select, link together, and elaborate his spectacle.

The ballets were appealing for several reasons. Theorists approved of them because they offered opportunities that conventional drama forms did not. Drama was concerned with the concrete, while dance could present ideas, allegories, and striking visual metaphors. They were delighted, too, because they could find classical precedent and source material in the pantomime performances of the ancient world, and particularly in the essay on dance by the satirist Lucian (ca. A.D. 125–190), who had professed to find the form aesthetically more satisfactory than tragedy. Lucian's work was therefore elaborated on, producing handbooks of classical themes and images suitable for ballet use. The aristocracy cultivated ballet because it provided them with a showcase in which they could display their wealth, talent, and physical grace. The ballets principally used amateur performers, with the nobles performing to their own peers, though professional ballet masters (usually Italians) were used from early on, and some professional dancers were eventually permitted to take part. The monarchy itself delighted in such displays, and Louis XIV, the Sun King (he acquired this epithet from one of his ballet roles), enjoyed performing, mostly in female parts, until middle age caught up with him. Finally, the ballets served a useful political end as ceremonies to entertain and impress visiting dignitaries, often with a topical diplomatic allusion worked into the plot. The expense alone was impressive, for staggering sums were spent on costumes and elaborate settings.

For an example we may look at a work that appeared in 1581, in the Salle du Petit Bourbon at the Louvre. It was designed by a naturalized Italian, Baldassarino di Belgioioso, who now worked under the French form of his name, Balthazar de Beaujoyeux. The occasion was a celebration of a royal marriage, and the work was entitled the *Ballet comique de la Reine.*

It should be noted here, at its first appearance, that the word *comique* in the French theater does not necessarily mean "comic." It implies rather a work that includes spoken dialogue. Thus, in French, actors, whether of tragedy or comedy, are *comédiens;* the French National Theater is the Comédie-Française; and opéra comique includes works like Bizet's *Carmen,* which, at least in its original form, contained spoken dialogue passages, as opposed to sung recitative. We shall find other applications of this word later on. The *Ballet comique de la Reine* was in fact a highly serious work, based on themes from classical literature and mythology.

The ballet began with the castaway Ulysses, running in fear from the enchantress Circe, who had changed his sailors into swine. Kneeling before the king (who, as in Italy, sat front and center of the audience), he begged for protection, making a flattering and anachronistic allusion to the contemporary glories of France. Circe followed, complaining that she had lost her prey. From the ceiling, in a mechanical cloud, descended the god Mercury, who in trying to aid Ulysses was himself entrapped by Circe. Mercury's son, Pan, the god of the woods and fields, promised his help. The goddess Minerva, appearing in a flying chariot, then led a concerted appeal to Jupiter, king and father of the gods, who descended from heaven in his own flying cloud. In the grand finale Pan, Minerva, and Jupiter combined their forces to lead an attack on Circe's palace. The enchantress was defeated, the prisoners released, and all knelt in homage to the king.

Around this simple plot was built a splendid show. The huge floor space allowed for mass movement of great complexity, and the action was periodically interrupted by dances of appropriate groups of mythological figures: sirens, tritons, and Nereids hauling a seashell chariot with the goddess Thetis in it; the satyrs who were Pan's companions; and the four Virtues, accompanied by deities both major and minor. Scenic units were set around the ground space. Directly opposite the royal throne stood Circe's palace, backed by a painted scene. On one side was a wood, on the other a "golden vault," which served both as stage setting and as a concealment for the musicians. Flying machines were rigged from the ceiling, and costumed stagehands brought in the endless procession of ornamental floats and chariots.

In this performance all sorts of theatrical traditions come together. The freestanding scenic units, each a self-contained setting, are reminiscent of the mansions of the Middle Ages, while the townscape backing Circe's palace reveals the Italian influence of perspective painting. In the climactic siege of Circe's castle we see a translation into ballet terms of the medieval tournament. The patterned movement of the *corps de ballet,* designed to be viewed from above, is consciously reminiscent of the dance of the Greek dramatic chorus in its orchestra: to this extent the king of France, like the high priest of Dionysus in Athens, had the *worst* seat in the house. And the flying machines, of course, display all the latest resources of Italian technology. Though there was no all-embracing proscenium arch, Pan was revealed to the audience by the dropping of a separate curtain.

The *Ballet comique de la Reine* was so costly that nothing quite so sumptuous was ever attempted again. However, it set a pattern and a standard for a long series of court performances, which attracted the talents of some of the most distinguished artists of the time. Though the emphasis was on music, dance, and spectacle, the scripts were often by men who had won literary distinction in other fields. Well-known dramatists were pressed into service, establishing a connection between these private performances and the public theater, which worked for the good and embellishment of both. We shall look at examples of this mutual influence later on.

ENGLISH MASQUES

In England the ballet style of entertainment was represented by the court masque, an entertainment linking songs and dances with a loose plot. The masque used subject matter and staging similar to those of the court ballet in France and the same social level of amateur performers. Queen Elizabeth enjoyed the masques, and her successor, James, was devoted to them, though the equally enthusiastic participation of his wife, Queen Anne, was marred by her no less enthusiastic devotion to strong drink.

The name of Ben Jonson has already been mentioned as a frequent writer of these masques, and we may appropriately look at his career as bringing to a crisis the increasing division of interest between the script and the stage design. In 1604 Jonson was commissioned to write *The Masque of Blackness* for Christmas at court. His designer was Inigo Jones, an English architect who had traveled widely in Europe and was rapidly introducing the Italian fashion in his homeland. Jones's masque sets regularly used the proscenium arch, each individually designed with appropriate motifs and usually displaying the title of the work on a central panel. *The Masque of Blackness* has the distinction of being the first such English work to use a front curtain. Before this time set changes were carried out in full view of the audience, though we have instructions for such alarming devices as making a loud noise at the rear of the auditorium or shouting "Fire!" to distract the spectators' attention. Jonson and Jones had a long and lucrative but cantankerous partnership.

The chosen subjects of the English masque, though classically oriented, also involved references to English history and the constant flattery of the monarch that was a regular element of the French ballet. The social and political symbolism of the English masque was apparent in its casting. Professionals played the low characters and courtiers the high, with the monarch lauded as the embodiment of justice and virtue and the bestower of order upon chaos. A partial list of Jonson's titles shows the prevailing mode of courtly allegory: *The Masque of Beauty, The Masque of Queens, Love Freed and Love Restored, The Vision of Delight, Pleasure Reconciled to Virtue,* and *Neptune's Triumph for the Return of Albion.*

Though productive, however, Jonson was not happy. His self-importance was offended by Jones's insistence on the primacy of the set, and a quarrel erupted between the two in which Jonson showed himself a master of the language of abuse:

> This is the money-got, mechanic age.
> To plant the music where no ear can reach,
> Attire the persons as no thought can teach
> Sense what they are; which by a specious, fine
> Term of you architects, is called Design:
> But in the practised truth, destruction is
> Of any art beside what he calls his.

The concept of the pictorial set, however, was now too deeply entrenched to be eliminated, and it was to remain a permanent feature of what its critics were to label "the new age."

London's "Private" Theaters

Though the lavish masque was, by economic necessity, an upper-class prerogative, its influence permeated to the lower social levels of the theater. Just as Kabuki, while professing antagonism toward Noh, absorbed and exploited many of its techniques, masque elements found a place in the popular playhouse. Shakespeare's *The Tempest,* for example, contains, besides flying spirits, a masque involving classical deities, song and dance, and magical scenic transformations. These things show the spirit of the public theater to come, and even in Elizabeth's reign managers were eyeing the possibility of establishing indoor houses, where more elaborate scenic effects would be possible and where plays could be staged for a more exclusive clientele.

BLACKFRIARS

As we have seen, the public playhouses were compelled to locate themselves in unattractive neighborhoods. The raffish nature of the South Bank was not calculated to attract the gentry, and because of the variability of English weather, open-roofed theaters had obvious disadvantages. A site within the city limits was more desirable to avoid the tedious river crossing and to place the theater on the doorsteps of the wealthier patrons. And the opportunity was created by a combination of entrepreneurial opportunism, dubious precedent, and legal ambiguity. The impulse came, indirectly, from the royal love of plays.

One of the features of Tudor London was the choir school, formed to provide a constant supply of boy singers for St. Paul's Cathedral, the Chapel Royal, and Windsor Castle. Here the boys were given a good general as well as musical education, and one of their duties was to present, perhaps several times a year, dramatic entertainment for Queen Elizabeth. This example gives us our first historical illustration of a recurring phenomenon in the theater, the periodic fashion for child actors; several famous examples occur as late as the eighteenth and nineteenth centuries.

With a widespread interest in the theater generally, the choirmasters were quick to see the possibilities for the boys' performances, not merely for the court but for the greater public. Richard Farrant, the master of Windsor Chapel, was especially active and had a keen eye for profit. But where could the boys' performances best be displayed? To build was politically inadvisable, for the hostility of London magistrates, even on this level, had to be reckoned with. It was better to rent and to find a site where performances could be given discreetly, without the fuss and publicity attendant on events in the public playhouse.

Blackfriars, the former monastery at the southwest corner of the city, suggested itself as a happy possibility. It had the added attraction of offering a legal loophole. As we have seen (p. 151), it was originally built as a religious foundation outside the city walls. Though the walls were later extended around it, it had continued to enjoy the status of a "liberty," and after the dissolution of the monasteries, it had come under the direct jurisdiction of the Crown. Thus although within the walls and easy of access, it escaped the attention of the civic authorities. An additional attraction, in Farrant's eyes, was that Black-friars had developed into a fashionable residential district providing exactly the kind of audience he was seeking. The converted monastery had already had some theatrical connections, housing the Office of Revels. By the time Farrant came upon it, it was leased out to private landlords. Taking a partner who already owned an interest in the building, Farrant leased space on the upper floors. One of the conditions of the lease, which turned out to be important, was that he should not sublet for twenty-one years.

The work of conversion went rapidly. Partitions were pulled down, creating a working space of about 40 feet by 20 feet, with a platform stage illuminated by chandeliers and chairs for the audience. Thus was created London's first "private" theater — though private only in the sense that it catered to a more exclusive, more monied audience. Wealthy patronage was essential, as the theater was expensive to run. Candlelight was costly — one of the most valuable perquisites of court officials at this time was the resale of candle ends. When Farrant died, he left a debt that was still unpaid years later. But under his operation Blackfriars ran with fair success, drawing on the boys of the Chapel Royal and Windsor. It opened in 1576 or 1577 — that is, at about the same time as the Theatre — and ran until 1580 without trouble.

Then the landlord complained. He had understood, he claimed, that the building was only to be used for very occasional, and truly private, performances. Now it was a full-fledged theater. He also found the structural alterations offensive and sought legal grounds for breaking the lease. Farrant died before the case could be decided, leaving his widow with the lease and the choirboys, of which she could make no use. She asked the courts for the right to dispose of them, but she seems to have gone ahead without waiting for formal permission, turning them over to William Hunnis. The theater continued in operation.

The landlord was still dissatisfied. Payments were not being met, and the property was sublet once more, thus breaking the terms of the initial agreement. This time the renter was Henry Evans, a lawyer who thought he could buy his way into a good thing. Evans was also able to use his own professional expertise to delay the increasingly complex litigation about who owned the building and what it was to be used for. Finally, Elizabeth herself, ever sympathetic to plays, intervened through the Earl of Oxford, himself a patron of the drama. The company was reorganized on a more reputable basis, with the children of St. Paul's added to the group, Evans retained as manager, and the lease presented to the novelist and playwright John Lyly (ca. 1554–1606).

LYLY'S INFLUENCE

Lyly was to literature what Inigo Jones was to stage design: a man who had constructed a highly elaborate art on a supposedly classical basis. His prose romance *Euphues* (1578–1580), slender in plot but richly decorated in style, flowery and ornate, had brought a new word, *euphuism,* into the English language. It represented the extreme of that richness in wordplay that so delighted the Elizabethans and became highly fashionable. Lyly's plays were of the same quality.

Alexander and Campaspe, played first at Blackfriars and on New Year's Day, 1584, in a private performance before the Queen, was a romance using characters from Greek antiquity. Plato, Aristotle, and Diogenes were depicted in it, but the main plot concerns Alexander the Great, who had fallen in love with Campaspe, a female captive brought home from the foreign wars. The artist Apelles, assigned to paint her portrait, falls in love with her too; and Alexander, in a burst of noble generosity, gives her to him. The plot, however, is merely a thread on which the author hangs a number of disquisitions, philosophical and otherwise. It is a play designed for the learned taste, with a number of jokes in Latin, which Queen Elizabeth was proud of speaking. We know how this play was staged at court, from the Office of Revels accounts. They list "players' houses" — that is, mansions — of canvas and wood, representing Alexander's palace, Apelles' studio, and a tub to show the traditional abode of Diogenes.

Lyly's work at Blackfriars was highly successful. The children's company had introduced a new element to the entertainment of Elizabethan London. Performed in surroundings at once more intimate and lavish than the public playhouses, the repertoire was designed for a coterie audience. Fashionable and well-educated spectators appreciated works that were satirical, contentious, heavily laced with in-jokes, and spiced with the erotic. But this success was

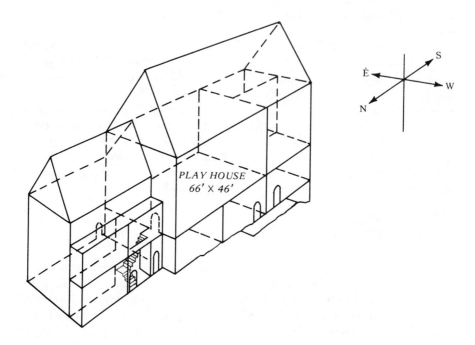

Burbage's Blackfriars Playhouse, an indoor theater in a former monastery.

terminated in 1584 by a new outbreak of litigation. The landlord finally had the theater closed and the building converted into tenements.

THE CHANGING FORTUNES OF BLACKFRIARS

So it stood until 1596, when James Burbage, looking for a new site when his Theatre lease in Shoreditch ran out, was tempted by the attractions of Blackfriars. This time he used another part of the building, what had originally been the dining hall of the monastery. Burbage combined several smaller rooms into an auditorium, 66 feet long by 46 feet wide, with, apparently, a ceiling high enough to accommodate two galleries. As in the boys' theater, the stage was lit by chandeliers. Actors may have been lodged in the rooms above. This theater, unfortunately, fell foul of the Blackfriars residents, who complained of the noise and the blockage of their streets by playgoers' coaches. A petition was brought before the privy council, who forbade the use of the theater for public performances, and Burbage and his partners concentrated their attention on the Globe across the river.

Blackfriars was still usable, however, for private performances, and in 1600 it was taken over by that same Henry Evans whom we have seen involved in the earlier company. Arguing that his original grant still empowered him to present children's plays, he went so far as to press suitable boys forcibly into his company. By these dubious means he put together a remarkable troupe that attracted some of the best writers of the time. Ben Jonson, who worked for them, leaves a moving tribute to a boy named Salomon Pary, who specialized in old men's roles and died at the age of thirteen. Shakespeare, whose Globe actors were commercial rivals to the Blackfriars boys, makes an ironic allusion to them in *Hamlet:*

> But there is, sir, an aery of children, little eyases, that cry out on the top of question, and are most tyrannically clapped for 't: these are now the fashion.

Then came disaster. Evans went too far in his attempts to recruit suitable talent, kidnapping the son of a country gentleman who was influential enough to strike back. The boy was released, but the father, furious with the theater, called down the full force of the law against it. For a while Blackfriars was closed. Evans, ever resilient, managed to reinstate himself, but the happy days were gone. His plays were blighted by political involvement. In 1604 Samuel Daniel's *Philotas* was suspect through possible connection with the Earl of Essex. In 1605 *Eastward Ho* was closed down as an anti-Scottish satire. In 1608 Chapman's *Conspiracy and Trial of Charles, Duke of Byron,* was resented as an insult to the French court.

Finally even Evans was glad to get out, and Richard Burbage agreed to take over Blackfriars as a winter house for the King's Men, with a syndicate of seven shareholders, including Shakespeare. In spite of renewed protests by the neighbors, it was protected by royal patronage and became very popular. Within this building some of Shakespeare's more elaborate plays were produced, including *The Tempest;* its mechanical effects were more elaborate than could be attempted in the public playhouse.

Blackfriars remained in use until 1642, a year of doom for the London theater, and then remained empty; it was pulled down in 1655, and the site was used for tenements. Its career, however, in a variety of hands, had been a long one and shows not merely the continuing political and social harassment against which the theater had to contend, but also how a more ornate and spectacle-oriented form of theater coexisted with the simpler staging of the public playhouse.

THE CLOSING OF THE THEATERS

We have referred, justly, to 1642 as a year of doom, for it was then that the English theater fell victim to political circumstances from which there was no easy escape. The reign of Charles I saw an increasing division between the King and the Parliament, culminating in the outbreak of civil war. England was geographically divided by its political sympathies. The South and East, the regions most economically advanced — including London — supported Parliament, while the North and West declared for the King. The universities were firmly royalist. Cambridge raised a large treasury for the King, only to have it seized by parliamentary forces; some Oxford colleges are poor to this day because they supported the losing side in the civil war. On September 2, 1642, as one of the emergency measures declared to be justified by the national crisis, Parliament closed the theaters. Plays were condemned as "too commonly expressing lascivious mirth and levity," and so unfit for "seasons of humiliation"; and at one stroke actors and playwrights found themselves without a living.

The Edict of 1642 was no isolated incident but the culmination of a series of brushes between the government and the stage, whose beginnings we have already seen in the reign of Elizabeth. Political resentment against unauthorized and seditious material was fanned by the increasing moral indignation of the Puritan faction who now controlled Parliament. There is no denying that the theater was not wholly free from blame. Post-Elizabethan drama shows an increasing concentration on the sexually titillating and the morally perverse: the plays of Marston and Webster take place in a world of festering corruption where murder and treachery are commonplace and virtue and innocence choked out of existence. Many who looked at these works shuddered. The censorious Puritan, Zeal-of-the-Land-Busy, whom Ben Jonson satirizes in *Bartholomew Fair* (1614) as going through the fairground and making moral objections to a puppet show, had a growing number of more deadly real life counterparts. To a good many people the theater appeared as both symptom and cause of moral disease, and they could quote the Christian fathers to prove it. Thus the theaters fell victim to the time.

They did not go without a struggle. In 1643 the players addressed a petition to Parliament, claiming that they were left without a means of livelihood. It was ignored. Some joined the army — as royalists, where their patronage lay. The King's Company of Blackfriars enlisted at once, selling off their costumes, props, and equipment. So did the Globe actors. As long as the royalist forces still had a secure base, some actors were able to find employment. Masques and plays were presented at Oxford, which was for a while the King's headquarters. Some even continued to act in London, but with vastly diminished opportunities and considerable risk.

In London the royal masque houses, which had long given offense because of the great expenses connected with such shows, were pulled down. In 1645 the great new masque house in Whitehall, begun eight years earlier and still unfinished, was demolished and the materials sold, as Parliament announced with politically inspired sanctimoniousness, "to pay the King's poor servants' wages." Some public playhouses staggered on, even after the edict. The Red Bull was particularly prominent, although frequently raided by parliamentary troops who seized the costumes and drafted the actors, and even members of the audience, into the army.

In 1647 plays were being acted quite openly at the Salisbury Court, the Cockpit, and the Fortune. The failure of the Act of 1642 to close the theaters completely is shown by the fact that it had to be reinforced by threats of demolition; in 1649 several theaters were torn down, though the Red Bull, among others, continued to play. Law records of the period show numerous complaints from theater landlords that their rent was not being paid and responses that the disturbances had diminished the companies' income. This continuous litigation is a sure sign that some performances were going on. The ban, in fact, had the same impact on the London theater that Prohibition had on the liquor trade in America of the 1920s. It did not mean that there was no theater; it meant that what there was could only be had illegally and tended to be of inferior quality. As instance of this bootleg drama, we hear of a heavily cut version of *A Midsummer Night's Dream,* concentrating on the antics of Bottom the weaver. Bearbaiting and similar entertainments were allowed to go on comparatively undisturbed.

Gradually the dispirited actors began to depart for the Continent, where the defeated royalists had settled. Charles I was captured, tried, and beheaded in 1649. His survivors fled across the Channel and bided their time at the French court, where a number of actors joined them. The French influence acquired at this period was to have an immeasurable effect when the English theater was allowed to resume. Other companies formed in the Low Countries and in Germany, among them one led by George Jolly, of whom we shall hear more later. They took their repertoire with them, some of it imperfectly remembered. Some of the more curious products of the theater of this troubled time are truncated and garbled versions of well-known scripts assembled from the faulty recollections of actors compelled to seek their fortunes abroad. *Doctor Faustus,* which had its genesis as a German folk tale, returned to its country of origin in Marlowe's version and was absorbed into the folk repertory in a puppet version that is still performed.

Theater in France

What the English exiles found in France was something quite different from the theater they had known at home. During the most prolific period of the Elizabethan drama, the French theater had been dormant. Political troubles and the threat of a civil war as devastating as that of the English had turned public attention to other things, and a general apathy had left the Hôtel de Bourgogne, in its new secular form, as the only playhouse in the capital. We should at this point glance at the topography of Paris, as we did at that of London, since the selection of theater sites and their social ramifications were no less important here.

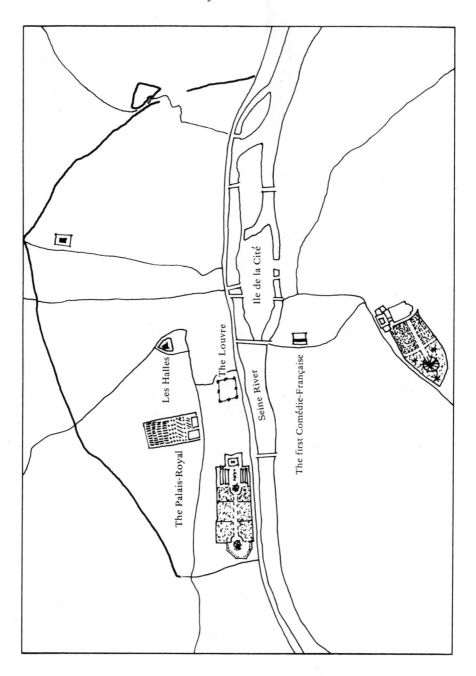

Paris in the reign of Louis XIV, showing the principal locations of theatrical performances: The Temple, near which stood the Marais; the Comédie-Française, home of the amalgamated companies; the Palais-Royal, home of Molière's company; the Louvre (court performances), and Les Halles, near which stood the Bourgogne.

In the second half of the seventeenth century Paris was still a medieval city, bulging out of its defensive walls and, though less overcrowded than London, housing a greater population than it could afford. By the end of the century, however, a rapid change had begun. Through the center of the city ran the Seine with its several islands. The smaller of these were joined to become a fashionable building site: the larger Île de la Cité, already graced with the medieval splendor of Nôtre Dame, saw much impressive new building, and it was joined to the Right and Left Banks by the Pont Neuf, a bridge remarkable in its time because it had no buildings on it whatsoever. On the Right Bank the existing palace of the Louvre was enlarged and embellished by a succession of monarchs. This palace itself, as well as the private mansions of princes of the church and state, had large halls that could be, and were, used for presentations of ballets and plays in the Italian manner. In the public sectors of the city a spate of town planning was clearing away the medieval squalor to build new walls, squares, and gardens.

THE PUBLIC PLAYHOUSES

The Hôtel de Bourgogne owed its site to such a clearance scheme. It stood, as we have seen, on land once occupied by an aristocratic town house and in a propitious location, on the fringes of the great covered markets of Les Halles, which had for long been the commercial heart of Paris and remained so until the 1960s. It thus had access to a large, floating population that had already developed its own tradition of street theater and could easily be tempted to see works more regularly performed. On one side, it was near one of the capital's more venerable churches, whose graveyard was a popular, if macabre, meeting place. On the other side, it was only a short distance from the fashionable quarter surrounding the Louvre.

France's senior playhouse, therefore, grew up unhampered by the social stratification that had cramped the theater in London. It also claimed the monopoly handed down from the days of its religious performances. Thus when, as in England, touring professional companies began to form, they were compelled, if they wished to play in Paris, either to rent the Hôtel de Bourgogne or to pay the managers a fee for the privilege of performing somewhere else. This arrangement provoked much resentment and frequent lawsuits. Some time elapsed before the monopoly was broken, and even then the Bourgogne retained a patriarchal authority that made it the most sought-after theater in Paris.

Its internal arrangements were simple, retaining the general shape of the other halls the company had used before acquiring a permanent home. The building was long and narrow, approximately 107 feet by 44 feet. Over half the floor space was given to the *parterre* (pit), where there was no fixed seating, though stools and benches could be placed according to need. Behind this rose the *amphitheatre,* the name clearly a relic of Roman usage and the shape perhaps

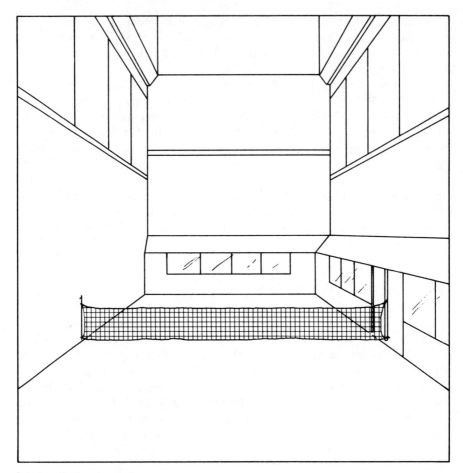

Interior of a tennis court.

remembering the open-air performances of the Middle Ages, providing a bank of steeply tiered seats with cramped accommodation and dubious visibility. On the upper level, running around three sides of the theater, were the *loges,* (boxes). This left a stage about 25 feet square, with proscenium arch and curtain. Stage and auditorium alike were illuminated by chandeliers, the ceremonial raising of which was the sign that the performance would soon begin.

The first serious commercial opposition to the Bourgogne was offered by a company locating itself in the recovered marshland in the northeast quarter of the city, which still went by the name of the Marais (marsh). This area was consciously chosen as a fashionable quarter by a group that was deliberately flouting the Bourgogne's monopoly and needed as much prestige as possible. The Temple of the Knights of Jerusalem had been built here, and some of the most elegant houses of Paris now stood in an area that had once been underwater. In France, as in England, theater companies sought subsidy and security by placing themselves under the protection of a member of the nobility, and the war between the new company and the Bourgogne became a game of theatrical power politics in which Cardinal Richelieu himself, the chief minister of Louis XIII and a prominent patron of the arts, finally intervened on the side of the newcomers.

The Marais company, after a series of moves, finally located itself in one of the most familiar types of buildings in fashionable Paris, an indoor tennis court. The year was 1629, and the choice of building produced a characteristic French theater shape. Indoor tennis was a game of some antiquity. Lawn tennis had, of course, not yet appeared; this game was a product of the nineteenth century. The indoor game was more complex, something like a combination of lawn tennis and squash; it was played in a long, narrow hall with windows high on the wall for safety's sake and a covered gallery down one side for spectators. A few such courts are still in use today. When the Marais company arrived, the game, though still common, was slightly past the peak of its popularity, and the conversion of a tennis court into a theater presented an appealing way for the landlords to augment their income. With a stage platform, the actors' basic necessity, erected at one end, and seating placed in the body of the hall, the conversion was quick and easy. This long, narrow shape, which echoed by necessity what the Bourgogne had already achieved by design, established a pattern to be followed by other French theaters and by the first new English playhouses built after the Restoration.

CLASSICAL INFLUENCES ON FRENCH DRAMA

What was staged in these theaters showed the influence of the classical spirit more clearly than anything yet done in England. So far we have been concerned chiefly with classical influences on the externals of play production. The French theater shows their impact on the ways plays were written. In England the theater had remained largely faithful to its medieval heritage. The French theater consciously turned its back on this heritage and followed another path, thereby setting up a schism between French and English drama that would not be bridged until the early nineteenth century.

Although the Hôtel de Bourgogne had kept its audiences over the lean years with a succession of popular farces, serious writers were increasingly intrigued with the revival of classical tragedy. In this they were stimulated by the spirit of the age. France, resurgent under an increasingly autocratic monarchy, saw itself as a new Rome, and it drew the parallel with frequency in literature, art, and sculpture. Louis XIII and his minister Richelieu, and Louis XIV after them, were very aware of the value of the arts, particularly drama, as a political device, with every impetus for associating the contemporary theater with the illustrious works of the classical past. These were models that could be followed. Not everyone read Greek, but the Latin tragedies of Seneca were available, not only in the original — they were widely studied, particularly in the Jesuit colleges — but also in French translation. And, finally, one of the great rediscoveries of the Renaissance, overshadowing Vitruvius, was what was taken to be an authentic book of rules for the composition of classical plays: the *Poetics,* by Aristotle. Up to this point the classical influences on later drama have revealed themselves mainly in the decoration and framing of the stage picture. In seventeenth-century France, however, we now see a conscious attempt to reconstruct the internals of classical tragedy, following what was assumed to be the ancient precedent.

We have already noted (p. 83) the importance of the *Poetics* in its own time, as the earliest extant study of the drama as an art in its own right. Its renewed importance in the seventeenth century was due not so much to what Aristotle said as to what his interpreters thought he said. He made certain observations on the state of drama as he knew it, or at least as he read it. His disciples, centuries later, chose to elevate these observations into cast-iron rules.

Most important in determining the shape and content of plays were the so-called Three Unities, time, place, and action. In Greek plays the first two had been only loosely adhered to, and time and place were manipulable according to need. Aristotle, indeed, hardly comments upon place, though those who read Greek plays for themselves could see that more often than not the tragedies confined themselves to one location. Even the Unity of action hardly existed for Euripides, who was quite capable of juxtaposing two different stories to make a thematic point. In neoclassical tragedy, however, the Unities became dramatic dogma.

When the curtain rose on the French stage, the audience saw a setting — almost invariably "a room in the palace" — which did not change for the duration of the play. All the action was confined within this room, and those events that logically had to happen elsewhere were reported by messengers.

The Unity of time presented some problems, mainly in defining what Aristotle meant by his suggestion that the action be encompassed by "a single revolution of the sun." Did he mean twelve hours or twenty-four? One critic argued for the former, on the grounds that most of our important acts take place by daylight. On the contrary, urged another, many significant events occur after dark. Generally speaking, French tragedy settled for a full day's span. This time, however, was limitation enough. It made impossible the expansiveness of Elizabethan drama. French critical theory could not accept a play like *Doctor Faustus,* whose action stretches over twenty-four years, or *Antony and Cleopatra,* where years of developing political antagonisms are compressed into a few hours' playing time.

Similarly, the Unity of action established a kind of tragedy directly antithetical to Elizabethan drama. It eliminated the subplot and rendered Shakespeare's complex interweaving of different actions impossible. It also insisted upon a distinction of genres and refused to tolerate comic figures, like the porter in *Macbeth,* who might be loosely attached to the main *tragic* action. By following supposed classical precedents, therefore, the French dramatists

The Hôtel de Bourgogne, Paris. (*left and middle left*) Overhead view showing disposition of loges, parterre, and stage. (*middle right*) Ground floor view, as seen by a spectator entering the main door. (*bottom left and right*) Stage with typical settings in place.

(*above*) Setting for *Pyramus and Thisbe,* Hôtel de Bourgogne. Note the means of illuminating the stage. (*right*) The love-duty conflict familiar in French neoclassical tragedy is seen in this modern production of *Bérénice.*

Molière's *The School for Wives,* in its most famous modern revival, with settings by Christian Bérard.

evolved a form far more limited in its possibilities than the Greeks themselves would have recognized.

It must be remembered, also, that though the French writers sought authority from Aristotle, their living examples came largely from Seneca, whose plays were notably static and conceived more as oratorios than drama. It was perhaps through reading Seneca that the French theater came to abandon the chorus, although it is the most characteristic feature of Greek plays. In Senecan tragedy the chorus, though still present, is of minimal dramatic importance, serving merely to bridge the gap between episodes. A contributory factor to the French avoidance of this device was undoubtedly economic. Greek tragedy was conceived in an environment where public participation was taken for granted, and the choruses were chosen from an ample supply of amateur volunteers. The French theater was a commercial institution where all participants had to be paid; and it is noticeable that, while choruses appear in the earliest French recreations of classical tragedy, they soon drop out. The last two tragedies of Racine, *Esther* and *Athalie,* based on biblical subjects, returned to the use of the chorus; but these works were written not for the commercial theater but for amateur performances in a fashionable girls' school, where there were no financial limitations on casting, and, indeed, every reason to provide parts for as many as possible.

FORM AND CONTENT OF FRENCH TRAGEDY

French seventeenth-century tragedy thus acquired a distinctive form and content, based on real and supposed classical precedent. Its subjects were often taken from classical mythology — sometimes direct adaptations of existing Greek and Roman plays — or from Greek and Roman history. Other subjects were possible, however. Some plays were based on biblical material — one of the few ways in which the religious dramas of the Middle Ages survived under the new regime — or on Christian themes from Roman sources. Thus Jean Rotrou (1609–1650) wrote *le Véritable Saint Genest (The True Saint Genesius),* a study of the Christian martyr who became the patron saint of actors, and Pierre Corneille (1606–1684) wrote *Polyeucte,* another study of Christian martyrdom under the late Roman Empire. Some plays dealt with foreign dynasties, achieving through geographical remoteness the same distancing effect that the classically inspired works achieved through time. Plays about the colorful history of the Turkish court were particularly popular. French interest in Turkey was high, and its palace revolutions and assassinations gave dramatists ample material to work with. Whatever the period and locale, the plays focused on the lives of kings, queens, and princes. The cast lists of French tragedy are socially exclusive, conspicuously lacking the mixture of royalty, nobility, and commoners that characterizes Elizabethan drama.

One recurrent device helped to fill the gap left by the disappearance of the chorus. This feature was the provision of a confidant for every major character: a lord- or lady-in-waiting who acted as a sounding board and "feed" for the principal. Thus the characters of French tragedy are regularly paired off, each principal with an appropriate counterpart, creating a pattern that, though useful, was to degenerate into a cliché of tragic composition. French tragedy did not restrict itself to the Greek three-actor rule, but scenes still tended to involve only small groups of characters, proceeding in a series of monologues and conversations without the mass effects possible to the Elizabethan stage.

The same restraint is observable in the onstage action. Like their classical exemplars, these are primarily plays of talk rather than movement. Death, violence, and indeed, any kind of abrupt action, though they have an important function in the plays, are kept offstage, outside the doors of the stage room. Their impact is realized through the resurrected device of the messenger speech; and as in Greek tragedy, some of the finest moments of the plays come in these extended narrations.

French tragedy, therefore, concerns itself with the response to actions rather than with the physical action itself. It is by no means actionless, but the action is in the mind and on the tongue. Perhaps the best illustration of this actionless kind of drama is in Racine's Bérénice (1670), which concerns itself with a chapter in Roman imperial history. Emperor Titus is in love with Bérénice, queen of one of the smaller Near Eastern kingdoms under Roman rule. She reciprocates his feelings. Titus's problem is one of national security. If he follows his natural inclinations and marries Bérénice, the resulting jealousies will upset the balance of Roman power in a crucial part of the world. What is he to do? The crisis comes to a sharp focus in a simple scene that finds Titus waiting in a room in the palace. On one side is a door that will take him to Bérénice; on the other is the door leading to the public, which is clamoring for him as emperor. His mental debate is thus crystallized in a moment of physical decision, and his taking the public door shows his sacrifice of private interests to the demands placed upon him as ruler.

CHARACTERISTICS OF FRENCH TRAGEDY

This simple, but critical, action serves to illumine some of the fundamental qualities of French tragedy. Titus's dilemma is that of most of the leading characters in French tragedy, the struggle between duty and desire.

One of the cardinal classical principles absorbed into the French drama was the concept that in all human affairs there is a right way, a guiding pattern that may not be immediately discernible, that may at times be obscured by the multiplicity of issues, but that nevertheless exists, is accessible to us by the use of our reason and intelligence, and is for us to follow. Humanity ideally should place itself in conformity with this pattern and not be led astray by more immediately appealing distractions. These distractions come, most obviously, from worldly desires and, most usefully for dramatic purposes, from the power of love.

Thus the archetypal pattern of French tragedy, explored in innumerable individual variations, is the conflict between love and duty. Sometimes, as in *Bérénice,* duty wins, resulting in the tragedy of individuals who have to be sacrificed or abandoned in the pursuit of a higher purpose. Racine's play ends with a sigh that such things have to be. Sometimes desire wins over duty, resulting in a different kind of tragedy, that of a human being whose inclinations have warped him into misjudgment; and as the leading characters of these plays are usually monarchs, their misjudgments may have widespread and devastating consequences. Racine's *Britannicus* (1669) gives us this side of the picture. It is about the Emperor Nero, who, as Roman historians attest, began his reign not as the monster of tradition but as a benign and able ruler. Racine's play shows the various influences to which the emperor is subject. He is under pressure from those around him: from Agrippina, his mother, jealously guarding her failing power; from Burrhus, his advisor, anxious to keep his royal charge on the right course; and from Narcissus, his evil influence. A potential rival to Nero is the prince Britannicus, who has an equal claim to the throne. The play is therefore about shifting palace plots and alliances, and the crisis is precipitated when Nero falls in love with Junia, the girl whom Britannicus intends to marry. His passion pushes him into irresponsibility. He falls an easy prey to the temptations of Narcissus and arranges to have his rival poisoned. (The poisoning, of course, takes place offstage and is reported by a messenger.) *Britannicus* closes with a gloomy look into the future, a hint that once this ideal ruler has taken his first false step, he starts to turn into the monster that history has remembered.

These considerations will perhaps suggest why neoclassical tragedy chose to concern itself primarily with kings, queens, and princes. This concern was not merely modish snobbishness. France was under the rule of the most autocratic monarchy that the Western world had known since Roman times, and the way in which monarchs chose to act, for better or for worse, was of immediate concern to most of the population. It is true that the king subsidized the theaters, and the audiences to whom the playwrights strove chiefly to appeal were aristocratic. Public success depended on noble patronage, and there was every inducement to write plays about the social milieu with which this prized audience was familiar. One might also note the way in which the king-figure is often invoked as savior and protector, and even as a deus ex machina to resolve plots in which he has no immediate concern. French tragedy provides instances of flattery of the monarch no less gross than those that appeared in the Jacobean masque.

This concentration on the monarchy, however, has a higher dramatic purpose. It is posited on the presumption that kings are not like ordinary people. Their power is vast; their influence is far-reaching. When an ordinary man goes wrong, the consequences may be disastrous but are limited to the wrongdoer and his personal circle. When the king errs, the whole country may suffer. Greater power involves greater responsibility and a sterner sense of duty. The conduct of the characters of French tragedy becomes tragic simply because they cannot allow themselves to behave like ordinary men and women. Racine habitually surrounds his principals with characters of lesser degree, representing the ordinary human point of view. But the king cannot afford to listen to them, for the consequences may be catastrophic. What we are dealing with here, then, is the principle of noblesse oblige, a standard of conduct that the royal participants must accept — or reject to their own loss and the loss of others.

These arguments also suggest why the insistence on the Unities, with their apparent restrictions on the scope of the drama, becomes an asset in the hands of dramatists who know what they are doing. True, there are occasional awkwardnesses. Sometimes there are obvious manipulations of the action to bring it into the compass of a single room; sometimes dramatists obviously grow restive and infringe upon the Unities enough to bring down critical wrath upon their heads. But on the whole, the new concept of staging is organically related to the subjects the theater now chooses to portray. Everything extraneous is pruned away, to focus upon the essential argument. The single setting creates a deliberately claustrophobic situation, with the passionate voices of debate reverberating more loudly in a closed space. By limiting the scope of the action, the French dramatists believed they were increasing its intensity, and, for the most part, they were justified.

LANGUAGE

Adherence to classical principles involved strict attention to form. As in classical architecture, order, symmetry, harmony, and proportion were all-important. Even the most casual reading of the plays shows how carefully these desiderata were involved. We have already commented on how cast lists tended to be constructed in matching pairs. One principal is matched against another, and each leading character has his or her confidant. This regularity is carried further into the structure of the plays. They tend to pivot about a central point, the moment of decision. Scene is balanced by scene, act by act, motif by motif. We often see what is, in effect, the measured pattern of the court ballet translated into verbal terms.

This symmetry extends itself to the language. The favored, though not invariable, verse form for French drama was the Alexandrine couplet, which derived its name from an early appearance in a medieval romance about Alexander the Great. This form involved both a longer line than the Elizabethan iambic pentameter (thus making particular demands on the actors' delivery and breath control) and the use of rhyme, which the Elizabethan writers had used only sparingly. In theory, each line of the couplet offers a complete thought. Words do not carry over from one line to the next, and the thought of the first line of the couplet is matched by the answering thought of the second, the responses being pointed by the rhyme. A delicate system of shifting internal stresses saves the pattern from monotony. Nevertheless, the Alexandrine, by its nature, displays more conscious artifice than the Elizabethan blank verse line, and a long speech is, by necessity, divided into a series of rhyming couplets. The following example comes from Racine's *Britannicus:*

> Je vous croirai, Burrhus, lorsque dans les alarmes
> Il faudra soutenir la gloire de nos armes,
> Ou lorsque, plus tranquille, assis dans le sénat,
> Il faudra décider du destin de l'état:
> Je m'en reposerai sur votre experience.
> Mais, croyez-moi, l'amour est une autre science. . . .

What we miss, therefore, is the swelling crescendo that Shakespeare could build into King Lear's speeches in the storm or into Henry V's appeal to his battle-weary troops at Agincourt. What we gain is a reinforcement of that sense of order and balance that governs the whole play. Line answers line with epigrammatic symmetry, just as character matches character and scene balances scene. Dialogue passages fall naturally into the rhythm of the Greek stichomythia. Characters converse in full and equal lines of verse.

Once again the use of so apparently restrictive a verse form may suggest that dramatists were imposing unnecessary limitations on themselves. Scenes of high passion have to be played in rhymed and measured verse. But here, as in other cases, the apparent limitation is turned, in skillful hands, into an asset. The contrast between the content and the form is productive. As we have noted, these plays are usually about the conflict between duty and desire, about human passions shackled by other imperatives. It is appropriate, then, that passionate sentiments should be harnessed within a rigid verse form, which has the same effect as channeling a running stream: the water flows faster between artificial boundaries.

In their choice of vocabulary the French dramatists showed a circumspectness dictated by both classical precedent and the social milieu for which they wrote. Language, like every other aspect of the production, was governed by considerations of decorum. It had to be appropriate to the station of the characters represented. Thus French tragedy — and to a certain extent French comedy also — notably avoids "common" words. This convention presents a further enormous difference from Elizabethan drama, where language fluctuates from the courtly to the mundane, from poetic conceits to the argot of the gutters, depending on the social standing of the characters and the requirement of the scene. Racine's dramatic vocabulary is noticeably sparse — some two thousand words as compared to Shakespeare's twenty-four thousand — though even he is sometimes given to courtly paraphrases. Though love is a dominant theme in Racinian tragedy, characters very rarely say that they are simply "in love." They pine, they languish, they expire from passion.

Components of the French Theater

In one important respect the French theater conferred benefits that the Elizabethans did not know. Its writers were treated almost from the beginning as men of literary stature. Their plays were eagerly discussed and studied, as literature as well as drama. Playwrights had their flocks of devotees and often basked in the favor of court appointments. As the Paris theaters were, directly or indirectly, subsidized by the throne, successful playwrights enjoyed greater prestige and financial security than they had for centuries. There might be occasional flurries of gossip about authors' private lives and more substantial scandals about particular plays and people, but on the whole this period had shed that aura of suspicion and downright hostility that haunted the Elizabethan theater. This is true of playwrights only: actors were another story, as we shall see.

PLAYWRIGHTS

Writers were attracted to the theater from various walks of life. Jean Racine (1639–1699) came to play writing out of a strict religious education. Pierre Corneille (1606–1684) began as a lawyer. The law contributed a number of writers. This connection seems to be a recurring one in the world of the theater, perhaps because the public practice of law has so many theatrical connotations. It was strong in France, through the law students' long-established tradition of producing plays themselves.

The monetary rewards of the theater were now greater. Corneille could ask, and receive, substantial sums for his work, and in this period, too, we see the tentative beginning of a royalty system. Increasing prestige, however, brought some corresponding disadvantages. Critical concern with the works presented made playwrights vulnerable to a large and influential body of academic opinion, which scrutinized each new offering in the light of established classical principles and awarded praise or blame. The establishment of the Académie Française by Louis XIII elevated critical dogma to a position from which it could shape the direction the theater was to take.

Pierre Corneille's *Le Cid,* which opened at the Marais in 1637, provided a cause célèbre whose repercussions have still not entirely died down. This play was a romantic tragedy based on the legendary Spanish hero. Don Rodrigue is in love with Chimène, but their romance is blighted by a quarrel between their respective fathers. Thus we have the familiar love-duty conflict. Don Rodrigue is bound by filial obedience to take his father's side, though this estranges him from the family of the girl he loves. He leaves to fight a spectacular battle — offstage — with the Moors, and he wins against overwhelming odds. The dilemma is reconciled at the last moment by the intervention of the king as deus ex machina, who announces that honor has been satisfied on both sides, and Rodrigue and Chimène are free to marry.

The play was a Paris sensation. It packed the house to overflowing. Critics, however, were antagonized, not so much because Corneille had broken the rules but because he had kept them in such a way as to make them ridiculous. So much incident is packed into *Le Cid* that the Unities are strained to bursting. Pamphlets were written, angry debates were held, Richelieu turned hostile, and the whole affair was passed to the Académie for judgment. Corneille's success was not diminished, and *Le Cid* remains one of the high water marks of French achievement. But the playwright's greater restraint in his later tragedies shows how sensitive he was to critical disapproval.

ACTORS

Actors, though they enjoyed much attention, did not share the same prestige as writers. Acting was still a beleaguered profession. A good deal of hostility came from the church — not universal, but powerful enough to be sporadically disruptive. The charge of immorality that has clouded the theater for much of its existence was widely evoked. Authors could cling to their distinction as men of letters, and individual actors could enjoy enormous personal popularity, but the profession as a whole, despite the royal patronage of the art, existed on sufferance. Actresses, now a regular feature of the French theater, were particularly vulnerable, and the equation between actress and prostitute, so frequently made, was particularly virulent at this time. The effect was to drive the actors in upon themselves. Acting companies became extended families, in which the members intermarried and brought their children up in the business. Many stayed with the same company all their lives, creating a group loyalty and an ensemble of tested quality out of which the playwright could successfully create his best work, though the major theaters raided each other periodically for star names, and there were some famous desertions.

THE NATURE OF FRENCH ACTING

The actor's most valuable professional attribute was his voice. The comparatively static nature of French tragedy threw vocal skills into prominence, for the voice was the chief means by which the actors could communicate with the audience. And just as tragedy created a special vocabulary, it also demanded, by the standards of the time, a special voice, which was not the diction of everyday but closer to a singsong recitative.

The vocal demands made on tragic actors were extraordinary. Montdory, for several years the star of the Marais and the original Don Rodrigue, suffered a partial paralysis, brought on by vocal overexertion, that drove him into retire-

ment. Montfleury, his counterpart at the Hôtel de Bourgogne, a grossly cor-
pulent actor whose voice was his main attraction, narrowly escaped the same
fate.

This doctrine of the special voice, which grew naturally out of the physical
conditions and critical preconceptions of the time, was to plague the theater for
many years to come. In the French theater it was justified on classical grounds
by the consensus of scholarship that Greek actors had delivered their lines with
a keen sense of musical intonation. It was justified in other ways by the social
pretensions of French tragedy. Here were characters operating in a milieu,
susceptible to moral imperatives, and talking in a language that were not those
of the ordinary world. It was only proper that their delivery should aim at
something higher than the level of ordinary speech. Like other aspects of the
neoclassical theater, however, the concept of the special voice outlived its time,
surviving as a meaningless cliché in a later generation. It was regarded as a
revolution when tragic characters first started to talk like ordinary human
beings.

SETTINGS AND COSTUMES

The settings and costumes of tragedy also contributed to the sense of moving
in a superhuman world. Although many of the plays were classical in inspiration and set, supposedly, against Greek or Roman backgrounds, little attempt
was made at historical authenticity. The tragic costume was still a formal
garment for acting in, not a dress that could have been worn at any time in the
street; its validity extended only as far as the walls of the theater. For male
costume the characteristic features were a bastardized Greco-Roman helmet,
hung with plumes, a breastplate worn over a pseudoclassical tunic, and boots
lacing high up the leg. Actresses in tragedy wore the high fashion of the day;
a regular accoutrement was the handkerchief, carried to point the scanty range
of gestures and useful in a theater where dim lights still prevailed. For men,
and even more for women, the weight of these costumes was a further restriction on mobility.

Stage settings represented a similar compromise. We have some designs for
the early Hôtel de Bourgogne that show that medieval spaciousness had not yet
been entirely eliminated. Here the Unity of place had not yet become insistent.
The various locations required by the play are represented simultaneously, in
the old mansion tradition but with the scenic elements now represented pictorially in the new Italian manner. A fragment of a sea is juxtaposed uneasily
against an architecturally painted flat piece. French logic rapidly found this
compromise unacceptable. More and more the stage came to show a painted
picture of a palace room, with classical architecture interpreted through French
eyes: a perspective back scene painted upon sliding shutters and framed by
wing pieces that conventionally indicated the walls.

A LIFE IN THE THEATER: MOLIÈRE

In the preceding chapter we used the life of Ben Jonson as a pattern for his time. In the French theater we may take as our example Jean Baptiste Poquelin Molière (1622–1673), whose life and career we know, for the most part, in intimate detail, though there are some perplexing gaps. Like Jonson, he was active in every aspect of the theater of his time. He was actor, manager, and writer; he worked both for the commercial theater and for the court. The abuses he suffered in his personal life show clearly how insecure was the status even of a favored practitioner of the theater. But above all, he was a master of French comedy, a form that we have not yet considered.

Jean Baptiste Poquelin, the son of a well-to-do upholsterer who held a minor court appointment, entered the theater in 1643. What made him forsake the family business for one more risky we do not know. He had no known theatrical experience, and the impulse probably came from a family distantly related to him, the Béjarts. Madeleine Béjart, who became his mistress, had been stage-struck from an early age and played small parts in the Paris theaters. The group of novices leased and converted a tennis court on the Left Bank. We still have the contract setting up the Illustre Théâtre and a detailed financial picture of the opening season. It was not a happy one. The site was unpropitious (even then the Left Bank had raffish associations), the authors willing to write for this new group were no longer fashionable, and the actors themselves were still learning their art. The Illustre Théâtre closed in bankruptcy, and Molière (who had by this time adopted his stage name) went into the provinces.

In the thirteen years that followed we know little of him. We can occasionally follow the course of his provincial tours. Some of the larger cities — for instance, Lyons — had good theaters, but, like the Elizabethan actors sent out of London by the plague, he must have learned rapidly to make the best of whatever temporary facilities the smaller communities offered. He must also have made contact with the touring Italian commedia dell'arte companies, for when he emerged as a playwright on his return to Paris, his first works were wholly in the Italian style.

The return came in 1658. By this time Molière had polished his own performing skills and somehow won influence. Under the sponsorship of the king's brother, the troupe performed two works at the Louvre: a tragedy by Corneille and one of Molière's own farces. The tragedy, which had been seen before in Paris, failed to please, but the farce was triumphantly successful, and Molière was given a theater. He spent the rest of his career under royal patronage, finally settling at the Palais Royal, which thus became, with the Hôtel de Bourgogne and the Marais, the third major theater of the capital.

One of Molière's company, La Grange, doubled as actor and bookkeeper, and his financial records give a detailed study of the company at work. Although the Palais Royal had the same subsidy as the Marais, overheads were heavy. Front-of-house staff included four box openers (ancestors of today's usherettes), a box office staff of two, and a janitor. Regular payments were made for a scene painter and a small orchestra, which could be increased at need for spectacular productions. Actors worked on a share basis, dividing each day's net receipts. Lighting, still by candles, and publicity were heavy expenses. Monthly takings varied enormously.

In the 1672–1673 season, November, always the most popular month, brought a peak audience of 7449. In March, just before the theater closed for the obligatory Easter recess, the attendance dropped to 3790. The company could rarely count on playing to a full house. In some ways the French theater had Elizabethan problems. Though theaters were now roofed, performances were still restricted to afternoons, as the negligible street lighting of Paris made later hours impossible. Thus audiences were mainly composed of those not bound by working conditions. There were also many freeloaders. Since these were royal theaters, any member of the royal household staff (and these were vast) had to be admitted without charge.

It was a dubious compensation that Molière, like other writers, could earn additional sums for private court performances. Louis XIV, who disliked the Louvre, had established his court at Versailles, far enough outside Paris to make a tiresome journey. For the greater part of his career Molière had to divide his energies between managing, writing, and acting for the commercial theater and fulfilling special commissions at court, often at absurdly short notice. He contributed plays, ballets, performers, and libretti to the increasingly elaborate festivities. It is clear that as he grew older, he often found himself in the humiliating position of which Ben Jonson complained, in which his writing was given second place to the settings and dances.

Molière's private life, about which we know a great deal, attests to the insecurities that still beset the theater. Madeleine was his mistress for years and a member of his company until she died. We can see her roles declining in importance as she aged, from leading ladies to *confidantes* and cameo character roles. Molière married another member of the Béjart family, a young beauty named Armande, and Paris gossip, stimulated by the rival Hôtel de Bourgogne, wove scurrilous stories around the relationship. It was alleged, in talk and print, that Molière had actually committed incest by marrying his own daughter by his cast-off mistress. This allegation was almost certainly untrue, though Armande's family connections still remain mysterious. The fact, however, that the story could be told at all and remain in currency for years shows how ready the public was to believe the worst of actors. Although the king might shower his favor on them, and although the public might go eagerly to plays, they would not meet with actors on terms of social equality. When, after Molière's death, his company was forced to relocate, it was almost impossible to find a parish in Paris that would accept them. Religious and social prejudice was still too strong.

Molière's death brought these issues into focus in another way. After suffering for years from a chest affliction, he finally succumbed in 1673, ironically, after performing in his own comedy *le Malade imaginaire* (*The Imaginary Invalid*). The priest did not reach him in time, and he passed away without receiving the last rites. The church therefore declared that since he had not renounced his profession, he must be classed with Jews and infidels and refused burial in consecrated ground. Only after a petition by Armande to the king was this decision reversed, and even then the funeral was carried out furtively, by night, with the bare minimum of ceremony.

MOLIÈRE AND FRENCH COMEDY

Molière's early career as actor embraced both tragedy and comedy. The former, however, eluded him, partly through his own attempts — ahead of their time and unacceptable to the audience — to reform the conventional tragic style in a more natural direction and partly through his own inadequacy. His weak chest gave him problems of breath control that his critics unkindly referred to as a "hiccup"; his inability to deliver Alexandrines in the manner expected is further testimony to the almost operatic expertise demanded of the tragic actor. His success in comic roles, however, was applauded, even by his enemies, and virtually all his own plays — certainly all the successful ones — were comedies.

The earliest works are based firmly on the commedia dell'arte, showing how totally this foreign spirit had permeated the French theater. Molière must have watched Italian companies during his years on the road, learned from them, and borrowed from them. Even after his return to Paris he retained this association, at one point sharing a theater with an Italian troupe and always being able to see them in Paris, where they remained for many years as the darlings of both the aristocracy and the greater public.

Le Médecin volant (*The Flying Doctor*), one of his earliest plays, shows the extent of this influence. A pair of thwarted lovers gives the play a rudimentary plot line, but the chief interest is in the grotesques — the senile, lecherous Gorgibus, who is simply Pantalone under a new name; the pompous rotund advocate, who is the Italian *dottore;* and the mainspring of the action, Sganarelle, a rascally servant in the best commedia tradition who masquerades as a doctor to bring the girl together with the man she loves. The short comedy is a compendium of *lazzi,* sight gags, and acrobatics, culminating in a sequence where Sganarelle has to play two people at the same time, appearing at an upstairs window in a lightning series of alternate disguises, arguing with himself, wrestling with himself, and finally begging himself for forgiveness. The only differences from commedia in this play are that the names are changed and that there is a written script.

The commedia style was to be the mainstay of Molière's career. It was just such a farce that earned him his theater in Paris, and almost to the end of his life, whenever his more adventurous comedies lost money, he returned to these short plays to restore his finances. He normally played the acrobatic roles himself, and he was still doing so when he died at the age of fifty-one, an old man by the standard of his time.

The commedia spirit also permeated his longer works, though in more subtle ways. Like every writer of his time, Molière was influenced by the classics. Several works of Plautus served as inspiration for his own: *Amphitryo* was adapted into *Amphitryon*, *Aulularia* (*The Pot of Gold*) into *l'Avare* (*The Miser*). He turned Terence's *Phormio* into *les Fourberies de Scapin* (*Scapin at His Tricks*), with much of the original translated verbatim.

Even where his sources are other than Italian, however, the commedia asserts itself, most noticeably in Molière's use of the concept of the mask. This feature was a vital part of the Italian comedy, serving to define characters into easily identifiable comic archetypes. Its use as a physical adjunct in the theater still survived through Molière's time, sometimes in unlikely places: the role of Madame Jourdain in his *le Bourgeois gentilhomme* (*The Self-made Gentleman*) was created by a male actor, Hubert, in a mask. More importantly, however, Molière retains the idea of the mask as a metaphor for social pretensions. In his more serious and psychologically penetrating comedies, the protagonists have put on masks to the world, which disguise their true natures and which often so restrict their vision that they cannot perceive the reality of their situation. Molière's ironic comedy stems from the contrast between the mask and the face, between the feigned image and actuality. His first Paris comedy, *les Précieuses ridicules* (*The Affected Young Ladies*, 1659), shows two young women so besotted by their fashionable intellectual pretensions that they have lost touch with the real world and are completely taken in by two servants masquerading as gentlemen. *Le Bourgeois gentilhomme* shows a nouveau riche retired tradesman so obsessed with his own pretensions to gentility that he falls prey to every shyster he meets, while remaining blind to the honest virtues of his own family.

The most conspicuous example of this method, and the most dangerously successful for its author, was *Tartuffe*, which had its first performance at Versailles in 1664 and afterward enjoyed a checkered history on the public stage. The title role is the spiritual director of a bourgeois household whose mask of pious humility conceals a greedy, lustful, and self-serving nature. He plots against his employer's well-being, destroys the harmony of his household, attempts to seduce his wife, and gains control of his possessions. He is stopped at the last moment by the all-seeing eye of the king, invoked (as so often in this period) as the champion and protector of his oppressed subjects. Although the Versailles performance was a success, the play was immediately interpreted as an attack on the Catholic Church and banned from the public stage. When private performances were attempted, the Archbishop of Paris threatened anyone who saw it with excommunication. The argument dragged on for years, until Louis XIV finally used his influence with the church hierarchy to allow all Paris to see the play they had been talking about. With its box office success thus guaranteed, *Tartuffe* went on to break all seating records.

Just as Molière was influenced, on one level of society, by the popular Italian comedy, he could not resist involving in his commercial presentations some of the spectacle with which he was accustomed to working at court. The balletic extravaganzas devised for Versailles and the other pleasure palaces of the nobility were compressed into the commercial theaters and, suitably abridged, presented for public consumption. Other authors besides Molière followed this trend, evolving a whole genre of "machine plays," which were essentially dramatic scripts embellished with all the latest mechanical devices of the theater, the latter usually in the hands of Italian artist-technicians who had exported their own branch of the art to Paris.

The Restoration and the New English Theater

The French drama that we have just described was what the exiled English monarchy and their supporters saw during their enforced stay in Paris, a kind of theater totally unlike the offerings of their own public playhouse but having many features in common with the Court before the outbreak of civil war. It is not surprising, then, that when the English monarchy was restored to the throne, after eighteen years, the theater of the new age should largely follow French patterns and forsake its own Elizabethan ancestry.

DAVENANT AND THE COMMONWEALTH

Even during the interregnum and the harsh climate that this created for the theater, some steps had already been taken in this direction. There were several people influential in theater circles who remained in England for the duration and who regretted the strictures of Parliament, not so much because they curtailed an art form but because they reduced their income. The most important of these was Sir William Davenant, who had been created Poet Laureate as successor to Ben Jonson in 1639 and had also been granted a patent to erect a playhouse for the performance of opera and plays. His efforts to bring these promises to fruition, even under a new and antagonistic regime, continued through the Commonwealth and helped to inaugurate the theatrical revival. Davenant was, by rumor, the illegitimate son of William Shakespeare. This was metaphorically, if not factually, true, for it was Davenant who was ultimately responsible for many of the bastardized versions of Shakespeare's plays that held the stage after the Restoration.

His interest in opera is significant. This art was new, fashionable, and lucrative. In contemporary Paris Jean Baptiste Lully (1632–1687), Molière's sometime collaborator and later rival, had succeeded in obtaining a monopoly of musical theater, which enabled him to close down the Marais and claim rights over any production involving more than a skeleton orchestra in the other theaters. Davenant was evidently anticipating the same kind of financial return in London, had not the violent change of government thrown theater under a cloud.

He was soon using his influence among Cromwell's supporters to find ways of continuing his profession. As we noted in Chapter 1, the theater is a hardy growth, impossible to eradicate completely. Even when banned, it continues to manifest itself under one pretext or another. Davenant was inventive in finding such pretexts. Theater, he argued, could be justified, even under the Puritan regime, if it could be made to serve educational or moral purposes; and musical theater ought in any case to be considered more as music than as theater proper and be exempted from the ban. (The latter pretext was often used by the persecuted theater in later years.) He began tentatively in 1656 with a private performance, a musical potpourri containing praise for the merits of opera, satire on the French court for harboring English exiles, and songs in honor of Oliver Cromwell, the Lord Protector. The authorities let this musical go by, and Davenant, emboldened, went on to a more substantial work, *The Siege of Rhodes*, offered, again, as a private performance in the autumn of the same year. This play, though still musical, had a connected plot, a tale of heroism and self-sacrifice, and it had the distinction of presenting the first woman known to appear on the English stage, Mrs. Coleman, who sang the role of Ianthe.

Davenant, restricted in funds and space, apologized in his prologue for the lack of elaborate effects. *The Siege of Rhodes*, however, was still elaborate enough. It continued, though in simplified and modified form, the devices of masque staging previously used at court, of which Davenant had personal experience. There was an ornamental proscenium, with front curtain; the stage was framed by wing pieces and backed by shutter scenes that opened in the middle, each piece running into the wings on grooves. The scenery was still not conceived as an illusionistic setting but rather as a decoration to the opera. Examination of the surviving set plot, the order of scenes, shows that scenes did not necessarily change when the locale was supposed to change but had a life of their own, independent of the action. In effect, the audience saw two shows at once, one given by the actors, the other by the scenery, which offered a succession of elaborate perspectives, sometimes depicting armies in battle as well as natural phenomena and using techniques borrowed from the French theaters of the time.

Inspired by the success of these semiprivate entertainments, Davenant urged the Commonwealth government to countenance public performances. In 1657 he addressed a memorandum to the secretary of state urging the value of plays in diverting the minds of the public, distracting them from treasonable activities and stopping the flight of the wealthy classes from the now joyless capital. He also offered to compose "moral representations" on subjects that would be useful as government propaganda. This he did in *The Cruelty of the Spaniards in Peru* (1658) and *The History of Sir Francis Drake* (winter 1658–1659). Both of these were public performances; both were operatic, consisting of historical tableaux enlivened with songs; and both were ostensibly designed to further the forthcoming war against Spain by dramatizing the less admirable periods of Spanish history.

MONARCHY RESTORED

In September 1658 Oliver Cromwell died. His government divided into factions and his successor proved incompetent. Sensing a growing revival of royalist sentiment, General Monk led Charles II back to England. Charles offered conciliatory terms for all but the regicides. Cromwell was burned in effigy, and the judges who had condemned Charles I to death were sentenced to the traditional, barbaric punishment of hanging, drawing, and quartering: "you shall . . . hang by the neck till you are half dead, and shall be cut down alive . . . and your belly ripped up and your bowels burst, your head to be severed from your body, your body shall be divided of into four quarters and disposed of as His Majesty shall think fit." We are prone to think of Restoration England as a time of wit, grace, and dalliance; it is as well to remember the savagery with which the new reign began and the financial stringency under which it had to operate. The period had its squalid side, which appears between the lines of the plays.

Public opinion was divided. Among the lower orders was still a vast residuum of Puritan sentiment that dictated an aversion to the theater. Among the aristocracy, however, it was a duty and a demonstration of political solidarity to react as vigorously as possible against the strict disciplines of the interregnum. Frivolity became a virtue, and it was inevitable, first, that the theater should return to a flourishing life and, second, that it should reflect the Frenchified tastes of the upper classes who now chiefly sponsored it.

Public performances of plays resumed immediately. Survivors of the former King's Company at Blackfriars refitted the old Cockpit Theatre in Drury Lane. Their principal actor was Thomas Betterton, destined to become one of the greatest actors of his age. In the same company the young Edward Kynaston, faithful to the Elizabethan tradition, continued to play women's roles. The old, partly unroofed Red Bull reopened. So did the renovated Salisbury Court. Over all these companies Sir Henry Herbert, Master of the Revels, asserted the powers he had laid down, but never formally relinquished, in 1642, claiming by virtue of his office the right of licensing plays and companies and receiving a fee for so doing.

But private enterprise and old offices were endangered by the patronage accompanying the new regime. Charles II, unable to reward his supporters with money, bestowed favors instead, often without regard to the contradictory interests thus created. In June 1660 warrants were issued to give a theater monopoly to Davenant (thus reasserting the patent granted before the war) and Thomas Killigrew. This situation created an obvious conflict of interest with

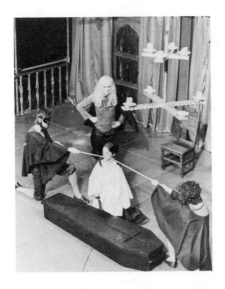

The English indoor playhouse: (*above left*) John Webster's *The Duchess of Malfi* as staged at Blackfriars. (*right*) A theater designed by Inigo Jones, possibly the Cockpit in London's Drury Lane: a compromise between the Elizabethan public playhouse and the seventeenth century French theaters. (*below*) Full-size reconstruction of the same stage in working use at the Bear Garden Museum, London.

Whitehall Palace, Westminster, in the reign of Charles I. The circular, spired building at the top is the private Cockpit-in-the-Court theater; immediately below it stands the indoor tennis court.

The large building on the right is Inigo Jones's banqueting hall, which housed the court masques and still stands; behind it, the tilting ground.

(*left*) Indoor tennis courts with their long, narrow halls both housed and served as models for theaters of the period. A Tudor structure from Hampton Court Palace still in use. (*above*) A setting for masques: Inigo Jones's banqueting hall, Whitehall Palace.

the Master of the Revels, who spent years in useless litigation trying to recover his lost prestige. Though seriously confused, the actors mostly sided with Davenant and Killigrew, who first created a united company out of the existing pool of actors and then split into two. Killigrew, taking the older players, established the King's Company, while Davenant, with the younger, including Betterton, founded the Duke's. These companies, protected by the royal patents, thus opened the only two licensed theaters in the capital — a restriction that tyrannized the London theater for the next two hundred years. After several moves, during which both companies occupied converted tennis courts in the French manner, they settled in more substantial quarters, Davenant in the Dorset Garden Theatre and Killigrew near Drury Lane.

RESTORATION PLAYHOUSES

The tennis court conversions were, of necessity, simple affairs. The buildings that succeeded them were not. Audiences, now primarily aristocratic, craved the more spectacular type of entertainment they remembered from prewar days and had seen abroad. Thus Restoration playhouses tended to develop along the lines laid down by Inigo Jones and Davenant rather than by Shakespeare and Burbage. The English theater had become a courtly art. Charles II was a keen patron. The two patent theaters, the Theatre Royal and the Duke's, were named after him and his brother, the Duke of York. The first English monarch to visit the public theater, he attended regularly, patronizing actors, selecting actresses for his mistresses, and often interfering in managerial disputes. He even lent state robes for use as costumes. Inevitably the court followed the example he set, the upper classes took their tone from the court, and the theaters dedicated themselves to satisfying the whims of their small but fashionable audience.

The playhouse took on a new shape, a compromise between the old public playhouse and the masque stage. Instead of the old open platform, the proscenium arch, with its picture frame concept, was now a regular feature. The old thrust platform was, however, partially retained in the form of a deep apron stage extending well outside the proscenium arch. This remained one of the most important acting areas. As lighting was still poor, actors tended to play as near the audience as they could. Scenes were often played out front while the elaborate stage picture was changed behind. During intermissions the audience would move up onto the apron. The actors entered it through proscenium doors, two on each side of the forestage, with windows or balconies over each. These balconies had a variety of uses. Sometimes they could be used for scenic purposes, with the balcony providing an upper level. When not so required, they could serve as audience seating — stage boxes for those who came not to see but to be seen. In some ways, too, the apron stage retained the presentational flexibility of the Elizabethan theater, providing neutral ground that could be successively reidentified as required. Characters could cross the forestage, go through one of the pair of doors, and appear immediately through the door adjacent; the scene would then be imagined to have shifted from outside to inside. On the apron, too, players could still work in intimate contact with the audience, acknowledge their presence, and respond to them.

Behind the proscenium, however, was another world, one in which the new ideas inherited from the continent held sway. Wing and shutter settings, as used in *The Siege of Rhodes,* grew more elaborate in the larger space now available. Instead of the shutters being grouped closely together, they could now be spaced more widely apart and so drawn open to reveal groups of players already in position. We have an example in William Congreve's *Love for Love* (1695), where shutters are used to give the effect of moving from room to room in a house. Here the plot concerns young Valentine, who is pretending madness in order to deceive his father Sir Sampson. The latter arrives at Valentine's lodgings to confront him and is met by his servant Jeremy in the anteroom. Jeremy says, "Mr. Scandal is with him, sir; I'll knock at the door." Then we have a stage direction: *Goes to the scene, which opens.* Clearly the shutters part to reveal Valentine and Scandal in the room within.

This simple example shows the almost cinematic fluidity that the Restoration stage could achieve by mechanical means. The scenery had become part of the action. Walls could open and disappear and settings change behind the actors. It will be recalled that we talked of the great flexibility of the Elizabethan stage, but this flexibility was achieved largely by the cooperative imagination of the audience. With the transformation to an illusionistic, picture frame stage, machinery must be called in to produce the same effect, a complex machinery worked by ropes and pulleys. Ex-sailors, habituated to rope work, often served as stagehands, directed by blasts on the stage manager's whistle. Here, it appears, is the origin of the theatrical superstition against whistling backstage: it might be misunderstood and provoke a scene change at the wrong moment.

RESTORATION THEATER: SHAKESPEARE REVISED

The characteristics of this new type of English stage become more evident in the handling of works not originally designed for it. Shakespeare's plays were still popular, and sixteen of them were revived by the two licensed companies, though in texts and productions greatly altered from what their creator had known. The neoclassical canons that had shaped the European stage now exercised their influence on England, not merely creating a new kind of original work but reshaping plays already written.

A typical voice of the time is found in the critic Thomas Rymer, who compared the classical theater with that of his own time and found the latter wanting. His *Short View of Tragedy* (1693) opened with an advocacy of restoring the classical chorus. He proposed an adaptation of Aeschylus's *The Persians* that would combine a classical framework with material drawn from English history:

the defeat of the Persians at Salamis is replaced by the defeat of the Spanish Armada, the setting is the court of the King of Spain, and the chorus composed of "fifteen Spanish grandees."

Like other critics, Rymer found Shakespeare lacking in classical restraint and dignity. His language was considered too vulgar, his plots too diffuse. Thus Restoration writers sought to tidy Shakespeare and make him conform to classical standards, creating versions that, in many cases, drove the originals from the stage for years. Davenant, who claimed Shakespeare's most notable works as his exclusive property, revised *Macbeth* to give it a classical symmetry that its author had not envisaged. The role of Lady Macduff, small in the original, was enlarged to counterbalance that of Lady Macbeth — the good woman matched against the bad. This approach was carried even further in Davenant's revision of *The Tempest*. This play contained the character of Miranda, a girl who has never seen any man but her father. Davenant introduced, to balance her, the character of Hippolito, a young man who has never seen a woman. Shakespeare's play had Ariel, a flying spirit, and Caliban, an earthbound monster; Davenant provided both with partners.

Some adaptations involved wholesale butchery. Davenant combined Shakespeare's *Measure for Measure* and *Much Ado About Nothing* into a single work, called *The Law Against Lovers.* Thomas Otway transferred *Romeo and Juliet* from Renaissance Verona to classical Rome and retitled it *The History and Fall of Caius Marius.*

Even where such major changes were not made, individual lines and words were altered in the sacred name of decorum. Hamlet was no longer permitted to say "I do not set my life at a pin's fee" but merely "I do not value my life" — a pin being a common object, not to be mentioned in the mouth of princes. Macbeth's contemptuous address to a cowardly messenger:

> The devil damn thee black, thou cream-faced loon,
> Where got thou that goose look?

is replaced by

> Now friend, what means thy change of countenance?

And the handkerchief that is the vital prop of *Othello,* and from which the whole web of tragic misunderstandings springs, is frowned upon as a commonplace object in everyday use, not suited to the dignity of tragedy.

Not all these versions excite derision. Some were sound, workable adaptations of old scripts to a new milieu, put together by practical men of the theater and able to hold their own on the stage. Colley Cibber, one of a prominent theatrical family, made an adaptation of *Richard III* with interpolated scenes and speeches from other Shakespearean historical plays, which remained the standard version for many years and which introduced lines that many have come to accept as original. Laurence Olivier's film of the play retained the famous "Off with his head! So much for Buckingham!" and "Now Richard is himself again," that came not from Shakespeare but from Cibber. Nahum Tate (*below*) A stage of 1660 with an elaborate changeable set. The proscenium arch is now a permanent feature: the wings slide in and out, and other scenic pieces can be lowered from the flies. (*right*) A cloud machine from John Purcell's opera *Dido and Aeneas*.

(*below*) Two scenes from Dryden's *Marriage à la Mode:* the tragic plot and the comic plot. (*right*) William Congreve's *Love for Love.* Staples of Restoration comedy were the seduction scene and the confrontation between the generations.

Model of Sir Christopher Wren's design for the Theatre Royal, Drury Lane, 1674.

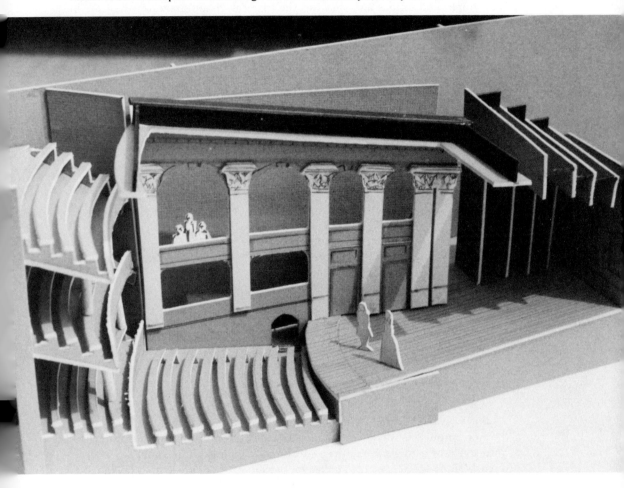

in 1681 rewrote *King Lear* in a version that has been seriously defended as solving many of the notorious difficulties of Shakespeare's text.

Many of the changes were made, however, not out of deference to classical principles but simply to accommodate the Restoration taste for spectacle. Davenant's *Macbeth* introduced several mechanical tricks. The witches, increased in number, sang, danced, and flew on ropes, and Banquo's ghost appeared through a trapdoor. *The Tempest* was a designer's delight, as it already included a masque and flying figures. The Restoration elaborated on these, adding dances of nymphs and tritons and showing the magical disappearance of the feast in Act Five with a "vanishing table" sinking through a trap. Shakespeare had already hinted at such an effect in his stage directions, and the Dorset Garden Theatre happily achieved it with the understage machinery that was one of its favorite devices. Thomas Shadwell wrote an operatic version that opened with a vivid presentation of a shipwreck: "The scene . . . represents a thick cloudy sky, a very rocky coast and a tempestuous sea in perpetual agitation. This tempest, supposed to be raised by magic, has many dreadful objects in it, as several spirits in horrid shapes flying down amongst the sailors, then rising and crossing in the air. And when the ship is sinking the whole house is darkened and a shower of fire falls upon them." *Richard II,* as revised and staged at Dorset Garden, used the disappearing table that was the *spécialité de la maison.* It was used in the scene of the deposed Richard in prison:

> (*A table and provisions shown.*)
>
> *Richard.* What mean my jailors by that plenteous board?
>   For three days past I've fed upon my sighs
>   And drunk my tears; rest, craving nature, rest.
>   I'll humour thy dire need and taste this food
>   That only serves to make misfortune live.
>
> (*Goes to sit. The table sinks down.*)

RESTORATION TRAGEDY

But revivals, however popular, represented only a portion of the Restoration theater output. Sensitive again to neoclassical promptings, writers launched into a vein of heroic tragedy that, superficially, has much in common with the French. It is written in heroic couplets, pairs of rhyming iambic pentameter lines, the English equivalent of the Alexandrine. It works on a superhuman level, exploring the extraordinary problems of kings and princes. Its plots turn on the conflict between duty and inclination. It prefers talk to violent action.

But while the works of Corneille and Racine have remained, at least in France, part of the living repertory, their English counterparts are no longer played, or even considered playable. It is illuminating to examine the reasons for this. The French tragedies, as we have seen, were rooted in the reality of the contemporary social situation. In England the days of the absolute monarchy were over. Nor had the classical form ever proved happily adaptable to the English temperament. The short life span of heroic tragedy shows how difficult it was to graft dramatic ideals so foreign in concept onto a theater tradition that had developed along such different lines. It remains a consciously artificial product, and its devices, far from being related organically to the whole, appear as literary affectations.

We may glance at one of the more extravagant of these works, the massive, two-part *Conquest of Granada,* by John Dryden. In many ways this author was typical of his age. Born in 1631, he had been educated at the University of Cambridge. Like many of his compatriots, he accepted the inevitability of the Commonwealth regime and, while it was to his advantage, supported it. In 1658 he wrote a poem eulogizing Oliver Cromwell, which was to cause him some embarrassment after the Restoration. Two years later he just as eagerly celebrated the return of Charles II. His first play, a comedy, appeared in 1663, followed soon after by *The Indian Queen,* a collaborative work and a rhyming heroic drama about the Inca and Aztec wars. Of this play the diarist Evelyn noted that the scenery was "the richest ever seen in England or perhaps elsewhere upon the public stage." Dryden followed this success with a sequel, *The Indian Emperor,* about the conquest of Mexico by Cortes, with several adaptations of Shakespeare, and with translations of Molière.

The Conquest of Granada appeared in 1669 and 1670. Following the fashion for the exotic already established by *The Siege of Rhodes* and Dryden's earlier plays, it was set in Spain toward the end of the Moorish occupation, tracing the victories of Boabdil and the triumph of the Christian forces under King Ferdinand and Queen Isabella. Its form was the rhymed heroic couplet, which at its best had the same virtues as the French Alexandrine. It embodied the balance and precise antithesis so admired in this age. Above all, it was tidy, imposing a regularity of form and order on the language, which was now preferred to the looser blank verse of Shakespeare, with its frequent resolutions. As in Racine's plays, characters can speak with epigrammatic succinctness:

> Ere he be trusted, let him then be tried;
> He may be false who once has changed his side.

> Love is a magic which the lover ties
> But charms still end when the magician dies.

> The brave own faults when good success is given,
> For then they come on equal terms to heaven.

In long speeches, however, the rhyme in English, even more obviously than in French, imposes an arbitrary closure at the end of each couplet. Characters tend to speak in a succession of epigrams, and the development of thought through a long speech is thereby rendered more difficult. This artificiality is most obvious in conversation, where characters neatly supply each other with rhymes. But the greatest difficulty, and one that has continually beset translators of Racine, is that English, being a less inflected language, is more limited in its rhymes than is French. English rhyme tends to become repetitive and predictable, and for this reason it has chiefly been associated with the lighter forms. Thus even when Dryden is at his most serious, the effect is often unintentionally comic.

For his characters Dryden begins with some traditional postulates about the heroic temperament. The hero is proud and keenly sensitive to real or supposed slights on his personal prestige. He has a strong notion of honor, which must not be trifled with. He is brave and chivalrous. Motivated by the call of duty, he may at times be defeated by passion or self-interest but always to his own detriment. His heroic stature resides, ultimately, in his ability to survive temptation and to sacrifice his own feelings to a nobler purpose. Thus *The Conquest of Granada* offers as its central character the warrior Almanzor, whose adherence to his principles is constantly threatened by the intrigues of lesser men and the tug of his passion for the beautiful Almahide. Whenever his personal honor is threatened by the faithlessness of his associates, he changes sides; he does this with considerable frequency throughout the two plays. His own dilemma is mirrored in a complex subplot, in which passion is allowed to win. Almanzor survives these hazards, though many of the minor characters fall by the wayside.

The failure of English heroic tragedy stems, perhaps, from its uneasy compromise between neoclassic principles and Shakespearean complexity. The one lesson its writers did not, on the whole, learn from the French was economy. Dryden's own *All for Love* is a conspicuous exception; here he takes *Antony and Cleopatra* and pares it down into a taut, sparing, and powerful play. By comparison, *The Conquest of Granada* is sprawling and prolix. So much happens, there are so many vicissitudes, that it is impossible to take the play seriously. Though the play has many fine moments, in totality it is more than faintly ridiculous.

PARODY OF TRAGEDY

Even Dryden's contemporaries recognized the absurdity of the heroic tragedy. In 1671 appeared one of the funniest parodies ever to hit the English stage, *The Rehearsal,* by George Villiers, Duke of Buckingham. It had probably been in the writing and in private circulation for several years, and it may have been several times revised. In 1671 it finally appeared before the public as a parody of heroic tragedy in general and of Dryden and *The Conquest of Granada* in particular. Showing a supposed rehearsal of a heroic tragedy taking place before the enthusiastic playwright and his critical friends, it parodies style, language, plot, and contemporary staging techniques. Inevitably, it contained a number of in-jokes — so many that a key had to be published in 1704 — but much of the humor is appreciable without the key. The plot is hideously complicated, involving two kings and two usurpers, and the epitome of absurdity. One of the characters says of it:

> For look you, sir, the grand design upon the stage is to keep the auditors in suspense; for to guess presently at the plot and the sense tires 'em before the end of the first act; now here every line surprises you and brings in new matter. And then for scenes, clothes, and dancing, we put 'em quite down everything that ever went before us; and these are the things, you know, that are essential to a play.

The last is a significant comment on the way in which the Restoration theater hoped to appear.

The play within the play is written in grotesquely affected and elevated language. Its principal character, Drawcansir, parodies Almanzor in *The Conquest of Granada:*

> Others may boast a single man to kill,
> But I the blood of thousands daily spill.
> Let petty kings the name of parties know
> Where'er I come I slay both friend and foe.

And there is a glorious burlesque of the conventional battle spectacles:

> (*Enter four soldiers.*)
>
> *1.* Stand. Who goes there?
> *2.* A friend.
> *1.* What friend?
> *2.* A friend to the house.
> *1.* Fall on.
>
> (*They all kill one another. Music strikes.*)

The dead soldiers then rise and dance. One of the characteristics of Restoration drama is its propensity to introduce songs and music, even at inappropriate moments, and the parody takes due note of this feature. *The Rehearsal* was the first fully fledged burlesque to appear on the English stage, and it helped to sound the death knell of heroic drama.

TRAGICOMEDY

That Dryden himself was sensitive to the absurdities of tragedy is shown by his turning to mixed forms. His *Marriage à la Mode* (1673) is an example of the genre of tragicomedy, which also had some vogue at the time. It has been said that these plays contained two casts who never met until the final act.

For *Marriage à la Mode* is a play divided in its allegiances. A tragic plot concerns the usurper, Polydamas, who rages in the tyrant's vein and searches for a long-lost child. There are two possible claimants, the boy Leonidas and the girl Palmyra, both reared in simple country fashion, both revealing elevated natures and talking as though born to the purple. The inevitable love-duty conflict follows. First Leonidas is recognized as the heir, but he cannot quell his love for Palmyra. Then Palmyra is identified as the more likely candidate, and we have the same problem in reverse: it is unthinkable that royalty marry a commoner. Then Leonidas discovers that he is in fact the son of the true king, and thus the rightful heir to the throne. The problem reasserts itself in more acute form. Leonidas's duty to his dead father and his country forces him to revenge himself on the usurper; but the usurper is Palmyra's father.

Interwoven with this tragic plot is a separate comic plot of amorous intrigue. Palamede has dishonorable designs on Doralice, which she is all too eager to reciprocate; Rhodophil has similar designs on Melantha. But Rhodophil is married to Doralice, and his friend Palamede is to marry Melantha. The friends are thus hard at work both to foil each other and to further their own plans; the complications multiply, culminating in a scene of quadruple misunderstandings, where both couples have assignations behind the terrace. Dryden, with sensual wit, extracts every possible variation from the situation. Nothing serious comes of these extramarital affairs, however. Adultery is never actually practiced, and Doralice makes an unaccountable reformation, preaching the virtues of marriage.

It is evident in the tragicomedy that we have left the lofty moralizing of tragedy for a totally different world, one of flirtatiousness, dalliance, amorous conquest, and sexual intrigue. And it was this world that Restoration audiences chiefly delighted in, both in their private lives and on the stage. Though Restoration tragedy has sunk without trace, Restoration comedy produced a series of sparkling, amoral works that enchanted their original audiences and have retained much of their appeal today.

Restoration Comedy

The Restoration audience, as noted, was a small one; too small, often, to fill both London playhouses simultaneously, so that a hit in one theater would leave the other empty. It was limited also in its spread of sympathies, being drawn mainly from the aristocracy and London gentry. These were people who either had been forced to compromise their royalist affiliations under the Commonwealth or had followed their monarch to exile. Both groups were loud in applauding the Restoration, to exculpate their own guilt or to celebrate the ultimate triumph of their faction, and both sought to demonstrate by their public behavior their solidarity with the new regime. Approval of the restored monarchy could best be shown by open reaction against everything that the Commonwealth had stood for. Solemnity was out and frivolity was in. Austerity was replaced by lavish display. Social glitter became a badge of political loyalty, and the theater, which had been one of the principal targets of Puritan resentment, now became one of the temples of the new spirit.

THE AUDIENCE

This obsessively worldly audience sought to see its own standards followed and its own world re-created in the playhouse; and this world was a small and superficially brilliant one. It was bounded by the mansions of fashionable hostesses and by the coffee shops in which smart society was accustomed to meet; by the royal parks that had now begun to adorn London, where, daily, the upper classes put themselves on show; by salons and masquerades, conversaziones and balls. As in any exclusive social group, not to know the approved members of the set was to be oneself unknown. This forced and brittle intimacy proved a breeding ground of gossip and passing romantic liaisons. The chief entertainment of society was itself. If we were to take the Restoration upper classes at their own valuation, we should have to assume that they spent half their time in seduction and the other half in talking about it.

When these people went to see a comedy (as usual, in closer touch than tragedy with the surface of life), they wanted to see themselves, not necessarily as they were but as they wished to appear, pursuing the same limited range of inclinations in a recognizable environment. Dramatists willingly responded to the demand, and the comic stage served as a mirror of the social aspirations of the time. Cynics might observe that in affairs of love Restoration tragedy represents the theory and comedy the practice. In place of the anguish of the neoclassic tragic hero torn between passion and honor, we see a comic world that reproduces the minuscule, ingrown world of its audience, peopling its plays with recognizable types of the time and finding an inexhaustible source of plot material in sexual intrigue. *Love* is the most familiar word in the titles of Restoration comedy.

THE CHARACTERS

These plays rapidly evolved their own gallery of stereotypes. The hero is the fashionable playboy, the young man about town, handsome, witty, well dressed, and sexually attractive. His success is measured by the number of his conquests. Etherege's *The Man of Mode* (1676) presents, under a significant title, a protagonist who is juggling several love affairs, faded and ongoing, simultaneously. No word of moral reproof is uttered. This situation is accepted as the natural state of things. Similarly, Valentine, the elegant hero of Congreve's *Love for Love* (1695), already has a bastard child before the play opens and suggests, in an appallingly casual throwaway line, that it should have been smothered long ago. For such men there are only two sins. One is poverty, which must be redeemed at all costs — by lying, stealing, or manipulation, never by working — for lack of money spells exile from the prized inner circle. In Congreve's *The Way of the World* (1700) one of the most powerful threats that old Lady Wishfort can make against young Mirabell is that she will ruin his credit with his tailor. Under the polished protestations of the plays, one often senses the despair of an upper class largely impoverished by the war and determined to keep up its standards at all costs. The other sin is dullness, which can never be redeeemed. A man retains his membership in this society by wit, and the plays reflect this. The dialogue crackles and sparkles, and characters never need pause for an instant to think of what to say next.

The hero's counterpart is the young lady of fashion, witty, attractive, beautifully dressed, willing to be wooed and won, and enjoying the elaborate ritual of seduction as much for its own sake as for the outcome. Women, however, labor under a burdensome restriction, for the double standard is rigidly enforced. The Restoration heroine, though she may be wanton, must appear chaste. Faithfulness in marriage is lauded in theory, ignored though it may be in practice. Reputation is a prized bauble, and a girl must present an innocent face to the world. Many of the more desperate complications of Restoration plots spring from the woman's desire to preserve appearances at all costs while still pursuing private pleasures, and plays bristling with sexual irregularity customarily conclude with lip service to the institution of marriage.

Some of the other regular characters have antecedents in earlier drama. The roaring, blustering, censorious father, doomed to be outsmarted by his scapegrace son, is as old as Plautus. So is the comic learned man, as exemplified by Foresight, the astrologer, in *Love for Love* — a man so engrossed in peering at the stars that he cannot see his wife cuckolding him under his very nose. The straitlaced husband victimized by his wife's amorous proclivities (for example, Pinchwife in Wycherley's *The Country Wife*) is already familiar from the commedia dell'arte, though acquiring sharper social relevance in the moral breakdown of the Restoration. More characteristic of his own time is the fop, who represents the ideal of the man about town carried to ridiculous excess. It is the mark of the fop that he lacks social judgment; he does not know when to stop. His clothes are extravagant, following the whim of every new style; his manners are affected; his tongue is never still. Serving as both butt and irritant, the fop in comedy usually ends as the victim of some ridiculous disaster.

In comedy, rustics are by definition inferior. For the London-centered audience the country was Siberia. Urban life was the only acceptable environment, and nature, when permitted to intrude at all, had to be tamed, regularized, and ordered, as in the great London parks. The comedies faithfully mirror this attitude. Settings are almost universally urban, with the salon and the coffee house as favorites. To be sent into the country is the worst punishment with which an errant wife or daughter can be threatened, for to live there means social extinction. Characters arriving in London from the country are ill dressed, ill spoken, and uncouth. This is true even of the country gentlefolk like Sir Wilful Witwoud in Congreve's *The Way of the World*. Miss Prue, the country relation in *Love for Love,* is an immediate source of amusement to the sophisticates. And Margery Pinchwife, for whom Wycherly's *The Country Wife* is named, acts as a homespun foil to the manipulations of the London society into which she is thrown.

For all their brilliance Restoration comedies present some problems for modern audiences. They are extremely long and are rarely revived without considerable cutting. A length of some four hours plus intermissions was not merely tolerated but expected by the original public. They went to the theater not merely to see a play but to have the opportunity to display themselves. The five-act comedies were designed to encompass extended intermissions during which the spectators swarmed all over the playhouse, including the stage, to mingle and converse. The mass of dialogue in the plays, also, often seems designed to accommodate an audience whose attention might not be fully on the action and who therefore needed to have a point or a joke made several times before it was heard by everybody. Furthermore, the convoluted plots and language, though appreciable by audiences who lived on daily acquaintance with similar social conventions, often seem willfully obscure to those bred in a different time. They seem *too* brilliant, *too* complex, *too* densely written, and modern audiences tend to be less concerned with social ephemera. To enter the world of Restoration comedy, therefore, may require as conscious an act of will as to enter that of neoclassic tragedy. Once in, however, the rewards and delights are more immediately apparent.

DEEPER ISSUES

Nevertheless, Restoration comedy may often plunge deeper and touch issues of more universal application. This tendency becomes more apparent as the period wears on and the carefree hedonism of the earlier years is replaced by a growing concern about the substance beneath the shimmering facade. Though drawing on the same body of material, authors vary in their moral stance. Some, like Etherege, openly admit the cynicism and corruption of the world in which they move and revel in it. For them the stage and society are virtually indistinguishable, preferring appearance to reality, the show to the substance, and good manners to good morals. Others take a more complex viewpoint, exploiting the follies of the age while subtly censuring them, or at least suggesting that there may be standards other than social success.

Conspicuous among these latter writers is William Congreve (1670–1729), who, beginning as a novelist, turned out a string of successful comedies, at least two of which still successfully hold the stage. His *Love for Love* seems at first sight to be the standard comic fare, and it was probably so taken by most of the audience. It has the usual gallery of characters. Valentine, the young man who has dissipated his fortunes, is in love with the heiress Angelica and is desperately trying to squeeze more money out of his father. The father, Sir Sampson Legend, is blustering and tyrannical; Sir Sampson's crony, old Foresight, is so immersed in his pursuit of astrology that his wife can cuckold him under his nose. Other characters include the man-hungry Mistress Foresight and her sister, the husband-hunting Mistress Frail; Tattle, the fop; and the rustics, Miss Prue from the country and Valentine's brother, Sailor Ben, who has spent all his life at sea. (One might notice how Congreve, following a tradition as old as Chaucer, gives his characters descriptive names.)

The plot follows the usual routine of intrigues, deceptions, and achieved or attempted seductions. But under this routine Congreve offers a subtle parody of the world he is portraying. He resists the temptation to make Miss Prue and Ben the usual easy targets. Rather, their unworldliness is used to make the social expertise of the rest somewhat ridiculous. Tattle, the fop, tries to seduce Miss Prue; she does not know how to be seduced; and he has to explain to her, in detail, the mechanics of how to conduct an affair:

> So, when I ask you, if you can love me, you must say no, but you must love me too. If I tell you you are handsome, you must deny it, and say I flatter you. But you must think yourself more charming than I speak you: and like me, for the beauty which I say you have, as much as if I had it myself. If I ask you to kiss me, you must be angry, but you must not refuse me. If I ask you for more, you must be more angry — but more complying; and as soon as ever I make you say you'll cry out, you must be sure to hold your tongue.

After this we cannot take the more polished seductions quite so seriously again.

Similarly, Sailor Ben's blunt honesty acts a foil to the pretensions and evasiveness of the others. Valentine himself realizes, near the end of the play, that all his elaborate deceits have got him nowhere. As a last, desperate alternative he tries honesty and finds to his surprise that he succeeds.

Congreve's later *The Way of the World* follows the same pattern. At the midpoint of the web of intrigue his hero and heroine, Mirabell and Millamant, engage in a candid and forthright discussion of what marriage means to them and what they expect from it and from each other. Though astute enough to sugar the pill, Congreve wrote against his world as much as for it.

Survivals

The masques, the ballets, the Serlian reconstructions, all belong to a vanished era that can now be reconstructed only for academic purposes, and then with difficulty. The world of lavish princely patronage that created them is gone forever, and we are no longer taught to sing and dance as a matter of social necessity. But the Teatro Olimpico still stands and can be visited; the Teatro Farnese in Parma is a living monument to the Renaisssance concept of scenic decoration; and occasionally, in the gardens of Versailles, *fêtes de nuit*, with ballets, fireworks, illuminated fountains, and orchestras playing, offer a glimmer of the spectacles that Louis XIV enjoyed.

Of the plays, the works of Corneille and Racine have been enshrined in the National Theater of France, but they do not travel well. The problems in translating them are enormous, and they are based on concepts difficult for today's larger theatergoing public to understand. *Phèdre,* however, is regularly revived in many languages. Molière's longer comedies have proved more adaptable. Though individual plays have come in and out of fashion, most of them are still available in performance. The shorter, commedia-influenced farces have had a more sporadic career. Ignored by scholars because of their apparent lack of literary merit, they began to be restored to the public in the 1920s and 1930s as part of the "pure theater" movement, and with the increasing frequency of French tours abroad, they have become more widely accessible. *Les Fourberies de Scapin* has had a successful reincarnation in London and New York as the musical *Scapino.*

As for the English theater, Restoration tragedy, with rare exceptions, has vanished from the stage; only *All for Love* is revived with any frequency. Although the Restoration revisions of Shakespeare have been replaced by the originals, something of the spirit that produced them still survives. The modern theater has seen several rearticulations of the Shakespeare histories, notably a compression of the three parts of *Henry VI* together with *Richard III* as a three-part *War of the Roses.* Restoration comedy enjoys a continual vogue, with Congreve's *The Way of the World* undoubtedly the most frequently revived play of its time.

7
An Age of Actors

A Time of Transition

The end of the seventeenth century is an appropriate point to take stock, for we are about to enter one of those periods when the theater marks time. During most of the eighteenth century, no crucial changes took place. The theater was content to live on its past, and the most noteworthy information concerns individual actors and their personal contributions to the art. This in itself is significant, and the reader will already have noticed how both the quantity and the quality of our information have changed. The French theater of the seventeenth century marks the first period in which we really begin to know actors as people.

Greek and Roman actors are known to us, if at all, only as names; medieval actors are mostly anonymous; even for the star performers of the Elizabethan theater we have little more than a few laudatory notices, too vague to be helpful

Growth of the provincial theater: the Theatre Royal,
Bristol, in its wharfside setting.

for historical purposes. We do know, however, the lives and careers of Molière's company — in more intimate detail than they, perhaps, would have wished — and this pattern continues in the centuries that follow. It is not simply a question of dealing with times nearer to our own and, therefore, having more surviving material for study. In the earlier period the theater was largely a matter of corporate effort, group activity, communal drive. From the eighteenth century on, the theater begins to reflect the individual contributions of those who participate in it. Personalities become more important. The style and character of a particular actor or playwright tend to determine what goes on in a particular theater at a particular time, and this in turn is reflected in the sorts of things that are written about them. Actors' biographies multiply. No one, as far as we know, wrote a detailed study of Polus, Alleyn, or Burbage. We do have such a study of Betterton. No one wrote a life of Shakespeare until many of the vital facts had been lost and the rest clouded by legend, but a biography of Molière appeared soon after his death, by someone who knew his milieu well and who had talked with those who knew him intimately.

As we look back at the development of the theater from its second beginning in the Middle Ages to the English Restoration, it is apparent that we have passed through another cycle similar to the cycle that we traced in the classical period. A theater that began as sacred has become secular; an amateur art has become professional; the presentational style has become representational, for even though the staging devices of Restoration comedy may seem conventional and artificial to us in the light of what the theater produced later, it was intended to be, and was seen as, realistic by the standards of its time. Congreve and his contemporaries thought of themselves as portraying London life as it actually was. Variations on this same cycle appear in the periods that follow but are less easily discernible. Up until now theatrical development has tended to be self-limiting, growing out of itself and only in a limited degree responsive to influences from outside. From this point on influences multiply. The world starts to shrink. What happens in France has a rapid effect on what happens in England and vice versa, and what happens in Germany is seized upon and imitated by other countries.

Morality and the Stage

Another revolution was occurring in the English theater, but a quiet one, determined largely by the changing nature of the audience and what it expected from the stage. As we have seen, Restoration comedy catered to a coterie audience by portraying its own circumscribed, glittering, amoral world. Designed for an aristocracy that lived by its own rules, the plays took no account of the far greater mass of the population who, indeed, hardly visited the theater at all. In the closing years of the century this segment began to be heard from and to revive — this time with greater reason — the kind of moral objections to the theater that had been voiced since the time of Plato.

COLLIER'S ARGUMENTS

Its loudest spokesman was a former clergyman, Jeremy Collier, whose frankness in political matters had debarred him from continuing in his vocation, who had already spent some time in prison, and who now launched a broadside against the depravity of the English stage. In 1698 he published a short but pithy tract with a long title, *A Short View of the Immorality and Profaneness of the English Stage, Together With the Sense of Antiquity upon This Argument.* It is usually referred to simply as *A Short View.* This tract appeared in the spring, to be followed in November of the same year by *A Defence of the Short View,* stimulated by the replies the earlier publication had provoked. Among a mass of pamphlets, lampoons, attacks, and counterattacks, these two works form our most important evidence for the moral objections to drama in general and Restoration comedy in particular.

In his introduction Collier outlines the topics to be discussed. "Their [i.e., the playwrights'] liberties in the following particulars are intolerable, viz. their smuttiness of expression, their swearing, profaneness and lewd application of scripture, their abuse of the clergy [to which Collier, as a defrocked clergyman, was especially sensitive], their making their top characters libertines, and giving them success in their debauchery." He attacks several playwrights by name, including Wycherley, Dryden, and Congreve, and he accuses their plays of presenting indecency and debauchery in so attractive a light as to seduce audiences into following the same path. He objects to the fact that many of the most indecent lines are spoken by women; he finds the frequent profanity of the plays disturbing, adducing, as he so often does, the ancients and arguing that if the Greeks treated their gods with such respect on the stage, Christians should do no less. "Have we not a clearer light to direct us, and greater punishments to make us afraid?" It is clear from this statement that he had not read Aristophanes, but few at this time had.

Reverting to the abuse of the clergy, he finds their use as comic butts intolerable: "These poets I observe when they grow lazy and inclined to nonsense they commonly get a clergyman to speak it. Thus they pass their own dullness for humour and gratify their ease and their malice at once." And, finally, he reflects on the lamentable condition of society as encouraged by the stage, taking the same view that some of the playwrights had done, though from a more censorious standpoint.

Collier was thus both serving as spokesman for the considerable residuum of Puritan sentiment and returning to the pre-Aristotelian view that the purpose of drama was to offer moral instruction. And the argument that followed echoed, in many ways, the debate between Aeschylus and Euripides in *The Frogs.*

CONGREVE'S REPLY

Among numerous replies, the most powerful came from Congreve himself. While admitting that what Collier had to say about the subject matter of comedy was factually true, he disagreed over the interpretation. Comedy, he insisted, portrayed vices in order to ridicule, not to provoke, them. "For men are to be laughed out of their vices in comedy; the business of comedy is to delight as well as instruct. And as vicious people are made ashamed of their follies and faults by seeing them exposed in a ridiculous manner, so are good people both warned and diverted at their expense." And again: "It were very hard that a painter should be believed to resemble all the ugly faces he draws." Among other responses, one of the wittiest is a direct satire of Collier's work called *The Immorality of the English Pulpit,* accusing the clergy of the very vices with which Collier had charged the playwright.

This argument has implications that extend far beyond its own time. It typifies the moral strictures that have continually been, and are still being, made against the performing arts, and the censorship it proposes is still advocated by those who object to sex and violence in films and television. Congreve's rebuttal is likewise still valid. Self-appointed censors, from Plato to the Revels Office to the Catholic League of Decency, have commonly concerned themselves with subject matter only. Certain subjects are, ipso facto, taboo. The concerned artist's reply has always been that subject matter that is in itself offensive may serve a serious moral purpose, depending on how it is treated. A play, book, or film about immorality is not necessarily a defense of immorality. In the succession of obscenity trials that still pass through our courts, and in the recurring question of whether a given work is purely pornographic or has "redeeming social purpose," the rival claims of Collier and Congreve may still be heard, rephrased but fundamentally unchanged. And after all these centuries, the question is still as hard to decide as it ever was.

THE INFLUENCE OF THE MIDDLE CLASS

In his time, however, Collier had the mass of public opinion with him. To a large extent he was right. The stage was undoubtedly profligate, and some writers did delight in obscenity for its own sake. Congreve, though not among them, was powerless to stem the tide. For what was happening was not merely an attack on the stage but a change in society generally. The Restoration represented the last fling of a gilded aristocracy able to impose its own standards on public manners and morals. The middle classes, becoming gradually richer, larger, and more influential, were now a factor to be reckoned with, and as they drifted back to the theater they had temporarily deserted, they demanded plays more appropriate to their own tastes and standards. These standards tended to be restrictive, for any social group is more possessive of what it has had to work for. The aristocracy, accepting its prerogatives as a matter of right, could afford permissiveness. The middle class, which had to labor to establish itself, could not. English drama rapidly begins to mirror these changes, not merely in the subject matter but in the settings of its plays.

Though impossible to define within arbitrary limits, the change is readily discernible. Collier's strictures had a rapid effect. We can see this in the works of Colley Cibber (1671–1757), actor, author, theatrical manager, and, in 1730, Poet Laureate. We have already noted his successful Shakespearean adaptations. Necessarily sensitive to public taste, he followed the trend to a moralizing, sentimentalizing comedy. *Love's Last Shift* (1696) remains one of his best-known works. Like its Restoration predecessors, it deals with an errant husband, but in this play the husband is eventually reconciled to his faithful wife. *The Careless Husband* (1704) shows a similar treatment of the marriage relationship. We see a willful and neglectful husband and an unfortunate wife; but the wife is treated sympathetically and sentimentally, and her husband is brought to see the error of his ways:

> Now, my dear, I find my happiness grow fast upon me; in all my past experience of the sex I found even among the better sort so much of folly, pride, malice, passion and irresolute desire that I concluded thee but of the foremost rank, and therefore scarce worthy of my concern; but thou has stirred me with so severe a proof of thy exalted virtue, it gives me wonder equal to my love. If then the unkindly thought of what I have been hereafter should intrude upon thy growing quiet, let this reflection teach thee to be easy:

> Thy wrongs, when greatest, most thy virtue proved,
> And from thy virtue found, I blushed and truly loved.

Sir Richard Steele (1672–1729) carried this process further, writing comedies free from even the suspicion of indecency and taking a strong moralizing tone. This pattern continues for most English eighteenth-century comedy. It is restrained, polite, and morally inoffensive. It is also, apart from a few exceptions late in the century, extremely dull and has not survived its own time. What the period had gained in morals, it had lost in wit.

A conspicuous and freakish exception is Henry Fielding (1707–1754), now far better known as a novelist but who began his career as a writer of farces and later of political satire. His attacks on the administration of Sir Robert Walpole so offended the government that it imposed, in 1737, a Licensing Act that was to inhibit the English theater for more than two hundred years.

THE LICENSING ACT OF 1737

The Licensing Act had two major detrimental effects on the theater. First, the act reaffirmed the status of the two patent theaters. One of these was the Theatre Royal, Drury Lane, which we have already noted. This still survives as the oldest working theater in London. Now the usual home-away-from-home of American musicals in the British capital, it still displays in its lobby a continuous list of managers from Davenant and Killigrew onward, which contains some of the most distinguished names in the history of the theater. The other patent, after a succession of political vicissitudes, had settled on the Covent Garden Theatre, built in 1732 in the heart of London's market district. Covent Garden still stands on the same site but no longer in its original form, the earlier building having been destroyed by fire. Now the Royal Opera House, it is operated by a generous state subsidy as the home of British opera and ballet. By the terms of the Licensing Act no further patents could be granted. Thus until the Theatre Regulation Act of 1843 broke the monopoly, there were only two legitimate theaters.

Various ways of evading these restrictions were tried, some of them successful. Several minor theaters already existed in London. These were still used for plays, but the plays were advertised as "musical concerts" or "rehearsals," thus satisfying the letter of the law, though not its spirit. This situation has given a term to the language. We still talk of the *legitimate* theater or, in American shorthand, *going legit,* to mean the spoken drama as opposed to musicals. Other expedients, which developed later in the century, included the advertising of "equestrian dramas," as though they were animal shows; they were, in fact, plays, with some of the characters on horseback. During the eighteenth century a continuing war was waged between the government and the patent holders on one side — the latter alive to the financial benefits of their monopoly — and the free-lance operators on the other; this war even extended to bans on acting in the fairgrounds.

Second, and far more serious, was the censorship of playscripts vested in the Lord Chamberlain, who had already exercised this office de facto for some time. Every script prepared for public performance now had to be submitted to him (in fact, to his chosen readers); he had the right not merely to delete any passages he considered offensive but to ban plays entirely. It will be apparent how readily a law that was originally created to serve political ends could be used to suppress freedom of expression on moral grounds, and its subsequent history shows how arbitrarily the Lord Chamberlain could exercise his powers to suppress material considered too offensive for the delicate ear of the British public.

Certain subjects were automatically taboo, and any suggestion of sexual impropriety was frowned on. Even the classics have not been immune. The revival of *Oedipus the King* planned by Sir John Martin Harvey in 1912 was initially disapproved on the grounds that it was a play about incest. It was seriously suggested that it could be done in Dryden's Restoration adaptation, as the language was sufficiently obscure to be inoffensive. In 1898 Bernard Shaw's *Mrs. Warren's Profession* was banned because it discussed the forbidden subject of prostitution. In more recent memory Noel Coward's *Private Lives* (1930) was suspect because it showed a love scene between two people married to other spouses, and Arthur Miller's *A View from the Bridge* (1955) was banned outright because of its implications of incest and homosexuality.

Directors asking their actors to improvise were under a constant threat of prosecution. Typically the theater found a way of evading censorship by creating private theater clubs, to which the audience paid a nominal membership fee: as private performances, these were then immune from the act. Once again the theater was compelled to ally itself with other, less reputable extralegal operations to ensure that its works could be performed, which did nothing to enhance its standing in the eyes of those who already considered it suspect.

After prolonged pressure, the act was finally repealed in 1968. With poetic justice the first production to open in a censor-free London theater was *Hair*. Walpole's legacy thus lay heavy on the British theater for a long time. Its only virtue was that it drove Fielding from the stage to the novel. Without the Licensing Act, we would never have had *Tom Jones*.

THE NEW MORALITY

The London theater thus gradually settled under the pall of middle-class respectability. We have already noted the changing moral tone of plays. Their settings and characters also reflected the shift of social values. Where Restoration comedy had been urban, later plays began to move their action into the country. George Farquhar's *The Beaux Stratagem* (1707), while still retaining much of the Restoration wit and sparkle, sets its action in a country house and judges London by country manners, rather than the other way about.

In any case, smart society itself was no longer London-centered. Other fashionable towns were opening up, notably the spas and watering places that attracted the gentry for cures and holidays. The organization of the theater followed this pattern. Important playhouses were in operation at such provincial centers as Bath and Bristol. A provincial circuit was created in which actors could try their wings before risking the London adventure, and the patent houses regularly sent out talent scouts to snap up likely talent.

One play which speaks clearly for its time is a middle-class tragedy, *The London Merchant* (1731), by George Lillo. Here the kings and queens of neoclassical tragedy have been deposed in favor of the bourgeoisie. It was a great success both in and after its own time despite its obvious defects — the strong, almost unbearable moralizing indulged in by its characters and its continual praise of middle-class virtues. To its original audience, however, these were not defects but the proper stuff of drama.

The London Merchant is the tale of a virtuous apprentice, destined for a happy and prosperous career until he is seduced from the paths of innocence by the wiles of a wicked woman. He is persuaded first to steal from his master, then to commit murder, and he ends on the gallows. Not the least difficulty of this play for modern audiences is its ponderous language. Here is Barnwell soliloquizing on his coming attempt at murder:

> A dismal gloom obscures the face of day; either the sun has slipped behind a
> cloud, or journeys down the west of heaven with more than common speed, to

avoid the sight of what I'm doomed to act. Since I set forth on this accursed design, wherever I tread, methinks, the solid earth trembles beneath my feet. Yonder limpid stream, whose hoary fall has made a natural cascade, as I passed by, in doleful accents seemed to murmur "Murder!" The earth, the air, and water seem concerned; but that's not strange; the world is punished, and nature feels a shock, when Providence permits a good man's fall.

At moments of passion Barnwell breaks into verse. Thus his gallows epilogue:

> Be warned, ye youths, who see my sad despair,
> Avoid lewd women, false as they are fair;
> By reason guided, honest joys pursue;
> The fair, to honor and to virtue true,
> Just to herself, will ne'er be false to you.
> By my example learn to shun my fate;
> (How wretched is the man who's wise too late.)
> 'Ere innocence and fame and life be lost
> Here purchase wisdom cheaply, at my cost.

The London Merchant is a tract in dramatic form, but contemporary audiences found its mixture of moralizing and sensational incident appealing. In its own time it became a favorite barnstorming piece, popular with touring companies, and it held the stage for years. It was to the eighteenth century what *The Spanish Tragedy* had been to the sixteenth and what *The Drunkard* was to be to the nineteenth, and there is no denying that even now it has extremely powerful moments. The temptress Millwood's condemnation of corrupt society for making her what she is has a surprisingly modern ring.

The French Stage and Its Actors

During this period the French theater developed along similar lines, both in its organization and in its material. In Paris, as in London, the playhouses were consolidated, though out of necessity rather than by design. By the end of the seventeenth century the three subsidized theaters had all fallen upon evil days.

DECLINE OF PROFESSIONAL COMPANIES

The Marais had fallen off sadly from the years of Corneille's ascendancy and the triumph of *Le Cid*. Though it had gained a second life from the spectacular appeal of "machine plays," even these were taken from it by Lully's insistence on his musical monopoly. Without the ballet interludes the machine plays were nothing, and the Marais lapsed into bankruptcy, finally being closed by order of Louis XIV.

Molière's former company fared little better. After the death of its guiding spirit in 1673, it struggled on for a while under the management of La Grange and Molière's widow Armande, playing revivals. Weakened by the defection of some of its best actors and evicted from the Palais Royal — by the machinations of Lully, whose influence at this time was all-pervasive — the company merged with the remnants of the Marais as the Troupe du Roi, at the Hôtel de Guénégaud on the Left Bank. Though Molière's work remained the basis of the repertory, they now felt strong enough to challenge the Hôtel de Bourgogne in its own domain of tragedy.

For a while cutthroat competiton reigned. When the Bourgogne presented Racine's *Iphigenie,* the Guénégaud countered with a rival version. When the Bourgogne produced *Phèdre,* Racine's last play for the commercial theater, the Guénégaud almost immediately riposted with Pradon's *Hippolyte et Phèdre,* provoking much discussion in artistic circles as to which version was the better. Pradon's version, for the moment, won — leading to unfounded accusations that his supporters had packed the Hôtel de Bourgogne to boo. But posterity has reversed this judgment, and *Hippolyte et Phèdre,* if remembered at all, is now printed merely as an appendix to a work regarded as the enduring masterpiece of French tragedy. This revival of the competitive spirit was, however, the last gasp of the rival theaters. The king's interest, which had proved the saving grace of the companies, was at a low ebb, and in 1680 they were merged into one, with a single state subsidy.

BIRTH OF THE NATIONAL THEATER

This event marked the true beginning of the National Theater of France, the institution now known as the Comédie Française. Each of the contributing companies brought the repertoire of its house dramatist: the Marais, Corneille; the Bourgogne, Racine; and the Palais Royal, Molière. The combination provided a company of twenty-seven, of whom seventeen were full shareholders; they played almost every day of the year, to moderate audiences. Free from the threat of competition, the combined troupe became predictable, safe, and respectable. In 1689 they moved to a 2,000-seat house in a converted tennis court. From 1770 to 1782 the company was in the Théâtre des Tuileries, next to the Louvre; from 1782 to 1793 they were in the Théâtre Français on the Left Bank; and finally, after a gap caused by the Revolution, they were back on the Right Bank again, a few minutes' walk from the Louvre, at the theater the Comédie Française still occupies today — which had the architectural distinction of being the first theater ever constructed on an iron skeleton.

The theater was at first under the direct control of the members of the royal family. For a while the wife of the Dauphin assumed the administration, going so far as to intervene in the distribution of roles. Throughout the vicissitudes of French politics, control remained vested in the government, and the Comédie Française is still, today, ultimately responsible to the appropriate minister.

The establishment of the National Theater worked for both good and ill. Its most beneficial result was that actors now enjoyed far greater financial security than they had ever known. The original distinction between *sociétaires* (shareholders) and *pensionnaires* (actors engaged on limited contracts) was retained. In the eighteenth century an actor was required to buy his place in the company, just as officers still had to buy a place in the army. If he could not afford the capital outlay, the amount was deducted from his salary, by installments. Financial security, however, did not guarantee social standing. A good deal of the traditional prejudice remained, to the extent that when Adrienne Lecouvreur, one of the leading actresses of the company, died in 1730, she was, like Molière sixty years before, refused Christian burial, and her body was flung out on a garbage heap.

TRAGEDY: REVIVALS

Even within the company the onset of officialdom brought its own hazards. State control encouraged a pedestrian approach to dramatic issues, and more and more the Comédie Française turned into a museum in which the masterpieces of the repertory were periodically revived in virtually the same conditions as those in which they had been created.

From one point of view this fidelity to tradition is admirable. It has produced in the French theater a continuity, lacking in its English counterpart, in which each revival is scrupulously numbered and recorded. We thus have a continuous performance history for Racine, Corneille, and Molière, which does not exist for Shakespeare, and the archives of the Comédie Française provide one of the best documentary sources in the world.

Against this, however, there evolved a distinct Comédie style, in which adherence to precedent became the dominant virtue. Innovation was distrusted and only grudgingly admitted. New plays were acceptable only if they conformed to established standards, and roles were distributed by seniority rather than in accordance with merit. This situation both diminished the quality of original output and perpetuated a style of presentation long after it would have withered in the more rigorous climate of the competitive, commercial theater. (It will be observed that the same factors operated in London; with only two official houses, there was little impetus for change.)

Paris, too, fell victim to the same bourgeois, sentimentalizing spirit that now dominated the English drama. Tragedy was represented by dutiful revivals of the past and by the works of Voltaire, which, though gaudier in their conception, remained faithful to established neoclassical principles. The difficulty was that Racine had already exhausted the limited possibilities of the form, and, given the spirit of the new century, all that remained was variation on familiar themes. Voltaire's first play, *Oedipe* (1718), was a clear Racinian imitation. In his later works, however, he did try to expand the scope of tragedy beyond the virtually obligatory love-versus-duty plot. *Zaïre* (1732), probably his best play and still occasionally revived, remains faithful to an old French fascination by being set among Turks; it deals, however, with the broader issue of the clash of Christian and Mohammedan sympathies at the time of the Crusades. Voltaire also developed the concept, suggested by Aristotle and already adumbrated in Racine, that tragedy should involve a purifying process, though specifically in terms of the characters involved. Some good would emerge from the suffering if the protagonist recognized his past errors and worked toward a change thereafter. This concept was to appeal to later dramatists, even those who deliberately set themselves outside the classical mold.

GENTEEL COMEDY

Comedy suffered a similar dilution of vitality. Much of Molière was now considered vulgar, and even *Tartuffe* had lost its shock value. Voltaire himself comments that no one now came to see a play that could once have been guaranteed to pack the house.

The spirit of commedia, which had so greatly influenced Molière, survived into the eighteenth century, but in chastened and muted form. The commedia players themselves, who had been established in Paris in 1570 and enjoyed almost continuous popularity thereafter, had suffered from the increasing sobriety of the latter years of Louis XIV's reign. In 1697 the new piety and the opposition of the Comédie Française provoked their dismissal. One of the saddest pictures in the history of the theater shows the once beloved characters, with their familiar masks and costumes, leaving the capital for exile. With the death of Louis XIV there was some court reaction against the severity of his closing years, and a new Italian troupe was invited back; it opened in May 1716 at the Palais Royal, once Molière's home, and later moved to the now deserted Hôtel de Bourgogne. Gone, however, was the agreeable anarchy, the spontaneity of improvisation. Though retaining their names and individuality, the commedia characters had been domesticated by the script.

Moralizing and sentimentalizing commedia was in order, and the acknowledged master of this new form was Pierre-Carlet de Chamblain de Marivaux. Like so many Paris writers, Marivaux came to the theater from the law. His first play, performed by amateurs in the provincial center of Limoges, reads like a polite version of Plautus. Similar themes were common in the novels of the time, some of which Marivaux wrote: young ladies separated from their parents in infancy and afterward restored; disguises, chance encounters, rambling, picaresque plots, and a gallery of servants commenting on the doings of their masters, together with an avoidance of any incident that might be construed as sensational.

Marivaux first began to produce plays professionally in 1720, and his connection with the commedia is obvious in his treatment and his choice of subject matter. *Arlequin poli par l'amour* (*Harlequin Polished by Love*, 1720), a one-act

(*top*) An English version of the tragedy of Phèdre. Although some of the old absurdities of heroic costume have gone, Phèdre's dress is still ornate, in the contemporary high style, and Hippolytus wears the pseudoclassical costume still thought proper for tragedies on classical themes. (*left and above*) Pantomime as respite from tragedy: Grimaldi, one of a famous family of clowns.

Set designs challenged the painter to produce
elaborate compositions. Setting by Thomas
Greenwood the elder, 1777.

comedy in prose, has been compared to Shakespeare's *A Midsummer Night's Dream* for its sense of fantasy, which replaced the original commedia anarchy. In four changes of scene it tells of a fairy, about to marry Merlin the magician, who falls in love with Harlequin and kidnaps him, in spite of the fact that Harlequin is himself in love with the shepherdess Sylvia. Harlequin finally defeats her plots, captures her magic wand, and leads all off the stage in a singing, dancing procession. The play contains much stage magic: the fairy has a ring that makes her invisible, and we may see in Harlequin the beginnings of the transformation from the quick-witted servant to the quick-fingered conjurer, a transformation that also manifests itself in the eighteenth-century English harlequinade. More important, Harlequin has been humanized. He is no longer a mere acrobat but has been endowed with delicacy and sensitive human feeling. The stage business consists mostly of *lazzi,* indicated in lengthy stage directions, but now articulated and made responsive to the needs of the plot — a reversal of the original commedia process whereby the rudimentary plot grew out of the *lazzi.*

In 1722 Marivaux wrote *la Surprise de l'amour (Love's Surprise),* a sentimental comedy concerned with the nuances and infinite perplexities of love. Master and maidservant, both left desolate by the deaths of their beloveds, leave Paris for the country, where they find themselves living near a man-hating countess and her manservant. After much hesitancy and reluctance, the master and the mistress are finally brought by their servants to confess their mutual admiration. Voltaire remarked of this comedy that the author "knew all the byways of the heart, but never found the main road." Nevertheless, this kind of *comédie larmoyante* ("tearful comedy") — what the English called sentimental drama or sentimental comedy — was appealing in its time. When so many subjects were no longer considered decorous on the public stage, what remained had to be explored in as much detail as possible.

COMMEDIA IN ITALY

The transformation of the commedia thus became an index of the theater of the time. In the country of the commedia's origin, a similar transformation occurred. Carlo Gozzi (1720–1806) placed the traditional characters in fairy tales, rich in scenic devices but usually with an obvious moral or an ironic commentary on characters and events of his own time.

Carlo Goldoni (1707–1793) took the same characters and moved them in a more sentimental direction. His avowed intention was to "substitute for the fantastic adventure plays of the *commedia dell'arte,* a regular comedy, written rather than improvised, without masks, without obscenities, without *lazzi,* horseplay, and mere buffoonery." His comedy was to be based on the close observation of life; his actors were required to stop building their performances on tradition and to examine real people. Whether he succeeded in this ambition is doubtful. He has never been given a proper chance. Though his output was enormous, only a small portion is still performed, and this usually to serve only as a foundation for the *lazzi* that Goldoni affected to deplore.

As true commedia was scriptless, Goldoni's plays represent our nearest approach to a vanished theatrical form, and the ease with which his scripts accept *lazzi* suggests that the tradition was too deeply ingrained in the Italian performing spirit to be easily eradicated. One of the most famous examples occurs in *The Servant of Two Masters* (1743), where Truffaldino serves dinner to his two employers simultaneously, each demanding his attention without knowledge of the other. As performed today by the Piccolo Teatro of Milan, it turns into a miracle of tumbles, pratfalls, and precise timing that may not be faithful to Goldoni but is as close to the essence of commedia as we are ever likely to get.

THE MOVE TOWARD NATURALISM

What general considerations emerge from all this?

First, we should be aware that we are watching the recurrence of something that has already happened in the history of the theater; that we are, in fact, observing another cycle, this time concerned not so much with the presentation of plays as with their subject matter. If we compare Marivaux and Goldoni with Molière, or with the commedia in its pure form, we see the same relationship as between the New Comedy of Menander and his Roman imitators and the Old Comedy of Aristophanes. In each case we see that an original abrasiveness, a frankness, a social awareness, has been replaced by a polite gentility, a conscious avoidance of giving offense. Formal components of the earlier comedy have been assimilated into a naturalistic context. Marivaux's *Surprise de l'amour* is based closely on stock items from the commedia repertoire, but these are now articulated and presented as natural behavior. Conspicuously, the monologue of Lelio, the master, concerning love and hate is not presented as a formal soliloquy but is punctuated by Arlequin's remarks; thus it is made to appear more like natural dialogue. Similarly, the *lazzi* of the double banquet in *The Servant of Two Masters* are not self-contained but are made to serve the functions of the plot. Generally speaking, we see a restriction to a more homespun world. We see a growing use of the pastoral motif, in which wild nature is tamed to provide an appropriately "pretty" background for delicate sentiments. We see, finally, the creation of a dramatic subworld of slaves or servants, who both imitate and comment upon the actions of their masters and influence their affairs.

Second, as subject matter and stage presentation are mutually influential, we see a growing realism in the staging of comedy. In the shift from Aristophanes to Menander, as already noted, the drama lost much of its frank communion with the audience. In Aristophanes the presence of the audience is taken for granted and continually acknowledged, most notably by direct address of the chorus to the audience in the *parabasis*. In Menander this never happens after the explanatory prologue, and in Plautus it occurs only for sudden, shock effects; it has become a special device, no longer a way of life. Molière's plays, though already performed behind a proscenium arch, still preserved some kind of awareness of the audience — particularly during the intermissions, which were occupied with commedia turns. In the silver age of eighteenth-century comedy, however, Goldoni can say, "Don't you see that it isn't right to address the audience? When he is alone on stage, the actor should pretend that no one sees or hears him; for this habit of speaking to an audience is an intolerable fault, that should not be permitted on any ground whatsoever." Actors, in short, were being asked to behave more naturally; and though this happens more conspicuously in comedy, we shall see how it begins to apply to tragedy, too. Comedy, as we have noted elsewhere, is the medium through which the reform of stage manners toward realism tends to come, since it draws its material more closely from everyday life.

Another aspect of the cycle is that an age of vital creative talent is succeeded by one of interpretive talent: a period of playwrights is followed by one of actors. So it was in the classical theater, when the fifth century that produced Aeschylus, Sophocles, Euripides, and Aristophanes was followed by one that produced the Artists of Dionysus. We see the same phenomenon in the years we are now considering: Shakespeare, Jonson, Molière, and Congreve are followed by a century in which the dominant figures are no longer playwrights but actors. But to study the actors' contributions, we must return for a while to the English Restoration.

Performers and the New Acting Style in Restoration England

The most significant innovation of this period is, of course, the use of actresses — known in Italy and France for at least a century before but appearing in England only at the close of the Commonwealth. If we speculate on why it took women so long to enter the stage, the answer seems to lie in prevailing social practices.

WOMEN AND THE STAGE

In fifth-century Greece women were, at best, second-class citizens. They had no voice in politics; they could not hold office; though an occasional priestly appointment might be given to a woman, for the most part even this was denied them. The prestige of the theater, on the other hand, was high. Its festivals were among the most important assemblies of the city-state, its actors enjoyed quasi-priestly status, and it was unthinkable, in Greek terms, that a woman should appear among them.

In Roman society the reverse was true. The status of women was much higher, that of the theater much lower, and the observances of polite society made it unthinkable for any woman to demean herself by taking part in such spectacles. The only women we know of who did so were mimes — who already belonged to the subworld — and, occasionally, women of the upper classes who, in the imperial decadence, went on the stage in a conscious flouting of convention, much as some members of the aristocracy offered themselves as gladiators.

In the Middle Ages, similarly, prevailing social patterns worked against the use of actresses. As long as cycle plays were presented by the guilds, the artisans and craftsmen could count their participation as approved guild activity, released time. No such recourse was available to the women. Further considerations seem to have been that the necessary time commitment was a long one and that the plays made demands on the performers' stamina that were thought to be beyond a woman's abilities. Thus though there is evidence for the use of women in the continental mysteries, examples are few and far between.

By the seventeenth century, however, actresses were accepted on the Italian and French stages, and when the royalist exiles returned to England, there seemed no good reason why they should not have them on the London stages, too. On January 3, 1661, the diarist Samuel Pepys, an inveterate theatergoer and observer of the social scene, noted "the first time that ever I saw women come upon the stage."

Pepys was a little behind the times. Even before the Restoration Mrs. Coleman had made her singing appearance in Davenant's *The Siege of Rhodes.* In 1660 Charles II's warrant to Davenant and Killigrew stipulated that henceforth only women should play female roles, to the end that plays might be "esteemed not only harmless delights but useful and instructive representations of human life."

Yet as in France, royal approbation could not eliminate centuries of prejudice. The profession, still considered degrading even for men, was especially so for women. No lady of respectable society dared contemplate a stage career, and actresses were drawn mainly from among those who were already beyond the social pale. Colley Cibber comments that "a lady with a real title, whose female indiscretions had occasioned her family to abandon her, sought a stage career." But she had to be refused because of family objections. Her attempt "to get bread from the stage was looked upon as an addition of new scandal to her former dishonor."

To counteract this social disapproval, actresses, married or not, regularly adopted the title of *Mrs.* (*Miss* then carrying the same implications as *mistress* does today). Many of them did little to improve the reputation of their profession, taking every opportunity to increase their earnings immorally and hoping to attract the nobility who frequented the playhouses or, if lucky, King Charles himself. Men from the audience regularly frequented the tiring house. Pepys comments, "But Lord! Their confidence! And how many men do hover about them as soon as they come off the stage, and how confident they are in their talk." In Pepys's time *confidence* meant what we would now call *brazenness;* and we have a vivid picture of the backstage as a convenient place for assignations.

The theater exploited the presence of women, as it has been prone to exploit every novelty, and their participation contributed to the increased sexiness and vulgarity of Restoration drama. By a complete reversal of Elizabethan practice, women were now used to play men's roles — what came to be known as breeches parts. In the Elizabethan theater it was convenient if justification could be found in the plot for putting women into men's clothes, as these roles were played by boys or young men anyway. In the Restoration theater the disguise formula had a new appeal: it enabled the actresses to show their legs. We even know of cases where women took every role in the play.

Colley Cibber insists that the use of women was one of the principal advantages of the Restoration theater over that of earlier times: "The characters of women in former theatres were performed by boys or young men of the most effeminate aspect. And what graces or master strokes of action can we conceive such ungain hoydens to have been capable of? The additional objects, then, of real, beautiful women could not but draw a proportion of new admirers to the theatre." They could, indeed, though sometimes for the wrong reasons. But this theatrical change of heart also offered new possibilities in the interpretation of female characters. We see an increased emphasis on women's roles; we see playwrights showing greater interest in feminine psychology; we see, in short, female characters becoming more feminine.

ACTRESSES

Some of these Restoration actresses have become legendary. Undoubtedly the most famous was Ellen (Nell) Gwyn, born in 1650 and, according to Pepys, "brought up in a bawdy house to fill strong waters to the guests" — in other words, a barmaid in a brothel. She began her theatrical career by selling oranges in the Theatre Royal. At age fourteen she was already an actress (we must remember that sixteen then was considered maturity), rapidly progressing from small parts to leads. Onstage she was known for her dancing and her breeches parts, but she also played the heroine and spoke the prologue in Dryden's *The Conquest of Granada*. Offstage she enjoyed another kind of fame — as mistress of various members of the nobility, culminating with Charles II himself.

Anne Bracegirdle, born about 1663, began by playing ingenue roles and then went on to tragic queens. She was admired in Shakespearean revivals, appearing as Desdemona in *Othello* and Ophelia in *Hamlet*. We have a charming contemporary tribute to her personal attractiveness: "She was of a lovely height, with dark-brown hair and eyebrows, black sparkling eyes, and a fresh blushy complexion; and whenever she exerted herself, had an involuntary flushing in her breast, neck and face, having continually a cheerful aspect, and a fine set of teeth; never making an exit, but that she left the audience in an imitation of her pleasant countenance." Fine teeth were an asset in a society that either never brushed them at all or cleaned them by the equally disastrous methods of honey or pumice. Gossip asserted that Anne Bracegirdle was the mistress of Congreve, for whom she created the roles of Angelica in *Love for Love* and Millamant in *The Way of the World.* She vehemently denied this rumor, proclaiming her purity to the world on a banner that accompanied her travels and bore the insignia C.V., standing for "Celebrated Virgin."

ACTORS

Actresses were still a novelty. In all his comedies Congreve holds back his female characters until an act has passed, presumably to keep his audience on tenterhooks of expectation. It would take a while for them to be completely assimilated into the theater. Thus it is to the men that we have to look for the continuity of the acting tradition.

Davenant, here as in other ways, provides a link between the prewar and postwar theater. Before the split between king and Parliament, he is said to have studied the actor Taylor in the role of Hamlet; after the Restoration he taught the same role to Betterton. This story has special interest because of the tradition that Taylor had originally been coached by Shakespeare himself. We have a similar story about the title role of Shakespeare's *Henry VIII:* "The part of the King was so rightly and justly done by Mr. Betterton, he being instructed in it by Sir William, who had it from old Mr. Lowin that had his instructions from Mr. Shakespeare." A system of acting, then, taught by the plays' author could still be used the better part of a century later, and in many ways the Restoration actors were in a similar position to Shakespeare's.

We have seen how the Restoration stage offered a compromise between the open platform and the proscenium, with its forestage still allowing intimate contact with the audience. We have seen, too, how one reconstruction of Elizabethan acting suggests that it was an extremely formal business, resting on a predetermined system of gestures and postures conveying specific meanings to an audience trained to the conventions. This formality certainly seems to have carried through into the new generation, producing handbooks for actors in which the range of possible gestures was described and illustrated. Heroic tragedy, like its French counterpart, imposed a formal, declamatory style, largely static, with a limited set of gestures accompanying a singsong recitative. Restoration comedy, with its emphasis on domestic intimacy, encouraged something more realistic — though here again we must remind ourselves that *realism* is a word with shifting meaning, and in acting, as in stage setting, what Restoration audiences found realistic would not necessarily appear so to us. However, the acting of the new age does seem to show, if not a revolution, at least a gradual shift from the old formality to a greater realism, and some hints of this change come from the career of Thomas Betterton.

THOMAS BETTERTON

Betterton's career was a long one. It began in 1659 in a company that included many survivors from the pre-Commonwealth theater. Betterton was thus an inheritor of the old tradition. He soon established himself in male leads, playing Hamlet in 1661, and his association with Davenant brought him a long list of important roles, both in new plays and in revivals. His repertoire ultimately embraced 178 roles, in such diverse fields as heroic drama, Jonsonian comedy, the comedy of manners, Beaumont and Fletcher's tragicomedies, Shakespearean tragedy, comedy, and history, and opera.

His most famous roles were Hamlet and Henry VIII; he was still playing the former at the age of seventy-four, though critics found him far too old for the part. He also played King Lear, though the play itself was not popular — even in its doctored form it was too rough and wild for Restoration susceptibilities and did not return to full favor until Garrick's time. Betterton's critics suggested that his success in Shakespeare was due mainly to his recapturing the flavor of the original conception. Three days before his death at the age of seventy-five he played a role in a Beaumont and Fletcher revival. When he died in 1710 he left behind a career that had spanned one of the major periods of transition in the English theater.

Contemporary comments on Betterton's acting are valuable not merely for what they tell us about him but for their implications for the usual practices of his time. For example, it was remarked that Betterton was unusual in remaining in character for the whole duration of the play, not just when he was speaking. We are told that many actors, on the contrary, relaxed once their own part was over, not even bothering to react to the replies to their own speeches but looking around at the audience until they heard the next cue, at which they snapped erect like soldiers and then, "like a caterpillar which has erected itself at the touch of a twig, shrink again to their crawl and their quiet, and enjoy their full ease until next rowsing." We are also told of Betterton's interest in paintings of historical scenes, which he studied for their value in play production: "[The painters] have observed a decorum in their pieces, which wants to be introduced on our stage: for they never place any person on the cloth who has not a concern in the action."

All this suggests that Betterton had an interest in the consistency of the role and in ensemble playing that was unusual in a theater that still regarded a play production as an assembly of individual performances, striking in themselves, but put together without any regard for the totality of the artistic effect. This individualism — every actor for himself — was to dominate the theater for a long time. The concept of the unified production, in which individual talents were subordinated to the concerted artistic purpose, was still in the future, and if Betterton was moving toward it, as these stories suggest, he was ahead of his generation.

Most of our information about the actor comes from Gildon's *Life of Betterton*, published in 1710 and including a treatise of doubtful attribution called *The*

Duty of a Player. Whether this treatise on acting was written by Betterton himself or by his biographer we cannot be sure. But it is closely related to Betterton's practice; and, as we have already noted, it is characteristic of the new interest in the theater that treatises on acting should be appearing at all. From Gildon and *The Duty of a Player* we learn a good deal about what most actors did and what Betterton did that was different.

We learn, for instance, that the delivery of most Restoration actors suffered from a monotony that Betterton avoided: his stage speech was "varied all along, like the divisions which a skillful musician runs upon a lute." We are told that most actors learned a system of gestures by rote. *The Duty of a Player,* indeed, lists many of these gestures in a catalog of emotions suitable for any role. To express triumph, the head was held high and the eyes fixed confidently ahead, the arms extended and held at an angle from the body. To show guilt, the eyes were cast to one side and the head bent low. Bashfulness was indicated by holding the arms close to the body and putting the hand to the mouth.

For the average actor these textbook instructions represented the sum of the art. Betterton evidently improved upon them by using them merely as a basis and by coloring his interpretations with a closer examination of nature. He was particularly interested in the eyes as an expression of character, and he told Gildon that the sick and old were slow in the turning of their eyes, that blinking often signified a timid nature, and that "eyes quiet and calm, with a secret kind of grace and pleasantness are the offspring of love and friendship."

We also learn about the individuality of his stage portraits and that all his Shakespearean characters were different — implying that his contemporaries used an all-purpose approach to standard roles, which he managed to transcend. We are given, therefore, a picture of Betterton as an actor who, while adhering to the largely formal concept of acting in his time, contrived to infuse it with an unprecedented emotional veracity. It would be some time before such an approach became the rule rather than the exception.

Betterton also made his mark in theatrical politics by leading a splinter group of actors disaffected with the patent theater managership. He eventually returned to the fold, but his venture looked forward to the pattern of paternalistic, more or less benevolent actor management that was to characterize the English theater in later years.

THE THEORETICIANS

In the years that followed Betterton's death, a spate of publications focusing on the central problem of the actor's art that had occupied Betterton — how much should be art and how much nature — shows how this issue was increasingly concerning theoreticians as well as practitioners and how, indeed, theorists could now expect to find a reading public for studies of a subject that, a generation before, few outside the profession would have taken seriously. Some of these works were French, some Italian, some English; but they were mutually influential, and the more important ones could be read in translation.

In 1719 Du Bos wrote *Critical and Historical Reflections on Poetry and Painting,* which included a study of the "theatrical representations of the ancients" and came down heavily on the side of art. It argued that the Greeks and Romans read their lines on the basis of a musical notation and that contemporary French tragic declamation was correct in following the same path.

This defense of the "special voice" school of acting, with its transcendence of everyday reality, was seconded by Luigi Riccaboni, whose theatrical career embraced several different disciplines and whose company we have already seen at work in Paris. Riccaboni (ca. 1676–1763) was the son of Antonio Riccaboni, the Pantalone of the commedia troupe in Modena, Italy. Luigi had gone on the stage at the age of sixteen. It is characteristic of his times that he found the traditional improvised performances lacking in artistic polish and preferred scripted plays in which the better actors were not hampered by those who were slower-witted. In 1716 he was in Paris, heading the troupe at the Hôtel de Bourgogne and acting for Marivaux; in 1728 he wrote a history of the Italian theater and a poem in six cantos on the art of acting. Ten years later came *Thoughts on Declamation,* which insisted on the need for art and study. Acting, he said, should be more than the reproduction of everyday behavior. It must be real life augmented by dignity and beauty. "Nature does not bestow the Polish upon the Diamond she forms; and it is Labor and Art which give it Lustre." Art derives its principles from nature but demands polishing. This theory was well suited to the smooth style of Marivaux and also to tragedy as then played, though it denied the spontaneity of the old commedia.

What gives Riccaboni's work a certain ambiguity, however, is the fact that while he champions artistic polish, he stresses at the same time the importance of feeling: "When right feeling is the master, it imparts the right feeling to the lines." This implication that the actor should work from the inside out, rather than from the outside in, was hailed by Constantin Stanislavsky, the nineteenth-century apostle of theatrical realism, as a precursor of his own theories. "I could kiss him!" Stanislavsky is said to have remarked. And indeed, Riccaboni seems to reverse his earlier comments with a remarkable defense of the natural manner: "All the world knows that Caesar, Hannibal, etc. were men like us; and everybody is persuaded that they felt their strongest passions, and performed their most heroic actions, in the same manner as the great men of our own age: yet the very spectators who are convinced of this, being prejudiced in their youth in favor of the bombastic manner of theatrical declamation, form their ideas of these heroes according to the appearance they make as performed by players; that is, men quite above the common level of mankind, with a manner of walking, speaking, and listening different from the rest of the world."

So the argument went on. Voltaire supported what he called the *pompeux* in tragedy; and we must remember that in French this word does not mean "pompous" but "ceremonious," "dignified." His contemporary La Motte, on the other hand, wanted a style close to actuality, which would abolish soliloquies and replace verse with prose. Comedy, he argued, had come closer to real life, and tragedy should do likewise. And playwrights began to write the kind of humanistic tragedy that La Motte talked of. In 1741 Paul Landois wrote *Sylvia,* a play about a man convinced of his wife's infidelity. We have already seen a cruder example of the same style in *The London Merchant.*

In 1747 Pierre de Saint-Albine published *le Comédien.* This work was soon translated into English as *The Actor,* revised, and retranslated into French in 1769. Saint-Albine's work is the first systematic critical treatise on "sympathetic imagination" in the actor. It states that he needs three things: first, good judgment; second, *le sentiment,* "sensibility," or the disposition to be affected by the passions — the actor must imagine that for the time being he really is the person he represents, weeping real tears as though suffering from real distress; third, he needs fire.

In part II of the work Saint-Albine lays stress on *truth.*

> The actor . . . if he would play his character with truth, is not only to assume the emotions which that passion would produce in the generality of mankind, but he is to give it that particular form under which it would appear, when exerting itself in the breast of such a person as he is giving us the portrait of. The rage of Achilles [i.e., the typical hero of classical tragedy] is very different from that of Chremes [the angry old father in Roman comedy].

Similarly, elsewhere he says:

> To exhibit true action in a part is to do everything allotted by the author to the character represented in a manner exactly conformable to what the person himself would or ought to have done in it, under every circumstance and in every situation through which the action of the play carries him.

Avoid declamation, he urges; rhyme is a danger. And then, after all this, Saint-Albine loses his nerve. Looking at the plays of his time, particularly those of Voltaire, he finds it hard to see how these could be played naturally, and he is forced to concede that there may be at times a major difference between art and nature.

Saint-Albine's work inspired another that has, perhaps unfairly, become much better known, *Le Paradoxe sur le comédien* (*The Paradox of Acting*), by Denis Diderot, begun some time in the 1770s, finished about 1778, and not published until 1830. Diderot had already proposed startling reforms in the theater, anticipating by a hundred years standard nineteenth-century practice. "Imagine a huge wall across the front of the stage, separating you from the audience, and behave exactly as if the curtain had never risen." Actors, he says, should turn their backs on the audience as the circumstances demanded and, above all, speak naturally. But after writing all this, Diderot, like Saint-Albine, reneged and swung back to the primacy of the intellect. He argued that the actor who plays from the heart rather than from the head "may give us a fine moment, or two; but would you rather have a fine moment, or a fine part?" The stimulus should come from the natural emotions, but art should remain in control. High art may even evolve when the actors are unsympathetic to the sentiments they express. Diderot illustrates this idea by a glorious parody of an actor and an actress who, between the lines of a passionate tragic scene, manage to carry on a private quarrel of their own.

Clearly the theorists could not make up their own minds. Their arguments are shifting, ambiguous, and confused. Those who defend the cause of art squeeze in a plea for greater realism, while those who advocate the primacy of natural responses urge, in the end, that these should be controlled by the intellect. This continuing dilemma is one that every actor has to solve for himself. No matter how realistic the performance, no matter how deeply the actor is immersed in his role, there must always be some part of the mind free to deal with extraneous circumstances: an unexpected response from the audience, a missed cue, a difficulty with a costume.

Behind these lengthy eighteenth-century arguments, however, lies something more particular to the time. The controversy is not really about the supremacy of one kind of acting over the other. Each has its place. It would be just as ridiculous to play Noh drama with the gestures of the street as to perform Arthur Miller with masks and hieratic gestures. What lies behind the arguments of Riccaboni, Saint-Albine, and the rest is the uneasy consciousness that play writing had moved on, while acting had largely stood still. A formal style that had evolved to cope with the demands of classical tragedy was no longer suitable for a more naturalistic drama. But the stage had grown lazy. Actors' behavior had become fossilized, with the same gestures and inflections handed down from generation to generation long after they had lost their artistic validity. Even stage groupings retained the old patterns, being governed by social protocol rather than dramatic expediency. Those individuals who recognized the problem, and tried to solve it by bringing their performances into greater conformance with nature, might be hailed by their audiences as creative geniuses, but they were often resisted by their fellow actors as sensationalists and upstarts, demeaning the grandeur that was expected from the tragic stage.

CHARLES MACKLIN

One of the livelier English actors was Charles Macklin, whose long, picturesque, and well-documented career illustrates the promise and the hazards that the eighteenth-century theater could offer. His exact date of birth is unknown, but, like Colley Cibber and Thomas Betterton, he was blessed with longevity, acting till he was nearly ninety, dying in 1797. Born and educated in Ireland, he revealed himself as a child prodigy in school performances. Moving to England, he became a touring actor, playing the Welsh and Midlands circuit that was regarded, with some justice, as the nadir of the provincial theater. From this hard apprenticeship he moved to the more prosperous surroundings of Bristol, a city that had grown rich on tobacco and slavery and whose elegant eighteenth-century playhouse still stands. He also played in Bath, a fashionable watering place, and from here he made the natural transition to London. His debut, in 1725, in Dryden's *Oedipus* failed to please because of his reluctance to conform to the accepted mode of tragic diction, and his ventures in the capital remained problematical, alternating with returns to Bristol and Bath. He finally settled at Drury Lane, playing small parts and undertaking some managerial responsibilities.

It was a bad time to be in London. The theaters were still smarting under the Licensing Act of 1737 and were torn apart by internal politics. A group of dissident actors had left Drury Lane to play in another house, and Macklin's career was hampered by his unwilling involvement in the struggle. It was hampered even more by his own violent temperament. A greenroom quarrel with a fellow actor ended in the actor's death. Macklin was put on trial, found guilty of manslaughter, and sentenced to be branded on the hand. After his discharge he returned to the company, only to fight with another actor, James Quin, one of the older school, whose pompous style we shall have occasion to note again. By now Macklin was playing a variety of roles: the First Witch in *Macbeth* (a long-standing theatrical tradition has one witch played by a man); Tattle, the fop, in Congreve's *Love for Love;* and another celebrated stage fop, Lord Foppington, in Vanbrugh's *The Relapse.* Restoration comedy continued to be played, though in emasculated versions to accommodate eighteenth-century propriety.

One of the uglier features of the theater of this period is the violence of the cheaper parts of the house. Theatrical riots were not unknown; we shall see them particularly in the career of David Garrick, an actor whom, for most of the time, the public idolized. Macklin was caught in one such disturbance in 1740, when the audience protested at the postponement of one part of the program. When the angry crowd swarmed onto the stage, Macklin ordered the trapdoors opened and summoned up the theater's thunder and lightning. Muttering, the crowd departed, though not before smashing the instruments of the orchestra and tearing up some of the seating.

Macklin now began to capture larger roles. His most famous, in a string of Shakespearean revivals, was Shylock in *The Merchant of Venice,* with the pompous Quin as Antonio. The performance must have been a revelatory clash of acting styles, for Quin was firmly wedded to the old declamatory methods, while Macklin was more concerned with the detail of the role and what made Shylock different from anybody else. Over the years Shylock had diminished (curious though it may seem to us) into a low comedy role. Macklin's predecessor, Thomas Doggett, had specialized in such parts and played Shylock in the same way. Macklin's interpretation, though still in the comic tradition, offered significant differences. He was concerned with the Jewishness of the character, with what distinguished him from the Christians in the play, and he examined at great length detailed studies of Jewish costume and character. He went so far as to read Josephus's ancient *History of the Jewish People,* and his attitude establishes him as one of the earliest scholarly actors, who saw in the interpretation of a role much more than the reading of the lines. A contemporary illustration shows Shylock in carefully observed Jewish dress rather than in ordinary eighteenth-century costume, as the fashion of the day dictated. This costuming is probably due to the impact of Macklin's performance.

Macklin's scholarly interests also established him as a teacher of acting. He insisted on the observation of nature as a necessity to qualify the formal style. He also wrote a manuscript on the actor's art. It is, unfortunately, lost, but some of his precepts are deducible from other sources. It seems clear that he disapproved of too much business on the stage, and thus he disliked his more famous contemporary, David Garrick, with whom he acted at Drury Lane and whose chameleonlike versatility he found unappealing. He disapproved particularly of what his contemporaries called "claptraps," sudden moves and pieces of business that did not spring logically out of the action but were calculated to jerk the audience into applause. Although Macklin was not what we should now call a realistic actor, he was on the way to becoming one within the context of his time. His method was to start from natural voice and gestures and then work his way up, by judicious heightening, until they reached the greater proportions necessary for the stage. Thus we still have acting considered primarily as art, but art increasingly informed by nature.

We must remind ourselves, however, that the rank-and-file actors did not share this vision. There was no general reformation of acting style. Many players were content to be artificial. Drama was still performed in modern dress — that is, contemporary dress rather than dress appropriate to the period the play was supposed to represent — and lines were generally intoned in a pompous and artificial cadence. That critics were becoming alive to the absurdity of this style we see from a contemporary description of Quin in *The Fair Penitent:*

> Quin presented himself upon the rising of the curtain in a green velvet coat, embroidered down the seams, an enormous full-bottomed periwig, rolled stockings and high-heeled, square-toed shoes: with very little variation of cadence and in a deep full tone, accompanied by a sawing kind of motion as he rolled out his heroics with an air of dignified indifference that seemed to disdain the plaudits that were bestowed upon him.

Tragedy was still held to demand a "great voice." Many players almost sang their parts, delivering them in a quavering recitative with syllables drawn out to give what they considered weight and dignity to the lines. This feature is shown in a parody of an anonymous actress in Congreve's only tragedy, *The Mourning Bride:*

> Mu-u-sick has Cha-a-arms to so-o-oth a savage breast,
> To so-o-often rocks or be-e-end the knotted oak.

DAVID GARRICK

But the individual reformers were making themselves felt, and Macklin was followed by the more famous David Garrick. Born in 1716, Garrick came from a provincial background and was intended for a business career. Bored with this field, he decided on the stage and joined a company playing in some of the more attractive provincial theaters. Here he soon made his mark in tragedy and comedy and also in the harlequinades (see p. 204), which were popular after-pieces to the more serious evening's fare. On October 19, 1741, he made his London debut as Shakespeare's Richard III, a part that was the regular test piece for actors of his time and, indeed, for most of the century that followed.

That Richard III was a test piece tells us something of what was expected from an eighteenth-century actor. In our time an actor is tested by his Hamlet, an introspective role in which the inner nature of the man has to be deeply explored before the character is exposed to the stage. Richard III, on the other hand, is an extraverted part. Richard is himself an actor. He shifts from role to role before the various people he wishes to convince or persuade; he is all things to all men, adopting whatever guise is demanded by his immediate circumstances. This versatility fitted the eighteenth-century concept of a stage performance, which ideally consisted of a series of brilliant moments, each perfect in itself but not necessarily having the connections that we should now look for. The reader will recall that we have already discussed eighteenth-century production as an assemblage of individual performances rather than as an ensemble, with each actor working for his own success rather than for the group as a whole. This concept extended to the individual role, which was seen as a succession of fine moments rather than a total entity.

In playing Richard, then, Garrick was measuring himself against accepted standards. But he brought something new to the role, and the novelty was in that kind of naturalness we have seen foreshadowed in Betterton and Macklin. The first thing that struck critics was the nature of his delivery.

> Mr. Garrick's easy and familiar, yet forcible, style in speaking and acting, at first threw the critics into some hesitation concerning the novelty as well as propriety of his manner. They had been long accustomed to an elevation of the voice, with a sudden mechanical depression of its tones, calculated to excite admiration and to entrap applause. To the just modulation of the words, or concurring expression of the features from the genuine workings of nature, they had been strangers, at least for some time.

Garrick was a great success, and the play was acted six or seven times, a long run for this period. Other theaters were deserted, and fellow actors were jealous. Quin remarked that "if the young fellow was right, he and the rest of the players had been all wrong." But audiences were happy with this breakaway from the old, heavy style.

Garrick's success took him to Dublin, whose prestigious theater regularly

(*below*) David Garrick, the most famous actor of his time, in the tent scene from Shakespeare's *Richard III*. Richard has been woken in terror by the ghosts of his victims. (*left*) Poster advertising benefit performance of John Gay's *The Beggars' Opera*.

imported the better London players, and then returned him to Drury Lane. His career soon became known as one of innovations. Not least of these was a revival of *Macbeth* pretty much as Shakespeare had written it. From 1665 to 1744 London audiences had known this play only in Davenant's neoclassical adaptation: heavy with music, interspersed with songs and dances, with the witches played as comic characters in high-pointed hats, and with additional ghosts and apparitions. Shakespeare's text came as a revelation and, to some, an unwelcome surprise. Quin objected to some of the language in the play, asking Garrick where on earth he had found such uncouth expressions. Garrick referred him to the original. In 1749 he also revived the original *Romeo and Juliet,* which had been driven from the stage for years by Otway's version. This production led to a stage war, as Covent Garden simultaneously mounted its own version of the play, with Garrick's rival Barry as Romeo. Since there were still only two authorized theaters, playgoing London had to see *Romeo and Juliet* or nothing. A contemporary verse, ending with a quotation from the play, summarizes the public annoyance:

> "Well, what's tonight?" says angry Ned
> As up from bed he rouses:
> "*Romeo* again?" and shakes his head.
> "Ah! Pox on both your houses!"

Garrick, however, was not above writing his own adaptations. He offered *A Winter's Tale* and *The Taming of the Shrew* in abridged three-act versions, and he altered Ben Jonson's *The Alchemist* to provide a larger role for himself. Nor was he averse to spectacle for its own sake. When George III was crowned in 1761, Garrick attempted to reproduce the coronation entire on the stage, opening up the back of the theater to the street so that audiences could see through to the real crowds and bonfires outside. This spectacle was enormously popular, and it ran for forty nights. The actors disliked it because "being exposed to the suffocation of smoke and the raw air from the open street, [they] were seized with colds, rheumatisms and swelled faces." Garrick also continued to play his harlequinades, in direct opposition to the pantomimes and spectacles of Covent Garden.

Audiences applauded Garrick's naturalness, and it seems clear that he toned down the grotesque excesses of his predecessors. However, he still excited audiences by the swiftness of his transitions. There is a story of Garrick entertaining friends at home by putting his head round the door and letting his face run, like a series of lantern slides, the whole gamut of human emotions. This story suggests what his stage performances must have been like.

The critics, too, were impressed by his naturalness, primarily of his costumes, and by his removal of many of the old absurdities of heroic dress. "The hero seldom sweats now under a nodding plume of swan feathers, and his face is no longer half hidden by an enormous bush of white horse hair." We are still not talking, however, about historical costume. Garrick played Macbeth in the uniform of a contemporary British general, and he caused a stir by coming onstage with one of the buttons of his waistcoat undone, to express the disorder of his mind. He afterwards claimed that this was an accident, and he did it up thereafter. But the fact that so trivial an incident should excite comment shows how hidebound the stage had become and how heavy a pall of tradition lay over most performances.

In one respect Garrick was a failure. He was not able to communicate his own concentration to some of his fellows. Other actors regularly stopped acting as soon as they stopped speaking, and Garrick's leading lady, Kitty Clive, used such pauses to acknowledge her friends in the stage boxes.

As manager, Garrick's innovations were less happy. In France an edict of 1760 had finally forbidden the seating of privileged spectators on the stage. In England the custom still persisted. Stands were erected on stage where the audience could sit, for a larger fee, of course, and one contemporary notes: "The battle of Bosworth Field [in *Richard III*] has often been fought in less space than that which is commonly allotted to a cock match." Even when the audience did not infiltrate onto the stage, it crowded the wings, interfering with the action. When Garrick was playing King Lear in Dublin and had reached the scene where Lear sleeps with his head in Cordelia's lap, a member of the audience walked out from the wings and threw his arms around the actress. Determined to eradicate this nuisance, Garrick urged that Drury Lane be enlarged to accommodate the same size of audience without impinging on the stage space, and this was done in 1762.

The expulsion of the audience from the stage provoked resentment. So did Garrick's attempt to eliminate a price concession. Theater bills then were long, usually including a five-act play plus several shorter pieces, and it had become the custom to allow the public in for half price after the third act of the main attraction. Garrick's abolition of this privilege provoked a major riot. One of the ringleaders stood up in a stage box and harangued the audience; Garrick, attempting to read his theater's balance sheet, was shouted down; and the crowd smashed benches and tore down chandeliers. It took four or five days to repair the damage, and the old prices had to be restored. Even the public darling was still very much at the public mercy.

Outside London Garrick was involved in the first celebration of what has now become an international event: the honoring of Shakespeare at his place of birth, Stratford-on-Avon. It took place in September 1769. Garrick was invited, among other luminaries, as the best living exponent of Shakespeare's work. The house in which Shakespeare had been born was decorated with transparencies showing a sun struggling through the clouds. An amphitheater was erected; there were speeches, tableaux, processions of Shakespearean characters in costume — everything, in fact, except the performance of a Shakespearean play. The event turned into a fiasco. Violent rain fell throughout, and the visitors were fleeced by the locals, who charged exorbitant prices for food and accommodation. Some of these comments still apply to the town that has now become the major center of Shakespearean performances in the world.

Garrick died in 1779. His career had given the theater a new dignity. He was buried in Westminster Abbey, England's most hallowed spot, under a monument to Shakespeare. His coffin was attended by a line of noble patrons and twenty-four of the principal actors of Drury Lane and Covent Garden.

Comedy Grows Robust: Richard Sheridan

In the later years of the eighteenth century two more bright spirits appeared to dispel the general blandness of the theatrical scene. One was Oliver Goldsmith, whose work is considered in detail in the Appendix. The other was Richard Brinsley Sheridan, playwright, politician, man-about-town, and Garrick's successor in the management of Drury Lane.

Sheridan was born in 1751 to a theatrical family; his father was Thomas Sheridan, who managed the Dublin theater that had once employed Garrick. Educated at one of England's best schools, he was despised as the son of a poor player, though his name is now preserved with pride in one of the school songs. A riotous youth culminated in his elopement with Elizabeth Linley, daughter of a celebrated musician, with whom he was later to collaborate in the theater. As poet, newspaper writer, and duelist, his name was constantly before the public.

In 1775 his first play, *The Rivals,* was produced at Covent Garden. It failed, but it was quickly rewritten and in its revised form won immediate success. Its failure was due to several reasons. It had a good cast, and Sheridan was able to write parts for actors whose individual strengths he already knew and who, in the manner of the time, had specialized in playing similar roles before. We are still talking of a theater where actors were typecast for most of their careers. But some of the cast were not trying. Shuter, who played the heavy father, was accused of not knowing his lines and attempting to fill the gaps with oaths and buffoonery. Lee, who played the comic Irishman, was pelted by the audience. Another problem was that the play was far too long — four hours — even in an age whose audiences had more stamina than our own. Finally, there is no doubt that the original script was too vulgar for refined taste.

Sheridan's attempts to bring some robustness back to comedy were hampered by the gentility of his times. One benefit of the Licensing Act of 1737 is that we have a copy of Sheridan's original script, submitted to the Lord Chamberlain for approval and preserved in the records. We can thus compare it with the revised version and see what changes were made. Most of the oaths and vulgarities were removed. Nothing was left that might offend a squeamish audience. And the play was considerably shortened; though it is usually cut still further in modern revival, it was no longer of abnormal length.

We are left, then, with a comedy in which Sheridan pokes fun at the sentimental fashion of his day. His heroine, Lydia Languish (another example of the English tradition of giving characters meaningful names), can love her suitor only when he presents himself to her as an impoverished army officer, not as the rich young gentleman he in fact is. Nourished on sentimental fiction, she cannot believe that love is real unless accompanied by suffering and hardship. In her guardian, Mrs. Malaprop, Sheridan created a character who has given a word to the English language — *malapropisms,* describing the grotesque deformings of the tongue to which she gives vent in the play. Here she is, in all her glory:

> Observe me, Sir Anthony, I would by no means wish a daughter of mine to be a progeny of learning. I don't think so much learning becomes a young woman; for instance, I would never let her meddle with Greek, or Hebrew, or algebra, or simony, or fluxions, or paradoxes, or such inflammatory branches of learning — neither would it be necessary for her to handle any of your mathematical, astronomical, diabolical instruments. — But, Sir Anthony, I would send her, at nine years old, to a boarding school, in order to learn a little ingenuity and artifice. Then, sir, she should have a supercilious knowledge in accounts; — and as she grew up, I would have her instructed in geometry, that she might know something of the contagious countries.

The Rivals was followed by *St. Patrick's Day,* a short piece Sheridan wrote for the actor Larry Clinch, to whom he was indebted for the ultimate success of his last work. Clinch was to celebrate his benefit, a cherished theater perquisite whereby an actor received the whole income, after expenses had been met, from one night's performance. Sheridan provided a piece that was designed to display Clinch's talents to the best advantage — and that, incidentally, reveals the qualities considered admirable in eighteenth-century acting. Its simple plot involves three distinct character impersonations for the leading actor, with rapid changes from one to another. The plays of this period were often designed to make the best of the contemporary acting style. The age was one that applauded rapidity of transitions and the versatility with which an actor could shift from one mood to another. Thus the comedies often allow the actor to demonstrate his versatility by successive impersonations within the role. In Goldsmith's *She Stoops to Conquer* the demure heroine, Kate Hardcastle, impersonates a barmaid. Young Absolute impersonates an army officer in *The Rivals,* and Sir Oliver Surface disguises himself first as moneylender, then as impoverished relative, in *The School for Scandal.*

Next came *The Critic,* Sheridan's equivalent of Buckingham's Restoration parody *The Rehearsal.* Like the earlier work, it is a spoof of the contemporary theater, taking the same format of a play within a play. In this case the work parodied is a historical drama, full of love, battle, and self-sacrifice, the sort of thing that audiences had been accustomed to seeing at Drury Lane and Covent Garden. In *The Critic* Sheridan shows how many of the conventions of neoclassical tragedy had lingered on to the point where they were ripe for parody. The love-duty conflict is reduced to absurdity. A Spanish prisoner, Don Fernando

(*above*) The library scene from
Sheridan's *School for Scandal*.
The bookshelves and vista are
simply painted on the rear
shutters, the stage is framed by
formal wingpieces, and
furniture is reduced to the bare
minimum. (*right*) The actor
grows in respectability.
Memorial to James Quin,
Garrick's former rival, with
epitaph by Garrick. Bath
Abbey, England.

Whiskerandos, is in love with the daughter of the governor who holds him captive. The daughter is thus placed in a burlesque of the position of virtually every heroine of heroic tragedy, and her father faces a similar dilemma — "The father softens, but the governor's resolved!" The daughter is provided with a confidante, who imitates every action of her mistress and even goes mad when she does — though in white muslin, as appropriate to her lower station, rather than in white satin, which was the daughter's dress. There is a duel, a totally irrelevant subplot, and a burlesque of the typical stage spectacle of the day in which all the effects go wrong; the play ends in complete disorder. *The Critic* is a parody of a kind of drama that was already in its death throes.

Sheridan's most enduring work was *The School for Scandal,* which opened at Drury Lane in 1777 and ran for a glorious twenty nights. It was played in the same theater three nights a week for several years, and it brought nearly twice as much to the box office as any play before it. Once again, Sheridan had the advantage of writing for a company he knew intimately. Several of his characterizations exploited the private personalities of the actors who played the roles, and, as usual, the company was cast in familiar and comfortable stereotypes. Much of the comedy is based on stock situations: the old man's problems with a young wife; the dissolute, though likable, young man who has run through all his money; the rich uncle from abroad who turns up, like a deus ex machina, in the nick of time to save the situation. The play defers to the tastes of its audience in its condemnation of vice and its ultimate championing of fidelity and virtue. But it has a wit and clarity that show how rapidly Sheridan had mastered the techniques of his art since *The Rivals,* while the vicious characters — the hypocritical brother who is a would-be seducer under the mask of virtue and the malicious gossips who give the play its title — are portrayed with a relish that equals the vigor and bite of Restoration comedy at its best.

Comparison shows, however, how much the world had changed. London was no longer the center of the universe, and Sheridan's characters embrace a broader social spectrum. In eighteenth-century comedy we are always conscious of a larger world outside the play; Restoration characters talk about each other. Both Goldsmith and Sheridan create a whole range of characters *outside* the play who are never seen but are talked about so vividly that they are almost as real as the characters before us.

The School for Scandal and *The Critic* were Sheridan's last considerable achievements in the theater. In spite of their box office success, Drury Lane continued to labor under financial difficulties, and Garrick, shortly before his death, lamented, "Poor old Drury, it will, I fear, soon be in the hands of the Philistines." Sheridan's versatile spirit, which could not be satisfied with any one activity for too long, sought a new outlet in politics. His play writing petered out in a translation of a tedious German drama, and while he was speaking in the Houses of Parliament in 1809, word was brought that Drury Lane had burnt down. Though it was soon rebuilt, Sheridan's interest in it had finished, and before long the reign of the patent theaters was itself to come to an end.

Eighteenth-Century Stage Design

Now is an appropriate moment to look at the way in which theater buildings had changed in the eighteenth century. The most marked feature of this period is the gradual disappearance of the apron stage. At Drury Lane the original deep apron with two pairs of proscenium doors on each side had been modified. The lower doors were transformed into stage boxes, the actors withdrew almost entirely inside the picture frame, and the audience was set at a greater distance from the action, establishing the deliberately artificial barrier identified as the fourth-wall convention. Drury Lane and Covent Garden, though still standing, have changed out of all recognition, but some provincial theaters in England still show eighteenth-century features. For example, the Theatre Royal, Bristol, still retains the main outlines of the original plans and even some of the original seating in its gallery.

For an eighteenth-century theater that has been reconstructed in entirety, we can look at the playhouse at Richmond, Yorkshire, which was built in 1788, fell into disuse in 1848, was used for various commercial purposes, and was triumphantly resurrected in 1963 to serve as a working reconstruction of the kind of theater for which Sheridan wrote. Its most remarkable feature, for the modern viewer, is its compactness. The whole building is barely sixty feet long, and its internal dimensions are equally divided between stage and auditorium. The theater has a pit with benches, two tiers of boxes running along each side, and an upper gallery.

Calculations from box office records show that, in its original operation, it must have seated some four hundred spectators. Less than half that number can be seated now. True, people in the eighteenth century tended to be shorter than they are today, but as contemporary cartoonists show, they were often fatter, and it seems almost incredible that such a mass of people could have been packed in without extreme discomfort. But an eighteenth- or even nineteenth-century audience did not ask for comfort. They were content to sit pressed close to their neighbors, happy as long as the play held their interest. When it failed to do so, content quickly vanished. It is easy to see how, in such circumstances, riots could erupt spontaneously and spread rapidly, with the destruction we have noted at Drury Lane.

The stage at Richmond shows that by the eighteenth century the apron has shrunk almost to extinction, with one proscenium door at each side. The main stage is slightly raked (sloping toward the audience) and provided with traps. Contemporary practice still preferred the shutter method for shifting scenes, with grooves set into the floor. and other provincial theaters retain vestiges of this. Lack of space at Richmond, however, probably favored the use of the painted drop scene, which in time would replace the shutters entirely. Stage and auditorium were still lit by candelabra, with the audience in light for the duration of the play. Gaslight, which first appeared in the London theaters in

1817, offered easier possibilities of control and of darkening the house while the stage remained lit. The Richmond Theatre was decorated in green, the traditional stage color, with the boxes in dark red. Actors note the intimacy of this theater. Although action is now largely pushed back behind the proscenium arch, actors playing downstage can reach out and shake hands with spectators in the adjacent boxes. It is easy to see why the stage "aside," lines delivered straight to the audience, survived as a stage convention for so long.

Contemporary illustrations from London and the provinces show us what stage settings were like and how much the stage picture, like the plays and the acting, had settled, for the most part, into dull routine. Up to about 1760 there was no question of creating specific designs for a particular play. Most theaters continued to use stock sets — palace, forest, garden, temple, prison — which were brought out when appropriate, or even sometimes when their appropriateness was hardly apparent. Each was composed on the same pattern, with a back scene (with shutters, as noted above, gradually replaced by drop cloths) and wing pieces moved by pulleys and winches, sliding in on grooves. For exteriors the wing pieces represented trees. For interiors the walls of the room were still conventionally indicated by parallel arrangements of wings. The box set, in which the walls of the room were realistically and solidly represented, enclosing the acting area rather than merely decorating it, was still in the future as a matter of general practice. We can look outside England to another restored theater, at Drottningholm, in Sweden, to see how mechanically elaborate such a theater could be. Here entire original sets have been preserved, and the complex arrangements of ropes and drums that have been reconstructed show that even in a tiny space the whole stage picture can change instantaneously.

Most theaters, however, had grown lazy. We see from pictures that companies tended to use whatever scene units were conveniently to hand, whether they were appropriate to the play or not. Critics were beginning to complain about incongruities: of sky borders used in what purported to be interior scenes, or of tree wings crowned with architecture. Stage carpenters often used any handy piece of scenery to fill gaps in the set. Changes, more often than not, were made in full sight of the audience by stagehands in their green theatrical livery or even in working clothes. Furniture, unless absolutely essential, was painted on the backdrop. A print of the original setting for *The School for Scandal* shows Joseph Surface's library, the key scene in the play, represented by the usual backdrop and wing arrangement with one chair, one screen, and a table and couch that have every appearance of being painted as part of the scenery.

Stage costuming was similarly uninventive. For most of the eighteenth century no attempt was made to achieve historical accuracy. Comedy, whatever its supposed period, was habitually dressed in the costume of the day. So was most tragedy. Occasional elements could be added to indicate special periods. Roman costume, for instance, was suggested by contemporary dress plus breastplate and helmet. We have a picture of Garrick in such costume, wearing the

The anatomy of an eighteenth century playhouse: the Theatre Royal, Bristol. (*above*) View from the rear of the pit toward the stage. Narrow aisles and cramped, uncomfortable benches. (*right*) Upper gallery, remnants of original seating.

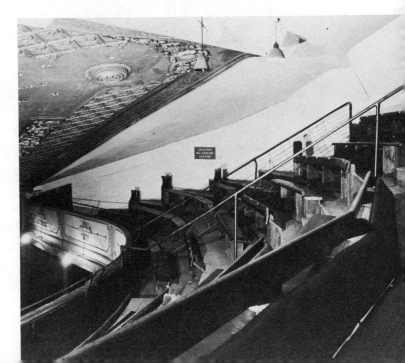

(*above*) Galleries, somewhat more comfortable than the pit, divided into loges. (*below*) Overhead machinery: shafts and drums for lowering cloud machines.

(*above*) Box book, charting patrons by name. This performance is a benefit, and some families have purchased whole blocks. (*right*) Eighteenth century scene change. The back scene, on painted shutters, slides apart in grooves on the stage; the sky pieces are lowered by winch and pulley; a liveried attendant shifts furniture on stage as the audience watches.

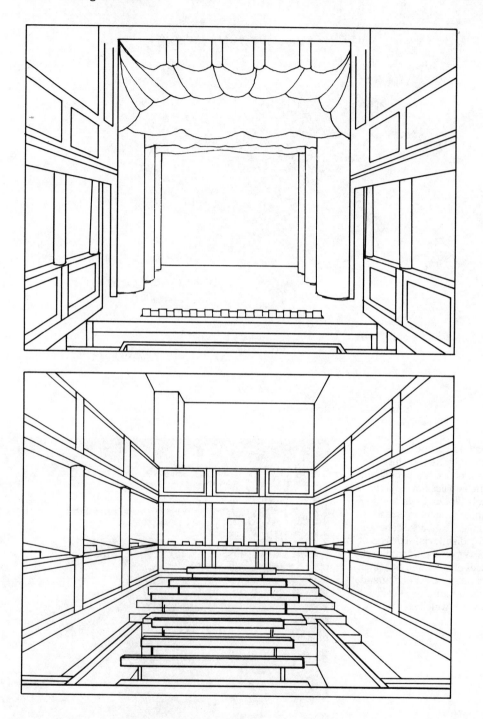

usual kneebreeches and stockings oddly juxtaposed with classical armor. Certain character types had developed their own traditional costumes. Orientals — the term was broadly interpreted — wore tight boots, breeches, a sash, a long coat rather like a dressing gown, and a high turban, usually augmented with plumes. Some Shakespearean characters had also acquired costumes of their own. An early eighteenth-century print of Falstaff shows him in Elizabethan ruff and cloak, with large floppy boots and, in defiance of contemporary fashion, wigless. His fellow actors, represented in the same scene, are dressed in the manner of the day.

Costuming for the actresses followed a similar line. Some women in Shakespeare wore distinctive costumes, but these were mainly the comic characters. And once again these costumes seem to have reflected a continuity of tradition in specific roles rather than any desire for period accuracy. In other parts actresses sought only to display themselves in the latest fashions. Thus the theater might present the curious spectacle of an actor playing Othello in "oriental" costume against a Desdemona in the latest mode, with the supporting cast in ordinary dress — or, even more alarming, a semi-Roman Antony with a contemporary Cleopatra. Again we see that the emphasis was still on the performers as individuals rather than on the unity of the stage picture. And the tradition has not entirely vanished from the modern theater. Programs may still note that a prominent leading lady is dressed not by the stage costumer but by a fashionable couturier. The latter part of the century saw individual attempts at historical accuracy. Macklin staged *Macbeth* in Scottish costume, and Garrick, though adhering for the most part to the conventional mode, presented an Old English *King Lear*. Any substantial change in costuming, however, had to wait until the 1820s.

(Facing page) The Georgian Theatre, Richmond, Yorkshire, 1788. (*top*) The stage end; (*bottom*) the audience end.

8
The Romantic Theater

Art and Politics

In Paris a *son et lumière* ("sound and light") spectacle is regularly given at the Cathedral of Nôtre Dame, which dominates the Île de la Cité in the middle of the Seine. Seated along the river bank, spectators see parts of the massive building picked out in light, as recorded voices describe its long construction and rich history. For most of the program the lighting effects are chaste and decorous; but as soon as the voices began to talk of Victor Hugo — the dominant figure of the French romantic movement, whose *The Hunchback of Nôtre Dame* has become inseparably bound up with the cathedral's legend — the whole structure is washed with red light, and fireworks flare into the evening sky. This is the effect that the romantic movement had on the arts generally and the theater in particular. It was an explosion, a revolt, a shock to the senses that broke decisively with the past and forced playwrights, actors, and audiences to look at the theater from new perspectives.

Edmund Kean.

315

Nor was it solely an artistic movement. The end of the eighteenth century was a period of violent change affecting both national governments and the life-style of the individual. Two major revolutions, in the American colonies in 1776 and in France in 1789, saw monarchical rule abolished in favor of a republican system. The political effect of these shattering changes was felt throughout Europe, though with less drastic consequences. England saw a revolution less obtrusive but no less insistent: the Industrial Revolution, which changed the face of the country and brought a new class of society into being.

Always a sensitive barometer of its times, the theater responded to these political and technological changes, evolving not merely new and appropriate subject matter for plays but new kinds of plays, marking as radical a break with the past as that between the French Republic and the hereditary Bourbon monarchy. It began to play, too, to a new kind of audience, different in its demands and larger in numbers — a change that, among other things, brought an end to the already moribund patent theater system in England. The theater also saw a critical revolution, changing the way in which the playwright was considered in relation to his work.

CHALLENGE TO AUTHORITY

We have seen the theater of the earlier eighteenth century as largely static, suffering from a torpor of complacency in which the inherited practices of the past were still cherished, more because of their venerability than because of any continuing merit. Against this background the efforts of individual innovators stand out, perhaps, more sharply than they would otherwise. To some extent, the theater had much in common with contemporary politics. In both areas, systems were preserved that had outlived their usefulness and that would crumble before any violent assault. In the revolutionary period, therefore, we see the same phenomena both off the stage and on and the same slogans and rallying cries being used interchangeably in politics and the arts. The age of the common man created a new kind of dramatic hero. A society that battled for liberty in its streets applauded similar sentiments from the stage; and in both spheres traditional authorities toppled before a new independence.

In the theater traditional authority was still represented by the doctrines of neoclassicism. These prescribed a kind of play that claimed its sanction from the ancients; whose structure could be analyzed in a rational, virtually mathematical way; and whose content, vocabulary, and delivery were regulated within limits that had become increasingly narrow, artificial, and restrictive.

To this authority the challenge of the American Declaration of Independence was directly applicable: "We hold these truths to be self-evident, that all men are created equal, that they are endowed by their Creator with certain unalienable Rights, that among these are Life, Liberty and the pursuit of Happiness." The first challenge that was taken up was the assumption of self-evident truths. It began to be argued, in the theater as in political life, that some things did not need to be proved, supported by authority, or rationally defended; they simply *were*. And one of these things was the dramatist's right of self-expression in any form that he saw fit.

Dramatically the movement began in Germany, with a marked breakaway from the doctrines of the French rationalists. At this time Germany was still an assemblage of independent kingdoms and duchies, united by a common language though not by a common political system. The romantic movement saw the beginnings of national unity in the arts, focusing on the Hamburg theater, which was founded in 1765 and became the German national theater two years later. Its first director was Gotthold Ephraim Lessing, whose series of essays on the art of the theater formulated the objections to the old school and gave the new movement a solid theoretical basis. Lessing advocated the primacy of inspiration in the creative artist. He should, he argued, be free to operate without the shackles of rules and conventions. "The one thing we can never forgive a tragic poet is coldness. If he arouses our interest, it does not matter what he does with the petty mechanical rules." It was not that Lessing believed *all* rules to be valueless. He held rather that they should not be considered universally valid and that each generation should feel free to formulate its own. Different ages must seek different patterns of dramaturgy. What was right for the Greeks in the fifth century B.C., or the French in the seventeenth century A.D., did not necessarily apply a hundred years later.

SHAKESPEARE RECONSIDERED

Lessing himself wrote plays, not so admirable as his theories, though still occasionally and reverentially revived in Germany. A spate of work shows how quickly the new drama, as advocated by Lessing, took hold and how playwrights had been chafing under the old restrictions. But here we find a paradox: that even a revolutionary age likes to dignify itself with illustrious examples from the past and to show that it is acting with noble precedent. Virtually every artistic movement, while loudly proclaiming the novelty of its aims, has also sought respectability by claiming distinguished antecedents; and this claim usually involves the resurrection of a long-dead name as the hitherto-unacknowledged hero of the new movement. (In exactly this way the French Revolution sought precedent from republican Rome, assuming its ideals and even its vocabulary, and comparing the overthrow of the Bourbons to the expulsion of the hated Roman kings.)

The model chosen by the romantics was, inevitably, Shakespeare, a dramatist of unquestioned eminence whose work had nevertheless been derided by the neoclassicists as sprawling, formless, and uncouth. But the qualities that urged the Restoration dramatists to rewrite Shakespeare's plays, and made Voltaire call him a barbarian, were precisely those that appealed to the new age. If Shakespeare wrote without considering the rules, this act was now a virtue. If he mingled tragedy and comedy in the same play, confusing the approved genres, this feature was now desirable precisely because the neoclassicists had *not* done it. If Shakespeare did not restrict himself to a courtly and decorous vocabulary, so much the better: the romantics wished only to sweep away all such clutter of their immediate past and return to an earlier freedom.

The exuberance of the theater as Shakespeare knew it therefore affects one romantic work after another. Some of the new plays clearly owe both their subject matter and their treatment to him; some are pastiches of the Shakespearean manner; but even those in which the influence is less obvious abandon the Racinian for the Shakespearean form, interweaving main plot and subplot, juxtaposing comedy and tragedy, and drawing on a broad spectrum of humanity rather than a narrow segment of it.

Romantic Drama in Germany

Much of the content of romantic drama is dictated by the spirit of contrariness. Anything the neoclassicists had not done now became the thing to do. In the older drama duty had ideally triumphed over desire, and the will of the individual was controlled by forces greater than himself. In the new drama the free will of the individual was paramount, and even when the individual was crushed by the system, it was now the system that was held to be at fault. Again we hear the echoes of the Declaration of Independence: life, liberty, and the pursuit of happiness were ideals voiced as loudly on the European stage as in the councils of Philadelphia. Inevitably these ideals were translated into a political context. The romantic hero tended to be a revolutionary, sometimes lowborn, sometimes an aristocrat forced into humble circumstances but pitting his virility and his liberated mind against the tyranny of the decadent political establishment.

GOETHE AND FAUST

In Germany Johann Wolfgang von Goethe (1749–1832) put Lessing's principles into practice. A man of omnivorous learning, he was known as a poet, scientist, and student of the occult arts — interests that manifested themselves in his best-known dramatic work. His enthusiasm for the theater led him into both play writing and the management of the Duke of Weimar's playhouse. In 1773 appeared his *Goetz von Berlichingen,* clearly modeled after Shakespeare, placed in a medieval setting and dealing with a revolutionary hero battling against the forces of oppression. In 1787 came *Egmont* — for which the German composer Beethoven wrote an overture — set in the Netherlands during the period of the Spanish Inquisition and showing the sufferings of a Catholic hero in opposition to others of his faith who imposed their beliefs too harshly.

Goethe's best-known work, *Faust,* appeared in two parts in 1808 and 1831.

It is of particular interest to us since its subject was already famous on the stage. Comparison with Marlowe's work shows how much of the Elizabethan spirit was absorbed by the romantics, but we can also find significant changes. Marlowe's *Doctor Faustus,* as noted earlier, was taken back to the country that had originally inspired it and was eventually reabsorbed in the German folk tradition as a puppet play, with Wagner, Faustus's assistant, replaced by Kasperl, a popular figure of low folk comedy. In the traditional puppet play, which is still performed, Kasperl has the last word. After Faustus has been taken down to hell, Kasperl enters the empty study and remarks, "What a terrible smell of sulphur!" It was when seeing this performance that Goethe was inspired to write his *Faust.*

Part one has two prologues. The first, rarely played, is set in the theater itself. Goethe comments humorously on the limitations of the stage as his generation knew it and the necessity for stretching these limits if he is to encompass the grand, cosmic design that he envisions. (One of the problems of *Faust* is that Goethe has stretched these limits a little too far. He admitted that in this play he was writing "against the theater rather than for it," and he makes demands of setting and action that, even with all the resources of modern technology, can only be shown with difficulty.)

The second prologue, which is the real prologue of the play, is set in heaven and is deliberately reminiscent of the techniques of the medieval mystery cycles, which may mislead us into thinking that this play is intended to be a Christian drama. It is not. God is shown among the archangels: Raphael, who speaks for the order of the cosmos; Gabriel, who represents the alternation of order and disorder; and Michael, who stands for storms and conflicts. From the beginning we are presented with the romantic conception of a universe governed not, as in classical thought, by a clearly defined and rational pattern, but rather by the tension of opposing forces. The tension is further illuminated by the argument between God and Mephistopheles, the polar opposition between good and evil, in which Mephistopheles is given permission to try to win Faust's soul. Faust thus becomes the representative of all humanity, and we are presented with a situation similar to the testing of Job in the Old Testament. (Archibald MacLeish, in his modern verse play *J. B.,* uses the same device, with God and the Devil represented as fairground barkers arguing over the Job figure, who is then put to the test in a circuslike environment.)

We then move, as in Marlowe's play, to Faust in his study. The scholar is shown protesting against the limitations of human knowledge. His impatience is contrasted with the smug acceptance of his disciple, Wagner. Oppressed with a sense of the futility of learning, Faust follows the romantic urge by seeking to identify himself with the essence of things, the very heart of nature, which does not need to be proved but simply is. Conjuring up the Earth-spirit, who represents this essential force, he is rejected by it; he has grown sterile, he is told, and has nothing in common with the eternal natural forces of growth and destruction. The scene moves to a more somber note. Faust toys with the notion that ultimate knowledge can only be found after death. He turns to thoughts of suicide and is about to take a phial of poison when he is interrupted by the Easter bells.

Once again we must beware of seeing Christian symbolism in a play that is dealing with other things. The bells, indeed, signify a resurrection, recalling Faust from his suicidal intentions. But it is not so much the Christian resurrection as the older, pagan concept of cyclical regeneration that lies behind the symbolism here.

Leaving his study, Faust moves outside the city gates and sees the crowd streaming, in response to the bells, out of the cramped and twisting streets, through the walls, and into the open countryside. Confinement gives way to a sense of liberation. The dark, labyrinthine alleys of the Middle Ages are touched by the sun of the Renaissance, and we are watching a tribute to people's quest for freedom rather than a celebration of Christ's victory over the tomb. Moved by this spirit, Faust longs to follow the call of nature, even beyond the setting sun, and he has his first glimpse of Mephistopheles, in the shape of a poodle dog.

Back in Faust's study Mephistopheles appears in human shape to make his bid for Faust's soul. Faust craves action. Man's purpose is to act: "In the beginning was the deed." Mephistopheles's destructive force is his championship of laziness, of inactivity. His aim is to lure Faust into that torpor of easily satisfied desire that will secure the destruction of his soul. There is talk of a bargain, supported by a chorus of sensual spirits. Mephistopheles leaves and almost immediately returns — perhaps an echo of his necessity in Marlowe's play to seek permission from Lucifer. Finally the bargain is sealed. What Faust asks for is a sense of challenge, the ability to try himself to the utmost. For him activity, the constant search, is the only good; to travel hopefully is better than to arrive. If Mephistopheles can satisfy this yearning, if he can quench this eternal striving of the human spirit, he will have won, and the following scenes show his successive attempts to achieve this goal.

Thus though the physical action recalls Marlowe's, the spiritual action moves in the reverse direction. In Marlowe's play Faustus committed his great sin, the intellectual sin of pride, first, and then he succumbed with increasing ease to the grosser and more carnal sins, ending with the sin of lechery. He sank from high aspirations to base. In Goethe's version we see the opposite. Mephistopheles begins by offering base temptations, in the hope that each in turn will satisfy Faust, but none of them does.

We begin with a scene in Auerbach's cellar, where Faust is offered the triviality and banality of a life that is concerned only with easily acquired creature comforts. He contemptuously rejects this life. Next he is offered the pleasures of sex. He is taken to the Witch's Kitchen to be transformed into a youth again. This scene is rich in symbolic references to the Reign of Terror that had followed hard on France's recent Revolution and that the rest of Europe had observed with horrified fascination. The breaking of a glass sphere and a crown signify the end of monarchy and order. Destruction is rampant. Faust, like civilization, must descend into chaos if he is to be reborn.

The rejuvenated Faust is offered Margaret, or Gretchen, a young girl who falls in love with him and is seduced by him. She stands as the prototypical heroine of this new kind of drama, in many ways Faust's counterpart, though on a more mundane level. Recall that the neoclassical drama, in its endless variations on the theme of duty versus desire, had come down firmly on the side of duty. To yield to love, in defiance of order and social propriety, could only bring disaster. For example, in the plays of Racine, which we considered in Chapter 6, Phèdre yields to her passion against the voice of conscience, destroys herself, and brings down others in her fall. Nero, lusting after a girl who is promised to his rival, transforms himself from a conscientious ruler into a tyrant. Romanticism takes the contrary view. If the call of the emotions is strong enough, they must be yielded to in defiance of all order and reason. Love is its own justification. So, like Faust, Margaret is a rebel. She sins, but with a grand and justifiable passion.

What is sufficient for her, however, does not satisfy her lover. He seduces her and moves on. Mephistopheles still has not won, though, for Faust has not yet found the total satisfaction that he craves. He is led into a witches' Sabbath, a Walpurgis Night that exemplifies the wild and restless cravings of his nature, and Margaret, though punished by the laws of men, is ultimately redeemed because of her selflessness. A girl who has given all in response to the dictates of nature cannot, in romantic eyes, be censured.

We may consider part one as a play complete in itself. Part two, which did not follow until years later, takes Faust into the realm of metaphysics. He wanders through Greece, meets Helen of Troy, and has a child, Euphorion, by her; he finally achieves his moment of total satisfaction but only by self-sacrifice, by devoting himself altruistically to the cause of others. So Mephistopheles has won — but really lost. Faust is still the master of his soul and has not allowed it to be trapped by enchantments.

Significantly, part two is only rarely performed and then, usually, as a dramatic reading. The scenic problems it creates are virtually insoluble. We may look at part one, however, for what it tells us about the essential features of romanticism — its splendors and longueurs, its merits and pitfalls, its flamboyant theatricality on the one hand and its challenge to theatrical practicality on the other.

Some characteristics will be obvious from what has already been said. We note, first, the hero as revolutionary — not, this time, in the political sense but as a rebel against traditional assumptions about life and against stale casts of thought. The image of the romantic hero, standing alone with all the world against him, moving to the beat of a different drummer with his eyes fixed on his own star, is always a powerful one in the theater. In minor key Margaret is no less a rebel, and her rebellion is ultimately justified. Faust, too, is vindicated at the end. Marlowe's protagonist was crushed, but Goethe's triumphantly survives. Second, we see the primacy of emotion over reason. What Faust is rebelling *against* is the world as it has been shaped and defined by people's minds; both he and Margaret respond to the calls upon them with instinct rather than with reason. Third, we see romanticism as a hymn of praise to the human spirit, to man's indomitable will and apparently ceaseless victories over both the traditional idea of divinity and the forces of the world in which he lives. We must remember that this age was not merely the one in which Mary Shelley wrote *Frankenstein,* testifying to our ability to create life; it was also the period of the invention of the steam engine, the puffing locomotive, which could be glorified by romantic painters as our triumph over a phenomenon of nature.

We notice, also, that the romantic drama tends to concentrate on periods of history different from those that had attracted writers in the past. Neoclassical writers turned to classical subjects, matter drawn from Greek and Roman history, or at least from periods in which the classical ideals were still manifest. Romantic drama looks more to the Middle Ages, a period about which little was yet known with any historical accuracy. Documents that would show the time to be one of political oppression and economic deprivation had still to be researched and annotated. People thought of the Middle Ages not as a time of incredible drabness and monotony, varied only by the appearance of death in its uglier forms, but as a kind of fairy-tale world, populated by knights in armor and forlorn but beautiful maidens, a picturesque world resounding to heroic deeds. This concept allowed the dramatists' imaginations to wander over unfamiliar territory; in addition, it provided another slap in the faces of the classicists, by treating a milieu they thought unworthy of their notice.

In form *Faust* is, like so many romantic plays, Shakespearean in the sense that it is diversified rather than contained. The action wanders from heaven to hell, study to tavern, city street to cottage, and the cast embraces everyone from the Almighty and his diabolical antagonist to village churls and gossiping old women.

What, then, are the failings? The most conspicuous problem of *Faust* is its length. In abandoning the other classical principles, the romantics had also abandoned the cardinal virtue of economy. If classical form was overthrown, there was no longer any need to restrict oneself within the compact five-act structure. If the artist was now free to indulge his inspiration without reference to the rules, there was no need for this inspiration to be confined within a given number of acts, or scenes, or lines — no reason for the play to stop at all until the inspiration gave out. Romantic plays therefore tend to be enormously long, and they are revivable for modern tastes only at the cost of brutal cutting. We are constantly reminded, in considering these works, of how much the romantics liked sheer quantity — of energy, of incident, of characters, of scenes, of lines spoken, of output in the artist. Restraint was cast aside. Lessing's dictum that every age needs *some* rules was forgotten in the enthusiasm to throw the old rules out. In the other arts we see the same phenomenon. Painting cultivates the huge canvas, blazing with color, filled with contrast, crammed with incident. Music looks for size and sensation: Berlioz, writing a piece for a giant orchestra with four conductors, does for the symphony hall what Goethe was trying to do for the stage.

THE PROBLEMS OF STAGING

The question of the scale of the enterprise brings about problems of staging. The romantic playwrights were so concerned with novelty, with reviving the stage by showing on it things that had never been seen before, that they were sometimes carried away by their own enthusiasm and failed to ask whether what they wanted to portray was feasible. Thus in *Faust* there is the problem of the poodle dog, who, if he is represented at all, has to move on cue; there is a short sequence involving a cabalistic sign above Faust's study door, which has to be gnawed by rats; there are the complex logistics of the witches' Sabbath scene.

The problem of staging was perhaps most acute in England. Here several romantic poets of unquestioned excellence turned their hands to the stage — Wordsworth, Keats, Shelley, Byron — but with notable lack of success. Their failure was largely due to their inability to accommodate themselves to the practical limitations of stagecraft. Although Byron's dramas, set amid Renaissance flamboyance or in periods previously considered outlandishly unworthy of dramatic attention, contained many fine passages and many powerful scenes, the word in the theater was that "Byron spells bankruptcy." His works were not only exorbitantly expensive to stage but, in the end, too dramatically unwieldy to hold the attention of audiences.

This problem is also the basic one of *Faust.* It could be easily produced in a theater that, like some of the earlier forms we have studied, relied on suggestion rather than presentation. Significantly, *Faust* has been most successfully revived in the modern theater in productions using imaginative, fluid settings created by lighting that can be controlled with an exactitude impossible in Goethe's time, and even Byron has been successfully revived in the twentieth century in pared-down versions using projected, rather than painted, sets. But in a theater that relied on paint and canvas, some of the playwrights' demands were impossible.

The scenic aspect of the stage was shaken out of its torpor by the demands now placed on it, and the surge of new material acted as a catalyst in promoting change. One simple but important difference between neoclassical and romantic drama is in where the action takes place. In the former it is usually indoors, within the conventional "walls" of the virtually obligatory palace room. In the latter much more action happens outdoors. Once man is shown as responsive to the forces not of society but of nature, it becomes desirable to show him in a natural environment and to display him as at one with the mountains, the seas, and the forests.

Thus romantic drama cultivates exteriors, and designers developed new ways of portraying them. While interiors still clung to the traditional backdrop-and-wing format, exterior designs moved toward a greater realism, which manifested itself in the use of three-dimensional forms rather than pictures painted on flats. And they became more elaborate. Instead of one drop, or a pair of shutters decorated with a vista, audiences now saw the stage space broken up into several planes with cut pieces and ground rows.

Once scenery had grown so elaborate, there was more need to hide the changes from the audience. The act drop came into greater use, and plays showed a growing tendency to alternate between painted drop scenes and elaborately built scenes behind them — a tendency particularly marked in Shakespearean production and reinforced by contemporary scholarly theories about the alternation between the main stage and the "inner below" (see p. 170).

A similar effect occurred with costuming. The departure from the conventional classical mode and the exploration of new periods of dramatic interest encouraged greater historical accuracy. Costumers began to feel that the dress should evoke the period and convey the excitement of the gaudy ages about which the dramatists preferred to write. This valuable reform communicated itself to other plays as well. The habit of playing Shakespeare in modern dress was gradually abandoned. In 1823 London saw a production of *King John* set and costumed after careful historical research and the consultation of authentic medieval documents.

THE PLAYS OF SCHILLER

Though *Faust* remains unique, Goethe's more worldly themes were echoed by another German, Johann Christoph Friedrich von Schiller (1759–1805), whose early life resembles the script for a romantic play. A deserter from the army, he lived under an assumed name, making his living as a court playwright and stage manager in the city of Mannheim. His first works are typical of his time.

Die Raüber (The Robbers), written in 1781, had as its hero one Karl von Moor, a type of German Robin Hood who flees to the forest to escape tyranny and becomes the captain of a band of outlaws. In its setting and characters *Die Raüber* is reminiscent of *As You Like It*. Karl is contrasted with his brother Franz, and the openness and sincerity of woodland life with the coldness and artificiality of the town. Schiller used the play to vent some of the dissatisfactions of his private life, and its implicit revolutionary sentiment made it an instantaneous European success. In 1784 came *Kabale und Liebe (Love and Conspiracy)*; this play has an urban setting, but it is no less revolutionary in its exposure of social inequity. The heroine Louise is the daughter of a town musician, one of the people; she loves and is loved by Major Ferdinand, the son of the aristocratic President von Walther. This nobleman is too proud to countenance the match, and as a result of his scheming both Ferdinand and Louise die.

Both these plays were prose works. For *Don Carlos* (1787) Schiller turned to verse, writing a tragedy of love and politics set in Spain during the despotic reign of Philip II. Philip's son, Don Carlos, is opposed to his father's policies and is in love with his young stepmother. Again the influence of Shakespeare is unmistakable. Don Carlos emerges as a character with much of Hamlet in him, given to brooding and introspection. He has his Horatio in the person of the Marquis de Posa, a devoted friend who eventually sacrifices his own life in an attempt to save Don Carlos. The sacrifice is in vain, and Philip hands over his son to the power of the Spanish Inquisition. But at least his conscience has been aroused, and there is some hope for his reign and for the country.

Perhaps Schiller's most interesting play, and certainly the one most often seen today, is *Maria Stuart* (1800), a drama about the life and death of the ill-fated Queen of Scots. Its fascination lies not so much in the fact that it is romantic but that so much of it is not; it represents a kind of watershed of dramatic theory, in which the playwright is torn between the old school and the new. The historical subject is a famous one, the conflict between Elizabeth, the Protestant Queen of England, and her Catholic first cousin, Mary, whom some held to have a prior claim to the throne.

English dramatists have traditionally idealized Elizabeth and underrated Mary. A European, however, was under no such obligation, and Mary's personal history was a gift to any romantic dramatist. She had an unhappy marriage and equally unhappy love affairs; she was suspected of complicity in the murder of her husband; and, above all, she was a persecuted princess, sent at last to the block by her powerful rival. It is typical of romantic drama that historical facts are treated with great freedom. Thus Schiller chooses to idealize Mary as others have Elizabeth. She is represented as a beautiful woman, still capable of inspiring passion. In fact, the Mary who went to execution was old before her time and completely bald. Schiller provides her with an admirer, an invented character, a young man deeply in love with her who tries to save her. And in one scene, which has been unfairly criticized for falsifying history, he brings the two queens face to face; in real life they never met. The irreconcilable split between them, in the play, turns out to be not one of politics but of personalities. Mary commits the unforgivable insult of calling Elizabeth a bastard. Thus the romantic Mary, the creature of impulse and passion, is contrasted with the cold, calculating, tyrannical Elizabeth, and it is obvious where our sympathies are supposed to lie.

To this extent, then, *Maria Stuart* is a romantic play. It deals with strong personalities and a highly charged emotional situation. Its action is diverse, moving from England to Scotland, from palace to prison. It treats of cruelty, passion, near escapes, and death.

In what sense is it still classical? Notably in its structure, which shows a symmetry scarcely less perfect than what we find in Racine. The focal point is

Act Three, where the two queens are brought face to face. Round this the other acts are balanced in subject matter. Act One is Mary; Act Two, Elizabeth; Act Four is virtually all Elizabeth; Act Five, virtually all Mary.

Other parallelisms occur within this main structure. Mary's life full of love is matched against Elizabeth's cold chastity. The plot devised by Mortimer, the young man in love with Mary, to save her life in Act Two is balanced by his suicide in Act Four. Mary's redemption by love, which exonerates the follies of the past, is contrasted with Elizabeth's characterization as a tyrant, in a manner parallel with the ending of *Britannicus*.

In language, too, the play tends to cling to the manners of the past. The diction sustains a high tragic style; dialogue is written in stichomythic pattern; the characters exclaim and ask rhetorical questions much in the French manner. This question of verse and language, and whether older styles could still serve the newer drama, was an important one and would become one of the critical issues of the romantic drama in France.

The Romantic Movement in France

It was, of course, in France that the battle between classic and romantic was fought with the greatest bitterness and intensity. In Germany the assimilation of new ideas had been painless. There had, after all, been no sustained classical tradition to combat against, and the theater profited from the movement toward German unity that applauded plays of political fervor and wished to see its own folk heroes dramatized. France was another matter. It was the home of Racine and Corneille, now enshrined at the Comédie Française. It was a country, moreover, that has always been prone to set up rules and standards for language and literature and been reluctant to see those rules broken — a country where the Académie Française enjoyed hardly less prestige than the writers whose work they blessed with official approval.

EFFECTS OF THE REVOLUTION

The shock of the French Revolution, however, had affected the arts, including the theater, as it had all other things. In this period of violence the old measured formality of the tragic stage could not escape disturbance. For a while the very existence of the National Theater, as a monarchically subsidized institution, was threatened, and the mobs, given a new and louder voice, preferred the enormous patriotic pageants celebrating the return of liberty and justice that were offered to them in the squares and public places.

The new Republic was alive to the value of spectacle and theater for political purposes, in obvious and less obvious ways. Much has been written on the emotional theatrical appeal of Napoleon for the public, the dramatic nature of his ceremonies and oratory, and, almost to the end, his unerring choice of costume. Napoleon (who governed France from 1804 to 1815) took lessons in movement from one of the leading tragedians of the day, a fact that did not fail to be remarked upon by British caricaturists.

After a brief hiatus, however, the Comédie Française was allowed to resume operation, though under a new name, the Théâtre de la République, and under severe restrictions. Any suspicion of performing politically unsound material was instantly punishable. Plays from the old regime that remained in the repertory had their texts changed to conform with the new times. Tragedy had typically dealt with kings and princes; now these were personae non gratae. Honorific titles were anathema; characters who had once addressed each other as *seigneur* now used the democratic *citoyen*.

Napoleon's defeat at Waterloo in 1815, and the restoration of the Bourbon monarchy, ostensibly also restored the status quo. But the French theater, like French society, had suffered too great a shock ever to be the same again. Just as French politics, for most of the next century, showed the revolutionary force still sputtering on and compelling the country to vacillate between republic and monarchy, so the French theater became a battlefield between the old style of drama and the new, a battle all the more bitter when the rival critical schools began to be identified with political issues. Louis XVIII, who was restored to the French throne in 1815, was noble but ineffectual, noted mainly for his corpulence; he had spent the years of the Reign of Terror and the First Empire walking his dog in the London parks. With his return, France welcomed with relief a respite from the series of crises through which they had passed since the Revolution. He presided, however, over a divided society. On the one side were the returning émigrés, seeking, for the most part unsuccessfully, to take up where they had left off; on the other were the partisans of the Empire. Both sides felt themselves humiliated by recent events. It was an age in which social standards were in the melting pot and party differentiations shifting and nebulous.

THE AUDIENCE

The greatest change, perhaps, in the French theater was in the nature of the audience. Those who had survived in Paris through the bloodbath of the Revolution, the coronation of Napoleon as emperor, and the glory of the foreign conquests that followed knew that they were witnesses of history in the making. Each day brought some new excitement. Public and private life had been transformed from dull routine to a succession of vivid, emotion-fraught incidents provoking fervent cheers or cries of terror.

The arts responded to this quickening pace. In painting the quiet genre pieces, the carefully composed classical groups, the mist-wrapped, nostalgic vistas were replaced by paintings of action recording the stirring succession of daily events. The painter David, who stage-managed the coronation of Napoleon, recorded on huge canvases the great moments of the emperor's life — and there were many of them. Napoleon's titanic personality was a living embodiment of the romantic dream. His defeat and death did not end the vision (in French popular prints Napoleon was canonized as a saint), and even after the Bourbon restoration there were still loud voices urging that France abandon the lumber of its traditional drama, as it had purged itself of its hereditary government. In such a climate anything that was new and exotic found adherents, and at least as far as French audiences were concerned, what was new and exotic was Shakespeare.

SHAKESPEARE: THE MODEL

In France up to this date Shakespeare had had little opportunity to be appreciated. Few had read him. In performance he had appeared only in mutilated versions, adapted, as in the English Restoration, to conform to classical taste. In the eighteenth century Voltaire, though sensitive to Shakespeare's virtues, still regretted his untidiness.

Shortly before the Revolution a minor dramatist named Ducis had made several adaptations for the Paris stage, adaptations that show how wide the gap in taste had grown. He wrote a greatly altered *Macbeth* and, in 1783, a *King Lear* in which Lear was not allowed to go mad, for contemporary censorship forbade that a monarch should descend to such impropriety. In 1792 came an *Othello* in which the protagonist was not represented as black, for fear that this would offend the audience, and in which Iago, Shakespeare's arch villain, was relegated to a minor role at the end of the play.

Then came Henri Beyle, writing under the name of Stendhal (1783–1842), now forever associated with the French romantic novel. In 1824 he published *Racine and Shakespeare,* the very title of which was a challenge and the substance of which contained a greater challenge — the argument that Shakespeare might be a more appropriate model for the drama of the new age than the neoclassicists whom every French person had been brought up to revere.

Read now, *Racine and Shakespeare* seems mild. Much of it is written in the form of a dialogue between a classicist and a romantic. Stendhal is careful not to deny the genius of Racine. He argues simply that his kind of drama has been superseded. "Is Caesar any less great a general because, since his campaigns against our ancestors in Gaul, the world has discovered gunpowder?" If Racine were alive today, he asserts, he would still follow rules but new ones; and it is ridiculous to expect drama still to pattern itself after models from a period of society whose language, manners, and ideals are now totally outmoded and completely foreign to us. He defines the romantic approach as that which deals with the contemporary pattern of life. "Romanticism is the art of presenting to the public literary works which in the context of contemporary customs and beliefs, are capable of affording the greatest possible enjoyment. Classicism, on the contrary, presents them with the literature which gave the greatest possible pleasure to their great-grandfathers." In this sense Stendhal argues that Soph-ocles and Euripides were, in their own time, romantics. They worked in the context of their age. But to imitate them after such a gap of years, and to claim that these imitations do not make nineteenth-century Frenchmen yawn, is classicism. For a stirring age, Shakespeare is the better model.

VICTOR HUGO

Hard on Stendhal's heels came another giant of the French romantic move-ment and, like Stendhal, better known now for his novels, Victor Hugo. Born in 1802 and looking back at a Napoleon he had never been able to know through clouds of glory, Hugo remained a confirmed Republican all his life — a fact that was to cause him no little trouble in the shift of French politics. He admired Napoleon as a champion of liberty and oppression; he was even able to tolerate his coronation as emperor on the grounds that the power gained by military conquest could be used to broaden the social revolution.

Like so many of his generation, Hugo saw the artistic and political reforma-tion as one. In the preface to *Hernani* (1830), his most notorious play, he announces: "This loud and powerful voice of the people, likened to the voice of God, declares that henceforth poetry shall bear the same motto as politics: TOLERATION AND LIBERTY." But before *Hernani,* whose explosive debut we shall consider later, came another play, *Cromwell* (1827), about the deposer of the English monarchy. And though *Cromwell,* a work of enormous length, was not performed but only read, it had a preface that stands as one of the prime documents of the romantic movement.

The preface to *Cromwell* is not so much a tract as a speech, delivered by a young man who has not yet learned when to stop. Going back before the dawn of civilization, it traces the various functions poetry has assumed in society, and its first salient point is that the drama of the Greeks chose not to represent the whole of life but only selected elements from it. "The purely epic muse of the ancients studied nature only in one aspect, mercilessly rejecting nearly every-thing in art which . . . did not relate to a certain type of beauty." To this selective paganism Hugo contrasts the broader scope of Christian art. "Chris-tianity unites poetry and truth. And, like Christianity, the modern muse will see things in broader perspective. She will perceive that not everything in creation is, in human terms, beautiful; that the ugly exists side by side with the beautiful, the deformed next to the graceful, the grotesque as the counter-part of the sublime, the evil with the good, the dark with the light." It is not the duty of art to correct God but to take life as it is, in all its fascinating variety.

Hugo uses the word *grotesque,* which becomes the key to his critical vocabu-lary. It expresses for him not necessarily the deformed, the twisted, the out-of-true, but rather the sharpness of contrast and richness of detail characteristic of the Gothic art in which heaven, hell, and purgatory shared the same friezes and in which saints and devils stood side by side; the art in which, though every-thing contributed to the general effect, each element was interesting and wor-thy of attention in itself. This attitude leads him naturally to the championship of Shakespeare: "Shakespeare *is* the drama; and the drama, which in the same breath embraces the grotesque and the sublime, terror and farce, tragedy and comedy, is the true character of the third age of poetry, the literature of today."

On this assumption Hugo goes on to attack the neoclassical posture as illogical, artificial, and stultifying. "We see how the arbitrary distinction be-tween genres crumbles rapidly before logic and taste." The comic grave diggers do not detract from the horror of *Hamlet.* Rather, they increase it. And the basic fault of neoclassical tragedy is that it has eliminated so much from the stage presentation that hardly anything is left to happen; everything that is really dramatic takes place offstage. "Instead of scenes we have recitations; instead of the striking stage picture, descriptions. Solemn characters inter-posed, in the manner of the ancient chorus, between the drama and ourselves come to report to us what is going on in the temple, the palace, the public squares, in such a way that we are often tempted to shout back at them: 'Really! Then why don't you take us along? We could surely have a good time there. It must be very agreeable to see!' To which they would no doubt reply: 'It might very well amuse or intrigue you, but that's not the point. We are the guardians of the Tragic Muse in France.' "

By being so restrictive, Hugo argues, the neoclassical drama falsifies the sense of life and bustling reality of the Greek drama. He points to a series of exciting, even lurid incidents in Greek tragedy that have no counterpart in their French imitations, and he draws up an indictment of the Three Unities, which he holds particularly responsible. Reality of place is for him an essential component of an exciting theater: "Characters, whether speaking or in action, are not the only ones who engrave on the spectator's mind a faithful image of the facts. The location where such a catastrophe has occurred becomes a terri-fying witness to it that we cannot do without." As for time: "The action forcibly compressed within twenty-four hours is as ridiculous as an action compressed within the lobby. Every action has its proper length, just as it has its own particular place." In any case, the Unity of time is illogical, since stage time does not equal real time: "and if twenty-four hours can be compressed in two, it would be logical for four hours to contain forty-eight." Against the Unity of action he claims that generations of critics have willfully misunder-stood what unity really means. "Besides, let us avoid confusing unity of action with simplicity. You can have a unity of the whole, without in any way rejecting subplots on which the principal action rests. It is merely necessary that the parts should be intelligently subordinated to the whole, never failing to bear on the central action . . . the unity of the whole is the law of theatrical perspective."

Corneille and Racine, Hugo points out, had not been confined by the rules.

Why should later generations be constricted by them? "Let us take a hammer to theories, poetics and systems. Let us tear down this outmoded stucco which masks the true face of art. There are no rules. There are no models. Or rather, there are no rules but the general laws of nature and those special laws which, for each work of art, result from the conditions appropriate to the subject at hand."

Cromwell, as we have seen, was not performed. But the spirit of its preface was abroad in the land. Shakespeare, the new god, was suddenly becoming available in France after centuries of neglect and misunderstanding. New translations made his works available to the reading public. And at about the same time English actors played Shakespeare in Paris. In 1829 Alfred de Vigny's French *Othello* saw the stage, the first faithful translation that audiences had been offered. So strong was the classical legacy that the word *mouchoir,* "handkerchief," was hissed, for the same reason that Restoration critics had sought to expunge it — because it was a vulgar word and unworthy of the dignity of the tragic stage.

ALEXANDRE DUMAS

In 1829 another young man made his romantic debut, Alexandre Dumas *père* (1802–1870), son of one of Napoleon's generals, later to reveal himself as a writer of prodigious industry and a man whose life-style was as tempestuous and emotional as the characters he portrayed. His play *Henry III and His Court* has the distinction of being the first fully fledged romantic drama in France. In it the seventeen-year-old author revealed the same flamboyance and inventiveness in melodramatic incident that he would later show in *The Three Musketeers* and *The Count of Monte Cristo.* Set in the Middle Ages, it dealt with courtly and marital intrigue during one of the more sensational periods of French history. It played for thirty-eight performances to good houses, in spite of the opposition of the classicists, and the publication rights were bought for the large sum of 6,000 francs.

Officialdom was alarmed, and the play was threatened with censorship on the grounds that it was a thinly disguised portrait of the present monarchy, but the duc d'Orléans himself came to Dumas's aid and convinced the government that its fears were ridiculous. Some of Dumas's warmest supporters were the actors and actresses of the Comédie Française, particularly Mlle Mars, its reigning queen, who realized what splendid parts the author was giving them.

Dumas went on to write other sensational successes, notably *The Tower of Nesle,* another medieval melodrama based on the bizarre career of Queen Margaret of Burgundy and her two sisters. Historical tradition credited them with nocturnal orgies on the morning after which the bodies of the young men forced to be their lovers were found floating in the Seine. Dumas's play deals with one youth who fortuitously escaped, lived to blackmail the Queen, and became her partner in crime and chief minister until their evil careers were cut short by the law.

HUGO'S HERNANI

The cause célèbre of romanticism, however, was not one of Dumas's plays but one of Hugo's, *Hernani,* which opened, and rapidly closed, at the Comédie Française in 1830. Set in sixteenth-century Spain, it tells of a young outlaw, handsome and brave, who opposes the claims of natural rights to inherited power. He is matched against Don Carlos, King of Spain, who is his rival in love as well as politics. Beneath the enmity, however, there is a genuine respect for each other's fine qualities, which makes them hesitate to take unfair advantage. Hernani will kill Don Carlos in a duel but in no other way. Eventually, lured to his death by other enemies, Hernani takes poison.

Hernani is a long play, packed with sensational melodramatic incidents — duels, concealments, forced marriage, attempted assassination. Its length and flamboyance alone were enough to alienate classically minded audiences already alerted by the *Cromwell* preface. Hugo, however, missed no chance to give offense. Though he is writing during the reign of the monarchy, his republicanism is blatant. The play pours scorn on conventional honors. One of the running jokes concerns a Spanish nobleman, a minor character, who ascends to higher and higher degrees of nobility through a series of pure accidents. The monarchy itself is represented as sinister and corrupt.

A good deal of Hugo himself also is revealed in this play. He has his own personal demon to wrestle with — his feeling of bewilderment and betrayal that his idolized Napoleon should have been so false to democratic principles as to have himself made emperor. The central act of *Hernani* tries to rationalize this action. Don Carlos has the opportunity to follow in the footsteps of Charlemagne, as Holy Roman emperor. And in one enormous monologue, set in a crypt, he communes with the spirit of the past, finally accepting the call to an imperial destiny as something that represents the voice of the ages and far transcends the petty rivalries of ordinary power struggles. So Don Carlos and Napoleon are redeemed.

Of many riotous opening nights in the history of the theater, that of *Hernani* remains one of the most famous. Before the curtain rose, the audience was already divided. The classicists had come determined to boo, the romantics — many dressed in deliberately outrageous clothing, as an additional offense — to cheer. It took only one line to start the riot — for, as another example of his revolutionary fervor, Hugo had dared to tamper with the structure of the sacred Alexandrine, cramming extra syllables into it. For much of the evening the noise in the auditorium was so great that the actors could not be heard. But some things penetrated, particularly those lines where the author's political sympathies seemed to be revealed. Hernani's ironic *"Oui, de ta suite, de ta suite, o roi, j'en suis"* ("Yes, follow you, my king! I'll surely follow you!") raised a howl from monarchists and antimonarchists alike.

But after its tumultuous opening, *Hernani* vanished from sight. It was too touchy a play to be revived in the troubled years that followed. The shock of the first night had become legendary, however. During the Paris Exposition of 1867, it was at last offered again. Its author, now no longer a brash young man but middle-aged and more circumspect, had taken care to remove all the lines that had given such offense in 1830 and to replace them with more innocuous sentiments. With one voice the audience chanted the originals.

It is hard for us now to reconstruct the impact of that first evening and to realize how an altered Alexandrine could have caused an artistic and social turmoil no less than that brought about, in our time, by the first exhibition of full frontal nudity on the stage. Yet for a theater that had grown stale, the shock was tremendous, and the romantics truly believed that the seriousness of the disease merited a drastic cure.

LEGACIES

Theatrical sensations, however, tend to be short-lived. The romantic movement, though it had adherents in other countries and spawned innumerable lesser melodramas, created no new theatrical epoch. Although Hugo's likeness eventually joined the paintings of Racine, Corneille, and Molière on the ceiling of the Comédie Française, he did not supplant them, and there have been many more subsequent revivals of *Phèdre* and *Le Cid* than of *Hernani*.

The most obvious legacy of the romantic drama has been in opera, and it is noticeable that, of the nineteenth-century works that still hold the musical stage, many are based on romantic plays. Works of strong situations and bold, uncomplicated emotions clearly lent themselves to the operatic form, while scenes of stage spectacle could be adapted for the chorus and the corps de ballet. Thus Goethe's *Faust* inspired Gounod's opera of the same name, which is, for all the popularity of its music, essentially a trivialization of the work, with the metaphysics vanishing, the love plot between Faust and Margaret, renamed Marguerite, made dominant, and the witches' Sabbath set to waltz time. From Schiller's *Kabale und Liebe* Verdi drew his *Luisa Miller;* from *Hernani,* an opera of the same name; and from another play by Hugo, *le Roi s'amuse (The King Takes His Pleasure),* one of the mainstays of the opera repertory, *Rigoletto.* (One might note that Verdi was also setting Shakespeare to music with *Macbeth, Otello,* and *Falstaff,* while Berlioz composed an operatic version of *Much Ado About Nothing.*) While these operas live on, most of the plays that inspired them have been forgotten.

Curiously, though, one of the most revived romantic dramas is one of the last manifestations of the movement: Edmund Rostand's *Cyrano de Bergerac,* first produced in 1897 when the theater had long moved on to other things.

Cyrano takes as its protagonist a real life figure, the swordsman, poet, and playwright who was a contemporary of Molière and perhaps his schoolfellow. It makes him a man whose admirable qualities are overshadowed by his sensitivity about his nose, which is abnormally long; it shows him forced to suppress his declaration of love for the woman he adores, Roxane, because she has eyes only for his young protégé; and after years of devoting himself selflessly to his rival's suit, his effort unites him with his love only at the moment of his death.

There is a pure showmanship in *Cyrano* of which Hugo would have been proud. The play opens with a representation, onstage, of a performance at the Hôtel de Bourgogne. It packs the stage with extras and crams a battlefield within the proscenium arch. Only a state-subsidized theater can afford to revive it now.

Yet for all its bravado, *Cyrano* is a sad play, written for a public still smarting from the defeats of the Franco-Prussian War, wanting to be reminded of lost glories but knowing in their hearts that ardor and high aspirations were not enough. (Significantly, Rostand's other best-known play, *l'Aiglon, The Eaglet,* is about Napoleon's son who died young.) Thus *Cyrano* is a romantic play chilled by the cold wind of reality. The heroine to whom Cyrano pays his lifelong devotion is a remarkably silly and vacuous woman; and we are left with a strong sense that not even the noblest ideals can stand up under the onslaughts of the pettiness of life.

What then had the romantics done? They had given the theater a much needed tonic. Young men all, they had infused their youth into a theater that had grown middle-aged and stale. Though they had few successors, they had at least shown that it was possible for the theater to look in other directions, and they opened the way for different kinds of exploration after them.

MELODRAMA

Some of the effects of romanticism, however, continued to be felt in the theater on its more popular levels. We have already mentioned melodrama as a form that shares several of romanticism's qualities; and since melodrama achieved great popularity in the late nineteenth century, it is worth exploring these affinities now.

Melodrama did for tragedy what the commedia dell'arte had already done for comedy. It simplified characters and issues, presenting plots in which the moral issues were clearly, not to say simplistically, defined, without halftones or shadings, and in which physical action took precedence over subtlety of thought and beauty of language. In melodrama good was always good and evil always evil. A string of exciting, though often implausibly contrived, situations placed the hero or heroine in predicaments from which they were able to extricate themselves only at the last moment by strength, superior moral qualities, or sheer luck. It was axiomatic that virtue should be triumphant, and mass audiences thrilled to fights, escapes, and natural disasters, staged with increasing scenic artifice as the century wore on.

Although the seeds of melodrama may be found far back in the theater's history — indeed, the form may be said to have originated with Euripides' stage versions of the more sensational Greek myths — it received a boost from the romantic movement that established it as one of the most popular forms of the nineteenth century. It was especially beloved by the working-class audiences for whom, with improved urban transport, the theater suddenly became accessible, whose importance was recognized in the proliferation of new theaters dedicated to their less literary tastes, and whose background, particularly in the United States, led them to prefer a form of drama in which visual excitement and close-packed action took precedence over the spoken word.

Melodrama thus represents another aspect of the opening up of the theater that characterizes the nineteenth century. It formed the staple of most companies' repertoires, and some of the finest actors of the time were not ashamed to divide their attention among melodrama, Shakespeare, and the "old comedies" — principally Goldsmith and Sheridan. The scripts, usually of slight literary merit, have been largely overlooked by historians. In performance, however, melodrama afforded the actor an opportunity for uninhibited histrionic display and the audience a chance to wallow in raw emotion uncomplicated by pretensions of literary grandeur. Similarly, the designer had every inducement to invention. An audience that could thrill to the swaggering of the bandit Robert Macaire on the French stage, or watch a train wreck taking place before their very eyes on the English or American, was too engrossed to lament the absence of polished verse or an abstruse intellectual theme.

Without literary manifestoes, without critical battles, melodrama propagated many of the qualities that the romantics had been at such pains to champion: the primacy of emotion over reason, the cultivation of the colorful, exotic, and bizarre, the absence of restraint. The form touched a nerve and brought popular audiences into the theater in a way that had scarcely been conceived in previous centuries. Until it was superseded by film, melodrama remained one of the greatest sources of mass enjoyment in the arts. Much of it was ephemeral. Much of it was ripe for parody, and it is through parody that melodrama is now chiefly remembered. But in its time it spoke with a strong, simple voice and addressed one of the theater's honorable functions, that of providing vicarious experience in lives that otherwise would have had no escape from the deadly monotony of industrial routine.

Romantic Acting

We have now looked at romantic stage design and romantic play writing. Was there anything that could be distinctively called romantic acting? Perhaps there was, and we can get an inkling of its quality from a comparison among figures prominent on the London stage around the turn of the century.

Two of them belonged to the same family. Roger Kemble, a strolling actor, had married in 1752 one Sarah Ward, whose father was actor-manager of a touring company. Kemble inherited the company from his father-in-law, and in 1755 he became the father of a girl, another Sarah, who was to become a famous actress.

SARAH KEMBLE SIDDONS

Like many born into the profession, Sarah made her stage debut as an infant, learning her trade in the rough-and-tumble of the provincial circuits. Though stars might be feted in London, social attitudes in some of the smaller towns had hardly changed since the sixteenth century. Local ordinances still frowned on players, who were often compelled to practice their profession by subterfuge, offering so-called concerts that were really plays. A typical program of the time announces a concert of vocal and instrumental music divided into three parts, with "exhibitions of elocution" during the intermissions. The intermissions, of course, were considerably longer than the concert.

In 1773 Sarah married a fellow actor, William Siddons, and with him she continued to tour the provincial centers. (One of them, Wolverhampton, now an industrial city but then considerably more rural, exhibited a notice prohibiting the performance of "any player, puppy or monkey.") Her growing success, however, attracted attention from the capital. Both Covent Garden and Drury Lane sent out their talent scouts, and Sarah Siddons eventually signed for the Lane under Garrick. She made her debut shortly after Christmas 1775, not too long after rising from childbed; nervous to the point of inaudibility and badly dressed, she made a poor impression as Portia in *The Merchant of Venice*.

Garrick's retirement broke all existing contracts at Drury Lane, and back went the Siddonses to the provinces. Her second attempt on London, however, in 1782, again at Drury Lane but this time under Sheridan, was a triumph. In 1783 she scored for a second time with what was hailed as a highly innovative Lady Macbeth. The most remarked-upon innovation seems to have occurred in the sleepwalking scene, when she put down her candlestick to leave her hands free for the attempts to wash the blood off them — a piece of business so slight that the fact that it was commented on at all shows how ossified the stage had become. It was also remarked of her that while still giving the traditional bloodthirsty impression of Lady Macbeth, she emphasized what evidence she could find of the tenderness and femininity of the character.

Sheridan, in his dilettante fashion, was a theatrical reformer, impatient with the orotundity of conventional stage delivery. Sarah Siddons, an actress of quick intelligence, responded to Sheridan's reforms, though she still adhered to rapid transitions and some of the old exaggerated gestures. One critic commented that her chief weakness was "a perpetual shaking of the head and turning of the chin." She devoted considerable study to each role, trying to present a coherent character rather than a series of brilliant but uncoordinated impersonations. Note how close we are coming to the modern concept of acting: the necessity for study, the consideration of the role as a unity, the creation of the character from the inside rather than the outside. It was noted of Sarah Siddons — again, a comment on the prevalent theater manners of her time — that she was still acting even when not speaking and seemed never to be conscious of the presence of the audience.

JOHN PHILIP KEMBLE

Her characteristics were shared by her brother, John Philip Kemble, who joined her in London in 1783, the year after her triumphant reappearance. Critics commented on the studious nature of Kemble's portrayals and, in particular, his slow delivery, which seemed to be "fetched from the schools of philosophy." They contrasted him with Garrick, who impressed an audience "from his skill in seizing and expressing with force and precision the first and most obvious view of his part." Kemble, on the other hand, was "more learned and more laborious"; his style was carefully worked out, where Garrick's was "impetuous, sudden, striking and versatile." Kemble seems to have been too laborious, and there was a stiffness in his acting that some found objectionable. The critic Hazlitt, in a famous comment, accused him of playing Hamlet "like a man in armor." But he could play with speed and agility when he wanted to, even performing in the harlequinades, which still offered a light afterpiece to a long and heavy evening.

It is significant that we rarely hear of his transitions, as we did for Garrick. Kemble had an idea of a constantly developing character performed with constantly developing intensity; the shifts from quiet to passion were never sudden. His diction showed similar care and earnestness, sacrificing speed to clarity of articulation. It was predictable that he would succeed as Hamlet but not as Richard III or Lear. Violence eluded him, and he was happier with the great and dignified Romans, Shakespeare's Coriolanus and Brutus.

Kemble's scholarly interests also led him into theatrical antiquities and period detail. We have already noted the 1823 *King John* as the first Shakespearean production on the London stage to use authentic historical costuming, taking immense trouble to create a correct period feeling. It was produced by Kemble's brother Charles, with designs drawn from historical sources by Planché.

The Kembles, then, who provided the theater with its reigning dynasty, survive in record as dignified, rather pompous figures — Sarah was so constantly "onstage" that she talked in iambic pentameters in private life — who deeply identified with their characters, in contrast to the earlier actors who were always conscious of themselves as players.

EDMUND KEAN

In complete contrast to the Kembles, the new century offered Edmund Kean, who, like so many in the romantic period, had a personal life as wild, unpredictable, and subject to emotional excess as any part he played. His parentage was doubtful, and his early stage career disastrous. Appearing as an evil spirit in attendance on the three witches in *Macbeth,* he tripped, fell, and toppled a whole line of waiting extras from the wings onto the stage. (He afterwards excused himself by saying that this was the first time he had appeared in tragedy!) He is also said to have annoyed Kemble by parodying him, which must have been easy to do. After a series of poorly paying engagements at the minor theaters, he finally bluffed his way into the patent houses with such success and lack of scruple that he was at one point under contract to both Drury Lane and Covent Garden at the same time.

Settling for Drury Lane, he made his first appearance as Shylock in January 1814. Kean was an unknown quantity, and the company was indignant at being asked to play with him. Kean had only one rehearsal, in which the others merely walked through their scenes. It should be remarked, though, that no revival of a known play would have had many more. Productions, like most acting practices, were standardized; an actor could expect to walk out of a major Shakespearean play in one theater and into the same play at another and find no surprises in setting or blocking; the other players would be in positions handed down by convention and tradition. Kean's treatment at Drury Lane, therefore, was not as abysmal as might now appear.

But it was still perfunctory, and only the prompter had a glimmering of what the real performance would be like. The audience knew, though, as soon as Kean walked onto the stage that they were in for a new experience. Kean had forsaken the traditional red wig, which had always given a comic cast to the part, for a black one. He was physically unprepossessing, short, stocky, with a harsh and husky voice, but on stage he blazed. This burning intensity characterized everything he did. The audience was as stunned later by his Richard III as it had been by his Shylock.

Critics were impressed by Kean's naked display of emotion, by the intuitive grasp he seemed to have of his roles (though, like most so-called intuitive actors, he worked hard to secure effects that were supposedly spontaneous). Some found his performances erratic and accused him of rehearsing a part rather than performing it, letting the intensity lapse between the high moments. Even his most famous plaudit — that "watching Kean act was like reading Shakespeare by flashes of lightning" — is a double-edged compliment; there were obscure moments between the flashes of brilliant illumination. But in the emphasis on his own personality, to which he adapted his roles rather than adapting himself to suit them, Kean showed himself a true romantic. "He stirred the general heart with such a rush of mighty power, impressed himself so vividly by accent, look and gesture, that it was as vain to protest against his defects as for French critics to insist upon Shakespeare's want of good taste."

Like other romantics — and, indeed, like the whole movement — Kean burnt himself out. He played as hard as he acted, pursuing a bohemian life-style in which he drank so hard that he was often carried home helpless. He acquired a tame lion cub, which he paraded through the streets; he became the leading member of the Wolf Club, a group so dissolute that even Lord Byron was shocked when Kean took him to a meeting.

The strain of his private life began to tell on his performances. The public was offended by his increasing incapacity to continue and demanded apologies from the stage. In an attempt to revive both his own fortunes and those of the continually ailing Drury Lane, he mounted a spectacular revival of *King Lear,* which utilized canvas forests bending to the wind and real hail and rain in the storm scenes. It was a triumph but one rapidly erased in the public mind by Kean's involvement in a lurid adultery case in the course of which his fatuous letters to the guilty lady were read in court and ridiculed in the popular press. Returning to the Lane to play *Othello,* he found the mob had turned out to boo. Drinking harder than ever, he was unable to speak his lines on the stage; thus he left the London stage as spectacularly as he had entered it, to eke out a miserable living in the provinces.

Alexandre Dumas, excited by Kean's personality, wrote a play about him, revised for the present century by so unlikely a figure as Jean-Paul Sartre, which was even turned into a musical. And Kean has continued to excite interest, not merely for his own performances but for the question his life so signally raises: how far is an actor involved in the characters he plays? To what extent is his personality his own, and how far is it submerged in other people? Can a man who, as a way of life, portrays the spiritual and emotional agonies of others escape such agonies himself?

This question of the involvement of the personality of the creator with his own creations is another of romanticism's legacies to literary criticism. According to traditional, Aristotelian standards drama was to be judged by its appropriateness to its genres. Tragedy and comedy, with their own strict definitions, were forbidden to mingle. Thus to criticize a work, one had to be able to fit it into the appropriate category. Romanticism suggested an entirely new approach. Now the personality of the creator became vitally important. Critics began to look at a work in terms of its author's life, to examine the extent of his personal involvement in the work, and to suggest that such factors had to be known before the work could be accurately evaluated.

The impact of the romantic movement on the theater was in some ways a negative one. It created few works of enduring value, and its adulation of the irresponsible playwright and the actor defying social propriety in the service of his Muse only served to exacerbate hostility against the profession. Some of the more extravagant romantic stereotypes have become ineradicably fixed in the public consciousness, to the theater's harm. On the positive side the movement brought about a long overdue housecleaning, sweeping away several centuries' accumulation of outmoded practices and stale traditions. After such a period of violent change, more temperate changes could be effected with less anguish.

9
Nineteenth-Century Realism

The Well-Made Play in France

We have seen how the romantic movement catered to those who found contemporary life dull after the succession of reverberant events through which they had passed; who mourned the disappearance of high ideals; who still longed for a flag to follow and a rallying cry. On the stage the re-creation of stirring passages from colorful periods of history provided a vicarious excitement, and in the auditorium and the daily journals the running battle between classicists and romanticists gave opportunities that could no longer be provided on the field of glory or in the barricaded streets. A literary cause was still a cause.

The romantic drama, however, was not the whole of theater. A large section of the public was weary of battles of any kind: even aesthetic controversy was too stimulating. This public was fatigued in spirit, desiring only to rest and be entertained. And it was a bourgeois public, clinging to the comfort of the

The solidity of Victorian theater building: Theatre Royal, Bath.

material security they had reconstructed from the debris of the Revolution, a public who had, in 1830, put on the throne a king who reflected their own way of life: Louis Philippe, a monarch of the middle classes, who walked the streets of Paris in an ordinary business suit, carrying an umbrella. For these people another segment of the theater performed the not dishonorable function of providing relaxation and escape. This was no time for a theater that offered a serious, critical view of contemporary society. What evolved, side by side with the effusions of the romantic drama, was the kind of work we have come to call the well-made play (*pièce bien faite*) the kind of play that bases its appeal on careful craftsmanship rather than on novelty of content, that follows predictable formulas, and that, while maintaining a sufficient level of theatrical excitement, offers no violent shocks and holds back from anything that might affront the audience's susceptibilities.

EUGÈNE SCRIBE AND VAUDEVILLES

The first distinguished practitioner of the French well-made play was Eugène Scribe, who was born in 1791 near Les Halles, the great commercial market of Paris and the district that had once produced Molière. When Scribe was seven, his father died, and his mother, whom he adored, worked hard to give him a good education and send him through law school. His life was therefore shaped by the solid bourgeois virtues of family devotion and hard work, and he faithfully reproduces these qualities in his plays.

He was already writing during his law studies, and his name first appeared before the public as a writer of *vaudevilles*. This word has acquired its own meaning in the context of American popular entertainment. For the French, though, it implied something rather different. The earliest meaning of *vaudeville,* going back to medieval times, was a popular song, with topical subject matter and usually satirical in nature. By the eighteenth century the theater knew a form called *comédie vaudeville,* short playlets, usually no longer than one act, with a few interpolated songs. They carried an aura of the fairground with them and were often salacious.

Scribe took this minor form and revivified it. It is significant of the popular taste of his time, and of the little that was demanded of the theater, that such a lightweight form could not merely be revived but become a box office success in the larger houses. Scribe gave the vaudevilles local color by populating them with characters from his own social milieu, the complacent bourgeoisie who increasingly filled the theaters. He purged them of satire and impropriety, keeping the humor light and entertaining but introducing a new skill in plot construction. He wrote middle-class plays for middle-class people, transforming works that had often been formless and haphazardly constructed into models of deft stage mechanics, which could be admired as one might admire a solidly built piece of furniture — and which had about as much effect on people's lives.

This kind of play obviously gives little scope for originality of theme or novelty of content. It is the craftsmanship that demands attention, the precision and implacable logic with which the plot is worked out. By its nature the play relies on stock scenes, characters, and events. It becomes the formula play, which traces its descent from the Greek New Comedy of Menander and its Roman imitations. The ingredients are the familiar ones of misunderstandings, jealousies, mistaken identity, and disguises. The characters are similarly conventional: hardhearted father, sentimental heroine, young lover, scheming servant. Where Scribe differs from previous practitioners of this form is in his emphasis on bourgeois morality. Where Plautus delights to show the old men fooled, Scribe declares himself on the father's side. He always defends the parent against the lover, prudence against rashness, and sound middle-class standards against romantic foolishness. The vaudevilles give no offense. They may be naughty, but they are never vicious; law and order are upheld.

INFLUENCE OF HISTORY

What is true of Scribe's vaudevilles remains true of his longer plays, which were much admired and were held up virtually as textbooks of dramatic method. He wrote several historical dramas, the fashion for which had already been encouraged by romanticism and which, in their own way, provided a means of escape; the nineteenth-century audience could contemplate the problems of the past with equanimity, secure in the knowledge that these matters did not touch their present.

The nineteenth century, indeed, shows a revival of interest in history in general and a change in historical method that itself influences Scribe's plays. Before this time history had been largely the study of ideas, and closely linked to philosophy and literature; it was not much interested in accuracy of sources or in sifting historical material. In the nineteenth century history first began to break away from other studies, severing its literary ties and establishing itself as an independent discipline. It began to interest itself in facts, to seek its own identity as an exact science, and to reconstruct the past as it actually was. Sources were now examined more strictly in an endeavor to separate historical fact from unreliable tradition. The past was reappraised, and a completely new view of whole periods was arrived at. This concern with hard fact reached its culmination, as the century wore on, in the establishment of archaeology as a rigid scientific discipline.

Such interests were not confined to the scholars. They had a wide popular appeal that was reflected in the arts. In literature the historical novels of Sir Walter Scott offered detailed reconstructions of specific periods; these novels both were inspired by historical research and inspired others to pursue historical studies. Scott's works were not only popular in England but were translated into a number of European languages, and they had an enormous vogue in Paris. In the visual arts the historical canvases of Eugène Delacroix were prominent.

In drama the romantic writers had already recognized the appeal of the more colorful periods of history, though they were less than faithful in their recon-struction of them. The dramatists of the new trend continued to be alive to the appeal but were more conscientious in reproducing period settings, dress, and manners. Thus the theater moved toward a much higher standard of realism in historical drama, something that could not fail to communicate itself even to plays with contemporary settings. Scenic rooms now looked like rooms; char-acters wore costumes that more closely resembled historical dress, and their actions on stage were much more conformable to those of real life.

PROPS AND FORMULA

One must notice, in the well-made play, the relatively little importance given to *character* (which, as we have seen, is formulaic and predetermined) and the much greater importance given not merely to plot but to the concrete objects around which the plot revolves — that is, the props. It is the props, not the characters, that become the focus of the action; it is the props that (in the manner of recognition-tokens in Plautine comedy) precipitate events.

Perhaps this emphasis on material objects reflects the materialism of the times. Perhaps it reflects the contemporary historical interest in things rather than ideas. Perhaps it demonstrates the way in which play writing was now regarded as a predictable mechanical exercise with virtually everything neatly foreseen and controlled by the dramatist and with very little stemming from the actors themselves, who, like walking props, simply went through the paces the dramatist had ordained for them. It remains a fact, however, that the props in the well-made play are usually the center of attention.

In any play, of course, props are important, but actors can usually improvise if one happens to be missing. In the *pièce bien faite* they are crucial, and their absence makes the scene impossible to play. For example, in Scribe's *A Glass of Water* the denouement is precipitated by the object that gives the work its title, and a pair of diamond earrings creates a chain of discoveries and misunderstand-ings. In one of the best-known plays by Scribe's disciple Victorien Sardou, *A Scrap of Paper,* one might almost call the main prop a principal character; it is a note — which is hidden, discovered, and passed from person to person in the play — that provokes a chain of complications.

In the well-made play the mechanics are everything. In a period that was increasingly leaning toward the exact formulations of science, there seemed no reason why drama should not be reduced to a science. Significantly, Sardou, when learning his craft, began by reading Scribe's plays. He would study two acts and then try to finish the play from his own imagination, working out the logic of Scribe's action. He then went back to the original, and if his version tallied with Scribe's, he considered that he had been successful.

The well-made play developed a formula: the posing of a question in Act One, a complication in Act Two, and its resolution in Act Three. Its virtues lay in its construction, its failings in its emptiness of content. It did, however, set a standard for the time, which other playwrights could not afford to ignore. Bernard Shaw some years later registered his contempt for the whole genre by labeling it *Sardoodledom* and calling Sardou's plays "clockwork mice." There is some truth in his remarks, as Sardou himself would have agreed. But several of the major figures in the theater, like Ibsen and even Shaw himself, took the framework of the well-made play and turned it to their own purposes, infusing it with a more vital content. Others reacted so strongly against it that they led the drama into different directions entirely.

LA DAME AUX CAMÉLIAS

One play of this school has established itself as a minor classic in its own right, while the rest have fallen by the wayside. This play is *la Dame aux camélias* (*The Lady of the Camellias*), popularly, though erroneously, known as *Camille.* The play, though faithfully adhering to the well-made philosophy, is still infused with enough personal feeling to give it a life of its own. It was the work of Alexandre Dumas (1824–1895), the younger (*fils*), son of the man whose sensational romantic dramas had set all Paris talking, who had once said of Dumas *père*, "My father was a great baby I had when I was very young," and who had tempered the romantic spirit he had inherited with a practicality of his own.

The younger Dumas was born, illegitimately, in 1824, and he saw little of his father in his early years. When Dumas *père* began to make money from his plays, he sent for the boy and had him educated. Dumas *fils* suffered much at school on account of his bastardy, acquiring a personal awareness of injustice and persecution that later was to influence his writing. He fell into his father's profligate way of life and was, by his own admission, 50,000 francs in debt at the age of twenty-four. In 1845 he began to write — plays, novels, and melodramas. Paris saw another revolution in 1848, which impressed him strongly. In 1852 he produced *la Dame aux camélias,* which was itself a kind of bastard, equally inspired by romanticism and the well-made play.

La Dame aux camélias first took shape as a novel and was later dramatized by Dumas in a spate of play writing designed primarily to pay off his debts. It came out of his own experience and his acquaintance with a girl called Alphonsine Plessis (or, as she preferred to call herself, Marie Duplessis), a leading figure of the demimonde during Dumas's wild youth. A country girl, she had come to Paris in 1839, where she established herself as a courtesan, acquiring a number of wealthy admirers including the composer Liszt. In 1844 she met Dumas, then only twenty; he idolized her but was not rich enough to keep her, and a year later they parted. In 1847 Marie died of consumption (tuberculosis). Dumas was out of Paris at the time but hurried back to see her furniture and belongings sold. She was buried in Montmartre, where it was for long the custom of Paris prostitutes to leave offerings on her grave in tribute to her as one of the leading lights of their profession.

The romantic drama remains enshrined in the operatic repertory. Scenes from three works by Giuseppe Verdi based on romantic originals. (*left*) *Don Carlos,* from the play by Schiller. (*right*) *Rigoletto,* based on Victor Hugo's *Le Roi s'amuse* (*The King Takes His Pleasure*). (*above*) *La Traviata,* based on *Camille,* by Dumas *fils.*

The incident remained everlastingly imprinted on Dumas's memory. He enshrined Marie in his novel and play as Marguerite Gautier, a fashionable courtesan with a host of glittering admirers, and he wrote himself into them as Armand Duval, the young man who falls in love with her. For the rest of the story he allowed himself a certain amount of wish fulfillment.

The dramatic version follows the established pattern of the well-made play. First we have the posing of the issue: Armand falls in love with Marguerite; she reciprocates, abandons her old way of life, and goes off to live with him in the country. Then comes the complication: Duval's father visits Marguerite during his son's absence and pleads with her to abandon him, as the notoriety of their association is ruining his daughter's marriage prospects. Marguerite, now established as the golden-hearted prostitute who rapidly becomes a cliché of fiction, reluctantly agrees and leaves a letter for Armand saying that she is returning to her Paris life. Note the customary reliance of the well-made play on props; the letter, left on the table for Armand to discover, becomes the focus of dramatic attention. Armand returns, discovers the letter, and is outraged. He follows Marguerite to Paris, and in a scene of the type that critics came to label the *scène à faire* — the obligatory scene made inevitable by the logic of the plot — he confronts and accuses her. In the last act Marguerite is dying. Armand's fat! :, realizing how wrong he has been in breaking up this true love, is at her bedside and has sent for his son, but the joyous reconciliation is cut short abruptly by Marguerite's death.

Dumas *père* wept when the play was read to him. The Paris censors were not so affected, and they banned it as an affront to public morality. What moved them most was Dumas's unprecedented action in taking his leading character from real life and only thinly disguising her under a change of name; Marie Duplessis was still uncomfortably alive in the memories of many of the theatergoing public. One might notice that this objection is a characteristic of the French theater of the time: the reluctance to involve the drama in any kind of contemporary action. With the aid of influential friends, however, Dumas secured a production, and the work was an immediate success. It should be noted, though, that when Verdi turned it into one of his most famous operas, *La Traviata,* he was faced with the same reaction; the first-night audience rejected it as too contemporary, and he was forced to push the setting back into the eighteenth century before his music could have a fair hearing.

Dumas himself lived to regret the success of his work. It had been written out of a youthful reminiscence, which he afterwards outgrew. Revolting, ultimately, against his father's free-and-easy way of life, he assumed a severe moral stance, which revealed itself in his later plays. Perhaps the most significant indication of his changing attitude was in a piece of stage business. In the original production of *la Dame aux camélias,* when the elder Duval entered to plead with Marguerite, he removed his hat. In the revivals Dumas never permitted this to happen on the grounds that Marguerite was not a lady.

Realism in England

In England in the first half of the nineteenth century, the state of the theater varied depending on where one happened to look. Remember that the changes we have noted on the English stage — the move toward greater control, toward a more consistent ensemble, toward greater realism of setting and costume — were largely confined to the principal London theaters. And even these showed some hostility to change and a tendency to cling to the outmoded, traditional ways. For example, Drury Lane was rebuilt in 1812 on a much larger plan, with seating rearranged on a circular sweep to secure better vision. In the architect's design the old proscenium doors were left out. But in the building as completed they were put back in on the insistence of the performers. In the provinces conservative pressures were even stronger.

Many companies were organized in much the same way as the plays, mechanically, into stock roles, so that there could be no fresh thought, no innovative casting, but merely the same routine characterizations and stage business. Here actors in Shakespeare might still be using, out of habit, laziness, and the mindless observance of tradition, the same inflections, line readings, and gestures that their predecessors had used in the Restoration.

Our critical appreciation of some classic works may have been unconsciously colored by the way in which these plays were customarily performed. *Macbeth,* for instance, was given in traveling repertory with the actor-manager in the lead and Lady Macbeth played by his wife, usually a middle-aged actress who was second-in-command of the company and played all the female heavies by right of precedence. This situation has given us a view of the character as a mature woman who dominates by her physical presence — a view not necessarily justified by the text, but one still so persuasive that any younger actress cast in the role has to fight to establish her credibility.

DICKENS AS EYEWITNESS

One of our best eyewitnesses and certainly the most amusing for the English provincial theater at this low ebb is Charles Dickens. Though primarily a novelist, he had a continuing and lively interest in the theater. An amateur actor of considerable talent himself, he had a number of friends in the profession, gave public readings of his own work (whose success has inspired imitators to the present day), and saw several of his novels pirated for the stage, where they attracted large audiences. Above all, he was a keen observer of the contemporary theatrical scene.

In *Nicholas Nickleby* he devotes some space to the activities of the Vincent Crummles troupe, a traveling company in the lower depths of the provincial circuit. We see at once how the company was organized, with the manager and his wife taking the choice roles and the rest divided among traditional "lines of business":

> A pretty general muster of the company had by this time taken place; for besides Mr. Lenville and his friend Tommy, there were present, a slim young gentleman with weak eyes, who played the low-spirited lovers and sang tenor songs, and who had come arm-in-arm with the comic countryman — a man with a turned-up nose, large mouth, broad face, and staring eyes. Making himself very amiable to the infant phenomenon, was an inebriated elderly gentleman in the last depths of shabbiness, who played the calm and virtuous old men; and paying especial court to Mrs. Crummles was another elderly gentleman, a shade more respectable, who played the irascible old men — those funny fellows who have nephews in the army, and perpetually run about with sticks to compel them to marry heiresses. Besides these, there was a roving-looking person in a rough great-coat, who strode up and down in front of the lamps, flourishing a dress-cane, and rattling away, in an undertone, with great vivacity for the amusement of an ideal audience. He was not quite so young as he had been, and his figure was rather running to seed; but there was an air of exaggerated gentility about him, which bespoke the hero of swaggering comedy. There was, also, a little group of three or four young men, with lantern jaws and thick eye-brows, who were conversing in one corner; but they seemed to be of secondary importance, and laughed and talked together without attracting any attention.
>
> The ladies were gathered in a little knot by themselves round the rickety table before mentioned. There was Miss Snevellicci — who could do anything, from a medley dance to Lady Macbeth, and also played some part in blue silk knee-smalls at her benefit — glancing from the depths of her coal-scuttle straw bonnet, at Nicholas, and affecting to be absorbed in the recital of a diverting story to her friend Miss Ledrook, who had brought her work, and was making up a ruff in the most natural manner possible. There was Miss Belvawney — who seldom aspired to speaking parts, and usually went on as a page in white silk hose, to stand with one leg bent, and contemplate the audience, or to go in and out after Mr. Crummles in stately tragedy. . . . Lastly, there was Mrs. Grudden in a brown cloth pelisse and a beaver bonnet, who assisted Mrs. Crummles in her domestic affairs, and took money at the doors, and dressed the ladies, and swept the house, and held prompt book when everybody else was on for the last scene, and acted any kind of part on any emergency without ever learning it, and was put down in the bills under any name or names whatever, that occurred to Mr. Crummles as looking well in print.

We see the manager's daughter born and brought up on the stage and deliberately kept young to pander to the sentimental fashion for child performers — the sort of theatrical apprenticeship served by the young Sarah Siddons. We see the typical offerings: Shakespeare, romantic melodramas pirated from the French, and shabby balletic divertissements. We see the company trying to maintain a pretense of gentility amid poverty and depending on the traditional benefit night to augment their meager earnings. Although this work is fiction, everything that Dickens writes can by paralleled from the contemporary stage. The Crummles troupe seems to be based on the Davenports, with whom Dickens traveled briefly.

In *Great Expectations* he gives an account of a performance of *Hamlet* in the dockyard town of Portsmouth:

> On our arrival in Denmark we found the king and queen of that country elevated in two arm-chairs on a kitchen-table, holding a Court. The whole of the Danish nobility were in attendance; consisting of a noble boy in the wash-leather boots of a gigantic ancestor, a venerable Peer with a dirty face, who seemed to have risen from the people late in life, and the Danish chivalry with a comb in its hair and a pair of white silk legs, and presenting on the whole a feminine appearance. . . .
>
> Several curious little circumstances transpired as the action proceeded. The late king of the country not only appeared to have been troubled with a cough at the time of his decease but to have taken it with him to the tomb, and to have brought it back. The royal phantom also carried a ghostly manuscript round its truncheon, to which it had the appearance of occasionally referring, and that, too, with an air of anxiety and a tendency to lose the place of reference which were suggestive of a state of mortality. It was this, I conceive, which led to the Shade's being advised by the gallery to "turn over!" — a recommendation it took extremely ill. It was likewise to be noted of this majestic spirit that whereas it always appeared with an air of having been out a long time and walked an immense distance, it perceptibly came from a closely contiguous wall. This occasioned its terrors to be received derisively. The Queen of Denmark, a very buxom lady, though no doubt historically brazen, was considered by the public to have too much brass about her; her chin being attached to her diadem by a broad band of that metal (as if she had a gorgeous toothache), her waist being encircled by another, and each of her arms by another, so that she was openly mentioned as "the kettledrum." The noble boy in the ancestral boots was inconsistent, representing himself, as it were, in one breath, as an able seaman, a strolling actor, a grave-digger, a clergyman, and a person of the utmost importance at a Court fencing-match, on the authority of whose practised eye and nice discrimination the finest strokes were judged. This gradually led to a want of toleration for him, and even — on his being detected in holy orders, and declining to perform the funeral service — to the general indignation taking the form of nuts. Lastly, Ophelia was a prey to such slow musical madness, that when, in course of time, she had taken off her white muslin scarf, folded it up, and buried it, a sulky man who had been long cooling his impatient nose against an iron bar in the front row of the gallery, growled, "Now the baby's put to bed, let's have supper!" Which, to say the least of it, was out of keeping.

THE BEGINNINGS OF REALISTIC DRAMA

From these doldrums the English theater rapidly and with considerable vigor reasserted itself. One of the prominent figures in the revival was T. W. (Tom) Robertson (1829–1871), who began his professional career as a writer of occasional pieces for the London papers and then gravitated to the stage. His journalism contains a number of amusing sketches of theatrical types, testifying to the extent to which the stage was still dominated by the patterns of the past.

His own first plays were still written in the spirit of romantic melodrama. More and more, however, he was drawn to the idea of total realism. He came to believe that the theater, in all aspects, should represent life as it was. The subject matter of drama should be drawn from real life — not a romanticized conception of life but life as actually lived. Characters should be shown performing real actions. Acting should be naturalistic; Robertson sought out actors prepared to abandon the old stereotypes and to draw their inspiration from real people. Settings should offer as exact a reproduction as possible of actual places.

Robertson was obsessed with the details of stage settings. He urged, for example, that the doors leading into a stage room should not be the usual makeshifts of lath and canvas but solid wood, with real doorknobs on them that could turn.

Most of what Robertson advocated, of course, was not original. Others before him had urged greater realism in writing, acting, and stage design. But Robertson was one of the first to coordinate these ideas and insist on the realism of the production as a whole. Before his time audiences could still see or hear onstage the inflections, the line readings, the movements, and the pieces of business that had been handed down in unbroken and unquestioned tradition for centuries. After him, not merely were actors compelled to rethink the basic premises of their profession, but audiences were led into a new appraisal of the function of the theater in their society. Robertson's best-known play, *Caste* (1867), for example, was an attack on the social injustice fostered by the English class structure. It is still occasionally revived, though much of its original sting has been lost.

In the organization of the theater Robertson stands out as one of the first figures that we can confidently label with the English term *producer* or the American term *director:* the artist charged with coordinating all the technical and physical resources of the production into a harmonious whole in which all elements worked toward a common end. This need for a guiding, controlling hand was in part called into existence by the growing complexity of the theater's resources. In part, also, it was an answer to a new vision of a stage production as a unified artistic statement, as a painting is, or a symphonic composition, rather than as a collection of individual performances.

SOCIETAL CHANGES AFFECTING THE THEATER

The speed with which realism caught on, not as a movement of the later nineteenth-century theater but as *the* movement, deserves some comment here. In looking at the theaters of earlier periods, we have seen movements limited largely by national boundaries and enduring unchanged for long periods of time. There have, of course, been influences: that of the French theater under Louis XIV on that of the English Restoration; the continuing and overwhelming influence of the English theater on that of the United States. On the whole, however, each nation has produced a theater that has been a law unto itself and responsive mainly to its own tradition.

When we reach the midpoint of the nineteenth century, this picture radically changes, reflecting the larger changes taking place in the world outside. This world was shrinking. Before the 1830s, travelers were still limited to the same means that a proconsul of the Roman Empire had used to survey his domains. Suddenly the horse was replaced by the steam locomotive; the steamboat narrowed the oceans; national and international postal systems hastened the interchange of news; and the eventual appearance of wireless telegraphy made communication instantaneous.

All these changes affected the theater. Any new play or significant production now had an impact far beyond its immediate community. Widespread touring became possible. Productions staged in one country could be seen by visitors and rapidly imitated in others. Thus we can now talk about *international* styles; and realism becomes *the* style, which dominates the theater for the rest of the century and in some respects for long after. Presentational theater tends to speak to a closed society and a limited audience, but realism is common currency.

We must also notice how a more mobile world changed the nature of playgoing. Improved transportation created a social revolution in the cities. It was no longer necessary to live within walking distance of one's work; the commuter age had begun. A population thus liberated could roam more widely in search of its pleasures, and one notices the multiplication of theaters in capital cities. In London the tyranny of the patent theaters, inaugurated with the Restoration and reaffirmed by the Licensing Act of 1737, was brought to an end in 1843. No longer was it necessary for plays at houses other than Covent Garden or Drury Lane to masquerade as lectures, animal shows, or musical entertainments. In Paris the boulevard theaters challenged the hegemony of the Comédie Française and attracted some of the leading dramatists of the time. As we pursue the development of the realistic movement in the theater, therefore, we must be aware that it was playing to an increasingly larger audience and that many of its leading practitioners were mutually influential.

GILBERT AND SULLIVAN

In England Robertson's work attracted a number of willing disciples, not the least of which was William Schwenk (later Sir William) Gilbert. This dramatist is now remembered principally as the librettist of the Gilbert and Sullivan operettas that were the high point of English musical theater in the 1880s and have won a permanent place in the world repertoire.

Gilbert, who came to the stage after writing for the London journals, teamed

(*below right*) Realistic Shakespeare: setting for Charles Kean's production of *Hamlet*. (*left*) The characters of swaggering melodrama were illustrated in popular prints. Smaller versions could be used to re-enact the plays in toy theaters, one of the favorite Victorian diversions. (*right*) Henry Irving in the popular melodrama *The Bells*.

The well-made play — like its characters, glossy and exquisitely tailored. A scene from Dion Boucicault's *London Assurance* as revived by the Royal Shakespeare Company, London.

with Sullivan in a temperamentally mismatched but artistically productive partnership that created a string of popular successes. He had worked with Robertson and found his ideas persuasive. Though his operettas usually involved a strong element of fantasy (a fact that Sullivan always resented), his productions, which he supervised personally, were insistent in their attention to realistic detail. One of his most powerful innovations was the integration of chorus and principals in a realistic pattern of action, something that had scarcely been attempted in the musical theater before.

His settings were realistically conceived and supervised by experts. *H.M.S. Pinafore* (1878) is set on the main deck of a British man-of-war. Gilbert went to naval authorities for authentic details of the ship's rigging and management. For *The Mikado* (1885), set in the Imperial Court of Japan, he found Japanese advisors on furnishings and deportment. *The Yeoman of the Guard* (1888), Gilbert and Sullivan's closest approximation to grand opera, was set before a reconstruction of the Tower of London.

As director, Gilbert was a rigid disciplinarian, testifying to the new spirit in the theater. He refused to allow any comic business, however funny, that was not relevant to the production as a whole, and he created an ensemble concept that was revolutionary in the musical theater of the time.

THE REALISTIC SHAKESPEAREAN PRODUCTION

The realistic spirit, of course, did not confine itself to new works. It also reilluminated old ones. Throughout this study we have regularly used Shakespearean revivals as an index of the changing state of the theater. A production of Shakespeare's *King John* in 1823, directed by Charles Kemble, stands out as a landmark in the British theater; it was the first revival to attempt complete historical accuracy of setting and costume. Its designer was J. R. Planché, also well known as a writer for the stage and, in 1834, as author of a history of British costume that remained a standard work for many years. He researched the period of John's reign (early thirteenth-century England) from medieval documents and illuminations, and he gave the production a historical authenticity that Shakespeare himself had never envisaged.

This example was rapidly followed by others. Charles Kean (1811–1868), son of the brilliant but dissolute Edmund, took over the management of the Princess's Theatre in 1851 and staged both Shakespeare and melodrama in lavish but historically accurate style. The set for the banquet scene of his *Macbeth* (1853) shows a vast hall, with an upper gallery, spread with tables, lit by torches, and framed by massive rafters and an immense rounded arch; Macbeth, downstage left, seen recoiling from the illuminated apparition of the dead Banquo, is backed by a mass of extras representing the guests at the feast. Many of the stage settings and costumes of this period, particularly those of Charles Kean, have come down to us through reproductions designed to be cut out, pasted on cardboard, and assembled as children's toy theaters. In these miniature replicas we can see something of the realism, and the flamboyance, of the mid-Victorian theater.

Another important figure from this transitional period was William Charles Macready (1793–1873), who in the earlier part of his career had been the only serious rival to Edmund Kean on the English stage. Having made his name in the patent theaters, Macready fought vigorously to free London from the restrictions that those theaters imposed, and in the new, more liberal climate he encouraged the reforms that were taking place all around him. He was the first to insist on full rehearsals for *everybody* engaged in the production, including all extras and crowd scenes. His own acting style was still inclined to be ponderous; he was prone to the affectation that has passed into theatrical legend as the "Macready pause," a weighty silence before some key word or phrase.

In the history of Shakespearean revival, however, the fullest attention must be paid to an actor of the next generation, John Henry Brodribb (1838–1905), who took, perhaps for obvious reasons, the stage name of Henry Irving. Irving's name became synonymous with the later Victorian theater. He was responsible for some of its most stunning productions, and by his character and personal achievements he did more to raise the status of the profession than any actor before him.

Irving's beginnings were inauspicious. He was tall and gawky — throughout his career cartoonists found it easy to caricature his physical appearance — and he had a stutter. To correct the stutter, he took elocution lessons, and these lessons fostered a growing interest in the stage. He began to appear first in amateur, then in professional, productions. After the usual apprenticeship of the provincial circuit, he appeared in London in 1866, playing a variety of roles in new melodramas and revivals of older comedies. In 1871 he made his first appearance at the Lyceum Theatre — with which his name was ever after associated — first in a Dickens adaptation that failed and then in a melodrama translated from the French under the title of *The Bells*. This play told the story of an innkeeper in a remote mountain village who murdered a rich, sleighborne traveler for his money and was thereafter haunted by the ghostly jingling of sleigh bells. Irving's electrifying performance in a trivial play drew all London, and it devastated Queen Victoria, who, having invited Irving to Windsor Castle for a command performance, was compelled to leave because her nerves were so affected.

Seven years later Irving assumed management of the theater where he had made his name. His career there was punctuated by splendid Shakespearean revivals that were the summation of the fashionable realistic style. He attracted notice by his rethinking of famous roles. His *Hamlet* was quiet and tender, his Shylock a somberly conceived performance that marked a radical break with the old, near-farcical tradition. On the other hand, in *The Merchant of Venice* Irving had the scenery become as important as the play. In Shakespeare's text Shylock's daughter Jessica elopes with her lover while a carnival fills the streets of Venice.

Irving interpolated a scene, wordless, in which Shylock is seen returning home after the elopement has taken place. He passes slowly across the stage, in the background the sunset silhouetting the familiar monuments of Venice. There follows a knocking on the door, louder and more frantic as Shylock begins to suspect the truth; and then come the reverberant cries of "Jessica! Jessica!" as he realizes that his daughter has left him.

Hamlet was staged with the same attention to local detail. The battlement scenes (in which the soldiers first discuss, and then see, the ghost) had a burning brazier, round which the soldiers clustered for warmth: the nights were cold in Elsinore. (It was objected against Irving, though, that he used the brazier to upstage his fellow actors by repeatedly pacing back and forth in front of it so that, from the audience's viewpoint, it flashed like a lighthouse. For all his insistence on verisimilitude and ensemble, Irving had a star actor's vanity.)

Realistic Shakespeare, however, had its own problems, and a growing awareness of these eventually brought an end to the style. One difficulty was that the constant scene changes made the productions monstrously long. The flexibility and swift pattern of action that were part of Shakespeare's dramatic scheme, and were encouraged by the physical conditions of his own theater, were now lost in a welter of realistic props and painted canvas. In addition, exactly *how* to stage Shakespeare realistically was often a matter of controversy. The history plays were easy enough. When Irving staged *Henry VIII* and played Cardinal Wolsey in it, he was dealing with historical characters located in a fixed and researchable period of time. Though Shakespeare had not envisaged a historically authentic setting for his play, it could be placed in one without violation of its spirit. And so it was with most of the tragedies: *Macbeth* could be plausibly located in a historically correct Scotland of the early Middle Ages, and *King Lear* in a primitive Britain. The occasional Elizabethan anachronism, like the striking clock in *Julius Caesar,* could be easily overlooked.

But the quest for historical accuracy ran into grave problems in design for other Shakespearean plays. What, for example, does one do with *A Winter's Tale?* Much of the action is set in a country that Shakespeare labels Bohemia but that he also specifies as having a seacoast; the geographical Bohemia is landlocked. Where, exactly, is the Illyria of *Twelfth Night,* and in what period does the play take place? The overwhelming tendency of these realistic productions of Shakespeare was to attempt to find concrete explanations for what, in the original, were only flights of the poet's fancy. Under this heavy-handed treatment many of Shakespeare's most imaginative passages became prosaic and dull.

Perhaps one of the most striking illustrations of this literal treatment may be seen in a production of *Julius Caesar* in which the director was greatly exercised by what he considered a problem in the battle scenes that make up the second half of the play. At one point the rival armies of Brutus and Cassius on the one hand and Antony on the other harangue each other bitterly. They do not come to blows. Why not? It was eventually decided that this Shake-spearean "problem" could be solved only by designing a set that showed the armies separated by a deep ravine. In that way the encounter could be made probable.

IRVING'S PRODUCTIONS

Though Shakespeare provided Irving with his most magnificent vehicles, the rest of his work is equally indicative of the state of the theater of his times. Following the pattern of his *The Bells* — a dynamic performance in a play of negligible *literary* merit — and ever aware of public taste, he presented a succession of works that became known as Lyceum melodrama — spectacular, sensational, and with great parts for himself. Typical of this genre was Dion de Boucicault's *The Corsican Brothers*, first written in 1852 and produced by Irving in 1880, the year after his successful *Merchant of Venice. The Corsican Brothers* uses a split time scheme to trace the divergent careers of two brothers; we see first an episode in the life of one, followed by a simultaneous event in the life of the other. It gave its name to a piece of stage machinery designed for one of its most impressive moments. An actor portraying a ghost stood on a belt concealed within a trap, which carried him upward and across the stage at the same time. This "Corsican trap" or "ghost glide" found many uses in the theater thereafter.

Even in his more serious productions Irving took every opportunity to ex-ploit new devices. In *Faust* Irving played Mephistopheles. For the scene in which Mephistopheles fights a duel with the brother of the girl Faust has seduced, he had metal plates set into the floor of the stage and wired for electricity. The charge ran up through corresponding metal plates set in the soles of his shoes, along wires concealed within the costume, and to his sword. When swords crossed, an electric spark was generated. It was one of Irving's favorite rehearsal jokes to step up the current so that his fellow actor received a violent shock.

Not the least of Irving's contributions to his art was his receipt of an honor that dignified the whole of his profession. In 1895 he received a knighthood from the hands of Queen Victoria. Knighthood for distinguished British actors is now commonplace. Irving's was the first, and his personal prestige did much to redeem the profession from the stigma of vagabondage under which it had labored since the reign of the first Elizabeth.

Irving's voice is still accessible to us. His career overlapped the invention of the phonograph, so that his rolling, reverberant "The bells!" has been preserved in wax, together with the voices of his colleagues and contemporaries. What *we* hear is a role conceived in the grand manner. The realism that terrified Queen Victoria would not be considered realistic by any audience today. It is an object lesson in the rapidity with which theater styles change.

The Realistic Movement on the Continent

On the continent of Europe the realistic movement made significant strides. One of its foremost exponents was George II, ruler of the duchy of Saxe-Meiningen in central Germany.

GERMANY AND THE MEININGER COMPANY

Germany was still not a unified country, and the numerous independent kingdoms and duchies with their own court theaters and orchestras were generous in fostering the arts. Duke George, who was deeply interested in the theater, had visited London as the guest of Queen Victoria and had been impressed by the productions of Charles Kean. As director of the Meininger company, he sought to infuse Kean's ideas into his own actors, break away from the traditional formality of the European stage, and create an ensemble in which every element would be subordinated to the concept of the work as a whole. Actors and technicians were regarded as equals in the combined operation. The star system was abolished, though not without some resistance from the actors and actresses involved. Members of the company might now expect to find themselves playing a leading role in one production and a walk-on in the next. This system has now become commonplace in resident and stock companies and may be seen in regular operation in the various state theaters of Europe, but it was revolutionary then in its threat to the traditional hierarchical pattern.

Audiences were especially enthusiastic over the Meininger crowd scenes, which substituted large crowds and swirling patterns of adroitly controlled stage movement for the old pattern of a handful of formally grouped extras. We have a contemporary account of the Meininger staging of a play dealing with the Roman invasion of Germany. Instead of the customary procession of spear-carrying extras from stage right to stage left, the audience was presented with a view of the *backs* of the apparently endless procession like a remorseless military machine, and they saw armor that had obviously been dirtied and battered in conflict.

Some argued that despite the great advance in realism offered by the Meininger, the productions were still not realistic enough. André Antoine, seeing them on tour in Paris, complained that although the crowds *moved* realistically, they did not *speak* realistically, and he urged that the crescendo of the crowd's roar should be orchestrated as carefully as their movement on stage. It was objected, too, that realistic actions were being performed against settings that failed to reach the same standards of realism: the Meininger forest settings still used flimsy canvas trees. Nevertheless, the company's influence was far-reaching and persuasive. In London it offered German-language productions of Shakespeare — *Julius Caesar* (with its obvious opportunities for crowd scenes), *Twelfth Night,* and *A Winter's Tale* — together with Schiller's romantic dramas *The Robbers* and *William Tell.* The company was also seen in the United States.

ANDRÉ ANTOINE IN FRANCE

André Antoine (1858–1943), whose comments on the Meininger are noted above, served his theatrical apprenticeship in a Paris dominated by the formula play. Born in the provinces, he had been brought to the capital while still young and had been an eyewitness of its brutal siege during the Franco-Prussian War. He combined a succession of odd jobs with a taste for the theater, eventually finding a place in the claque at the Comédie Française. The claque, which traces its origins to Roman times and still functions in the opera houses of Europe and America, was a group of applauders paid to provoke clapping and cheers, at appropriate moments, from the general audience. This meant, at least, that Antoine saw a lot of plays done in the traditional manner. He even auditioned for the company himself but was rejected because of his poor voice.

Growing dissatisfaction with the complacency of the national theater and enthusiasm for the realistic movement urged him, in 1887, to start a company of his own. It was called the Théâtre Libre, the Free Theater, a title that has been borrowed by innovative groups all over the world ever since. Though it was located in a remote and unpropitious quarter of the city, it excited widespread attention by both the novelty and the quality of its offerings. Its opening bill included a play by Emile Zola (1840–1902), a writer whose name was already notorious in Paris for an intransigent honesty that explored the seamier side of life untouched by the fashionable novel and the well-made play. *Jacques Damour* dealt with a husband, believed dead, who returned to find his wife remarried; it was set in the back room of a Paris butcher's shop. Antoine filled the set with real furniture that bore the marks of hard use; it was, in fact, his mother's, which he had borrowed out of financial necessity. And the acting method was completely new. Antoine did something that theorists had talked about as long as a century before but that no one had yet put into practice: whole scenes were played with the actors' backs to the audience. The impression of an actual room, in which characters went about their business in a real environment ignoring the presence of the audience, was complete.

ZOLA'S NATURALISM

This mention of Antoine and Zola introduces a new concept into the theater, a by-product of realism and often confused with it: *naturalism.* Zola, whose work so happily adapted itself to Antoine's staging innovations, was recognized as the leading figure of this movement in France and, indeed, as its founding father. What was this movement, and what principles did it espouse?

Though Zola was the most prolific French naturalist, he had good company: the Goncourt brothers, Alphonse Daudet, Guy de Maupassant — all of them, like himself, novelists who also wrote plays or whose novels were adapted for the stage. Zola's most important contribution was his proclamation of naturalistic theory. Influenced by contemporary science and philosophy, he argued for a rigorous determinism in human behavior and hence in the arts that professed to depict such behavior. Character for him was determined by environment and heredity and therefore could be studied by the same processes that zoologists were now bringing to bear on animal evolution. A play or novel was a controlled experiment. The subject must be studied in its environment and that environment portrayed in exact detail so as to show its effect on character.

In the novel this principle implies that a great deal of time must be devoted to description. *Thérèse Raquin* (1867), Zola's most famous work, relates the story of a sordid back-street murder in Paris. Much space is given to a description of the characters' milieu, the dark, moldering room in which they live, with an intent to show that, given their surroundings, they could not be other than what they are. It followed that when *Thérèse Raquin* was transposed to the stage — as several of Zola's works were, though he wrote little original material for the theater — the setting was of prime importance. Decor replaces description, and we come back to the new function of the designer, that of creating an accurate environment rather than a mere decoration, of bringing into being a vital element of the play.

Zola was himself fully conscious of the power of stage design, and he urged playwrights to take advantage of true-to-life settings:

> Is not stage decor a continual description, which can be much more exact and much more powerful than a novelistic one? After the settings so powerful in their depth, and so astonishing in their verisimilitude, that we have recently seen in our theaters, we can no longer deny the possibility of evoking the reality of a milieu on the stage. It is up to the dramatists to make use of this reality. Let them provide the characters and the action; the designers, working from their directions, will provide the descriptions, as exactly as is found necessary.

Note this new insistence on decor and action as equal components in an organic whole. The setting no longer provides merely a decorative background for the players and a frame for the action. It enfolds the action. It contains it. It dictates it.

In acting, too, Zola provided the theory, Antoine the practice. Annoyed by the conventional declamatory delivery of most French actors, the novelist accused them of sacrificing the ensemble effect on the altar of personal vanity. It was true: the star-by-seniority system of the establishment theaters, in which a succession of distinguished players had imposed their whims and personalities on companies and scripts alike, had not merely encouraged such abuses but had made them appear laudable. Not that Zola denied the contemporary theater any virtue: indeed, he praised the well-made playwrights — Sardou, Dumas *fils,* Augier — for their acute observation of the social milieu. What he distrusted was the pasteboard nature of their characters and the artificiality of their plots. From his kind of theater he demanded a sterner sense of purpose. He asked that characters in a play be real people of flesh and blood, placed in a clearly defined environment that was true to life and that was shown to determine their lives and actions. He asked that characterization be psychologically accurate. And finally, harking back to the precepts of French classical drama — we have seen how the theater constantly repeats itself — he argued for the virtues of simplicity. Cut the action down to the bone; make it striking and important. Write grandly, so that people will notice, but with subjects taken from everyday life. Avoid frivolity; forsake unnecessary complications. *Faire vrai, faire simple, faire grand:* "Make it real, make it simple, make it big."

We see, then, how — conspicuously in the French theater — the techniques of realism could be used for quite contradictory purposes, reflecting the great division in French (and indeed in all European) society as the nineteenth century drew to its close. On the one hand, realism dressed the glossy dramas that delighted the fashionable audiences. On the other, it gave vividness and authenticity to a welling drama of social protest. But in its concentration on the more desperate aspects of the human condition, naturalism found itself forced to modify the terms of realism and stress some things at the expense of others.

What most obviously differentiates naturalism from the other realistic modes is its scientific detachment and its pessimism. In a sense it revives some of the feeling of Greek tragedy, suggesting that people are the victims of inexorable laws over which they have no control and which they cannot even begin to understand. Thomas Hardy, the English naturalistic novelist, ends his most famous book with a sentence that might have been framed by Aeschylus: "The President of the Immortals had finished his sport with Tess."

Zola's slogan suggests that naturalism was already pushing toward a new form of expression. *Faire vrai* was by now virtually taken for granted in the theater, so rapidly had the realistic movement established itself. *Faire simple* was a natural, perhaps inevitable reversion to older principles of the French theater that had never, in spite of the romantics, completely lost their hold, and a necessary reaction against the prolixity and diffuseness involved in Hugo's cultivation of the grotesque. *Faire grand,* however, suggests something else: an enlargement, a distortion of certain features of the drama, to make them more apparent, more meaningful, more effective; and this development was one that an arm of the theater was soon to take to an extreme.

HENRIK IBSEN

Other dramatists outside France began to use the realistic theater to address contemporary ills. We remarked earlier (p. 147) that representational staging — of which we have now reached the perfected form — is best adapted to deal with immediate issues, where it can convince the audience of the reality and urgency of what it sees. The dramatist who most conspicuously employed these techniques to investigate the problems of contemporary society was a Norwegian, Henrik Ibsen. He was born in 1828 in a country that had only recently acquired independence and a sense of national purpose; until 1814 Norway had belonged to Denmark. Liberated in the aftermath of the Napoleonic wars, it was now in the process of establishing its artistic freedom, setting up its own theaters and encouraging native writers.

Ibsen's early career was bound up with this nationalist movement. Critics wedded to romantic theories might claim Ibsen as an example of a man whose life was reflected in his works. Raised in a provincial lumber town, he suffered greatly when his father's bankruptcy led to ostracism by local society. Though his early poems may exaggerate the hardships and indignities of this period, it is noticeable that the figure of the undischarged bankrupt recurs in several plays of his maturity, and a preoccupation with what is now called the generation gap may stem from the widening rift between himself and his parents.

Leaving home in 1850, Ibsen arrived in the city then called Christiania, now Oslo, with a play already written. It was, appropriately, a revolutionary subject, *Catilina,* drawn from Roman history and previously treated by, among others, Ben Jonson and Dumas. In its study of a man who tried to overthrow the government, it showed Catilina's better nature unable to dominate his darker side. Ibsen and a friend published it at their own expense; it failed, and the many unsold copies were used by a grocer as wrapping paper. So much for romantic beginnings.

But revolutionary sentiments in Ibsen were still dominant. After a period of writing political satires in verse and prose, he was offered the position of stage manager and *dramaturg* in the new theater at Bergen, the self-proclaimed Norwegian Theater, whose emphasis was on native work. The term *dramaturg,* though familiar in the European theater, has not yet had widespread American usage. It means, roughly, "literary manager." The *dramaturg* has the responsibility for editing old scripts and developing new ones, for assembling appropriate background material, and for overseeing all literary manifestations of the theater program. Ibsen was to spend six formative years in this function, gaining a practical knowledge of the theater and sharpening his own dramatic skills from his growing knowledge of the work of others.

Native output did not equal patriotic fervor, and the Bergen theater relied heavily on foreign importations. While there, Ibsen mounted 145 plays, of which 75 were French and 21 of these by Scribe. He came to admire the well-made plays for the same reasons that Zola had — their superb theatrical craftsmanship — and their form, though not their content, influenced his later work.

In 1864 Ibsen won a small literary scholarship that permitted him to travel abroad. During his European voyages he wrote several plays that were really dramatized epics; they are long, complex, and difficult to produce, and for that reason they are rarely revived. Among them was *Peer Gynt* (1867), in which a Norse folk hero engages on a long, picaresque journey, emblematic of life, among humans, trolls, and satirical representations of foreign countries; and *Emperor and Galilean* (1873), a play about Julian the Apostate, which calls for a volcanic eruption on stage. These works were products of a stay in Italy. In Germany, perhaps appropriately, he turned to work of stricter form and more immediate social content — the plays of ideas that made his name notorious in Europe and America and on which his fame chiefly rests.

Ibsen adopted the techniques of the well-made play and employed them for a more serious purpose. His social dramas follow the Scribe-Sardou pattern precisely: an initial situation is created, followed by a complication, a *scène à faire,* and a resolution. Abandoning the froufrou of polite entertainment, however, Ibsen used this tested formula for subjects that made his audiences wince.

The first of his social dramas to attract attention outside Scandinavia was *A Doll's House,* written and published in 1879 and acted in Copenhagen soon afterwards. In 1889 it was seen in London, in 1894 in Paris, and wherever it went, it caused a stir.

The theme of the play is the place of woman in society. Ibsen takes the fourth wall out of a family home and shows us a marriage. On the surface it is a perfectly happy and normal one. The husband is apparently kind and considerate; he keeps his wife well provided for; he is an honorable and upright man. His wife, apparently, is behaving as the marriage code instructs her — loving, honoring, and obeying her husband, caring for her three children. Ibsen plunges into this situation and exposes its true values.

One of the first things we hear is that the wife, Nora, is living a lie. In earlier days she had been forced to borrow money to take her husband abroad for his health. She had pretended to borrow this from her father, but it had really come from another man, now one of her husband's subordinates who is threatened with the loss of his position. To get the money in the first place, she had forged her father's name on a document. Her creditor knows this and now threatens her with exposure unless she uses her influence over her husband. But her husband is a man of high principles and he remains adamant; the employee is dismissed. Nora, caught in the consequences of her own lie, finally confesses, and her husband is wounded by her deception. But the bond is returned. The husband, concerned more with his own position than with his wife's distress, jubilantly announces "I am saved!" and is ready to forgive and forget.

This scene is where the play, if written by Sardou, would have ended. All the ingredients of the well-made play are here: the importance of props and material objects — the bond itself, the letter in which the dismissed employee reveals Nora's guilt to her husband; the existence of a secret, which is exposed as the play proceeds; the obligatory confrontation scene. Taken by themselves these elements are somewhat melodramatic and unconvincing. Ibsen, however, uses them only as his framework. He does *not* end the play with forgiveness and reconciliation.

What interests him is the relationship between husband and wife: the false position in which the two of them have been placed by the constraints of conventional society and which allows such a fundamental misunderstanding to grow and fester in the context of an apparently happy marriage. Nora is presented as a woman of her time, forced into a subordinate position by a male chauvinist society, childish, impractical, existing only to be protected. When we first see her, it is as a child among her own children, playing around the Christmas tree to her husband's condescending delight. What happens in the course of the play is that Nora grows up. She recognizes that all her life she has been merely a plaything to men — first to her father, then to her husband. The crisis has forced her to develop a sense of individual responsibility. She has never been an essential part of her husband's life, only a picturesque accessory. Ibsen is arguing that such a marriage is outwardly in accordance with the law and the dictates of polite society. Inwardly it is a sham. For the woman it is spiritual suicide, and the degradation of the wife diminishes the husband's stature too.

So carefully is the texture of domestic life depicted that the melodramatic quality of individual incidents is no longer noticeable. So convincing was Ibsen's portrayal of a marriage that the audiences were shocked. This play seemed to reach into their own homes and threaten the foundations of society. At the end of *A Doll's House* Nora leaves her husband and her children. What will happen to her we do not know. Ibsen simply leaves us with the sense that she will try to make her own way, to establish herself as an independent human being, and then, perhaps — a very faint perhaps — return to her home and family. But there is an awful finality about the slamming of the street door, which is Nora's only response to her husband's desperate appeal, and which contemporary audiences found the most shocking thing in the play. Sardou, in *Let's Get a Divorce,* had made an elegant diversion out of the breakup of a marriage and, of course, brought husband and wife happily together at the end. Ibsen treats a similar situation as a real and tragic possibility. He wrote, reluctantly and under strong commercial pressure, a new ending for foreign production in which Nora *did* come back, but the memory of the original was ineradicable.

The social impact of *A Doll's House* has diminished with time, yet it is still offered as a contemporary problem play in countries where women's rights are insecure — India, Greece, Japan — and even in the now more enlightened West it remains in the repertory as a work of considerable power in its own right. Not the least remarkable thing about it is its demonstration of the new stagecraft, the way in which setting is a concomitant of action. Some of the most effective moments of the play depend upon the setting rather than the actors: the Christmas tree, at first proud but later bedraggled; the letter rattling through the door; and the final door slam that signals Nora's departure.

Ibsen's subsequent plays confirmed his reputation as a dangerous writer challenging the pillars of orthodoxy. *Ghosts* (1881) tackled the unmentionable subject of social disease. *An Enemy of the People* (1882) turned to the corruption of a whole community. In this play the central character, Stockmann, is a doctor who has discovered that the public medicinal baths, on which the economy of his hometown is based, are polluted. As a man of science, bound to pursue the truth at whatever cost, he breaks this unwelcome news to the authorities. Immediately the community closes ranks against him. Stockmann's brother, the mayor, argues that the discovery must be hushed up for the good of the town. Thus the baths assume a wider implication: Stockmann's crusade is not merely against their pollution but against the pollution of the whole body politic. At first he is supported by the newspapers, but they too are motivated by self-interest and fall silent. In the end the very processes of democracy are called in to muffle the voice of truth. Act Four takes the form of a public meeting. Stockmann has secured a room to address the people. But before he can begin the mayor and other dignitaries appear; they go through the forms, elect a chairman, prevent Stockmann from delivering his speech, and finally have him declared an enemy of the people by public acclaim. Arthur Miller considered this play to be so valid in his own time that he rewrote it for twentieth-century America.

Just like the naturalistic dramas, however, Ibsen's social dramas sometimes contain hints that the realistic method is too restrictive and that the theater is starting to move in new directions. *The Wild Duck* (1884) has been seen by some critics both as a satire by Ibsen upon himself and as a tentative shift toward a different style. We are introduced to the Ekdal family, consisting of four people, all of whom have suffered at the hands of the wealthy merchant Werle. The old father has served a prison sentence that should have fallen on Werle himself. Gina, the wife, had been Werle's mistress. Hjalmar, her husband, was married to Gina and set up in business as a salve to another man's conscience. As for Hedvig, the young daughter, her parentage is dubious. All are living a secret, but to some purpose; they have shaken off the past and have made a good life together.

Into this family comes Gregers Werle, the old merchant's son. He has quarreled with his father, and his self-appointed mission is to open the family's eyes to the truth of their situation. An idealist, he has no conception of the harm he is causing. By exposing the former relationship between his father and Gina, by showing Hjalmar the deception underlying his life, he believes he is setting him on his feet. In reality he is taking away from him the whole support of his existence. The only results that Gregers achieves are catastrophic. Hjalmar indignantly leaves his wife who, he feels, has deceived him, but he promptly comes back, a doubly pathetic failure. Hedvig shoots herself. Gregers remains deaf and blind to the harm he has done.

What Ibsen seems to be telling us here is that truth is not always necessary or helpful, and that some part of life must be founded upon illusion. *The Wild Duck* was, significantly, a play of Ibsen's middle life, a time when youthful idealism begins to make way for compromise. The play contains one cryptic feature: the wild duck of the title, which has been crippled in a hunt and which now, unable to fly, lives as a pet in the attic. What does it represent and to which character is it supposed to be related? It is clearly a symbol, but of what? Critical opinions differ, but the device looks forward to a later period in Ibsen's life, identified with his return to Norway, when he forsakes pure realism for a more symbolic drama. This period, in turn, presages one of the major movements of the twentieth century in its shift away from the realistic stage.

THE CULMINATION OF REALISM: STANISLAVSKY

For what is generally acknowledged as the culmination of the realistic movement, both in play writing and in staging, and a force that is still a mainspring of the modern theater, we must look to Russia and the work of Constantin Stanislavsky (1863–1938). Stanislavsky came to his perception of the theatrical art by devious means. One of his early ventures, oddly enough, was in a Russian production of Gilbert and Sullivan's *The Mikado.* His name has become synonymous, however, with the ultimate expression of the realistic approach, both in acting and in stage design. In 1898 he founded, with Vladimir Nemirovich-Danchenko, the Moscow Art Theater and mounted a series of productions that had repercussions all over the world.

Stanislavsky's treatment of Shakespeare demonstrates his method. We may study his approach to one play, *Othello,* for which he has left a full analysis and promptbook. We need look only at the first scene to see how comprehensive the realistic conception was. *Othello* is set in Venice, and the opening scene takes place before the house of Brabantio, a wealthy Venetian nobleman. Othello, the Moorish general who has led the Venetian armies to victory, has married Brabantio's daughter. This marriage offends both Brabantio and Roderigo, a young and foolish gallant who is in love with the girl himself. Also estranged from Othello is Iago, the general's lieutenant, who is angry that he has been passed over for promotion. In the first scene Iago and Roderigo are together; the older man is working on the younger one and plans to use him as his cat's paw in a plot to gain revenge.

Shakespeare's text makes it clear that we are in a street and that Brabantio's house is somewhere in the background. In the original production this setting would have been indicated simply by the regular architectural components of the Elizabethan playhouse. In the eighteenth century we would have seen a vista of Venice painted upon shutter scenes, and in Irving's Lyceum the same kind of painterly effect would have been expanded to a huge backdrop.

Stanislavsky, however, rebuilds a slice of Venice on the stage. Set back from the proscenium arch are Brabantio's house and those adjoining, built in three-dimensional relief. Between them and the audience runs not a street but the canal demanded by topographical accuracy. Stanislavsky gives detailed instructions for obtaining this effect: there should be a loose floor covering with currents of air passing under it to make ripples. On the canal rides a gondola (on wheels) with Iago and Roderigo in it. Stanislavsky's scrupulous reconstruction of detail extends so far as to suggest that the gondolier's oar shall be made hollow and partially filled with water, to reproduce that splashing sound so evocative of Venice.

What is most remarkable about the *Othello* promptbook, however, is the way in which this same attitude extends itself to the characters. Roderigo has a fairly small part in the play, yet Stanislavsky fills pages with a reconstruction of his past and the events that have brought him to this point. He suggests that Roderigo was the son of a wealthy merchant family and thus had means and leisure to amuse himself. He followed the usual pleasures of the smart set and was generally welcome there, if only on account of his money. One morning, returning from an all-night debauch, he saw Desdemona — the girl who is now Othello's wife — in a passing gondola. He was immediately infatuated with her, followed her at a distance, and spent a fortune on flowers, which he dropped in her way along the canal. Desdemona was amused and flattered by his presumption, but her interest went no further. (All of this, we must remember, is nowhere mentioned in the play.) Now she has married Othello. Hence Roderigo's frustration and anger, which make him a willing partner in Iago's schemes.

Just as Stanislavsky surrounds the actors with a real environment, he creates a wider context for the lines that they speak and the roles that they play. The text is now seen only as *partial* evidence for a character. To fill this out, the actor must go outside the play to reconstruct for his character an imaginary offstage past, an offstage present, and perhaps an offstage future. And all these must be related with psychological probability, so that the lines spoken on stage are merely the momentary utterances of a whole being with a life extending far beyond the play itself.

By the time Stanislavsky came to the theater, acting had achieved a style that most thought realistic. Stanislavsky himself was dissatisfied. He felt that what was accepted as stage realism touched the outward aspects only and suffered from lack of inner conviction. His method was to work from the inside out, to ask his actor to reconstruct a state of mind appropriate for the character and, from this, to develop the walk, actions, mannerisms, and pattern of speech that such a character would possess. The play's text was thus regarded as a casebook, giving various key moments in the character's life; it was for the actor to work them into a whole.

To do this, the actor was instructed to search his own mind, to reach back into the "emotive memory" for associations that might illumine the character's behavior. In many cases these associations were easily forthcoming. We have all of us, at some time, fallen in love, felt an insult, suffered the death of someone near to us. In other cases the state of mind had to be arrived at by analogy, and Stanislavsky was fecund in providing examples. How, an actor asked, could he reconstruct the thought processes of a murderer, when he had never been one? Stanislavsky asked him to remember how he felt when he swatted a fly. The text was scrupulously analyzed and dissected. Every sentence, every word, every inflection was seen as the end process of a mental state, what actors call the subtext, or reading between the lines.

With such elaborate preparation, it followed that the rehearsal process was a long one. Stanislavsky's productions became notorious for the length of time it took to mount them. Actors worked for months on the script before they were allowed to translate the words into action. Sometimes they grew restive under this discipline. One of the most amusing stories of the Stanislavsky regime is of the actor who, driven berserk by the monotony of being asked to examine, yet again, a text he already knew inside out, screamed "I know my lines!", threw the script away, and chased the director round the theater, forcing him to seek refuge in the men's room. But on the whole, actors relished the support that the system gave them and the new level of theatrical truth to which they could now aspire.

This kind of acting is the polar opposite of that with which this book began — the presentational style, developed for theaters that were only a step away from ritual. There the emphasis was on acting from the outside in. The actor revealed his character to the audience by carefully chosen and manipulated *external* features — mask, costume, codified gesture — each with its own predetermined connotations. Some evidence suggests that the classical Greek actor, before going on stage, sat down to contemplate his mask. The regular practice of Noh and Kabuki actors is still to spend some time in front of a full-length mirror before beginning the performance. Stanislavsky-trained actors, on the contrary, spend time in *mental* preparation — or even appropriate physical preparation — to get themselves into the right frame of mind for the role. They may improvise dialogue, in character. They may even, in extreme cases, run around the theater if their character is required to enter out of breath and in haste.

The influence of the Stanislavsky system or "the Method," as it has come to be known in the United States, has been far-reaching. In this country it has been most notably propagated by the Actors' Studio conducted by Lee Strasberg in New York, with which many of the famous names of the American stage and screen have at some time been associated. It is still — though its influence has weakened somewhat in recent years — the foundation of most American actors' training, and its values have been justly recognized. Its impact has been most obvious in the film, which encourages intimacy and introspection. Sybil Thorndike, a senior British actress trained in the classical school, once found herself acting in a movie with Marilyn Monroe, a representative of the new generation with Actors' Studio affinities. She remarked afterward that during the filming, her young colleague appeared to be totally haphazard and undisciplined, but when the finished product was shown, "I was the old ham, and she was completely natural."

The Method has some problems that are the counterpart of its merits. There are difficulties in applying it to plays written for an earlier, more extraverted style. Sometimes these problems may be solved by indirection. Lee Strasberg, when asked by this author how he would apply the Method to Racine, replied, "I would ask the actors to imagine they were nuns and priests."

But there is, perhaps, a deeper problem. Many of the plays that now form

The Gilbert and Sullivan operettas were insistent on realistic staging. A scene from *The Pirates of Penzance*.

(top and above left) Stage realism: the Moscow Art Theater production of Chekhov's The Cherry Orchard (1904), directed by Constantin Stanislavsky. Scenes from Act II. (above right and below) The Moscow Art Theater production of Chekhov's Three Sisters (1901), directed by Constantin Stanislavsky. (below) Act II. (above right) The finale. Masha (above at left, below in white blouse) is played by Chekhov's wife, Olga Knipper.

the classic repertory do not give the Method-trained actor answers to the questions he has been taught to ask. How much does Aeschylus tell us about Agamemnon *as a person?* Extraordinarily little. And dramatists may often sacrifice logic and psychological plausibility to immediate theatrical effect. One of the most provocative analyses of Shakespeare has been by a psychiatrist, Ernest Jones's *Hamlet: A Psychiatric Study.* But it remains debatable how far a character from a play can be treated as if he were a real person.

In the realm of pure technique, too, the Method has its dangers. Actors sometimes cultivate introspection to the exclusion of audibility; they play for their fellow actors, and though their feeling for the part may be correct, they cannot project it to the audience. Again this problem is less of a danger in film, where the demands on the actor to project are minimal. The cameraman and sound technician do this for him. On the stage the older virtues are sometimes neglected for the newer truth. And the Method has produced its own mannerisms. Marlon Brando's performance in Elia Kazan's film *On the Waterfront,* with its pregnant silences and groping after words, was hailed as staggeringly realistic. A few years later the veteran Helen Hayes asserted that all Brando had done was to resurrect the Macready pause.

Diderot's paradox still holds. The question of how much is art and how much technique still varies with the individual actor and the play. Some of the greatest actors swear by the Method; others have been untouched by it. Sarah Bernhardt, the most powerful actress of her time, who could still move huge audiences to tears in ingenue roles when she was an old lady with a wooden leg, could play a masterly tragic scene while intermittently hissing abuse at a stagehand in the wings. Laurence Olivier could break off a conversation, toss away a cigarette, and go on to give the performance of his life as Richard III. However mentally involved the actor may be with his role, some portion of his mind must still be free to deal with exigencies. From time to time experiments have been conducted that represent Stanislavsky's conception carried to its ultimate: the hypnosis of actors to make them believe they truly are the people they represent. Adequate documentation is not yet available, but the results could be fascinating.

To return to Stanislavsky's own theater, it should be clear now that his concern with the detailed realism of stage setting, and of every aspect of the production, was not merely in accord with his times but was the logical accompaniment of his concern with the veracity of the actor. If acting was, indeed, being, if the actor was to think of himself as a real person, engaging in real events, then nothing on the stage should be permitted to jar this perception. The setting, like the acting performance, had to evolve from the situation, not merely reproducing the characters' social milieu but echoing their moods and sending out those vibrations that real houses acquire from the people who live in them. Just as what happened outside the stage action was as important to the characters as what happened in it, so aspects of the setting that scarcely registered with the audience were treated as carefully as those that did. Stanislavsky once ordered the backs of some scenic pieces to be painted. His stage manager argued, "But the audience can't see them." "Yes," said Stanislavsky, "but my actors can, and it bothers them."

CHEKHOV AND INDIRECT ACTION

Just as Antoine found Zola, a writer who shared his theater aesthetic, so Stanislavsky found Anton Pavlovich Chekhov (1860–1904). The Moscow Art Theater produced a range of works from European classics to contemporary plays, yet it is with Chekhov's drama that it has become most closely identified. In some ways this identification has been misleading, as Chekhov disagreed violently with Stanislavsky over artistic matters. For all that, the Moscow Art Theater productions of his plays have come to be regarded as definitive.

Anton Chekhov's father was a serf, freed a few years before the boy was born. The family ran a small grocery store in the provincial town of Taganrog, which gave Chekhov several experiences in common with Ibsen — early privation, the restriction of small-town life, and, in time, family bankruptcy. He eventually came to Moscow with a medical scholarship, which for a while supported the whole family. It was at this time that he began to refer to his family as a "benignant tumor" and to feel the lack of personal freedom obviously experienced by many of his characters, whose lives hang on decisions made by others. He began to write short stories for magazines as a way of adding to his income; he also wrote two full-length plays, neither of which was successful. Several one-act plays that he wrote at this time are still frequently produced, particularly *The Bear,* a short farce about a widowed lady clinging to her grief and an outrageous neighbor turned wooer who reconciles her to the idea of remarriage.

Gradually Chekhov came to take his writing more seriously, though he continued to practice as a doctor almost all his life. While still in his early thirties he had made enough money to buy a large estate. His most interesting and innovative work was done in the last few years of his life, the period when he became involved with the Moscow Art Theater. The four plays on which his reputation as a playwright rests were all produced there; there were other productions in other theaters, but it is the success of the Moscow productions that is remembered. The first, *The Seagull,* was produced in 1898, and the last, *The Cherry Orchard,* in 1904. Chekhov's wife, whom he married late in his life, was an actress from the Moscow Art Theater. He died soon after the production of *The Cherry Orchard.*

Although his dramatic output was not extensive, Chekhov was interested in the theater and in play writing all his life. His early one-act pieces, with their safe, conventional structure, were spiritually kin to Scribe's vaudevilles. Then came a long gap, and when he tried again, with *The Seagull,* he used a different technique. This is generally referred to as "indirect action": that is, the dramatic events take place offstage, and the play consists of the reactions of the characters to these events in their lives.

Such a play, achieving its effects by oblique means, demanded a new technique of production and was only really successful when staged by a director who understood the implications of Chekhov's method. Chekhov read *The Seagull* to a circle of his friends and found their reaction so disappointing that he never repeated the experience. *The Seagull* was compared unfavorably to the works of Dumas and Sardou for its lack of obvious dramatic incidents.

The first stage production, at St. Petersburg, was a total disaster. Two years afterward the Moscow Art Theater requested it. At first Chekhov refused, and only after several letters did he agree to allow Stanislavsky to direct it. This time the approach was completely different. Rehearsals were preceded by weeks of intensive preparation in which the actors discussed the play as a whole and the roles of their characters in it.

For Chekhov this approach was not merely preferable but essential. In the well-made play the rhythm is obvious, the climax self-evident. A formulaic work responds to formulaic methods of production. In Chekhov's more delicate and allusive text, the realization of events gradually impinges on the audience's consciousness through the characters' subsequent discussions. The rhythm is not obvious. The director has to search for it and impose it, in the same way that a conductor does for a symphony. (It is no accident that the rise of the interpretive symphonic conductor in music parallels the emergence of the interpretive director in the theater.) And several equally valid interpretations are possible. Subsequent directors have found in Chekhov's plays things quite different from what Stanislavsky did; Chekhov himself, on more than one occasion, considered Stanislavsky's approach to be wrongheaded. But the play requires interpretation of some sort and, whatever happens, must not be allowed to drift.

The Seagull may be considered a representative Chekhovian play in that apparently nothing happens. What Chekhov's friends objected to is true: it lacks the conventional plot structure, the forward movement with a clear objective. We have seen something like this form before — in neoclassic tragedy, where all the important events happen offstage and the characters merely respond to them. But in Chekhov there is no unity of action. Rather, we have a multiplicity of characters and actions, a multiple focus that seems to belong to the novel rather than to the play. But in this apparently formless, actionless drama there are in reality many conflicts. One is between Treplev, the young writer son, and Madam Arkadin, his brilliant actress mother. It is a struggle for money, for literary reputation, for Treplev's freedom of expression; his problem is to define himself in the shadow of the relentless matriarch. Another conflict occurs for Masha, the young girl who is in love with Treplev, but she recognizes the problem as hopeless; she decides in the end to marry her second choice, a schoolmaster.

The Seagull contains a play within a play, written by Treplev to shock his mother. It is his declaration of independence, conceived in terms of art. The play fails, because no one is prepared to see it for what it is. Madam Arkadin dismisses it contemptuously as decadent poetry. Others in the party claim they cannot understand a word of it. Masha is interested in it only because she loves the author. Chekhov is clearly telling us something here about his view of the contemporary stage. For most people art is decorative illusion. Treplev tries to distinguish between art as it is conventionally accepted and art as it should be; he fails.

But Chekhov touches on some other issues here. One, which will be given louder voice in the twentieth-century theater, is the theme of noncommunication. Here are people bound by ties of family and affection, moving, moreover, in a literary and artistic world where people are *supposed* to communicate — and yet there are barriers between them; they cannot truly speak to one another. All, too, are struggling in their own way for security — by clinging desperately to what they have or by trying to establish some solid foundation for existence. This aspect of the play is sharpened by the era of its composition. Chekhov lived in a society that was rapidly changing and in which the erosion of the vested privileges of the aristocracy would be followed, in a few years, by the Russian Revolution.

Of all Chekhov's work, however, *The Three Sisters* (1901) provides the best example of the new kind of drama and the value of the Chekhov-Stanislavsky combination. Like *The Seagull,* it seems relatively formless; like that play, too, it contains several independent plot lines.

The play is set in a house in a provincial town, where the sisters of the title, together with their brother, live. Olga, the oldest, is twenty-eight and a schoolteacher. Masha, the second, is married to a teacher. Irina, the youngest, is twenty and a working girl. Irina has three suitors; two are young officers from the garrison stationed in the town. She is in love with neither of them but likes one somewhat better than the other. The third is the sixty-year-old regimental surgeon, who has an unhealthy attachment to her.

Well-educated, intelligent, and recently orphaned, the sisters are bored by their life in the provinces. Their brother is their hope of escape. He is expected to become a professor and take the family back to Moscow, but he recently has married a local girl of a lower social class, who is still an outsider in the household when the play begins. Another officer is introduced, just posted to the town. His name is Vershinin, and he claims to have known the family in Moscow years ago. Though he is a married man with children, he and Masha soon fall in love.

In the third act a fire occurs in the town, and in the crisis the various plots come to a climax. Masha becomes Vershinin's mistress. The brother's wife asserts her domination over the household, and Irina reluctantly decides to marry one of her suitors. The news comes that the regiment is to be transferred to a remote part of the country.

Act Four takes place in the following fall. A good deal has happened and, typically, we hear about the events weeks later through the reactions of the characters involved. Olga has become the principal of the school where she was teaching and has given up her dream of going to Moscow. She has grown to accept the reality of her situation. Masha's husband has been promoted, and her lover has left town. She too will stay and accept her life. Irina's intended husband was provoked into a duel by the rival suitor and killed — offstage. She plans to stay and teach, like Olga.

What binds these plots together is the idea of Moscow. For the sisters the capital is the solution to every problem. Their dream of going there reduces everything about them to triviality. In consequence they are continually led to devalue the present reality. Only at the end of the play, when the dream is abandoned as unattainable, do the girls develop some maturity and begin to work out their destinies in the world they actually inhabit.

Chekhov saw the real drama of life as being performed "in that ordinary flow when things are left to themselves and nothing happens." The everyday pattern of life was thus for him not merely a setting or the background against which exciting and extraordinary things took place. It was the central area of his drama. The events become the details, the details the events. By the same token, the feeling of the play comes through in what is not said rather than what is said — in the silences rather than in the conversations, in the reactions rather than in the events. For this reason *The Three Sisters* is not a satisfactory play to read. Chekhov was disappointed in the first reading by the Moscow Art Theater. So were the actors. They complained that there were no good parts and that nothing happened. Stanislavsky's guiding hand, however, transformed the play into a moving experience. His promptbook for the original production has survived and shows how the director constructed a whole world around the text.

In Stanislavsky's interpretation every detail becomes important. The smallest thing tells us something about the people who live in this house. What stands out most vividly is the use of realistic offstage sound effects. Sound effects are something we have scarcely noticed in the theater before, but they now become powerful weapons in the director's armory. In Act One, when the mood is still optimistic and Moscow an attainable reality, we hear birds singing outside and Andrei, the brother, playing a sonata in another room. In Act Two, when Andrei's plebeian wife has taken over, the mood changes. Instead of the sound of birds outside, drunken singing is heard from the tavern down the street. The look of the room has changed, too. Andrei's wife has filled it with her own concerns. A child's bedclothes and toys are strewn over the set. To show the gap between the dream and the reality, Stanislavsky punctuates the conversation of the lovers, Masha and Vershinin, with distracting noises. A mouse is heard scratching in the room — a familiar nuisance in nineteenth-century Russia. Andrei is heard fidgeting outside. He plays the violin for a while and then does some carpentry. While talking to Masha, Vershinin plays with a clockwork toy — Petruschka, the traditional Russian clown figure with cymbals, who clatters an ironic commentary on the characters' aspirations.

LEGACY OF STANISLAVSKY

Stanislavsky's contribution to the theater represents the summation of several movements that had rapidly been gaining impetus throughout the nineteenth century: the shift to a more realistic style in acting, the growing realism of the stage picture, and, most importantly, the vision of the director as an integrator of effects and as an equal partner with the author in the artistic enterprise. His directorial approach as well as his system of actor training were enthusiastically welcomed and imitated far beyond Russia.

In Moscow the Art Theater still functions today, and his name is inseparably associated with it. Long after realism had lost its vogue, and the theater had moved in other directions, Stanislavsky's legacy was cherished without question. We have noted various theater forms that, for one reason or another, have been preserved far beyond their normal life span. The Noh theater of Japan is one, and the D'Oyly Carte Opera's staging of the works of Gilbert and Sullivan is another. To this number must be added the Moscow Art Theater. Although many who grew up with the institution went off in other directions, it retained the characteristics that had made its name: the front curtain still bears the sea gull that has been its symbol since the production of Chekhov's play.

Until very recently, on its European tours the Moscow was still displaying to the Western world productions that might have been directed by Stanislavsky himself. A London critic, after seeing *The Three Sisters,* noted that the realism of the whole was so overwhelming that even apparent lapses could be justified. At one point, he wrote, there was the offstage noise of a military band. The effect was not handled as deftly as Stanislavsky would have liked. Instead of the change in volume that one would expect as the band moved on or the wind changed, the level was constant throughout. And yet, the critic said, instead of criticizing the effect as badly managed, he was so absorbed in the realism of the total effect that he found himself asking, "I wonder why that band is standing so long on the next street corner?"

American Spectacular Realism

The examples we have just considered — Antoine, Zola, Ibsen, Stanislavsky, Chekhov — may be called purposeful realism, a technique harnessed to a higher purpose. It must be pointed out, however, that the general run of the commercial theater was happy to cultivate realism for its own sake. Often the stories of these plays were slight. What mattered was the skill and lavishness with which they were mounted. The result was a popular theater we might call spectacular realism. Audiences paid to see the real world represented on the stage. They applauded the execution rather than the author. They were delighted by stage depictions of natural phenomena, disasters, and historical periods re-created in rich detail. Although the American theater will be considered separately in Chapter 11, it is appropriate to anticipate here and look at some striking examples from the New York stage, for the cult of spectacular realism flourished most conspicuously on this side of the Atlantic.

One of its most successful proponents was David Belasco (ca. 1854–1931), author, director, and entrepreneur. A flamboyant figure, he produced himself as carefully as his plays, regarding himself as high priest of the theater to the extent of wearing clerical garb and haranguing visitors from a kind of pulpit constructed in his office. The works he produced were sensational in their time.

The Girl of the Golden West (1905) was a melodrama set in gold-mining country, with a scene in which the wounded hero, hiding in the rafters, is nearly betrayed by his blood dripping onto the stage below and ending with a near lynching and an exciting rescue. *Madame Butterfly* (1900) capitalized on the surge of interest in Japan, which after centuries of self-imposed isolation had only recently reopened communications with the Western world. Its heroine is a Japanese girl who marries an American officer, not realizing that he regards her only as a temporary amusement. When he returns to Japan with an American wife, she kills herself. The high point of Belasco's production was a long, wordless scene in which Butterfly, learning that her husband's ship is back in harbor, waits through the night for him to visit her. It was a tour de force of stage lighting: audiences saw the stage pass through all the subtle variations from evening through darkness to dawn.

The plays themselves have vanished from the stage, but they have won permanence in musical versions. Giacomo Puccini, who was developing a new style of verismo (realistic) opera, adapted both *The Girl of the Golden West* and *Madame Butterfly,* and the latter — in which a humming chorus replaces Belasco's famous light changes — has become a staple of the opera houses of the world.

In 1902 Belasco produced *Du Barry,* a play in five acts and eight spectacular scenes. The audience was treated to a fete in the gardens of Versailles, with Du Barry flaunting herself in an elaborate pavillion downstage with a panorama of the palace, its statues, and fountains stretching into the distance behind her, and a guillotining in a Paris public square, with which the play ended.

But even Belasco's work paled beside the production of General Lew Wallace's *Ben Hur* (1894), whose popular blend of Christianity and melodrama had already made it a phenomenal success as a novel. Those familiar with later film versions of the work may find it hard to conceive that all its spectacular scenes were originally mounted on the stage. *Ben Hur* involves, among other things, a scene on board a Roman galley that is engaged in a sea fight; the galley is destroyed, and the hero, at this point one of the galley slaves, saves himself and the Roman commander on a tossing raft. Breathless spectators *saw* all this; the raft bobbing up and down on canvas waves while, in the distance, the battered galley plunged to the depths. Even more spectacular was the chariot race, in which Ben Hur defeats his supercilious rival. Two four-horse chariots were set side by side downstage, headed toward the audience. On cue the horses were set to gallop — on strong wooden treadmills, so that they seemed to be racing neck and neck into the auditorium. Simultaneously, on panels surrounding the stage, a panorama of the racecourse was set in motion, so that the chariots seemed to be passing a sea of faces. It did not matter that the play was trite and the dialogue the worst kind of historical fustian. The horses were what the audiences came to see.

As might be guessed, the realistic movement in the theater brought about a surge of inventiveness in stage machinery, leaning on a rapidly advancing technology to cope with the elaborate effects that were now required. Theaters expanded both above and below the stage. They grew fly lofts into which whole scenic units could be hauled straight up out of the audience's sight. They developed wagon stages, huge rolling platforms on which full settings could be mounted in advance and rolled into place during a momentary blackout — or, in the more advanced cases, brought up on lifts from the understage area.

But most important of all was the advance in stage lighting. Gas, which had already been developed to ensure considerable delicacy of control, was replaced by the even more versatile electricity. Belasco was famous for his innovations in the color, control, and positioning of light. Even before the invention of the incandescent bulb in 1879, he had been experimenting with silk screens to change the color of light onstage. He also claimed to be an innovator (though those who worked with him have disputed this claim, asserting that here, as elsewhere, he stole the ideas of others) in what is now known as front-of-house lighting — hanging instruments in the auditorium, along the balcony level, to give more interesting angles. In time this effect did away with the line of footlights running along the front of the stage and left nothing interposing between the audience and the perfectly composed stage picture.

The realistic movement, which dominated the nineteenth century, was so persuasive and so easily acceptable that it has distorted many people's ideas about what the aims of the theater should be. Most critics of the time, and some long afterwards, fell into the trap of assuming that realism was the theater's perfected form and that the theaters of earlier periods had merely been struggling with crude and fumbling approximations of the ideal that the nineteenth century had achieved. Theater historians wrote condescendingly of the Greeks, the medieval players, and the Elizabethans, and tried to force them into a realistic mold. Because of realism's tenacious hold on the new media of cinema and television, several generations of audiences have found it difficult to comprehend that the realistic mode was a late-appearing and temporary phenomenon, and cannot easily come to terms with works designed for a more presentational theater. Every movement, however, carries within it the seeds of its own destruction. Even at the height of realism's vogue, many artists were becoming aware of its limitations, and the twentieth century reveals how this discontent was translated into action.

10
Twentieth-Century Diversity

Film and Theater

One reason for the popularity of the realistic theater, as exploited by Belasco, Wallace, and their kind, was that it provided wish fulfillment for the audience. If they could not go out into the world or back into history, the stage brought the world and history to them. Its enchantment only began to fade when another medium was discovered that could do the same thing better.

BIRTH OF FILM

While *Ben Hur* was running in New York, George Méliès, a Parisian master of stage magic, was already experimenting with ways of improving his theatri-

Bernard Shaw continued to treat contemporary social problems in plays realistically conceived. *Candida* illuminates the reciprocal demands of marriage.

cal devices by translating them to film. In 1896 Thomas Alva Edison's kineto-scope opened timidly on Broadway. The curious could peep into a box and watch a moving picture. In France the Lumière brothers developed the projec-tor, which brought the picture out of the box and showed it to a larger audience on a screen. At the Paris Exposition of 1900 crowds were already watching a primitive forerunner of the talkies — a film of Coquelin, leading actor of the Comédie Française, in speeches from *Cyrano de Bergerac* with the text played simultaneously on a wax recording.

The new medium made a humble entrance. It saw itself as subservient to the theater. Leading figures of the stage despised it as a passing fad, a mechan-ical toy — until they realized its potential for preserving their performances and enlarging their public. When Sarah Bernhardt graciously permitted herself to be filmed, the medium became respectable.

In the early ventures, however, the camera was merely a recording instru-ment. It confined itself to filming the stage play, unchanged — but, of course, without sound — from the viewpoint of a spectator sitting front row center in the stalls. But as early as 1903 the movies had shown that they could beat the contemporary theater at its own game. *The Great Train Robbery,* appearing in that year, not only set a precedent by telling a connected story but did so with a realism that surpassed Belasco's wildest dreams. When audiences ran scream-ing from the nickelodeon because a train seemed to be rushing straight at them and ducked when a gun was pointed at their heads, the days of realistic spectacle on stage were numbered.

As the new medium began to flex and grow, it divorced itself from the proscenium arch entirely. The camera found that it no longer needed to restrict itself to stage sets. It could move outside and film the real world — or at least sets built especially for it, with a verisimilitude that the theater could not equal and on a scope that no playhouse could contain. *Ben Hur* could stagger the theater audience with eight horses and a moving panorama. When David Wark Griffith, a mere fifteen years later, produced *The Birth of a Nation,* he threw the whole magnitude of the Civil War across the screen.

This film was followed in 1916 by *Intolerance,* which expanded the poten-tialities of the screen still further by telling four interwoven stories, set in different historical epochs, and staging them with a magnificence that still, after years of Hollywood superspectacles, confounds the imagination. One se-quence called for the reconstruction of the city of Babylon. The research that went into this project was itself staggering. Three copies of every known book on the period were purchased, one for reference and the others to be reassembled into a giant comprehensive scrapbook. When completed, the set spread over 254 acres. It had walls and columns 90 feet high, topped by giant statues of elephants — on Griffith's insistence, though there was no historical precedent — which brought the highest point of the set to over 140 feet. The banquet hall for the royal feast, again constructed in meticulous Babylonian detail, could comfortably seat five thousand people. Griffith displayed these wonders to his audience by shooting from a camera platform over 100 feet high. No wonder that the theater suddenly felt itself diminished. *Intolerance* cost $1 million to make, a phenomenal sum at the time; it has been estimated that to re-create it now with the addition of a sound track would cost thirty times this amount.

Ben Hur, too, forsook the stage for the more extravagant splendor of the movie screen. The first film version, advertised in 1907 as "sixteen magnificent scenes with illustrated titles," was made cheaply at a nearby racetrack. But in 1925 came an elaborate production starring Ramon Novarro as Ben Hur and Francis X. Bushman as Messala and costing the then unheard of sum of $3 million. A whole stadium was built for the race, which was made extraordinarily exciting by mounting a camera on one of the chariots, thus thrusting the audience into the heart of the action. The *New York Times* reviewer was most taken by the galley scene, for which three fully operative ships were built. Ignited for the battle sequence, these ships nearly caused a real disaster and an international incident when three of the crew were temporarily lost at sea. Farewell to canvas waves and painted backdrops: realism, clearly, had found its natural element.

MOVIES' EFFECTS ON THEATER

The advent of the movies thus affected the live theater in two ways. One was to draw off a continually larger proportion of the popular audience, who found this new form of entertainment cheaper, more accessible, and in many ways more satisfying. It took some time for the full impact of this shift of allegiance to be realized, but those actors who had once scoffed at the movies soon saw the necessity of joining them. The presence of a movie house in any town of size spelled, first, the end of the touring shows and then, finally, the decline of the settled companies. There was still a large enough audience to maintain the theater, but its nature had changed. It tended now to be drawn from a much smaller segment of the population; the mass audience had deserted to the new medium.

Since that time many attempts have been made to reestablish the theater in the popular domain, but they have usually failed, particularly since the advent of television. In France in 1911 the Théâtre Ambulant Populaire, the People's Traveling Theater, made motorized forays across the country, stopping at key centers, assembling trailers into a playhouse, performing, and then moving on. With low-priced tickets for popular appeal, the first season played thirteen provincial cities in three months to sell-out houses. But by the second season the novelty had worn off.

A more recent attempt in London illustrates how radically theatergoing habits have changed. In the early nineteenth century most of London's theaters were located in the upper-class West End. The early nineteenth century saw the development of the East End, London's dockside, which soon had an enormous population of its own. Theaters sprang up in this district and were soon catering to 63 percent of the total audience capacity of London. This theatrical subculture produced no widely acclaimed stars; its productions were reviewed almost entirely in the local press and never mentioned in the grander London dailies; its output, though ranging from slapstick farce to Shakespeare, was mainly melodrama.

Side by side with these popular theaters were the music halls, where crowds packed into tiny spaces to hear a string of singers and comedians. It was an unsophisticated audience, an artisan audience, but a vital one. And it was this audience that defected to the movies. The theater had become redundant in one of its traditional functions: that of providing cheap, popular escapist entertainment. In the 1950s one London director, Joan Littlewood, made a determined effort to restore this audience to the theater. She produced works that were deliberately provocative and slanted toward a blue-collar audience in the hope of reestablishing a people's theater. Ironically her work was rejected by the audience she hoped for but seized on with acclaim by the West End, which made it a commercial success. And Joan Littlewood's experience has been the common one of the twentieth century. In the United States less than 2 percent of the population goes to the theater.

The other principal effect of film on theater was more positive. By taking over one of the theater's possibilities, the movies forced it to reappraise the others. What the movies did for the theater, the still camera had already done for painting.

When photography was invented, it at once made representational art redundant. Realistic canvases no longer dominated the galleries of the world. Now that the photograph could show total realism — and better than a painting ever could — the painters began to study new approaches. A growing movement argued that the function of art was to get *behind* the surface and to bring out underlying patterns and relationships. Cézanne (1839–1906), for example, sought to reduce nature to its basic geometrical components and to suggest things that the ordinary eye could not see. Other artists worked in terms of light and the way it is reflected or absorbed by solid objects. Others deliberately distorted human or natural subjects, the more powerfully to convey their essence. These antirealistic developments took much art out of the popular domain. Viewers had to reappraise their standards, as the artist had his, and a major time lag developed between each school of art and its popular acceptance. Artists spoke initially to a smaller, more select clientele, who, if not informed, were at least willing to be informed, and the public was expected to go halfway to meet the painter.

In the theater the same thing happened. Realism, though not discarded, lost its dominance. Doubtless this would have happened anyway. One can already sense, toward the end of the nineteenth century, a feeling that the limits of realism had been reached and that it was time to push on in other directions. Film merely accelerated the process.

With the turn of the century came a wave of experiments. Sometimes these experiments revealed a genuinely new theatrical philosophy associated with contemporary developments in the natural or social sciences. Psychiatry had a visible effect upon the theater; so did the Communist Revolution. More often, these new movements probed the theater's past, to rediscover elements that may be defined as purely theatrical — the mask, the use of ritual gesture, the sung or chanted chorus. Each movement won adherents, enjoyed a brief life, and gave place to another. Most of them assumed a sophisticated, knowledge-able audience, willing and ready to meet the theater halfway. Thus it is no longer possible, as in the past, to talk of a single movement dominating a substantial period of time. The twentieth-century world moves too fast for that. What we have is a century of disunity; and this chapter will do no more than identify some of the principal movements and suggest their origins and consequences.

The Continuance of Realism

Though realism was displaced in the theater, it was not abandoned. Main-stream commercial drama continued in the realistic mold. Some of the old arguments were still valid.

In the English-speaking theater Ibsen's probings of the social conscience inspired several successors. Sir Arthur Wing Pinero (1855–1934), one of the most successful playwrights of his time, wrote a string of popular, though mechanically contrived, farces, still effectively revived as period pieces, and a number of more serious works that touched — though with Victorian, some-times elephantine, delicacy — on aspects of the social malaise. *Trelawny of the Wells* (1895) deals with the life of actors, still largely considered as social outcasts, and what happens when one of their number crosses social boundaries and marries into society. *The Second Mrs. Tanqueray* (1893), a bulwark of the provincial theater long after its London run, treats delicately of a couple who have been "living in sin." John Galsworthy (1867–1933) used a realistic format to deal more vigorously with aspects of social injustice. His *The Silver Box* (1906) is the case study of a cleaning woman victimized by suspicion of a theft that she has not committed. But by far the most outspoken, most successful, and best-publicized playwright of his time was George Bernard Shaw.

GEORGE BERNARD SHAW

Shaw (1856–1950), like Congreve, Sheridan, and Wilde, was an Irishman who made his mark on the English theater. Educated in Dublin, he moved to London at the age of twenty, first as a novelist but soon as a critic reviewing books, plays, and music with equally caustic fervor. His political sympathies led him to the Fabian Society, an intellectually inspired socialist movement of the 1880s, and throughout his career his politics remained inextricable from his art.

Shaw was one of Ibsen's warmest and loudest advocates. In 1891 he published *The Quintessence of Ibsenism,* arguing that Ibsen was fulfilling the dramatist's prime function of pointing the way and exposing the social and moral evils of his time. Both Ibsen and Antoine were making an impression on England. Ibsen's *Pillars of Society* had already been produced in London in 1880, in a translation by the critic William Archer; Shaw, among others, heralded this attempt and agitated for "bringing the English theater into some sort of relation with contemporary culture." Coining the term *Sardoodledom* to express his contempt for the trivial content of the average well-made play, he craved a theater that would have more serious concerns.

In 1891 the Independent Theatre was organized in London and presented Ibsen's *Ghosts,* followed the next year by Shaw's first play, *Widowers' Houses. Mrs. Warren's Profession,* written in 1893, was banned under the provisions of the still powerful Licensing Act because it dealt with the forbidden subject of prostitution. It did not see the stage until 1902, and then only as a private production. In 1905 it was produced in the United States — which had no Licensing Act — amid a flurry of lawsuits and moral indignation. One reviewer alleged that "the audience, some members of it paying as high as $25 for the privilege, found that the same thing . . . might have been obtained at a much lower price and with far less difficulty from any of the garbage cans along the street."

Shaw reveled in this opprobrium, which was to be leveled at his plays for most of his career. A mischievous iconoclast, he knew that when he offended people they took notice, and he insisted that he used the theater only as a lecture platform, to preach certain moral or social truths and reach the largest possible audience. This attitude is reminiscent of the Greeks. Shaw had much in common with Euripides, both in his use of rhetoric and in his love of shock effects, and with Aristophanes, in his delight in satirizing contemporary values. It is scarcely an exaggeration to say that Aristophanes' *parabasis,* in which the chorus directly addresses the audience, lives again in the argumentative prefaces that Shaw attached to his published plays. His Irish relish for argument, sharpened by political experience, led him to fill his plays with debates. Shaw's characters can never resist an argument, even when it seems dramatically inopportune. *Man and Superman* (1903) contains a scene where Spanish bandits, waiting for their prey, sit down and discuss rival systems of government. And the debate element grew noticeably more predominant as Shaw's career advanced.

Three things, however, keep Shaw's plays from being mere talk and give them lasting dramatic interest. One is objectivity. He does not write a tract and is quite fair about expressing opposing points of view. The second — and something that distinguished him from European naturalists, although his philosophy was in many ways akin to theirs — is his sense of humor. While

Ibsen's and Zola's works were notable for their prevailing gloom, Shaw wrote comedy. Third was his remarkable ability to write plays that appealed to an audience on two quite different levels. To the average theatergoing audience many of them seemed merely ingeniously constructed comedies. For those with eyes to see, however, these comedies revealed an insurrectionist spirit, all the more dangerous for being touched with wit. A gushing lady once said to the author, "Mr. Shaw, you are a very funny man." Shaw replied, "The funniest thing, Madam, is that I am completely serious."

This combination made Shaw not only one of the most provocative but also one of the most commercially successful playwrights of the twentieth century. Although the Independent Theatre folded in 1897, it was replaced in 1899 by the Stage Society, of which Shaw was a leading member. And his commercial success was inaugurated by the production at London's Court Theatre, from 1904–1908, of eleven of his plays under the direction of Harley Granville-Barker, whose innovativeness in the theater rivaled Shaw's own.

Two examples will illustrate Shaw's method. *Arms and the Man* (1894) opens with a situation that suggests Ruritanian operetta. The action passes in a country in the Balkans. A war is in progress, and the heroine, Raina, is set before us as a young girl with romantic notions of military glory. Her dreams center on her fiancé, Major Sergius Saranoff, who has just led a dashing cavalry charge. Shots ring out, and a soldier climbs the balcony into her bedroom. He is Captain Bluntschli, one of the fugitive enemy, who forces Raina to conceal him. Having set up this apparently romantic situation, Shaw then proceeds to demolish it and, with it, all conventional notions of military heroism. Bluntschli is a cynic with a keen eye for self-preservation. His pouches are stuffed with chocolate, not ammunition, because he never knows where the next meal will come from. The antitype of the romantic figure, he praises the universality of the flying instinct: it is quite natural, he insists, to run away. Raina is at first repelled by his shattering of her girlish dreams. As the contrast between Bluntschli and Saranoff is developed, however, she and her family become more and more fascinated by the man's practicality and common sense. In his company Saranoff loses luster. The magnificent cavalry charge turns out to have been an accident: Sergius's horse ran away with him. At the end of the play Bluntschli is smuggled out of the house in disguise, headed for Switzerland and his prosaic trade of hotel keeping. It is presumed that Raina, whose attitude to war and life has now completely changed, will ultimately join him. To Shaw's disgust *Arms and the Man* was turned into an operetta in his lifetime, under the title of *The Chocolate Soldier*. The musical version exploited the romantic trappings of the play and ignored its hard center. The original, however, is still regularly enjoyed, both as an expertly contrived comedy and as an exposure of a recurrent type of human folly.

In *Candida* (1895) Shaw turns to the institution of marriage, which fascinated him as it had Ibsen. He was constantly preoccupied by the problem of the family and the personal and economic pressures that it creates. *Mrs. Warren's Profession* had discussed material necessity and sexual relationships from the standpoint of prostitution. For Shaw, however, marriage could be even worse than prostitution, imposing on women a drudgery without recompense. He saw many women as slaving for their families without the freedom of an independent income. Thus *Candida* investigates the balance of power and need between a husband and a wife. Like Ibsen in *A Doll's House,* Shaw takes an apparently happy marriage and exposes its foundations. The husband, James Mavor Morell, is a clergyman, a pillar of the community, a reformer. Candida is the wife whose daily drudgery makes it possible for him to continue his good works. Shaw does not weaken his case by making the husband a tyrant and exploiter. Morell loves Candida and idolizes the married state. In the course of the play, however, he is gradually brought to realize that he is a parasite feeding upon his wife's endeavors. The catalyst in the action is a young poet, Marchbanks, who enters the household, falls in love with Candida, and pleads with her to go away with him. Instead of drudgery, he offers her a free existence, unhampered by domestic toil. Candida, at the end, announces that she will give herself to the weaker of the two. Morell is shattered when he thinks that this means the end of his marriage. He is even more shattered when he realizes that Candida means himself.

It is difficult to identify Shaw with any one group, for his impish perversity tended to carry him in all directions. Ultimately, however, he must be reckoned as a naturalist; his plays increasingly reveal his belief in what he calls a "life force," manifesting itself in biological necessity to which individuals must eventually succumb. The outward expression of his plays is completely realistic. Shaw wanted to be author and director, too. He has become notorious for his enormous stage directions, prescribing setting, furniture, costume details, manners, and stage movement, even what the actors should be thinking — anything that he thinks crucial to the meaning of the scene. He had a disconcerting habit of appearing at rehearsals of touring companies to correct their pronunciation.

Throughout his long life he remained an intentionally provocative figure, espousing such diverse causes as eugenics and the reform of English spelling and offending orthodoxy by his claim that he was a better playwright than Shakespeare. His last play, *Shakes versus Shav,* written for marionettes, shows a puppet Shaw triumphing over his illustrious rival. After the inevitable eclipse that comes over every successful writer after his death, his plays have once again become a staple of the world repertory, and several festivals have been established in his honor.

NOEL COWARD

The other face of realism, the well-made play designed for entertainment only, continues to be seen in a steady stream of works. Its most brilliant exponent on the English-speaking stage has been Noel Coward (1899–1973), solely a product of the commercial theater, who, while admitting that he had only "a talent to amuse," produced a succession of elegant comedies whose craftmanship has stood the test of time and won for them the status of minor classics.

Coward's plays are about nothing. *Private Lives* (1931), written when the economic depression had fallen over the Western world and fascism was looming in Europe, is a deft quadrille for two sets of married partners who change combinations. *Blithe Spirit* (1941), written when the German bombs were raining down on London, might have been written twenty years earlier, so divorced is it from any of the harsher realities of the time.

It seems clear that the well-made play will always be with us and that realism will continue to be a part of the theater. It is encouraged, indeed, by the theater's rivals, film and television, which have so indoctrinated mass audiences in the realistic mode that they find it hard to come to terms with works adopting different approaches.

Distortion of Reality: Strindberg

One movement broke sharply from the limitations of the realistic method and had a brief but vivid impact on the European stage: expressionism. It may be seen most clearly in the work of another Scandinavian playwright, August Strindberg (1849–1912).

Strindberg began as a naturalist. He had contacts with both Zola and Antoine, and he sent the manuscript of one play, *The Father,* to Zola for comment. Zola read it with qualified praise, and it was accepted for production at Antoine's theater, though it did not actually appear there until it had been seen in a number of other places first. Like Ibsen, Strindberg was preoccupied with the problems of marriage. This obsession stemmed in part from the unhappy circumstances of his own life. An affair with another man's wife led to marriage, but when his wife took up acting, they became estranged and he divorced her. At the age of forty-four he was married again, to a twenty-year-old girl. This marriage, too, ended in divorce. His third marriage, to the Norwegian actress Harriet Bosse, when he was fifty-two and she twenty-three, lasted for a year.

Strindberg thus had ample material in his own life to explore the man-woman relationship. It was, too, a subject of current controversy, extending far beyond the stage and already reflected in such plays as *A Doll's House.* Strindberg, however, took an attitude different from Ibsen's. He had no patience with the modern woman who insists on living a man's life to the abandonment of her natural womanly function. Strindberg takes the naturalist stance in arguing for a larger imperative: the future of the race and the duty of the woman to make a home in order that the line be preserved. Ibsen's Nora had stood up for the independence of the individual. Strindberg wrote a story, also called *A Doll's House,* which is a parody of Ibsen's play. The hero is having trouble with his wife, who has come under the influence of a meddlesome bluestocking. Their home life is destroyed. The wife sends her husband a copy of Ibsen's play, hoping this will solve their problems. The husband reads but cannot understand it. Why not a doll's house? Nora is a fool; why should she leave? He eventually restores harmony by engaging in an affair with his wife's friend; this shock restores the wife's femininity, and she returns home.

EARLY WORKS

This story, though it may be read unsympathetically today, shows Strindberg's concern with biological priorities — what is important for a man and a woman is determined by the conditions of their being. *The Father* (1887) treats the same circumstances from a gloomier point of view, undoubtedly colored by the author's own experience. In the play life is a battle, a struggle for the survival of the fittest — a battle both of brains and of natural instincts. Strindberg really uses only part of Zola's formula, *faire grand.* He elevates a story of domestic discord into something of more universal significance. The husband in the drama does not even have a name but is referred to simply as "the Captain." His quarrel with his wife, Laura, is the eternal one between masculinity and femininity, focused on the question of their child. Laura's cruelest weapon is the hint that the child may not be his own. Both are bound by the laws of their own natures, reaching out for love and happiness but helpless against their destructive impulses. Strindberg uses sex, but not as the French well-made play had used it. There it was a means of intrigue, a device for initiating certain romantic entanglements; the characters in these plays tended to be unmarried. Strindberg is interested in something more fundamental: in sex both as bond and as weapon, in what brings people together and what keeps them from achieving full harmony in that union.

The woman's biological necessity is to be a mother. Thus Laura is driven to destroy her husband to preserve her child. For her, a husband is only the means to an end. As mother, she can feel affection for the Captain. As wife, she cannot be wholly his, for love implies strife. It is the mother-child relationship that dominates the play. At its end the Captain, tormented to desperation, is lured into a straitjacket by his old nurse, who makes him see himself as a child again.

Strindberg is already exaggerating, distorting for effect. The seeds of expressionism are already latent in this play, as Zola saw when he complained that Strindberg's characters philosophize too much, that they are creatures of reason rather than natural impulse. But this savage portrait of female machinations has enough truth in it to be effective. Woman is seen in man's life as both protector and potential torment. The struggle is one between instinctive, hereditary forces and the more civilized qualities that the Captain has — his intelligence, his speculation, his propensity to doubt, which eventually destroys him. Strindberg saw the play as an intensely personal document and was afraid that he had revealed too much of himself on stage.

Objectively, *The Father* is a statement of certain laws of life that it is useless to combat. Man tries to raise his children in his own image and is cheated. He only sows the seed. It is the woman who controls the rearing. The strong conquer the weak, and only the fittest survive. Once again naturalism, despite its obvious affinity with contemporary evolutionary theory, reaches back across the ages to align itself with the universal imperatives of Greek tragedy. The struggle between patriarchy and matriarchy echoes the issues of Aeschylus's *Oresteia*.

In mid career Strindberg suffered a long period of mental illness. His work after this crisis shows a marked change of direction, clearly indicated in his autobiographical writings. His earlier autobiography, *Son of a Servant* (1866), is a naturalistic document. It is concerned with the larger pressures, the formative factors upon the individual: heredity, from father and from mother; the influence of the nurse in early childhood; the parents' economic circumstances and their view of life; school, teachers, friends, siblings. After the crisis his writing about himself becomes more fragmentary and subjective, and a similar change is seen in his later plays.

EXPRESSIONISM

These plays, and the whole art movement of which they are but one example, have been categorized as *expressionistic,* and the term needs careful explanation. Just as naturalism had been linked with contemporary scientific thought, expressionism can be identified with new developments in philosophy: a concentration not on the external facts but on the nature of the inner self; the emergence of subjectivist theories, particularly as represented in the new science of psychology; and an exploration of the mind in the hope of revealing the secrets of life. It was now being suggested that the subconscious may be intuitively aware of things that are inaccessible to our waking consciousness, and that things that may seem trivial in the pattern of our everyday lives may weigh more heavily beneath the surface.

Once again we may seek a parallel in the visual arts and compare Strindberg's change of direction to the breakaway from academic painting and the offerings of new insights by painters such as Cézanne and van Gogh. When he broke down nature into certain basic shapes, Cézanne was not merely offering a new way of looking at the world around us or a simplification of nature. Rather, he was suggesting the existence of another world, a harmony parallel with nature, a second reality achieved through distortion and exaggeration. Similarly, van Gogh distorts and exaggerates the appearance of natural objects to express his own powerful feelings, producing paintings that illustrate not so much the world about him as his own mental state.

Expressionism does the same thing in the theater. It digs beneath the surface. It seeks for what is *really* important and expresses it. It takes a key element and exaggerates and distorts it until we are conscious of nothing else. It brings our subconscious onto the stage.

A DREAM PLAY

It follows that the expressionistic drama commonly takes the pattern of the dream, in which the mind breaks loose and our inner concerns are more conspicuously revealed; we see an apparently formless progression of incidents, in which elements from the sense-perceptible world mingle with manifestations of our inner consciousness. Indeed, Strindberg's best-known work in this genre is called *A Dream Play* (1902).

Note that the play only appears to have the disorderly, haphazard quality of dream life. The dramatist does not abandon control. In reality *A Dream Play* is carefully structured. The juxtaposition of incidents is formulated to produce certain resonances so that, although a point may not be specifically made, the audience is left with an impression, an association of ideas.

The plot is simple. Its basic situation is the examination of the human condition through the eyes of a visitor from another sphere — a device that Swift, for example, had exploited in *Gulliver's Travels*. The daughter of the Hindu deity Indra assumes human form and makes a journey through the world. She becomes the mistress of an Officer, through whom she meets a Lawyer. The Lawyer marries her, and she bears him a child. Finding life with him intolerable, she sets off with her first love on a tedious and unprofitable journey. She meets a Poet, with whom she finds a temporary happiness; when the Lawyer grows importunate, she retires from the world.

Around this simple story line Strindberg weaves a complex web of images and associations. Indra (representing Strindberg's growing interest in the exotic and occult) embodies the basic tenets of most Eastern philosophy: the idea that our stay in this world is one of a series of reincarnations, which we must endure with suffering, and the idea of ultimate deliverance through the transcending of the material world and the identification with the world spirit, the supreme good. Thus the pilgrimage of the Daughter of Indra, and her ultimate return to a higher sphere, represents the necessary progress of the human soul. In the various people that she meets we are also made aware of another cardinal principle of Eastern religion, that of the One and the Many. The god Brahma, by dismembering himself, created the material world. The eternal godhead thus produces the diversity of nature. All natural phenomena derive from the same source and will, in the perfection of time, return to the same source. But disunity is imperfection. The scattered elements of the divine are warped and distorted because they represent only one part of the divine nature.

In the play the idea of a cyclic universe, passing through periods of suffering to ultimate regeneration, is expressed in a striking visual image that dominates the stage: a castle, which we see at the beginning rooted in dung and which gradually grows until at the end it bursts into a glorious flower. The idea of unity and diversity is expressed in characters who are, at the same time, many and one, different aspects of the same personality. Apart from the Daughter of Indra, there are four principal characters: the Officer, the Lawyer, a Quarantine Master, and the Poet. These represent four aspects of a person, aspects that we all, from time to time, assume. The Officer is the romantic hero; the Lawyer, the bickering husband; the Quarantine Master, the merciless critic; the Poet, the lover of beauty, who in this imperfect world comes closest to the ideal.

The Daughter of Indra is first seen outside the Growing Castle. In the Castle is the Officer, who permits her to take him into the outside world — a motif perhaps derived from Strindberg's own life and the guilt he felt from his self-imposed isolation. We then move to an opera house, where the Officer is waiting for his beloved Victoria. The stage, like the dream, plays tricks with time. The wait is endless; the Officer grows old; Victoria never comes. He finally insists on breaking in and opening a mysterious door marked with a cloverleaf symbol, which stands for the secrets of the universe. The police prevent him from breaking in, and he demands to see a lawyer. The door remains onstage, unopened, to symbolize the enigma of existence.

The focus shifts to the Lawyer, who has grown ugly through exposure to human pain. We see his humiliation in an academic degree ceremony, where he is first passed over, then crowned with thorns. The Daughter of Indra decides to join him in order to experience marriage, the supreme joy of human existence. But the marriage turns sour, and she is willing to run away with the Officer when he comes to rescue her.

Together the Officer and the Daughter of Indra embark upon a journey, which is cheated of its promise. Aiming for Fairhaven, they reach instead the Channel of Shame. Here they meet the Quarantine Master, a satirical self-portrait of Strindberg himself. He tells us that to forget himself he has taken up playacting and become a merciless critic of others. A pair of lovers falling under his jurisdiction is mercilessly fumigated: the girl is the Officer's lost love, Victoria. The Poet is there; and at this point the three men are obviously one, different aspects of the human condition. The Officer feels jealousy over the girl he loved. The Poet feels compassion. The Quarantine Officer is obliged to disinfect, in his capacity as national watchman.

The journey resumes but things still go wrong. Desiring to escape, the Daughter of Indra retraces her steps. Once more the dream pattern asserts itself: as in a dream, events begin to unwind backward. The Daughter returns with the Poet through a montage of former scenes and incidents until she is back at the forbidden door. The Officer is still there, young again, and waiting for Victoria. The Daughter offers to unlock the door and reveal to the Poet the mysteries of life. When it opens, there is nothing inside. Then the Daughter offers to communicate the secret, but she is interrupted by the Lawyer, who presses his claims and the needs of their child. Prevented from giving the Poet the ultimate answer, she shakes the dust of earth from her feet. At that point fire breaks out and the characters appear one by one to cast into the flames those things that they have prized on earth. As the Daughter ascends, the budding flower on the castle summit bursts into full bloom.

A Dream Play is a curious combination of the obvious and the cryptic, of some symbols that are transparent and of others that are hopelessly obscure. Many incidents, themes, and objects are obviously drawn — as in dreams —

from Strindberg's own life and the everyday features of his Scandinavian environment. Seeing the Officer waiting hopelessly at the stage door, we remember Strindberg's unfortunate involvements with actresses. In the Lawyer's house an old servant doggedly and remorselessly papers over the windows. This task was regularly done in Scandinavian houses in winter, but in the play it becomes a symbol of isolation, of shutting out the larger world, and of the ingrowing frustrations of marriage. The Officer is drawn out of the Castle, the prison of the soul, by his contact with the Divine. He then becomes the Poet, who is nearest to the Divine.

A Dream Play is about the mysteries of life, apparently insoluble. Behind the closed door there is no answer. Some of the answers that the world has traditionally suggested are present, but they are either dismissed or seen as only part of the larger, vaguer pattern and liable to be misunderstood. For example, a momentary vision of Christ is seen by the frustrated travelers, anticipating the same device used by Kafka in *The Castle. A Dream Play,* then, represents the quest for other patterns in the drama besides those of conscious awareness.

Strindberg's impact on the world theater was not as immediate as that of Ibsen (the first American production of *A Dream Play* did not come till 1926) and was necessarily more limited because of the unprecedented demands that he was making on the stage. A sense of strain is apparent in his stage directions. Strindberg was clearly hampered by the technology of a theater that had been developed for realistic purposes. Although he organized his own theater, the Intiman, for the production of his plays, it is only recently that stagecraft, particularly with its advances in lighting and projections, has been able to provide the ambience that his work requires.

Strindberg was, in fact, ahead of his time, demanding many of the devices soon to be accessible only through film. Nevertheless, the fragmentary pattern of the play and the deliberate shattering of the space-time continuum had their effect on plays and productions of a later generation. Although the movement was more evident in Europe, expressionism had, in Elmer Rice and Eugene O'Neill (see pp. 463 and 464), its exponents in the United States. On a more popular level, Arthur Miller's *Death of a Salesman* shows an action vacillating between past and present and creates a picture of the protagonist's mental state in which dead characters have as much immediacy as living ones.

In its scenic manifestations expressionism cultivated the same distortions it encouraged in its subject matter. Settings were unnaturally compressed or tilted; the phenomena of the material world were shown awry (as in a dream). Actors' makeup was exaggerated to express their essential nature; for example, we note the ugliness of the Lawyer, which is dwelt upon at length in *A Dream Play*. Again, these techniques found imitators, sometimes in unexpected places. In one of Stanislavsky's early exercises in drama school, he made an appearance as a Dramatic Critic, with lurid makeup and a quill pen curled between his teeth.

Such devices have been preserved on film. Expressionism had a powerful effect on the early German cinema, which favored the abnormal and bizarre. Its twisted, leaning sets and harsh, angular lighting further distorted by unusual camera angles may still be seen in such products of the silent cinema as Paul Leni's *Waxworks* (1924) and Robert Wiene's *The Cabinet of Doctor Caligari* (1919) — the latter telling a subjective story through a madman's eyes. Even the American commercially oriented Frankenstein series of the 1930s used deliberately tilted walls and distorted doorways to create an atmosphere of menace and horror.

Simplification of the Shakespearean Stage

Now that we have seen how the twentieth-century theater availed itself of the new psychology, we may consider how it treated more traditional material. Irving's realistic style of Shakespearean production did not disappear entirely. Indeed, it remained standard in the commercial theater for years, and a few directors still cultivate the realistic approach. In many respects Irving's spiritual descendant in the second half of the twentieth century has been Franco Zeffirelli, whose meticulously detailed and historically authentic productions have been seen both on stage and film. Nevertheless, the attendant disadvantages — notably the sacrifice of speed and flexibility to the creation of elaborate stage pictures — provoked a challenge, which in turn inspired a reappraisal of how Shakespeare had used his own stage.

THE PRODUCTIONS OF WILLIAM POEL

Prominent in the movement to free Shakespeare from the tyranny of the designer was William Poel (1852–1934), who grew up in a London where Irving *was* the theater. He saw the great actor in *The Bells* and found its sensationalism revolting, nor was he any more impressed by the lavish Shakespearean productions at the Lyceum. On the contrary, he found himself more moved by other theater disciplines — by the visiting French companies who appeared in London playing their own classical material and by the Italian actor Salvini, who played an emotional *Othello* there on tour. He admired the latter not only for the naturalness of the performance but for its evidence of close study of the text.

Poel then went on the stage himself. He first joined Charles Mathews, whose more intimate style of playing he admired, and went on to work for other groups, including one touring company still working in conditions reminiscent of the eighteenth century, where the actors pooled their savings, shared the manual labor of moving from town to town, and were continually on the verge of bankruptcy. The acting lessons that Poel received in this environment made him all the more inclined to criticize contemporary productions, and his bookish inclinations continually led him back to the text and to the historical

(*above and left*) The violent reaction against naturalism. Expressionistic works such as Strindberg's *Dream Play* distorted sets and characters and made demands on the theater which only modern technology has been able completely to fulfill. A modern production is illustrated here. (*right*) Realism, though often simplified, continued to dominate the twentieth century theater. The opera box scene from Gaston Baty's staging of Flaubert's *Madame Bovary*.

The simplification of the stage. Set designs by
Gordon Craig (*above*) and Adolphe Appia (*right*) are
conceived as arrangements of basic architectural
shapes.

circumstances of Shakespeare's time. His growing conviction that the spirit of Shakespeare lay in the language rather than in any scenic embellishments led him to organize a series of dramatic readings. In 1879 he formed a group called The Elizabethans who toured the country with recitals of the plays in costume. Of necessity their scenic arrangements were of the simplest, and Poel retained the same approach when he came to mount full productions.

In 1881 Poel staged *Hamlet* at St. George's Hall in London, on a bare, draped platform. Though not the first such experiment, it created much excitement; here was the play restored to something like the physical conditions for which it had been written. Poel continued to research the features of the Elizabethan stage and see how they could be adapted to the contemporary theater situation. In 1893 came the foundation of the Elizabethan Stage Society and the production of Shakespeare's *Measure for Measure,* a work hardly known to Victorian playgoers. Other actors came to scoff at what they thought would be an arid antiquarian exercise, but they left impressed by Poel's integrity and obvious intelligence. What they had seen was a reconstruction of the Elizabethan public playhouse, imperfect in detail and hampered by having to be framed within a conventional proscenium stage but still restoring to the play a dimension that Irving's productions lacked — the collaborative, creative imagination of the audience. *Twelfth Night* followed. It was attacked by William Archer (the critic and translator of Ibsen, see p. 388), who argued that such productions were for scholars and dilettantes and no longer for the public audience. Nevertheless, it provoked a fruitful controversy about what the Elizabethan stage really looked like and how accurate Poel's reconstruction was, which has continued unabated to this day. More rarities followed: *A Comedy of Errors,* played in a setting Shakespeare would have recognized, one of the Inns of Court; Marlowe's *Doctor Faustus,* which had not been seen on the stage in living memory; *The Two Gentlemen of Verona; Troilus and Cressida;* and John Ford's almost forgotten Jacobean tragedy, *The Broken Heart.*

Poel did not, however, confine himself to Shakespeare and his contemporaries. He also brought to London the early Indian drama *Shakuntala,* Molière's tragicomic *Don Juan,* seen for the first time in English, Milton's *Samson Agonistes,* and Schiller's romantic historical drama *Wallenstein.* Most importantly, he rediscovered the medieval morality play *Everyman* and restored to the stage one of the finest works of the early English drama. It was played outdoors in a gray stone medieval quadrangle; Death was appropriately chilling, dressed in medieval fashion as a skeleton with drum and trumpet; and it was the only one of Poel's productions to make money.

Although Poel's productions were only a fringe activity in their own time, their influence has been widely acknowledged. Not only did he encourage a new way of looking at Shakespeare, but by his insistence that plays are inseparable from the circumstances of their original production, he inspired a collaboration between scholarship and the theater that has continued to bear fruit.

Not everyone would agree that the only way to present Shakespeare is on the

kind of stage that he knew. Nevertheless, this view has had powerful proponents. In England Ronald Watkins has staged a series of successful productions
in Elizabethan conditions and under natural light. In the United States the
Ashland, Oregon, Festival Theater has offered since 1935 summer seasons
embracing, over the years, all the plays in the canon, staged in the open air and
on an elaborate Elizabethan replica — though in this case, since the plays are
given at night, also with all the resources of modern stage lighting. The effect
has been refreshing. Although theater historians may squabble over the details
of the reconstructions, the gain in speed, immediacy, and imaginative flexibility cannot be denied.

THE DESIGNS OF EDWARD GORDON CRAIG

Another challenge to Irving's method was delivered by a theater artist who,
like Poel, was antagonized by him and yet began by being far closer to him,
Edward Gordon Craig (1872–1966), the son of Irving's leading lady Ellen
Terry. First appearing on the stage as a child actor, he joined Irving's company
at the Lyceum in 1899 and remained with it for nine years. Here his interest
gradually shifted from acting to design and production. After designing some
productions for his mother, he moved to Europe, where he remained for the
rest of his life, staging plays for several prominent theaters and publishing his
theories and designs in a journal, *The Mask,* and in several books that attracted
widespread interest within the profession.

Like Poel, Craig reacted against the vogue for smothering Shakespeare's
plays in scenery. His method, however, was not to restore the conditions of the
Elizabethan stage but rather to use the technical means available to the modern
theater, particularly the resources of stage light, to create an environment that
was both flexible and suggestive; that would work in terms of mass, light, and
shadow rather than of painted detail; and that would convey the *mood* of the
scene rather than any specific locale. Ideally, he argued, Shakespeare could only
be staged in the theater of the mind. But if the plays were to be performed,
they should be given settings that would release the imagination rather than
constrict it.

Craig accordingly designed an all-purpose stage set composed of basic
shapes — screens, cubes, levels, columns — that could be reassembled in various ways and, under changing lighting, give a multitude of different effects.
His published designs for Shakespearean and other plays were both praised and
criticized — the latter particularly by fellow designers, who complained that
though Craig's ideas looked all right on paper, they could never be realized
within the limitations of the ordinary theater.

One of Craig's most famous and controversial designs was for the sleepwalking scene in *Macbeth,* where Lady Macbeth, haunted by guilt for the murder of
the king, is watched by a doctor and her gentlewoman as she desperately tries
to wash the imaginary bloodstains from her hands. Craig set this scene on a

spiral staircase twining round an immense column towering into the upper darkness. Lady Macbeth is halfway up the stairs; the others are at the bottom, watching her: the characters are dwarfed by the simple but majestic scenic conception. The American designer Lee Simonson complained that if this set were built according to the scale of the human figures, it would need a proscenium arch higher than any theater in the world.

It is true that — though he was practical enough to patent his designs — Craig's realizations of his settings disclosed unexpected technical difficulties. In 1912 Stanislavsky invited him to direct *Hamlet* for the Moscow Art Theater. Craig designed a setting of movable screens that would form new combinations as the action progressed and be moved by stagehands positioned behind them. Opening night was disastrous. The stagehands had been insufficiently drilled, and the screens collapsed against each other and ripped. It is only fair to add, however, that when these mistakes had been remedied, the production ran for a considerable time.

CRAIG'S CONTINUING INFLUENCE

Craig's chief importance was not so much in his own work as in the influence he had on others. The concept of a moving, adaptable stage, approximating the flexibility of Shakespeare's own through modern technology, has come to dominate contemporary Shakespearean production. This revolution may be clearly seen in the history of the Shakespeare Memorial Theater at Stratford-on-Avon, England, which, after its unhappy debut as a center for bardic pilgrimage in Garrick's time (see p. 302), has come to offer productions attracting hundreds of thousands of visitors annually from around the world.

The first production of a Shakespearean play, to celebrate his birthday, occurred at Stratford in 1864. A permanent theater followed, and the festival in its present form was inaugurated in 1879. This first theater was of typical Victorian design, and its productions, in keeping with the spirit of the times, were heavily realistic — even to the extent of standing stuffed stags about the stage for the Forest of Arden in *As You Like It*. In 1926 the building was destroyed by fire (and Bernard Shaw sent a telegram of congratulations). Its replacement, opened six years later, was of happier construction, though its 1930s modernity has dated and it is now known locally as "the jam factory." Inside, however, it has undergone a series of reconstructions, showing an increasingly more flexible approach to Shakespearean production. The drop curtain was removed, and an apron stage was pushed out toward the audience. Entrances leading from beneath the auditorium made it possible for crowds to surge onstage from under the audience's feet. An improved revolve made sets more mobile. The most recent tendency has been to break up the floor into stage lifts, which can rise or sink in various combinations to rearrange the levels of the acting area.

The revolution in stage design, of which Craig's work was an early example, did not, of course, confine itself to Shakespeare. We can see the same transition in another of the major festival theaters, the Festspielhaus in Bayreuth, Germany, opened in 1876 and devoted to the production of Wagnerian opera.

Wagner had sought to create an environment in which his works could be seen at their best, and the Bayreuth theater was, in its time, revolutionary. There were no galleries. All seats in the house, on rising tiers, directly faced the stage. Conductor and orchestra were in a sunken pit, the famous "mystic gulf," so that there was nothing between the audience and the opera.

What happened on the stage was highly realistic, according to directions prescribed by Wagner himself and rigidly adhered to after his death. His operas draw their material from Germanic legend. They call for such effects as the forging of a magic sword, the slaying of a dragon, airborne Valkyrie, and the destruction by fire of Valhalla. As originally conceived, these effects were shown to the audience with all the artifice that the stage machinery of that time could contrive. But Wagner, like Shakespeare, eventually proved susceptible to the new staging.

The Swiss designer Adolphe Appia (1862–1928), using an approach similar to Craig's, advocated light as a substitute for paint and showed how, for example, the forest in Wagner's *Siegfried* could be suggested more effectively, and more simply, by bare platforms dappled with the projected shadows of leaves, creating a pattern of light and shade through which the characters could pass. Although Craig and Appia used similar technical means, they differed in emphasis. Craig saw the actor as dominated by the set, as simply one component in the total mise-en-scène (stage setting). Appia subordinated the set to the actors, to give them prominence and scope.

After World War II, when Bayreuth was reestablished as a festival center, this kind of setting came to dominate. Gone were the painted rocks, the canvas backdrops; in their place were bare, tilted platforms, with all the necessary effects suggested by light. Some audiences have found such settings too austere. They have complained, for instance, that when, in *Lohengrin,* the text calls for the knight to sail on his mysterious quest mounted on a swan, it is not enough to have him followed by a moving shaft of light upon the stage. Nevertheless, the change has been largely beneficial, concentrating the attention on the action and the music rather than on the stage mechanics.

Similar manifestations appeared in France. At the Théâtre du Vieux-Colombier Jacques Copeau (1878–1949), whose cry was "give me a bare platform," developed a stage, for the production of the classics, that used a combination of simple, permanent architectural elements, in the manner of the Elizabethans or the fifth-century Greeks. His pupil Charles Dullin (1885–1949) similarly cultivated, in his Théâtre de l'Atelier, a "theater of the imagination," in which movable screens provided the principal decor and masks and dancing were incorporated into the action. Enthusiasm for the new movement also appeared in the United States, as we will see in Chapter 11.

Rediscovery of the Theater's Past

It will be apparent that many of these new movements were not new at all. They represented a return to principles centuries old, principles the theater had once employed exclusively and then abandoned — for example, the whole notion of presentational theater, in which settings are not shown but merely *suggested* and in which the audience is always conscious that it is undergoing a theatrical experience. Some of these rediscoveries were unconscious. Modern directors and designers had simply arrived, from a different starting point, at the same solutions that earlier cultures had evolved for themselves. Others, like Poel's reconstruction of the Elizabethan stage, were totally conscious; and one of the characteristic features of this period is the way in which the theater begins to dig back into its own past and find contemporary applications for conventions that had lain abandoned for centuries.

REVIVAL OF THE NOH FORM

One rediscovery was a matter not so much of time as of geography. We have seen how Japan developed distinctive forms of presentational theater that the Western world had never been allowed to see. With the reopening of Japan to foreign influence in the late nineteenth century, this long-sequestered art gradually became accessible. Not only could Western visitors now see Noh and Kabuki on their home ground, but Japanese performers displayed their work in Europe to audiences who found themselves strangely stirred by what they could not fully understand.

Particularly responsive to the possibilities of Noh was the Irish poet and dramatist William Butler Yeats (1865–1939). The increasingly bitter struggle for Irish independence from England had drawn him into the theater, partly against his will. As poet he preferred to speak with a private voice. As Irishman and patriot he could not ignore the loud public voice of the theater. His letters reveal his discontent at having to sit through so many mediocre Irish plays, badly written and performed but still claiming an audience because of their nationalistic sentiments. In 1899 he cofounded the Irish Dramatic Movement, which by 1904 was housed in Dublin's Abbey Theatre, a breeding ground for native playwrights working mostly in the realistic vein. Yeats's own inclinations led him in other directions, and when he was introduced to Noh, he seized upon it eagerly as a way of combining the intimacy of the poem with the immediacy of the theater. He saw how it could appeal to a select, initiated audience, without the brashness and vulgarity of the commercial theaters, and began to adapt the legends and history of his own country to Japanese forms.

Yeats did not reproduce the conditions of Noh drama exactly but sought rather for an intelligent transposition that would convey their essence. His "plays for dancers" were designed to be staged in salons, in drawing rooms, in the homes of friends. As in Noh, the settings were minimal. A cloth, ceremonially unfolded, both denoted the beginning of the play and defined the limits of the action. Yeats used narrators, as a reduction of the chanting Noh chorus, and a small number of musicians. The actors were masked, and the culmination of the play was a dance.

Typical of Yeats's early works is *At the Hawk's Well* (1916), which dramatizes an episode from the life of the legendary hero Cuchulain. The play's first words are "I see in the eye of the mind . . ."; the narrators conjure up for us a rocky island, somewhere in the mists of the end of the world, where there is a well whose waters give perpetual youth. But the waters rarely flow. An old man has spent years on the island waiting to drink, but always when the waters run, he misses them. To this island comes Cuchulain, also questing for the magic water. But the Hawk who is the well's guardian reveals herself as the spirit of the place and performs a dance to distract him. Then the cry of warrior women is heard far off, and Cuchulain runs to fight with them, neglecting perpetual youth for the immortality of glory. The old man is left by the dry well, and the play closes with a lament:

> He might have lived at his ease
> With an old dog's head on his knees,
> Among his children and friends . . .

By the time he wrote *Purgatory* in 1938, Yeats had fully assimilated the Noh spirit. This play is set in a more modern Ireland, the country that Yeats had grown up in, with its great, decayed houses, relics of more prosperous days, and its once proud families impoverished. It is set in front of a mansion gutted by fire; the only other scenic object is an ancient tree, reminiscent of the gnarled pine that forms the conventional background for Noh. There are only two characters (again Yeats observes the Noh restrictions), an old tinker and his bastard son. The tinker was once heir to the house, son of his mother's mismarriage with a groom. But his father had squandered the family property and finally burnt the house down in a drunken rage, during which the boy killed him. Then the boy went on the road, turned tinker, and fathered his own son, whom he now brings back to the house that might have been his. *Purgatory* is a drama of reminiscence. As the old man evokes the past, we see the shadows of his mother and his drunken father at the window. At the end the tinker stabs his own son, both as an act of penance and to ensure the end of a line that has decayed.

Though it lacks the climactic dance, this short play — it is only twenty minutes long — has all the simplicity, the compression, and the power of Noh. It uses the same basic device — two characters, who serve as answerer and inquirer — and the same themes — the journey and the reawakening of the past. At the same time, the characters stand for something far vaster than themselves — or even than the decline of modern Ireland. In the repeating rivalry between father and son, we see the cyclic conflict of youth and age. The characters are important not so much in themselves as for what they stand for;

The stylization of the stage and the depersonalization of the actor revived interest in puppetry both as medium and inspiration. One of its most elaborate forms is the *bunraku* theater of Japan.

(*right*) The stage simplified by necessity. Post-revolutionary deprivations in Soviet Russia reduced settings to their bare mechanics. A constructivist set for an operetta by Offenbach. (*above*) Theatrical anarchy. Jarry's *Ubu Roi* in a modern production by Peter Brook.

and in this aspect Yeats aligns himself with a contemporary school of drama known as *symbolist,* in which the characters are seen as manifestations of the higher force that lies unseen around us and controls our lives. The symbolist theater, which thus depersonalized the character, leaned heavily on the mask, which now returns to the twentieth-century theater as a viable dramatic device.

RETURN TO GREEK TRAGEDY

The revival of interest in Greek drama at the end of the nineteenth century has already been noted (see Chapter 2, p. 68). We should look at it again here, however, as it brings together several people who have already appeared in this chapter.

William Poel, whose interests were widespread, ventured into Greek theater with a production of *The Bacchae.* Unfortunately it was too timidly conceived. When Agave entered with what was supposed to be the bleeding head of Pentheus, the head was represented by a plaster cast.

The two men who did most to restore Greek drama to the professional stage were Gilbert Murray and Harley Granville-Barker. Both had contacts with Bernard Shaw. Murray is said to have served as the model for Cousins, the drum-playing professor of Greek in Shaw's *Major Barbara,* and Granville-Barker staged several of Shaw's plays. The influence was probably mutual: we have already noted how Shaw brought back to the stage a sense of drama as debate that was as much Euripidean as it was Irish. Murray prepared several translations of the plays, which made them accessible to the larger public for the first time in comprehensible, playable English. Granville-Barker, with Murray's collaboration, staged them in his seasons at London's Court Theatre, thus offering Greek tragedy side by side with the newest and most provocative offerings of contemporary European dramatists. The very old had suddenly become very new. Yeats, in Ireland, was corresponding with Murray and translating and staging his own versions of Sophocles. Thus audiences were reminded of such devices as the use of the mask and the chorus, instruments that other playwrights hastened to borrow.

T. S. Eliot (1888–1965) restored poetic and religious drama to the stage in a series of plays whose borrowings from the Greek are obvious. In 1935 came *Murder in the Cathedral,* dealing with the martyrdom of Thomas à Becket. Though its subject matter is Christian, its affinities are Greek: Eliot not only uses a chorus of the Women of Canterbury but turns the four knights who murder St. Thomas into a virtual *parabasis,* addressing the audience directly and explaining their actions. The play was written not for a proscenium theater but for Canterbury Cathedral, and Eliot takes full advantage of this setting to return to a presentational style in which the barriers between actors and audience are broken down. At the play's midpoint the audience is actually assumed into the drama as a character, just as the Greek audience could be (see p. 47). When Thomas preaches his Christmas sermon from the pulpit, the audience becomes the congregation. In *The Family Reunion* (1939) Eliot took inspiration from Aeschylus's *Oresteia,* showing the murderer protagonist in a country house setting, with his family used as a chorus device and the pursuing Eumenides seen at the window.

In France the classical theater had never disappeared from sight. Even so, the first half of the twentieth century saw a new surge of interest and a spate of new plays based on classical models. Prominent in the movement was Jean Cocteau (1889–1963), whose new version of *Antigone* was staged by Charles Dullin at the Atelier in 1922. In 1932 came *la Machine infernale* (*The Infernal Machine*), a modern version of *Oedipus the King.* Cocteau's play begins earlier than Sophocles' and shows Oedipus's meeting with the Sphinx; the chorus is represented by an amplified offstage voice.

The most famous, and most frequently played, French adaptation of Greek tragedy is Jean Anouilh's *Antigone* (1943), in which Sophocles' story of resistance to authority is colored by the German occupation of Paris during World War II. Here the chorus is a single figure, who opens the play by introducing the various characters to the audience and then steps back, ironically, to watch them go through their motions.

Director as God, Actor as Puppet

We must return now to Edward Gordon Craig for another important aspect of his work that we have not yet considered: his theories about the function of the director. The Moscow collaboration of Craig and Stanislavsky over *Hamlet* (see p. 402) brought together two men who saw directorial control as vital to the dramatic experience.

DEVELOPMENT OF THE DIRECTOR'S ROLE

In some of its aspects the role of the director was as old as the theater itself. In the earliest manifestations that we can trace, there was always someone in charge. The Greek theater had its *choregus,* who supervised, or delegated, the training and equipping of the chorus, while the artistic unity of the play was largely the responsibility of the dramatist himself. As we have seen (p. 51), early Greek tragedy was, for all practical purposes, a one-man theater, in which the poet was his own composer, designer, choreographer, and chief actor, selecting and training his assistants but taking the brunt of the performance upon himself. Even in the fifth century B.C., however, these functions had begun to diversify, and by the time of Aristophanes we already see the emergence of specialists in the mounting of plays, distinct from the author.

As the operations of the theater grew more complex, the need for a controlling hand was evident. The medieval theater had its *maître de jeu,* who exercised a largely administrative function in assembling the components of this massive public enterprise and controlling the mechanics of the production. Any artistic control, however, must have been largely out of his hands, as the performances were governed by traditional rubrics that were followed without change or question from year to year.

The professional Elizabethan theater had its bookholder, whose function, again, was largely mechanical. His duty was to see that the actors had their parts, to prompt them when they forgot, and to arrange the necessary entrances and exits. In the highly pressured conditions of the public playhouse, there must have been many actors who never saw the play whole. This emphasis on the individual performance, as opposed to the artistic unity of the whole work, spilled over into later ages. As late as the nineteenth century, in the haphazard conditions of the touring star system, there were still actors who could be thrust on the stage more or less secure in their own lines but with only the vaguest idea of what was happening around them.

The first inkling of a change, and the earliest recognizable attempts to subdue this collection of individuals into an ensemble, comes with the generation of Garrick (Chapter 7). At this period, too, we see the earliest experiments at creating a unified costume style, in contrast to the disparate, every-actor-for-himself tradition that had preceded. Technological advances in the theater made clear the need for one controlling hand, and the growing vogue for historically authentic, stylistically coherent productions brought the director as we know him into existence. Often, however, the director was still the actor-manager, who would control every aspect of the production but still build it around himself. The emergence of the director as a distinct theater artist, who controls the production but does not appear in it, is largely a phenomenon of the twentieth century.

CRAIG'S THEORY

Craig carried this vision of the director to an extreme. He argued that the director should be solely responsible for everything that happens on the stage, thus producing in the theater the same one-to-one relationship that exists in the other arts: the painter to his canvas, the composer or conductor to his symphony. To this end, he said, the director should possess all the requisite theatrical skills. He should design the play as well as stage it. He should have the literary perception to determine the play's meaning and the technical ability to train and instruct his actors.

Craig's own career, indeed, was a continual attempt to realize his own vision. He designed for his own stage productions, and he saw the creation of an environment, and the behavior of characters within that environment, as inseparable components of the same artistic impulse. This attitude necessarily led him to restrict, or even to deny, the individual contribution of the actor. In one of his most provocative statements he asserted that the actor should abnegate his individuality entirely and become an *übermarionette,* a "superpuppet," in the director's hands. Though this was naturally resented by actors and has always been regarded as an extreme, even eccentric view, it was in tune with developments elsewhere. We have noted Stanislavsky's interminable rehearsals — often equally resented by actors — until every nuance of the work had been explored and set, and his definition of the director as *interpreter,* disclosing patterns in the play that the actors might not perceive, or agree on, by themselves.

THE PUPPET THEATER

Craig's theory of the *übermarionette* necessitates a look at the role of the puppet in the theater. In a period that was consciously reviving purely theatrical, presentational devices, the puppet, like the mask, underwent a substantial reappraisal.

Puppetry is at least as old as the theater itself, and, like the theater, its earliest manifestations seem to have been connected with ritual usages. In antiquity, worshipers were impressed by moving, speaking statues of the gods. Puppets were also used as substitutes for human figures when the act of worship turned away from human sacrifice or when the divine figure was held too sacred to be represented by a living being: we have already seen the use of the marionette in the French medieval church (p. 117).

For centuries in Europe the puppet theater flourished side by side with the living art. It lent itself naturally to the character simplifications of the commedia dell'arte, a major influence on the development of the Punch and Judy show. In eighteenth-century England puppet troupes regularly took the latest London successes around the provinces to places that actors themselves could not reach easily.

The puppet theater aligns itself most happily with the presentational style and significantly, as Western acting became more realistic, puppetry declined. Equally significantly, in the Far East, where the theater has preserved the presentational style in its most extreme form, puppetry has never declined but exists on the same level of regard as human acting. For a school of acting that is psychologically oriented, and where the actor explores his inner self to find his motivations for the role, the puppet, having no psyche, is by definition inferior. For the presentational method, where all the emphasis is on externals, the puppet is the perfect actor, for it is all externals. Thus the 1920s and 1930s, which saw the return of presentationalism to the theater, also saw the rediscovery of puppetry as a serious art form. It was recognized that the puppet performs the same function as a mask — is, indeed, an extension of the mask — in enlarging a character beyond the bounds of the merely individual, to present either a heroic abstraction or a caricature.

Craig, therefore, in asking for an *übermarionette,* was not degrading the actor. Far from it. He was asking that the actor harness all his skills in the service of the work and subjugate his own ego to the ensemble effect. Also, he was asking that the actor look for ways to project characters who were larger than life, who had an added dimension, just as Craig's sets took simple forms and enlarged them into an overwhelming statement. Some playwrights had already come to this perception independently. Maurice Maeterlinck (1862–1949), a Belgian and the leading European exponent of the symbolist school, had written several plays for puppets. Yeats, in one of his periodic fits of frustration with the limitations of the realistic actor, had suggested that actors be placed in little carts and wheeled about the stage, so that they could leave their movements to others and concentrate on the thought and the verse. Craig's last stage work was written for puppets, and many artists since his time have refined the puppet for poetic, symbolic, or satirical purposes.

THE AGE OF THE DIRECTOR

Though actors may not have found Craig's theories sympathetic, directors did. There followed a spate of productions in which actors were stripped of their individual personalities to serve the directorial concept — by putting them in masks or heavy, masklike makeup; by concealing them in all-enveloping costumes; or by subordinating them to systems of movement and choreography that expressed the director's vision of the play.

Although the concept of the director's function has now retreated, in the live theater, from this extreme position, Craig's vision of the director as supreme creator has found its logical home in the film, where, in current theory, the director is regarded as *auteur* and the actors merely as the components of his art. Interestingly enough, Craig's set designs also found a natural home on the screen, where there were space and money enough to create environments on the scale he had envisioned.

We have seen how, over its history, the theater has tended to alternate between the age of the dramatist and the age of the actor. The twentieth century added a new factor to this cycle, the age of the director. Some directors were identified with a specific style, which always stamped its mark on their productions, so that the theatergoing public could tell one director from another as easily as, in the past, they could tell a performance by John Philip Kemble from one by Edmund Kean. Others changed styles to suit their material.

One of the most prominent of the latter school was Max Reinhardt (1873–1943), whose eclectic directorial approach both utilized contemporary movements and reached back into the theater's past. Born in Vienna, Reinhardt spent some years as an actor in Austria and Germany before emerging as a director in 1903. Responsive to the theories of Craig, he sought to demolish the tyranny of the author over the theater, to break down the confines of conventional theater forms, and by using new kinds of space and working on a vast scale, to reintegrate the audience with the theatrical production in a way that had scarcely been attempted since the Greeks.

One of his most notable productions was Greek: *Oedipus the King,* staged originally in a circus ring in Vienna in 1910 and later in a similar setting in Berlin, with enormous crowds, rigorously choreographed, representing the plague-stricken people of Thebes, and the audience surrounding the action. In Salzburg Reinhardt used a riding school; in Venice he took over a section of the city, with canals, to mount a production of Goldoni (see p. 286), re-creating commedia dell'arte techniques.

Although he found no lack of backers, and was always able to realize his most extravagant visions, opulence was not necessarily his aim. He staged some productions in baroque ballrooms lit by chandeliers and with no more setting than a single screen. For other works he cultivated the extreme stylization and economy of the oriental theater. To re-create the community spirit of the Middle Ages, in which whole portions of the town were periodically given over to the production of religious plays, he founded in 1920 the Salzburg Festival, using the magnificent baroque facade of the cathedral as a background for *Jedermann,* an adaptation of the medieval morality play *Everyman.* His interest in the Middle Ages also produced a popular pseudomedieval drama, *The Miracle,* first staged at Olympia, London — a site more often used for displays of military exercises and for trade fairs. Here the audience was placed in a vast cathedral setting with great stained glass windows looking down upon the central acting area.

Reinhardt's flair for the obviously dramatic, and for devices that left audiences gasping, caused him to be sought by the commercial theater, for which he directed a number of productions ranging from classic works to light opera. His production of *Helen* for C. B. Cochran, one of London's most astute commercial managers, was famous for its all-white set, something that had never been seen in the theater before.

In 1933, under the threat of Nazi persecution, Reinhardt left Europe to take up permanent residence in America, where he turned his attention to film. His movie version of *A Midsummer Night's Dream,* with its unusual casting of the young Mickey Rooney as Puck and James Cagney as one of the mechanicals, its trick photography, and its endless chains of fairies circling haunted trees, can still be seen as at least a partial monument to the wealth of his rococo imagination. A better record is preserved in his promptbooks — meticulous records of his productions with every movement and every crowd action scrupulously annotated — that are now enshrined in the Reinhardt Institute at Salzburg.

Reinhardt was accused by his critics of vulgarizing the theater, but his productions were widely imitated, and their influence can still be seen in Europe, particularly in the Austrian theater that was his first home. His work was a watershed of contemporary developments, not merely demonstrating the ascendancy of the director but summarizing all that was new, vital, and exciting in the theater before World War II.

Radical Reactions to Realism

We must turn now to a movement that, like so many, had its origins in the reaction against the realistic theater of the nineteenth century and has had a continuous, though sometimes confusing, history to the present day. Most of its exponents have been French; and perhaps only in a country that has constantly championed logic, order, and reason could there have arisen a counter-movement cultivating illogic, anarchy, and absurdity.

ANARCHY: ALFRED JARRY

While the commercial theater championed the well-made play, a literary subculture was deliberately breaking the taboos of theatrical and social convention simply for the sake of breaking them. The novelist de Maupassant and his circle, for example, were engaging in private, transvestite theatricals in which they thumbed their noses at established mores.

The first public manifestation of this subversive, anarchic movement came in December 1896, at the Théâtre de l'Oeuvre in Paris. The usual bourgeois audience had assembled, drawn to the announcement of a new play but having no notion of what they were going to see. They might have been alerted if they had noticed that the settings were by Toulouse-Lautrec, whose own life-style was considered by his aristocratic family to be a continual affront to decorum and whose paintings and posters revealed a fascination for the seamier side of society and the entertainment world: pictures of prostitutes and cabaret singers, which were themselves a sardonic commentary on the pretensions of the time. The curtain went up; a fat, grotesque figure waddled down to the footlights and delivered the single word *"Merdre!"* which is almost, but not quite, the most familiar vulgarism of the French language. English translations have rendered it variously as "Shitrr!" and "Pschitt!" It was a word that would resound throughout the evening, a schoolboy insult, delivered directly to the audience, which set the tone for the play and made this first night an iconoclastic event, the like of which had scarcely been seen in the French theater since the opening of *Hernani*.

The play was *Ubu roi* (*King Ubu*), and the author was the twenty-three-year-old Alfred Jarry, who had prefaced the performance with an announcement from the stage. In this statement he made plentiful allusion to marionettes. He defined actors simply as "big puppets" and his leading character Père Ubu as a simple character into whom the audience could read as many complex allusions as they wished. Simplicity, said Jarry, in a pseudophilosophical jargon that concealed a deep truth, is complexity.

Ubu roi indeed had its origins in the puppet form and particularly in the French popular tradition of the *guignol* shows, still regularly seen in the public parks and featuring an anarchic character much like the English Mr. Punch.

Jarry's play was born out of a blend of this tradition and the miseries of his own childhood. As a schoolboy, Jarry had been victimized by an unpopular physics teacher, M. Hébert, and he retaliated by writing with friends a puppet satire that ridiculed the common enemy. Called *les Polonais* (*The Poles*), it showed its central character, under the name of Père Hébé, suffering all kinds of indignities as king of an imaginary Poland. (The name obviously suggests the later Père Ubu, though there are other possibilities.) *Ubu roi* was the direct offspring of this puppet version and brings us back again to the importance of the puppet in the theater.

In his debt to the *guignol* Jarry was instinctively responding to the same impulse that inspired later, more formally pronounced theories: the dehumanization of the actor, the desire to reduce the complexity of the stage and return to single, simple issues. This is what the puppet theater, in its popular form, has always been able to do. Its European development has revealed a striking similarity of folk forms in different cultures, with the evolution of a central anarchic figure, impatient of restraint and placed in various conflict situations. Such are the English Punch, the Greco-Turkish Karaghoz, the German Kasperl and Hanswurst, the Russian Petroushka, and the Italian Pulchinello. One line of theory, indeed, would derive all these figures from the ritual conflict asserted to be the origin of all drama, and would suggest that this hypothetical beginning has survived, in its purest form and free from the complexity of literary associations, in folk art.

The French Guignol is a true representative of the type, making his first appearance in Lyons around the end of the eighteenth century and given local color as a representative of the people, a Lyonnais silkworker, shrewd and not easily fooled, scornful of false pretenses, inclined to drunkenness and revelry — in short, an unruly figure who, as a puppet, could say and do things that would never have been permitted on the living stage.

On this Jarry hangs his play. *Ubu roi* is a guignolesque response to the pressures of life, and Père Ubu is used to flay the establishment. A pseudoliterary coloration is applied by an adaptation of the plot of *Macbeth*. Père Ubu begins as a noble high in esteem at the Polish court. He leads a conspiracy against the king, kills him, and is finally removed by the king's young son. But the world in which Ubu moves is a purely fanciful one, full of schoolboy puns and crude allusions.

This play is iconoclastic, destructive both of social and dramatic conventions. Society is seen through the eyes of the acquisitive man, motivated by pure greed and bowling over everyone who stands in his way. The staging, like the theme, was reduced to the uttermost simplicity. Whole crowds — for instance, the Polish and Russian armies, who fight a pitched battle in the course of the play — were reduced to a few figures. A rapid succession of scenes flashed past before a permanent backdrop representing the changing seasons. The language alternated between gutter slang and flights of mock Shakespearean rhetoric. At the end, when Ubu, defeated and dethroned, still strutted around the stage as the quintessential survivor and delivered the nonsensical

(*above and right*) Two scenes from *Marat/Sade* by Peter Weiss, directed by Peter Brook: a virtually bare stage, close actor-audience involvement, and actors required to improvise.

The loneliness of existential man as portrayed in absurdist drama. Samuel Beckett's *Krapp's Last Tape* is written for a single actor and a tape recorder.

closing line, "After all, if there weren't a Poland, there would be no Poles," the audience was totally outraged. What they had seen had been destructive not merely of all propriety but of all the laws of the theater.

Jarry wrote two sequels, *Ubu cocu* and *Ubu enchaîné* (*Ubu Deceived by His Wife* and, with an allusion to Aeschylus, *Ubu Bound*). These plays attracted less attention, but the original work has been revived a number of times, in both human and puppet form. Its bizarre, deliberately provocative nature, and its emanation from a mentally unbalanced, suicide-prone alcoholic, should not blind us to its affinities with works of greater contemporary note and apparently more serious purport. In his reduction of life to simple basic issues, Jarry was equating himself with the expressionists, whose works trimmed everyday existence of its superfluous details, concentrated on fundamental urges and forces, and stripped characters of their individuality by identifying them by titles rather than names (for example, Strindberg's Officer, Lawyer, and Poet in *The Dream Play*). The deliberate naiveté of the folk puppet form was a means to this end, and an example of what the modern director Peter Brook, surveying puppetry in other lands, has called "rough theater": a kind of drama that, by avoiding the theater's more sophisticated appurtenances, creates a primitive excitement and reduces dramatic action to its fundamentals.

DADA AND SURREALISM

For some time *Ubu roi* remained a lonely example, a solitary shock. The disintegrative philosophy embodied in this drama was, however, given vast emphasis in the years that followed. The traumatic effect of World War I — which devastated Europe, toppled kingdoms, made millions look into the face of violence, and brought the established social order to its knees — brought in its wake an equally destructive movement in the arts: a discontent with traditional values, a cynical desire to wallow in destruction, to demolish Europe's literary monuments no less surely than its architectural monuments had been flattened by German bombardment. Amid the rubble of postwar Europe was heard the angry cry of a new nihilism. "What!" wrote André Gide. "While our fields, our villages, our cathedrals have suffered so much, our language is to remain untouched! It is important that the mind should not lag behind matter. It has a right, it too, to some ruins. Dada will see to it."

Dada was the name elected for this movement. It means, literally, "hobbyhorse." It is also one of the first utterances of baby talk, and the aim of its proponents was to reduce the arts to childish babbling, to intellectual chaos. Though its vogue was mercifully short, it helped to bring to birth another movement that, though similarly concerned with the fragmentation of the world that had till then been known, took the more positive approach that new perceptions could arise out of the chaos: that by reassembling the pieces in a different order, one could gain a fresh vision of the component parts. This movement, later known as surrealism, was concerned with what lies over and above the real, and it had its most familiar manifestations in painting.

Surrealism sought, as Jarry had, to shock; it desired, as Dada had, to annihilate traditional thought patterns. But its constructive side was its attempt to bring about a new awareness by showing familiar objects in unfamiliar situations. The paintings of Salvador Dali showed human bodies slotted to contain bureau drawers: he announced that by doing this he hoped to prompt the viewer into thinking again about the nature of the bureau drawer and the human body. Dali also projected what would now be called a happening: gigantic loaves of bread would be baked, smuggled in, and discovered simultaneously in the centers of principal European cities.

In the theater surrealism provided a fertile period of experimentation. One of its principal exponents was Jean Cocteau (1889–1963), whom we have already seen (p. 409) as reviving Greek concepts on the modern stage. Cocteau worked in many forms, no sooner achieving mastery of one than abandoning it for another. His surrealist experiments in the theater were given scope by Sergei Diaghilev (1872–1929), one of the most remarkable entrepreneurs of his time.

Born in St. Petersburg, Diaghilev had been actively promoting the Russian arts in Paris. After successfully organizing two exhibitions of painting there, he introduced a Russian ballet troupe in 1909, which became a focus for the artistic world in the years that followed. Diaghilev, like Reinhardt, was eclectic. Virtually every contemporary movement was mirrored in his productions. He not only kept faith with the past, by producing sumptuous versions of established classical ballets, but he encouraged any experiment that would excite an audience. Fashionable painters were called in to design his sets, many of whom had never worked in the theater before.

In one sense the Diaghilev seasons represented the end of an age, the last fling of the painter in the theater, for the settings tended to be individual drops, enormous canvases against which the dancers performed. In his profitable cultivation of modernity, however, Diaghilev helped to popularize new approaches. His instruction to Cocteau, "Astonish me!" has become famous. Cocteau did, by creating the ballet *Parade* (1917) with his own script and the decor by Pablo Picasso. The characters included a Chinese conjurer, an American girl, acrobats, and a horse: the music introduced the sound of dynamos, boat sirens, typewriters, and airplanes. Picasso's cubist, all-enveloping costumes reduced the dancers to automata.

In 1921 Cocteau created another work that belongs both to ballet and to the legitimate theater. *Les Mariés de la Tour Eiffel* (*The Wedding Party on the Eiffel Tower*), an amalgam of play, pantomime, and dance with music by Les Six, a group of modish, innovative composers that included Milhaud and Honegger. Like *Ubu roi, les Mariés* professes a deceptive simplicity, a return to the diversions of childhood. On closer investigation it follows the principles of surrealism by shedding new light on the commonplace.

The setting is that most familiar of French landmarks, the monument to nineteenth-century bourgeois aspiration. The vast metal construction that had been implanted on the Paris scene for the Exposition of 1889 had at first been derided as a monstrosity of modern engineering but had since become accepted, on equal terms with Nôtre Dame and the Arc de Triomphe. Cocteau's backdrop showed the Tower but from a new angle and in unfamiliar perspective. Similarly, the wedding party whose gathering provokes the action is the most traditional and familiar of French bourgeois functions. But it is constantly punctuated with surprises. A racing cyclist speeds past, having apparently lost his way on the Tour de France. The photographer summoned to take pictures of the wedding group produces a succession of unexpected creatures from his camera. "Watch for the birdie!" he cries at intervals, ducking under his concealing hood. But what comes out is never a birdie, at least not in the expected sense. On one occasion it is an ostrich; on another, it is a lion. The General, a member of the wedding party, who has been in Africa, snorts, "It's a mirage!" But the lion eats him.

Cocteau so confuses our notion of reality that we are no longer sure what is a mirage and what is not. In this apparently juvenile jeu d'esprit, Cocteau is concerned with the difficult distinction between appearance and reality, between the fictional and the historical event. By forcing his actors and dancers into outrageous, and obviously theatrical, costumes, he compels us to an awareness of the difference between our inner selves and the roles we adopt in that convenient fiction we call society. Society itself, with its rituals and ceremonies, is seen as a kind of theater, in which the role becomes the accepted reality, the visible truth.

Most of these surrealist offerings have now vanished from the stage, though we may note one other that is still occasionally revived: Guillaume Apollinaire's *les Mamelles de Tirésias* (*The Breasts of Teirésias*, 1917). This work draws its inspiration from Greek legends of the blind prophet who is a recurrent character in fifth-century tragedy. According to one story, he has been in his time both man and woman, a bisexuality inflicted on him because of some insult to the gods. Apollinaire revives this myth, links it to contemporary French concern with the declining birthrate, sets the action in the country of Zanzibar (which has no more geographical reality than Jarry's Poland), and shows Teiresias as the center of a one-woman population explosion. The leading character is eventually unsexed by the disappearance of his breasts, which are drawn out of his costume and revealed as balloons. The people of Zanzibar are represented on the stage by a single actor, a one-man crowd scene.

LEGACIES OF SURREALISM

What then emerges from the surrealist drama? Much of it is now unintelligible, and it was designed to be unintelligible, or at least to be intelligible only to a limited inner group. Like any new art movement, it attracted its share of phonies — the more so in this case because the deliberate removal of traditional theater disciplines created an environment in which anything could be accepted and enjoy a temporary vogue. And as we saw happening in the first effusions of the romantic drama, the delight in rule breaking for its own sake produced its share of trivial, unstageable works. The surrealist movement, did, however, embody some distinct principles that dictated much of the course of subsequent drama.

First, and most obvious, is its destructive attitude toward conventional patterns and ideals. *The Wedding Party on the Eiffel Tower* turns the solidarity of French middle-class married life into chaos. *The Breasts of Teiresias* takes its cue from contemporary social movements — the population crisis, the emancipation of women — to strike at the fundamentals of society by reversing the sexes. Often the plots of these plays are familiar from earlier dramatic styles but reduced to banality by being placed in a different frame of reference. For instance, Raymond Radiguet in *The Pelicans* (1921) takes a story of domestic strife and love intrigue and makes it absurd by the casual way in which it is treated.

This aspect of the avant-garde made an impact far larger than would at first be supposed through its assumption into the popular media. Surrealist art was a major influence on billboard advertising. And the demolition of social conventions was made apparent to millions who had never heard of Dali or Cocteau through the movies of the Marx brothers, who are canonized by surrealist theorists as supreme exponents and popularizers of the school. When Groucho appears as head of an imaginary state in *Duck Soup* and reduces politics to anarchy; when, as college president in *Horse Feathers,* he sings, "Whatever it is, I'm against it"; when he shatters conventional notions of courtship and romance by sending flowers to a woman with instructions to write "I love you" on the bill; or when, after having wined and dined the same lady, he peers at the check and sneers, "It's outrageous! If I were you, I wouldn't pay it!" he is performing the same reductio ad absurdum as Jarry's Ubu and manifesting the same nihilistic stance as the Dadaists.

Second, we note a growing impulse to turn away from pure drama to other theatrical forms: to dance, to vaudeville, to mime, to conjuring, to circus. Part of this impulse stems from a desire to confront the audience more vividly and to break down the traditional actor-audience relationship in the theater. Equally, however, this emphasis on the more transitory performing arts represents a philosophical concern with the ephemerality of things. Life is a show. We arrive, we put up our tent, we give our performance, we depart into the darkness. Thus actors are seen more and more as pure *performers* — the antithesis of Stanislavsky's approach — and certain obvious clichés appear, notably the image of the world as a great circus, which is used and overused by many plays of this era and still occasionally makes its return to the theater.

Third, there is an emphasis on the difficulty — indeed, the impossibility — of communication as it has been generally understood. How can we say "we know"? And how can we convey what we know to someone else? Everything is subjective; each of us has a different perception of the same object. The same words have, for each of us, a different set of associations. (Contemporary philosophy, with its emphasis on semantics, was investigating the same questions.) Anouilh wrote a touching little play called *Humulus le muet* (*Humulus the Mute*) in which a young man is unable to tell a girl he loves her because he can only speak one word a day. Other plays accentuate this problem by abolishing language altogether or reducing it to a meaningless collection of words and symbols.

Fourth, to find some means of communication, however rudimentary, among the fragmentary, dissonant, and meaningless nature of everyday experience, we see a growing use of myth and symbol to touch the collective memory. This trend, in great part, encourages the return to Greek themes, to fundamental myth patterns that strike a common chord in human awareness. Thus we have Apollinaire's recourse to the Teiresias figure and Cocteau's *Oedipus* and Cocteau's recurrent use of the Orpheus story in his plays and films. We see, too, a growing use of ritual, as providing a meaningful pattern where language has abdicated. Hence, by highly sophisticated means, the theater begins to return to the conditions of its earliest being.

THEATER OF THE ABSURD

It was the problem of noncommunication in an increasingly complex and terrifying world that chiefly concerned the dramatists of the next generation: those who had lived through World War II, with its spiritual and material impoverishment, its genocide, and its ultimate threat of total annihilation. Their response was to declare the world absurd, a place in which no logic or pattern could be found, where the most one could hope to do was to continue, to survive. Hence the name given to the movement, the *absurdists*.

As early as Aristophanes, playwrights had professed to find the world absurd. What distinguished the postwar movement, with its legacy from surrealism, was its use of the means themselves made deliberately absurd. Eugene Ionesco (1912–), a Rumanian playwright working in Paris, posed the crucial questions in his journal:

> What a flood of images, words, characters, symbols, figures, signs, all at the same time and meaning more or less the same thing though never exactly the same, a chaotic jumble of messages that I may perhaps end by understanding but which tells no more about the fundamental problem: what is the world? What is it that is all around me? Who am I? Is there an "I" and if there is an "I," where am I going? What am I doing, what am I doing here, what am I to do? I have been asking myself these questions from the beginning. I have always been at the foot of the wall. I have always been in front of a locked door. There is no key. I am waiting for the answer, whereas I ought to provide it myself, to invent it. I keep waiting for a miracle, which does not come. Presumably there is nothing to understand. But one's got to have a reason, to find a reason. Or else to lose one's reason.

Perhaps the easiest point of entry to Ionesco's work is through one of his later, longer plays, conceived in an apparently more realistic mode, *Tueur sans gages* (*The Killer,* 1959). Written in Ionesco's middle age, and a personal response to his consciousness of growing older, it discusses the most preposterous riddle of all, the question of why we die.

Ionesco sets his hero Berenger (a kind of twentieth-century Everyman, who appears elsewhere in his work) in what seems to be an ideal city, beautifully planned, with walks, fountains, spacious streets — an apparent paradise on earth. There is one flaw, though. In this city lurks a killer, whom the police are unable to catch. Every day bodies are found floating in the river. Berenger is led to hunt this murderer and eventually finds himself face to face with him, just as Everyman in the medieval play confronts death, or as Doctor Faustus confronts an eternity of damnation.

But we have a difference here: the earlier plays were concerned with a wider metaphysical system in which death was part of the grand design; in *The Killer* there is no design. Death is annihilation, complete and incomprehensible. The murderer is presented as a giggling imbecile who does not know why he does what he does. In a monologue of enormous length Berenger appeals to him on all the grounds that human reason has devised: patriotic, religious, political, humanitarian, logical, illogical. All are received with the same manic chuckle. What are we to do? The same question is asked by Everyman and Faustus; they are given an answer. In *The Killer* there is no answer. Life is absurd because it is absurd.

Given this assumption, our human posturings become ridiculous. What do we do while waiting for the end to come? Social behavior becomes ridiculous; we are merely devising games to pass the time. Language becomes ridiculous. What is the point of pretending to communicate when there is nothing to communicate about?

Ionesco's first work, *la Cantatrice chauve* (*The Bald Soprano* or *The Bald Prima Donna,* presented in 1950 as an "antiplay"), is concerned primarily with this use of language. The story of the inspiration for the dialogue is now famous. Ionesco took it from an English-French phrase book, a frequent source of humor but here serving a larger philosophical purpose: language, with pompous solemnity, only recounts what is perfectly well known already. We are offered a parody of conventional social drama, leaning heavily — and perhaps with deliberate borrowing — on familiar nineteenth-century patterns, such as Pinero's social farces, used here as an attack on the mechanized, dehumanized world in which habit has become a substitute for thought and all true individuality has disappeared. We see two families, the Smiths and the Martins, who go through the meaningless social gestures, the rituals of identification, but who can no longer talk because they can no longer think. Individuals become interchangeable. Someone brings up the name of Bobby Watson: the identifications of this character proliferate until *everyone* is called Bobby Watson. Individual identity is meaningless. Ionesco returned to this question in the longer play *Rhinoceros*

(1960) in which all the characters but the ubiquitous Berenger are turned into the same pachydermous, indistinguishable animals.

Just as human identity is forfeit, so language loses its meaning by repetition. In Ionesco's *la Leçon* (*The Lesson,* 1951) a nervous pupil visits a professor. What begins as a conventional play is distorted into absurdity as the professor begins to be carried away by his own theories of language. The girl comes more and more under his dominance, and he finally kills her. One critic has seen this play as a demonstration of the perversion of language and rhetoric for the uses of power, drawing a parallel from the Nazi experience. Another finds the professor's nonsense speech to be another demonstration of the impossibility of communication: the pupil's frame of reference seems to be mathematical rather than linguistic, though even this is limited. The only communication possible is through the use of violence.

In their staging, Ionesco's plays demand bizarre, haunting images — a corpse that grows until it fills the apartment, an empty room gradually filled to the walls with empty chairs — surrealistic flourishes in which the author's impish humor found full vent. His contemporary, Samuel Beckett (1906–   ), took a different path, conveying his vision of a bleak world by increasingly more austere staging. *En attendant Godot* (*Waiting for Godot,* 1955) sets its two principal characters in a barren landscape, talking in circles and waiting for a visitor who never comes. Their dialogue has echoes of vaudevillian patter: they are entertaining themselves while keeping their purposeless vigil. Significantly, one of the most acclaimed productions of this play was in the United States with the veteran burlesque comic Bert Lahr in the main role.

In subsequent plays Beckett limited his characters even more severely, confining them in wheelchairs, placing them in garbage cans or coffins, or half burying them in sand. In this staging he was following, for his own ends, one of the cardinal principles of French classical drama, in which the plays are virtually actionless and the characters have little to do but talk. The austerity of Racine's stage is carried even further by Beckett, the talk is increasingly simplified and refined (a characteristic perhaps influenced by the fact that Beckett was writing in an acquired language: an Irishman, he chose not to write in his original tongue), and the language itself becomes increasingly repetitive and meaningless. Ultimately Beckett so reduces the dramatic action that he writes *Act Without Words* — in which a silent figure interacts, to his continual frustration, with inanimate objects — and the reductio ad absurdum of this kind of drama: a brief performance in which the audience watched the curtain rise on an empty stage, pause for a moment, and then fall again.

Like the surrealist dramas of the interwar period, these plays have had an effect far beyond their immediate audiences. When *Waiting for Godot* was originally offered to prominent actors of the London theater, it was contemptuously rejected. Within a few years those same actors were involved in other plays based on the same premises and employing the same technical means. The view of human existence as meaningless has been applied, by hindsight, to the classics. A production of Shakespeare's *King Lear* at the University of Hawaii set the play in a landscape blackened and devastated by nuclear war; Peter Brook's more recent production of the same work created an arid world devoid of human responsibility and compassion, in which the individual can only hope to suffer and endure.

Theater as Politics

We have pursued the history of surrealism and the absurd to the present time because it represents the developing theatrical expression of a distinctively twentieth-century mode of thought. Now we must return to look at certain other important developments between the two world wars.

The most conspicuous of these developments occurred in Russia, where the postrevolutionary theater notably reversed one twentieth-century trend. When in the rest of the world the mass audience was defecting from the playhouse to the cinema, the Russian theater underwent a vast expansion and created a hitherto untapped popular audience for plays. The reasons for this expansion were primarily propagandistic. Official desire to instruct the masses not only kept the best of the old companies in existence but created new ones: by 1940 there were nearly 400 professional theaters in Russia, together with countless amateur and community groups.

The shock of revolution affected the staging of plays as well as their content. Most of the new audience was theatrically illiterate and had to be reached by simple and direct means. Experiments proliferated. The older, introspective style of Stanislavsky was no longer applicable. Plays now had to be taken to places where there were no proper buildings and no possibility of using realistic sets. An additional factor here was the impoverishment of the arts, as indeed of the country generally, in the early Soviet years.

Out of this economic necessity a pseudostyle was born, which has come to be distinguished in histories of stage design as constructivism — a style that was really no more than a practical response to financial stringency. Instead of full sets audiences saw the skeletons of sets: the bare bones of the stage decor with the minimum necessary for the physical requirements of the play. The substructure of platforms was left open, columns were represented by laths nailed into place, and the mechanics of construction were blatant.

As always the theater made a virtue out of necessity, and some directors, already in revolt against Stanislavskian realism on artistic grounds, found in these forced circumstances an agreeable challenge. One of the most prominent directors of the new school was Vsevolod Meyerhold (1874–1942), who had received his early training at the Moscow Art Theater, where his stylistic experiments were in conflict with Stanislavsky's own vision. He had therefore already begun to work in other theaters, reducing stage design to its essentials: a bare platform, no proscenium arch, no curtain, and actors performing against abstract designs.

During the Revolution Meyerhold was appointed head of the theater section of the Commissariat of Education, whose purpose was to provide theatrical propaganda for the masses. He took this opportunity to develop his highly individual style still further, ripping out the theater walls to show bare brick and building against this background to open up new uses of stage space. Architects who worked with him recall his desire to integrate stage and auditorium as the Greeks had done. Entrances were made through the audience. On one occasion Meyerhold brought a truck down the aisle, arguing that if you could have horses on stage in *Don Quixote,* the mechanical equivalent should be permitted in the modern theater. His actors were asked to work in three dimensions; *vertical* space now became an area they could use. Meyerhold's production of Ostrovsky's *The Forest* set a play of the old regime in a new environment. Characters climbed ladders and swung from a trapeze.

In deference to the age of the machine and the industrial collective, the theater itself became a machine, and the actors a group of highly drilled technicians assembled in a productive pattern of physical skills. Note how, again, the drama begins to align itself with other modes of performance, rediscovers a nonliterary theater, and adopts the direct presentational methods of the circus. Actors were no longer giving an illusionistic performance. The actor, indeed, had himself become a machine. Meyerhold's theory of biomechanics, which asked actors to translate inner emotion into overt physical action, went back to the athletics and tumbling of the commedia dell'arte. Stanislavsky, directing a romantic love scene, asked the actor to concentrate on his mental preparation. Meyerhold sent a romantic lover onstage down a playground slide, to show the urgency of the impulse that motivated him.

Meyerhold's best-known production was of another prerevolutionary play, Gogol's *The Government Inspector* (1836). A satire on bureaucratic corruption, it had originally been frowned on as potentially provocative, but it won reluctant approval because it amused the czar. To the new regime its theme was obviously more attractive. A penniless young schemer drifts into a provincial town that is nervously awaiting government inspection. The townsfolk, assuming him to be the inspector traveling incognito, wine, dine, and bribe him. Just after he has departed, loaded with their money — and the officials breathe a collective sigh of relief — a telegram arrives: the real inspector is coming.

Meyerhold's production used a bare stage backed by a row of doors to show the frenetic activity of the town administration. First one door opened, to reveal an official with a bribe, then another, and then another, in a cumulative effect of mechanical repetition. At the end the telegram was blown up to enormous size, with the officials jigging and dancing in front of it like demented puppets.

Always the emphasis was on finding what was important and revealing it to the audience in unambiguous terms. For a projected, but unrealized, production of *Othello,* Meyerhold wanted to begin the play with Desdemona's handkerchief, spotlit on a black velvet ground. Thus a simple, mundane object would be given the prominence that it deserved, as the symbol of Othello's jealousy and catalyst of the tragic action.

Meyerhold later became politically suspect and vanished from sight; the supposed date of his death was only reluctantly revealed by the Soviet authorities in 1958. His system of actor training, however, with its emphasis on physical skills, has had its impact on the later theater. Peter Brook, in his production of *A Midsummer Night's Dream* (1970), placed his actors on a set that Meyerhold would have recognized: bare walls and trees indicated by coiled wire. And instead of the usual illusions of stage magic for the fairy scenes, he turned his Puck into a juggler and acrobat.

Besides innumerable legitimate theater productions, the Soviet regime encouraged mass spectacles, living recreations of recent history, in which whole sections of the population were involved. *The Storming of the Winter Palace,* staged in St. Petersburg (now Leningrad) against the buildings where the real event had happened, was reminiscent of the pageant dramas of the French Revolution and created a fusion of dramatic interest and patriotic enthusiasm that had scarcely been equaled since Aeschylus's production of *The Persians* in 472 B.C. Theater and life had once more come very close together.

Similarly, the new totalitarian regime in Germany staged mass spectacles that professedly took their inspiration from ancient Viking ceremonial, as part of Hitler's design to reaffirm the unity of the Nordic race. Held in open-air theaters recalling those of ancient Greece, they used military displays and mass recitations to whip the audience into a fervor. No less carefully staged were the party rallies at the Soldiers' Field outside Nuremberg, with Hitler dramatically isolated on a spotlit central podium, the ranks of his followers bellowing their scripted enthusiasm, and a massive audience on surrounding bleachers. Reinhardt's circus staging of *Oedipus the King* and Hitler's management of Nuremberg had much in common.

The Assault on the Audience

Earlier in this chapter we stressed the dichotomy of twentieth-century theater: on the one hand, its continuance as an entertainment medium, producing a stream of situation comedies and light musicals, expertly conceived but void of serious content; on the other, its emergence as an agent for political and social reform, as a form for debate, and as a pulpit for preaching. In this latter aspect the theater increasingly sought means to transform the passive audience into a more lively contributor. Sometimes this involvement was sufficiently achieved by the nature of the material presented, as at Dublin's Abbey Theatre, where controversial subjects, realistically staged, not infrequently provoked abuse and outright violence from the audience. More often the shift in the theater's purpose was marked by a change in the stage form, abolishing the fourth wall and confronting the audience directly, making them partners in the action instead of witnesses to it. Just as theatrical techniques crossed over into politics, the mechanics of the party meeting or political rally were adopted by the theater. We have seen how many of the modern movements redefined the limitations of stage space and urged a more extraverted approach upon their actors; the audience could now expect to be harangued from the stage no less than from the speaker's rostrum.

EPIC THEATER

In Germany, as in Russia, political ferment bred a committed theater. In the unrest consequent on World War I, numerous propaganda troupes were formed to play at workers' meetings, out of which evolved a kind of theater known as *epic*. The term is potentially misleading, for its popular definition as "heroic" does not apply; the output of this movement was often conspicuously unheroic. For a more accurate definition we must go back to Aristotle, who distinguishes epic poetry from tragedy in terms of structure. While tragedy is restricted in time and action, the epic (for example, Homer's *Iliad*) has greater scope. Its looser, more extensive scheme allows it to embrace a greater time span and a wider range of incidents and places. Thus epic theater, in the German sense, comes to be used for a more casual linking of events, a type of dramatic narrative that rejects the traditional conventions of plot and substitutes a sequence of actions that need not be related strictly to one another.

For its exponents, however, epic theater was more than a structural revision. Each segment became a political or social lesson in itself, and the elements used to break up the plot were aimed directly at the audience: film, song, projected titles and slogans, statements from the stage. In many ways the theater borrowed, to educate an unsophisticated audience, devices that had already been tried and tested with just such an audience in the film, the music hall, and the *café chantant*.

In 1927 Erwin Piscator (1893–1966), a disciple of Max Reinhardt and, like him, ultimately a refugee to America, staged an epic production of *The Good Soldier Schweik.* This adaptation of a famous satirical novel of World War I told the story of an innocent drafted into the Austrian army, subjected to the rigors of training and the horrors of the battlefield and maintaining to the last a gullible belief that his superiors were always right. To convey the pace of the action and the rapid succession of short scenes, Piscator installed a moving belt to bring on characters and scenic units, and using film as film had in its early days used the theater, he projected animated cartoons as a background to his actors, to suggest the monstrous inhumanity of the military machine. Schweik, coming up for his medical examination, faced a cartoon doctor magnified to enormous size, typifying the "little man" against the overbearing military bureaucracy. By its nature epic theater was adapted to subjects of greater scope than the conventional theater could handle. On his return to postwar Germany, Piscator directed a massive, episodic staging of Tolstoy's *War and Peace*.

BRECHT'S ALIENATION EFFECT

Bertolt Brecht (1898–1956) followed Piscator's example in both choice of subjects and production methods. He saw the theater as essentially engaged with society, a medium for transmitting and illuminating the political and social currents of the day. And he demanded an audience that would be similarly engaged: not passively enjoying or admiring but prepared to render objective judgment on what the play was talking *about* and to carry this judgment away with them to inform their working lives. Consequently, Brecht opposed all theatrical illusion that lulled the audience into forgetting that the play was a play. This philosophy led to his formulation of the *Verfremdungseffekt*, "alienation effect," a series of related devices that periodically jolted the spectator into an awareness of what he was seeing, moments of estrangement rather than total empathy. By *alienation* Brecht did not mean making the audience hostile to the play. Rather, he implied a sense of critical detachment, a stepping back to look at familiar objects in a new and unfamiliar way; he wanted the audience to view the play as an object lesson rather than as a vicarious experience. To quote one of Brecht's own examples: "To see one's mother as a man's wife, one needs an alienation effect. This is provided, for example, when one acquires a stepfather."

So, like other innovators for other reasons, Brecht set about abolishing the trappings of the representational theater. His productions removed the proscenium and curtain in favor of a bare platform. The lighting units were exposed and used, as in a sports arena, for sharp illumination rather than for realistic effect. Sets were reduced to the minimum necessary for the play to make sense. Brecht was insistent that the sparse environment remaining should show natural textures, not those of stage artifice: that it should be, in other words, not realistic but real. Props similarly were reduced to significant and necessary objects, with the shabbiness of hard use — like Antoine's furniture, deriving from the real world and not the theater paint shop. Thus the setting, while providing the necessary environment for the action, became a functional unit that secured the necessary estrangement in the audience by its lack of pretense and the exposure of its mechanics. The audience was continually reminded that they were watching a play.

Similarly, Brecht asked of his actors that, while creating consistent and believable characters, they should from time to time enforce a critical detachment on the audience by stepping out of character, to remind them that they were actors and that this was only a play. This technique occurred most obviously in the songs that punctuated the action. Here Brecht borrowed heavily from the techniques of the cabarets, which served as an informing image for his plays that was no less powerful than the public debate had been for the Greeks or the sermon for the medieval morality play. The songs also served to bridge the gap between the theater and the world outside. Tuneful, pungent, acerbic, they reminded the audience of other milieus and connected the sociopolitical content of the plays with what was being said and sung elsewhere.

As a background for the stage Brecht usually called for a projection screen. The screen allowed him another means of alienation, by punctuating the action with projected titles, slogans, or photo montages that would both relate to the play and give it a wider frame of reference. These images also served as another way of limiting empathy with the characters, by showing them as mere components in a larger scheme of things.

It was some time before Brecht's presentational techniques won wide acceptance outside their own country. The English-speaking theater was particularly slow to respond. In the United States, where Brecht spent the war years, he was suspect for his Communist sympathies, and his attacks on conventional social patterns were resisted as insidious. In the British theater, still largely dominated by realism and the well-made play, he was dismissed even after the war as crude and sensational. This initial hostility, however, was rapidly replaced by adulation. As the work of Brecht's company, the Berliner Ensemble, became more widely known, he was hailed as the greatest theatrical innovator of our time.

As so often happens, however, the innovations represented only a rediscovery of once familiar techniques. The device of periodically estranging the audience from the action by punctuating it with song was fundamental to the Greek experience. Brecht himself was fully conscious of his debt to older forms of presentational theater, particularly those of the Orient. He learnt much from the Chinese actor Mei Lan-Fang, adapting Eastern techniques of stylized makeup and movement and symbolic gesture for use in his plays. Many of his plays are themselves consciously derivative from earlier theaters: *Antigone* from the Greek; *Trumpets and Drums* from Farquhar's late Restoration comedy *The Recruiting Officer; The Threepenny Opera* from Gay's *The Beggar's Opera,* a work of the early eighteenth century that ridiculed contemporary operatic pretensions by setting new lyrics to popular ballads; *Coriolanus* from Shakespeare. Yet all these were reworked in terms of Brecht's own social vision and presented with stark immediacy to a politically conscious audience.

Perhaps Brecht's most characteristic work, and the one by which, after *The Beggar's Opera,* he is most widely known in the West, is *Mother Courage,* appropriately epic in its scope and subject matter. Set in the Thirty Years' War, which swept over most of Europe in the early seventeenth century, its action spans years of time and moves among Sweden, Poland, and Germany. Its central character is a *vivandière,* owner of a traveling canteen wagon, who follows the armies and makes her living by selling food and drink to the troops. Victimized by both Protestant and Catholic armies in turn, she is deprived of all her children, one by one; even her mute daughter Kattrin is shot for trying to give a signal to the enemy. Through all this Mother Courage survives, expounding her cynical materialist philosophy against the background of war and concerned only with keeping her business going. The principal scenic motif of the original production was a revolving stage, which turned against Mother Courage as she hauled her wagon, thus showing her continually plodding on but always remaining in the same place. Projected titles and nine songs punctuated the action: the sympathy evoked by the deaths of individuals was offset by the objective stance, which showed the hardness to which material necessity reduces us. The audience could at the same time feel sympathy for Mother Courage and be repelled by her.

THEATER OF CRUELTY

Revolutionary though Brecht's approach might have been, he still worked largely in the methods of the traditional, literary-dominated theater. Ibsen would have recognized the components of his art, though not the way in which these components were put together. Simultaneously another movement was growing up, which sought to abolish the literary aspect altogether and to assault the audience by more primitive, more urgent means, appealing to the collective subconscious by a more fundamental manner of communication that struck the spectators to the roots of their being.

We have already seen (p. 421) how the French avant-garde theater between the wars was abandoning language as inadequate and relying instead on ritual and symbol. A strong theoretical basis for this endeavor was provided by the French actor and director Antonin Artaud (1896–1948), who, in 1938, published his collected essays as *The Theater and Its Double*. Inspired by a troupe of Balinese dancers presenting their traditional masked art and the sense of ritual involvement this induced in the audience, he formulated his theory of a "theater of cruelty" that would embrace the audience in a collective experience, loosening their inhibitions and effecting a catharsis by releasing the inner consciousness. In this view the text, if there was a text at all, became merely the starting point for the theatrical event. Actors were free to depart from it, to improvise upon it, to find ways of appealing to the audience directly and drawing them, literally, into the action. Physical gesture, mime, dance and gymnastic patterns took precedence over speech.

Often the actors surrounded the audience or made forays among them, addressing individuals directly or even physically assaulting them. The old distinction between acting space and audience space no longer existed. Usually the theater — which might as well have been a public hall, a church, or a gymnasium — simply provided an environment in which the audience sat or stood where they could, and they might at any moment find themselves in the center of a developing action. The means used to break down the audience's self-consciousness were often deliberately shocking and provocative. Stage nudity, once taboo, became commonplace. Abused, harangued, and subjected to a barrage of obscenities, the spectators were expected to abandon their restraints and become participants in the collective experience. In the United States and Europe the best-publicized exponent of this approach has been the Living Theater, a group organized by Julian Beck and his wife Judith Malina, who described themselves as producing not a play but a series of "magical experiences."

Such experiments have had variable success. At their worst, the desire to shock has developed a self-consciousness of its own, embarrassing the audience and, ultimately, the actors, and at the lowest ebb they are indistinguishable from pornography. The most effective manifestations seem to be those that retain an artistic unity through some recognizable literary affinity. *Dionysus in '69,* performed in an East Side garage in New York, went for inspiration to Euripides' *Bacchae,* rearticulating the text, demanding audience participation, and making a gymnastic exhibition out of the action to recreate the ritual savagery that underlies the literary tragedy.

Sometimes the techniques of the theater of cruelty have been harnessed productively to more conventional productions. *The Persecution and Assassination of Marat, as Performed by the Inmates of the Asylum at Charenton under the Direction of the Marquis de Sade,* more conveniently known as *Marat-Sade,* by Peter Weiss (1964), has lent itself conspicuously to such treatment. It shows a key event of the French Revolution as a play within a play, performed by a cast of lunatics; the lunatics spill over the stage into the auditorium, involving the spectators and identifying with them. In the same way Peter Brook's production of Seneca's *Oedipus* for the National Theatre of Great Britain in 1968 began with actors in the aisleways mingling with the audience as they took their seats, moved through a sequence of horrifying actions (Jocasta in this version committed suicide on stage by thrusting a sword into her womb), and ended with a ritual dance around a giant phallic symbol on the stage.

The Cycle Begins Again

We have seen the history of the theater as moving not in a regular linear progression but in a series of cycles, continually turning back upon itself and rediscovering its past. In the late twentieth century we seem to have reached the end of an enormous cycle, for contemporary experiments suggest that the theater is consciously returning to the rituals that were its genesis. The theater has always been a sensitive register of the needs and wishes of the public that it serves, and it is, perhaps, significant that when ritual is being supplanted in so many areas of life — the ritual of marriage by cohabitation, the rituals of the church by apathy without and reconstruction within, even the ritual of family dinner by the cafeteria — the need for ritual should reassert itself so strongly on the stage.

Even the most apparently anarchic manifestations of the modern theater have re-formed, in the end, about discernible patterns of language or action. In the arid world of Beckett's *Waiting for Godot,* the dialogue imitates the patter of the vaudeville act; in *Rosencrantz and Guildenstern Are Dead,* Tom Stoppard's backstage view of Hamlet, the characters communicate with each other through games. When society seems to be falling apart, and the traditional patterns are no longer imposed upon us, we seem to feel the need to invent patterns for ourselves. Thus on the experimental fringe of the contemporary theater, we see artists working not with the abolition of language but with its substitution by an esoteric, sacerdotal tongue that will communicate with its audience on the psychic level. In New York, Greek tragedy has been returned to ritual by deliberate use of languages unfamiliar to the bulk of the audience: ancient Greek, Latin, or even invented. At his center for theater studies in the Middle East, Peter Brook works with mime, chorus, and ancient Persian texts to produce theatrical experiences that will be more profound because they avoid the common currency of communication, evoking the mystery at the heart of things and asking actor and audience to participate in a shared, common emotional experience, a rite. If the priest was the first actor, there are signs that the actor may once again become the priest.

11
The American Experience of Theater

The Early Years

When seen as part of the world picture, the history of the American theater must necessarily seem brief and largely derivative. This brevity is counterbalanced by a remarkably vigorous growth and the development, during the twentieth century, of distinctive American forms that have gone abroad to make their mark in other countries.

COLONIAL ADVENTURES

As the earliest settlements on the eastern seaboard were English colonies, it was inevitable that the English theater should shape the development of the American. Its origins were wholly English and slow to appear. The Jamestown settlers, who made their landfall in Virginia in 1607, were of the generation of

A reconstructed Early American stage curtain.

Shakespeare and Marlowe, but they had no time for plays. In their new home, surrounded by hostile natives, starved and ravaged by disease, they could think only of immediate survival. The Plymouth settlement of 1620 was no less beleaguered; in any case, these first New England colonists shared the religious sympathies of those who closed the London theaters in 1642, and it would be years before an actor dared to show his face in Boston.

As the colonies took root and flourished, the first signs of a theater began to appear, but even in the more enlightened South, it was potentially suspect. In 1665, as Restoration comedy made its mark in London and Molière established his ascendancy in Paris, three young men of Accomac County, Virginia, were arrested for acting a play written by one of them, called *Ye Beare and ye Cubbe.* They were found not guilty, but the first original play recorded on American soil vanished without trace. By the turn of the century we have records of other, scattered, amateur performances. The governor of New York wrote a play, and students of the College of William and Mary in Virginia delivered a "pastoral colloquy." Although religious prejudice against the theater was still powerful, a popular desire for it was growing evident. Even in Puritan Boston recognizable dramatic elements began to creep into public festivities, and a strolling company located itself under the equally austere shadow of Philadelphia, but outside the city limits. The city itself was penetrated in 1749 by a professional company headed by Walter Murray and Thomas Kean, who used a converted warehouse. In 1750 the same company was in New York and in 1751 in Williamsburg, Virginia, foreshadowing the age of touring that was to be so marked a feature of the American scene.

A major impetus was given by the arrival, in 1752, of a company organized in London by William Hallam. Its nucleus was made up of his own family, in the manner of the day. The Hallams had received their training on the English stage; one of William's brothers had been engaged in the unfortunate fight with Macklin (see p. 297), which led to his death. They exaggerated their achievements, as actors are prone to do. At best their London careers can only have been mediocre. Though they boasted of connections with Garrick, they sprang from the class of rank-and-file actors whom Garrick eclipsed, and almost certainly they practiced the hackneyed, artificial style of acting that he and Macklin attempted to reform. The colonies were still terra incognita in the theater world and offered no hope of profit or reputation sufficient to lure star players from the patent houses of London. For many years the shape of the American theater was dictated by those who could not make it in the motherland.

Nevertheless, the Hallams' voyage was a brave venture, though even they were daunted as they saw the virgin forests on the coastline and wondered where, in this wilderness, they would ever find an audience. Discretion led them to Virginia, whose more relaxed life-style and claim to cavalier ancestry had already given hope to would-be actors. In Williamsburg was a playhouse, probably the same one built for the Murray-Kean company the year before, and the Hallams opened with *The Merchant of Venice* in September. We know their repertoire: it was a sampling of contemporary London taste.

In addition to *The Merchant of Venice,* of which Macklin had become the definitive London exponent, Shakespeare was represented by *Hamlet, Othello,* and *Richard III;* the last, in America as in England, was to become the standard bravura piece for actors and the accepted test of a newcomer's ability. Also included were Farquhar's *The Beaux' Stratagem,* a late example of the Restoration comic style, already mild by comparison to its predecessors and probably additionally refined to suit the new moral sensibility, various examples of the fashionable sentimental comedy; and that grand old barnstormer *George Barnwell,* or *The London Merchant* (see p. 279), which combined impeccable moral instruction with lofty rhetoric and a dash of sex and crime. Among the farces chosen for short afterpieces were one of Garrick's own, *A Miss in Her Teens,* and imitations of Molière.

Conjectural reconstruction of the Williamsburg playhouse suggests a building modeled after the smaller English provincial theaters of the time, like the Richmond, Yorkshire, building described at length on pages 307–308. We can assume, then, a limited stage space, a cramped and usually packed auditorium, and the conventional wing-and-shutter scenic arrangements. Significantly, although many of the structures of colonial Williamsburg have now been rebuilt and restored to an approximation of their original condition, the historical site still offers no reconstruction of the theater. It has been proposed several times to rebuild a working copy of a typical eighteenth-century playhouse, yet the economic conditions of the modern theater forbid it; the audience capacity would be simply too small. It was once seriously suggested that the playhouse should be built, but with a removable facade so that a larger audience could be accommodated in the open air. During the bicentennial years of 1976 and 1977, however, several university theaters, where economic factors were of less consequence, built reconstructions of the kind of theater the Hallams knew, with benches in the pit and narrow balconies, to revive appropriate plays from the period. Williamsburg does have a theater now, but it is purely modern in genesis, offering an open-air spectacle based on local history.

Outside Williamsburg, the companies could not hope to find themselves so fortunate. On tour they could expect to play in inns or barns with the minimum of scenery and only an arbitrary differentiation between the acting area and the audience. Late colonial America was repeating, for reasons of its own, the patterns of theater history at large: plays come before buildings. When, reluctantly, permanent theaters began to be built, they tended to be flimsy structures.

Largely, however, there was no real impetus to build. The principal towns were still small, the audience was limited, and there was no competition, for the Hallam company, in its various manifestations, dominated the market for years. Against initial opposition they played successful seasons in New York, Philadelphia, and Charleston; then they sailed for the nearby British colony of

Jamaica. Here their career was nearly blighted by the death of Lewis Hallam, William's brother and the company manager, but amalgamation with another English troupe led out by David Douglass returned them to America with confidence.

The years before the War of Independence saw permanent theaters built in several important towns, notably the Southwark Theater in Philadelphia, which opened in 1766. Built of wood on a lower story of brick, it looks, in conjectural reconstructions, not unlike a Quaker meetinghouse. It had a long and distinguished history, and some parts of the original structure were still standing until 1912.

Now the theater had to fight a new enemy: the lack of time and money, for the colonies were absorbed in greater urgencies. War with Britain was imminent. The Continental Congress, in October 1774, passed a decree reminiscent of the parliamentary ban in London over a century before, discouraging "every type of extravagance and dissipation" and, specifically, plays. The stern mood of the times was not propitious to further theatrical expansion. Cannily, the Hallam-Douglass troupe — which had already, sniffing the prevailing wind, changed its name to the American Company — sat out the war in Jamaica.

ENGLISH INFLUENCE

Nonetheless, substantial inroads had already been made. In some ways the American companies were duplicating the contemporary English experience — the same plays, the same acting styles, the same arrangement of stage space. The Hallam-Douglass troupe was made up according to the traditional system of "lines of business" that we saw in the London theater of Goldsmith and Sheridan (see p. 303), and actors could expect the same types of roles in any play that was offered.

In other ways the colonials were reliving the English experience of a century before. Hostility to the theater on religious grounds, which had largely disappeared — at least in London — was still rampant in America and was to remain a strong force in some parts of the country for many years. American audiences, too, had grown up without a theatrical tradition. They were new and raw, and they had to be broken in. London audiences were hardly models of civility, liable to riot on occasion; still the everyday bad manners of American audiences continued to be criticized for years.

This rough environment bred an impatience with certain traditional theater practices, and as we shall see, the fact that an American tradition had to be created had important consequences for the development of a native drama. The actors were compelled, in self-defense, to various shifts and subterfuges to allay popular suspicion. Here, as in provincial England, plays were disguised as "moral representations." The average actor still tended to be stigmatized. As yet, no Garrick dignified the profession, and no equivalent of Westminster Abbey existed in which to bury him. We are still talking of a narrow, divided, sparsely settled country; of a New England where the western frontier meant Deerfield, Massachusetts, with its attendant dangers; and of a people with little inherited taste and little opportunity or time, so far, to develop tastes of their own.

INDEPENDENCE AND EXPANSION

During the revolutionary war, such scanty theatrical activity as there was was confined mainly to the soldiery and chiefly to the British, who, during their occupation of Boston, presented plays in Faneuil Hall. The city had enacted stern antitheater laws in 1750, but the military, encouraged by General Burgoyne, reversed the trend. Once again, this phenomenon is reminiscent of English conditions a century before and the performances at royalist headquarters at Oxford while the cavalier armies were losing the war in the country.

With the end of hostilities the American Company returned from Jamaica, and in a more optimistic period, with a burgeoning population, it continued to dominate the scene. New troupes grew up to cater to the growing demand, better actors came out of England, and most important, new theaters started to be built that were the equal of the finest in the English provinces.

New York had not yet become the focus of theatrical activity, and in Philadelphia the Chestnut St. Theater opened in 1794. Here the stage was 36 feet wide and 71 feet deep, spacious compared to what the prewar actors had been used to. An abbreviated apron looked out on a curving horseshoe-shaped auditorium. In the pit, rows of benches stretched from wall to wall. Here, as in some English theaters, there were no side aisles, which must have contributed to the restiveness and discomfort of the spectators. Over the pit hung three tiers of boxes, which, though elegantly designed, offered only restricted viewing. The stage was lit by oil lamps capable of being dimmed — presumably by baffles — and the auditorium by chandeliers: it was still regular practice to leave the auditorium in full light during the performance. Fire was an ever-present hazard, and in 1820 a conflagration destroyed the scenery.

Recalcitrant Boston also had its theaters by this time. While earlier attempts to stage full plays had been halted by law, the Federal Street Theater opened in the same year as the Philadelphia house, and the two were apparently of similar design. It did not, at first, do well; nor did a second Boston theater, the wooden Haymarket, which began its short career two years later.

New York had its Park Theater, managed for a time by William Dunlap and John Hodgkinson, a combination of talents that showed how much the American stage, even after independence, owed to England. Hodgkinson (1767–1865), English-born, had acted in Bristol (see p. 296) and toured the provincial circuits with Sarah Siddons. In 1792 he crossed the Atlantic to join the American Company, the temptation probably being the opportunity to play the leading parts that had been denied him at home. Early reports describe him as a handsome, dashing actor, though he seems later to have gained weight and lost appeal. Dunlap (1766–1839), acclaimed as the father of the American drama, was born in America but had spent some time in England studying to be a painter. His acquaintance with Shakespearean and contemporary drama there bore fruit on his return to the United States. In 1796 he became one of the managers of the American Company, and with Hodgkinson, opened the Park two years later. This theater, housing the American Company until 1805, was criticized by some as an ugly house, but it had certain architectural advantages. The boxes were cantilevered, needing only slim supports, which radically improved the sight lines. Its main curtain abandoned the traditional green for blue mohair with a gold fringe. Fire destroyed it in 1820, but it was rebuilt on similar lines, with four tiers of boxes and a seating capacity of some two thousand.

The touring company of the early days was now giving way to permanent companies located in the principal cities, though touring as a way of life was to reappear in the American theater at a later date and on a far larger scale than the pioneers could have dreamed of. Many of the actors were still English-trained, but increasingly America was now breeding its own. The transition is seen in the history of the Jefferson family, one of America's first theatrical dynasties. Thomas Jefferson (1732–1807) had acted in London for Garrick and also had managed a theater in the provinces. His son Joseph (1774–1832) came to the United States in 1795, where he acted in New York and Philadelphia. Joseph Jefferson II (1804–1832) worked as both actor and scene painter. Joseph Jefferson III (1829–1905), who made his stage debut at the age of four, became one of the most famous actors in the country, eventually completing the cycle by playing the role of Rip Van Winkle, with which his name was inseparably associated, in London.

THE PLAYWRIGHTS

As well as creating its own actors, the American theater could now lay claim to its own playwrights. The first native work professionally performed was Thomas Godfrey's blank verse tragedy, *The Prince of Parthia,* which had its premiere in Philadelphia in 1767. A turgid, derivative work, full of the clichés of the debased classical style, it was soon followed by better.

Royall Tyler (1757–1826) wrote the first American comedy, *The Contrast.* Performed in New York in 1787, it has the manner of Sheridan's *The School for Scandal* but with a distinctively American coloration. In keeping with the spirit of the times, British manners are ridiculed as hypocritical and effete, while the virtuous hero, Colonel Manley, is a hero of the Revolution. The play contains a tribute to George Washington, whose name headed the subscription list when the work was published, and it sets a precedent by introducing the stage Yankee as a major character. Manley's servant, Jonathan, has the rugged independence of his master. He even despises the title "servant," and he serves as the model for innumerable American characters after him who evolve into a distinctly American theatrical type, the hardheaded, short-spoken New Englander with a shrewd eye for business and a distrust of affectations. The Revolution also inspired several patriotic pieces, including a re-creation of the Battle of Bunker Hill. (Though the events are American, this trend follows the English pattern; we must remember that Garrick's Drury Lane, in the same period, was reduplicating contemporary events on stage.)

Undoubtedly the most prolific and the most successful playwright was William Dunlap, whom we have already noted as manager. Inspired by *The Contrast,* he went on to write at least sixty-five plays. Some of these were adaptations from the German of August Kotzebue, a contemporary of Schiller, whose fashionable success in his own day has been totally forgotten since. His romantic dramas were played all over Europe, and one of them, *The Spaniards in Peru,* was adapted by Sheridan for Drury Lane under the title of *Pizarro.* Dunlap's version of the same drama had over two hundred productions in the United States. He also adapted other French and German authors. *André* (1798) had more immediate inspiration. It is the well-known story of the British agent involved with Benedict Arnold, captured and executed by the American side in the revolutionary war. The initial audience response was tepid, partly because the play lacked spectacle but also because, in spite of a good deal of flag-waving, its patriotic spirit was thought to be inadequate. Dunlap rewrote it as *The Glory of Columbia: Her Yeomanry,* in which guise, with the addition of patriotic songs and a representation of the Battle of Yorktown, it had a long life.

Actors and Their Stages

Although native talent had begun to appear, foreign importations continued to dominate the American theater. The United States had won its political independence, but its arts were still dominated by European, mainly by English, influences. In 1773 audiences had seen *She Stoops to Conquer* a few months after its premiere in London. After the war, they were still watching the standard repertoire of Shakespeare and contemporary successes. Although the United States had passed its first Copyright Act in 1790, international copyright was still far in the future. Any English work could be played in the United States without payment to the original author. As late as 1880 Gilbert and Sullivan had to open *The Pirates of Penzance* in London and New York simultaneously to establish American copyright for their work.

The English tradition, which had shaped the beginning of the American theater, died hard. Many, albeit reluctantly, conceded it a superiority over the native product. It was older, tried and tested, and more sophisticated. In some ways the American experience echoes that of Rome with Greece, showing a

Information on the early American playhouses has largely vanished. For the Bicentennial, the State University College, Oneonta, New York, built a rural eighteenth century playhouse, based on contemporary English models, and staged typical plays from the eighteenth and nineteenth century repertoire. (*right*) The intimacy of the theater is seen in this view of the boxes from the stage.

(*above*) Looking down from the side galleries. Spectators in the pit often complained of assaults from those seated above. Note the seating on benches. (right) Skeleton of an early American playhouse: the pit, galleries, and side boxes.

The first successful American comedy: Royall Tyler's *The Contrast*. Sheridanesque elegance in a republican setting. Note the footlights illuminating the stage and the setting composed of wings and drop. This is the Mall from Act III.

Rip Van Winkle: Joseph Jefferson III's star vehicle and one of the most successful American plays of the nineteenth century. (*above*) Rip's home. (*right*) The Catskill mountains.

newer, larger, and increasingly more powerful culture accepting the dramatic standards of another time and place because it was still too young, too busy, to develop standards of its own.

COOKE AND KEAN

In the aftermath of independence, English actors still came over, and now that the market was larger and more secure, the quality of the imports improved. One of the greatest box office attractions was George Frederick Cooke, who had acted with Sarah Siddons and John Philip Kemble in England and had a reputation for erratic brilliance. Reckoned to be one of the finest portrayers of villainy who ever appeared on the stage, his alcoholic propensities made every performance a risky proposition. He did well in his first season, when he opened at the Park in the inevitable *Richard III* and then went on to Philadelphia. Dunlap accompanied him and kept him reasonably sober. His Iago in *Othello* was also much admired, and Cooke found himself surrounded with American fans, applauding the repetition of his London successes. The second season went less well; Cooke had started drinking again. His alcoholism led to altercations with the audience and a sad end to a promising career. Cooke died in New York, and Edmund Kean, who followed him to America after the War of 1812, erected a monument there to his memory.

Kean, himself hardly a model of sobriety, made his American debut in 1820, playing a Shakespearean repertory. Critics found his lack of physical stature unappealing, but they were bowled over by his fiery performances as Richard, Shylock, and Lear, and they gave him the same tumultuous welcome that had marked his debut in London: indeed, a better one, for London had not liked his Lear at all, finding it deficient in nobility. These American successes paved the way for a series of English stars to come. They also helped to undermine the permanent company system in the United States, for when traveling stars were a guarantee of box office success, why should the residents try to cultivate their own?

One noticeable feature of the American theater of this period is the demand for greater stage realism, occurring perhaps earlier, and certainly louder, than it did in Europe. We find critical objections to inadequacies of setting and costume, to the arbitrary placement of actors on the stage, to illogical arrangements of entrances, and to such conventional devices as soliloquies and asides. Such things, as we have seen, were largely the product of the aristocratic tradition in the European theater, and they had been kept in currency by the weight of tradition long after their natural life had expired. America had no aristocratic tradition. Democracy was the great leveler in the theater as in public life. Audiences were impatient with mannered acting, and they wanted plays performed in ways that they could understand. Not the least reason for the success of Cooke and Kean was their sheer energy. Romantic players both, they had broken with the stale traditions of their own country. It was their robustness that endeared them to Americans.

EDWIN FORREST

America produced its own robust actor in Edwin Forrest (1806–1872). Philadelphia-born, he made his debut in his hometown at the age of fourteen, and he made his name in a series of powerful roles that owed much to the influence of Edmund Kean. Some critics found his performances lacking in style; one called him an animal. But the public loved him.

Seeking plays to complement his personality, he instituted a competition for original work, which produced one of his greatest successes, *Metamora*. Forrest opened this play in 1829 at the Park Theater, where he had first appeared three years earlier, and continued to play it for nearly forty years. *Metamora,* by John Augustus Stone, had a professedly indigenous subject; its hero is an Indian chief leading his tribe in conflict with the white settlers. Actually, the tragedy owed little to observation of native mores. Metamora is seen as an ideal type, the American version of the Noble Savage, and he delivers long, heroic speeches that owe more to the European theater than to the American frontier. Nevertheless, the play was extremely popular and lasted longer than the author, who, after a series of disappointments, committed suicide.

CHAPMAN AND THE SHOWBOAT

Meanwhile, the real frontier was pushing outward. Where the settlers went the theater followed, rediscovering a sense of adventure and improvisation that recalled the colonial days. One of those who beat new paths, and in doing so created an American institution, was an Englishman, William Chapman (1764–1839). His early training had inured him to the road. In England he had worked for Muster Richardson, the country's leading traveling showman, who took his tent shows around to the fairs that were still annual institutions in many parts of the country. By presenting legitimate drama, he was in defiance of the law, for the Theatre Licensing Act was still in full force. Nevertheless, Richardson played for years on the fringes of the capital, offering melodramas liberally laced with ghosts and duels, the popular pantomimes, and panoramas.

With this experience behind him, Chapman sailed for America, acted for a while in New York, and then headed for the newly opened-up southwest. Where there were no good roads, it was easiest to travel by water, and Chapman is credited with the introduction of the American showboat, taking productions — usually melodramas — down the Ohio and Mississippi rivers. There was no front man, no advance publicity. The boat moored when and where it could, at any settlement that promised an audience; a flag was raised and a trumpet blown. The audience clambered into the long, narrow auditorium to see what might be their only entertainment for months; and the following morning the boat sailed on. When it reached New Orleans, at the mouth of the river, it was demolished, the company returning upstream by steamboat to begin the cycle again.

Chapman's success inspired many imitators, some of them fly-by-night operators, but none rivaled the original's prestige. In later years the paddle-driven showboats, larger and more resplendent, became a feature of southern life: Jerome Kern's musical, *Showboat* (1928), later turned into a film starring Paul Robeson, is a tribute to their romantic past. One or two showboats still house theaters in the United States, but they are shore-bound; the voyaging days are over.

THE PLAYHOUSE IMPROVES

Meanwhile the permanent theaters were becoming more numerous and more commodious. The Bowery Theater in New York was built in 1826. Two years later it burned to the ground, the first of a series of fires and rebuildings. Seeking a mass audience, it was so addicted to blood-and-thunder melodrama that it became known as the Bowery Slaughter House. Its most sensational production was *Mazeppa, or The Wild Horse,* ostensibly derived from a poem by Lord Byron about a youth who, convicted of adultery, was bound to a wild horse that ran through the landscape until it dropped of exhaustion. A version had already been staged in London at the Coburg Theatre, an obscure house that drew a large local audience for its melodramas. What attracted the American audience was not the poetry but the spectacle: a real horse pursued by wolves (represented on a moving canvas panorama), climbing crags and precipices (ramps with painted fronts), caught in a thunderstorm (trees toppled by ropes from the wings), and attacked by an eagle (dropped from the flies and compared by captious critics to a turkey vulture). *Mazeppa* was one of the first of a string of popular and profitable melodramas that continued to draw crowds until the advent of the cinema.

But if the democratization of the theater was revealing itself in its choice of subject matter, it also began to be apparent in theater architecture. The St. Charles Theater in New Orleans, built in 1843, not only had a large stage that made it suitable for spectacle but also had a lack of boxes; in the most European of American cities, the European differentiation of seating had disappeared.

A further impulse to spectacle was given by the appearance of gas lighting. In this feature America may have anticipated Europe. London's Lyceum claimed to be the first to light the stage by gas in 1817, though it had already been used in the auditorium elsewhere. The Chestnut St. Theater in Philadelphia, however, claimed to have gaslight in 1816, whether for the stage or the auditorium is not clear. The St. Charles in New Orleans lit the auditorium with 176 gaslights in a central chandelier. As there was still no public gas supply, the theaters had to manufacture their own on the premises. Curiously, remote control was now available; yet the habit of leaving the auditorium lit for the performance prevailed for several years.

Audience manners had not improved with their surroundings. There were still complaints of noisy and unshaven patrons, of the spitting of tobacco juice, and of assaults on the audience in the pit from the balconies above.

A BROADER TASTE DEVELOPS

By midcentury, then, the American theater had broadened its appeal to embrace distinct levels of taste. On the one hand, the standard European classics continued to make up the bulk of the repertoire with the occasional addition of new American plays of merit. One of the most popular of these was *Fashion* (1845), by Anna Cora Mowatt, a comedy with a distinct family resemblance to Tyler's *The Contrast* of the century before. Once again, American honesty and forthrightness are contrasted with European affectation; this time it is French, not English, manners that are ridiculed. *Fashion* not only enjoyed long runs in its time but has been periodically revived ever since.

On the other hand, spectacular melodrama was a growing force. It could justify itself both by European precedent and financial success. The romantic period had left its legacy of melodrama to England, Germany, and France; fights, adventures, thwarted lovers, villainous adversaries, ghosts, hairbreadth escapes. In America plays that relied more on incident than dialogue appealed to the increasing waves of immigrants for whom the literary drama was, in every sense, a foreign language. It acquired its representative characters, vernacular cousins of the Yankee servants in the more polite drama, such as Mose, the fire boy, a distinctive Bowery type. Mose prefigured the amiable weakness of Mayor LaGuardia; he loved to follow fires. He also loved to fight, but underneath his rough exterior he had a heart of gold.

Melodrama could also be harnessed to pious purposes. W. H. Smith's *The Drunkard*, which appeared in Boston and ran for a hundred performances, was a temperance tract in dramatic form. It became a national success, joining that select group of plays, like Kyd's *The Spanish Tragedy* and Lillo's *George Barnwell*, that combine the worst elements of the theater of their time and yet manage to catch the public fancy. *The Drunkard* is still occasionally revived today, though only for laughs.

FURTHER EXPANSIONS

At this time the arena for American actors expanded. English actors still visited, but the traffic was now turning the other way, on one occasion with disastrous results. Edwin Forrest appeared in London on two occasions. His first visit in 1836 met with some success, but his return in 1845 was greeted with hostility. Rightly or not, Forrest saw in this the hand of William Macready (see p. 357) trying to put down a foreign competitor. Macready was a tactless man, and he seems to have transferred his rivalry with Kean to Kean's disciple. Macready was no stranger to Forrest's country, having made his first appearance there in 1826, and 1849 saw him in New York again, playing at the fashionable Astor Place Opera House, which had opened two years before.

Forrest's supporters saw this visit as an opportunity to revenge themselves for the English treatment of their favorite. Tickets were distributed to those prepared to hiss, and Macready, appearing as Macbeth, was greeted with a barrage of hostility that stopped just short of open riot. The performance was abruptly terminated, and Macready supposed that his American engagement was over. Unfortunately, he was persuaded to remain, largely by New Yorkers who had their own reasons for disliking Forrest, and on the night of May 10 he appeared as Macbeth again. This time the audience was more evenly divided. Macready's supporters cheered him, Forrest's booed. A larger crowd was gathering outside, hurling stones at the police and trying to force their way into the theater. The troops were ordered out, and though the cavalry was routed, the infantry, after an abortive bayonet charge, began to fire into the mob. The death toll for the night was twenty-two, and Macready never appeared in America again.

By midcentury the American theater had expanded further still. The first playhouse in California was the Eagle in Sacramento, opening in the fall of 1849 and catering to the mass audience of the gold-rush years. It was a primitive structure with canvas walls and a sheet metal roof, and it held about four hundred people. Its melodramatic offerings capitalized on the appearance of actresses, for women were a rarity in California. San Francisco did better with three theaters offering more solid comfort.

Another part of the country had been opened up by the Mormon trek to Utah in 1846. The Mormons conspicuously did not share the distrust of the theater found in other religious groups. On the contrary they saw it as an instrument for good. One of the legends of the great trek tells of the bust of Shakespeare, never jettisoned while more and more possessions had to be discarded as the way grew harder. In 1861 Brigham Young erected the Salt Lake Theater, which he ran as a model business enterprise. He even insisted on putting all his daughters on the stage, although only one had any sign of talent. The theater in Salt Lake City stood until 1928, when it was torn down. Theatrically, however, Utah is still one of the most active states of the Union, for plays are still cultivated in the Mormon church for teaching purposes. Brigham Young University at Provo has five theaters in constant use.

THE BOOTH FAMILY

The theatrical dynasty that straddled the Civil War years and, for one reason and another, became one of the best-publicized families in America was the Booths. Their origin was English. Junius Brutus Booth (1796–1852) had been seen as Richard III at Covent Garden, and though first attempting to rival Kean, he ended by playing supporting roles to him. In 1821 he visited America where, with brief exceptions, he remained for the rest of his life; he died on a showboat tour of the Mississippi and was buried in Baltimore.

Booth had a large family, many of whom died young. His second surviving son, Edwin (1833–1893), far outclassed his father, and he became the greatest actor of his time. At the age of eighteen he had already risen from small parts to play Richard III. It is indicative of the way in which the theatrical world was opening up that his first big success was in San Francisco and that he was soon appearing in Australia and London. Forrest was still alive, and there was a clear distinction between the two styles. Booth lacked the older actor's muscularity, but he had an intellectual sensitivity that was especially appealing in the role of Hamlet and a shrewd sense of theatrical effect that helped him in the more extravert, flamboyant parts. When playing Richelieu in Bulwer-Lytton's historical melodrama of that name (a role already made famous by Macready and Forrest), he contrived an electrifying effect in delivering the "curse of Rome." Booth lifted his condemnatory hand, rising on tiptoe underneath his cardinal's robes; simultaneously the others on the stage sank to their knees. It looked as though the cardinal had grown to giant stature.

John Wilkes Booth (1838–1865), Edwin's younger brother, has earned his place in history for a different reason. Scholars still dispute about the reasons for his assassination of President Lincoln in 1865. One school of thought, supported by recent psychiatric studies, suggests that the killing was the product of a warped mind stimulated by Booth's growing sense of his inferiority in a profession dominated by his father and brother. Another argument, periodically reappearing with new "evidence," suggests that Booth was merely the agent for a larger political conspiracy involving some of the most prominent names of the time. At all events, no performance that John Wilkes Booth ever gave won him as much attention as the one that he interrupted on the evening of April 14, 1865, soon after Lee had lain down his command at Appomattox.

The handsome theater in Washington was managed by John Ford; the play, *Our American Cousin* (whose character, Lord Dundreary, gave his name to a style of whiskers), was performed by a company headed by Laura Keene. This woman, English-born, became one of America's more emotional actresses and one of its most successful managers. *Our American Cousin* opened in New York in 1858, and its long run helped to establish that city as the country's theatrical center. During the early years of the Civil War, Laura Keene's theater was the only one that remained open.

The comedy gained a different kind of fame when it was punctuated by a shot and Booth's cry, "Sic semper tyrannis." In the national shock caused by the assassination, felt again when Lincoln's funeral train made its slow, melancholy progress across the country, the odium inspired by John Wilkes Booth spilled over into the theater at large. John Ford and his brother were arrested as possible accomplices. Edwin Booth was booed the first time that he reappeared on stage. The modern reconstruction of Ford's theater keeps the memory alive. It is now used for happier purposes, including the annual American College Theater Festival. *Our American Cousin* is still periodically revived, either for its own worth or for its historical associations, sometimes with a pause to mark the moment of Lincoln's death.

Toward Spectacle

Edwin Booth's popularity was not eclipsed for long. In 1869 he opened a theater built for him in New York with a production of *Romeo and Juliet;* Mary McVicker, who later became his second wife, played the female lead.

THEATER MACHINERY

Booth's Theater had a number of innovations in construction. The raked stage, sloping slightly toward the audience, which had been standard practice up to this time, disappeared; the apron and proscenium doors were gone; the stage boxes had been almost entirely eliminated. Onstage the settings showed the full force of the realistic movement that was sweeping the theater of the time. Wing pieces were still used, but they no longer slid in grooves. Instead they were set irregularly and supported (as is still contemporary practice) by braces. A high stage house allowed whole scenic units to sink beneath the stage and be rapidly replaced by others. Settings were elaborate, three-dimensional, and lit with the greater subtlety made possible by gas. Booth's Theater even advertised electric light — before it was officially invented!

The mechanical ingenuity of Booth's Theater was further improved upon by the Madison Square, which opened in New York ten years later. This theater had a sophisticated elevator stage that weighed forty-eight tons yet took only forty seconds to move into position. It was the brainchild of J. Steele MacKaye, manager, director, inventor, actor, and dramatist, who had studied in Europe and had already brought new French methods of actor training to the New York stage. MacKaye's own play, *Hazel Kirke,* which opened the new theater, was a melodrama that pleased the audience more than it did the critics. It was later given over to traveling companies that took it across the United States. MacKaye's grandiose vision later projected a "Spectatorium" for the Chicago World's Fair of 1893. It was designed, in anticipation of today's multimedia spectacles, to present the voyage of Columbus for an audience of ten thousand spectators. Financial difficulties prevented its completion — a pity, for it would have fitted well into the world of plasterboard wonders on Chicago's South Side, of which the Museum of Science and Industry is the solitary survivor.

DIRECTORS

The courses of the English and American theaters were now established on separate, though parallel, lines. On both sides of the Atlantic an increasingly complex theater technology created the need for an all-powerful directorial personality. Steele MacKaye certainly answered this description; so did David Belasco, whose meticulously realistic productions have already been described (see p. 379). Another man who merited the title was Augustin Daly (1838–1899), who began as a dramatic critic and later turned to management in New York, opening the Fifth Avenue Theater in 1869 and Daly's Theater ten years later; 1893 saw another Daly's Theater in London.

Daly offered both Shakespeare and melodrama. His principal actress was Ada Rehan, who starred in revivals of the English classics and whose most memorable role was Katherine in *The Taming of the Shrew*. Daly's productions were mounted with a strong sense of realism but also with a heavy managerial hand that paralleled Irving's in London. Texts were cut and speeches altered and transposed — largely, it was said, to suit the personality of Miss Rehan. But to Daly's credit, he also liberated his company from the old lines of business, creating a freshness of interpretation and more versatile players.

In any case, the old method of building up a company was on the wane. The habit of importing visiting stars had destroyed the resident companies by reducing the local actors to supporting roles. In the later nineteenth century the prevailing pattern was more and more to send whole plays on tour. With the linking of the Union Pacific and Central Pacific Railroads at Promontory, Utah, in 1869, it became possible to make an unbroken journey from Omaha to Sacramento, and before many years had passed, a true coast-to-coast link was available. In 1876 one company broke a speed record by closing a production of *Henry V* at Booth's Theater, New York, on June 1 and reopening in San Francisco four days later. The theatrical center was now firmly established in New York; its perimeter was limited only by the oceans.

MELODRAMA

On the more popular level, melodrama continued to exercise its hold. *Mazeppa,* the equine drama, was revived in California in 1863 with the additional fillip of a woman in the title role. The actress was Adah Isaacs Menken, who went on to repeat her triumph in New York, where she scandalized audiences and drew large crowds by giving the illusion of appearing virtually naked. In fact, she was respectably covered in a flesh-colored, skintight costume.

Another kind of spectacle was provided by the emergent American musical. In 1866 at Niblo's Garden in New York audiences were delighted by an extravaganza called *The Black Crook,* which had originated as an ad hoc piece designed to make use of an unemployed ballet troupe. Its plot combined the trappings of Gothic romances with fairy tales and memories of *Faust;* its closest equivalent is the traditional British Christmas pantomime. Its scenery was splendid. It made lavish use of flying machinery, and above all, it was a leg show: a contemporary illustration shows a group of somewhat muscular young ladies preparing to make their descent from the heavens.

UNCLE TOM

One melodrama in particular, with a distinctively American subject, became a saga in its own right, establishing a number of records and, at least in one respect, changing the pattern of the American theater: it claimed to be the first stage work with sufficient popularity to dispense with the traditional afterpiece. This play was *Uncle Tom's Cabin,* first appearing in 1852 as a novel by Harriet Beecher Stowe. Intended as a factual account of the conditions of slavery in the southern states, its fictional coloration gave it an appeal that mere statistics would never have had. Its author was afterward embarrassed by its fame and by the legend that it had precipitated the Civil War. (In truth, the antislavery issue was not raised until some time after the war had started.) As she shared the still not uncommon prejudice against the theater, she was especially embarrassed by attempts to dramatize her novel.

At first, indeed, the embarrassment was widely shared. The story, it was felt, touched on too delicate a political issue, and the first stage version, which appeared five months after the book, was withdrawn after only eleven performances. This judgment was soon reversed. Mrs. Stowe's permission was not given, nor was it asked. Inadequate copyright protection left the stage rights open, and in September of the same year a version by George Aiken was seen in Troy, New York. A year later it opened in the metropolis and was an immediate popular success, inspiring rival versions and, eventually, a host of touring companies.

Uncle Tom's Cabin had something for everybody. In dealing with a burning social issue, it provided fuel for the abolitionist cause. To this extent, it defies dramatic criticism, for it becomes impossible to separate the play from the events that inspired it. Its closest twentieth-century parallel may be *The Diary of Anne Frank,* which dramatizes the Nazi racial persecutions in Europe. Both plays have been accused of cheapening a serious issue for the sake of dramatic effect. Both made the issue comprehensible by reducing it to simple, human, individual terms.

Though the language and devices of *Uncle Tom's Cabin* may seem stilted and melodramatic now, they were the popular dramatic parlance of the time. For those who cared less for the issues than the melodrama, the play still had enough to offer. There was the exciting chase of Eliza and her child as she leapt from ice floe to ice floe across the frozen river into abolitionist Ohio. Later managers added bloodhounds, which appeared in neither Aiken's version nor the original novel. The cruel Simon Legree fitted perfectly into the melodramatic stereotype of the stage villain. There was the tear-jerking death of little Eva. And finally, with poetic justice, came the ascent of Uncle Tom to heaven, surrounded by angels and glory.

Uncle Tom's Cabin was a godsend to the touring companies who lived on it for years. It became not so much a play as an institution, gradually divorcing itself from the general current of the theater and acquiring some of the trappings of the medicine show or circus. Some versions even advertised "two Uncle Toms, two little Evas." Translated into many languages, it has been staged as a song-and-dance extravaganza and several times filmed. The contemporary American musical, which has a way of remembering its own, enshrined it in *The King and I* (1951) in an episode where the English governess of the King of Siam's children has them entertain their father with "The Little House of Uncle Thomas," translated into oriental dance theater.

Popular Entertainments

Another popular manifestation combining the circus arts with drama came with the advent of the Wild West shows. After the initial horrors, privations and unbearable monotony of pioneer living had been defeated and forgotten, the American public happily accepted a romantic picture of life in the great expanses of the West that it has never abandoned.

WILD WEST SHOWS

Exhibitions of western phenomena, more or less accurate, had been popular since the early nineteenth century. Indians were on show in the East from 1827, demonstrating war whoops and tribal dances. In 1837 Philadelphia boasted an Indian Gallery with *tableaux vivants,* and London saw the same kind of show three years later with a local cast. Phineas T. Barnum, the quintessential American showman, was exhibiting Indians in 1841.

John Clum, in 1876, assembled the first traveling Indian show, with scenes of camping, fighting, sending smoke signals, and scalping. (The latter atrocity had been introduced by the British in New England; later generations conveniently forgot this and attributed it to the savage Red Man.) Clum's show ended with the victory of the Indians over the whites, a surprising finale in the context of the times and never destined to be repeated. Gone was the Noble Savage of *Metamora*. Indians, once represented in plays and novels as exotic, were now regularly depicted as savage.

Between 1870 and 1890 nearly four thousand yellow-backed novelettes professed to describe frontier life. Public interest centered on William F. Cody, whose largely self-made myth was propagated by Buntline's spurious autobiography *Buffalo Bill.* This work appeared in serial form in 1869, and three years later Cody was pestered by Buntline to appear on stage in person. He finally agreed to star in *Scouts of the Prairie,* worked up by Buntline in three days, and in several similar border dramas that followed.

The financial return from these enterprises seemed inadequate when compared with the vast sums that other showmen were making. Barnum took in half a million dollars in 1879. Cody therefore introduced his Wild West Exhibition in open competition. This combination of circus, rodeo, and drama leaned almost entirely on physical action. A parade type of introduction of the principal characters was followed by demonstrations of Indian skills and encampment life. Then came a battle, a chase, and an escape, with Cody demonstrating his skills in riding and marksmanship. The show ended with the staging of some natural disaster or display of Indian treachery in which the whites inevitably triumphed.

The affinity between the Wild West Exhibition and *Mazeppa* on the one hand, and Steele MacKaye's Spectatorium on the other, is a close one, showing the same love of spectacle and mechanical devices. In the later history of the shows their connection with the legitimate theater became even more evident. Cody hired one of the former scene painters for Charles Kean to design his sets, and he embarked on an English tour that involved $40,000 worth of scenery. He continued to tour Europe and America until the mid nineties, when his popularity declined and the Wild West Show dwindled into an afterpiece to the circuses it had once rivaled. Cody's legend, however, remained strong, and the American musical enshrined him as a major character in *Annie, Get Your Gun* (1946).

MINSTRELS

In minstrelsy Americans romanticized, and condescended to, another element of their heritage whose reality was less agreeable to contemplate. Utilizing songs derived from the black slave culture of the South, the art found its beginnings in 1830, when Thomas Rice developed a blackface song-and-dance act and a character named Jim Crow, with which he toured throughout the United States and Europe.

In the 1840s this genre developed to involve whole companies and a standardized pattern of performance. The players with their instruments — banjos, tambourines, bones, and one-string fiddles — formed a semicircle, with the compere, "Mr. Interlocutor," in the center. Songs and soft-shoe dances were interspersed with comic dialogues between Mr. Interlocutor and the "end men." In America the most popular troupe was the Christy Minstrels.

Soon imported to England, the minstrel show became popular family entertainment in London, playing in St. James's Hall, Piccadilly, rather than at a regular theater. Gilbert and Sullivan attested to its appeal by paying it the honor of parody. In their *Utopia Limited* (1893), set in a mythical island, the king and his court deliver one number as a mock-minstrel chorus. While the minstrel show professed to find its roots in the black culture, many of the later performers were whites in blackface.

The form has largely disappeared in America, but it had its effect on other arts. The Amos 'n' Andy cross talk act of radio and television reflected the traditional insulting patter of the end men. In England the form has had some modern exponents, notably the Kentucky Minstrels seen on BBC television in the 1940s, and the Black-and-White Minstrels of the 1960s, though the latter, when transferred to the live stage, used prerecorded sound to which the performers merely synchronized their movements.

BURLESQUE

Then there was burlesque. In its strict sense the word implies a parody of some serious work, and so the form can trace its origins to the Greek satyr play (see p. 61). The desire for such relief seems to be instinctive in the theater and produces later examples in the Japanese *kyogen,* which offered comic entertainment between Noh plays, and the English harlequinade (p. 204). The Duke of Buckingham, Henry Fielding, and Richard Brinsley Sheridan all in their time wrote burlesques of contemporary tragedy. The English nineteenth-century theater was rich with them; in France parodies of classical subject matter were popular.

In America the earliest examples were of this type, consisting mainly of Shakespearean parody. Other elements were soon introduced, notably dancing girls, scantily clad according to the standards of the time, who turned the burlesque show into a more risqué entertainment. *The Black Crook* belongs as much to burlesque as to the legitimate theater. In 1868 a company with the strangely modern title, Lydia Thompson and Her British Blondes, became the rage across the country.

In its staging, burlesque's distinctive feature was a runway, designed to carry the girls among the audience and often imitated in the modern theater for more serious enterprises. Later burlesque lost most of its literary associations and became a loose combination of monologues, skits, and chorus numbers. The closing sketch, in which all the comics participated, could still sometimes be a parody of some serious play, the plot line of which was faintly discernible amid the slapstick and pratfalls: *Antony and Cleopatra* was one of the favorite subjects.

The fraternity of burlesque performers, traveling from theater to theater and gradually building an extensive repertoire of skits and business, produced a kind of indigenous commedia dell'arte. In the business the gags and situations became public property. Every performer knew them and could put a string of them together to suit any time span or occasion. In 1951, when Phil Silvers starred in a musical called *Top Banana,* tracing the career of a burlesque performer, much of the material was assembled in rehearsal from the players' memories of their own backgrounds.

Burlesque went on well into the twentieth century. The best-known company before World War I was Minsky's in New York. With the introduction of striptease, however, it gradually degenerated into a girlie show, raunchy and profane, with all the true burlesque lost and the comics reduced to filling in between the strippers. One famous burlesque house lingered on in Washington, D.C., for many years. In Boston in the early 1970s, a new house, ironically called the Pilgrim, opened but survived for only a few months.

In its prime burlesque provided a training ground for innumerable comics who later brought this expertise to other forms. When the first silent film comedies were made, the robust physical humor of burlesque was found to transfer effortlessly to the new medium and to provide an endless supply of comic routines and business. Fred Karno's *Mumming Birds,* which brought Charlie Chaplin to the United States and gave him his entry into film, was, though English, presenting the same type of material that American popular audiences were already familiar with: exaggerated character types, grotesque costumes, and broad sight gags performed with apparently effortless physical expertise. Thus a dying tradition fed directly into a new and vital one. Without burlesque there probably would have been no Mack Sennett, famous for his Keystone Kops.

A ROMAN PARALLEL

This brief and necessarily incomplete survey of the popular theater-related arts shows a vast audience growing up apart from the traditional theater, and it suggests certain historical parallels. While it may seem invidious to compare the American experience with the ancient Roman, similarities are obvious. Both cultures began by adopting wholesale the already perfected works of another time and place together with the literary and artistic standards that produced them. Both after a short time developed a mass audience that turned away from the literary drama to more accessible, because more extraverted, forms of entertainment. The American burlesque comics are the Roman mimes, the Wild West shows are the counterpart of the Colosseum, with the spectacle though without the blood. In both cases the same factors seem to have applied: a large country and a mixed, polyglot population, which only slowly, and never completely, acquired a sense of national identity.

In one respect, of course, the American experience has been considerably healthier. Whereas in Rome the serious theater dwindled and died, in America it has remained very much alive. But the fact remains that in America the theater has become increasingly a minority experience. When legitimate plays were all that could be had, the people flocked to them. But burlesque, vaudeville, film, and, later, television drew the crowds away. The adulation lavished on a Booth or a Forrest cannot be matched in the theater today, and the mass hysteria of the Astor Place riots now surrounds rock groups, not actors playing Macbeth. Many people living in the country now have never seen a live play; for them *theater* means *movie house;* and this trend can be seen emerging distinctly in the later nineteenth century.

THE ENTERTAINERS

Some actors, by the force of their personalities, could still appeal to all levels of taste. Joseph Jefferson III, the last of the name (see p. 440), built an unusual career by identifying himself almost entirely with one role that he refined and perfected over most of his life. Introduced to the stage at the age of four as the partner of "Jim Crow," he spent years in the touring theater, finally joining the company of Laura Keene. In 1865 he appeared for the first time in a stage version of *Rip Van Winkle.* Washington Irving's original short story told of the New York Dutch eccentric who went hunting in the Catskills, met the dwarfish incarnations of Henrik Hudson's crew, and returned to his village to find that years had mysteriously elapsed — while he had slept, the American Revolution had taken place. The stage version, under Jefferson's urging, increasingly elaborated this story with a melodramatic plot in which Rip returns, a changed man, just in time to foil a scheme to dispossess his family. *Rip Van Winkle* was an enduring success in America but more coolly received in London. In 1881 Jefferson wrote that he had already played it twenty-five hundred times, and he was to go on playing it until his retirement in 1904.

Charlotte (Lotta) Crabtree (1847–1924) appealed to literary-minded audiences through her adaptations of Dickens and to the crowds through song, dance, and an endearing, youthful personality. Lotta had a colorful and in some ways bizarre career. Taken to California when six years old, she was taught to sing and dance by the fabulous Lola Montez, who had herself started her career as an exotic dancer in London and whose association with King Ludwig of Bavaria rocked one of the thrones of Europe. This unlikely crossing of paths was providential. As a child actress Lotta sang and danced around the mining camps, and in 1865 she braved New York. Dickens provided her most enduring success.

The Dickens novels had been frequently adapted for the stage, without profit to the author. Lotta starred in a musical version of *The Old Curiosity Shop,* in which she doubled in the roles of Little Nell and the Marchioness. This doubling was made possible by Dickens's love of complex plots. The novel contains two interwoven stories, one of the innocent, abused grandchild of an inveterate gambler, and the other of a gamine rescued from a life of domestic drudgery by an amiable ne'er-do-well, Dick Swiveller. When Dickens wrote of the death of Little Nell, he wept, and the whole of England wept with him.

In the stage version much of the pathos is gone. The antics of the Marchioness have precedence, and most of the other characters are simplified to dramatic stereotypes. The musical element is slight, scarcely integrated with the plot. Nevertheless, Lotta was able to show her versatility against a background of attractive scenes, including an elaborate depiction of an English fairground with Muster Richardson's tent. Retiring in 1891, she was one of those rare beings in the theater who had made, and kept, a fortune; the Crabtree Trust is still in existence to help young entrants into the profession.

Another successful entertainer, William Gillette (1855–1937), wrote and acted in convincing melodramas that combined exciting action with sharply observed supporting detail. His *Secret Service* (1895), still occasionally revived, is one of the best plays about the Civil War. The setting is Richmond, under siege by the federal army. In the opening scenes the social life of the threatened southern capital is cleverly invoked: the parties that are still being given, though without food and drink; the shabbiness of the girls' dresses; the brave pretense that the old way of life is going to endure. Into Richmond comes a northern spy with orders to seize the telegraph office and frustrate the Confederate forces by sending false messages. To fulfill his plan, he pretends to fall in love with the daughter of the Confederate general but ends by doing so in earnest. Discovered, he is about to be shot when orders arrive to hold him as a prisoner of war, and the action closes with the promise of a happy ending.

In 1899 Gillette wrote *Sherlock Holmes* to capitalize on the worldwide popularity of Conan Doyle's character, the first true detective hero of fiction. All the familiar characters are there: Holmes, with his violin, penchant for disguises, and cocaine addiction; Dr. Watson, a more serious character than the amiable buffoon portrayed in the movies, whose life at one point is in danger; and the arch villain, Professor Moriarty, controlling his network of crime from his elaborately protected hiding place. Gillette's Holmes is more active and less cerebral than the character in the novels. At one point he is bound in a riverside cellar by Moriarty's henchmen (including that beloved character of the melodramatists, a lascar) and is about to be gassed to death. One surprising twist derives from nothing in Conan Doyle's short stories: Holmes falls in love, a feature sometimes viewed with disapproval by aficionados. It was thought at one time that the play would not outlive its leading actor, but recent revivals in London and New York have shown that while some of the language has become dated, the work remains remarkably effective. Gillette was another one who did well on the stage, retiring at the end of his career to a castle in Connecticut.

Commercialism Versus Innovation

The coming of the twentieth century saw the theater as big business in America. Vaudeville and the legitimate theater were controlled by circuits that divided the country among them. In the period 1895–1896 a group of powerful managements combined their holdings to create a group known as the Syndicate, which imposed its terms on actors and directors over most of the United States. Although this monopoly was eventually broken, much of the theatrical output has been determined by the larger commercial interests, which prefer the predictable to the adventurous and proven formulas to brave experiments. Consequently, here, as in Britain, the mainstream commercial theater continued to be served by a stream of light comedies, musicals, and popular melodramas conceived in the realistic mode.

EUROPEAN STIMULUS AND INNOVATIVE THEATER

To counterbalance this fare came visits from plays and companies that were causing a contemporary stir in Europe. Ibsen's *A Doll's House* was seen in New York before it appeared in London. Shaw's *Mrs. Warren's Profession,* banned by the British censorship, found a hearing in America. The Moscow Art Theater came here on tour, though the artistic success of the visit was vitiated by political hostility. The Abbey Theatre of Dublin visited, as did Copeau with his new conception of a sparse stage decor, which greatly influenced some American designers. The London theater was well represented, sending over actors and productions in a steady stream that has continued unabated to this day.

In response to this stimulus as well as in reaction against commercial pressures the United States developed, in the 1920s and 1930s, several independent theater groups of its own, sometimes forming about the works of one playwright, sometimes ranging widely in their choices, but equally concerned with introducing new material and new concepts of staging. The European influences were not merely reflected but absorbed so that the United States could at last lay claim to an innovative theater that was distinctively its own and to playwrights who found audiences around the world.

Many of these playwrights eventually won support from the commercial theater, to its lasting credit. For those that did not, the country was vast and diverse enough to produce audiences for every kind of theatrical experiment. One of the phenomena of recent years has been the multiplication of little theater groups in every major city, sometimes playing to only a hundred people in a church basement but still reflecting the interest and vitality of a sizable playgoing public. The inroads made by film and television have been serious, and playgoers now form only a tiny percentage of the population, yet the theater in all its forms remains a living art.

COMMERCIAL COMEDY

In the commercial theater light comedy has become the staple of entertainment, and American authors have been recognized as expert practitioners of this form. Between the two world wars the best and certainly the most prolific comic writer was George S. Kaufman (1889–1961), a painfully shy and melancholy hypochondriac who wrote best when collaborating with other writers. Kaufman won a reputation as the best play doctor of his time, and his name on the bills was the nearest thing that Broadway knew to a guarantee of box office success.

Despite these achievements, he had little luck with writing on his own. He seemed to need a partner who could impose some form and discipline on Kaufman's abundant wit. Significantly, some of his best writing was for the Marx brothers, who had no discipline at all and who used his lines as the basis for their own brilliant improvisations. With collaborators he produced a series of expertly tailored comedies that still hold their own on the stage.

Kaufman sought no higher purpose than to entertain. "Satire," he said in an often-quoted remark, "is what closes on Saturday night." His plots and characters, therefore, tend to be divorced from the mainstream of life and draw their humor from a clash of eccentricities in carefully circumscribed situations. Several of his plays are drawn from the show business milieu in which he moved. Two comedies are set in the movie world whose mystique and larger-than-life personalities exercised a growing fascination on the American public. *June Moon,* which Kaufman coauthored with humorist Ring Lardner in 1929, is set in a music publisher's office.

One of Kaufman's works demands a special note, as it offers a slice of American theater history. *The Royal Family,* written with novelist Edna Ferber in 1928, is Kaufman's half-mocking, half-affectionate tribute to the Barrymores, the reigning theatrical dynasty of his time. Lionel, John, and Ethel Barrymore had each made a name in the serious theater. John, in particular, combined the looks of a matinee idol with an aptitude for Shakespeare, and his Hamlet and Richard III were regarded among the great performances of the period. His later career, weakened by laziness and ravaged by drink, tailed off in a series of embarrassing small parts in movies and on radio. In their play Kaufman and Ferber enshrine the family as the romantic idols they once were, with Ethel seen as the grande dame who, dogged to the last, dies onstage to the sound of applause from the next room, and with John as the dashing hero of the screen whose love affairs force him to leave Hollywood and nearly precipitate a European war.

Kaufman's best-known play, *The Man Who Came to Dinner* (1939), is similarly based on show business personalities that he knew — writer Alexander Woollcott, the Marx brothers, Noel Coward — but it is far more than an in-joke, continuing to amuse, after forty years, audiences who may never have heard of the originals. Somewhat more serious is *Dinner at Eight* (1932), also with Edna Ferber and later made into one of the best movies of the decade, a study of the personal and business involvements of a mixed group of guests assembled for a fashionable dinner party. Kaufman also ventured into musicals: *Of Thee I Sing* (1931), a spoof of campaign politics, is still frequently revived in election years. Written with Morrie Ryskind, with songs by George Gershwin, it won a Pulitzer Prize in 1932.

Kaufman's comedies have now, like those of Noel Coward in England, won the status of minor classics. At this remove in time they show qualities that seem to be distinctive of modern American comedy: the sense of the work as a product carefully shaped by commercial considerations to appeal to a known market; a polish that may sometimes degenerate into slickness; and a preference for the snappy one-line joke over the gentler, more gradual humor of developing character and situation.

This latter characteristic, perhaps deriving from the influence of vaudeville, is clearly to be seen in the work of Kaufman's modern counterpart, Neil Simon (1927–   ). Simon's plots are negligible and his characterizations perfunctory at best. Like the nineteenth-century masters of French farce, he assembles a group of unlikely characters under the same roof and allows them to strike sparks off one another. *Barefoot in the Park* shows a newly married couple in an excessively inconvenient apartment, under frequent threat from an interfering mother-in-law and an eccentric neighbor. *The Odd Couple* has a compulsively tidy man sharing living quarters with his equally untidy friend. The humor of the plays is all in the lines. Simon, with an ear for language as acute as Congreve's, so polishes his dialogue that we willingly surrender logic and consistency to laughter.

To compare Simon to Kaufman, however, is to become aware of one overriding characteristic of contemporary American theater: the way in which economic considerations have shaped the writing of plays. In Kaufman and Lardner's *June Moon,* one of the large cast is the house pianist at the music publisher's office. At the end of one act, he wanders back to his piano to find it occupied by the window cleaner who is picking out a tune with one finger. With a shrug the pianist wanders over to the windows and starts to clean them. The window cleaner is only needed in the play for this one joke, but in 1929 the theater could still afford an actor to play this tiny part. In the 1970s, this is no longer possible. The expense of commercial productions has so multiplied over the years that, outside the musical theater, small casts have become virtually obligatory.

This phenomenon is not, of course, confined to America. The Welsh actor Emlyn Williams recalls in his autobiography that his first appearance on the professional London stage was as an apprentice in a dramatization of the diaries of Samuel Pepys. He made his entrance at the beginning of the play, spoke one line, and had the rest of the evening to himself. This short role would be considered insane extravagance today.

It is on Broadway that the effects of higher production costs and higher salaries for actors have been most clearly marked, resulting in a succession of one-set, two-actor plays and, most recently, a fashion for solo performances. Simon's comedies, though not so attentuated, still show the marks of economic attrition, with one set and some half-dozen characters.

Eugene O'Neill

At the other end of the spectrum stands Eugene O'Neill (1888–1953), a writer anything but safe and predictable, whose experiments ran counter to every formula for commercial success and yet whose death left him as one of the most admired and most performed American playwrights of the century.

EARLY YEARS

O'Neill's background was theatrical. His father, James O'Neill (1847–1920), was a popular romantic actor, trapped, like Joseph Jefferson III, in a single role: in this case the hero of a dramatization of Dumas *père*'s *The Count of Monte Cristo*. Opening in this spectacular production in 1883, he continued to play it for most of his life, though without the freshness that Jefferson, to the end, injected into Rip. For all this, O'Neill had a huge following, and he used his prestige to help destroy the power of the Syndicate.

Eugene O'Neill was born while his father was playing on Broadway, and he spent his early years in and out of theaters. In 1910 he went to sea; the impact of these early voyages remained with him for the rest of his life and provided the subject matter for his first plays. Four years later saw him back in the United States and working with a group that foreshadowed the growing interest of American universities in the theatrical process: Professor George Pierce Baker's '47 Workshop at Harvard, which offered not merely instruction but production opportunities to some of the strongest play-writing talents of that generation.

O'Neill's earliest plays were one-acters drawn from his experiences at sea, and his first work to have professional production was another maritime drama, *Bound East for Cardiff*, staged in 1916. It was produced by the Provincetown Players, an experimental group of actors and playwrights working at the Wharf Theater on the northern tip of Cape Cod. Later moving to New York, the group continued to produce O'Neill, introducing him first to Greenwich Village and then to the larger metropolitan audience.

O'Neill's first play to make a public stir was *Beyond the Horizon,* presented in special matinee performances on Broadway in 1920. A study of blighted lives set in rural New England, it shows a young man who gives up the life of voyaging and discovery that he has always dreamed of to marry the girl who loves him. Resigning himself to life on the farm, he sees his youth wither like the grudging fields, his dreams fade, and the girl for whom he made this sacrifice lose her charm and freshness and become a stranger to him.

Beyond the Horizon won the Pulitzer Prize for that year. Critics saw it as a naturalistic play and hailed O'Neill for allying himself with what seemed at that time the most powerful and persuasive European movement. Naturalistic the play perhaps is, with its sense of larger imperatives dominating individual lives, its preoccupation with marriage as a destructive force, and its ambiguous perception of the face of love. Naturalistic, too, is its concern with environment and with the bleak countryside that imposes bleakness on its settlers.

EXPRESSIONISM

O'Neill's next work, however, showed that he was not to be bound by any one school or mode of thought. Achieving in his early career the same radical shift of styles that Strindberg had found in the middle of his, he wrote *The Emperor Jones* a year later, using expressionistic techniques to fragment human life according to the pattern of the dream and plumb not merely the individual but the racial subconscious. His protagonist, a Pullman porter, rises by murder to become the self-proclaimed emperor of a tribe of "bush-niggers"; in a sequence of eight short scenes we see him haunted, Macbeth-like, by the apparitions of his own guilt. The dreamlike manipulations of time carry him back to scenes from the Afro-American past: the slave ship, the auction block (set as a stark silhouette against a blank sky), and the voodoo-haunted Congo where the fugitive is hunted by the throbbing drums, insistent, menacing, and ever louder.

The Hairy Ape (1922) is a work in the same vein, about a ship's stoker, Yank, sneered at as an animal by society, alienated from that society, and after a period of agonizing, futile revolt, reduced to the level of the beast with which he was identified. O'Neill's play is perhaps a more easily comprehensible example of the aims and techniques of expressionism than the European works in this genre (see p. 393), for we see these techniques evolving as the play is in progress. *The Hairy Ape* begins as a realistic drama, in a stokehold setting colored by the author's experience at sea. Language and characters are still those of the ordinary world. The protagonist's disintegration begins when a woman passenger, a visitor from the other world of the upper decks, makes the insulting comparison. From this point the inner workings of the stoker's mind begin to dominate the stage and the action assumes the unreal quality of a hallucination, falling into the same sequences of stark, apparently unrelated images that we have seen in Strindberg's *A Dream Play*. In one scene the stoker's attempts to revenge himself, or at least to make some impression on the society whose upper echelons ignore and reject him, is shown in a Fifth Avenue scene in which he hurls himself against a crowd of faceless, smartly dressed automata, but he rebounds without making any impact.

This play shows the first instance of O'Neill's use of the mask, which the European theater was simultaneously rediscovering. One might note, however, that where the mask in earlier theater cultures had been a flexible and versatile instrument, an extension of the actor's personality rather than a suppression of it, in the twentieth century it has often been used as O'Neill uses it here: to suggest faceless anonymity. In the Fifth Avenue sequence the smartly tailored, bespatted gentlemen are all masked. By this point in the twentieth century the concept of acting as an inner-motivated art had acquired such ascendancy that the mask, though frequently seen in the modern theater, was regarded more as a deprivation than an asset. By taking away the actor's face, which has become his chief means of expression, the mask is seen as reducing him to something less than human. Thus, though it can be profitably used for scenes such as the one in *The Hairy Ape,* it has become a dead thing and one that its ancient practitioners would hardly have recognized. O'Neill involved the mask even more deeply in his later plays *The Great God Brown* (1926) and *Lazarus Laughed* (1928), though here again the mask tends to be used merely as an empty simulacrum, a concealment, without life or conviction of its own.

Other American writers had made forays into expressionism. The most prominent was Elmer Rice's *The Adding Machine* (1923), which, like *The Hairy Ape,* offered a study of the dehumanization of the individual in modern society (the same theme, incidentally, taken up by Charlie Chaplin in *Modern Times*). In Rice's play life is ruled by numbers. The principal character, Mr. Zero, is an accountant. His friends are Mr. and Mrs. One, Mr. and Mrs. Two, and so forth. Zero, replaced in his work by an adding machine, goes insane and murders his employer. As he kills him, the office setting revolves, and numbers and spots of blood are projected on the walls. He is tried, condemned, and executed; the trial is staged in a room whose walls lean at bizarre angles, with the characters starkly isolated in spotlights. After his death Zero goes to the Elysian Fields, but his spirit has been so diminished by the drudgery of his earthly life that he can take no pleasure from his liberation. Condemning Elysium as frivolous and immoral, he finds his only joy in operating a gigantic adding machine, the keys of which are seen to dominate the stage. Proving inept even at this, he is returned to earth in a bitter parody of the Buddhist doctrine of continual reincarnation, with the knowledge that his new life will be even more tedious, mechanical, and trivial than the old.

Although expressionism, as an exploitation of the new psychology, exercised some fascination over playwrights, it had small commercial appeal. *The Hairy Ape* and *The Adding Machine* achieved some popularity at a time when socialism was fashionable, and the former had a successful production in the Soviet Union, but the only work in which expressionism reached a mass audience was a musical, *Lady in the Dark* (1941), by Moss Hart, with music by Kurt Weill. Hart (1904–1961) was already well established as a writer of popular comedy. He had begun his career as one of George S. Kaufman's collaborators. Weill (1900–1950), one of the many distinguished refugees from the European theater during World War II, had composed astringently tuneful scores for Bertolt Brecht. This somewhat unlikely team found justification for bringing scenes of the inner consciousness onto the stage by having them emanate from a psychiatrist's couch. An expressionist work was thus made palatable to the popular audience by being set within a realistic frame, and the musical won even greater popularity when filmed in 1944 with Ginger Rogers in the lead.

But without such tempering, expressionism in America proved an unprofitable venture. In *Street Scene* (1929) Elmer Rice, though retaining the sympathy with the materially exploited and spiritually deprived that characterizes *The Adding Machine,* returned to a wholly realistic format. The setting — solid, sordid, and with the appearance of having been built brick by brick on the stage — was the facade of a tenement building, a background of sound effects underscored the reality of the urban milieu; and the characters, revealed in brief, apparently casual encounters and speaking the language of every day, were drawn directly from life. *Street Scene,* though winning the Pulitzer Prize for that year, offered nothing that would puzzle or offend the general theater-going public. Years after it was written, it served as the basis for a television series of the same name.

OTHER EXPERIMENTS: NATURALISM AND CLASSICAL DRAMA

O'Neill also retreated from expressionism, though he continued to experiment in other ways. *Desire Under the Elms* (1924) returns to the landscape and the naturalistic concept of *Beyond the Horizon.* Set in a New England farmhouse, it shows a farmer, made unforgiving and despotic by his puritan morality and his years of labor, a stern and lonely figure deserted by his elder sons; his new young wife, on whom he hopes to beget an heir he can raise in his own mold; and the love growing up between the wife and her stepson, the only one of the brothers who has stayed at home. Critics professed to find the play morally obnoxious, but they could not deny the skill with which O'Neill evoked the sense of place and the oppressiveness of the harsh New England locale, which forced the characters in upon themselves and precipitated the crisis. This environment was brilliantly evoked by Robert Edmund Jones's stage setting, which showed an end-on view of the farmhouse, with moving panels as required to display the rooms within. Thus the set became a partner in the action, a cage in which the characters were so confined that they could only beat upon and hurt one another.

This naturalistic treatment continued to dominate most of O'Neill's later work, though with one conspicuous exception, *Strange Interlude* (1928), in which he not only defied commercial requirements by writing a play five hours long but, as in his use of masks, went back to the theater of an earlier time for his central dramatic device. On this occasion he resurrected the stage aside, in which characters step out of the action to address themselves directly to the audience and reveal their true feelings.

The aside is a venerable stage device. It had made its first appearance in Greek tragedy, and by the seventeenth century it had become firmly entrenched in dramatic dialogue. For an illustration of the traditional use of the aside, we may look at a scene from Sheridan's *The School for Scandal,* where the hypocritical Joseph Surface is given a letter by the honest steward Rowley, informing him that his uncle is about to visit him:

Joseph. So he says. Well, I am strangely overjoyed at his coming. — (*Aside.*)
   Never, to be sure, was anything so damned unlucky!
Rowley. You will be delighted to see how well he looks.
Joseph. Oh! I'm rejoiced to hear it. — (*Aside.*) Just at this time!

In the realistic theater, which built the "fourth wall" between the actors and the audience, the aside was rapidly discarded. In *Strange Interlude* O'Neill revives it in extended form — no longer brief interjections but sustained monologues in which his characters reveal the workings of their minds. It is as though, as in Chekhov, the characters came forward periodically to voice the subtext that informs their scripted lines. *Strange Interlude* is really two plays going on at the same time: the drama of outer action, in which the characters relate to each other, and the drama of inner action, in which they relate to the audience; this situation accounts in large measure for the play's extraordinary length. Audiences were puzzled by the device, and it found few imitators — though Groucho Marx immediately parodied it in *Animal Crackers*.

O'Neill, however, did not cease to test his audience's stamina. In 1931 he brought out a play in fourteen acts that took six hours to perform. Called *Mourning Becomes Electra,* it took its inspiration from the *Oresteia* trilogy by Aeschylus. We have already noted the vogue in the 1920s and 1930s for rewriting Greek tragedy. We have also remarked on the affinity between Greek tragedy and the naturalistic drama (see p. 363). Both invoke a higher power: the Greeks, their implacable gods and a fixed and unshakable destiny; the moderns, the no less rigorous sanctions of evolutionary force, biological necessity, and environmental conditioning.

O'Neill transplants Agamemnon and Clytemnestra from Argos to his favorite New England territory, renames them Ezra and Christine Mannon, and shows the implacable demands that crush them, though the presiding deity is no longer Zeus but Freud. The period is immediately after the Civil War. Ezra has come home, on the winning side, to a wife who has been living in adultery with his cousin David. Christine's passion typifies the urges by which this family is doomed. She poisons her husband and is killed in turn by their son Orin and daughter Lavinia (Orestes and Electra). Lavinia is already jealous of her mother as a rival for her father's love; when the murder has been done, Orin seeks expiation in his sister's arms. Thus the whole family is mordant, ingrown, incestuous. The crimes they commit are not imposed upon them from above, as in Aeschylus's grand design, but evolve from the festering desires of their own natures. At the end of the play Lavinia shuts herself within the empty, pillared mansion, to pass her life in brooding bitterness. The Mannon house is but a grander version of the claustrophobic farms of O'Neill's earlier plays.

Aeschylus had conceived the *Oresteia* as a universal drama, of which the family feud was merely the starting point. His human characters are not important in themselves but only as pawns in the grand design. Although *Mourn-*

ing Becomes Electra was extravagantly praised at the time, it was soon objected that O'Neill had trivialized the original and that the sexual urge, however compulsive, was no equivalent of the cosmic forces that shape the Greek play. Certainly O'Neill's work is most pretentious where it is most obviously derivative. The author asked his actors to assume masklike expressions. He periodically introduces a chorus of New England townspeople, chief of whom is the caretaker Seth, whose occasional use of traditional song is probably intended to approximate the effect of Greek choral odes. He substitutes Greek Revival architecture for the fifth-century *skene,* and in the closing sections of the play he imposes a symbolic function on the doors. The play's language has also been criticized as unworthy of the subject: sparse, naturalistic, and colloquial, where that of Aeschylus was rich, metaphorical, and rhetorical. We might say, however, that O'Neill has chosen to write only part of Aeschylus's tragedy, and that his choice has produced a work with its own cumulative intensity, more apparent in the performance than in the reading.

ARGUMENT OVER POETIC VERSE

The debate over O'Neill's dialogue in *Mourning Becomes Electra* revived the old argument that certain subjects, by their lofty nature, require a special voice, in language if not in delivery, and this in turn raises the question of how far poetic drama may be justifiable on the modern stage. This same debate was held again over the works of Maxwell Anderson (1888–1959), a commercial playwright greatly concerned with the use of verse in the theater. His first success, *What Price Glory?* (1924), dealing with the American army in World War I, was wholly realistic in language and conception. Later he turned to a series of historical dramas, including *Elizabeth the Queen* (1930), *Mary of Scotland* (1933), and *Valley Forge* (1934), which showed a conscious striving for a heightened style and a theatrically viable poetic language. In 1935 came *Winterset,* his most discussed work, based on the celebrated Sacco-Vanzetti case of 1920–1927.

Sacco and Vanzetti, two impoverished immigrants living in Massachusetts, had been accused of the murder of a watchman and convicted and executed on what many thought was insufficient evidence. It was widely argued in liberal circles that the defendants had been victimized for their radical political sympathies, and the case continues to excite interest and reappraisal to this day. Anderson, fictionalizing the event as the Romagna case, gains dramatic distance by setting his play thirteen years after the execution and reassembling the characters principally concerned in it: a professor who has been conducting his own private investigations and has discovered that one important witness was never asked to testify; the witness himself, who now lives with his father and sister in a New York tenement; the gangster who had actually committed the crime; the son of the executed man; and the presiding judge, anxious to reassure his conscience. All these people are drawn to the tenement. The son provokes a disclosure of the real murderer, leaving the judge a broken man (there are echoes of *King Lear* here), and the gangster is driven into further murders to conceal the truth.

Anderson's treatment attempted to elevate this issue to the stature of Shakespearean tragedy and to probe the nature of truth and justice in a fallible, self-seeking world. His borrowings are blatant: *Winterset* introduces the equivalent of Banquo's ghost from *Macbeth* as well as the star-crossed lovers of *Romeo and Juliet*. Liberal critics complained that where the play could have been a scathing indictment of the prevailing social system, it was content to attribute the blame to the stars. Those whose criticism was more dramatically than politically oriented found that *Winterset* never came near to answering the large questions it had raised. And although the blank verse of the drama attracted considerable admiration at the time, it has since been dismissed as verbose and pretentious.

Winterset, significantly, has had few revivals. The question raised by its form is the opposite of that provoked by *Mourning Becomes Electra:* can a mundane action be dignified and universalized by recourse to verse? Shakespeare could achieve this dignity. But the later history of *Winterset* suggests that the gap between the poetic tradition and the modern stage has grown too wide to be bridged. Poetic drama has had a small place in the contemporary American theater. Even Archibald MacLeish's *J. B.,* a modern verse retelling of the Book of Job, though successful when first produced, has had few important revivals, and contemporary poets of stature have tended to confine their theatrical efforts to reworkings of the classics, where the lyric voice is held to be more appropriate.

LATER WORKS

Two other works must suffice to show the breadth of O'Neill's achievement. *Ah Wilderness!* (1933) was the only truly happy play that he wrote, a nostalgic comedy, set against the background of small-town America in 1906, that deals affectionately and humorously with the problems of adolescence. We are introduced to the family: the father, the editor of the local newspaper; the older son, a brash undergraduate of Yale; the younger, discovering the romantic poets, first love, and himself, simultaneously; Uncle Syd, the amiable family drunk; and Aunt Lily, who might have married him but never did. Amid Fourth of July picnics and fireworks, the younger son is introduced to the perils of drink and worldly temptation, but he clings to his teenage affection for the girl next door. Even in this totally realistic comedy, O'Neill cannot resist two of his favorite devices: the sea and a soliloquy, spoken at the water's edge, which voices all the impatience and restlessness of youth and the desire for adventure and escape. Were O'Neill's name not firmly attached to this work, it would be difficult to believe that he had written it; in 1959 it was turned into a musical, *Take Me Along.*

Anderson and his contemporaries perhaps attracted more attention than they would otherwise have done, because O'Neill was in temporary eclipse. Many wrote him off as finished. He was, however, only in seclusion, composing an elaborate play cycle, most of which was destroyed upon his death in 1953. Of the remnants the most significant has been *Long Day's Journey into Night* (1956), another work in which O'Neill tested the stamina of his audience. One critic, recognizing the autobiographical tendency always evident in the author's work, has commented cynically that *Ah Wilderness!* represents a good day in the O'Neill family, *Long Day's Journey into Night* a bad one. The same concerns reappear: drunkenness, the problems of parental authority, the dreams of youth, the disillusion of middle age. But the later work, confining the characters, thinly disguised as the Tyrone family, in a single, decaying setting, offers no hope or comfort. We see the actor-father clinging to the memory of lost glory, the elder brother attempting to obliterate his inadequacy in drink, the helpless and incapable mother, and the consumptive younger brother, O'Neill himself. Each, by the end of the play, is given a long, brutal, and excoriating monologue in which they flagellate themselves and those around them. The work is a summary of hopelessness, lost causes, and declining standards.

O'Neill's long, powerful, and erratic career in many ways sums up the history of the modern American theater. We see the various new influences, successfully or unsuccessfully absorbed; we see the return, again and again, to the naturalism that has become the prevailing American mode; we see the dramatist's concern with the stress, malaise, and neuroses underlying a society apparently confident and prosperous. We see, particularly, how little the commercial theater has had to do with all this. Although O'Neill has achieved several successful commercial revivals since his death, his work was originally fostered by smaller groups outside the system: by the Provincetown Players, by the Theater Guild, which was formed in 1919 to encourage the production of distinguished but noncommercial plays, and later by the Circle-in-the-Square Theater, off Broadway, which had the courage to launch *Long Day's Journey into Night* when most commercial producers shunned a work that so affronted conventional playgoing habits.

The Theater and Social Awareness

The stock market crash of 1929 and the subsequent Depression, which lasted until the United States entered World War II, affected the theater in several ways. With money limited and production possibilities curtailed, the commercial theater was as hard hit as any other business enterprise. It reacted, predictably, in two directions. Some of the productions of the depression years were as glossily escapist as anything that had gone before, catering to an audience that sought a few hours' respite from the cares of every day. But there also emerged

Eugene O'Neill's original theater, Provincetown: model in the Provincetown Museum.

For much of its life the American
theater took from England. In
the twentieth century, it has
given to the world. Eugene
O'Neill's *Long Day's Journey
into Night* (*above*) and his *The
Iceman Cometh* (*right*), about a
group of derelicts in a bar.

a string of works dealing with the problems of the impoverished and demonstrating the continued strength of American playwrights in treating, frankly and naturalistically, crises of confidence both national and individual.

DEPRESSION YEARS

One successful depiction of the lives of the urban poor, Elmer Rice's *Street Scene,* has already been noted. Though it preceded the Depression by a few months, it marked the coming of a trend. In the climate of the times a number of playwrights, using the same realistic terms, addressed themselves to similar problems. In 1933 came a work that, for right or wrong reasons, was to achieve a status similar to that of *The Drunkard: Tobacco Road,* Jack Kirkland's dramatization of the novel by Erskine Caldwell.

Tobacco Road is set among the poor whites of rural Georgia. It shows the Lester family, rotted by generations of promiscuity and inbreeding and assailed by poverty and a growing hopelessness that reduces them to a torpor in which they can barely make a motion to prevent the destruction of their lives. The old grandmother is a nagging burden, an additional toothless mouth to be fed. Jeeter, head of the family, has scarcely the energy to steal. The son continually whines of his persecution by inanimate objects: "that ol' wall" destroys the ball he is aimlessly bouncing, "that ol' tree" tears a fender off the car that, in a brief moment of glory, he has managed to acquire. One daughter has a harelip; another endures the slavery of a loveless marriage. The mother's fondest dream is to have a new dress in which to be buried. The harelipped daughter is sexually frustrated; there are hints of incest, which gave the play a lurid reputation from the beginning and led some critics to dismiss it as offensive. Finally, the Lesters have their farm sold out from under them; their home, squalid though it was, has gone; and the only one of the family who finds a glimmer of salvation is the prettier daughter, who escapes to the uncertainties of the big city.

Critics could not make up their minds whether *Tobacco Road* was written tongue in cheek. Certainly it is easy to play as farce, and its long stage life was largely due to the fact that audiences came to regard it as a raunchy comedy. Played straight, however, it is still a moving document of the waste of human beings.

In 1935 came *Awake and Sing!* by Clifford Odets, a study of Jewish family life in the Bronx. Like *Tobacco Road,* it is a play about survival, though here the characters have more energy to fight the inevitable. The son is an incipient Marxist; the daughter leaves her husband to find happiness, however temporary, with a racketeer lover. Odets himself went on to become a highly paid Hollywood screenwriter, a condition that he illogically resented. *Awake and Sing!* was produced by the Group Theater, a new organization that modeled itself on Stanislavskian principles and from which a number of famous names emerged. The same year also brought Sidney Kingsley's *Dead End,* focusing on children growing up in the waterfront slums and distinguished by a realistic setting of which Belasco would not have been ashamed.

John Steinbeck's *Of Mice and Men* (1937) moved the action further west and used the Depression as a background for a moving story of human frailty and dependence. Two ranch hands, drifting from place to place, find a job that gives some promise of security. George is nimble-witted, opportunistic, sharp; his companion, Lennie, is a giant of a man, mentally defective and with a history of uncomprehending violence. His simple mind craves things to love, but he always loves too hard. His caresses end by killing, and the tiny objects of his affection — a mouse, a puppy — always die. Lennie is totally dependent upon George; George is hardly less dependent on Lennie, for he too needs someone to love. The pair have a dream of one day owning their own place, of working for themselves without having to obey a foreman's orders. It is this dream that keeps them going; they talk about it with a lyrical intensity made more painful by being constrained into the forms of ordinary, simple language. But the boss's wife comes too close to Lennie; he strokes her lovely hair, the inevitable happens, and, like the puppy, she is strangled. Lennie is shot, and George is left alone, without even the consolations of their dream. *Of Mice and Men* is not a doctrinaire play. Like Steinbeck's novel *The Grapes of Wrath*, it offers no cure for social ills. But perhaps for this reason, and because it is more concerned with people than with economic theory, it remains one of the best plays to come out of this bleak period in American history.

THE FEDERAL THEATER PROJECT

The Depression did more than give playwrights a new source of subject matter. It produced a new kind of theater and the hope, for a brief time, that the arts might acquire the same kind of state subvention that they had long enjoyed in European countries. Actors, playwrights, composers, and designers had been as hard hit as the rest of the community, and Franklin D. Roosevelt, who was elected president in 1932, felt it as necessary to create work for them as for any of the unemployed labor force.

The Works Progress Administration, created in 1935, gave impetus to the Federal Theater Project, under the direction of Mrs. Hallie Flanagan. Its aims were twofold: to provide employment opportunities in the theater, and thus take as many professionals as possible off relief, and to make theater available across the country at little or no admission cost. At its inception the Project funded not only actors' salaries but a large part of the production expenses. As the programs became more solidly established, it was found that production cost could be met from income.

At its greatest extent the Federal Theater employed ten thousand people and operated theaters in forty states. The altruism and intelligence of this enterprise, however, were always tempered, and eventually subverted, by political caution. One of the professed desires of the program was to encourage new

American play writing, but Congress found itself more and more alarmed by the kind of plays that were being produced. Revivals of standard classics were usually (but not always) politically innocuous. So were T. S. Eliot's *Murder in the Cathedral* and Mike Todd's production of *The Hot Mikado,* a swing version of Gilbert and Sullivan's operetta, which offended only D'Oyly Carte purists. More dubious was Sinclair Lewis's *It Can't Happen Here,* a dramatization of his novel about a hypothetical fascist movement in the United States. Though hailed by Hallie Flanagan as a demonstration of " 'the free, inquiring, critical spirit' which is the center and core of a democracy," it was felt in some quarters to show a dangerous interest in politics on the part of a theater that was now itself under the wing of the government.

Nor did the Living Newspaper offer political reassurance. Originating in New York, it provided dramatized documentaries of contemporary issues, similar to the activist theater movement in Soviet Russia and the propaganda groups in Germany that evolved the epic theater style (see p. 428). In its method of presentation the Living Newspaper adopted, or spontaneously reinvented, a number of epic theater techniques and grafted them onto existing newspaper practices: the head office was managed by an editor in chief and had a staff more like that of a magazine than a theater.

Its first production, an examination of Mussolini's invasion of Ethiopia, was banned by the State Department before it could have a public showing. This move was an omen of things to come. *Triple-A Plowed Under,* which surveyed the problems of the American farmer, was allowed to go forward but inspired much controversy. The *Triple-A* of the title was the New Deal's Agricultural Adjustment Administration, created to alleviate the crisis in food production but subsequently invalidated by the Supreme Court. Employing news reports and verbatim statements by public figures, the production dramatized the problem in a series of short, vivid scenes, interwoven with full-screen projections of statistics and newspaper headlines and accompanied by loudspeaker commentary. The Living Newspaper was attempting to create the same immediacy in the theater that the March of Time newsreels brought to the movie house. Its material, however, was explosive. *Triple-A Plowed Under* showed a wheat burning by protesting farmers. Suspected of Communist sympathies, it provoked anger from the conservative elements in the audience; and in continuation of a pattern familiar in the history of the theater, the political authorities sought to repress what they considered a dangerous stimulus to unrest and subversion. *Power* (1937) again brought Supreme Court decisions into question in connection with the Tennessee Valley Authority, with the members of the Court represented by large, impassive masks. (Compare the comments on O'Neill's use of masks, p. 463.) *One Third of a Nation* (1938) dealt with the slum problem.

The political attacks on these productions were largely unfair. Although the Living Newspaper advocated massive governmental intervention in major problem areas, it went no further than the New Deal had already undertaken to do.

But Roosevelt's administration was itself sufficiently controversial for its opponents to see the productions as a contributory annoyance, and the odium inspired by the stage documentaries spilled over onto the Federal Theater as a whole. In 1937, *The Cradle Will Rock,* a satirical musical by Marc Blitzstein about management-union relations in the steel industry, was suppressed by order of the WPA. The actors staged the show anyway, without scenery or costumes, but this act of interference, together with the resignation of a number of prominent theatrical personalities who found themselves unduly harassed by the government, marked the effective end of the Federal Theater movement.

ORSON WELLES

One of the more flamboyant figures brought to the public eye in this period was Orson Welles (1915–   ). Exploiting his precocious talent, Welles had already bluffed his way into Dublin's Abbey Theatre. Returning to the United States, he directed innovative revivals of the classics for the Federal Theater, including an all-black *Macbeth* that substituted Haiti and voodoo for Scotland and medieval witchcraft in an attempt to reinterpret the play in terms of modern images that would have the same effect on a modern audience as the conditions of Shakespeare's production had on its original public. Lady Macbeth's guilt-ridden hand washing, for example, was translated into the native woman's ritual of scrubbing clothes by hand at the water's edge. This work was followed by Marlowe's *Doctor Faustus,* in which Welles himself played the leading role. Mephistopheles's first appearance was as a pair of enormous, stabbing eyes illuminated on the backdrop. In his human incarnation he was played by Jack Carter, a black actor, with his head completely shaved. The Seven Deadly Sins were represented by rod puppets manipulated from stage boxes, a device imitated by several productions since.

On leaving the Federal Theater over the Marc Blitzstein incident, Welles founded, with his colleague John Houseman (1902–   ), the Mercury Theater, dedicated to plays from the classic repertoire reinterpreted with relevance to the contemporary scene. Its most famous production was Shakespeare's *Julius Caesar,* staged with deliberate allusions to current European politics. In some ways it was reminiscent of Russian techniques: the drop curtain remained up for the entire evening, the stage was stripped to the brick walls, and the principal scenic unit was a large platform from which Caesar, Brutus, and Mark Antony harangued the crowds in a manner similar to that of Hitler's Nuremberg addresses or Mussolini's speeches from his Roman balcony. Costume was modern dress (thus the theater, for different reasons, reverted to the practice traditional before Garrick's time) and, in a period when shirts black or brown denoted political affiliations, many of the characters were dressed in a resemblance of contemporary fascist uniform.

In some ways Welles's *Julius Caesar* was an oversimplification of Shakespeare's play, for to present Caesar as a fascist dictator cuts away the complexity that Shakespeare had built into his study of a critical political situation. Nevertheless, it had an urgency that more conventional productions lacked, and it marked the coming of a fashion, to which the modern theater is still responsive, for translating Shakespeare into idioms more easily accessible to the general audience.

Welles's subsequent career soon took him from the theater into other fields. He won international notoriety for his radio production on Halloween 1938 of H. G. Wells's *The War of the Worlds,* which applied Living Newspaper techniques to a fictional situation and convinced a surprising number of the American public that their country had been visited by a Martian invasion. Moving to Hollywood, he used several of his former Mercury Theater actors in *Citizen Kane* (1941) and *The Magnificent Ambersons* (1942), which have become established as classics of the modern cinema.

Acceptable Conventions

In design, as in play writing, the mood of the American theater remained primarily naturalistic, and until the Depression it was still economically possible to build sets in lavish realistic detail. There were some exceptions, though.

THE STAGE SETTINGS

Robert Edmund Jones (1887–1954), whose interest in theater was fostered by Professor Baker's Harvard Workshop and who went on to collaborate with Eugene O'Neill, cultivated an austerity clearly influenced by the new movements in Europe. As a student he had been able to watch Max Reinhardt at work, and he brought back to the United States a more selective and symbolic style. In 1915 he designed a production of *The Man Who Married a Dumb Wife,* by Anatole France, staged on Broadway by the English director Harley Granville-Barker.

Although the play was set in the Middle Ages, Jones turned away from period architecture to devise a setting in primary colors and simple geometric shapes, light, open, and, as he felt, evocative of the spirit of the comedy rather than a literal reproduction of its historical environment.

His most controversial design, with strong expressionistic influences, was seen in 1921 for a production of Shakespeare's *Macbeth* starring Lionel Barrymore. Jones's stark setting reduced the environment to Gothic arches leaning out of a black void, moving forward, à la Gordon Craig, as Macbeth's career progressed, leaning more steeply as the characters were menaced, and being successively removed to show the protagonist's eventual isolation until only one arch remained on an otherwise empty stage. Periodically three huge masks were suspended over the action, to suggest the witches and the power of fate over the lives of individuals. The settings were as controversial as the production; Lionel Barrymore deserted the live theater for the movies, and Jones's subsequent designs, including those for O'Neill, offered a simplified realism more acceptable to the general audience.

Norman Bel Geddes (1893–1958) was another designer whose vision of a more open, flexible stage had to be reconciled with what commercial audiences would accept. His project for Dante's *Divine Comedy,* conceived in 1921 but never produced, envisaged an amphitheatral construction with monumental, steeply rising tiers of steps, which would change, according to the principles laid down by Appia, under shifting patterns of light. But his setting for Reinhardt's New York production of *The Miracle* was a massively realistic reconstruction of a medieval cathedral, similar to what had been seen in London, and his waterfront slum for Kingsley's *Dead End* was dressed in detail no less true to life than what was currently being achieved by the movies.

Firmly on the side of realism was Lee Simonson (1888–1967), already noted as one of Gordon Craig's sternest critics. In his writings Simonson argued, perversely, that the theater had *always* tried to be realistic, and had been hampered only by technical limitations; that the ancient Greek theater, for example, had used masks and exaggerated costumes only to give an illusion of realism to spectators sitting far back in the huge auditorium. A somewhat similar approach to works from the past was taken by Donald Oenslager, whose work for the contemporary theater was typified by his setting for Steinbeck's *Of Mice and Men.* His setting for a play by Plautus envisages what is essentially a modern street scene with Roman trappings, including wall posters advertising the coming chariot races.

THE PLAYS

The days of the elaborately realistic set were numbered, if not by changing tastes at least by economics. In *Ah, Wilderness!* O'Neill could still assume a theater capable of staging a light comedy with several full interior settings and — for one short scene only — an exterior showing a seashore with a ruined boat. With increased costs and dwindling income, such lavishness was no longer possible. (The effect of economics on reducing the casts of American plays has already been noted; see p. 461). Orson Welles's street clothes production of *The Cradle Will Rock* and his austere *Julius Caesar* at the Mercury Theater represented not so much an artistic manifesto as — like similar bare stage movements in the past — a recognition of hard times. Significant of this new trend was Thornton Wilder's (1897–1975) *Our Town,* which opened in New York in 1938.

Our Town is, for several reasons, an unusual play. A presentational work in a theater conditioned to realism, it has nevertheless enjoyed continued commercial success. It affects a simplicity so deceptive that, while it has been staged by virtually every high school in the country, Tyrone Guthrie, one of the world's most distinguished directors, claimed that he could never cast it adequately from the professional actors available.

Our Town is set in Grover's Corners, New Hampshire, and traces the intertwining, undistinguished lives of its inhabitants: the boy's first drugstore date with the girl he eventually marries; the preparations for the wedding day; the young wife, who dies in childbirth; the church organist, who drinks; the young brother, who dies of a ruptured appendix at Boy Scout camp. We are taken into the lives of these families and made part of their unassuming world. But the play has no setting beyond a few pieces of furniture and a ladder. The houses are imaginary. There are no properties. Actors pantomime newspapers, dishes, or whatever the action requires; the stage has the bareness and unpretentiousness of a rehearsal. Presiding over the action is the Stage Manager, who addresses the audience directly and functions as a kind of one-man Greek chorus, describing the setting and the characters and from time to time wandering into the action.

By divesting the stage of all superfluous detail, Wilder was able to invest ordinary lives with extraordinary qualities. Part of the reason for the play's consistent appeal is that audiences everywhere have been able to see in it something of their own lives, backgrounds, and youthful experiences. We have noted earlier that one of the prime qualities of the presentational theater is that it universalizes individual experience.

Audiences brought up on realism were surprised at the ease with which they could accept the presentational conventions. And here, as in presentational theater elsewhere, Wilder is able to play tricks with space and time and show things that the realistic theater could not. The last act of *Our Town* is set in the graveyard, where the tranquil dead, secure in a world that the living cannot understand, are joined by the young wife whom we first saw as a girl in high school. She asks to go back to her past and relive the days on which she was happiest. Though permitted to do so, she can only watch, without intervening. In each case her knowledge of what is to come spoils the enjoyment of the moment, and she returns, wiser, to the other dead, content to let the living world take its course.

Our Town remains unique, an extreme example of presentational techniques in the modern commercial theater. But many American plays and settings of recent times have followed its example partway, employing a selective realism that may suggest a house by a bed, a chair, and a venetian blind and profit from a corresponding flexibility that naturalism forbids.

Such an attitude is seen in the work of Arthur Miller (1915–). His first successful play, *All My Sons* (1947), was a traditionally structured, Ibsenian, realistic drama about a wartime manufacturer convicted of producing defective airplane engines, whose burden of guilt permeates and corrodes his family. Two years later came the work that has been called the definitive American tragedy, *Death of a Salesman*.

In this play we see Willy Loman (his surname is, perhaps intentionally, significant) with his wife Linda and his two sons; we trace Willy's declining confidence and fortunes in middle age: the cheap affair in a hotel room that costs him the affection of his favorite son, Biff; the loss of his job; the suicide attempts that eventually succeed. Poignantly interwoven with these grim details are scenes from a happier past, when Willy was younger and successful, when the car was new and when Biff was a high school football star. Just as past and present are entwined, the dead can mingle with the living. A recurrent visitor is Willy's brother Ben, a model of the success that Willy will never be, a revenant who taunts, cajoles, and, ultimately, urges Willy into suicide.

The setting designed for the original production seemed to be a naturalistic environment, but it soon revealed itself to be something other. Walls opened or became transparent to reveal scenes from Willy's past. Similarly, though individual characters and vignettes were conceived within a realistic framework, Miller had universalized his characters by pruning away unnecessary detail. Though Willy is a salesman, for example, we are never told what he sells, and the brief final scene around his graveside is written as a formal litany in which the members of his family voice their inner thoughts about the dead man.

In its concern for the little man, *Death of a Salesman* remains true to the social awareness of American plays of the 1930s. Its protagonist is a visible failure, a man of no consequence except to his immediate family, whose life is seen to be founded on sham and self-deception; yet, as Linda says, attention must be paid to such a person. In its structure, however, the play combines an almost Greek sense of inevitability, marked by the recurrence of particular motifs, with an observance of the poetry in everyday dialogue and the lyrical importance of small, humdrum things. One of the most pathetic scenes is when Willy, jobless and rejected, plants seeds in his lonely garden at night, hopelessly pursuing an unfulfilled dream at the end of a life that has been full of them.

Tennessee Williams (1911–   ) used similar devices in *The Glass Menagerie*, his first stage success, which appeared in 1945. Like *Death of a Salesman,* it moves productively between past and present. We see the Wingfield family through the eyes of the son, Tom, who acts as a chorus figure and looks back at the past to evoke scenes from his youth. We see Amanda, his mother, clinging pathetically to memories of a vanished gentility and anxious that her daughter should have a "gentleman caller"; Laura, the daughter, withdrawn into her own world and seeking comfort in the collection of glass animals that gives the play its title; and Tom himself, increasingly estranged from his family and finally leaving it to make some sort of life for himself. Although Williams's first drafts of the play were rejected as unstageworthy and undramatic, *The Glass Menagerie* has established itself as an American classic.

The New Face of Naturalism:
Edward Albee

Neither *Death of a Salesman* nor *The Glass Menagerie* was typical of its author's work. Most of Miller's later plays were conceived in a more realistic vein, though *A View from the Bridge* (1955) used a quasi-chorus figure to frame the action and draw morals from it, and the largely autobiographical *After the Fall* (1964) juggled space and time to juxtapose the story of a disastrous marriage with larger world issues. Miller speaks to the postwar society, which he sees as preoccupied with material ends to the exclusion of spiritual values. His central characters wrestle with problems of conscience and integrity in an age that has little time for such things. Williams also is concerned with the problems of the individual in society, though his protagonists are usually more flagrant outsiders, persecuted, often in violent and horrible ways, for daring to depart from the accepted norm.

ABSURDISM

Edward Albee (1928–   ), who emerged as the most distinctive dramatist of the 1960s, may be seen as a modern example of the way in which the American theater has tended to develop. With Albee, as with O'Neill, there is an early, experimental phase in which a new fashion is pushed to its limits to see how much it will bear. With O'Neill it was expressionism. With Albee it was the theater of the absurd.

His first works were one-acters, clinging to the coattails of the contemporary European movement. *The Zoo Story* (1959), written for two characters on a park bench, confronts a respectable member of society who has middle-class inhibitions with a young derelict who has no inhibitions at all. Their mutual antagonism moves from taunts and insults to ultimate senseless violence. *The Sandbox* (1959) and *The American Dream* (1960) bring together various American stereotypes in a bizarre picture of the superficiality of contemporary society.

Absurdist drama, however, had a limited life in the American theater, despite several successful examples. American dramatists came late into a movement whose limitations had already been recognized in Europe. Absurdism purports to show the meaninglessness of life by *being* meaningless. But once one has done that, there is nothing left to do except to design increasingly rococo variations on the same theme. While there are infinite ways of being meaningful, there is only one way of being meaningless. Ionesco, the high priest of the French absurdists, had come to this realization independently. His later, longer plays, though retaining absurdist elements, are more conventionally structured and conceived in a more naturalistic mode.

MODIFIED NATURALISM

So in the American theater, as in the modern theater generally, after the inevitable excesses of any new movement, the pendulum swings back to a modified naturalism — though one that has absorbed whatever of lasting value the new movement produced. So it was with O'Neill, so too with Albee. After the wildness of experiment comes a settling down, an observable refinement. (Compare, for example, the intemperance of early surrealism with the later plays of Beckett doing far more with far less.) The maturing artist realizes that he need no longer shock an audience into attention; he can secure his effects by more subtle means. It is a process through which every playwright, from Shakespeare downward, has passed. Thus *Who's Afraid of Virginia Woolf* (1962) not only shows a shrewd commercial awareness by being written for four characters and a single set — and by being conceived in a deceptively naturalistic mode that makes it acceptable to a larger audience — but turns these apparent restrictions into an asset.

The setting is a faculty house on a small college campus. The characters are George, a middle-aged professor of history; Martha, his wife, the college president's daughter; Nick, a younger member of the faculty; and his wife, Honey. In a night of hard drinking that vacillates wildly among vacuity and boredom, bitter quarrels, and sexual provocation, these four tear away at one another, revealing the pretenses on which their lives are based. Albee's absurdist affinities are still evident when he explores marriage in terms of the games people play. Ritual patterns, which may in themselves be meaningless, serve as a link between couples. Party games, which begin as a ritual to hold the group together, end in hurt and torment: "get the host" and "hump the hostess."

The drunken evening, in which inhibitions are successively removed (Albee labels one act "Walpurgisnacht") exposes the fictions that people build up around themselves to make life bearable. George and Martha expose themselves in recriminations about a dead child, who turns out never to have existed; this fiction was simply one of the pretenses forged by the couple to patch over the fissures in their life together. Containing this quarrel, the house becomes a cage, a prison, from which the quartet cannot escape — or do not want to, because even in violence and abuse there is some contact, while outside yawns the empty void. A cardinal mistake made when the play was filmed was to open up the action and take one scene out to a roadside diner. Onstage the claustrophobia imposed by the single setting is an essential ingredient in the action. The characters have to stay and lacerate one another. There is nowhere else that they can go. Finally, beaten and exhausted, they have passed through the turmoils of the night — but for what? A certain honesty; a truer perception of themselves and of one another. But there is small joy in this honesty, and little hope of comfort.

A Delicate Balance (1966) carries this dramatic refinement even further, though with a larger cast and more complex relationships. One could almost analyze Albee's plays in terms of the liquor consumed. In *Virginia Woolf* the characters gulp bourbon and scotch; Martha's constant cry is "Drink up!" In *A Delicate Balance* they sip anisette and cognac, very dry martinis, and vodka and orange juice. This comment is not frivolous. It is evident from the beginning that we are moving in a more refined world in every sense; the world of the title, of delicate balances; a world where all real feeling has been replaced by sensibility. We are shown a middle-aged suburban couple, Tobias and Agnes, coping with the problems in their lives by keeping them at arm's length and refusing to be troubled by unpleasant realities. The opening dialogue between husband and wife explores ideas delicately, tentatively, handling them as one would handle puffballs, which, if touched too roughly, will explode. They shy away from real emotions, real contact. They skirt around unpleasant subjects. "We are cozy here," says Agnes. They are; but only because they have chosen to exclude anything that might ruffle the coziness.

As we are introduced to the rest of the family, we realize the delicate fabric that holds the group together. Claire, Agnes's sister, is an alcoholic. Julie, the daughter, is an unstable girl who has just returned home from the breakup of her fourth marriage. Here, as in Ibsen's *The Wild Duck,* we see a group of people essentially empty, who can live together only by denying so much and accepting the convenient fiction for the reality. All their lives are flawed, all lack something.

Like *Virginia Woolf,* this play is deceptively naturalistic. Beneath the surface lurk other, stranger dramatic patterns. One of the familiar aspects of surrealism is the way in which characters, individuals, blur into the mass and take on each other's attributes. This is what happens here. Sexes are reversed. Agnes plays the dominating, masculine role, while Tobias is more feminine. Julie's last husband was homosexual.

Claire is the character who stands out, for her particular method of escape has given her an ability to see and speak the truth, which the others lack. Her name is meaningful; Claire suggests clairvoyant, and she functions as Cassandra does in *Agamemnon,* uttering truths the rest prefer to ignore. She sees things clearly and recognizes her own way of life for what it is.

The family's apparent serenity is disturbed by the arrival of two friends, Harry and Edna, seeking sanctuary because they are afraid. Here is another absurdist element. We are never told what they are afraid of. They do not know. They are simply "afraid." Their plea for protection against this unnamed menace, their assumption that people have claims on one another, threatens the delicate balance. Adjustments have to be made, and people begin to look at one another in a different light. Tobias, sitting up all night in the all-too-familiar living room, summarizes the situation in a beautifully contrived monologue in which he describes the way ordinary objects take on new appearances when seen at a different time or in an unusual frame of reference.

Harry and Edna depart as abruptly as they come. The fear is over, and they go back to their own home. Left to themselves, the family members try to readjust to their old life together. Agnes, with an optimism that conceals an inner desperation, presides, smiling, over the breakfast table with the assertion that everything will go on as before. Tobias says simply, "We do what we can." But what can we do? Julie is already on the verge of seeking security in that alchoholism that has comforted Claire. Albee has shown us the neuroses and insecurities that underlie our common lives. He is as clearly the spokesman for his generation as O'Neill was for his.

Black Theater

Given that so many countries have contributed to the population of the United States, it is strange that the various ethnic and linguistic groups have developed so little theater of their own. Spanish plays were being performed on the West Coast long before the landfall of the *Charming Sally,* which brought the first English actors to the colonies, but they contributed nothing to the mainstream of American theater development. Only in recent years have companies been formed to cater to the Hispanic population. Around the turn of the century a Yiddish theater flourished in New York, performing for a limited but faithful audience and developing a flamboyant style all its own, but this theater has long ceased to exist. The black theater movement is a conspicuous exception to this general trend, starting late but rapidly developing its own actors and writers and a distinctive body of subject matter.

BEGINNINGS

The American theater has always seen a sprinkling of plays with black protagonists, but these roles were normally played by white actors. It was years before a black played the title role in *Uncle Tom's Cabin.* The first seems to have been Sam Lucas, a famous member of a minstrel troupe, who in 1877 took the role with a touring company in Richmond, Kentucky, and thirty years later was cast in the first movie version. Even the minstrel shows, which claimed descent from the slave songs of the South, were usually composed of white performers in blackface.

Far earlier than this, however, a group of determined black performers had attempted to break the white monopoly of the theater. In 1816 a Mr. Brown (his first name is unknown) rented a house in lower Manhattan and offered entertainment for the local black population. This venture was so successful that in 1821 he built a theater called the African Grove, in what was by then New York's chief black neighborhood, since rechristened Greenwich Village. Holding between three and four hundred people, the theater sardonically reversed prevailing practice by marking off a special area at the back for whites.

The company was only semiprofessional (Mr. Brown was a former ship's steward; one of the stars was a waiter), but the repertoire, apart from such antislavery classics as the eighteenth-century *Oroonoko,* was primarily Shakespearean. James Hewlett became the first black Othello in the year of the theater's opening, and the company also produced a distinguished *Richard III.*

Despite the condescension apparent in contemporary reviews, the African Grove was good. In fact, it was too good. Alarmed by the success of this new rival, nearby theater managers hired toughs to take seats in the segregated section and jeer the performances — something that the local hoodlums were already prone to do. The subsequent riots provoked police intervention, which closed the theater, though not before the company had given, defiantly, *The Drama of King Shotaway.* A play about a slave insurrection in the island of St. Vincent was thus seen four years before slavery was abolished in the state of New York, and it was a foretaste of the polemic tone that black theater was to take in its later development.

The most distinguished black actor of the century was hardly seen on the American stage at all. This was Ira Aldridge, who probably acquired his earliest experience at the African Grove but, convinced that America offered no opportunity for a black, left the country shortly thereafter, never to return. Beginning at the Coburg Theatre, London, under an assumed name, Aldridge went on to achieve a remarkable career in England and Europe. Although the color bar in London's fashionable West End theaters worked against him, he won a large East End following, appearing in several antislavery plays as well as in leading Shakespearean roles. Othello was, of course, a natural choice, and he continued to play the part until his death in 1867. But he also played Macbeth, Shylock, and King Lear, in white makeup, and after 1852 he began to take his repertoire to Belgium, Germany, Austria, and Switzerland, and eventually as far as Sweden, Russia, Poland, and Yugoslavia. Hailed as the African Roscius, he was loaded with European honors, and he acted with some of the leading players of his time.

GROWTH

Distinguished though Aldridge's career was, it had little impact on the United States theater. He died in Poland as a British subject, and few Americans had ever heard of him. The black theater in his homeland had to wait nearly a century for its resurgence. Individual performers had made their names in vaudeville but found it harder to command attention in the legitimate theater. When they did so, it was in plays written and produced by whites. Black companies such as the Lafayette Players attracted local audiences, but it was not until 1917 that leading critics began to rank them on a level with white performers. That year saw the production of three plays by Ridgely Torrence at the Garden Theater, New York, with an all-black cast. George

Jean Nathan, the most prominent critic of the day, named two of them, Opal Cooper and Inez Clough, among the top ten performers of the year. In 1920 Charles Gilpin was a brilliant individual success in the title role of O'Neill's *The Emperor Jones* and caused a flurry among reactionaries by being invited to the New York Drama League Dinner.

In 1930 came Marc Connolly's *The Green Pastures,* a white man's play retelling the Bible story in terms of the southern black culture. Modern black playwrights tend to condemn this work as condescending and derogatory. In its time it provided a triumphant vehicle for black actors in the grimmest days of the Depression. Richard B. Harrison, who played "De Lawd Gawd Jehovah," was over sixty-five when he was given the role, and though he had spent years traveling as a voice teacher and elocutionist, he had never set foot on the legitimate stage before.

Connolly's play has not aged well. Its racial arrogance is no longer tolerable, and the affected naiveté of the writing and production soon grows wearing. De Lawd miraculously lights his cigar without mechanical aid, (the stage direction reads, "Gabriel remains unimpressed by this minor miracle"), and Heaven is presented as a celestial fish fry. In its time, however, *The Green Pastures* was controversial because it took a whole black company into theaters where black audiences were denied access, and Harrison himself lost considerable prestige when he broke a company strike against segregationist policies in the nation's capital.

The Federal Theater provided other opportunities for black actors in the Depression, which in normal times might have been harder to come by. John Houseman, Orson Welles's collaborator, headed a black company in Harlem. Welles's own Haitian production of *Macbeth* has already been commented upon (see p. 475). Welles had always been attracted by the theatrical vitality of black performers; in a Paris production of *Doctor Faustus* he cast Eartha Kitt, whom he termed "the most exciting woman in the world," as Helen of Troy. With the demise of the Federal Theater, however, the black actor's impact on the larger audience was again postponed. By way of compensation came *Porgy and Bess* (1935), with music by George Gershwin, based on an earlier straight play, *Porgy,* which had already had long runs in London and New York. Gershwin's work, which had immediate success, is still regularly revived; what it showed in the 1930s, however, was that audiences were far readier to accept blacks in musicals than in serious drama.

One artist who made the transition from musical to serious theater — and who, like Ira Aldridge, enjoyed his greatest success abroad — was Paul Robeson. The son of a New Jersey pastor who had been a fugitive slave, Robeson sang his first concert in 1925 and became world famous for his performance in the film of *Show Boat* (1936). In 1943 he opened in *Othello* on Broadway, in a record-breaking production of 296 performances. He was declared persona non grata in 1949 for his Communist politics. In 1959 he triumphantly re-created his Othello in Shakespeare's birthplace and became the first black performer in Stratford's history to take this part.

CONTEMPORARY DRAMA

The number of black artists in the theater and other fields of entertainment was steadily growing; yet there was still a lack of black writers and of plays specifically directed toward black concerns. The burgeoning civil rights movement and the activity of the National Association for the Advancement of Colored People (NAACP) brought such plays into being; not surprisingly, many of them were polemic in nature.

James Baldwin (1924–   ), also distinguished as a novelist, professed open scorn for such works as *The Green Pastures,* claiming that they offered only cartoon stereotypes of the black experience. He argued, too, that there could be no true relationship between black and white beyond the merely physical. His best-known play, *Blues for Mister Charlie* (1964), based on a racial murder in Mississippi, was infused with anger. A freewheeling, loosely constructed work, it intertwines past and present, and several different stories, in a castigation of white prejudice.

The same rage is apparent in the work of LeRoi Jones (1934–   ), who later took the name of Imamu Amiri Baraka. *Dutchman* (1964) is set in a subway car "in the flying underbelly of the city" and shows a quarrel rising to manic intensity and ending in murder, somewhat in the manner of Ionesco's *The Lesson* or Albee's *The Zoo Story.* A young white girl taunts a middle-class black man, reviling his speech, his manners, his education, and his virility in an attempt to reduce him to the beast she is convinced he is. When he defends himself, she produces a knife and stabs him. The other passengers watch without intervening, drag the body down the aisle, and throw it from the moving car. As the play ends the girl is closing in on another black victim. *The Slave Ship* (1967) is a work of larger scope, using the ghastly brutality of the slave trade as a metaphor for the black condition generally. Baraka later shifted his interest to guerrilla theater, in which he headed a workshop at Yale.

These plays dressed their invective in some novelty of form. A significant proportion of contemporary black theater has chosen to address racial problems in theatrically familiar ways, adopting the three-act structure and the naturalistic mode that have characterized most modern white theater. Thus we see here a pattern visible at other moments of theater history: one finds, commonly, that form and content do not change together; playwrights with a novel or unpalatable argument to present find that it will have a better hearing if presented in a manner with which audiences are already familiar. Thus Euripides, who wrote shatteringly untraditional plays, remained faithful to the outward conventions of his medium, and both Ibsen and George Bernard Shaw used accustomed forms to deal with revolutionary issues. This situation perhaps explains why, despite continual appeals to black Americans to remember their African heritage, and despite the increasing amount of work being done on oral traditions and dance dramas and their place in African society, traditional African conventions have had no discernible effect on contemporary American plays. (The best play about the black experience using masks and ritual is by a Frenchman: *The Blacks,* by Jean Genet.)

At present it seems that black writers are too concerned with the importance of what they have to say to risk any adventuresomeness in the way they say it. Such experiments may come as the movement takes more solid hold. For now, though, we are left with naturalistic plays by black authors, which examine the problems of blacks in a white-dominated society or the problems of blacks among themselves. For example, Lorraine Hansberry's *Raisin in the Sun* (1954) deals with money problems and shifting family relationships in a black household, and *The Sign in Sidney Brustein's Window* (1964) deals with a protagonist so involved in political issues that he loses touch with those close to him. Lonnie Elder's *Ceremonies in Dark Old Men* (1969) is set in a Harlem barbershop used as a cover for illegal activities. Ed Bullins's *The Pig Pen* focuses on the involvement of the black intellectual, forsaking naturalism in a climactic fantasy scene involving a grotesque caricature of a white cop, while his *Clara's Old Man* shows another black intellectual unable to grasp the realities of life about him. Charlie Russell's *Five on the Black Hand Side* (1970) is a comedy about the personal revolt of a housewife and mother against the conservatism of her husband.

Though the body of material is still comparatively small, certain distinctive themes, characters, and settings have begun to emerge. Most notable is the importance of the matriarch, a dramatic affirmation of the reality of life in many black families when, with the man unemployed (discrimination against black men has been even greater than that against black women), the wife's resourcefulness and industry hold the group together. The black activist, distributing pamphlets or seeking donations, often appears — sometimes, interestingly enough, as a comic intruder, with little relevance to the main plot. And the barbershop is coming to be a locale as familiar as the chocolate house in Restoration comedy.

Interestingly, too, racism no longer necessarily dominates the action. Though most plays still contain the obligatory jeers at whitey, the authors' main concerns are with other things. Although racial anger may have been the spur that brought the contemporary black theater into being, an increasing number of plays have an interest extending beyond their immediate time and audience, and we are witnessing not merely the emergence of a separatist black theater but a growing black involvement in *all* theater. For instance, in the late 1970s Joseph Papp, one of New York's liveliest producers, has revived the spirit of the original African Grove in a primarily black ensemble to perform the classics.

The American Musical

So far little has been said in this book about the musical theater, because it has usually tended to take a different path from the spoken drama and to operate in more specialized ways. At the beginning no such rift existed. For the Greeks, and for other cultures, music and drama were inseparable; in

Sanskrit they are the same word. But as early as the Roman theater the musical element had already largely disappeared. Plays might continue to be enlivened by songs, but music drama proper, after being lost for centuries, eventually emerged as an independent form.

OPERA AND OPERETTA

Opera began in Florence in the late sixteenth century, when a group of composers set themselves to reconstructing what they considered to be the musical declamation of Greek tragedy. These classical connections, however, were soon forgotten. By the seventeenth century opera had become a fashionable art in its own right and a serious rival to the spoken drama. In Europe it remains a popular art: in Italy it may be found everywhere; in Germany any town with pretensions to importance has its own opera house and local company. In England and the United States this situation has never existed. Opera has always been regarded, in Dr. Johnson's famous phrase, as an "exotic and irrational entertainment," appealing to a restricted audience. Particularly in the United States opera has been largely cultivated for its snob appeal, as a badge of class. The name *opera house* dignified cramped and squalid theaters across the country, which had never seen an opera in their lives. The Metropolitan Opera of New York, though it plays to huge audiences of genuine music lovers at home, becomes more of a social occasion than a performance on its provincial tours.

The English-speaking world has, however, from time to time produced more popular kinds of musical theater. This activity has never been more obvious than in the United States today, to such an extent that it is no longer possible to talk of the musical as a thing apart. Musicals dominate Broadway, and from there they have spread across the world, which recognizes them as the distinctive American art form of the twentieth century. They have created the need for actors who are singers and dancers, too; the actor who neglects these other arts is seriously limiting his chances in the modern American theater. Serious composers from Claudio Monteverdi in the sixteenth century to Richard Wagner in the nineteenth have tried to reintegrate music and drama in a total theatrical experience, but appreciation for their works has remained confined to a limited segment of the public. The American musical has achieved such a fusion on a more popular level, and some are regularly performed in European opera houses with the same care and skill that is lavished on a Mozart score.

American interest in musicals first became evident in the nineteenth century, with such works as *The Black Crook* and Lotta Crabtree's *Little Nell and the Marchioness* and in the mania for Gilbert and Sullivan operettas that swept the country. Through the 1920s and 1930s most American musicals remained largely derivative, sometimes echoing Viennese operetta, sometimes exploiting the native musical idiom, but retaining thin, conventional plots that served merely as an excuse for music and dancing and were even emptier of content

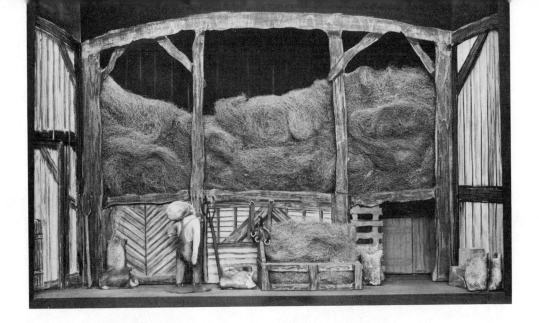

(*top*) The drama of the Depression. Design by Donald Oenslager for John
Steinbeck's *Of Mice and Men*. Realism selectively adapted. (*bottom*) The Black
theater movement has produced social problem plays realistically conceived. A scene
from *Ceremonies in Dark Old Men*.

American popular entertainment revived in the musical; Buffalo Bill's Wild West Show provides the setting for *Annie Get Your Gun.*

than the commercial well-made plays of the period. One of the most prolific scriptwriters was, in fact, an Englishman, P. G. Wodehouse, who settled in the United States as a naturalized citizen.

MUSICALS AND SOCIAL AWARENESS

One of the first signs of change came with *Show Boat* (1928), by Jerome Kern and Oscar Hammerstein II. This musical was not merely a tribute to a famous American institution; it had a complex and partly serious plot given equal importance with the music. With some daring for the time, it touched upon the issue of miscegenation: a white actor in the showboat company declares that he has Negro blood rather than allow his wife, who really has such heredity, to be victimized by southern laws against interracial marriage. The leading character, a riverboat gambler, is by no means the conventional musical comedy hero. Characterized as hedonistic and irresponsible, he deserts his wife, returning at the end of the last act to find his daughter a grown woman. And the show's most famous song, "Ol' Man River" (which in the film brought instant fame to Paul Robeson), is, under its romanticism, a deeply felt complaint against the oppression of blacks by whites.

That such sentiments could be voiced without protest in musicals, when they would have provoked controversy in a straight play, and that, in the social context of the times, black performers were much more easily accepted in musicals than in serious drama, suggests something about the nature of the musical form itself. In the theater music has always given license, making it possible to sing and do things that would not be permitted in spoken plays. This situation seems to exist because music translates the action to another sphere of being, takes it out of the real world and isolates it to an extent that audiences feel it can do them no harm. Numerous examples demonstrate that you can sing what you cannot say. The music of most nineteenth-century operas ennobles plots that, by themselves, would seem trivial and irrational even by the standards of their times. When Johann Strauss wrote his most famous operetta, *Die Fledermaus,* the work was almost rejected in advance by the official censors, who saw some passages as satire on the Russian aristocracy. The audiences who heard it in the theater merely came out humming the waltzes. Gilbert's libretti for the D'Oyly Carte operettas contain scathing parodies of individuals and institutions, which defied the censorship of the time but were insulated from protest by Sullivan's music. Thus the musical form traditionally granted certain dispensations and a freedom to innovate, of which the American theater was to take full advantage.

In 1940 came a musical with a very unappealing hero, the astringent *Pal Joey,* with music by Richard Rodgers and lyrics by the brilliant, erratic Lorenz Hart. This story of a nightclub proprietor content to serve as a gigolo, and the wealthy society woman who kept him, had originally only a limited success, though it justified itself in numerous revivals later. The musical usually, and rather unfairly, credited with being the first in America to deal responsibly with adult issues is Rodgers and Hammerstein's *Okalahoma!* (1943). Based on a straight play, Lynn Riggs's *Green Grow the Lilacs,* it was sponsored by the Theater Guild, which normally concerned itself with more sober fare, and astonished them by making a fortune. Set amid the sheepmen-cattlemen wars that accompanied the beginnings of the state, it combined an endearing rural innocence with apparently discordant elements that a 1920s musical would not have recognized: a subplot involving a morose, sex-obsessed ranch hand who is driven to shoot himself. It won wide praise for its choreography. A clear signal that the musical had come of age was the employment of Agnes de Mille, who had made a reputation in serious ballet, to direct the dances in *Oklahoma!*

SPECTACLE

The war and immediate postwar years were boom years for the musical, as the shows provided color and spectacle in an otherwise drab and austere period of American history, and produced several works that have become established as modern classics of the genre — all by Rodgers and Hammerstein. *Carousel* (1945) was based on *Liliom,* a play about a drifter who redeems himself after death, by the Hungarian dramatist Ferenc Molnar, and would have been the first musical to include God in the cast if the authors had not had second thoughts at the last moment. *South Pacific* (1949) again touched on miscegenation and race relations; an American nurse on the fringes of the battle zone falls in love with a wealthy, attractive white planter, but she is at first repelled when she finds he has children by a native girl. Its best-remembered song is "Some Enchanted Evening" but its most powerful, "Carefully Taught," has the line, "You've got to be taught to hate and fear."

Succeeding decades have seen the musical ranging far and wide for materials and the translation of major literary works into the new idiom with the same enthusiasm that Restoration playwrights brought to the adaptation of Shakespeare and sometimes with the same mind. *Hello, Dolly* is known to millions who have never heard of Thornton Wilder and his original play, *The Merchant of Yonkers.* Lerner and Loewe's *My Fair Lady,* one of the most successful musicals of all time, was adapted, after the author's death, from Shaw's *Pygmalion,* not merely vastly enriching the Shaw estate but creating a situation in which, when the original play was revived some years after the musical, a member of the audience in all seriousness complimented the leading lady on having had the wit to stage *My Fair Lady* without the music.

Shakespeare has served as the basis for several musicals, notably *Kiss Me Kate* (1948), a version of *The Taming of the Shrew* that included a good deal of the original in it; many in that audience, laughing at Shakespeare, would never willingly have gone to see a production of that author in the theater. Leonard Bernstein's sensitive and witty version of Voltaire's *Candide* (1953) did badly on its first appearance, when the satire was lost under an opulent production, but it did far better in a simpler revival some years later. At the other end of the literary scale, comic strips provided the material for *Li'l Abner* (1956), *Superman* (1966), and *Annie* (1976). Between these extremes almost every conceivable author has been represented, from Chaucer to Conan Doyle.

In production, musicals have encouraged a scenic inventiveness that has often been ahead of what would have been permitted in the serious theater. Once again, music gives license; mass audiences have accepted in musicals theatrical conventions and departures from naturalism that they would have rejected in straight plays. Also, the musical is allowed a budget enjoyed by few straight plays, and musicals remain one of the last holdouts of spectacular showmanship on the modern stage.

Finally, the musical has repaid America's debt to Great Britain on which the country launched its theatrical beginnings. Not merely have successful American musicals been regularly transported to London, thereby reversing the traffic of two centuries, but the success of this distinctively American form has inspired many British imitations, good, bad, and indifferent — musical adaptations of Dickens, Thackeray, and Jane Austen and a rock opera version of *Othello,* side by side with original works, and staged with the same expertise and scenic inventiveness that characterize the American examples. Staging a musical has been called "the most professional activity in the world." Certainly, with enormous budgets the stakes are high. But in this area, at least, the theater has continued to appeal to a popular audience that deserted the spoken drama years ago.

12
The Ways and Means of Theater

Theater Organization

NATIONAL THEATER SYSTEMS

A national theater is, by definition, largely subsidized out of taxation with moneys received either from the government directly or through appropriate agencies. One of the oldest and most distinguished in the world is the French national theater, the Comédie Française, whose origins have already been described (p. 281).

FRANCE

The Comédie Française is unique in retaining a system of organization that goes back, in its essentials, to the Middle Ages. Its history has been virtually

National Theatre of Great Britain, London.

unbroken, beginning with the monopoly of sacred drama awarded to the Confrérie de la Passion, continuing through the royal patronage of the three principal Parisian theaters in the seventeenth century, and evolving, in 1680, into the united company that remained for years under strict monarchical control and whose pattern is still retained in the present system. The theater suffered a brief dissolution during the French Revolution, but Napoleon, on his way to Russia, took time to rewrite its constitution.

It remains a cooperative society, into which new actors are admitted, according to merit, as *pensionnaires,* with limited contracts. After a short or long probation period, they may then be accepted as full members, *sociétaires,* though the number of these remains constant, and a new *sociétaire* may only be elected when a previous member has resigned or died. *Sociétaires* are expected to pledge themselves to the organization and to remain for a minimum of twenty years. Acting engagements in other theaters or in films may only be undertaken with the approval of the Comédie (though certain members, notably Sarah Bernhardt, have been sufficiently confident of their value to the company to work elsewhere whether approval was given or not). On retirement, *sociétaires* are entitled to a pension. Funding of the theater, and thus a large measure of control, is ultimately vested in the Ministry of Fine Arts.

The Comédie Française is housed in the Théâtre Français, an elegant eighteenth-century foundation that, despite numerous redecorations and alterations, still retains much of its original character. More recently the Odéon, on the Left Bank, has been taken over as an ancillary, government-subsidized theater, playing its own classical repertory interspersed with more modern works. The professed aim of both theaters is to provide a home for the French classics and to make them available, at low cost, to as wide a cross section of the public as possible. Thus although orchestra stalls tend to be as expensive here as in any commercial theater, there is a large block of low-cost seating. School matinees are regularly played and have become part of the French schoolchild's educational experience, and cheap seats are always available, on a last-minute basis, for students.

The advantages of the system lie in giving actors a far greater measure of security than the commercial theater can provide, in establishing a company that can work together for long periods on a regular basis, and in presenting an ever-changing repertory of the best classical and modern drama. The corresponding disadvantages are the creation of a museum atmosphere, which tends to resist innovation, and a susceptibility to political interference both external and internal. Positions within the company hierarchy, for example,   jealously guarded. It has not been unknown for a *sociétaire* to refuse to take a role previously assigned to a *pensionnaire,* on the grounds that this role was beneath his or her dignity. The oldest established member of the company, the doyen, tends to acquire disproportionate influence, which may affect the allotment of roles and the choice of repertory. Political pressure from above was clearly evident in the student riots of the 1960s, when the offerings at the Odéon became a target for militants. Occupying the theater, they published a manifesto declaring that the traditional arts were dead and that the only true theater was guerrilla theater; they also invaded the scene and costume shops, destroying the Odéon's valuable collection. When Jean-Louis Barrault, the theater's director, attempted to prevent this action by personal intervention and appeals to the authorities, he was removed from his post as a sop to the dissidents.

For all its shortcomings, however, the Comédie Française remains a monument to the national dramatic achievement. Like all monuments, it has its detractors, and some of the most exciting movements in the French theater have been led by those who were infuriated by the Comédie Française and all it stood for. Even in this way, however, the institution has performed a useful function — by adhering to a certain style of performance against which other styles can be measured. Even those who have broken away from the institution proclaim their debt to it and their lasting affection for it.

AUSTRIA

By way of comparison one may consider the Austrian National Theater, whose activity is chiefly located in Vienna. The first German-speaking national theater was established by the Emperor Joseph II in 1776, and the Viennese system now comprises two opera houses and two legitimate buildings. It is significant of national priorities that the larger opera house, the Staatsoper, located near the city center, was one of the first buildings to be reconstructed after the devastation of World War II, with the enthusiastic approval of a population, many of whom were without adequate housing.

Of the legitimate theaters the older is the Burgtheater, Emperor Joseph's eighteenth-century foundation, which under the imperial regime was more concerned with opera and ballet. Musical drama is still performed here, but a large part of the repertoire is now made up of plays from the classic, baroque, and romantic periods, including numerous translations of foreign classics.

The modern government, continuing imperial patronage, subsidizes 80 percent of the theater's operating costs. In 1975 the theater personnel included, besides the director and the *dramaturg,* 16 stage directors, 14 designers, and an acting company of 143. Just after World War I a second house, the Akademietheater, was opened, using largely the same personnel as the original theater. It is thus possible to go to the Burgtheater on one night, and the Akademietheater on the next, and see several of the same actors in two different plays, often alternating as leads and walk-ons. Tickets for all four state-supported theaters are available from central locations, and, as in Paris, a large block of seats is available at low prices.

The Austrian theater seems to have escaped some of the abuses of the French system. Although it produced its own doyens, who attracted large personal followings, and although the wieght of tradition is sometimes apparent (the influence of Max Reinhardt is still visible, even over the break of World War II), the offerings remain fresh and lively — perhaps because Austria, with a less distinctive dramatic tradition of its own, has always been forced to be more eclectic in the choice of material.

GREAT BRITAIN

The evolution of a British national theater has been typically more laggardly and more circuitous than that in other countries. First seriously mooted in 1848, the project was heartily endorsed in 1904 by William Archer, the translator-critic (see p. 388), in a publication entitled *Scheme and Estimates for a National Theatre*. In 1938 George Bernard Shaw contributed money for the purchase of a site. A site was, in fact, chosen, and a foundation stone laid, but the straitened postwar economy delayed further progress. Some twenty years after Shaw's gift, the critic Kenneth Tynan had himself photographed in full Victorian mourning dress on the site of a national theater that seemed likely never to materialize.

However, Great Britain, with its habit of doing things indirectly, had already evolved what was, to all intents and purposes, a de facto national theater in the shape of the Old Vic. This institution had a long and curious history. Founded as the Royal Coburg Theatre, on the south bank of the Thames, it opened in 1818 with a program typical of its time: a melodrama, a harlequinade, and a ballet. Its location made it unpopular with upper-class theatergoers, who remained faithful to the West End. Nevertheless, it had an enthusiastic following and featured such performers as Edmund Kean and Ira Aldridge.

Remodeled in 1833 as the Royal Victoria — hence the affectionate diminutive by which it is still known — it lasted as a melodrama house until 1880, when it was bought by Emma Cons, an energetic crusader for temperance, who reopened it as the Royal Victoria and Coffee Tavern, a place where workers might find cheap family entertainment without the temptations of strong drink. Later under the management of the founder's niece, Lilian Baylis, this entertainment was supplemented by films, opera, and, in 1914, performances of Shakespeare, to whom Miss Baylis was passionately devoted. Under her strong, if idiosyncratic control, the theater went on to devote itself to Shakespearean seasons interspersed with occasional revivals of other classics, and it attracted some of the best acting and directing talent in England.

Though small, inconveniently located, and with archaic facilities — including a raked stage that successive generations of designers have cursed and a scene shop so small that room for building and storage has to be found elsewhere — the Old Vic became recognized as the repository of the classical tradition in the English theater. Though the building itself was badly damaged by the German bombing in World War II, the company continued to work together in other locations. A triumphant reopening in 1950 inaugurated a period in which the Old Vic, with Laurence Olivier and Ralph Richardson dividing the leading roles, represented the peak of dramatic achievement at home, and it received similar recognition on its tours abroad.

Meanwhile, support for a national theater was growing. The war years had seen the formation of the Council for the Encouragement of Music and the Arts (CEMA), which created a climate of favorable public opinion for government subsidy of the arts generally. Thus in 1946 was formed the Arts Council of Great Britain, which was at last able to transform the dream of a national theater into reality. Under the direction — inevitably — of Laurence Olivier, the company made its first home at the Old Vic. A new theater was planned but delayed several times through lack of funds. Finally, in 1976 it opened on London's South Bank, not far from where Shakespeare's Globe had originally stood. It contained three playing areas under the same roof: a 1,160-seater house with a thrust stage and the audience surrounding the action on three sides, which makes it particularly suitable for Elizabethan drama; a smaller proscenium theater, more suitable for realistic drama and seating 890 spectators; and a 400-seater space for experimental drama that can be rearranged in any number of ways. With the establishment of the National Theatre, Olivier, who had already been knighted, outdid Irving by becoming the first British actor to be admitted into the peerage.

The British National Theatre recognizes several commitments. One, of course, is to the English classics in general and to Shakespeare in particular. Many works have been offered that would scarcely be possible in a commercial theater, including the two parts of Marlowe's *Tamburlaine* and a number of plays by minor Jacobean dramatists. Equally, however, the theater feels bound to encourage new dramatists and stages a growing number of successful original works. It also has a literary manager — the equivalent of the European *dramaturg* — responsible for commissioning new translations and adaptations and looking into hitherto unexplored areas of dramatic activity. Kenneth Tynan, during his tenure of the post, encouraged productions of several dramas from the Spanish Golden Age, which had been undeservedly neglected by the rest of Europe.

In such operations Britain has the advantage of being a small country. Most places are within a few hours' journey from London; audiences can travel in from the provinces, and actors can accept temporary work elsewhere in the knowledge that they are never far from their home base. Censorship, the traditional enemy of the British theater, has virtually disappeared — as it has, indeed, in most countries of the non-Communist world (in the state-run theaters of Soviet Russia, it is all the more oppressive for not being officially admitted). The British system, however, still has to operate under financial restraints. Government funding is limited and must be shared with the Royal Opera, the ballet, and a host of smaller activities. Cuts in production budgets, therefore, regularly threaten to curtail the season, and some of the best actors find the salaries pitifully small compared to what they can make in the commercial theater or in movies.

The American Commercial Theater

The United States has no national theater. The nearest it has so far come to this was the ill-fated Federal Theater Project of the 1930s, which foundered under political attack. Thus the task of preserving the classical repertory has fallen to festival and regional theaters, many of them subsidized by federal monies through the National Endowment for the Arts. Apart from a few productions linked to star names, like the John Barrymore or Richard Burton *Hamlet,* the commercial theater has refused this charge, and individual attempts to create a classical repertory system within the commercial framework have had little success. Eva Le Gallienne, whose Civic Repertory Theater opened in New York in 1926, was a rare exception. The enterprise ran six years with productions of Shakespeare, Molière, Chekhov, Goldoni, and more modern writers who had been rejected by Broadway as uncommercial.

BROADWAY

The American commercial theater has turned art into industry, and, like any industry, it seeks the greatest possible return for money invested. Since the mid nineteenth century it has been centered in New York, though a proven success may be duplicated in other major cities and touring companies may eventually take a work across the country. In New York itself the pattern of the season is dictated by the theater owners.

Since the 1920s the number of theaters available has substantially declined. Those remaining are so eagerly competed for that new production may find itself forced into a theater of the wrong shape and size or have to wait months to find a theater at all, and any production must pay its way from the beginning or find itself evicted. This situation effectively prevents the development of a repertory system or the kind of extended season that a national theater may plan, in which the losses on one production may be (hopefully) offset by the profits on the next. Commercial productions are ad hoc affairs, with the cast and production staff selected for one work only; when the production closes, they may never work together again.

In the 1920s, the producer would normally expect to finance the production himself. Astronomically rising costs have now made this impossible. Most productions today are financed by a consortium, and the backers naturally demand some assurance that the work will be marketable, either because it features known names or because it caters to a demonstrated popular taste. Money is commonly raised by backers' auditions, in which the work is read or sung in as appealing a format as possible. Sometimes workshop productions are arranged, with minimal financing, or a new work may be staged out of town, often in a summer theater where costs are small and audiences guaranteed, as a prelude to Broadway presentation: Neil Simon's *Barefoot in the Park* began in this way and went on to become a Broadway hit.

Once the production is financed, cast, designed, and rehearsed, it normally tries out in several other cities before risking Broadway exposure. Philadelphia, New Haven, and Boston have become established as tryout cities. The process is long and expensive but necessary, allowing the company to assess audience reactions and to make whatever changes seem to be desirable. Some shows are almost completely rewritten, and sometimes recast, during the tryout tours. Some, because of unfavorable audience response, never reach Broadway at all, as the producers find it cheaper to cut their losses by abandoning the work on tour than to risk a financial disaster by opening in New York with anything less than a tested success.

The show's fate on Broadway is largely decided by a handful of critics, who, many feel, have acquired disproportionate influence. Their approval guarantees a prosperous run of many months; their disapproval, that the show may close in a few days. Thus has arisen the hit-flop mystique of the contemporary commercial theater. There is no way in which a production may sustain itself on moderate audiences and hope to pick up more with time. Broadway economics forbid it, for there is always another production waiting to get in. A rare handful of productions have been successful despite critical disapproval, and New York newspaper strikes, in which the critics' voices have been stilled and audiences have been drawn by word of mouth, have sometimes brought unexpected results, but on the whole a show must succeed instantaneously, or it has failed. The consequences have been predictable. Broadway openings have steadily diminished in number and become increasingly conservative, with musicals, despite their expanded budgets, still regarded as the safest risk. New playwrights and untried actors now find it impossible to penetrate the Broadway scene.

OFF-BROADWAY

One productive result of this situation has been the growth of off-Broadway, theaters operating on the fringes of the main commercial area, in smaller spaces but with less ground rent and overheads, thus making experiment more feasible, though on a limited budget. We have already seen how O'Neill owed his reputation to such little theaters. From the early 1950s off Broadway offered a succession of distinguished works, some of which were eventually transplanted to the commercial theater. The Theatre de Lys, in Greenwich Village, revived *The Threepenny Opera,* Brecht's sardonic rewriting, with music by Kurt Weill, of an eighteenth-century ballad opera by John Gay. *The Threepenny Opera* appealed on various levels. It had good tunes; one of them, "The Ballad of Mack the Knife," became the number-one popular song in America, and number two in England, in 1959. Set in a world of thieves, murderers, and prostitutes, it offered a view of the human power struggle and the fight for survival, sympathetic to audiences suffering from postwar disillusionment. And for those still romantically inclined, Brecht's amoral protagonist still retained some of the endearing bravado of Gay's highwayman hero Macheath. Tennessee Williams's *Summer and Smoke*, which had failed on Broadway, had a triumphant revival, arena style, in a converted nightclub: the theater, the Circle in the Square, went on to establish itself as one of New York's most exciting companies. *Cat on a Hot Tin Roof*, a later Williams play, drew the approval of leading critics, not merely for the script but for the forced economy of the production. Another off-Broadway theater, the Phoenix, founded in 1953, offered successful productions of the world's classics under leading American and British directors, with occasional works by innovative newcomers.

Eventually off Broadway, like Broadway itself, became the victim of rising costs and was forced to adopt a more conservative posture. Thus in the 1960s came off-off-Broadway, using spaces even more remote and budgets even more restricted. Here experiment still proliferates, some valuable, some deplorable, most of it amateur in the best and worst senses — for though writers and actors can find the freedom off-off-Broadway to create as they please, they can rarely hope to support themselves. The La Mama group, founded in 1961 by Ellie Paine, won an international reputation with productions that moved away from the conventional script to more abstract compositions of dance, ritual, and mime. Of the new playwrights the more prominent have been Sam Shepard, who combined drama with rock music in *Operation Sidewinder* (1970) and *The Tooth of Crime* (1974); Paul Foster, whose *Tom Paine* (1968) used two actors to play different aspects of the leading character and left many scenes to the actors' improvisation; Lanford Wilson, with *The Rimers of Eldritch* and *The Madness of Lady Bright;* and Ronald Ribman, who demonstrated the versatility of the off-off-Broadway movement by writing, in 1966, *The Journey of the Fifth Horse*, a charming dramatization of a Russian short story, largely conventionally structured and with an almost romantic appeal.

Other Theater Groups

The growth of off- and off-off-Broadway theaters represents a challenge to the traditional pattern of theater economics. While the nineteenth century was dominated either by state-subsidized companies or the established commercial system, the twentieth has devised other possibilities. In a country as large as the United States, such responses have taken a variety of forms, depending largely on local community interest. Although the theater-going audience has proportionally diminished, the ways in which plays may be brought to the public — through festival, regional and university theaters, through community theater and summer stock — have markedly increased.

FESTIVAL AND REGIONAL THEATERS

As noted earlier, while Broadway is motivated by commercial opportunity and the fringe theaters are increasingly concerned with experiment for experiment's sake, the task of preserving the classical repertory has fallen increasingly on regional theaters. Established as nonprofit organizations, these theaters enjoy considerable subsidy from federal or local sources and thus are able to plan extended seasons with companies who may expect to work together for a considerable period of time.

One of the most famous regional theaters on this continent is Canadian: the Shakespeare Festival Theater at Stratford, Ontario, which has served as a model for similar institutions elsewhere. It was founded in 1953 by a local businessman who believed that a town called Stratford should own some connection with Shakespeare, persuaded others to help finance his beliefs, and brought out the eminent British director Tyrone Guthrie, whose Shakespearean productions were world famous, to discuss the feasibility of the project. The first season, in a theater still largely built of canvas, opened with Guthrie's production of *Richard III,* with Alec Guinness in the title role. Enthusiasm was so great that the temporary playhouse was soon replaced by a permanent structure designed by Tanya Moseiwitch and one of the handsomest theaters in North America.

Stratford has gone on to establish itself as one of the great festival theaters of the world. The present operation no longer confines itself to Shakespeare, though this remains the staple of the repertory; other productions have included Sophocles, Congreve, Shaw, Wilde, Brecht, and a dramatization of Dumas's *The Three Musketeers,* given either in the main theater or in a converted cinema downtown. Stratford prides itself on creating a sorely needed center for Canadian actors, who regularly take productions on regional tours, and on evolving a distinctively Canadian Shakespearean style, though box office considerations still dictate the engagement of leading British and American actors.

Years before the foundation of Stratford, a Shakespeare festival had been in operation at Ashland, Oregon. Like Stratford, it found its beginnings in local enthusiasm. Angus Bowmer, a professor at the state college, discovered, in a local park, an abandoned Chautauqua site, which he found to have the same dimensions as Elizabethan London's Fortune playhouse (see p. 168). The rest of the story has become Ashland legend. Bowmer persuaded the town authorities to finance a limited summer Shakespeare season. They agreed, only on condition that they could also stage boxing matches, anticipating that the profit from these would make up the inevitable loss on Shakespeare. It was the Shakespeare that made the profit, and the boxing matches that lost. From these humble beginnings Ashland has gone on to build a permanent open-air theater in the park, which has offered the entire Shakespearean corpus several times, with the history plays in chronological sequence. Plays by other Elizabethan dramatists, such as Ben Jonson's *Volpone* and Beaumont and Fletcher's *Knight of the Burning Pestle,* have also been given. More recently, the addition of an indoor theater has made year-round operation possible, with handsomely mounted productions of the world's classics.

Stratford and Ashland rely on tourists for a large part of their audience. Other regional theaters cater to a more local, though no less devoted, clientele. The Guthrie Theater in Minneapolis was founded by Tyrone Guthrie after his successful Stratford enterprise; once again the stage was designed by Tanya Moseiwitch, in an auditorium holding 1,441 spectators. Plays are given in rotating repertory and have ranged from a complete production of Aeschylus's *Oresteia* (later taken to New York) to contemporary French-Canadian work. Although a system of internships for young actors and trainee directors was frustrated by the professional unions, the Guthrie retains close ties with the Department of Theater Arts at the University of Minnesota, thus giving the advantages of professional contacts in an academic situation. And like the national theaters of Europe, it has pursued an ambitious educational program, touring productions to high schools, colleges, and smaller communities to build an enthusiastic audience for the living theater.

In Washington, D.C., the Arena Stage opened in 1950 in a converted movie house, then moved to a disused brewery affectionately known as the Old Vat. This building in turn was replaced in 1961 by a purpose-built theater dedicated primarily to the production of new American plays, American premieres of important European works, and revivals of the classics with a contemporary slant. In Atlanta the Memorial Arts Center, after a disastrous opening in 1969 with a revival of Purcell's rarely produced *King Arthur,* has settled down to a more conventional classical program, though without the benefit of a permanent repertory company.

Most cities of any size in the United States can now boast similar institutions: The Alley Theater in Houston, the American Conservatory Theater in San Francisco — whose productions of *Cyrano de Bergerac* and *The Taming of the Shrew* have been nationally televised — the Barter Theater in Abingdon, Virginia, the Cleveland Playhouse, Chicago's Goodman Theater, the Mark Taper Forum in Los Angeles. Many other theaters of similar prestige throughout the country draw large audiences, but still, in the present economic climate, they are unable to exist without external support. It is a tribute to the farsightedness of federal, state, and local authorities, and to the excitement that living theater still generates in a television age, that such support continues to be given; for it has become apparent that, like museums, libraries, art galleries, and symphony orchestras, the serious theater cannot survive without public funding.

In recent years the regional theater movement has also gained strength in Great Britain. Before the advent of television, many towns supported local repertory companies. Though these displayed varying degrees of talent, and generally clung to an unadventurous repertoire, they commanded a good deal of loyalty and affection within the community. As soon as unlimited entertainment began to be piped into people's homes, many of these companies were threatened with insolvency. Lately, however, there has been a significant change. Public funding has revivified older theaters and created new ones in key provincial centers. Cities such as York, Birmingham, Leeds, and Nottingham operate expertly designed and staffed civic playhouses, which bring both classics and provocative new works to large audiences. The Arts Council, in addition, periodically sponsors tours that take productions to smaller communities that would otherwise have no access to them.

ACADEMIC THEATER

One of America's most significant contributions to the theater arts has been its recognition of their rightful place in the universities. At various periods drama has played an important role in education, notably in the Jesuit colleges of Europe, which preserved a dramatic tradition that threatened to vanish elsewhere. It took some time, however, for this concept to be established in the English-speaking world.

The senior British universities, Oxford and Cambridge, still maintain a traditional antagonism to theater studies. Although proposals for an inclusion of drama in the curriculum and for a university theater have been made from time to time, the discipline has always been rejected as lacking intellectual rigor. Paradoxically, although theater has remained an extracurricular activity, Oxford and Cambridge have become recognized training grounds for aspirants to the profession. The Oxford University Dramatic Society, the Experimental Theatre Club, and their Cambridge equivalents offer a number of productions annually, which are reviewed by leading critics. Individual colleges have their own dramatic societies presenting familiar and original work; professional directors have been brought in to work with student actors. And for a while Cambridge even had a group producing original musical comedies, at least one of which was given a professional London run. This background has produced some of the more prominent names in the contemporary British theater: Peter Brook, Peter Hall, Emlyn Williams, Kenneth Tynan, John Wood. As in the days of Elizabeth I, the senior universities, against their will, have fed a stream of talent into the professional theater.

It remained for American universities, however, to make this connection a formal one. Here, too, there was an initial hostility. One of the first to argue that theater schools had a place in the universities was George Pierce Baker, Professor of English at Harvard, whose influence on the young Eugene O'Neill has already been noted. He was revolutionary in arguing that the class should study not merely dramatic texts (which was already being done, in various languages) but the whole mechanics of production that gave those texts life on the stage. Faced with academic obduracy, Baker was compelled to restrict himself to a course in play writing, listed as English 47. This course produced a number of distinguished alumni and, in 1913, was supplemented by the '47 Workshop, an extracurricular group in which students could acquire production skills by staging works written in the course. Continuing hostility prompted Baker's move to Yale, where his Workshop became the basis for the

Graduate School of Drama and eventually the Yale Repertory Company, a professional group working in an academic situation. Baker's dream of a department of drama at Harvard still remains unrealized, though the university did construct the Loeb Drama Center, an efficient theater complex with a small permanent staff for use by various student groups and visiting companies. Ironically, the Yale company, its career terminated in New Haven, has since moved back to Harvard.

Other, younger universities, unimpeded by Harvard's weight of academic tradition, embraced the theater more readily. A substantial movement, starting in the 1930s and gaining rapid impetus, has added dramatic arts to the curriculum of nearly every university and college in the country.

Considerable variation exists in individual programs. Some emphasize academic studies over production, while others are virtually conservatories, training actors, directors, and designers for the professional stage, with academic courses reduced to a minimum. Some of the best-equipped theater buildings in the country are on university campuses; so are some of the worst. Production programs also vary greatly. Most departments recognize conflicting claims on their attention: the necessity to produce standard classics, the need to supplement and illustrate readings done in other courses, and an equally strong need for airing the more unusual works that are hardly ever available commercially. Some universities, by contrast, concentrate on primarily commercial fare, arguing that this is the material their students will have to perform when they enter the profession. Alternatively, it is argued that the university theaters provide one of the few remaining avenues by which new plays can be brought before the public, and they have a duty to concentrate on these. Such differences in practice and philosophy are aired through a national society, the American Theater Association, which publishes its own journal and sponsors festivals and conferences.

The American lead has been followed in Great Britain. Since the early 1950s several important provincial universities have added drama departments of their own, modeled on American lines though usually with a smaller production program.

Universities have thus come to play an important part in the pattern of theatrical activity, both serving their own areas and feeding into the profession. Many distinguished practitioners have, in fact, preferred to work in the universities. Although actors are, by definition, young and comparatively untrained, production standards, unimpeded by union regulations, restrictions on hours, and the necessity to show a profit, are often very high indeed. The university theaters offer, also, a range of productions and production methods with which the commercial theater cannot hope to compete.

One must note, also, the ways in which such activity has influenced the course of scholarship. Seeing a play performed is a vastly different experience from reading the script, and writing about the theaters of the past has become more practically oriented since opportunities for seeing the plays have become more plentifully available. The department of drama, ideally, offers a synthesis of theory and practice, the one informing the other.

SUMMER STOCK

Another distinctively American phenomenon is summer stock, which now operates across the country, often, though not always, caters to the tourist trade, and has revived the concept of the resident company to present a number of plays for a limited season. The theaters vary from fully equipped permanent playhouses to converted barns. The summer seasons are often tests of endurance, requiring a different play to be presented each week; actors may therefore find themselves rehearsing one play in the morning and another in the afternoon and performing a third at night.

Many of these companies are shoestring operations, with actors doubling as scene crew, house staff, and box office help. A few, more substantial, offer apprenticeship programs to fee-paying students, which may provide an introduction to the professional theater. Although the productions are usually confined to musicals and standard Broadway fare, the companies are often interesting fusions of young professionals, college students, and amateur talent. Time and resources for productions, however, are skimpy, and the summer stock circuit has unfortunately been recognized as a last resort for fading Broadway and movie stars on their way down.

COMMUNITY THEATERS

Most communities have their own dramatic groups. Some enjoy civic funding, or at least have salaried professional directors. Most are recruited from local, amateur talent, and the standard varies from the good to the abysmal. Some of the best are to be found in major centers of the entertainment industry, particularly in California, where they draw on trained personnel who find themselves artistically frustrated in their professional careers and see the community groups as a useful vehicle for self-expression. Some of the worst remain true to Sinclair Lewis's grim depiction of a small-town amateur performance in *Main Street.*

For all this the community theaters, with a national organization and a monthly journal, represent a groundswell of public interest whose value cannot be denied, and it must be remembered that many of the important developments in the contemporary American theater began with small groups just like these, debarred from, or alienated by, the commercialism of Broadway and staging plays in whatever circumstances they could simply for the love of the art.

Contemporary Theater Design

Many theaters now functioning date from the nineteenth or early twentieth century and thus retain the architectural characteristics of a period when proscenium staging was the inevitable mode. This is particularly true of the commercial theaters. Over the past quarter century many have been demolished, but only a few new houses have been built. Though equipment has been modernized, architectural remodeling is prohibitively expensive, and there is no impetus for such remodeling in theaters that do not serve a permanent company. Thus the commercial theater, already inclined to adopt a conservative posture for economic reasons, has been further constrained by being forced to operate in a format now considered by many to be out of date. Normally the most that can be done to break out of the enclosing proscenium arch is to bridge over the orchestra pit and perhaps the front rows of seats, or to throw a walkway out into the auditorium, though even such limited alterations are frowned upon if they deprive the theater of revenue or infringe fire regulations.

SCENIC APPARATUS

For the most part, then, commercial theaters, and a good many others, still offer conditions in which Sir Henry Irving or Joseph Jefferson III would feel immediately at home. The dominating feature is the proscenium arch, which we have seen develop since the sixteenth century as a picture frame to enclose the production, with its drop curtain and, in modern times, the additional asbestos curtain required by law for public safety. Immediately in front of the proscenium usually lies the orchestra pit; few of the older theaters now have apron stages of any size. Access from under the stage is provided by trapdoors.

The scenic apparatus also reflects the state of the art as it had already developed by the middle of the nineteenth century. *Teasers* and *tormentors,* horizontal and vertical masking pieces, may be used to adjust the size of the proscenium opening. Just inside the proscenium is the *light bridge,* to carry lighting instruments, which may, of course, be supplemented by freestanding lamps at floor level or by lighting from the front of house. Above the stage, and easily discernible from outside as a projection above the roofline, is the *scene house,* with a *gridiron* or *grid* from which scenery can be lowered to stage level and into which it can be hauled out of sight. Scenery thus handled is said to be *flown.* Many theaters still cling to the nineteenth-century practice of flying scenery by means of hand-held ropes, counterbalanced by sandbags or lead weights. Others have moved to more sophisticated electrical systems. If the height of the grid is insufficient, scenery may be raised vertically as far as it will go and then *tripped* — pulled horizontally by another set of lines.

Most theaters also have a scene dock, a large storage space to one side, where scenery not in immediate use may be stacked, though one of the commoner complaints about older theaters is that the storage space is never large enough: the old Metropolitan Opera House in New York was often forced to stack sets outside, in the alley, during a heavy season. The scene dock may also hold other mechanical devices already familiar to the nineteenth-century theater, particularly the *wagon stage,* a large platform rolling on castors that can quickly be moved into place with a set already built on it. American musicals, with their many short scenes and rapid pattern of action, have tended to use multiple wagon stages to reduce shift time to a minimum.

Theaters more elaborately equipped may have a *revolving stage,* or even concentric revolves capable of turning in opposite directions. In the main stage or suspended under the revolve itself may be found power-driven elevators, capable of raising sizable platforms to stage height and so increasing the flexibility of scene changes.

Note that all these devices, like the proscenium stage itself, were originally designed to facilitate the mounting of realistic productions. Thus, as so often happens, theater architecture has a dominant influence on the nature of the works performed; the continued use of such theaters has helped to keep the realistic style in currency, long after its natural term might otherwise have expired.

STAGES

It will be remembered from Chapter 10 that the first act of the theatrical revolutionaries of the 1920s and 1930s was often to tear down the traditional appurtenances of the proscenium theaters in which they were forced to work, to create a new, less inhibited relationship between the actors and the audiences. Theaters built since that time reveal the effect of these ideas in their structure. The most familiar manifestation of new theater design today is the *thrust stage,* which abridges the proscenium arch or demolishes it entirely and projects the stage into the auditorium so that the audience may surround it on several sides. Tanya Moseiwitch's design for the Stratford, Ontario, Festival Theater is of such a type.

Though its immediate inspiration may derive from Max Reinhardt's experiments in the Grosses Schauspielhaus, the Stratford thrust stage clearly looks back to earlier theater forms. A stage designed primarily for Shakespeare seeks to re-create the openness and flexibility of the Elizabethan public playhouse without archaeological pedantry. The actors are pushed forward into immediate contact with their audience, and the swift pattern of action may ebb and flow upon the stage without architectural impedances. Since the auditorium rises in steep tiers, the construction is also reminiscent of Greek theater practice, making it ideally suitable for Guthrie's 1954 production of *Oedipus the King,* with characters formally robed and wearing stylized masks. The film of this production, still widely shown, gives little idea of the effectiveness of the original stage version, which was placed in a setting similar in all essentials to the original Greek concept. Moseiwitch's later design for the Guthrie Theater in Minneapolis followed the same general lines, though with an asymmetrical thrust stage and auditorium. The Chichester Festival Theatre in England and the Olivier Theatre in the British National Theatre complex are other impressive examples of the same type.

Thrust stages have also appeared on a smaller scale, particularly in university and college theaters. One variant is the *caliper stage,* which extends the acting area on either side of the auditorium, so that the audience may find itself outflanked on right or left by the stage action.

The values of such theaters for the presentational style are obvious. They also return the plays of earlier periods to an equivalent of the acting space for which they were composed. But just as the proscenium stage is uneasy with nonrealistic plays, so the thrust stage presents problems for plays representationally conceived. The audience may be too close for comfort; a good deal of drama, from the eighteenth century onward, presupposes a spatial distance (and, hence, an aesthetic distance) between the action and its spectators, and to obliterate this distance may impair the effect of the play.

Realistic plays on thrust stages also pose distinct problems for designers. The proscenium stage, as we have seen, was at its best when showing interiors. But realistic interiors on thrust stages are difficult: not only is there usually no overhead grid, but box sets are rendered invalid by virtue of the different sight lines. Such playwrights as Chekhov and Ibsen, therefore, lose on the thrust stage something of the claustrophobic effect their works were intended to have when framed by the proscenium.

With the thrust stage the audience surrounds much of the action; with the *arena stage* it surrounds all of it. Though less in evidence than the forms discussed above, arena theater has its enthusiastic proponents, who trace its uses back to some of the most important periods of theater history.

Even more than the thrust stage, the arena stage bestows intimacy. Actors and audience are linked in a corporate presence; wherever the actors are placed on the stage, the audience is also close at hand. Arena staging therefore develops a particular intensity in the actors, for they are always in the picture; there is no way in which they can cheat or relax.

For the director, working in an arena has a sculpturesque quality, rather than the picture frame quality that the proscenium stage bestows. Any grouping or movement must have meaning and plastic value for everyone, though no two sections of the audience ever see exactly the same composition. For the designer the arena presents even greater problems than the thrust stage. Hanging sets, or standing units above a certain height, cannot be used, for they would block the sight lines for some part of the audience. Thus arena stage design is often conceived largely in terms of a patterned floor, built sets are reduced to a minimum, and interiors are indicated mainly by the placement of furniture.

As with the thrust stage, fully realistic plays are the most difficult to present in this medium. So are physical farces, in which it is essential that all the audience should see the same effect at the same time. Arena works best with the kind of play that can capitalize on the facility of direct address to the audience and create its settings in the imagination rather than in actuality. In the professional theater the best-known stages of this type are New York's Circle in the Square — which after twenty-one years of distinguished off-Broadway operation (see p. 502) moved to a new Broadway location and uses a three-quarters arena — the Alley Theater in Houston, and the Arena Stage in Washington, D.C. Tufts University in Massachusetts has one of the oldest arena stages in the country.

These forms do not exhaust the possibilities. Multiform theaters, whose acting and seating spaces may be rearranged to suit varying production needs, are becoming more common. Oxford University proposed such a design, on a historical basis, in its aborted project for a university theater; it consisted of modular units that, put together in various ways, would resemble theater structures at key periods of history. On a more practical level the multiform concept has been used for the Vivian Beaumont Theater in the Lincoln Center, New York — a site that, it was once hoped, would be the base for a national company — and in the black box familiar on many college campuses. Here the theater is basically a room with walls painted a neutral color and some provision for hanging lights. Risers for the audience may be moved at will, and the acting space be turned into arena, thrust, or even proscenium as the play requires.

It seems clear that, as the theater is more and more required to seek alternative premises, the formal separation of actors and audiences hallowed by nineteenth-century practice is fast breaking down. A number of modern productions (see p. 431) have so dispersed the action among the audience that not merely do no two spectators ever see exactly the same thing, but it becomes impossible for any one spectator to see everything. The introduction of the proscenium arch to the French public playhouse of the seventeenth century imposed a frame on the action and a single point of view, in an age when such things were implicit in social and political philosophy. The dispersed playing areas increasingly familiar in our time, with information handed out piecemeal and apparently at random, speak to an age concerned with the fragmentation of knowledge and the impossibility of absolute judgments.

Theater Personnel: Actors

Actors are the lifeblood of the theater. For centuries the theater managed well without a director, and from time to time, by choice or necessity, it has dispensed with scenery or costumes. But without actors there can be no play.

Despite this fact, actors are the most abused members of the profession. For long regarded as social outcasts, they have also had to endure financial privations. These reached their lowest point in the touring system, which dominated the American theater in the nineteenth century. At the mercy of unscrupulous managers, actors might find themselves penniless and stranded hundreds of miles from home if the show had failed to turn a profit. For the rank and file of the profession, conditions were little better in the larger centers. Though successful stars could write their own contracts, their humbler colleagues worked long hours for miserable stipends, could expect little sympathy in an overcrowded profession, and had small redress under law. Working conditions, especially on tour, were often abysmal. Actors could expect to give ten performances a week, to rehearse without compensation, and to pay their own traveling expenses.

ACTORS' UNIONS

The earliest attempts to improve the actors' lot by collective action occurred in England, when Henry Irving became the first president of the Actors' Association in 1891. It was American actors, however, who first brought these attempts to fruition with the foundation of the Actors' Equity Association in 1913. Its demands were fair and simple; a minimum wage, a maximum of eight performances a week, free Sundays, and a limit on unpaid rehearsal time. The managements, then at the peak of their power, responded with imperious contempt. "Acting," proclaimed Lee Shubert, "is more nerve than skill," and he went on to suggest that actors were well paid for what they did, when most of them could not expect to earn $10 a week in any other occupation.

These disagreements came to a head in the actors' strike of 1919, which closed thirty-five theaters in New York alone together with others in Boston and Chicago, played havoc with the touring circuit, and cost $500,000 a week for the month it was in force. Managements were driven to new heights of fury. David Belasco snarled, "Starve the actors out!" George M. Cohan, creator of *Yankee Doodle Dandy* and the reigning darling of the musical stage, was adamant to the last, refusing to join Actors' Equity even when its victory was won. The union, with consummate graciousness, permitted him to continue to appear, the only professional actor of the period without an Equity card. British actors followed suit by organizing a similar strike the year after and forming their own Equity Association in 1929. Both organizations, as recognized trade unions in their respective countries, have become the authorized mouthpiece for their members. In recent years British Equity has become increasingly concerned with the granting of work permits to foreign actors, while its American counterpart has campaigned vigorously for the desegregation of the stage. In 1943 American Actors' Equity, in collaboration with the New York Public Library, established the Equity Library Showcase as a medium for exposing new talent.

What no equity association could do, however, was create new jobs. Periodically, gloomy statistics are published. Unemployment of American actors, after the balmy days of World War II when the USO show tours created an enormous market, has hovered between 80 and 90 percent. In 1971 the average annual income of the American actor from all sources was $2,500. This situation has created something of an ambivalence. As a trade union Equity on both sides of the Atlantic has felt a duty to create a closed shop in the interests of its members. As representing an artistic enterprise, however, it feels an equal need to encourage new talent. Attempts to limit the membership by raising dues have caused unfavorable comment from within the profession.

For various reasons, then, the acting profession is a difficult one to enter. Assuming equal degrees of training and competence, pure chance often plays the deciding role. Orson Welles once claimed that he could form an entire repertory company from actors, at least equal in talent to established stars, who had never been lucky enough to be noticed. Actors thus prize personal contacts in a profession that is overpopulated and often anonymous. In a world where careers are so often decided by chance, actors are also, as a group, intensely superstitious. The theater has always been riddled with superstitions. *Macbeth*, a traditionally unlucky play, must never be quoted backstage. Actors refrain from wishing one another good luck, for fear that the reverse may follow. And the theater is perhaps the only profession in the world whose members regularly sit down and talk about their disasters, presumably in the expectation that such discussion will propitiate the evil spirit.

TRAINING

Actors may secure their basic training in several ways. In America the universities provide increasingly elaborate programs. Alternatively, the student may enroll in specialist schools, of which the Conservatory Theater in San Francisco and the Juilliard School in New York are only two of the most famous. Great Britain, which offers fewer university opportunities, has its equivalents in the Royal Academy of Dramatic Art (RADA), the London Academy of Music and Dramatic Art (LAMDA), and several others only slightly less prestigious.

Though individual programs vary, the student may expect to spend his or her first years in mastering the essential instruments of the actor's craft, voice and body. Traditional programs introduced the student to scene work from the beginning. Today increasing emphasis is given to physical exercises, including gymnastics and tumbling, designed to liberate both body and mind; to group work, in which students learn to interact with one another without scripts; and to various improvisation exercises. Much of this new approach has developed from the theatrical experiments of the earlier part of the century: teachers are as much interested in what the student *feels* as in what he *shows*. Scene work and vocal exercises come later. The student will also learn such auxiliary skills as theatrical fencing and period dancing. Throughout, however, the emphasis is on ensemble work. And from time to time the students are exposed to public performance, both to learn the kind of awareness that only stage exposure can give and to provide a shop window for their talents.

AUDITIONS AND REHEARSALS

For the graduate who prefers a university environment, the next step may be to audition for such organizations as the University Resident Theater Association (URTA), which brings students and professionals together in joint companies on a number of campuses. For those who determine to approach the profession directly, there remains a virtually obligatory residence in New York and the endless round of casting calls in the hope of finding an opening.

At any stage of an actor's career, auditions are critical; the actor is expected to reveal his or her personality and ability in the space of a few minutes and in competition with perhaps hundreds of others trying out for the same few roles. Auditions are so crucial, in fact, that special classes and workshops have been developed to teach actors how to deal with them and to make the best possible impression in the shortest possible time. General auditions may leave the choice of material to the actor, though often specifying one classical and one modern passage. After the initial selection, some may be called back to read for particular roles; in this case the actor must already have developed a view of the part, without the benefit of direction and rehearsal. This view may be quite different from the one that develops during the production process, but directors are more interested, in the early stages, in assessing an actor's intelligence and potential than in whether the audition reading agrees with their own conception of the part. Auditions are just as crucial for the director as for the actor, since it may never be possible to rectify an early mistake in casting.

Early rehearsals are, necessarily, tentative, for the actors are exploring not merely their roles but one another. Some come in with the parts already memorized, others wait until at least the basic moves and business have been worked out. In any event, rapid memorization is essential for an actor, and most soon acquire the skills of learning large quantities of dialogue at short notice. A prompter is always present during the early stages of rehearsal. One traditional method, still in common use in Mediterranean countries, is to use the prompter as a learning device; the prompter recites the lines, and the actors repeat them after him. In the days before general literacy this method was much more common than it is now; but still, for actors who are trained to it, it remains surprisingly effective. Some actors have adopted the modern equivalent of recording their lines and cues and playing them continually until they are fixed in the memory.

Rehearsals, however, involve much more than the mechanical problems of memorization. Since Stanislavsky, the actor has been trained to ask questions, and the most common question is "Why?" What motivation does the character have for saying a particular line, for making a move? Is it consistent with other things he has said or done, and if not, why? What lies *behind* the line — in other words, what is the character thinking; what is the subtext? Under the director's guidance, and with the other actors' assistance, such questions are gradually thrashed out. When working in a period play, the actor may need to research the character's life and times. Even apparently irrelevant questions become important. What does the character eat? What is her or his employ-ment? How does the character spend the day? The answers are assembled into a composite pattern of behavior, with the aim of presenting a character who is logical, credible, and consistent. Although the actor may be confronted period-ically with problems that have to be worked out in purely mechanical terms — a quick entrance, a tricky piece of business, a response to a sound or a light cue — the mechanics must be assimilated until they become unconscious. Questions of relationship are worked out by the actors together. What do I think of you? What do you think of me? For there comes a time when the actor ceases to think of the character as a being apart — the two have become one.

One of the actor's major problems in any production is to retain the sense of freshness and discovery that marked the rehearsals. Long runs, though they offer financial security, may mean artistic disaster, for staleness sets in, reducing the role to a nightly mechanical repetition. Most actors of standing have clauses in their contracts ensuring that they will not be required to remain with a role for more than a given time, for apart from the dangers of boredom, long runs may mean professional death. An actor may become identified with one partic-ular part and find that the world has passed him or her by. For this reason some directors are now prone to encourage continual improvisation within the pat-tern of the production to keep the invention fresh. And many actors prefer the repertory system, because it gives them a chance to distance themselves from the play for a few days periodically, do something else, and come back to it with new eyes.

Today's actors set a high value on their individuality. Though working in situations involving the closest cooperation and teamwork, they are aware that their careers, in a competitive profession, depend on qualities that distinguish them from their peers. The résumé of roles played, accompanied by photo-graphs and favorable notices, becomes the actor's most treasured possession and a passport to further employment.

In the nineteenth century the stock company system encouraged imitation. Often the actor could find no training outside the company itself. Joining as a neophyte, he or she would proceed from walk-on to increasingly more impor-tant roles, learning by doing and by observing. This system in itself discour-aged innovation and experiment; for every Edwin Booth, there were fifty imitators. Today, with much greater diversity of training and experience, the actor feels a need to be justified as an independent artist: to question what is not understood, to resist what does not seem artistically valid, and to make a personal contribution to the creative process. Actors' egos, so derided outside the profession, grow as a natural defense against professional pressures.

Directors

The responsibility for composing these individual and disparate talents into an artistic whole, and devising a working compromise between the demand for personal expression and the needs of the ensemble, falls to the figure known in the American theater as the *director*. (The British theater has traditionally used the title *producer,* thereby causing some transatlantic confusion, though the current trend is to follow American usage. In Europe the title is *régisseur.*)

INTERPRETIVE FUNCTION

We have seen the director as a figure slow to evolve in the theater but now established as one of its essential components, with the responsibility not merely of unifying the actors' individual contributions but of overseeing every other element of the production also. Thus the director's function is partly mechanical and partly interpretive.

The mechanical function — supervision of rehearsals, arranging entrances and exits, disposing the actors about the stage — has always existed in the theater, although its holders have gone by different names. The interpretive function is new. With some plays it is still minimal. A commercial Broadway comedy such as *Barefoot in the Park* hardly needs to be interpreted. It states its own terms, and the directorial function is reduced largely to traffic control on the stage and the devising of appropriate business. Dealing with plays of the stature and complexity of *Hamlet, Phèdre, A Doll's House,* or *The Cherry Orchard* is another matter. Here the director functions first as critic. What is the play about? What did it mean in terms of the society for which it was written, and how have its values changed for the audience of today?

Such questions were rarely asked even a century ago. Audiences went to see individual displays of histrionics, not a concerted enterprise, and were content to ignore deficiencies in minor roles as long as the star was satisfactory. Though they might be offered different interpretations of leading roles, and eagerly discuss the rival merits of Booth's and Forrest's Hamlet, they could rarely expect a different interpretation of a whole play. Sets, costumes, and business were standardized; apart from the personality of the star, productions were virtually interchangeable.

The emergence of the director has brought about a major change in thinking. In theater, as in literature and the visual arts, the critical revolution has been such that point of view has become all important. Each major production of a standard work is now expected to be unique and to offer a fresh approach to the illustration and orchestration of its dramatic content. The question of interpretation has thus become paramount, and the same work may bear entirely different interpretations depending on the time, the situation, the audience, and the director's own evocations.

SOME EXAMPLES

Consider, for example, Shakespeare's *Henry V*. A superficial reading suggests that this play is simply a dramatization of certain events in fifteenth-century history: the English claim to the French throne, exacerbated by deliberately provocative French behavior; the declaration of war and the English invasion of France under the personal leadership of a monarch who inspires his small force to a decisive victory over the frivolous, degenerate enemy; and the establishment of peace by the marriage of state between Henry and the French princess Katherine. In short, it would be easy to dismiss this play as a heroic chronicle designed to flatter English pretensions, particularly for the audience of Shakespeare's time who saw themselves as heirs to this grand tradition.

But if this were all there were to the play, why should it deserve revival four centuries later for audiences who have no vested national interest in recording the battle of Agincourt? Attempting to answer this question prompts a deeper reading, which brings to light certain complexities and resonances that transcend the simple pattern of events. It appears that Shakespeare's Henry is not so simple a figure as one might first have supposed.

The ardor and heroism of the battle speeches are undeniable. Side by side with this, however, we see signs of a calculating nature, of brutality, even, in dealing with opponents both at home and abroad. (Are these part of Henry's essential nature, or are they forced on him by events? This point is where interpretation begins to enter the picture.) We see a study of the problems of the leader and the hard decisions that distinguish him from one who merely follows orders. We see, too, Shakespeare reflecting on the way in which wars come to be fought. *Henry V* begins with a scene involving the leaders of the church, whose personal interest in a foreign war — it will take the king's mind off ecclesiastical taxation — becomes manifest. And at the end of the play Shakespeare, in his description of a ravaged France, is clearly ruminating not merely on this war but on all war and the horrors that it brings to the civilian population. Thus *Henry V* becomes a play of much wider significance, and any particular production of it will be influenced by the prevailing attitude of the times.

Consider now two quite different interpretations. The first is the film directed by Laurence Olivier in 1944, with himself in the title role, and still considered to be one of the finest transpositions of stage drama to the screen ever made. When it went into production, Great Britain had been at war for four years, during which fears of almost certain defeat had slowly been replaced by a more hopeful upturn in military fortune. The mood of the times cried out for a patriotic stimulus. (Olivier, in fact, had been released from military service precisely for this purpose.) In the small group of battered soldiery huddled under the walls of Harfleur, and urged to a last, triumphant effort by their king, the audience recognized themselves as they had been after Dunkirk and as they hoped to be in the future.

Thus Olivier's production from the beginning emphasized the patriotic qualities of the work. The scheming prelates were reduced to comic figures, sputtering ineffectually on the fringes of the main action. Henry's declaration of war on France was shown as a straightforward, manly response to the insolence of foreigners. After the Battle of Agincourt the long roster of the French dead, followed by the tiny English casualty list, was recited as a demonstration of native valor and resourcefulness against overwhelming odds. And Henry's wooing of the Princess Katherine, at the end of the play, was played with charm and appeal; the dauntless conqueror showing that he was still a man, after all.

It is instructive to contrast this film with productions staged later in the period of postwar disillusion, when patriotism and the merits of foreign entanglements were being increasingly called into question; when America was itself engaged in an unpopular war, resented by a large part of its population; and when Olivier's attractive simplification of Shakespeare's text was no longer timely. In a production at the American Shakespeare Festival in Stratford, Connecticut, the less palatable elements of the play were stressed at the expense of the heroism. Here the passages illustrating Henry's brutality, which Olivier had either cut or glossed over, were given heavy emphasis. In the production's most striking image the roll call of the Agincourt dead was played from the viewpoint not of the survivors but of the fallen. As the names were read, the stage became full of silent, white-masked figures, the dead as mute accusers of the living who had killed them. Finally, in the wooing scene Henry appeared not as a romantic hero come to claim his lady and having endearing difficulty with his French but as a thug, dispensing with all ceremony and affection to secure a desirable political end.

Both productions used the same text, the same characters. But the interpretations could not have been further apart. Each selected from the range of possibilities inherent in the script and chose what to stress and what to play down. It will be apparent that in such a case the director does not merely need the appropriate critical and scholarly apparatus to determine what the range of possibilities may be; he is also required to make a personal statement, which is evident in his choice.

Henry V presents a fairly simple example of varying interpretations. In other plays the range of possibilities may be much wider. We have seen how, in Chekhov, the director is compelled to create a pattern in a script that seems uncoordinated and formless, and how Chekhov and Stanislavsky differed over what the pattern should be. *The Cherry Orchard* emerges as a very different play, depending on where the director's sympathies lie: with the improvident aristocracy who are losing their land or with the man of the people who inherits and intends to convert it. *Hamlet,* by the same token, has received almost as many interpretations as it has had directors.

In working with an original script, the director may become a full partner in the creation of the work. It is generally recognized that the playwright is not the best director of his own play; normally it is safer to entrust this work to someone who can take a more objective stance. Some playwrights refuse categorically to be involved in the staging. The Scottish author James Bridie, when asked what one of his plays meant, replied, "Why ask me? I only wrote it!" At the other extreme stand writers like Shaw, who held firm views on every aspect of the production.

More playwrights belong to the latter camp than to the former, which can sometimes produce conflict between author and director. The Chekhov-Stanislavsky quarrel has already been mentioned. Closer to our own time is the collaboration between Elia Kazan and Tennessee Williams. When Kazan directed Williams's *Cat on a Hot Tin Roof* (1955), a closely argued study of family relationships among a dominating father, an alcoholic son, and a nymphomaniac daughter-in-law, he insisted on such sweeping changes that the play was largely rewritten during the rehearsal. Unhappy with alterations that he felt had been forced on him, Williams responded in the only way still open, short of staging his own production: by publishing his original script and the amended version side by side. Comparison reveals the extent of Kazan's contribution, affecting not merely individual characterization but the whole thrust of the play.

SETTING AND COSTUME

Once the interpretation has been decided, it must be planned in terms of the means available. The director will have strong ideas about the setting wanted and the kind of statement it should make. Though this setting will be worked out in detail with the designer, and sometimes considerably modified, it will normally still be faithful to the director's original conception. The same is true of the costumes.

Increasingly in the contemporary theater the director's interpretation of a period play will involve setting it in a period other than that for which it was originally written. Though such a transposition may reflect only directorial eccentricity, or the desire to be different at all costs, there are usually valid reasons for it: the director may feel that the associations conjured up by a particular period make his interpretation more accessible to today's public.

Thus we have seen *Hamlet* set in every period from early Scandinavian to the present day. Tyrone Guthrie once set *Troilus and Cressida,* Shakespeare's bitter, cynical study of the Trojan War, in the uniforms of 1914–1918, to make what he considered the play's central point: the decline of an effete, decadent aristocracy before a brutal, despotic militarism. The Trojans were thus dressed as operetta figures in Ruritanian uniforms, plumed, braided, and bespurred, and Helen of Troy delivered one speech sprawled across a grand piano, with a glass of champagne in her hand. The Greeks, by contrast, were uniformed as Junkers, with spiked helmets and enveloping cloaks, which gave the impression of a faceless, impersonal military machine. Jan Kott's iconoclastic production of Euripides' *Orestes* at Berkeley, which saw the play as a study of alienated youth in conflict with a remote and unsympathetic establishment, dressed Orestes and

Pylades in black leather and sent them on stage on motorbikes. Orson Welles's *Julius Caesar* (see p. 475) interpreted Roman power politics in the light of contemporary fascism, and his *Macbeth* substituted voodoo for witchcraft, while *Dionysus in '69* set Euripides' *Bacchae* amid the modern drug culture.

Conversely, some productions have sought to convey the universality of the theme by using costumes derived from several periods, or no period at all. Kenneth Tynan's production of *The Beaux' Stratagem* dressed each group of characters in the costume of a different century. John Gielgud once played King Lear in abstract costumes against a setting of mobiles and nonrepresentational sculpture, and later in his career he directed Richard Burton in a *Hamlet* where all the actors wore rehearsal clothes.

Such changes are not merely freakish. They show the director functioning as *translator;* for each period of the theater develops its own grammar and vocabulary, comprehensible to its immediate audience and provoking certain predictable responses but, for a new audience in a different age, needing elucidation to obtain the same effect. Ideally, then, the director should be a scholar also, with a knowledge of how the theater of past ages worked and of what has to be done to translate these devices into terms a modern audience will understand.

ACTION AND CHARACTERIZATION

Decisions on interpretation, with their consequences for setting and costume, belong to the planning stage. They will be made, at least in broad outline, before the play is even cast. As soon as the actors are available, the director's task is to translate his concept into actuality. The action must be shaped into patterns of stage movement that reinforce the text and express, in visual terms, the points the director feels the text is making. This process (known as *blocking*) normally occupies the early days, or even weeks, of rehearsal. How should the characters be placed in relationship to one another? How can their personal relationships be illustrated by their positions on the stage? Who is the most important character in a scene, and how can this character's importance be shown by his or her own movements or the movements of others? Where does the focus lie? How can the stage picture be arranged so that the focus can shift, at need, from one character to another?

Some directors present themselves at the first rehearsal with the blocking for every scene already worked out on paper, or at least in their minds. Max Reinhardt was famous for this; his production books contained the plan for the whole production, complete to the smallest detail, so that there was nothing left for the actor to do but follow directions. This conception of the director as autocrat, fashionable in the 1920s and 1930s when the novelty of the director's position led inevitably to overemphasis, has been considerably modified in the modern theater, though many directors still like to have the basic patterns of movement worked out in advance. Laurence Olivier, when working as director rather than actor, preferred to read the play through while moving pieces on a model of the set to show the actors where they were to stand. Increasingly, however, the rigidity of such a blocking process is giving way to a more fluid interaction between actor and director. Peter Brook records how he went to one of his first rehearsals, which involved directing a procession, with every move and position worked out on paper. Face to face with the cast, he found himself confronting not a mass of interchangeable units but a crowd of individuals, whose differences in size, shape, and personality immediately suggested a whole range of possibilities that he had not even been aware of before. He immediately threw away his carefully prepared notes and started again from scratch.

In today's theater, therefore, the director — given that there is time available — may adopt a more leisurely and exploratory approach, allowing the actors to find their own way through a scene and move as their instinct prompts them. Though the director may offer stimulation and encouragement and suggest other possibilities that the actors may have failed to discover for themselves, the final patterns of movement and business may not be set until close to performance time.

Similar situations evolve with the development of character. The director may have strong ideas about what motivates the characters and their relationships to one another, but usually he refrains from imposing them. Such conclusions are more meaningful if the actors can be led to arrive at them by themselves, and the rehearsal process becomes a period of exploration, in which the whole concept of the play may change.

Every production has its own peculiar chemistry from the mixture of the personalities involved, and new perceptions may be generated by the group spontaneously as they wrestle with their common problems. Directors have often had some actor training; they should at least know how an actor feels and works, so that they can utilize the actor's contribution creatively. Today's director is rarely a tyrant, imposing an ironclad vision of the play on others. Rather, his or her function is to act as a clearinghouse for the contributions of the cast and the other creative personnel involved, within the general conceptual framework of the production, approving and elaborating on some things and rejecting others if they are not consonant with the main intent.

REHEARSAL

Thus the rehearsal process tends to fall into two phases. The first is to break down the play into its component parts. Once the director has established a general line of approach, the action is analyzed to discover how each act and scene contributes to the whole. Scenes are further dissected into units of action, to reveal the through line and the most important movements of each, and the process continues through individual speeches, lines, and words.

Actors take time to explore, to test different line readings and compare their effectiveness. Suggestions from the group may be taken up, tried out, expanded, and accepted or discarded. (One of the conspicuous trends in contemporary theater is to evolve not merely the production but the *script* from the rehearsal process, with the actors working in a collective endeavor under the director's guidance.)

The process is unpredictable. A long and complex scene may take shape almost instantaneously, or half an hour may be spent in deciding the correct reading of two words. Accidents of rehearsal may incorporate themselves in the scene and suggest a whole new line of approach. For these reasons directorial purists have always argued that the process should continue as long as possible; Stanislavsky's endless rehearsals have already been mentioned, and there are still directors who rehearse until the play is ready to open by its own momentum. Commercial pressures, however, normally limit such self-indulgence; though at the other end of the scale, the weekly grind of summer stock may eliminate the possibility of fruitful exploration completely.

The second phase of rehearsal consists of putting the pieces back together, with the director coordinating them and controlling emphasis and tempo, so that each element has its proper importance in the general scheme. Sometimes the director has to yield authority to others. Few directors, for example, are experienced choreographers, and musicals normally have a separate dance director. (Some choreographers, however, have found a new career as directors.) Stage fights also require specialist supervision. But it remains the director's function to integrate these elements and lay down the broad lines of what the dance, or fight, should accomplish.

As the rehearsals near their end, directorial interruptions become fewer, as the actor must be allowed to adjust to the rhythm and pacing of the play. Entire scenes and acts may be played without comment, though notes at the end of each rehearsal period will suggest additional refinements and improvements. As the props, costumes, sets, and lighting are added, new problems appear, and it is the director's task to help the actors to assimilate these with minimal disturbance.

Once the play opens, the director's function is largely over, though even at this stage further rehearsals may be called, and changes made, in the light of audience reactions. The director, if no longer an autocrat, is at least the midwife of the theater, with the responsibility of using his or her own talents to help others bring a production to birth. Standing outside the production, the director can continue to watch it with an objective eye and keep all the elements in balance. Improvisation may be encouraged, even insisted upon, to create scenes that go beyond those written and thus inform the script with broader, deeper character awareness. Such improvisation may even continue into the finished production, leaving room for the actors to explore and keep their freshness when an audience is present. The test of a good script, and a good production, is how long it can continue to grow and mature after the play has opened, and directors, no less than actors, are alive to the dangers of stultifying, meaningless repetition.

All this is not to deny that there are still directors who have their recognizable trademarks or who stamp their personality, indelibly, on any production that they do. But the personality cult so prevalent among directors in the early part of this century has now largely vanished, and the best director, like the best designer, is the one who effaces his or her own contribution and leaves the feeling that the play has spoken for itself.

Designers

The designer is sometimes responsible for both set and costumes, and many designers are equally competent in both areas. More often, the functions are divided, as each is an elaborate and time-consuming process with its own techniques and problems. Like the director, the set designer has increasingly come to be regarded as an important creative artist.

In the past the designer was often anonymous. Though a few great names, such as Bibienas in Italy or Inigo Jones in England, stand out, the scene painter was usually ignored in an actor-oriented theater. Even the great backdrop painters of the nineteenth century are now little more than names to us, though with hindsight we recognize them as artists of major accomplishment. With the increasing emphasis on the visual aspects of production (Elmer Rice has made the point that the theater of the past was directed largely to the ear, that of the twentieth century to the eye), the designer has come into his own. Stage designs are now collected, exhibited, and recognized as art. Since Diaghilev harnessed some of the finest talent in Europe to provide the decor for his ballets, painters have felt it no degradation to design for the stage. But as the designer's prestige has increased, so have opportunities narrowed. In America the limited openings in the professional theater have enforced a closed-shop policy far more exclusive than that for actors, with notoriously difficult entrance examinations to the union to which many are called, but few are chosen.

DESIGNER AND DIRECTOR

Design embraces the entire visual aspect of the stage production. It therefore offers a statement that should complement the director's own, an all-embracing metaphor that speaks to the audience of the play's central concerns. A production may exist without a designer, but it cannot exist without design. To do away with scenery, to strip the theater down to brick walls and a bare platform, is itself an act of design, for it immediately suggests a particular relationship between the action and the audience. A scene played with a single chair and an empty stage still involves a design choice; what sort of chair should it be, and where, exactly, should it be set on the stage? The more limited the design elements, in fact, the more acute the designer's choices have to be, for when a single scenic unit makes the visual statement for the whole play, it is essential that this statement be a valid and meaningful one.

Just as each production of a major work is now assumed to be a unique artistic statement, so each stage design is conceived as making its own unique statement, compatible with the director's vision. This is not to deny that settings may perform a long tour of duty, both in the lower and the higher reaches of the theater. The days of the stock set are by no means over. Summer theaters and the smaller repertories acquire units that perform multiple service over several seasons. Designing for opera has become so expensive that the same setting may be held over for a new production of the work in the same house or be shipped to other houses; a set originally designed for a production of *Don Giovanni* in New York is quite likely to turn up next season in Seattle or Dallas. We are talking here, however, about designs freshly conceived for a specific production; and the genesis of such designs is in discussions between the designer and director.

Just as the director's creative vision must be controlled by certain fixed points in the script, so the designer's approach must be conditioned by certain given elements in the action. Does the locale require separate acting levels? Is the acting area expansive, providing room for large crowd scenes, or small and confined? Are there any mandatory elements without which the action cannot make sense? *Hamlet,* for example, whatever the approach to the production, posits a place where Polonius can conceal himself prior to his assassination and something to serve as the grave where Ophelia is buried. Sheridan's *The School for Scandal* involves a picture gallery, which is so important to the plot that some way must be devised of at least suggesting it. Feydeau's farce, *A Flea in Her Ear,* demands a revolving bed.

The designer will attend the first meeting with such matters in mind. How these elements will be arranged, however, and the style in which they are to be presented, are open questions. Sometimes the directorial concept imposes a certain approach from the beginning. A Stanford University production of *Antony and Cleopatra,* for example, envisaged all the characters as representing different organs in the human body; given this datum, it became the designer's responsibility to devise a setting to support this concept. Alternatively, the first discussion may be exploratory and mutually influential. The designer may already have strong ideas of his own that the director is willing to accept. He may suggest technical possibilities, or limitations, that the director was unaware of. Thus director-designer discussions proceed like director-actor discussions in rehearsal, with each side contributing ideas until a mutually satisfactory solution has been found.

Ideally, director and designer share the same vision, and the design is an organic part of the production process, an extension into pictorial and architectural terms of what the director seeks to accomplish with his actors on the stage. We have already seen several examples of this. Gordon Craig's Shakespearean designs, however impractical, convey the essence of the scene by significant arrangement of mass, light, and shadow. In the sleepwalking scene in *Macbeth*, Lady Macbeth is isolated, driven in upon herself, by her ineradicable guilt. Craig's famous design (see p. 401) shows the character physically isolated, a tiny moving figure against a massive, towering pillar that suggests the weight of the pressures upon her. Robert Edmund Jones's designs for the same play (see p. 476) make a fluid contribution to the production with their system of arches that move, multiply, and dwindle according to the protagonists' fortunes. In the more recent theater Jo Mielziner used scrims to suggest the cloud of memory that hung over Williams's *The Glass Menagerie* and Miller's *Death of a Salesman*.

THE STAGE DESIGN TAKES SHAPE

The designer, then, seeks an appropriate visual image, a style, that will evoke the concept of the production. Inspiration may be historical, involving close study of architecture and decorative modes of the past. It may come from the works of a particular painter — art history is an important part of a designer's training; or it may be purely theatrical in nature, exploiting the range of available stage devices for their own sake. Whatever the choice, the design makes a comment on the action and sets up certain expectations in the minds of the audience.

Designs take concrete form either as color sketches or as models. The former are usually preferred, as they are easier to make and adequate for most purposes. Models may be necessary when the design presents particular architectural or constructional problems, and they are an undoubted asset to the director, who can use them to block the scene in three dimensions.

Once the design has been approved by the director and production staff, the next step is to prepare working drawings. This is the point of no return. Though it may be possible to eliminate elements after this stage, it is rarely possible to add anything or make major alterations. The designs are reduced to plan form, to ensure that they fit into the space available. Most important for the director is the *ground plan*, which gives a scaled-down view of the stage floor, with all steps and elevations marked and all furniture in place. This plan is helpful in blocking the action of the play. For his or her own purposes the designer will often also prepare a vertical section drawing, to ensure that there are no sight-line problems — in other words, that the set can be seen from all points in the auditorium. For traveling shows this issue can be crucial, as no two theaters have the same dimensions or proportions. In the nineteenth century, touring companies often found that their scenery would not fit a particular stage and had to use whatever was available locally. Even today major tours, like that made annually by the Metropolitan Opera, have to make considerable adjustments from one theater to another.

As well as the plans, the designer also prepares detailed working drawings to show the construction of each scenic unit. These units are then built in the *scene shop.* As noted earlier, proscenium theaters have perpetuated methods of scene building already familiar in the nineteenth century, particularly the box set and the backdrop. The basic unit for interior sets is still the *flat,* a wooden frame normally 5 feet wide and 14 feet high, covered with linen, canvas, or similar material and painted. Other dimensions are possible, though these are ultimately limited by the maximum width of the covering material commercially available. In any case the theater prefers to standardize so that flats can then be reused in other combinations. Flats can be lashed together with cleats and ropes from behind, to give the appearance of a solid wall, and supported on the stage floor by weights and braces. Doors or windows can be inserted in them, and their profiles can be changed by trim pieces. Most theaters carry a stock of such units, which can be assembled in various ways. The designer's original sketches, therefore, may be determined by what is available. Backdrops are first drawn to scale, then enlarged to full size on canvas hung over a *paint frame,* which can be raised or lowered for the convenience of the painters. Most theaters also carry a set of risers in standard sizes, which can be raised on legs of various heights in any desired configuration.

We saw earlier how escalating costs spelled the end of the elaborate naturalistic set. Even on the proscenium stage, therefore, designers may simply suggest the locale, without depicting it completely. This is even more true on thrust and arena stages, where sight-line problems are multiplied and solid walls are no longer possible. (For this reason designers often prefer thrust or three-quarters round stages over full arenas, giving them at least one wall in which to make a scenic statement and giving the play an anchor in time and place.) Thus a hanging cornice may serve to indicate a wall and define the limits of a room, and a window necessary for the action may hang in open space.

Difficulties of scene shifting on an uncurtained stage have encouraged the revival of techniques developed in earlier, less mechanically complex periods of the theater. Thus, once again, the theater feeds upon its own past and has once more learned how to utilize the simultaneous settings of the Middle Ages or the composite architectural set that can be used in various patterns to suit the requirements of the action, with the modern advantage of stage lighting to define and isolate particular areas according to need. Advances in lighting techniques have also encouraged the use of *projections* to replace elaborate built sets. The projections have obvious advantages, particularly for the fluid, poetic play, but they create their own problems in the relative placement of light sources, screens, and actors.

In most theaters the actors cannot use the set until late in the production process. Sets are being built while the actors are in rehearsal. Often, given the usual pressures of space and time, the rehearsals cannot even take place onstage but are held in some other building that offers roughly equivalent space. Here the ground plan is translated into lines taped on the floor, to indicate where walls, steps, and entrances are. When the set is finally assembled, the cast may have only a few days to adjust to the realities of the stage. During rehearsals the designer normally keeps a watchful eye, to ensure that the action remains compatible with the set as planned. Even so, a number of last-minute adjustments have to be made as the actors learn how long it takes to go up a real flight of stairs instead of marks on the floor or learn the logistics of moving backstage from one part of a complicated set to another. For this reason the setting is usually put in place as soon as the basic units are finished, with details and final painting to be added as time allows.

COSTUME DESIGNERS

The costume designer, like the set designer, is now recognized as an individual creative artist. Once again the process of evolution was a long one. For most of the theater's history stage costume was real costume: actors wore the same sort of clothes that they would have worn in everyday life, sometimes with the addition of conventional elements to give a rudimentary indication of the style of the period. This tradition of actors providing their own costumes has not entirely vanished. Even twenty years ago it was still assumed that an actor had an adequate modern wardrobe, including evening dress, and in summer stock and the smaller repertory theaters actors may still wear their own clothes.

Even with the development of a historical consciousness in the early nineteenth century, most costumes were still not purposely designed for specific productions. Rather, they were associated with particular roles, and they would see service throughout an actor's career, often being handed down through several generations of the same family. Some productions still use costumes drawn from stock. Professional costume houses carry large collections, including full sets of costumes for shows — usually musicals — in current demand. Costumes purposely made for major productions may end up in such houses and have a long life as rental properties. When costumes are hired — as they are in most high school and some university and professional productions — the work of the costumer becomes largely mechanical: filling in measurement forms, making any small adjustments necessary when the costumes arrive, maintaining the costumes during the run, and returning them in good order. In most major productions, however, costumes are now specially designed by a process similar to the design for the set.

The first step is, as before, consultation with the director. This step presupposes a thorough reading of the play and an estimate of the problems involved. For the costumer this process is demanding, as it entails a knowledge of each separate character. It is not merely necessary to establish country and period. Each costume must tell the audience something about the character who wears it.

Here the director's views are essential before any detailed work can be done, as there may be overriding considerations that affect the whole costuming concept of the play. A director who sees *Macbeth*, for instance, as a study in violent, primitive society may ask for costumes crudely cut in rough textures, using furs, hides, and materials suggesting hand-beaten metal and bone. (Orson Welles's film of *Macbeth* took this approach, dressing the characters in pelts, giving Macbeth a square crown, and setting the action among rough-hewn stone walls dripping with moisture.) Alternatively, the director may see *Macbeth* as a play about cynical power politics, an exercise in Machiavellian statecraft: this concept suggests more elaborate, sophisticated costumes, closer to the period in which Shakespeare wrote the play than to the one in which he set it. Sometimes a costuming concept may be designed to bring a particular actor into prominence. When Judith Anderson, following a tradition of distinguished female players of the role, appeared as Hamlet, every member of the cast was dressed in red, with the exception of Hamlet himself, who wore black. Once the general approach has been decided, a range of possible variations within this approach remains. The director staging a Restoration comedy in period costume may ask for the complexity of line and detail to be exaggerated if he is most concerned with period manners. If the production is to emphasize action and the fast-moving story line, a more simplified, clean-cut version of Restoration costume will be called for.

On this basis the designer prepares a sketch for each costume. A permissible color range is worked out in collaboration with the set designer, to ensure that there will be no clashes. Within the costumes themselves color and texture can suggest relationships. To set an all-black Hamlet against an all-red court, as Judith Anderson did, stresses from the beginning the isolation of the central character; to dress the whole court, except for the king and queen, in mourning, as some other productions have done, suggests a different balance of sympathies and isolates Gertrude and Claudius. Color, then, can suggest groupings and alliances; texture can suggest basic character attributes, rougher, homespun materials indicating one kind of character, glossier fabrics another. The costume designer therefore needs a strong historical sense and the facilities for research to determine what kinds of fabrics were worn in particular periods and how they were cut, but departures from strict authenticity may be licensed by artistic effect.

The practicality of costumes is another urgent consideration, dictating some substitution of materials. Stage armor is an obvious case in point. Real metalwork, even if it could be provided in today's conditions, would be impossibly heavy. In the seventeenth century stage breastplates were made out of painted canvas; the modern theater uses plastics. But even in ordinary costumes weight must be taken into consideration. An actress wearing forty pounds of Restoration costume is obviously going to find her movements inhibited. Most costumers, therefore, seek a working compromise between authenticity and utility. Even then the cast may need to learn how to work in costume. Actresses used to blue jeans need training in the wearing of an eighteenth-century skirt, which affects both walking and body posture. Corsetry essential for the correct period line may affect movement and breath control. Equivalents are therefore provided early in the rehearsal process to ensure that the transition to full costume is not too severe.

Most theaters have their own fully equipped costume shop. The costume designer may be a trained pattern maker and cutter or have assistants with these skills and a staff of seamstresses to execute the designs. Fittings are carried out during the rehearsal process, but, like the set, the finished products are rarely available until the last few days. Some designers hold a costume parade, to check their work without other distractions. Others study the costumes in action during the first dress rehearsals and make any last minute changes that seem necessary then. Even in a short run costume maintenance is an important consideration. Stage costumes get dirty easily and need periodic laundering; trim comes loose, seams need to be restitched, and fasteners must be replaced. When the play closes, the costumes are returned to stock, to be reused, recut, or adapted for later productions.

Just as economic pressures and new kinds of stagecraft have placed limitations on the set designed, so the costumer has often been led to *suggest* period rather than to depict it accurately. A full-scale Shakespearean production may need a budget far larger than the theater can afford. (Orson Welles, in his film of *Othello,* was forced to set one scene in a Turkish bath because his money had run out.) Thus the modern theater has increasingly returned to a presentational mode of costuming, echoing conventions of the past and paralleling the return to presentational sets and staging. The Gielgud-Burton *Hamlet* in rehearsal clothes has already been noted. Al Pacino appeared in a production of *Richard III* in which only Richard wore historical costume; the rest of the cast wore modern dress. A popular expedient is to devise a basic performance uniform — leotards, sweaters, or jeans — over which simple, interchangeable costume elements are worn to suggest period and character. Thus the modern theater, out of a new necessity, reverts to an approach to costuming developed long ago by the fifth-century Greeks or the performers of the medieval mysteries.

LIGHTING DESIGNERS

The basic function of stage lighting is to illuminate the actors. For centuries this was its only function. As long as the means were restricted to candles or oil lamps with no possibility of central control, only rudimentary effects were possible. It is in this area that modern technology has made its most conspicuous contribution to the theater. Otis Skinner, a star of the American stage at the turn of the century, reflects in his autobiography on the astonishing changes that had occurred in his lifetime. At the beginning of his career:

> Electrical lighting had not been invented; when the gas man had lighted the "borders" at seven-thirty P.M. with torch and long pole, and his "foots" in front of the curtain, and turned them "down to the blue," all illumination was ready, except for the calcium lights of blended gas from the red and black cylinders. . . . The scene today, lighted in chiaroscuro worthy of a Rembrandt, would have seemed an incredible attainment in my beginnings. But now the soft mellow

beauty of stage lighting has evolved so gradually from those hot wiggly little wires of the first incandescent lights that it is not a matter of wonder to an audience how these things have come about.

But the lighting praised by Skinner would seem crude by today's standards. The *lighting designer* now functions as a creative artist, and even the smaller theaters are capable of being lit with considerable sophistication. Instruments commonly in use are variants of a few basic types. The *ellipsoidal reflector spotlight* produces a narrow, hard-edged beam that can travel long distances with little loss of intensity and so is chiefly used to illuminate acting areas from front-of-house (i.e., over the audience) positions. It can also be fitted with a *gobo,* a lightweight metal cutout that allows it to project patterns. The *Fresnel spotlight* produces a softer, more diffused light with a beam adjustable in width and capable of being cut down further by *barn doors,* hinged metal panels mounted in front of the lens. This light is used for broader washes, and, as it produces some spill, it is normally mounted behind the proscenium. General lighting can also be achieved with *striplights,* lines of bulbs mounted in a trough and wired in several circuits. The *ellipsoidal reflector floodlight,* or *scoop,* is used primarily to light backdrops or sky cloths, as its conical reflector gives a smooth wash of light over a large area. There are also various specialty instruments, the most familiar being the *follow spot,* pivoting on a stand and with an iris device to give a variable aperture.

Using combinations of these instruments, the designer can fill the whole stage with light or illuminate only a tiny portion of it at will. *Intensity* is controlled by dimmers operated from a central board with a clear view of stage. In many theaters the old, manually operated resistance dimmers, worked by throwing a large handle, have been replaced by boards of increasing electronic sophistication and, most recently, with computer memories, which can have a series of cues punched into them and execute them on command. *Color* is achieved through gelatine or plastic filters, in a wide range of hues, slid into metal frames mounted on the instruments. Thus lighting can contribute its own statement to the production and, like the set, must be planned to follow the directorial concept.

As lighting is closely linked to action, a detailed plot is not normally worked out until rehearsals are in an advanced stage, though the approximate positions of the instruments may already have been noted. The lighting designer sits through several rehearsals, checking angles for the key lights of each scene and ensuring that all acting areas are covered. A detailed plot is then produced, with each instrument listed separately according to its position. Lights are hung — a necessarily long and tedious process — and during subsequent rehearsals intensities are set and angles adjusted in consultation with the director. Every change is noted on a *cue sheet,* which is indispensable to the smooth running of the production.

A separate light rehearsal is often held, without the actors, to ensure that all the cues are understood by the staff operating the control board and that all are mechanically possible within the time permitted. If the light plot is a simple one, this rehearsal may be dispensed with or a cue-to-cue rehearsal substituted, in which actors play only those parts of the scenes where light changes are involved. Synchronizing lighting with action is, again, inescapably tedious. Actors particularly dislike such rehearsals, as the continued interruptions prevent them from concentrating on their roles, and many repetitions may be necessary before each cue is right. Once set, the cues are entered by number in the stage manager's promptbook, while the lighting crew retains the detailed breakdown of what each cue entails.

The Stage Crew

The performance that the audience sees is merely the visible portion of a larger and more complex pattern of activity, which has to be planned and rehearsed as carefully as anything that happens on stage.

STAGE MANAGER

Supervising and coordinating the backstage operations is the responsibility of the *stage manager,* whose function changes as the production takes shape. In rehearsal the stage manager works as the director's immediate assistant. It is his or her task to post rehearsal calls and to ensure that actors know when they are needed in the schedule; to lay out the rehearsal space, working from the designer's ground plan; and to provide equivalents of the furniture required for each scene. (The actual furniture, like the set, is usually not available until late in the process.)

As the director blocks each scene and works out movement and business with the actors, the stage manager keeps a careful record in an annotated promptbook. As the rehearsal process is a fluid one, and different patterns of action may be tried out and discarded, it is essential to keep a continuing record of every decision made.

At the same time notes are taken of all props demanded in the action, with queries about any special problems these may present. Many of these props are predictable from a reading of the script, but others may suggest themselves as the production evolves. It is the stage manager's responsibility to ensure that these ideas are practical and that their consequences are thought through. The director, caught up in the immediate inspiration, often has no time or inclination to consider all the ramifications of a particular idea. For example, the director may devise a piece of business in which money changes hands between two characters. The stage manager will want to know how much money; whether it is notes or coin; where it comes from and where it goes. If the play is a costume play, do the costumes have practicable pockets? This question must be ascertained from the costume designer. Is the money loose or in a purse? How large is the purse, and what is it made of? All these details must be foreseen, so that there will be no last-minute problems or surprises. Thus the promptbook becomes a meticulous record of the entire physical aspect of the production, noting all cuts and changes in the text and the nature and placement of all material objects.

In rehearsal the stage manager normally doubles as prompter, though the need for this, it is hoped, disappears after the first few rehearsals. And once the actors no longer have scripts in their hands, the manager provides rehearsal props, which serve as working substitutes until the real things are available. As set, lighting, and sound effects are added in the technical rehearsals, the stage manager notes all cues and changes, with the appropriate light or sound levels. Thus the promptbook becomes the master plan for the complete production.

Once the play has opened, the stage manager assumes total control. Both actors and technicians work under the stage manager's authority. It is his or her responsibility to post sign-in sheets for each performance and to check them to ensure that all personnel are in the theater; to authorize changes or replacements if an actor is sick or missing; and to call the cast at appropriate intervals before the performance. Normal calls include at least half an hour to curtain time, five minutes, and places, when every actor should be in position to go on. The callboy who was such a familiar feature of the nineteenth-century theater, calling actors individually from their dressing rooms for each scene and calling them back at the end of the play for applause, has now largely vanished, his place being taken by intercom systems.

Onstage before the curtain goes up, the stage manager runs a check on all the lighting instruments, then retires to a point of vantage to coordinate the various stage crews. As each curtain, light, or sound cue approaches, first a warning, then the cue itself is given. At moments of intense stage activity, the stage manager may therefore be relaying instructions to several people at once, working from the promptbook that has already been compiled. It is also the stage manager's responsibility to record the timing of each performance, to note any accidents, breakages, or unusual circumstances, and to see that the appropriate personnel are notified to deal with them.

Thus stage management is a profession within the theater at least as demanding as that of the director, calling for particular training and skills and requiring both a strong sense of personal discipline and the ability to enforce discipline on others. As the director rarely remains with the production for the length of the run, the stage manager becomes the director's surrogate, ensuring that the production remains true to the original concept both in intent and practice.

THE CREWS

Subordinate to the stage manager are various other functionaries with responsibility in particular areas. The *property master* or *mistress* heads a crew that procures all props in the stage manager's list and places them for performance.

Some props may have to be specially designed; this procedure is at least supervised by the set designer, to ensure coordination with other design elements. Others are bought, borrowed, or found. Most theaters carry a remarkable selection of miscellaneous objects providing a classified stock from which props can be drawn to suit most occasions. Placement is crucially important. Personal props — those that the actor carries as part of the costume, such as spectacles, canes, handkerchiefs, or rings — are usually handed to the person who uses them and become her or his responsibility. Others may be preset on stage before the performance or during scene changes. Props brought in during the action are laid out near the appropriate entrance and returned to the same spot after use. The prop crew lists and checks each single object both before and after performance.

The *stage crew* is responsible for shifting sets and furniture. They work to a pattern of activity that has been carefully programmed by the stage manager during rehearsals, to ensure that everyone has an assigned task, that all mechanical problems have been foreseen, and that changes can take place in the minimum time possible. As this task may involve simultaneously flying one set and dropping in another, turning a revolve, and moving large pieces of furniture, the work must be choreographed as meticulously as a ballet; a well-trained crew can execute complex changes in a few seconds.

The *light crew* divides itself into distinct groups. Control board operators, working to the stage manager's cues, execute the lighting plan made up by the director and lighting designer. This task may take one operator or several, depending on the complexity of the control board and the play. Other crew members work on the floor or in light galleries with individual instruments, shifting or refocusing them at need. One of the most familiar manifestations of these lights is the *follow spot,* once common in the legitimate theater but now confined to musicals, which accompanies a particular performer. In repertory, where the light plan changes daily, every instrument may have to be rehung and refocused between performances.

The *sound crew* performs a similar function with background music and offstage noises, though the sophistication of modern tape recording has simplified this operation to the point where it can usually be handled by one person at a control board. Timing and sound levels have already been set in rehearsal, and electronic devices allow the recorder to move to each new cue automatically.

MODERN ECONOMIC PROBLEMS

In the commercial theater it is now sadly recognized that these ancillary functions have come to dominate the production process. The powerful stagehands' union enforces wage demands that take much of the production budget, and it also insists on minimum crew requirements and strict demarcation of jobs, which create severe practical difficulties. Broadway productions rehearse in semidarkness because to use more than the bare permitted minimum of rehearsal lights would require the paid presence of a professional electrician, even if he had no other function than to turn a single switch on and off, for union stipulations prevent anyone else on the staff from doing this. This division of labor, though originating in a laudable desire to provide adequate working conditions and salary in a hazardous and underpaid profession, has resulted in redundancies, featherbedding, and needless duplication, which contribute not a little to the theater's economic problems. Stagehands' strikes have closed performances; even the Comédie Française was once forced to spend a summer under canvas in the Tuileries Gardens because a strike had made its regular theater inoperable.

We have noted how small casts and limited scenic demands have been enforced on the theater by today's economic conditions, but the same restrictions cannot be applied backstage. William Gibson, who wrote an ingenious two-character play with a single setting, called *Two for the Seesaw,* afterward published an account of the production process under the title of *The Seesaw Log,* in which he ruefully noted that for these minimal requirements, with no change of scenery needed, the unions insisted on a stage crew of nineteen people. Nonunion houses, including most university theaters, can escape these demands; but even so, trained backstage personnel are sufficiently in demand that they can often command higher salaries than the actors.

Appendix

Diary of a Production

This book has endeavored to suggest the multiplicity of problems and processes — historical, aesthetic, and practical — that are involved in a theatrical production. It has been suggested that, although certain *general* laws are discernible in the theater, their application must vary, as no two productions ever come to function in exactly the same conditions. The purpose of this appendix, therefore, is to document the course of one specific modern production in detail, both to show these general principles at work and to illustrate how strongly local and particular circumstances may affect the play in performance.

The Play

The play we will consider is *She Stoops to Conquer,* a five-act comedy by Oliver Goldsmith (ca. 1730–1774), first performed at Covent Garden Theatre, London, in 1773. Like a number of the more brilliant British writers, Goldsmith was an Irishman. Encouraged by some of the most distinguished men of his time, he demonstrated his versatility in the novel (*The Vicar of Wakefield*) and the poem (*The Deserted Village*) as well as on the stage. He entered the London theater at a time when it was in the doldrums. Its audience was predominantly middle class and determinedly genteel; its preferred fare was mild domestic comedy calculated to provoke polite amusement without any hint of shock or scandal. Goldsmith, revolted by this complacency, sought to revitalize comedy by introducing broader humor and parody of contemporary sensibilities.

His first comedy, *The Good Natured Man* (1768), was condemned by the audience as vulgar chiefly because of one scene. A young man, in the process of having his household goods seized for debt, tries to conceal the presence of the bailiffs from guests he has invited to a formal party. He disguises them as naval officers; and the humor arises from their attempts to pass themselves off as members of polite society. The scene reads pleasantly enough, but tamely now. That it was taken as an affront by its first audience tells us plainly how straitlaced the London theatergoing public had become. *She Stoops to Conquer* had a happier first reception, though some critics hissed what they found to be the coarseness and improbability of the plot. It has, however, survived as a staple of the English comic stage, and though time has dimmed its revolutionary luster, it is still applauded as a work of high spirits and ebullient comic eccentricity.

At this point the reader should turn to the play, which is plentifully available in a number of editions. The following synopsis is intended only as a quick reference guide to the action.

ACT ONE

We are introduced to the household of Squire and Mrs. Hardcastle in a remote part of rural England. Hardcastle is entirely happy with his rustic, uneventful surroundings and with his old-fashioned house, which looks "for all the world like an inn"; his wife has higher social pretensions and longs for the life of the big city to which she feels she is naturally suited.

There are two children. Tony Lumpkin, Mrs. Hardcastle's son by a previous marriage, is an unschooled, happy-go-lucky youth whom everyone calls "a booby"; his love of mischief precipitates the various misadventures that make up the plot. Kate Hardcastle, the daughter of the house, is of marriageable age. Her father tells her that he has an eligible suitor, one Marlow, son of his old friend Sir Charles Marlow, and that the young man is to visit the house imminently. Kate confides her news and apprehensions to her friend Constance Neville, living under the same roof and Mrs. Hardcastle's ward. Constance is an heiress in her own right, but her fortune, in jewels, is being held by Mrs. Hardcastle in the hope that she will marry Tony and so keep the legacy in the family. Constance, however, has her own preferred suitor, George Hastings, who is (by the sort of coincidence so beloved by this kind of comedy) young Marlow's closest friend.

(*top*) Marlow and Hastings abuse Hardcastle's hospitality. (*left*) The coach ride: Constance, Mrs. Hardcastle, Tony Lumpkin. (*right*) The successful wooing; Kate and Young Marlow with their fathers in the background.

Tony Lumpkin is seen in his favorite surroundings, the tavern, with his rustic drinking partners. Marlow and Hastings arrive. They have lost their way and ask directions to Hardcastle's house. Tony, to play a trick on his stepfather, sends them to the house under the pretense that it is an inn, where they can spend the night before proceeding to their proper destination.

ACT TWO

Back at the house, Marlow and Hastings arrive. They believe what Tony has told them, that this is an inn and Hardcastle the landlord. We learn several things about Marlow in the opening conversation that have already been hinted at earlier in the play. Marlow, though free enough with women of a lower class, is totally ill at ease with those from polite society. He does not know what to say to them, and the forthcoming interview with Kate, the prospective bride he has never seen, fills him with terror.

Hardcastle's attempts to make the two young men welcome are rebuffed by them. They still take him for a landlord with pretensions above his station, and he is enraged by their cavalier attitude to his hospitality. Constance catches Hastings alone and enlightens him about the mistake. They dare not tell Marlow, as his natural timidity would drive him away at once if he found he had committed so gross a social blunder. They resolve therefore to continue the deception of the inn, and they tell him that Kate has just arrived there as a traveler.

Marlow's first unwilling encounter with Kate is disastrous. He stammers; he is at a loss for words; he cannot bring himself to look her in the face. She is amused by his excessive shyness, but she thinks he is still worth the trouble of winning. Hastings has ingratiated himself with Mrs. Hardcastle and seeks an opportunity of eloping with Constance — who does not want to leave without her jewels. Tony is only too willing to help them solve their problem.

ACT THREE

Hardcastle and Kate discuss Marlow, and they discover that they are apparently talking about two different people. Kate finds him impossibly timid, her father finds him an arrogant boor. They decide to investigate further. Tony enters with Constance's jewels, which he has stolen from his mother's room so that Hastings and Constance may elope. Hastings runs off with the jewels to hide them.

Kate discovers Marlow's mistake from her maid, and she decides to improve upon it by passing herself off, in another dress, as the barmaid of the supposed inn. Marlow, completely taken in, tries to seduce her, and Kate learns very quickly that her suitor is not always as timid as he first appeared to be.

ACT FOUR

Hastings has given Marlow the jewel box to keep safe. Marlow, still under the original delusion, has taken special precautions by giving them to the "landlady" for safekeeping. Mrs. Hardcastle thus has the jewels again, and Hastings's elopement is temporarily doomed. Hardcastle finally erupts in fury at the behavior of his guests, and it begins to dawn on Marlow that he has made a terrible mistake. Mrs. Hardcastle discovers, by an intercepted letter, the plot between Tony, Constance, and Hastings. All are discomfited; Constance is to be taken off to another aunt, to be kept virtual prisoner.

ACT FIVE

But Tony has another plan. Pretending to drive Constance and Mrs. Hardcastle to their proper destination, he really leads them a wild-goose chase and brings them back, at dead of night, to their own garden. Hastings and Constance run off together. Mrs. Hardcastle, convinced that she is on a lonely heath and menaced by dangerous highwaymen, gradually learns the truth of her situation.

The arrival of Marlow's father precipitates a solution. Marlow has been won over by the charms and virtue of the girl he supposed to be the barmaid, and he asks for her hand in marriage. He is aghast to discover it is really Kate, but the two fathers persuade them to make a match. Constance and Hastings return and are forgiven. Tony is allowed to come into his manhood and emancipate himself from his mother, and all ends in rejoicing.

Thus the play. In many ways it has the classic pattern of farce. It depends upon a ridiculous premise, which is then carried with remorseless logic through a series of complications to a resolution. (Goldsmith's critics found the premise too implausible to be acceptable, in spite of the author's insistence that it was based on an episode from real life. For contemporary concern with decorum, probability, and propriety, see Chapter 7.) The play's humor is based on confrontations between characters of sharply contrasting types, and much of it (as in the scene on the supposed heath) is physical.

The Circumstances of Production

She Stoops to Conquer was given as the third in a summer season of four plays. Each play had a rehearsal period of two weeks, followed by a two-week run; but these overlapped, so that for most of the season the company was rehearsing one play in the daytime and performing another at night.

As the four plays were of widely different types and directed by people with radically different approaches, the greatest problems for the cast were in making rapid adjustments and in not letting the day's rehearsals spill over into the evening performance: "changing gears," as one actress put it. Thus while rehearsing *She Stoops*, the company was performing Jean-Claude Van Itallie's *A Fable,* a work evolved originally out of group performance and demanding from the actor a highly introspective style that was a complete contrast to the extraverted humor of Goldsmith. While performing *She Stoops*, they were rehearsing *R,* a new play by C. V. Peters, which used a nightclub format to present the personal history of a psychopathic killer. The versatility demanded by this sort of season is one of the theater's greatest challenges, and as the company consisted of a mixture of young professionals and drama students, the challenge was particularly severe.

An associated problem in such a season is that the company is selected to cover as well as possible the casting demands of all four plays, with the larger roles distributed as fairly as possible among them. For any particular play, then, the casting may be less than ideal. The intensive rehearsals demanded during this season were also an important factor. Normally actors rehearsed from ten to five, with an hour's break for lunch — though this hour was often taken up by such necessary nuisances as costume fittings, posing for publicity pictures, and the like. Most of them had to be back in the theater by half-past six to make up and prepare for the evening's performance. Alternate Sundays (i.e., those in the middle of a run) were free, but weekends before a new play opened had to be taken up by technical rehearsals. By the third production of the season, therefore, fatigue was increasing. The normal procedure in such cases is to cover new ground in the morning, while the actors are still fresh, and to use the afternoons for repetition of things already accomplished. But on more than one occasion rehearsals stopped only because the cast was simply too tired to work any further. It is a tribute to Goldsmith's exuberance, though, that the further the rehearsals proceeded, the more enlivened the actors became; the bounce and sparkle of the comedy gave them a second wind.

Directorial Concept

In such a season, with limited rehearsal time, as much as possible must be worked out in advance. A more generous rehearsal schedule would have permitted the director and actors to work through scenes from scratch and from different points of approach; this one did not. A point of approach had to be predetermined, at the cost of lessening the contributions of the actor and increasing those of the director.

As we have seen, every play in revival presents its own problems. These usually involve re-creating, for a modern audience, things the original audience took for granted and enabling the spectator to understand the world in which these dramatic events took place. *She Stoops* offers two well-known, and interrelated, problems of this kind.

COPING WITH LANGUAGE

The first and most obvious is the language of the play. Goldsmith wrote beautiful English prose; but it is eighteenth-century English prose, ornate, intricate, with an artfully balanced symmetry of clauses. Here, for example, is Marlow's farewell to Kate, just before he discovers who she really is:

> It must not be, madam. I have already trifled too long with my heart. My very pride begins to submit to my passion. The disparity of education and fortune, the anger of a parent, and the contempt of my equals, begin to lose their weight; and nothing can restore me to myself but this painful effort of resolution.

This language is not the kind in which we now converse, even in our most formal moments. Modern actors often have trouble in finding their way through it; modern audiences have difficulty in understanding it if it is delivered at anywhere near the speed that was originally intended. This matter of speed is a constant problem in a variety of plays from the classic English repertory — Shakespeare, Restoration comedy, Goldsmith, Sheridan — and the problem is compounded by geographical distance as well as the distance of time. British ears are still, by tradition and habituation, more accustomed to this kind of speech pattern than American ears are. British audiences are, at any rate, more familiar with their own classical repertory. American audiences, accustomed to different rhythms, tend to lose their way if addressed in this kind of language at the British tempo. To slow down, on the other hand, invites boredom. American productions of Restoration comedy have a noticeably longer playing time than their British equivalents.

Something can, however, be done about the language. More meaningful equivalents can be substituted for words now archaic. (The opening line of the play is a case in point. Mrs. Hardcastle complains, "Mr. Hardcastle, you are very particular." *Particular* meant, for Goldsmith, what we should now express by *extraordinary, odd,* even *eccentric,* and there is some justification for changing the word to retain the sense.) Excess verbiage can be pruned without doing undue violence to the play. Several acting versions in print do exactly this, and the present production used one of them as a starting point.

Actors can be taught to handle the language; and often the problem of what now appears to be excessive formality in conversations between father and daughter, or lady and suitor, can be solved by making the style of address not less but more formal. For example, consider the interchange between Hardcastle and Kate about her proposed new husband:

> *Hardcastle.* And, to crown all, Kate, he's one of the most bashful and reserved young fellows in all the world.
> *Kate.* Eh! You have frozen me to death again. That word *reserved* has undone all the rest of his accomplishments. A reserved lover, it is said, always makes a suspicious husband.

Hardcastle. On the contrary, modesty seldom resides in a breast that is not enriched with nobler virtues. It was the very feature in his character that first struck me.

Here the actors were instructed to treat the formal lines as if they were moral maxims lifted from a book of familiar quotations: to parody, in effect, their own formality. This technique has been used in other modern revivals of *She Stoops,* and it often works.

SOLVING PROBLEMS OF TIME AND PLACE

The language, however, is only part of a deeper problem. Like a good deal of English comedy from Shakespeare to Noel Coward and beyond, *She Stoops* is predicated upon a class structure that has never been part of American life and is rapidly ceasing to be part of the English experience. Each character in the play has a sharply defined social station, which dictates language and behavior, particularly, behavior with respect to others. Marlow gives offense because he treats Hardcastle as an innkeeper and applies to him the kind of language and behavior that a gentleman would normally use to the lower orders. Hardcastle is enraged because he finds *demanded* from him, as a right, that same hospitality that he is perfectly prepared to extend to social equals. Marlow's embarrassment in Kate's presence is caused by the fact that she is on his level; his freedom with Kate the barmaid is permitted by the presumption that she is not. (This is, incidentally, surely Goldsmith the Irishman making fun at an English phenomenon; the reticence that Marlow refers to as "the Englishman's malady" is still very much part of the English character.) Hardcastle's servants are comic because they behave more like family than hirelings. They unclass themselves. Mrs. Hardcastle similarly becomes grotesque because she seeks to unclass herself; she is country gentry pretending to be city gentry, and Goldsmith's audience would have noted the distinction.

This kind of stratified society, with its shades and subdivisions and nuances, no longer exists. Yet its equivalent must be provided if the play is to make sense. The solution chosen here was to transplant the play to an environment in which the relevant social distinctions could be made more broadly and clearly: to change the date slightly and set it not in rural England but in even more rural New England — in Massachusetts of the 1760s. (The actual date of the play, 1773, was avoided as coming too close to the War of Independence.) Thus the contrast developed was not between various kinds of English manners but between English and simpler, less elaborate colonial manners. Marlow and Hastings remained two very English young men, but the Hardcastle family spoke, in varying degrees, with a New England accent, particularly Tony Lumpkin.

Once this fundamental decision had been made, it turned out to have a number of side benefits. Not the least was the question of place references, which had to be changed to conform to the new location. For example, when Hastings is ridiculing Mrs. Hardcastle's social pretensions while pretending to applaud her, he says, in the original text: "I concluded you had been bred all your life either at Ranelagh, St. James's, or Tower Wharf." These are all contemporary London references, and the point is that while St. James's is the haunt of polite society, Tower Wharf is part of London's dockland and the lowest of the low. Mrs. Hardcastle does not know the difference. These references fall flat before an American audience. They have little to say even to an English audience now. But in the new environment they can be replaced with Boston references that were immediately meaningful (the production took place just outside Boston), and the joke became fresh again.

Another gain was thematic. Goldsmith, as we have noted, intended this play, in some sense at least, as a revolutionary work. He wanted to open windows and let some fresh air into the stuffy, overpolite drawing room comedy of his time. (One has only to read the work of Goldsmith's rivals to realize how stilted comedy had become.) Although much of the action takes place in Hardcastle's house, there is always a sense of the outdoors, of a fresh wind blowing. The American environment assisted this with the sense of a New World emancipation blowing away the cobwebs of Old World manners. Kate, in particular, emerged as a kind of new woman, managing, contriving, fending for herself in a way certainly not typical of English girls of her time. The change of costume from lady of the house to barmaid (which gives the title of the play its meaning) came to signify a refusal to be bound by existing conventions, a willingness to cross social barriers, if any good could be obtained thereby.

In the initial thinking about the play, this kind of contrast — outdoors versus indoors, the unrestrained life versus the restricted, outspokenness versus inhibition — came to be more and more important. It communicated itself to the physical staging of the work. One of the most important incidents takes place offstage: the coach ride in which Mrs. Hradcastle becomes hopelessly lost. Why not *show* this? Why not have the actors construct at least a suggestion of a coach from existing furniture and ride it, so that the audience could see what the characters later talked about?

The supplementing of the verbal with the physical became important in other ways. As it stands, Marlow's embarrassment scene with Kate is almost entirely verbal and depends on niceties of language and social consciousness that are difficult to communicate to a modern audience. The impulse, then, was to make this scene more visual too, to give Marlow obvious physical embarrassment, which would convey, through sight, the same sense that the original audience received through sound. How could we give Marlow some physical awkwardness? Clumsiness? Knocking things over? The same line of thought applied to other scenes in the play, giving rise often to a broader kind of humor than Goldsmith originally intended but still faithful to the spirit of the work.

Set and Costume Design

Here another kind of transposition had to be made. Goldsmith wrote for the picture frame theater in which stage settings could be changed behind a curtain with considerable ease. The present production took place in an arena theater, where changes were nowhere so simple and the only form of concealment was darkness. It was decided to make capital out of this difficulty by turning the scene changes into part of the show. For instance, the sense of open-air freshness already alluded to would be suggested at the very beginning of the play by showing Hardcastle and his wife in the fields: Hardcastle shooting, in his element; a pheasant dropping from the skies; Mrs. Hardcastle reacting in horror to this grossness and starting her complaints about her lack of smart society. Then they move into the house — or rather, the house moves around them. As the dialogue continues, servants bring in a table, chairs, a bench, a fireplace; out of the bare stage a room evolves. The other changes were designed after the same principle.

As the production was itself taking place in New England, local color was easily obtainable. The set and costume designer made visits to Lexington and Concord to study textures, architectural styles, construction, and disposition of the furniture in surviving period houses. All the furniture was specially built, and once the decision to show the coach had been taken, the size and nature of the individual pieces were worked out, as it were, backward. The designer began by working out a coach shape, with appropriate dimensions to hold two passengers and a driver and then, considering the furniture as building blocks, evolved the number of pieces in the shapes and sizes necessary.

The most difficult scene to design, for more than one reason, was the tavern. As Goldsmith's script stands, this scene is very short, but it demands a complete change of setting (which is never used again) and a number of small-part players who never appear elsewhere in the play. Nevertheless, it is vital to the plot. In Goldsmith's time actors were badly paid and extra players easy to come by. This company was strictly limited; as it was, Goldsmith's landlord had to be turned into a landlady, as the cast had one extra woman and no extra men. (One of the recurrent problems in reviving older plays is the way in which more stringent theater economics have limited the casting possibilities.) After a good deal of discussion, a solution was found that kept the essence of the scene but trimmed away the superfluities. At the scene transition Hardcastle's room was cleared; a tavern sign was lowered; a window at one end of the arena lit up, showing silhouettes in period costume, waving tankards; and the audience saw, as it were, the tavern from the outside rather than the inside. The preliminary chatter, cut to the bone, and Tony's song were heard offstage; Tony entered shouting back at his cronies; and the subsequent discussion with the Landlady, Marlow, and Hastings took place "outside" on the empty stage.

Thus a scenic concept evolved that was simple and fluid. The designer wished to provide more visual elaboration and suggested the use of projection screens, with appropriate slides to frame the various locales. This idea was agreed to in principle, and she eventually evolved a system of four projectors and screens at key points around the arena, changed simultaneously by remote control from the light booth. Slides of period furniture and decoration surrounded Hardcastle's house; these changed to more rustic vignettes for the tavern and a whole series of outdoor shots for the coach ride. Simple though the basic concept was, it took two weeks of hard work from a staff of eight to build the furniture and prepare the slides.

Costumes, mercifully, were less burdensome. As the theater had recently staged a series of new works to celebrate the country's bicentennial, a number of appropriate costumes were already in stock, to be used as they were or adapted. The most important costumes, however, still had to be made from scratch, and this task involved three weeks' work for the costume designer and two assistants. Fortunately, this play was the only elaborate costume play of the season: *A Fable* used street clothes, which took little time to prepare.

Rehearsals

In the nature of the business, rehearsals do not proceed with the precision of a military maneuver. The director normally arms himself with a schedule of what he hopes to achieve at each session, and actors are called to rehearse specific scenes; but each working day may differ markedly from the prediction. Far from being continually creative, much of the rehearsal process is occupied with tiresome and frustrating repetition. For every moment of inspiration, there are long periods of necessary boredom. The following merely summarizes what was, in actuality, a complex, enervating and fragmented process.

DAYS ONE AND TWO

The morning was occupied with the first reading, to familiarize the actors with the main lines of the play, clear up any problems of meaning or pronunciation, give cuts, and suggest, very generally, the basic lines of approach. Some of the cast already know the play well. Others have only read it cursorily. But even at this early date the actors' personalities begin to mingle with, and color, those of their characters. (From this point in these notes, characters' names will also be used for the actors who play them.)

The reading is relaxed and uneventful. One worry is disposed of: within the limits of the company the casting is obviously as good as it can be; no major errors have been made. Other small worries appear. Hastings misreads "open the campaign" as "open the champagne." Everyone laughs, but the mistake is symptomatic; Hastings several times makes similar errors and obviously is far less at ease with this kind of language than the others.

The director makes a few elementary suggestions. He asks for a strong feeling of family warmth between most of the characters in the play — not merely in the obvious cases of Kate with her father or with Constance but between Hardcastle and the servants, and even (under the superficial crossness and teasing) between Tony and his step-relations. This warmth will make the breaches of hospitality and decorum that occur more vivid and incisive. The director also suggests that Marlow should cultivate a stammer for his moments of embarrassment. Marlow tries this indiscriminately; he still has to settle on which specific letters will give him trouble.

Blocking begins in the afternoon and continues through the next day. The purpose of this blocking is to establish the principal movement patterns of the play and the key positions for each scene. With so tight a rehearsal schedule it is essential to give the actors a scheme they can hold onto, but the director emphasizes that this scheme is not meant to be rigid. As work continues, actors should feel free to improvise on this scheme and change it where they have justification. At this stage a great deal is only sketched in. Even the text is fluid, as some of the topical allusions have yet to be found. Some moments are only indicated, moments that will take a great deal of time to work out fully later on ("Here we do the coach ride."). But by the evening of the second day, everyone knows, more or less, where they are supposed to be, where the exits and entrances are, and what the principal business is. Everyone has been present to watch these blocking rehearsals. The full cast will not meet again for some days to come. Every move and entrance is painstakingly plotted by the stage manager in the master promptbook so that any query can be instantly checked.

DAYS THREE THROUGH SIX

The company goes back to the beginning of the play and works, in detail, individual scenes or groups of scenes. Most actors still work with book in hand through day five. Kate and Marlow have their lines by day four. Hastings still has trouble with the language. Several times the rehearsal stops while his lines are explained to him or paraphrased in modern idiom so that he can grasp the sense of them.

As always, the script gives no real indication of the problems that arise in rehearsal. Some long and complex scenes fall into place easily, almost automatically. Kate and Constance complement each other perfectly in voice and behavior. The early scene between them, in which they discuss their matrimonial ambitions, is from the beginning warm and intimate, exactly right. At other moments the rehearsal may hold up for half an hour over one line or movement.

Actors are busy trying to find images for themselves, often from sources quite outside the play, to help them illuminate their characters. Tony first fixes on Huckleberry Finn, but he finds that this image makes him too slow, rustic, and stupid. He is worried by the fact that Tony, although called a clod and a bumpkin by everyone, in fact devises the key stratagems of the plot. After a good deal of heart searching and several changes of direction, he settles on Puck, a malign mischief maker. From this point his performance becomes much more physical; he jumps, climbs, throws himself about the stage, strikes attitudes. Mrs. Hardcastle, whose performance has to be more stolid, begins to worry that he is upstaging her in their scenes together; but, in fact, she acts as a useful foil to him, and the combination is good. Marlow similarly displays a good deal of physical inventiveness, particularly in the embarrassment scene, which he enjoys. The director has devised a culminating piece of business in which he gets his foot stuck in a tankard that has been left on the stage from the previous scene. This business is very funny, but it is going to present more problems than anything else in the play. The stage manager's promptbook becomes a mass of changes and erasures.

As the books leave the actors' hands, working props are brought in — approximations to objects currently being built or procured, which the actors will not have till the last stages of rehearsals. Actresses wear long rehearsal skirts from the beginning — necessary because they have to accustom themselves to the limits of movement their costumes will inflict. Kate, especially, has a typically modern American girl's stride, which has to be curbed into shorter, more delicate steps.

Real props begin to appear, and none too soon. Marlow's tankard gives problems. His foot will not remain stuck in it. It is lined to make it tighter; the foot still comes out. (On one occasion the foot and the stuffing come out.) The jewel box, for some mysterious reason, will not stay shut. Mechanical details suddenly become very important. But the cast remains in high spirits. They enjoy the play and are continuously inventive.

DAYS SEVEN THROUGH NINE

Individual scenes are pulled together into acts, and the director is concerned largely with continuity and timing. Scripts are now banished, and no prompting is permitted. (It is hardly ever necessary; only a few lines are missed.)

On days eight and nine two complete run-throughs of the play are done. These are immensely fatiguing for the actors, but they are necessary not merely for continuity but for the technical staff, who have to see the play complete before sound and lights can be properly set. On the evening of day nine, during the performance of A Fable, a near-disaster strikes. Kate gashes her arm on a steel pipe, part of the set. She applies a tourniquet and goes on to finish the performance (of such stuff are actors made). She then faints and is taken to the hospital to have four stitches put in her arm.

DAY TEN

This day is Sunday, a nonperformance day. The set, complete except for a few details, is assembled in the theater. Lights are hung and angled, a dreary and time-consuming process. The cast is called for the evening, and the first technical rehearsal occurs. Costumes are worn, but without makeup. Kate is under heavy sedation and her arm is so painful that many of her moves cannot be played as they were rehearsed. The sleeves of her costumes have to be lengthened to conceal the bandage.

This detail, however, is merely an additional problem. Technical rehearsals are traditionally disastrous; the present one is no exception. This is the occasion when, for the first time, all the elements of the production come together. However carefully effects have been planned on paper, they have existed to this point only in the mind's eye. Now they must be realized, and what evolves is, at best, only an approximation to the finished production. The projectors have been badly hung, so the slides are only half seen; one fails so that the slides are not seen at all. It takes far longer to shift the furniture than anyone has calculated. Carefully plotted patterns of movement disintegrate because actors are preoccupied with their costumes or sound and light cues. The rehearsal staggers on from one cue to another and does not end until long after midnight.

DAY ELEVEN

Morning and afternoon are spent redoing scenes that have not gone well. There are two in particular: Marlow's seduction of the supposed barmaid and his farewell to her, before her true identity is revealed. After a good deal of reblocking and discussion, it turns out that the seduction scene is not working because it is too busy: the actors are so mobile — Marlow chasing Kate all over the stage — that no one has time to listen to the words. The director simplifies the scene, reducing the movement to half; it works better. The farewell scene is more difficult, because it is a question of mood, not movement. Marlow is embarrassed by it. The elaborate profession of love he has to deliver is out of keeping with his modern susceptibilities. The scene is played through several times, but it still does not come together.

In the evening comes a rehearsal under full performance conditions with full costume and makeup. The actors are now fairly used to their costumes, though some aspects of the set still bother them: there is less space than they antici-pated, and some moves have to be curtailed or changed. Makeup is generally good, though some must be adjusted: Mrs. Hardcastle's is not artificial enough — she needs to look more like "mutton dressed as lamb"; Hardcastle is too pallid — he needs more of a ruddy, outdoor look.

At this stage the production is wholly under the control of the stage man-ager. She calls the cast and gives the sound and lighting cues from the booth. The director is relegated to the sidelines and does not intervene in the rehearsal; he merely gives notes at the conclusion. Act One goes well. Act Two is chaotic. For no reason the actors appear unable to work together. Lines are missed; there is no ensemble sense. One scene goes much better than expected: Marlow's farewell. In costume the actor gains the panache that, in his own clothes, he lacked. His rehearsal embarrassment is forgotten.

DAY TWELVE

During the day the cast again works on specific scenes. The one that demands attention this time is the scene where Mrs. Hardcastle intercepts Hastings's letter to Tony. It is a scene with a great deal of intricate movement, which has to be worked out as carefully as a ballet. The company goes through it again and again; finally Constance freezes out of sheer fatigue, and the rehearsal has to stop.

In the evening comes the final dress rehearsal. All the projectors are adjusted, and the slides show in the proper places. The furniture shifting takes far less time than the day before. All the play goes well; Constance has recovered her spirits and her voice. There are a few people in the audience, and they laugh. This reaction is invaluable; most of the actors have been working so long that they have forgotten how funny the lines were when they first read them. It is a good rehearsal, and everyone is pleased.

DAY THIRTEEN

The day is one of rest; it is first night. The first performance achieves a full house and much laughter, which often catches the actors unawares. During the next few nights, they will learn to adjust to it. Marlow's embarrassment scene earns laughter and a round of applause. After all the trouble in rehearsal with the tankard, the effect will never fail in performance. The coach scene, too, gets applause. Everyone is happy.

From this point throughout the run, the production continues to change in subtle ways. No two audiences are the same or laugh in exactly the same places, but the high spots of the play are known, and the actors can work on them. A two-week run is not long enough for the production to fossilize. The technical effects become smoother — second nature now. Marlow continues to experiment, particularly in the embarrassment scene. Some things work, some do not, but the scene is solid enough to permit such variations.

CONCLUSION

Such is a play production; and this case is fairly typical. Some things are preplanned, others are last-minute inspirations. Some are deliberate, some are accidents. Some ideas come from the director, some from the actors, some from a creative fusion of both. And some come from other sources altogether — it was the costume designer who, seeing the play for the first time while at dress rehearsal, suggested two pieces of business that were at once embodied and turned out to be exactly right. Perhaps the true measure of a production is the extent to which it can still change and grow in detail while maintaining a recognizable shape. It is this corporate, mutually responsive effort that distinguishes theater from any other art.

Acknowledgments (*continued from page iv*)

Photo Alinari, pp. 102, 108 (bottom)

Josef Meier, Black Hills Passion Play, p. 132 (bottom)

University of Bristol Theatre Collection, pp. 133, 134, 166, 167, 309, 310, 311. Model by Richard Southern, p. 311

Oregon Shakespearean Festival, Ashland, Oregon, p. 148. Dwaine Smith, p. 174. Bill Bayley, p. 175

Museum of London, pp. 155, 254

Culver, p. 175

Dionisio Minaggio, The Feather Book. Milan, 1618. Blacker-Wood Library of Zoology and Ornithology, McGill University, Montreal, p. 201

Arena Theater, Tufts University, p. 202 (bottom)

University of Lancaster, Nuffield Theatre Studio, pp. 236, 237, 399 (bottom). Model by C. M. Fogarty, p. 235. Reconstruction by Keith Sturgess, p. 253 (top). Photograph by Ivor Dykes, p. 259 (top)

Morris Newcombe, pp. 236 (bottom), 354 (bottom), 416, 417

Greater London Council Architects Dept., p. 253

Carroll Durand, p. 261

By permission of the British Library, p. 284 (top)

Harvard Theater Collection, pp. 284 (bottom), 300 (top), 314, 355 (top), 471

Crown Copyright, Victoria and Albert Museum, p. 285

Walker Art Gallery, Liverpool, p. 300 (bottom)

Louis Mélançon, New York Metropolitan Opera Archives, pp. 346, 347

Colonial Theater, Boston, p. 371

By arrangement with the Bakhrushian Museum, Moscow, USSR, pp. 372, 373

Junius Hamblin, pp. 434, 442, 443

University Theatre, Rarig Center, University of Minnesota, p. 490

Bibliography

CHAPTER 1

General Introductions to the Theater

Brockett, Oscar G. *The Theatre: An Introduction.* 4th ed. New York: Holt, Rinehart and Winston, 1979.
Kernodle, George. *Invitation to the Theatre.* New York: Harcourt Brace Jovanovich, 1967.
Whiting, Frank M. *An Introduction to the Theatre.* 4th ed. New York: Harper and Row, 1978.

General Histories of the Theater

Brockett, Oscar G. *The Theatre: An Introduction.* 4th ed. New York: Holt, Rinehart and Winston, 1979.
Nicoll, Allardyce. *The Development of the Theatre.* 5th ed., rev. New York: Barnes and Noble, 1976.
Roberts, Vera Mowry. *On Stage: A History of Theatre.* 2nd ed. New York: Harper and Row, 1974.
Southern, Richard. *The Seven Ages of the Theatre.* New York: Hill and Wang, 1961.

551

CHAPTER 2

Arnott, Peter D. *An Introduction to the Greek Theatre.* New York: St. Martin's Press, 1959.

Arnott, Peter D. *The Ancient Greek and Roman Theatre.* New York: Random House, 1971.

Bieber, Margarete. *History of the Greek and Roman Theatre.* Rev. ed. Princeton, N.J.: Princeton University Press, 1961.

Conacher, D. J. *Euripidean Drama: Myth, Theme and Structure.* Toronto: University of Toronto Press, 1967.

Murray, Gilbert. *Aeschylus: The Creator of Tragedy.* 1940. Reprint. New York: Greenwood, 1978.

Spatz, Lois. *Aristophanes.* Boston, Twayne, 1978.

Webster, T. B. L. *Greek Theatre Production.* London: Methuen, 1956.

Whitman, Cedric. *Sophocles: A Study of Heroic Humanism.* Cambridge, Mass.: Harvard University Press, 1951.

CHAPTER 3

Beare, William. *The Roman Stage: A Short History.* London: Methuen, 1950, 1965.

Casson, Lionel, ed. *The Plays of Menander.* New York: New York University Press, 1971.

Duckworth, George E. *Nature of Roman Comedy: A Study in Popular Entertainment.* Princeton, N.J.: Princeton University Press, 1971.

Segal, Erich. *Roman Laughter: The Comedy of Plautus.* Cambridge, Mass.: Harvard University Press, 1968.

CHAPTER 4

The Medieval Theater in England and Europe

Frank, Grace. *Medieval French Drama.* Oxford: Oxford University Press, 1954.

Nagler, Alois M. *The Medieval Religious Stage: Shapes and Phantoms.* New Haven: Yale University Press, 1976.

Nicoll, Allardyce. *Masks, Mimes and Miracles.* New York: Harcourt Brace Jovanovich, 1932.

Salter, Frederick M. *Medieval Drama in Chester.* Darby, Penn.: Folcroft, 1973.

Southern, Richard. *Medieval Theatre in the Round.* New York: Theatre Arts Books, 1975.

Wickham, Glynne. *The Medieval Theatre.* New York: St. Martin's Press, 1974.

Noh Theater

Arnott, Peter D. *The Theatres of Japan.* New York: St. Martin's Press, 1969.

Keene, Donald. *No: The Classical Theatre of Japan.* New York: Kodansha International, 1966.

CHAPTER 5

The Elizabethan Theater in London

Beckerman, Bernard. *Shakespeare at the Globe, 1599–1609*. New York: Macmillan, 1962.

Bradbrook, Muriel C. *Themes and Conventions of Elizabethan Tragedy*. London: Cambridge University Press, 1952, 1960.

Chute, Marchette Gaylord. *Ben Jonson of Westminster*. New York: Dutton, 1953.

Hodges, C. Walter. *The Globe Restored: A Study of the Elizabethan Theatre*. New York: Coward McCann and Geoghegan, 1968.

Hotson, Leslie. *The First Night of the Twelfth Night*. Darby, Penn.: Folcroft, 1954.

Nagler, Alois M. *Shakespeare's Stage*. New Haven: Yale University Press, 1958.

Styan, J. L. *Shakespeare's Stagecraft*. London: Cambridge University Press, 1967.

Watkins, Ronald. *On Producing Shakespeare*. 2nd ed. New York: B. Blom, 1964.

Wickham, Glynne. *Early English Stages*. 2 vols. New York: Columbia University Press, 1959, 1963.

Commedia dell'arte

Ducharte, Pierre Louis. *The Italian Comedy*. Translated by Randolph T. Weaver. London: Harrap, 1929.

Lea, Kathleen M. *The Italian Popular Comedy: A Study in the Commedia dell'Arte*. 2 vols. Oxford: Clarendon Press, 1934.

Nicoll, Allardyce. *The World of Harlequin*. London: Cambridge University Press, 1976.

Smith, Winifred. *The Commedia dell'Arte*. Rev. ed. New York: Columbia University Press, 1965.

CHAPTER 6

The Court Ballet and the Masque

Lees-Milne, James. *The Age of Inigo Jones*. London: Batsford, 1953.

Nicoll, Allardyce. *Stuart Masques and the Renaissance Stage*. New York: Harcourt, Brace, 1938.

Orgel, Stephen. *The Illusion of Power: Political Theatre in the English Renaissance*. Berkeley: University of California Press, 1975.

Silin, Charles. *Benserade and His Ballets de Cour*. 1940. Reprint. New York: AMS Press, 1977.

London Theater

Smith, Irwin. *Shakespeare's Blackfriars Playhouse: Its History and Its Design*. New York: New York University Press, 1964.

The Theater in France

Arnott, Peter D. *An Introduction to the French Theatre*. London: Macmillan, 1977.

Lawrenson, T. E. *The French Stage in the Seventeenth Century*. Manchester, Eng.: Manchester University Press, 1937.

Turnell, Martin. *The Classical Moment: Studies of Corneille, Moliere and Racine*. London: H. Hamilton, 1947.

English Restoration Stage

Hotson, J. Leslie. *The Commonwealth and Restoration Stage*. Cambridge, Mass.: Harvard University Press, 1928.
Krutch, Joseph Wood. *Comedy and Conscience After the Restoration*. New York: Columbia University Press, 1949.

CHAPTER 7

Burnim, Kalman A. *David Garrick, Director*. Carbondale: Southern Illinois University Press, 1973.
Nicoll, Allardyce. *History of Early Eighteenth Century Drama*. London: Cambridge University Press, 1925.
Nicoll, Allardyce. *History of Late Eighteenth Century Drama*. London: Cambridge University Press, 1927.
Pedicord, Harry William. *The Theatrical Public in the Time of Garrick*. Carbondale: Southern Illinois University Press, 1954.
Price, Cecil. *Theatre in the Age of Garrick*. Totowa, N.J.: Rowman, 1973.

CHAPTER 8

Houghton, Norris, ed. *The Romantic Influence*. Laurel Masterpieces of Continental Drama. Vol. II. New York: Dell, 1963.
Maurois, Andre. *Titan: A Three-Generational Biography of the Dumas*. Translated by Gerard Hopkins. 1957. Reprint. New York: Greenwood, 1971.

CHAPTER 9
General

Abrahams, Doris Caroline. Pseud. Caryl Brahms. *Gilbert and Sullivan: Lost Chords and Discords*. Boston: Little, Brown, 1975.
Irving, Laurence H. S. *Henry Irving: The Actor and His World*. New York: Macmillan, 1952.
Rowell, George. *The Victorian Theatre: 1792–1914*. 2nd ed. London: Cambridge University Press, 1979.
Southern, Richard. *The Victorian Theatre: A Pictorial Survey*. New York: Theatre Arts Books, 1970.

The Well-Made Play

Arvin, Neil Cole. *Eugène Scribe and the French Theatre, 1815–1860*. Cambridge, Mass.: Harvard University Press, 1924.
Stanton, Stephen, ed. *Camille and Other Plays*. New York: Hill and Wang, 1957.

Chekhov and Ibsen

Meyer, Michael. *Ibsen: A Biography.* New York: Doubleday, 1971.
Rayfield, Donald. *Chekhov: The Evolution of His Art.* New York: Barnes and Noble, 1975.
Shaw, George Bernard. *The Quintessence of Ibsenism.* 1913. Reprint. New York: Hill and Wang, 1957.
Styan, J. L. *Chekhov in Performance.* London: Cambridge University Press, 1978.

Stanislavsky

Stanislavsky, Constantin. *An Actor Prepares.* Translated by Elizabeth Reynolds Hapgood. New York: Theatre Arts Books, 1973.
Stanislavsky, Constantin. *Stanislavsky on the Art of the Stage.* Translated by David Magarshack. New York: Hill and Wang, 1962.

CHAPTER 10

Benedikt, Michael, and Wellwarth, George E., eds. *Modern French Theatre: The Avant-Garde, Dada and Surrealism.* New York: Dutton, 1966.
Brockett, O., and Findlay, R. *Century of Innovation.* Englewood Cliffs, N.J.: Prentice-Hall, 1973.
Brook, Peter. *The Empty Space.* New York: Atheneum, 1978.
Craig, Edward. *Gordon Craig: The Story of His Life.* London: Gollancz, 1968.
Esslin, Martin. *The Theatre of the Absurd.* Rev. ed. New York: Overlook Press, 1973.
Fergusson, Francis. *Idea of a Theatre.* Princeton, N.J.: Princeton University Press, 1968.
Gorelik, Mordecai. *New Theatres for Old.* 1940. Reprint. New York: Octagon, 1975.
Heilpern, John. *Conference of the Birds.* Indianapolis: Bobbs-Merrill, 1978.
Houghton, Norris. *The Exploding Stage: An Introduction to Twentieth Century Drama.* New York: Weybright and Talley, 1971.
Purdom, Charles Benjamin. *Harley Granville-Barker: Man of the Theatre, Dramatist and Scholar.* London: Rockcliff, 1955.
Roose-Evans, James. *Experimental Theatre.* New York: Avon, 1971.
Schechner, Richard. Introduction to *The Living Book of the Living Theater.* Greenwich, Conn.: New York Graphic Society, 1971.
Speaight, Robert. *William Poel and the Elizabethan Revival.* London: Heinemann, 1954.
Willett, John. *Theatre of Bertolt Brecht: A Study From Eight Aspects.* Rev. ed. New York: New Directions, 1968.

CHAPTER 11

Hewitt, Barnard. *Theatre U.S.A.: 1668 to 1957.* New York: McGraw-Hill, 1959.
Hornblow, Arthur. *History of the Theatre in America.* 2 vols. Philadelphia: Lippincott, 1919.
Moody, Richard. *America Takes the Stage.* Millwood, N.Y.: Kraus Reprint Co., 1955.
Moody, Richard. *The Astor Place Riot.* Bloomington: Indiana University Press, 1958.

CHAPTER 12

Brockett, Oscar. *The Theatre: An Introduction.* 4th ed. New York: Holt, Rinehart and Winston, 1979.

Gillette, Arnold S., ed. *Stage Scenery: Its Construction and Rigging.* 2nd ed. New York: Harper and Row, 1972.

Gillette, J. Michael. *Designing with Light: An Introduction to Stage Lighting.* Palo Alto, Calif.: Mayfield, 1975.

Mielziner, Jo. *The Shapes of Our Theatre.* New York: Potter, 1970.

Southern, Richard. *Changeable Scenery.* London: Faber and Faber, 1952.

Index

557